W9-BMS-788

THE Enduring Vision

A HISTORY OF THE AMERICAN PEOPLE

VOLUME I: TO 1877

Concise Seventh Edition

PAUL S. BOYER
University of Wisconsin, Madison

CLIFFORD E. CLARK, JR.
Carleton College

KAREN HALTTUNEN
University of Southern California

SANDRA MCNAIR HAWLEY
San Jacinto College

JOSEPH F. KETT
University of Virginia

ANDREW RIESER
State University of New York, Dutchess Community College

NEAL SALISBURY
Smith College

HARVARD SITKOFF
University of New Hampshire

NANCY WOLOCH
Barnard College

WADSWORTH
CENGAGE Learning

Australia • Brazil • Japan • Korea • Mexico • Singapore • Spain • United Kingdom • United States

WADSWORTH
CENGAGE Learning

Dedicated to the memory of Sandra Hawley

The Enduring Vision: A History of the American People, Volume I: To 1877, Concise Seventh Edition

Paul S. Boyer, Clifford E. Clark, Jr., Karen Halttunen, Sandra McNair Hawley, Joseph F. Kett, Andrew Rieser, Neal Salisbury, Harvard Sitkoff, Nancy Woloch

Senior Publisher: Suzanne Jeans

Senior Sponsoring Editor: Ann West

Senior Development Editor: Tonya Lobato

Assistant Editor: Megan Chrisman

Editorial Assistant: Patrick Roach

Senior Media Editor: Lisa Ciccolo

Marketing Coordinator: Lorreen Towle

Marketing Communications Manager: Glenn McGibbon

Senior Content Project Manager: Jane Lee

Senior Art Director: Cate Rickard Barr

Manufacturing Planner: Sandra Milewski

Rights Acquisition Specialist, Image: Jennifer Meyer Dare

Rights Acquisition Specialist, Text: Jennifer Meyer Dare

Production Service: S4Carlisle Publishing Services

Cover Designer: Yvo Riezebos, RHDG

Cover Image: Keys, Mary (19th c.e.) *Lockport on the Erie Canal,* 1832. Watercolor on paper. Munson-Williams-Proctor Arts Institute/Art Resource, NY.

Compositor: S4Carlisle Publishing Services

© 2013, 2009 Wadsworth, Cengage Learning

ALL RIGHTS RESERVED. No part of this work covered by the copyright herein may be reproduced, transmitted, stored, or used in any form or by any means graphic, electronic, or mechanical, including but not limited to photocopying, recording, scanning, digitizing, taping, Web distribution, information networks, or information storage and retrieval systems, except as permitted under Section 107 or 108 of the 1976 United States Copyright Act, without the prior written permission of the publisher.

For product information and technology assistance, contact us at
Cengage Learning Customer & Sales Support, 1-800-354-9706

For permission to use material from this text or product, submit all requests online at **www.cengage.com/permissions**. Further permissions questions can be emailed to **permissionrequest@cengage.com**.

Library of Congress Control Number: 2011935137

Student Edition:

ISBN-13: 978-1-111-84103-4

ISBN-10: 1-111-84103-9

Wadsworth
20 Channel Center Street
Boston, MA 02210
U.S.A.

Cengage Learning is a leading provider of customized learning solutions with office locations around the globe, including Singapore, the United Kingdom, Australia, Mexico, Brazil, and Japan. Locate your local office at **international.cengage.com/region**

Cengage Learning products are represented in Canada by Nelson Education, Ltd.

For your course and learning solutions, visit **www.cengage.com**.

Purchase any of our products at your local college store or at our preferred online store **www.cengagebrain.com**.

Instructors: Please visit **login.cengage.com** and log in to access instructor-specific resources.

Printed in Canada
1 2 3 4 5 6 7 15 14 13 12 11

Emerging Partisanship 153
The Whiskey Rebellion 154

■ The United States in a Wider World, 1789–1796 155
Spanish Power in Western North America 156
Challenging American Expansion, 1789–1792 156
France and Factional Politics, 1793 157
Diplomacy and War, 1793–1796 158

■ Parties and Politics, 1793–1800 159
Ideological Confrontation, 1793–1794 160
The Republican Party, 1794–1796 160
The Election of 1796 161
The French Crisis, 1798–1799 162
The Alien and Sedition Acts, 1798 162
The Election of 1800 165

■ Economic and Social Change 165
Producing for Markets 166
White Women in the Republic 167
Land and Culture: Native Americans 168
African-American Struggles 170

8

America at War and Peace, 1801–1824   174

■ The Age of Jefferson 175
Jefferson and Jeffersonianism 175
Jefferson's "Revolution" 176
Jefferson and the Judiciary 176
Extending the Land: The Louisiana Purchase, 1803 178
The Election of 1804 179
Exploring the Land: The Lewis and Clark Expedition 180

■ The Gathering Storm 181
Challenges on the Home Front 182
The Suppression of American Trade and Impressment 183
The Embargo Act of 1807 184
James Madison and the Failure of Peaceable Coercion 185
Tecumseh and the Prophet 186
Congress Votes for War 188

■ The War of 1812 188
On to Canada 188
The British Offensive 190
The Treaty of Ghent, 1814 190
The Hartford Convention 191

■ The Awakening of American Nationalism 191
Madison's Nationalism and the "Era of Good Feelings," 1817–1824 192

John Marshall and the Supreme Court 192
The Missouri Compromise, 1820–1821 193
Foreign Policy Under Monroe 195
The Monroe Doctrine, 1823 195

9

The Transformation of American Society, 1815–1840   198

■ Westward Expansion 199
The Sweep West 199
Western Society and Customs 200
The Far West 201
The Federal Government and the West 201
The Removal of the Indians 201
Working the Land: The Agricultural Boom 204

■ The Growth of the Market Economy 204
Federal Land Policy 204
The Speculator and the Squatter 205
The Panic of 1819 205
The Transportation Revolution: Steamboats, Canals, and Railroads 206
The Growth of the Cities 208

■ Industrial Beginnings 209
Causes of Industrialization 209
Textile Towns in New England 210
Artisans and Workers in Mid-Atlantic Cities 211

■ Equality and Inequality 211
Urban Inequality: The Rich and the Poor 211
Free Blacks in the North 212
The "Middling Classes" 213

■ The Revolution in Social Relationships 214
The Attack on the Professions 214
The Challenge to Family Authority 215
Wives and Husbands 216
Horizontal Allegiances and the Rise of Voluntary Associations 217

10

Democratic Politics, Religious Revival, and Reform, 1824–1840   220

■ The Rise of Democratic Politics, 1824–1832 221
Democratic Ferment 221
The Election of 1824 and the Adams Presidency 222
The Rise of Andrew Jackson and the Election of 1828 223

Jackson in Office   224
Nullification   225
The Bank Veto and the Election of 1832   227

■ The Bank Controversy and the Second Party System, 1833–1840   228
The War on the Bank   228
The Rise of Whig Opposition   229
The Election of 1836   229
The Panic of 1837   230
Log Cabins, Hard Cider, and a Maturing Second Party System   231

■ The Rise of Popular Religion   232
The Second Great Awakening   232
Eastern Revivals   233
Critics of Revivals: The Unitarians   233
The Rise of Mormonism   234
The Shakers   234

■ The Age of Reform   235
The War on Liquor   235
Public-School Reform   236
Abolition   237
Women's Rights   240
Penitentiaries and Asylums   241
Utopian Communities   242

11

Technology, Culture, and Everyday Life, 1840–1860   245

■ Technology and Economic Growth   246
Agricultural Advancement   246
Technology and Industrial Progress   247
The Railroad Boom   248
Rising Prosperity   250

■ The Quality of Life   250
Dwellings   251
Conveniences and Inconveniences   251
Disease and Health   252
Popular Health Movements   253
Phrenology   254

■ Democratic Pastimes   254
Newspapers   255
The Theater   255
Minstrel Shows   256
P. T. Barnum   257

■ The Quest for Nationality in Literature and Art   257
Roots of the American Renaissance   258
Cooper, Emerson, Thoreau, Fuller, and Whitman   258
Hawthorne, Melville, and Poe   260

Literature in the Marketplace   261
American Landscape Painting   263

12

The Old South and Slavery, 1830–1860   265

■ King Cotton   266
The Lure of Cotton   267
Ties Between the Lower and Upper South   268
The North and South Diverge   269

■ The Social Groups of the White South   271
Planters and Plantation Mistresses   271
The Small Slaveholders   272
The Yeomen   273
The People of the Pine Barrens   273

■ Social Relations in the White South   274
Conflict and Consensus in the White South   274
Conflict over Slavery   275
The Proslavery Argument   275
Violence, Honor, and Dueling in the Old South   277
The Southern Evangelicals and White Values   278

■ Life Under Slavery   278
The Maturing of the Plantation System   278
Work and Discipline of Plantation Slaves   279
The Slave Family   280
The Longevity, Health, and Diet of Slaves   281
Away from the Plantation: Slaves in Town and Free Blacks   282
Slave Resistance   283

■ The Emergence of African-American Culture   285
The Language of Slaves   285
African-American Religion   285
Black Music and Dance   286

13

Immigration, Expansion, and Sectional Conflict, 1840–1848   289

■ Newcomers and Natives   290
Expectations and Realities   290
The Germans   292
The Irish   292
Anti-Catholicism, Nativism, and Labor Protest   293
Immigrant Politics   294

■ The West and Beyond   295
The Far West   295

Far Western Trade 295
Mexican Government in the Far West 297
The Texas Revolution, 1836 297
American Settlements in California, New Mexico, and Oregon 298
The Overland Trails 299

The Politics of Expansion, 1840–1846 300
The Whig Ascendancy 300
Tyler and the Annexation of Texas 301
The Election of 1844 301
Manifest Destiny, 1845 302
Polk and Oregon 303

The Mexican-American War and Its Aftermath, 1846–1848 304
The Origins of the Mexican-American War 304
The Mexican-American War 306
The War's Effects on Sectional Conflict 307
The Wilmot Proviso 309
The Election of 1848 309
The California Gold Rush 310

14

From Compromise to Secession, 1850–1861 · 313

The Compromise of 1850 314
Zachary Taylor's Strategy 315
Henry Clay Proposes a Compromise 316
Assessing the Compromise 317
Enforcement of the Fugitive Slave Act 318
Uncle Tom's Cabin 318
The Election of 1852 320

The Collapse of the Second Party System, 1853–1856 320
The Kansas-Nebraska Act 321
The Surge of Free Soil 321
The Ebbing of Manifest Destiny 322
The Whigs Disintegrate, 1854–1855 323
The Rise and Fall of the Know-Nothings, 1853–1856 323
The Republican Party and the Crisis in Kansas, 1855–1856 324
The Election of 1856 326

The Crisis of the Union, 1857–1860 327
The Dred Scott Case, 1857 327
The Lecompton Constitution, 1857 328
The Lincoln-Douglas Debates, 1858 329
The Legacy of Harpers Ferry 331
The South Contemplates Secession 331

The Collapse of the Union, 1860–1861 332
The Election of 1860 332
The Movement for Secession 333
The Search for Compromise 334
The Coming of War 335

15

Crucible of Freedom: Civil War, 1861–1865 · 337

Mobilizing for War 338
Recruitment and Conscription 338
Financing the War 340
Political Leadership in Wartime 341
Securing the Union's Borders 342

In Battle, 1861–1862 343
Armies, Weapons, and Strategies 343
Stalemate in the East 345
The War in the West 347
The Soldiers' War 349
Ironclads and Cruisers: The Naval War 350
The Diplomatic War 351

Emancipation Transforms the War, 1863 352
From Confiscation to Emancipation 352
Crossing Union Lines 353
Black Soldiers in the Union Army 354
Slavery in Wartime 354
The Turning Point of 1863 355

War and Society, North and South 357
The War's Economic Impact: The North 357
The War's Economic Impact: The South 358
Dealing with Dissent 359
The Medical War 360
The War and Women's Rights 361

The Union Victorious, 1864–1865 362
The Eastern Theater in 1864 362
The Election of 1864 363
Sherman's March Through Georgia 364
Toward Appomattox 365
The Impact of the War 366

16

The Crisis of Reconstruction, 1865–1877 · 369

Reconstruction Politics, 1865–1868 370
Lincoln's Plan 371
Presidential Reconstruction Under Johnson 372

Congress Versus Johnson 373
The Fourteenth Amendment, 1866 373
Congressional Reconstruction, 1866–1867 374
The Impeachment Crisis, 1867–1868 375
The Fifteenth Amendment and the Question of
  Woman Suffrage, 1869–1870 376

Reconstruction Governments 378
A New Electorate 378
Republican Rule 380
Counterattacks 380

The Impact of Emancipation 382
Confronting Freedom 382
African-American Institutions 383
Land, Labor, and Sharecropping 385
Toward a Crop-Lien Economy 386

New Concerns in the North, 1868–1876 387
Grantism 388
The Liberals' Revolt 389

The Panic of 1873 390
Reconstruction and the Constitution 391
Republicans in Retreat 391

Reconstruction Abandoned, 1876–1877 392
"Redeeming" the South 392
The Election of 1876 393

Appendix   A-1

Declaration of Independence A-1
Constitution of the United States of
  America A-3
Amendments to the Constitution A-9
Presidential Elections, 1789–2008 A-14

Index   I-1

Maps

The Peopling of the Americas   4

Locations of Selected Native American Peoples, 1500 C.E.   12

Europe, Africa, and Southwestern Asia in 1500   20

Major Transatlantic Explorations, 1000–1542   27

The Spanish and Portuguese Empires, 1610   29

European Imperial Claims and Settlements in Eastern North America, 1565–1625   33

Chesapeake Expansion, 1607–1700   41

English Migration, 1610–1660   47

The Caribbean Colonies, 1670   56

European Colonization in the Middle and North Atlantic, c. 1650   59

Main Sources of African Slaves, ca. 1500–1800   74

Immigration and British Colonial Expansion, to 1755   75

European Occupation of North America, to 1750   82

The Seven Years' War in North America, 1754–1760   93

European Territorial Claims, 1763   96

The War in the North, 1775–1778   125

The War in the West, 1776–1782   126

The War in the South, 1778–1781   128

Federalist and Antifederalist Strongholds, 1787–1790   144

Indian Land Cessions, 1768–1799   169

The Louisiana Purchase and the Exploration of the West   180

Major Battles of the War of 1812   189

The Missouri Compromise, 1820–1821   194

The Removal of the Native Americans to the West, 1820–1840   202

Major Rivers, Roads, and Canals, 1825–1860   207

The Election of 1828   224

The Election of 1840   231

Railroad Growth, 1850–1860   249

Distribution of Slaves, 1820 and 1860   270

Internal Slave Trade, 1810–1860   281

Trails to the West, 1840   296

Major Battles in the Texas Revolution, 1835–1836   298

Oregon Boundary Dispute   304

Major Battles of the Mexican-American War   308

The Compromise of 1850   317

Bleeding Kansas   325

Secession   334

The War in the East, 1861–1862   346

The War in the West, 1861–1862   349

Gettysburg, 1863   356

The Final Virginia Campaign, 1864–1865   364

The Reconstruction of the South   375

The Barrow Plantation, 1860 and 1881   385

Southern Sharecropping, 1880   387

Charts, Graphs, and Tables

The Election of 1824   **223**

Value of Cotton Exports as a Percentage of All U.S. Exports, 1800–1860   **267**

Growth of Cotton Production and the Slave Population, 1790–1860   **268**

Slave Ownership, 1860   **275**

German, Irish, and Total Immigration, 1830–1860   **291**

Comparative Population and Economic Resources of the Union and Confederacy, 1861   **344**

The Reconstruction Amendments   **377**

The Duration of Republican Rule in the Ex-Confederate States   **392**

Preface

Much has changed in America and the world since we began planning *The Enduring Vision* for college survey students more than twenty-five years ago. Some of these developments have been welcome and positive; others deeply unsettling. This new Concise Seventh Edition fully documents all of these changes for today's new generation of students, as well as the continuities that offer reassurance for the future.

Vision and Goals

The Concise Seventh Edition builds on the underlying strategy that has guided us from the beginning. We want our history to be not only comprehensive and illuminating, but also lively, readable, and true to the lived experience of earlier generations of Americans. Within a clear political and chronological framework, we integrate the best recent scholarship in all areas of American history. Our interest in social and cultural history, which shapes our own teaching and scholarship, has suffused *The Enduring Vision* from the outset, and it remains central. We integrate the historical experience of women and men of all regions, ethnic groups, and social classes who make up the American mosaic.

As we pursue these purposes in this Concise Seventh Edition, we welcome Karen Halttunen to the team of authors. A distinguished historian of nineteenth-century American social and cultural history who teaches at the University of Southern California, Professor Halttunen brings impressive strengths to our mission.

New Interpretations, Expanded Coverage

This edition of *The Enduring Vision* brings the work fully up to date, incorporating major developments and scholarship since the previous edition went to press. We have included the best of the new political history, stressing the social, cultural, and economic issues at stake in political decisions and debates. Religious history remains an important focus, from the spiritual values of pre-Columbian communities to the political activism of contemporary conservative Christian groups. We again offer extensive coverage of medicine and disease, from the epidemics brought by European explorers to today's AIDS crisis, bioethics debates, and controversies over health-care financing.

As with previous editions, we have added a number of new chapter-opening vignettes, including new vignettes on Edmund Ruffin, a fanatical defender of the South and slavery, and Martin Luther King, Jr. These vignettes introduce a central theme of the chapter and remind us that, in the last analysis, history involves the choices and actions of individual men and women.

Streamlined Organization

In our continuing quest to make the text clear and reader-friendly, we have rear-ranged some sections and reorganized some chapters. The post–World War II chapters, in particular, have been heavily reorganized to consolidate topical coverage and tighten the narrative. We have edited rigorously but without sacrificing any sub-stantive material. As a result, we have reduced the total number of chapters from thirty-two to thirty-one and shortened the text by about 10 percent.

Understanding history requires a firm grasp of geography, and *The Enduring Vision* has always emphasized the significance of the land in the interplay of histori-cal events. Our extensive coverage of environmental history, the land, and the West is fully integrated into the narrative and treated analytically—not simply "tacked on" to a traditional account. An upgraded map program offers maps that are rich in information, easy to read, and visually appealing.

Visual Resources and Features

Based on the positive feedback we have received from readers, we have maintained the layout of the previous edition. Our one-column format allows for seamless inte-gration of images and a smoother narrative flow. Each chapter begins with Focus Questions that correspond to the major sections of the chapter to give students a preview of the key topics to be covered. These questions are briefly answered at the end of the chapter in the "Chapter Summary." All maps in the text have been rede-signed to be more visually dynamic and engaging; each map also features a corre-sponding online interactive map. Throughout the chapters, students get assistance from key terms that are boldfaced in the text and defined in the margins; "Checking In" boxes at the end of each section summarize the key points in that section.

Supplementary Resources

A wide array of supplements accompanies this text to help students master the mate-rial and guide instructors in teaching from *The Enduring Vision,* Concise Seventh Edition. For details on viewing or ordering these materials, please consult your Cengage Learning sales representative.

Instructor Resources

PowerLecture CD-ROM with ExamView® and JoinIn®. This dual platform, all-in-one multimedia resource in-cludes the Instructor's Resource Manual, authored by Ken Blume of Albany College of Pharmacy and Health Sciences; the Test Bank, authored by Volker Janssen of California State University, Fullerton; Microsoft® PowerPoint® slides of lecture outlines as well as images and maps from the text that can be used as offered, or customized by importing personal lecture slides or other material; and JoinIn® PowerPoint® slides with clicker content. Also included is ExamView, an easy-to-use assessment and tutorial system that allows instructors to create, deliver, and customize tests in minutes. Instructors can build tests with as many as 250 questions using up to twelve question types; using ExamView's com-plete word-processing capabilities, they can enter an unlimited number of new ques-tions or edit existing ones.

eInstructor's Resource Manual. This manual has many features, including chapter themes, lecture suggestions, directions for using print and nonprint resources, and additional instructional suggestions. This manual is available on the instructor's companion website.

WebTutor™ on Blackboard® and WebCT®. With WebTutor's text-specific, preformatted content and total flexibility, instructors can easily create and manage their own custom course website. WebTutor's course management tool gives instructors the ability to provide virtual office hours, post syllabi, set up threaded discussions, track student progress with the quizzing material, and much more. For students, WebTutor offers real-time access to a full array of study tools, including animations and videos that bring the book's topics to life, plus chapter outlines, summaries, glossary flashcards, practice quizzes, and weblinks.

CourseMate. Cengage Learning's History CourseMate brings course concepts to life with interactive learning, study, and exam preparation tools that support the printed textbook. Watch student comprehension soar as your class works with the printed textbook and the textbook-specific website. History CourseMate goes beyond the book to deliver what you need! History CourseMate includes an integrated eBook; interactive teaching and learning tools, including quizzes, flashcards, videos, and more; and EngagementTracker, a first-of-its-kind tool that monitors student engagement in the course. Learn more at **www.cengagebrain.com.**

CourseReader for U.S. History. CourseReader offers a way for instructors to build customized online readers for their courses. By selecting documents from a rich database of primary and secondary sources, including many from the Gale collections, instructors can create their own reader to match the specific needs of their course. An Editor's Choice developed for *The Enduring Vision* provides a useful starting point. Go to **Cengage.com/coursereader** for more information.

Student Resources

CourseMate. For students, CourseMate provides an additional source of interactive learning, study, and exam preparation outside the classroom. Students will find outlines and objectives, focus questions, flashcards, quizzes, primary source links, and video clips. In addition, CourseMate includes an integrated *The Enduring Vision* eBook. Students taking quizzes will be linked directly to relevant sections in the eBook for additional information. The eBook is fully searchable and students can even take notes and save them for later review. The eBook links out to rich media assets such as video and MP3 chapter summaries, primary source documents with critical thinking questions, and interactive (zoomable) maps. Students can use the eBook as their primary text or as a companion multimedia support. It is available at **www.cengagebrain.com.**

Book Companion Site. This website for students features a wide assortment of resources to help students master the subject matter. The website includes a glossary, chapter outlines, flashcards, crossword puzzles, tutorial quizzes, focus questions, and weblinks. Throughout the text, icons direct students to relevant exercises and self-testing material located on the student companion website.

Cengagebrain.com. Save your students time and money. Direct them to **www .cengagebrain.com** for additional choices in formats and savings and a better chance to succeed in your class. *Cengagebrain.com,* Cengage Learning's online store, is a single destination for more than 10,000 new textbooks, eTextbooks, eChapters, study tools, and audio supplements. Students have the freedom to purchase a-la-carte exactly what they need when they need it. Students can save 50 percent on the electronic textbook, and can pay as little as $1.99 for an individual eChapter.

Wadsworth American History Resource Center. Wadsworth's American History Resource Center gives your students access to a "virtual reader" with hundreds of primary sources, including speeches, letters, legal documents and transcripts, poems, maps, simulations, timelines, and additional images that bring history to life, along with interactive assignable exercises. A map feature including Google Earth™ coordinates and exercises will aid in student comprehension of geography and use of maps. Students can compare the traditional textbook map with an aerial view of the location today. It's an ideal resource for study, review, and research. In addition to this map feature, the resource center also provides blank maps for student review and testing.

Rand McNally Atlas of American History, 2e. This comprehensive atlas features more than eighty maps, with new content covering global perspectives, including events in the Middle East from 1945 to 2005, as well as population trends in the United States and around the world. Additional maps document voyages of discovery; the settling of the colonies; major U.S. military engagements, including the American Revolution and World Wars I and II; and sources of immigrations, ethnic populations, and patterns of economic change.

Reader Program. Cengage Learning publishes a number of readers, some containing exclusively primary sources, others a combination of primary and secondary sources, and some designed to guide students through the process of historical inquiry. Visit **Cengage.com/history** for a complete list of readers.

Custom Options Nobody knows your students like you, so why not give them a text that is tailor-fit to their needs? Cengage Learning offers custom solutions for your course—whether it's making a small modification to *The Enduring Vision* to match your syllabus or combining multiple sources to create something truly unique. You can pick and choose chapters, include your own material, and add additional map exercises along with the Rand McNally Atlas to create a text that fits the way you teach. Ensure that your students get the most out of their textbook dollar by giving them exactly what they need. Contact your Cengage Learning representative to explore custom solutions for your course.

Acknowledgments

Any book, and this one in particular, is the result of the hard work of many people. In preparing this Concise Seventh Edition, we benefited from the critical readings of many colleagues. Our sincere thanks go in particular to the following instructors and teachers: Vanessa de los Reyes, Gateway Community and Technical College;

Eva Mo, Modesto Junior College; Donald Trotter, Johnson Bible College; Jason McCollom, University of Arkansas; Charles Hubbard, Lincoln Memorial University; Verdis Robinson, Monroe Community College; Nicolas Rosenthal, Loyola Marymount University; and James Gillispie, Sampson Community College. As always, the editorial staff at Cengage has been outstanding. Particularly deserving of thanks are Ann West and Tonya Lobato, and also Roxanne Klaas of S4Carlisle Publishing Services. On behalf of everyone associated with *The Enduring Vision* over the years, Andrew Rieser expresses his condolences to the family of co-author Sandra McNair Hawley and dedicates this volume to her memory.

CHAPTER 1

Native Peoples of America

TO 1500

Kwakwaka'wakw Sun Transformation Mask,
Northwest Coast

Courtesy, National Museum of the American Indian, Smithsonian Institution #D115235

CHAPTER PREVIEW

The First Americans, c. 13,000–2500 B.C.E.
*How did environmental change shape the
transition from Paleo-Indian to Archaic ways
of life?*

Cultural Diversity, c. 2500 B.C.E.–1500 C.E.
*What were the principal differences among the
Native American cultures that emerged after
2500 B.C.E.?*

**North American Peoples on the Eve
of European Contact**
*What common values did Native Americans share
despite their vast diversity?*

American history began thousands of years before the arrival of Europeans. The earliest Native Americans lived in small hunter-gatherer bands, but as they spread across North and South America they adapted to a wide variety of regional environments. Consequently, their cultures diverged and diversified. Indian bands and communities ranged from a few dozen to thousands of members, with a large range of social structures. Hunters and gatherers, as well as farmers and fishers, depended on a wide variety of food sources. Nonetheless, many Indian cultures demonstrated common characteristics amid great diversity.

1

THE FIRST AMERICANS, C. 13,000–2500 B.C.E.

How did environmental change shape the transition from Paleo-Indian to Archaic ways of life?

Precisely how and when the Western Hemisphere was settled remains uncertain. Although many Indians believe that their ancestors originated in the Americas, most scientific theories point to the arrival of peoples from northeastern Asia during the last Ice Age (c. 33,000–10,700 B.C.E.), when land linked Siberia and Alaska. As the Ice Age waned, Native Americans adapted to environments that ranged from tropical to frigid and developed diverse cultures that nonetheless had many elements in common.

Peopling New Worlds

Monte Verde, Chile Site of human habitation by 12,000 B.C.E.

Bering land bridge Link between Northeast Asia and far Northwest North America during late Ice Age

Scientists now believe that the earliest migrants from Asia traveled by boat along the coastline around 13,000 B.C.E. Recent archaeological finds at **Monte Verde, Chile,** reveal evidence of human habitation by 12,000 B.C.E. Later migrants reached the Americas by crossing the **Bering land bridge** and fanned out in the interior as melting glaciers opened the way for eastward and southward migration.

Most Native Americans descend from these early migrations, but a later surge of migration brought Athapaskan (ath-a-PAS-kan)-speaking peoples to the Americas about 7000 B.C.E. Their descendants include the Apaches and Navajos. The arrival of non-Indian Inuits, Aleuts, and Eskimos after 3000 B.C.E. completed the peopling of the Americas.

Paleo-Indians Earliest peoples of the Americas, 13,000–8000 B.C.E.

Most **Paleo** (PAY-lee-oh)-**Indians** lived in small bands of fifteen to fifty people. The band lived together for the summer but split into smaller groups of one or two families for fall and winter. Although they moved constantly, they remained within informal boundaries except when they traveled to favored quarries to obtain jasper or flint for making tools. Here they encountered other bands, with whom they traded and joined in religious ceremonies. Most Paleo-Indians practiced **reciprocity,** the mutual bestowing of gifts and favors rather than competition for resources.

reciprocity Mutual bestowing of gifts and favors rather than competition for resources

By 9000 B.C.E. many big-game species, including mammoths and mastodons, had vanished. Paleo-Indian hunters contributed to this extinction, as did a warming climate and environmental changes. Human beings were major beneficiaries of these changes.

Archaic Societies

Climatic warming continued until about 4000 B.C.E. with dramatic effects for North America. Sea levels rose, flooding the shallow continental shelf, and glacial runoff filled the Great Lakes, the Mississippi River basin, and other waters. As the glaciers receded northward, so did the cold, icy arctic or subarctic environments that had covered much of what is now the United States. Treeless plains and evergreen forests yielded to deciduous forests in the East, grassland prairies on the Plains, and desert in much of the West. An immense range of plants and animals covered the landscape.

Archaic peoples Native Americans from 8000–2500 B.C.E.

The **Archaic** (ar-KAY-ick) **peoples,** as archaeologists term native North Americans from 8000 B.C.E. to sometime after 2500 B.C.E., lived off wide varieties of smaller

Chronology

c. 13,000 B.C.E.	People present in America
c. 10,500–9000 B.C.E.	Paleo-Indians spread throughout Western Hemisphere
c. 9000 B.C.E.	Extinction of big-game mammals
c. 8000 B.C.E.	Archaic era begins
c. 7000 B.C.E.	Athapaskan-speaking peoples arrive in North America
c. 5000 B.C.E.	First domesticated plants grown
c. 3000 B.C.E.	First maize grown in Mesoamerica
c. 3000–2000 B.C.E.	Eskimo and Aleut peoples arrive in North America
c. 2500 B.C.E.	Archaic societies yield before diverse cultures; first maize grown in North America
c. 1200 B.C.E.	Poverty Point flourishes in Louisiana
c. 400–100 B.C.E.	Adena culture flourishes in Ohio Valley
c. 250 B.C.E.	Hohokam culture begins in Southwest
c. 100 B.C.E.	Anasazi culture begins in Southwest
c. 100 B.C.E.– 600 C.E.	Hopewell culture thrives in Midwest
c. 1 C.E.	Rise of chiefdoms on Northwest Coast and in California
c. 100–700	Teotihuacán flourishes in Mesoamerica
c. 600–1400	Mayan kingdoms flourish
c. 700	Mississippian culture begins; Anasazi expansion begins
c. 900	Urban center arises at Cahokia
c.1000	Norse attempt, and fail, to colonize Vinland
c. 1200	Anasazi and Hohokam peoples disperse in Southwest
c. 1200–1400	Cahokia declines; inhabitants disperse
1428	Rise of Aztec empire
1438	Rise of Inca empire
1492	Christopher Columbus reaches Western Hemisphere

mammals, fish, and wild plants rather than big game. Greater efficiency in hunting and gathering permitted larger populations to inhabit smaller areas. In rich areas, such as the East and Midwest, large populations lived in villages for virtually the entire year. For example, a year-round village that flourished near present-day Kampsville, Illinois, from 3900 to 2800 B.C.E. supported 100 to 150 people. Its residents procured fish and mussels from local lakes to supplement the deer, birds, nuts, and seeds available in the surrounding area.

Over time, Archaic Americans sharpened distinctions between women's and men's roles. Generally men fished and hunted while women foraged for wild plant products. However, both genders apparently served as religious healers. As they foraged for wild plants, gatherers—usually women in North America—gradually learned how to manipulate their environments to favor plants that produced food and medicine. They then developed tools for digging and grinding, as well as effective methods of drying and storing seeds. Agricultural societies began domesticating wild animals such as sheep, goats, and cattle as early as 8000 B.C.E., but the Americas lacked large animals suitable for domestication; by the time Native Americans began farming, the only animals they found suitable for taming were llamas, turkeys, guinea pigs, and dogs, which seem to have been omnipresent in human societies as early as 30,000 B.C.E. This not only limited food sources but also forced American Indians to rely primarily on human power for carrying goods and dragging loads.

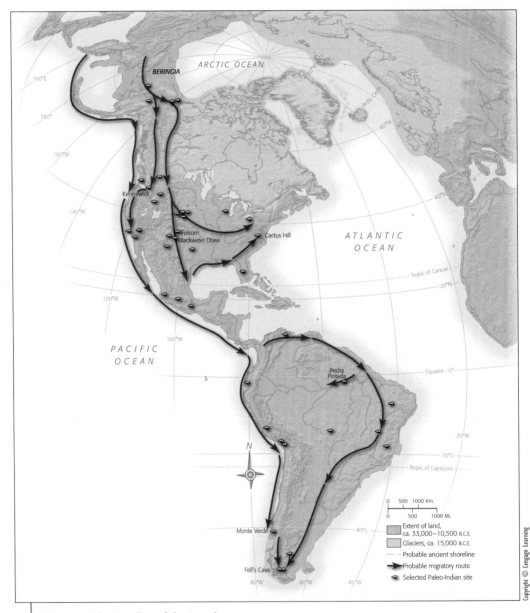

Map 1.1   The Peopling of the Americas

Scientists postulate two probable routes by which the earliest peoples reached America. By 9500 B.C.E., they had settled throughout the Western Hemisphere.

⬛ Interactive Map

The most sophisticated of these early farmers lived in highland valleys in **Mesoamerica,** particularly Tehuacán (teh-wha-CAHN). By 3000 B.C.E. they were cultivating squash, gourds, beans, chili peppers, and fruits. At the same time Tehuacán farmers began the long process of domesticating a lowlands plant called teosinte, which ultimately became maize (maze), or corn. Maize agriculture spread rapidly; by 2500 B.C.E. maize was cultivated as far north as modern New Mexico and as far south as the Amazon basin.

At the same time, Indians in the Andes were already cultivating potatoes, while their counterparts along the Pacific coast harvested squash, beans, and peppers. Initially these domesticated plants constituted only a small part of the Native American diet, essentially a supplement to meat, fish, and wild plants. Centuries would pass before stable societies based primarily on agriculture emerged.

CHECKING IN

- Historians believe that most Native Americans descended from Northeast Asian peoples who arrived in the Americas from around 33,000 to 9000 B.C.E.
- Paleo-Indians, the earliest peoples of the Americas, lived in small groups and were mainly hunters.
- Climatic warming created favorable environments for expansion, including the emergence of agriculture by 5000 B.C.E.

Mesoamerica Roughly, land extending from modern Mexico to Colombia; Central America plus Mexico

CULTURAL DIVERSITY, C. 2500 B.C.E.–1500 C.E.

What were the principal differences among the Native American cultures that emerged after 2500 B.C.E.?

After 2500 B.C.E. many Native Americans moved far beyond the ways of their Archaic ancestors. The most far-reaching changes occurred among peoples whose environments permitted them to produce food surpluses by cultivating crops or by other means. Intensive farming radically changed the environment, and larger populations linked by trade and religion evolved into formal confederacies, and even hierarchical states joined by political and religious systems.

Mesoamerica and South America

Mesoamerican farmers rapidly developed sophisticated agricultural systems, improving both the quality and the quantity of their crops. In turn, the higher yields and improved nutrition led to the emergence of maize-based farming societies throughout Mesoamerica during the next eight centuries. According to geneticist Nina Fedoroff, the development of maize "arguably was the first, and perhaps man's greatest, feat of genetic engineering."

By 2000 B.C.E. some Mesoamerican farming societies were trading surplus crops to their nonfarming neighbors. Trade led to the development of wealthy and powerful urban centers that dominated surrounding communities. These chiefdoms generally dominated relatively small areas, but some developed into centralized states complete with taxes, public works, and armies. The capital of the largest early state, Teotihuacán (tehoh-tee-whah-KAHN), about fifty miles northeast of modern Mexico City, housed a population of one hundred thousand people. At its center was a complex of pyramids over which towered the

Sun Pyramid, Teotihuacán

Built over several centuries, this pyramid remained the largest structure in the Americas until after the Spanish arrived.

Sun Pyramid, the largest structure in the Americas prior to the arrival of the Spanish. From 100 to 700 C.E., Teotihuacán dominated the Valley of Mexico, with trade networks extending throughout modern Mexico; its influence on the religion, government, and culture of its neighbors was enormous.

As Teotihuacán declined, the Maya (MY-uh) rose. Living in kingdom-states that flourished from southern Mexico to Honduras, the Maya developed a highly accurate calendar; a numerical system; and a system of phonetic, hieroglyphic writing. Mayan codices (singular, codex)—formed from bark paper glued into long folded strips—recorded religious ceremonies, historical traditions, and astronomical observations.

In the fifteenth century two powerful empires emerged: the Aztecs of Mexico and the Inca of Peru. In 1428 the Aztecs began asserting control over Lake Texcoco in the Valley of Mexico and its surrounding communities. After 1450 Aztec expansion became increasingly bloody, as Aztec priests maintained that their gods demanded to be served human blood and hearts; warriors sought captives for human sacrifice.

Tenochtitlán (teh-knowtch-teet-LAN), the Aztec capital, at its peak had some two hundred thousand inhabitants. At the center of the city was a massive temple complex. The Aztecs borrowed freely from other Mesoamerican societies, taking writing from Teotihuacán and the calendar from the Maya. To support the capital's population, the Aztecs developed intensive agriculture based on artificially created islands anchored in Lake Texcoco; Aztec engineers developed an elaborate irrigation system to provide fresh water for both people and crops.

The Aztecs collected taxes from conquered peoples living within a hundred miles of the capital; from those farther away, they exacted tribute. Aztec trading networks extended far from Tenochtitlán, reaching as far north as the American Southwest. However, by the early sixteenth century rebellions had flared up within the Aztec empire.

Far to the south, the Inca empire was expanding as well. After 1438, Inca conquests created an empire that stretched along the Andes and its adjacent areas. The Inca were highly successful farmers, producing enormous quantities of potatoes, maize, beans, and meats. They constructed terraced irrigation systems on their uneven terrain, perfected freeze-drying and other preservation techniques, and built a vast network of roads and bridges.

However, the arrival of the Spanish would destroy both empires.

Richard Alexander Cooke III

The Southwest

The Southwest (the modern American Southwest and most of northern Mexico) is an arid region of diverse landscapes; however, various peoples managed to establish stable supplies of water there and become farmers. Although maize had reached the Southwest as early as 2500 C.E., large agricultural societies did not emerge until the introduction of drought-resistant strains of the plant around 400 B.C.E. The two most influential of these were the **Hohokam** (ho-HO-kum) and the **Anasazi** (an-uh-SAW-zee).

Hohokam culture emerged in the third century B.C.E. when ancestors of Pima and Tohono O'odham Indians began farming in the Gila (HEE-la) River and Salt River valleys of southern Arizona. The Hohokam people built elaborate canal systems for irrigation that enabled them to harvest two crops each year. The construction and maintenance of the canals demanded large, coordinated workforces. The Hohokams therefore built permanent villages of several hundred residents, and many such communities were joined in confederations linked by canals. The central village in each confederation coordinated labor, trade, and religious and political life for all.

The Hohokam way of life drew on Mesoamerican materials and ideas. From about the sixth century C.E., the larger Hohokam villages had ball courts and platform mounds like those in Mesoamerica, and ball games became major public events. Mesoamerican art influenced Hohokam artists, who used clay, stone, turquoise, and shell. Archaeologists have found Mesoamerican items, such as rubber balls, macaw feathers, and copper bells, at Hohokam sites.

Anasazi culture originated during the first century B.C.E. in the Four Corners area where Arizona, New Mexico, Colorado, and Utah meet. Although they adopted village life and agriculture late, the Anasazis expanded rapidly in the eighth century C.E. and came to dominate a wide area. Modern Pueblo Indians are descendants of the Anasazi.

The Anasazis had a distinctive architecture. They constructed their early dwellings, round pit houses, in the shape of **kivas** (KEE-vahs), the partly underground, circular structures where Anasazi men conducted religious ceremonies. Anasazi-style apartments and kivas are characteristic of the architecture of the modern-day Pueblo Indians of the Southwest.

From the tenth through the mid-twelfth century, an unusually wet period, the Anasazis expanded over much of today's New Mexico and Arizona. Village populations grew to a thousand or more. In **Chaco** (CHAH-ko) **Canyon** in northwestern New Mexico, a cluster of twelve villages forged a powerful confederation numbering fifteen thousand people. Perfectly straight roads radiated from the canyon to satellite pueblos up to sixty-five miles away. The builders carved out stairs or footholds in the sides of steep cliffs. The canyon was a major trade center, importing and exporting a wide range of materials from and to Mesoamerica, the Great Plains, the Mississippi Valley, and California.

Devastating droughts in the late twelfth and thirteenth centuries destroyed classic Anasazi culture. Suddenly, the amount of farmland was drastically reduced for a population that had grown rapidly during the preceding centuries. The Indians abandoned the great Anasazi centers and scattered. Other large agricultural

Hohokam Early agricultural society of Southwest

Anasazi Pueblo culture that dominated Southwest from 100 B.C.E.–1200 C.E.

kivas A large chamber, often wholly or partially underground, in an Anasazi and later a Pueblo Indian village; used for religious ceremonies and other purposes

Chaco Canyon Center of powerful Anasazi confederation, 900–1200 C.E.

communities, such as those of the Hohokam, also dispersed when droughts came, clearing the way for the arrival of the nonfarming Navajos and Apaches at the end of the thirteenth century.

The Eastern Woodlands   Long before they developed agriculture, Indians of the Eastern Woodlands, the vast forests from the Mississippi Valley to the Atlantic coast, experimented with village life and political centralization. By 1200 B.C.E. about five thousand people had concentrated in a single village at Poverty Point on the Mississippi River in Louisiana. Two large mounds flanked the village, and six concentric embankments—the largest over half a mile in diameter—surrounded it. During the spring and autumn equinoxes, a person standing on the larger mound could watch the sun rise directly over the village center. Solar observations formed the basis for these Indians' religious beliefs as well as for their calendar.

Poverty Point lay at the center of a large political and economic unit. It imported quartz, copper, obsidian, crystal, and other sacred materials from long distances and distributed them to nearby communities. These communities almost certainly supplied the labor for the earthworks. The Olmec peoples of Mesoamerica clearly influenced the design and organization of Poverty Point. The settlement flourished for only three centuries and then declined, for reasons that are unclear. A different **mound-building culture,** the Adena, emerged in the Ohio Valley in the fifth century B.C.E. Adena villages rarely exceeded four hundred inhabitants, but the Adena people spread over a wide area and built hundreds of mounds, most of them containing graves that reflected an individual's social standing.

> **mound-building culture**
> Eastern Woodlands societies, which flourished from 1200 B.C.E.–1400 C.E.; included Poverty Point, Adena, Hopewell, and Mississippian

During the first century B.C.E., Adena culture evolved into a more developed and widespread culture known as Hopewell. Hopewell ceremonial centers, which were larger and more elaborate than those of the Adena, mushroomed along the Ohio River and Illinois River valleys. Some centers contained two or three dozen mounds within enclosures of several square miles. The graves of the elite contained elaborate burial goods: freshwater pearls, copper ornaments, mica, quartz, and other sacred substances. Hopewell artisans used raw materials from throughout America east of the Rockies. Through trade networks the Hopewell influence spread to communities as distant as places in modern-day Wisconsin, Florida, and New York.

The people who created the sophisticated Hopewell culture were primarily hunter-gatherers, not farmers. Although they did grow some crops, agriculture became a dietary mainstay for Woodlands people only between the seventh and twelfth centuries C.E.

The first full-time farmers in the East were the Mississippians, who lived on the flood plains of the Mississippi River and its major tributaries. Their culture, beginning sometime around 700 C.E., blended elements of the Hopewell culture and ideas from Mesoamerica with their own traditions. Mississippian towns, containing hundreds or even thousands of people, were built around open plazas like those of central Mexico. Religious temples and elite residences stood atop large mounds next to the plazas. Religious ceremonies focused on worship of the sun as the source of agricultural fertility. Chiefs claimed to be related to the sun, and when they died, wives and servants were killed to accompany them to the afterlife. Artisans produced sophisticated work in clay, stone, shell, copper, and wood, largely for religious and funeral rituals.

By the tenth century most Mississippian centers were part of larger confederacies based on trade and shared religious beliefs. Powerful "supercenters" and their chiefs dominated these confederacies. The most powerful confederacy revolved around the magnificent city of **Cahokia** (ka-HO-kee-uh), near modern St. Louis; its influence extended from the Appalachians to the edge of the Plains and from the Great Lakes to the Gulf of Mexico.

Cahokia Major mound-building "supercenter," which existed from 900–1200 C.E.

After 1200 C.E. Cahokia and other valley centers experienced shortages of food and other resources. Densely concentrated societies had taxed a fragile environment with a fluctuating climate. Competition for suddenly scarce resources led to debilitating warfare, and survivors fled to the surrounding prairies. By the fifteenth century, their descendants lived in villages linked by reciprocity instead of coercion.

The Spanish later encountered them as the forerunners of the Cherokee, Creek, and other Southeastern Indian peoples.

The Mississippians profoundly affected native culture in the Eastern Woodlands. They spread not only new strains of corn and beans but also the techniques and tools to cultivate them. However, northern New England and the upper Great Lakes had growing seasons too short for corn to become a reliable crop.

Cahokia Mounds: Historic Site, painting by William R. Iseminger

Cahokia Mounds

This contemporary painting conveys Cahokia's grand scale. Not until the late eighteenth century did another North American city (Philadelphia) surpass the population of Cahokia, c. 1150.

Woodlands tribes employed slash-and-burn techniques, which were environ-mentally sound as well as economically productive. Indian men systematically burned hardwood forests to form open expanses of land. The grass and berry bushes that flourished there attracted deer and other game, and some areas of the ash-enriched soil were planted in corn, beans, and pumpkins. After several years of abundant harvests, yields declined, and the Indians repeated the process on another area; ground cover eventually restored the fertility of the abandoned areas, permitting the Indians to return.

Nonfarming Societies Along the Pacific coast, from Alaska to southern California, improvements in the production and storage of food enabled Indians to develop more settled ways of life than their Archaic forebears. From the Alaskan panhandle to northern California, natives spent brief periods each year catching salmon and other fish. The Northwest Coast Indians dried and stored enough fish to last the year, and their seasonal movements gradually gave way to settled life in permanent villages of cedar-plank houses. On the Columbia Plateau, Indians built villages of pit houses and ate salmon through the summer. They left these communities in spring and fall for hunting and gathering.

By 1 C.E. many Northwest Coast villages numbered several hundred people. Trade and warfare strengthened the power of chiefs and other leaders, whose families had greater wealth and prestige than commoners. Leading families proclaimed their status in elaborate totem poles depicting supernatural beings linked to their ancestors and in potlatches, ceremonies in which the Indians gave away or destroyed much of their material wealth. The artistic and architectural achievements of Northwest Coast Indians awed Europeans.

At about the same time, Indians farther south, along the coast and in the interior valleys of what is now California, began to cluster in villages of one hundred or more people. Acorns dominated their diet, supplementing game, fish, and plants. After the fall harvest, Indians ground the acorns into meal, leached them of bitter tannic acid, and then roasted, boiled, or baked the nuts before eating or storing them.

The end of the Archaic period produced little change in the forbidding aridity of the Great Basin, encompassing present-day Nevada, western Utah, southern Idaho, and eastern Oregon. However, the area continued to support small hunting-and-gathering bands.

To the east of the Great Basin lay the grasslands of the Great Plains, which were too dry to support large human settlements but ideal for herds of game animals such as antelope, deer, and elk. Primary among the Great Plains animals were the buffalo, which served nomadic hunters as an ambulatory supermarket. In addition to meat, buffalo provided hides for clothing and tipis, as well as bones and horn for tools and arrowheads; Indians used most other buffalo parts as well. Following the great herds on foot, nomadic tribes killed individual animals with spears and arrows, but also stampeded hundreds at a time over cliffs. Despite such wasteful practices, humans were so few in number that they had no significant impact on the buffalo population before the arrival of the Europeans. There are no reliable estimates of the number of buffalo that roamed on the Great Plains, but they may well have numbered in the tens of millions.

In western Alaska, the Aleuts arrived around 3000 B.C.E., bringing with them sophisticated tools and weapons from their Siberian homeland. Most importantly, the Aleuts introduced the bow and arrow to the Americas. Over several thousand years, they spread eastward across Canada as far as Greenland.

The first verified contacts between Europe and America came when the **Norse** colonized Greenland in the 980s. The Norse traded with the Aleuts for furs and walrus ivory. In 1001 Leif Ericson led a group of Norse who planted a small settlement in **Vinland,** now known as Newfoundland. However, the Norse quickly settled into a pattern of hostility with local Indians. By 1015 the Norse had abandoned their Vinland settlement, although the Greenland settlements endured almost until the end of the fifteenth century; Europeans would later reap, at the expense of the native peoples, the fruits of a "new world."

Norse Also known as Vikings, a warrior culture from Scandinavia

Vinland Site of first known attempt at European settlement in the Americas

CHECKING IN

- Powerful states, such as the Maya, Aztec, and Inca empires, developed in Mesoamerica and Peru.
- Pueblo society, featuring sophisticated agriculture and irrigation, developed in the Southwest.
- The Eastern Woodlands saw an increase of mound builders in Mississippian centers such as Cahokia.
- Along the Pacific coast, nonfarming societies flourished.

NORTH AMERICAN PEOPLES ON THE EVE OF EUROPEAN CONTACT

What common values did Native Americans share despite their vast diversity?

In 1492 the Western Hemisphere numbered about 75 million people, clustered thickly in Mexico and Central America, the Caribbean islands, and Peru. Between 7 and 10 million Native Americans lived north of Mexico. Sparse nomad populations inhabited the Great Basin, the high plains, and the northern forests. Denser concentrations, however, thrived along the Pacific coast, in the Southwest and Southeast, in the Mississippi Valley, and along the Atlantic coast. Speaking many diverse languages and dialects, these people constituted several hundred Indian nations and tribes.

Despite the vast diversity of Native American cultures, they shared many characteristics. Kinship, reciprocity, and communal control of resources lay at the base of Indian societies, while trade ensured that the bow and arrow, ceramic pottery, and certain religious practices existed in almost all Indian societies.

Kinship and Gender

Kinship and gender cemented societies north of Mesoamerica together. Ties to cousins, aunts, and uncles created complex patterns of social obligation.

Kinship bonds were more important in Indian society than the bonds within **nuclear families,** that is, among married couples and their children. Indians did not necessarily expect spouses to be bound together forever, but kinship lasted for

nuclear families Married couples and their children

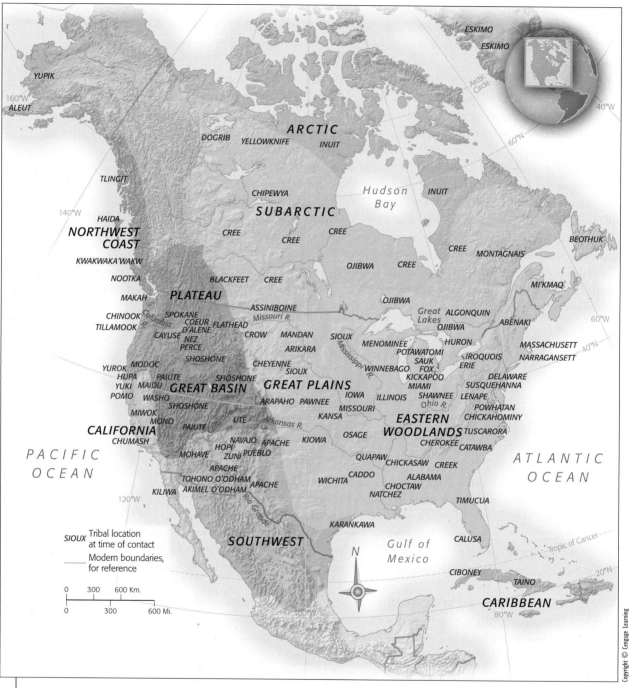

Map 1.2 Locations of Selected Native American Peoples, 1500 C.E.

Today's Indian nations were well established in homelands across the continent when Europeans first arrived. Many would combine with others or move in later centuries, either voluntarily or because they were forced.

Interactive Map

life. Customs regulating marriage varied, but strict rules prevailed. In most cultures young people married in their teens, generally after a period of sexual experimentation. Strong ties of residence and deference bound each couple to one or both sets of parents, producing what social scientists call **extended families.**

In some Native American societies such as the Iroquois, the extended families of women took precedence over those of men. A new husband moved in with his wife's extended family. The mother's oldest brother was the primary male authority figure in a child's life. In many ways, a husband and father was simply the guest of his wife's family. Other Indian societies recognized men's extended families as primary, while still others did not distinguish sharply between the status of male and female family lines.

extended families Families that consist of several generations living together

In addition, kinship was the basis for armed conflict. Indian societies typically considered homicide a matter to be resolved by the extended families of the victim and the perpetrator. If the perpetrator's family offered a gift that the victim's family considered appropriate, the question was settled. If not, the victim's kin might avenge the killing by armed retaliation. Chiefs or other leaders intervened to resolve disputes within the same village or tribe, but disputes between members of different groups could escalate into war. Densely populated societies that competed for scarce resources, as on the California coast, and centralized societies that attempted to dominate trade networks through coercion, such as the Hopewell culture, experienced frequent and intense warfare. However, warfare remained a low-level affair in most of North America. An exasperated New England officer, writing of his efforts to win Indian allies in the early seventeenth century, described a battle between two Indian groups as "more for pastime than to conquer and subdue enemies." He concluded that "they might fight seven years and not kill seven men."

Among almost all agricultural Indians except those in the Southwest (where men and women shared the work), women did most of the cultivating. With women producing most of the food supply, some communities gave women more power than European societies did. Among the Iroquois of what today is upstate New York, for example, women collectively owned the fields, distributed food, and played a major role in selecting chiefs. In New England, women often served as *sachems*, or chiefs.

Courtesy Milne/Photographer's Choice/Getty Images

Big Horn Medicine Wheel, Wyoming
The medicine wheel was constructed between three and eight centuries ago as a center for religious ceremonies, including those relating to the summer solstice.

Manitou Powerful spiritual force that Algonquian-speaking Indians believed pervaded all of nature; other Native American languages had comparable terms

Spiritual and Social Values

Native American religions revolved around the conviction that nature was alive, pulsating with spiritual power—**Manitou** (MAN-ih-too) in the Algonquian language. A mysterious, awe-inspiring force that affected human life for both good and evil, such power united all nature in an unbroken web. Belief in supernatural power led most Indians to seek constantly to conciliate all the spiritual forces in nature: living things, rocks, water, the sun and moon, even ghosts and witches.

Native Americans had several ways of gaining access to spiritual power. One was dreaming; most Native Americans took seriously the visions that came to them in sleep. They also sought access to the supernatural by using physical ordeals to alter their consciousness. Young men gained recognition as adults through a vision quest—a solitary venture that entailed fasting and waiting for the appearance of a spirit that would endow them with special powers. Girls went through comparable rituals at the onset of menstruation, to initiate them into the spiritual world from which female reproductive power flowed. Entire communities often engaged in collective power-seeking rituals, such as the Sun Dance (see Chapter 17).

Native Americans reinforced cooperation with a strong sense of order. Custom, the demands of social conformity, and the rigors of nature strictly regulated life and people's everyday affairs. Revenge was a ritualized way of restoring order. Failure to restore order could bring ominous consequences—blind hatred, unending violence, and, most feared of all, witchcraft. Indians would share this dread with both the Europeans and the Africans they would encounter after 1492.

The principle of reciprocity remained strong. Although it involved mutual give-and-take, the purpose of reciprocity was not equality, but the maintenance of equilibrium and interdependence among individuals of unequal power and prestige.

Most leaders' authority depended on the obligations they bestowed, rather than on coercion. The distribution of gifts obligated members of the community to support them and to accept their authority. In the same way, powerful communities distributed gifts to weaker neighbors who reciprocated with tribute in the form of material goods and submission.

CHECKING IN

- Kinship ties bound virtually all Native Americans.
- In most Native American societies, gender roles were clear: women farmed and men hunted.
- Native Americans lived in a world permeated by spiritual power that they could tap into through various rituals.
- Indian societies generally demanded cooperation and order from their members.
- Reciprocity dominated political and social relationships among individuals and between leaders and their followers.

Chapter Summary

How did environmental change shape the transition from Paleo-Indian to Archaic ways of life? (page 2)

Ancestors of most Native Americans reached North America from around 33,000 to 10,500 B.C.E., during an Ice Age when Asia and North America were directly connected. Warming weather facilitated the spread of these Paleo-Indians and granted them access to a wide range of food sources that could support large populations. Climate change also contributed to the extinction of many of the large animals that might have threatened early Americans.

KEY TERMS

Monte Verde, Chile *(p. 2)*
Bering land bridge *(p. 2)*
Paleo-Indians *(p. 2)*
reciprocity *(p. 2)*

What were the principal differences among the Native American cultures that emerged after 2500 B.C.E.? (page 5)

From 2500 B.C.E. to 1500 C.E. diverse Native American societies based on agriculture proliferated and adapted to widely varying environments. Among the most prominent were the centralized Mesoamerican societies, such as the Maya and the Aztec; the Inca of the Peruvian Andes; the Pueblo societies of what is now the southwestern United States; and the Eastern Woodlands mound builders of Hopewell, Adena, and Cahokia. Nonfarming societies like those of the Pacific Northwest also prospered. The vast grasslands of the Great Plains were home to nomadic hunters dependent on the great buffalo herds.

What common values did Native Americans share despite their vast diversity? (page 11)

Despite their diversity, the majority of these societies shared several common characteristics. In most, kinship played a critical social and political role, with extended families assuming greater importance than nuclear families. Gender also played a major role in organizing most societies, with women doing the farming and men primarily hunting. Indians believed that nature was spiritual as well as physical and sought to live in accord with the supernatural. Most people sought orderly societies and relied on reciprocity to maintain stability.

Native Americans never saw themselves as a single people. It was Europeans who emphasized differences between themselves and the Indians, a name bestowed by Christopher Columbus, who thought he had landed in the Indies. This new America, in which people were categorized according to continental ancestry, was radically different from the one that flourished for thousands of years before 1492.

KEY TERMS continued

Archaic peoples *(p. 2)*

Mesoamerica *(p. 5)*

Hohokam *(p. 7)*

Anasazi *(p. 7)*

kivas *(p. 7)*

Chaco Canyon *(p. 7)*

mound-building culture *(p. 8)*

Cahokia *(p. 9)*

Norse *(p. 11)*

Vinland *(p. 11)*

nuclear families *(p. 11)*

extended families *(p. 13)*

Manitou *(p. 14)*

CourseMate

Go to the CourseMate website at **www.cengagebrain.com** for additional study tools and review materials—including audio and video clips—for this chapter.

CHAPTER 2

The Rise of the Atlantic World

1400–1625

CHAPTER PREVIEW

African and European Backgrounds
What major changes were reshaping the African and European worlds in the fifteenth and sixteenth centuries?

Europe and the Atlantic World, 1440–1600
What was the Atlantic world, and how did it emerge?

Footholds in North America, 1512–1625
How did European exploration, conquest, and colonization of North America begin?

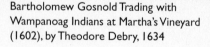

Bartholomew Gosnold Trading with Wampanoag Indians at Martha's Vineyard (1602), by Theodore Debry, 1634

Courtesy of the John Carter Brown Library at Brown University

At ten o'clock on a moonlit night the tense crew spotted a glimmering light. At two o'clock the next morning came the shout "Land! Land!" It was October 12, 1492. At daybreak Christopher Columbus went ashore, the royal standard of Spain fluttering, knelt to give thanks, and rose to claim for Spain the island that he named San Salvador.

Columbus's meeting with the Tainos marked the first step in the formation of an Atlantic world. After 1492, peoples from Europe, Africa, and North and South America became intertwined in elaborate webs of trade, colonization, religion, and war. These interchanges constantly challenged customary ways of thinking and acting. They also led to far-reaching environmental changes, as not only people but also plants, animals, and germs crossed the Atlantic in both directions, a process known as the "Columbian exchange." European nations sought to increase their wealth and power by conquering and exploiting the inhabitants of the Americas, whom they deemed uncivilized.

In much of what is now Latin America, the arrival of the Europeans led to conquest. In the future United States and Canada, however, European mastery came more slowly; more than one hundred years would pass before self-sustaining colonies were established there.

■ AFRICAN AND EUROPEAN BACKGROUNDS

What major changes were reshaping the African and European worlds in the fifteenth and sixteenth centuries?

When the Atlantic world emerged in the fifteenth and sixteenth centuries, enormous changes were engulfing the Atlantic basin. In the Americas, some societies rose, others fell, and still others adapted to the new circumstances (see Chapter 1). In both West Africa and western Europe, a market society emerged, and wealthy merchants financed dynastic rulers trying to extend their domains.

Western Europe's transformation was thoroughgoing. Its population nearly doubled, wealth and power changed hands, and new modes of thought and spirituality challenged established systems. Social, political, and religious upheaval accompanied a brilliant explosion of creativity and innovation.

West Africa: Tradition and Change

Before the beginning of Atlantic travel, the only link between sub-Saharan Africa and the Mediterranean was a broad belt of grassland, or **savannah,** which separated the desert from the forests to the south. Here caravan trade stimulated the rise of kingdoms and empires whose size and wealth rivaled those of any in Europe.

savannah Rich grasslands where West African civilizations prospered

The richest grassland kingdoms rose in West Africa, with its ample stores of gold. Chief among these in the fifteenth century was Mali, whose Muslim rulers enjoyed access to a network of wealthy Muslim rulers and merchants. Mali's wealth rested on the careful cultivation of trade, dominated by gold and slaves, and its fame extended throughout Africa, Europe, and the Middle East.

Gold had recently become the standard for all European currencies, and demand for the precious metal soared. Thousands of newcomers flooded into the region later known as the Gold Coast, and new states emerged to claim their share of the gold trade.

To the south of the savannah empires lay a region of small states and chiefdoms. During the first millennium C.E., Islamic states arose in Senegambia (seh-nuh-GAM-bee-ah), at Africa's westernmost bulge, and in Guinea's (GINN-ee) coastal forests. The best-known state was Benin (BEH-nin), where artisans fashioned magnificent ironwork for centuries.

Near the Congo River still farther south, four major kingdoms had arisen by the fifteenth century. The most powerful of these kingdoms was Kongo.

West African leaders wielded sharply different amounts and kinds of political power. Grassland emperors claimed semigodlike status, whereas rulers of smaller kingdoms depended on their ability to persuade, to conform to custom, and

Sankore Mosque, Timbuktu, Mali
Sankore was one of three great mosques built during the fourteenth century when Timbuktu became the center of Islamic worship and learning in West Africa.

Jenny Pate/Robert Harding World Imagery/Corbis

sometimes to redistribute wealth justly among their people.

In West Africa, kinship groups knit societies together. Parents, aunts, uncles, distant cousins, and those who shared clan ties formed networks of mutual obligation. In centuries to come, the tradition of strong extended families would help enslaved Africans to endure the breakup of nuclear families by sale. The region's high mortality rate from famine and tropical disease epidemics was a driving force behind marriage. Children were an essential part of the labor force, contributing to a family's wealth by increasing its food production and the amount of land it cultivated. Men of means frequently married more than one wife in order to produce more children; women generally married soon after puberty.

Both men and women farmed. Vast amounts of land and a relatively sparse population enabled African farmers to shift their fields periodically and thus maintain high soil quality and productivity. In areas of coastal rain forest, food crops such as yams, sugar cane, bananas, and eggplant flourished; so, too, did cotton. On the grasslands, cattle raising and fishing complemented the cultivation of millet, sorghum, and rice.

By the fifteenth century the market economy took in many small farmers, who traded surplus crops for other food and cloth. Artisans wove cotton or raffia palm leaves, made clothing and jewelry, and crafted tools and religious objects.

Religion permeated African life. People believed that another world lay beyond the one they perceived through their five senses, a world to which the souls of most people passed at death. Deities spoke to mortals through a variety of means, including priests, dreams, "speaking shrines," and magical charms. West African religions emphasized the importance of continuous revelations; consequently, there was no fixed dogma or hierarchy like those that characterized both Islam and Christianity. African religion also emphasized ancestor worship, venerating ancestors as spiritual guardians. Religious motifs saturated African art. West Africans used their ivory, cast-iron, and wood sculptures in ceremonies reenacting creation myths and honoring spirits. A strong moralistic streak ran through African folktales. Oral reciters transmitted these stories in dramatic public presentations with ritual masks, dance, and music of complex rhythmic structure. West African art and music powerfully influenced twentieth-century art and jazz.

Chronology

c. 1400–1600	European Renaissance
c. 1400–1600	Coastal West African kingdoms rise and expand
1440	Portuguese slave trade in West Africa begins
1488	Bartolomeu Días reaches the Cape of Good Hope
1492	Christian "reconquest" of Spain; Columbus lands at San Salvador
1498	Vasco da Gama rounds the Cape of Good Hope and reaches India
1517	Protestant Reformation begins in Germany
1519–1521	Hernán Cortés leads conquest of the Aztec empire
1519–1522	Magellan's expedition circumnavigates the globe
1532–1536	Spanish conquest of Inca empire
1534	Church of England breaks from the Roman Catholic church
1539–1543	De Soto attempts conquests in southeastern America
1541–1542	Cartier attempts to colonize eastern Canada
1558	Elizabeth I becomes queen of England
1565	St. Augustine founded by Spanish
1585–1590	English colony of Roanoke established, then disappears
1588	England defeats the Spanish Armada
1598	Oñate founds New Mexico
1603	James I becomes king of England
1607	English found colonies at Jamestown and Sagadahoc
1608	Champlain founds New France
1609	Henry Hudson explores the Hudson River
1610–1614	First Anglo-Powhatan War
1614	New Netherlands colony founded
1619	Large exports of tobacco from Virginia begin; House of Burgesses, first elected assembly in English North America, established in Virginia; first Africans arrive in Virginia
1620	Plymouth colony founded
1622–1632	Second Anglo-Powhatan War
1624	James I revokes Virginia Company's charter

Among Africans, Islam appealed primarily to merchants trading with Muslim North Africa and to grassland rulers eager to consolidate their power. By 1400, Islam had just begun to affect the daily lives of grassland cultivators and artisans.

European Culture and Society

When Columbus reached the Americas in 1492, Europe was approaching the height of a cultural revival known as the **Renaissance,** a rebirth of classical Greek and Roman culture. Intellectuals and poets believed that their age marked a return to the ideals

Renaissance "Rebirth" of classical Greek and Roman culture that swept Europe from the fifteenth to the seventeenth century

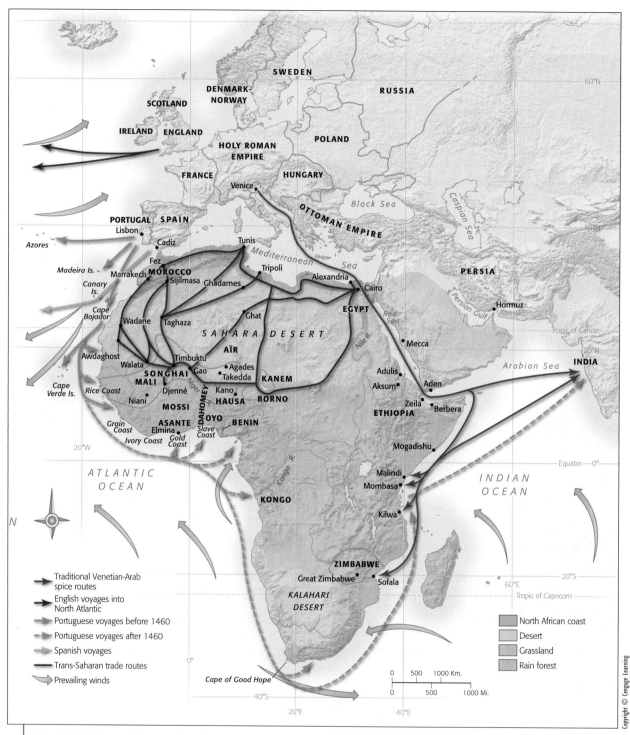

Map 2.1 Europe, Africa, and Southwestern Asia in 1500

During the fifteenth century, Portuguese voyages established maritime trade links between Africa and Europe, circumventing older trans-Saharan routes. Several voyages near the end of the century extended Europe's reach to India and the Americas.

Interactive Map

of the ancient Greeks and Romans. The writings of Muslim, Eastern Orthodox, and Jewish scholars provided a treasure trove of ancient texts in philosophy, science, medicine, geography, and other subjects. Scholars strove to reconcile Christian faith and ancient philosophy, to explore the mysteries of nature, to map the world, and to explain the motions of the heavens. Renaissance painters and sculptors created works based on close observations of nature and attention to perspective.

At the same time, European society quivered with tension. The era's artistic and intellectual creativity stemmed partly from intense social and spiritual stress, as Europeans groped for stability by glorifying order, hierarchy, and beauty. A concern for power and rank, or "degree," dominated European life in the fifteenth and sixteenth centuries. Gender, wealth, inherited position, and political power affected every European's status, and few people lived beyond the reach of some political authority's claim to tax and rule. But this order was shaky. Conflicts between states, between religions, and between rich and poor threatened the balance, making Europeans cling all the more eagerly to order and hierarchy.

Change lay at the heart of these conflicts. By the end of the fifteenth century, strong national monarchs in France and England had unified their realms and reduced the power of both the nobility and the Catholic church. On the Iberian Peninsula, the marriage of King Ferdinand of Aragon and Queen Isabella had created the Spanish monarchy and a unified Spain.

Between 70 and 80 percent of Europeans were peasants. Taxes, rents, and other dues to landlords and church officials were heavy. Poor harvests or war drove even well-to-do peasants to starvation.

By 1600 dramatic growth was driving up the population to 100 million. Food supplies, however, did not rise as rapidly. Peasant families survived on pitifully low yields of wheat, barley, and oats. Plowing, sowing, and harvesting together, they also grazed livestock on jointly owned "commons." But with new land at a premium, landlords, especially the English gentry, began to "enclose" the commons, thus making them private property. Peasants with no *written* title to their lands were particularly vulnerable.

Environmental factors worsened peasants' circumstances. A "little Ice Age" began in the fifteenth century and lasted more than four centuries, drastically reducing the food supply. Hunger and malnutrition were widespread, and full-scale famine struck in some areas. Population growth led to increased demand for wood and thus to deforestation of large areas; the subsequent disappearance of wild foods and game accelerated the exodus of rural Europeans to towns and cities.

Although numerous, European towns usually contained only a few thousand inhabitants. London, a great metropolis of 200,000 people by 1600, was an exception. Large or small, towns were dirty and disease ridden, and townspeople lived closely packed with their neighbors. People of the times saw towns as centers of opportunity, and immigration from the countryside swelled urban populations.

The consequences of rapid population growth were particularly acute in England, where the population doubled from 2.5 million in 1500 to 5 million by 1620. Some members of the gentry grew rich selling wool; however, because of technological stagnation, per capita output and household income among textile workers fell. In effect, more workers competed for fewer jobs as European markets for English cloth diminished and as food prices rose. Land **enclosure** aggravated

enclosure English practice of fencing off what had been common grazing land; left many peasants impoverished

unemployment; large numbers of unemployed workers and displaced farmers wandered the countryside, seeming to threaten law and order. A handful of English writers began to speculate that overseas colonies could serve in effect as a safety valve.

As in the New World and Africa, traditional society in Europe rested on long-term, reciprocal relationships. Reciprocity required the upper classes to act with self-restraint and dignity, and the lower classes to show deference to their "betters." It demanded strict economic regulation, too, to ensure that sellers charged a "just" price—one that covered costs and allowed the seller to profit but barred him from taking advantage of buyers' and borrowers' misfortunes or of shortages to make "excessive" profits.

Yet the ideals of traditional economic behavior had been withering for centuries. By the sixteenth century, nothing could stop the practices of charging interest on borrowed money and of increasing prices in response to demand. New forms of business organization, such as the **joint-stock company,** the ancestor of the modern corporation, steadily spread. Demand for capital investment grew, and so too did the supply of accumulated wealth. Gradually, a new economic outlook arose that justified the unimpeded acquisition of wealth and unregulated economic competition. Its adherents insisted that individuals owed one another only the money necessary to settle each market transaction. This "market economy" capitalism stood counter to traditional demands for the strict regulation of economic activity to ensure social reciprocity and to maintain "just prices."

joint-stock company Forerunner of modern corporation; way to raise large sums of money by selling shares in an enterprise

Sixteenth- and seventeenth-century Europeans were ambivalent about economic enterprise and social change. A restless desire for opportunity kept life simmering with competitive tension. However, even those who prospered still sought the security and prestige of traditional social distinctions, and the poor longed for the age-old values that they hoped would restrain irresponsible greed.

Fundamental change in European society could also be seen in the rising importance of the nuclear family. Each member of the family—father, mother, children—had specific roles. The father exercised supreme authority; the wife bore and reared children, and assisted her husband in the unending labor of providing for the family's subsistence. Children were laborers from an early age. The family was thus the principal economic unit in European society and the household, the primary social organization. Those who lived outside a household were viewed with extreme suspicion and became easy targets for accusations of theft or even witchcraft.

Europeans frequently characterized the nuclear family as a "little commonwealth." A father's authority over his family supposedly mirrored God's rule of Creation and the king's over his subjects. According to a German writer, "wives should obey their husbands and not seek to dominate them. . . . Husbands . . . should treat their wives with consideration and occasionally close an eye to their faults." Repeated male complaints about "wives who think themselves every way as good as their husbands" suggest that male domination had its limits.

Religious Upheavals

Although predominantly Christian by 1400, Europe was also home to significant numbers of Muslims and Jews.

Although Jewish and Muslim European minorities shared Christians' worship of a single supreme being, based on the God of the Old

Testament, hatred and violence often marred their shared history. For more than three centuries, European Christians had conducted Crusades against Muslims in the Middle East; each side saw the conflict as "holy war" or "jihad" and labeled the other "infidel." Ultimately, ambitious rulers transformed religious conflicts into wars of conquest. At the same time as the Catholic empires of Spain and Portugal drove Muslims from their territory, the Islamic Ottoman empire conquered much of the Balkans and menaced Central Europe. In 1492, the Spanish completed the "reconquest" of the Iberian Peninsula from Muslims and forced Jews to convert or leave.

The medieval Christian church taught that Christ had founded the church to save sinners from hell. Every time a priest said Mass, Christ's sacrifice was repeated, and divine grace flowed to sinners through sacraments that priests alone could administer—especially baptism, confession, and communion. In most of Europe the "church" was a network of clergymen set apart from laypeople by ordination into the priesthood and by the fact that they did not marry. The pope, the "vicar (representative) of Christ," topped this hierarchy.

The papacy wielded awesome spiritual power. Fifteenth- and sixteenth-century popes claimed the authority to dispense extra blessings, or "indulgences," to repentant sinners in return for "good works," such as donating money to the church. Indulgences also promised time off from future punishment in purgatory. Given people's anxieties over sin, indulgences were enormously popular.

However, the sale of indulgences provoked charges of materialism and corruption. In 1517 Martin Luther, a German friar, attacked the practice. When the papacy tried to silence him, Luther broadened his criticism to include the Mass, priests, and the pope. His revolt sparked the **Protestant Reformation,** which changed Christianity forever.

Protestant Reformation Split of reformers from Roman Catholic church; triggered by Martin Luther

To Luther, the selling of indulgences was evil not only because it bilked people but also because the church did harm by falsely assuring people that they could "earn" salvation by doing good works. Luther believed instead that God alone chose whom to save and that believers should trust only God's love, not the word of priests and the pope. Luther's own spiritual struggle and experience of being "reborn" constituted a classic conversion experience—the heart of Protestant religion as it would be preached and practiced for centuries in England and North America.

Later reformers also abandoned Catholicism. For example, the French theologian **John Calvin** insisted on the doctrine of predestination, in which an omnipotent God "predestined" most sinful humans to hell, saving only a few to exemplify his grace.

John Calvin Early Protestant theologian who believed in "predestination"

Despite their differences, Protestants shared much common ground. Reading the Bible became an essential element of faith; translations into living languages made the Bible accessible, and the newly invented printing press allowed for wide circulation. Protestantism thus fostered education. Protestants also rejected the idea that priests had special powers; each individual had to assume responsibility for his or her own spiritual and moral condition. Finally, many Protestants felt displaced by the rapidly changing European world and yearned for greater simplicity. Thus, Protestantism condemned the replacement of traditional reciprocity by marketplace values.

Challenged by the rise of Protestantism, the Catholic church displayed remarkable resilience. Indeed, the papacy vigorously attacked church corruption and combated Protestant viewpoints. This Catholic revival, known as the Counter-Reformation, created the modern Roman Catholic church.

The Reformation also split Europe geographically. Many northern and western European areas, including England, most of the German states, the Netherlands, and parts of France, became predominantly Protestant; most southern European states—Portugal, Spain, and Italy—and most of France remained Roman Catholic.

The Reformation in England, 1533–1625

England's Reformation began when King Henry VIII, anxious for a male heir, tried to annul his marriage to Catherine of Aragon. When the pope refused to do so, Henry persuaded Parliament to annul the marriage and then to proclaim him "supreme head" of the Church of England (the Anglican church).

Religious strife troubled England for over a century after Henry's break with Rome. Under his son Edward VI (ruled 1547–1553), however, the English church veered sharply toward Protestantism. Then Henry's daughter Mary assumed the throne in 1553 and tried to restore Catholicism, in part by burning several hundred Protestants at the stake.

The reign of Mary's successor, Elizabeth I, who became queen in 1558, marked a crucial watershed. Most English people were now Protestant; *how* Protestant was the question. A militant Calvinist minority, the **Puritans,** demanded wholesale "purification" of the Church of England from "popish abuses." As Calvinists, they affirmed salvation by predestination, denied Christ's presence in the Eucharist, and believed that a learned sermon was the heart of true worship. They wished to free each congregation from outside interference and encouraged lay members to participate in parish affairs.

Puritans English followers of Calvin, dissenters from established Church of England

Puritanism appealed mainly to the growing middle sectors of English society—the gentry, university-educated clergymen and intellectuals, merchants, shopkeepers, artisans, and well-to-do farmers. Self-discipline had become central to both the worldly and the spiritual dimensions of these people's lives, and from their ranks would come the settlers of New England (see Chapter 3). Puritanism attracted few of the titled nobility, who enjoyed their wealth and privilege, and few of the desperately poor who struggled for mere survival.

Queen Elizabeth distrusted Puritan militancy until the pope declared her a heretic in 1570 and urged Catholics to overthrow her. By courting influential Puritans and embracing militant anti-Catholicism, Elizabeth maintained most Puritans' loyalty. After her death, however, religious tensions came to a boil.

Under Elizabeth, most Puritans expected to transform the Church of England into independent congregations of "saints." However, Stuart monarchs James I (ruled 1603–1625) and Charles I (ruled 1625–1649) bitterly opposed Puritan efforts to eliminate the office of bishop. Nonetheless, they quietly tolerated Calvinists who did not dissent loudly.

CHECKING IN

- In the fifteenth century the West African savannah fragmented politically, and Islam gained a foothold.
- From the fourteenth to seventeenth centuries, Europe was undergoing major changes. The Renaissance, the rise of nation-states, population growth, the emergence of a market economy, and the Reformation set the stage for territorial expansion and conflict.
- In the throes of religious transformation, Reformation England saw the rise of Puritanism.

EUROPE AND THE ATLANTIC WORLD, 1440–1600

What was the Atlantic world, and how did it emerge?

The forces transforming Europe reverberated beyond that continent. In the fifteenth and sixteenth centuries, monarchs and merchants organized imperial ventures to Africa, Asia, and the Americas. Europeans proclaimed that their mission was to introduce Christianity and "civilizations" to the "savages" and "pagans" in alien lands—and to increase their own fortunes and power. Both the transatlantic slave trade and the colonization of the Americas grew out of this new imperialism, and the cascading exchanges that resulted created a new Atlantic world.

Portugal and the Atlantic, 1440–1600

Merchants realized that they could increase their profits by trading directly with Asia and Africa. Leading the shift from a Mediterranean to an Atlantic world was Portugal.

Improved maritime technology permitted this European expansion. In the early fifteenth century, shipbuilders added the triangular Arab sail to their heavy cargo ships, creating a highly maneuverable ship, the caravel, to sail the stormy Atlantic. Further, the growing use of the compass and astrolabe permitted mariners to calculate their bearings on the open sea. Hand in hand with the technological advances of this "maritime revolution," Renaissance scholars corrected ancient geographical data and drew increasingly accurate maps.

Led by **Prince Henry "the Navigator,"** Portugal was first to capitalize on these developments. Henry encouraged Portuguese seamen to pilot their caravels farther down the African coast searching for weak spots in Muslim defenses and for trade opportunities. By the time of Henry's death, the Portuguese had built a profitable slaving station at Arguin; shortly afterward, they had penetrated south of the equator. In 1488 Bartolomeu Días reached Africa's southern tip, the Cape of Good Hope, opening the possibility of direct trade with India, and in 1498 Vasco da Gama led a Portuguese fleet around the cape and on to India. For more than a century the Portuguese remained an imperial presence in the Indian Ocean and the East Indies (modern Indonesia). Far more significantly, they brought Europeans face to face with black Africans and an already flourishing slave trade.

Prince Henry "the Navigator"
Member of Portuguese royal family who encouraged exploration of Africa and searched for routes to Asia

The "New Slavery" and Racism

Slavery was well established in fifteenth-century West Africa, as elsewhere. The grassland emperors as well as individual families depended on slave labor. However, most slaves or their children were absorbed into African families over time. In contrast, first Arabs, and then Europeans, turned African slavery into an intercontinental business.

In 1482, the Portuguese built an outpost, Elmina, on West Africa's Gold Coast, but they continued to rely primarily on African-controlled commercial networks. The local African kingdoms were too strong for the Portuguese to attack, and black rulers traded—or chose not to trade—according to their own self-interest.

© Trustees of the British Museum

**African View
of Portuguese,
ca. 1650–1700**

A carver in the kingdom
of Benin, on Africa's
west coast, created this
salt holder depicting
Portuguese officials
and their ship.

"new slavery" Harsh form
of slavery based on racism; arose
as a result of Portuguese slave
trade with Africa

Treaty of Tordesillas
Agreement in which Portugal
and Spain divided between
them all future discoveries in
the non-Christian world

The coming of the Portuguese slavers changed West African societies. Small kingdoms in Guinea and Senegambia expanded to "service" the trade, and some of their rulers became rich. Farther south, in modern Angola, the kings of Kongo used the slave trade to consolidate their power and adopted Christianity.

Europeans had used slaves since ancient Greece and Rome, but ominous changes took place once the Portuguese began making voyages to Africa. The **"new slavery"** was a high-volume business that expanded at a steady rate as Europeans colonized the Western Hemisphere and established plantation societies there. The "new slavery" had two devastating consequences. First, it became a demographic catastrophe for West Africa and its peoples. Before the Atlantic slave trade ended in the nineteenth century, nearly 12 million Africans would be shipped across the sea. Slavery on this scale had been unknown since the Roman Empire. Second, African slaves were subjected to new extremes of dehumanization. In medieval Europe, slaves had primarily performed domestic service, but by 1450 the Portuguese and Spanish had created large slave-labor plantations on their Atlantic and Mediterranean islands. Using African slaves who toiled until death, these plantations produced sugar for European markets. Enslaved Africans became property rather than persons of low status, consigned to endless, exhausting, mindless labor. By 1600 the "new slavery" had become a brutal link in an expanding commerce that ultimately would encompass all major Western nations.

Finally, race became the ideological basis of the "new slavery." Africans' blackness and alien religion dehumanized them in European eyes. As racial prejudice hardened, Europeans found it easy to justify black slavery. European Christianity, moreover, made few attempts to soften slavery's rigors. Because the victims of the "new slavery" were physically distinctive and culturally alien, slavery became a lifelong, hereditary, and despised status.

To America and Beyond, 1492–1541

The fascinating, contradictory figure of Christopher Columbus (1451–1506) embodied Europeans' varied motives for expansion. The son of an Italian weaver, Columbus became obsessed by the idea that Europeans could reach Asia by sailing westward across the Atlantic. Combining an overestimation of Asia's eastward thrust with an underestimation of Earth's circumference, he concluded that the world was much smaller than it actually is and that the open-sea distance from Europe to Asia was roughly three thousand miles, not the actual twelve thousand miles. Religious fervor led Columbus to dream of carrying Christianity around the globe, but he also hungered for wealth and glory.

Europeans had ventured far into the Atlantic before Columbus: besides the early Norse, fifteenth-century English fishing boats may have reached North America's coast. What distinguished Columbus was his persistence in hawking his "enterprise of the Indies" around Europe's royal courts. In 1492 the rulers of newly united Spain, Isabella of Castile and Ferdinand of Aragon, accepted Columbus's offer, hoping to break a threatened Portuguese monopoly on Asian trade. Picking up the westerly trade winds, Columbus's three small ships made landfall within a month off the North American coast at a small island that he named San Salvador.

Word of Columbus's discovery fired Europeans' imagination. It also induced the Spanish and Portuguese to sign the **Treaty of Tordesillas** (tore-day-SEE-yuss)

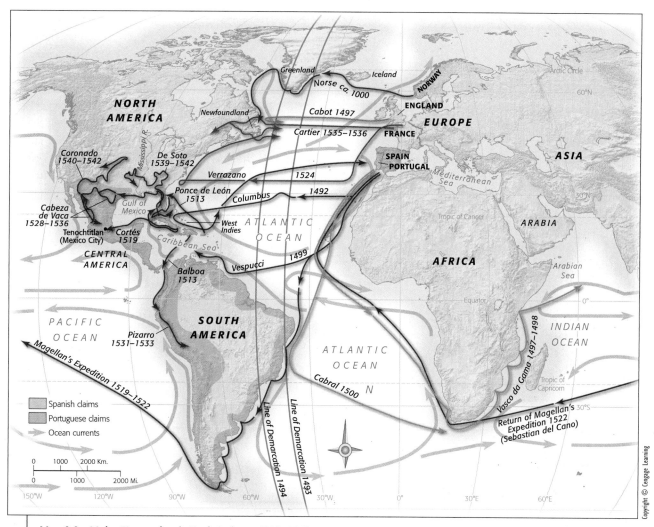

Map 2.2   Major Transatlantic Explorations, 1000–1542

Following Columbus's 1492 voyage, Spain's rivals began laying claim to parts of the New World based on the voyages of Cabot for England, Cabral for Portugal, and Verrazano for France.

Interactive Map

in 1494, dividing all future discoveries between themselves. Columbus made three further voyages, in the course of which he established Spanish colonies but never fulfilled his promise of reaching Asia. In 1506 he died a bitter man, convinced that he had been cheated of his rightful rewards. Meanwhile, England's Henry VII (ruled 1485–1509) ignored the Treaty of Tordesillas and sent an Italian navigator known as **John Cabot** westward across the northern Atlantic in 1497. Cabot claimed Nova Scotia, Newfoundland, and the rich Grand Banks fisheries for England, but he vanished at sea on a second voyage. Eighty years would pass before England capitalized on Cabot's voyage.

The more Europeans explored, the more apparent it became that a vast land-mass blocked the western route to Asia. In 1500 the Portuguese claimed Brazil, and

John Cabot Italian explorer who established English claims to the New World

uanen delantera Ce enpecaron adenostar conpala
Gras muy feas, diciendole que sera muger delos espa
ñoles y que combidal sehauiaconfederado y concierto

En tanto aprieto como los españoles, y despues fue
ron los q lleuaron la peor parte pues muy pocos dellos
boluieron a tlaxcala como adelante dire mas

Spanish Conquistadors vs. Aztec Defenders
After the Spanish conquest, a Mexica (Aztec) artist recalled this moment before the disastrous smallpox epidemic destroyed the Indians' ability to resist.

other voyages outlined a continuous coastline from the Caribbean to Brazil. In 1507 a publisher brought out a collection of voyagers' tales, including one from the Italian Amerigo Vespucci (ves-POO-chee). A shrewd marketer, the publisher devised a catchy name for the new continent: America.

Getting past America to Asia remained the early explorers' goal. In 1513 the Spaniard Vasco Núñez de Balboa crossed the narrow Isthmus of Panama and chanced upon the Pacific Ocean. In 1519 the Portuguese mariner Ferdinand Magellan, sailing under the Castilian flag, began a voyage around the world through the stormy straits at South America's southern tip, now named the Straits of Magellan. He crossed the Pacific to the Philippines, only to die fighting with natives. One of his five ships and fifteen emaciated sailors returned to Spain in 1522, the first people to have sailed around the world.

Spain's Conquistadors, 1492–1526

Columbus was America's first slave trader and the first Spanish *conquistador* (cone-KEES-ta-dohr), or conqueror. On Hispaniola he enslaved native people and created *encomiendas* (en-cohmee-EN-dahs), grants for both land and the labor of the Indians who lived on it. He also ignited the New World's first gold rush. Indians were forced to hunt for gold and to supply the Spanish with food. The gold rush quickly spilled from Hispaniola to Puerto Rico, Jamaica, and Cuba.

As disease, overwork, and malnutrition killed thousands of Indians, Portuguese slave traders supplied shiploads of Africans to replace them. Although shocked Spanish friars sent to convert the Native Americans reported the Indians' exploitation, and King Ferdinand attempted to forbid the practice, no one worried about African slaves' fate. Missionaries joined most other colonizers in condemning Africans as less than fully human and thus beyond hope of redemption. Blacks could therefore be exploited mercilessly.

Spanish settlers were soon fanning out across the Caribbean in pursuit of slaves and gold. In 1519 the young nobleman **Hernán Cortés** (core-TEZ) (1485–1547) led a small band of Spaniards to the Mexican coast. Destroying his boats and enlisting Indian allies, he marched inland to conquer Mexico.

Hernán Cortés Spanish conqueror of Aztec empire

Upon reaching the Aztec capital of Tenochtitlán (see Chapter 1), the Spanish were stunned by its size and wealth. The Spanish raided the imperial palace and treasury, melting down all the gold they could find. But the Aztecs regrouped and recaptured the city. Then an epidemic of smallpox, which the Aztecs and other Indians were ill equipped to resist, plus reinforcements from Cuba, enabled Cortés to defeat the Aztecs. By 1521 the Spanish had begun to build Mexico City on the ruins of Tenochtitlán. Within twenty years, Central America lay at the Spaniards' feet. Thus was New Spain born.

Over the remainder of the sixteenth century, conquistadors and officials established a great Spanish empire stretching from Mexico to Chile. The Inca empire represented the most important conquest, thanks to smallpox and Inca unfamiliarity with European weapons. The human cost of the Spanish empire was enormous. When Cortés landed in 1519, central Mexico had been home to between 13 and 25 million people. By 1600 the population had shrunk to 700,000. Peru and other regions witnessed similar devastation in the greatest demographic disaster in world history.

The Columbian Exchange

The Spanish conquest came at enormous human cost. Disease, not war or slavery, was the greatest killer. Native Americans lacked resistance to European and African infections, especially the deadly, highly communicable smallpox. From the first years of

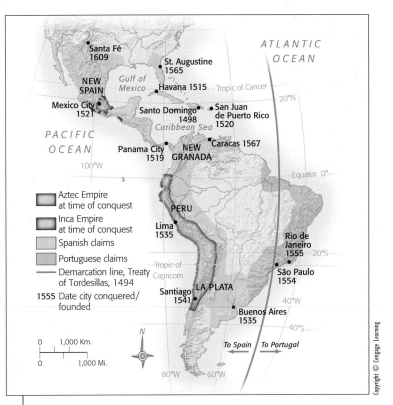

Map 2.3 The Spanish and Portuguese Empires, 1610

By 1610, Spain dominated Latin America, including Portugal's possessions. Having devoted its energies to exploiting Mexico and the Caribbean, Spain had not yet expanded into what is now the United States, beyond outposts in Florida and New Mexico.

 Interactive Map

"Columbian exchange"
Exchange of people, plants, animals, and disease within the Atlantic world as a result of European voyages

contact with Europeans, terrible epidemics decimated Indian communities. In the West Indies the native population vanished within a half-century, and disease opened the mainland for conquest as well.

The **"Columbian exchange"**—the biological encounter of the Old and New Worlds—went beyond deadly germs. Europeans brought horses, cattle, sheep, swine, chickens, wheat, coffee, sugar cane, and numerous fruits and vegetables with them, as well as an astonishing variety of weeds. African slaves carried rice and yams across the Atlantic. The list of American gifts to Europe and Africa was equally impressive: it included corn, white and sweet potatoes, many varieties of beans, tomatoes, squash, pumpkins, peanuts, vanilla, chocolate, avocados, pineapples, chilis, tobacco, and turkeys. European weeds and domesticated animals often overwhelmed indigenous plant life and drove away native animals, especially in North America. Settlers' crops, intensively cultivated on land never allowed to lie fallow, frequently exhausted American soil. Nonetheless, the worldwide exchange of food products enriched human diets and made possible enormous population growth. Today, nearly 60 percent of all food crops worldwide trace their roots to the Native American garden.

Another dimension of the emergence of the Atlantic world was the mixing of peoples. Within Spain's empire, a great human intermingling occurred. From 1500 to 1600 about 300,000 Spaniards immigrated to the New World, 90 percent of them male. A racially mixed population developed, particularly in towns. Spaniards fathered numerous children with African or Indian mothers; most of the former were slaves. Such racial mixing would occur, although far less commonly, in French and English colonies as well.

The Americas supplied seemingly endless wealth for Spain. West Indian sugar plantations and Mexican sheep and cattle ranches enriched many. Much of Spain's wealth, however, was dug from the silver mines of Mexico and Peru. After 1540, enormous amounts of silver flowed across the Atlantic, far more than the small Spanish economy could absorb, setting off inflation that eventually engulfed Europe. But, bent on dominating Europe, Spanish kings needed even more silver to pay for their ships and armies. Several times they went bankrupt, and in the 1560s their efforts to squeeze more taxes from their subjects provoked revolt in Spain's Dutch provinces. In the end, gaining access to American wealth cost the Spanish dearly.

CHECKING IN

- In the fifteenth century, Portugal undertook African exploration, beginning the creation of the Atlantic world.
- By 1600, a "new slavery" based on race arose.
- Early explorers, such as Columbus, Balboa, and Magellan, reached the Americas.
- The Spanish conquered Mexico.
- The "Columbian exchange" transported food, animals, drugs, and germs between Europe, the Americas, and Africa.

FOOTHOLDS IN NORTH AMERICA, 1512–1625

How did European exploration, conquest, and colonization of North America begin?

Spain's New World wealth attracted other Europeans. Throughout the sixteenth century, they sailed the North American coast, exploring, fishing, trading for furs, and smuggling. But, except for a Spanish fort at St. Augustine, Florida, all sixteenth-century attempts at colonizing North America failed. Unrealistic dreams of easy wealth and pliant Indians brought French, English, and Spanish attempts to grief. Only the ravaging of the Indians by disease, declining Spanish power, and rising French, Dutch, and English power finally made colonization possible.

In 1607–1608 the English and French established permanent colonies. By 1614 the Dutch had followed. Within a generation, North America's modern history took shape as each colony developed an economic orientation and its own approach to Native Americans.

Spain's Northern Frontier

The Spanish built their New World empire by subduing the Aztecs, Inca, and other Indian states. The dream of finding even more wealth drew would-be conquistadors to lands north of Mexico.

Earliest came Juan Ponce de León (wahn PON-say deh lee-OWN), the conqueror of Puerto Rico, who trudged through Florida in search of gold and slaves twice, in 1512–1513 and in 1521, and then died in an Indian skirmish. The most astonishing early expedition began when three hundred explorers left Florida in 1527 to explore the Gulf of Mexico. Indian attacks whittled their numbers until only a handful survived. Stranded in Texas, the survivors, led by Cabeza de Vaca (cuh-BAY-zuh deh VAH-cah), moved from Indian tribe to tribe, at first as slaves, then later as traders and medicine men. They finally made their way south to Mexico in 1536.

As de Soto roamed the Southeast, the Southwest drew others with dreams of conquest, lured by rumors that the fabled Seven Golden Cities of Cíbola (SEE-bow-lah) lay north of Mexico. In 1538 an expedition sighted the Zuñi (ZOO-nyee) pueblos and assumed them to be the golden cities.

For decades after these failures, Spain's principal interest in the lands north of Mexico lay in establishing a few strategic bases in Florida to keep out intruders. In 1565 Spain planted the first successful European settlement on mainland North America, the fortress of St. Augustine. Spanish missionaries moved north from the fortress to establish religious missions as far north as the Chesapeake (CHESS-uh-peak) Bay, but Indian resistance and epidemic disease ended their efforts shortly before 1600.

Meanwhile, in the 1580s, the Spanish returned to the southwestern pueblo country, preaching Christianity and scouting for wealth. In 1598 Juan de Oñate (oh-NYAH-tee) led five hundred Spaniards into the upper Rio Grande Valley, where he proclaimed the royal colony of New Mexico. When Acoma Indians refused his demands for provisions in December 1598, Oñate ordered massive retaliation. In January, Spanish troops captured the pueblo, killing more than eight hundred inhabitants. Oñate then forced surviving men to have one foot cut off and sent them, along with women and children, to become servants.

The new colony barely survived. In 1606 the Spanish replaced Oñate because of his excessive brutality. Determined to succeed, by 1630 Franciscan missionaries had established more than fifty pueblo missions stretching along the Rio Grande and had converted about 20,000 Indians.

Colonizing Canada

France made its first attempt at colonizing North America in 1541, when ten ships sailed into the St. Lawrence Valley. Having alienated many of the Indians along the St. Lawrence in two previous expeditions, Jacques Cartier built a fortified settlement on Indian land and thus ended all possibility of peaceful Indian-French relations. Steady Indian attacks and harsh winters drove the French off within two years.

George H. H. Huey

Navajo View of Spanish Colonizers

This pictograph (a painting or drawing on rock) was sketched in the early colonial period in Cañón del Muerto, Arizona.

In 1562 French Huguenots (HYEW-guh-nots) (Calvinists) made the next French attempt at colonization, establishing a base in modern South Carolina. Two years later they founded a settlement in Florida, which the Spanish quickly destroyed. These failures, as well as a civil war between French Catholics and Huguenots, ended France's first attempts at colonization.

Meanwhile, French and other European fishermen worked the teeming Grand Banks off the coast of Newfoundland. Going ashore to dry their catch, French sailors bartered with Indians for beaver pelts; by the late sixteenth century, as European demands for beaver hats soared, a French-dominated fur trade blossomed.

Most traders, unlike explorers or colonizers, recognized the need for reciprocity in dealing with Native Americans; consequently, trade flourished. Glass beads were a mainstay of this trade, for Indians believed that the beads possessed spiritual power comparable to that of quartz, mica, and other sacred substances. To deter potential competitors, the French dispatched Samuel de Champlain to establish the colony of New France at Quebec in 1608. Familiar with Indian politics and diplomacy,

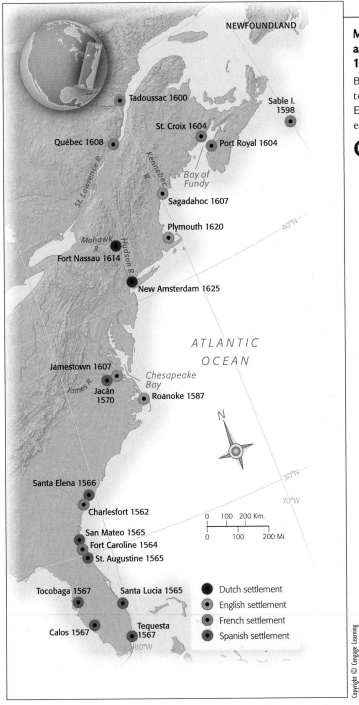

Map 2.4   European Imperial Claims and Settlements in Eastern North America, 1565–1625

By 1625, four European nations contended for territory on North America's Atlantic coast. Except for St. Augustine, Florida, all settlements established before 1607 were abandoned by 1625.

 Interactive Map

Champlain built alliances with the Montagnais (MON-tan-yay) and Algonquins (al-GON-kwins) of the St. Lawrence and with the Hurons of the lower Great Lakes by promising to help them defeat their enemies, the Mohawks.

In July 1609 Champlain and Indian allies encountered a substantial Mohawk force near the southern tip of Lake Champlain (which the explorer had named for himself). In the ensuing Battle of Lake Champlain, more than fifty Mohawks died and a dozen were captured. The battle marked the beginning of a deadly era of trade, diplomacy, and warfare. Through their alliance with the Hurons, the French gained access to the thick beaver pelts of the interior in exchange for European goods and protection against the Mohawks and other Iroquois. These economic and diplomatic arrangements defined the course of New France's history for the rest of the seventeenth century.

England and the Atlantic World, 1558–1603

When Elizabeth I became queen in 1558, England, a second-rank power, stood on the sidelines as Spain and France grappled for European supremacy. Religious division and domestic instability preoccupied the English. They hoped to cure the country's economic woes by founding colonies overseas, but Spain blocked the way.

Meanwhile, England's position in Ireland had deteriorated. By 1565 English troops were fighting to impose Elizabeth's rule throughout the island, where a Protestant English government was battling Irish Catholic rebels aided by Spain. In a war that ground on through the 1580s, English troops drove the Irish clans from their strongholds and established "plantations," or settlements, of Scottish and English Protestants. The English resorted to a "scorched earth policy" of starvation and mass slaughter to break the Irish spirit. Elizabeth's generals justified these atrocities by calling the Irish "savages." The Irish experience gave England strategies that it later used against North American Indians, whose customs, religion, and methods of fighting seemed to absolve the English from guilt in waging exceptionally cruel warfare.

England had two objectives in the Western Hemisphere in the 1570s. The first was to find a northwest passage to Asia, preferably one lined with gold. The second, as Sir Francis Drake said, was to "singe the king of Spain's beard" by raiding Spanish fleets and cities. The search for a northwest passage proved fruitless, but the English did stage spectacularly successful and profitable privateering raids against the Spanish. The most breathtaking enterprise of the era was Drake's voyage around the world in 1577–1580 in quest of sites for colonies.

In 1587 Sir Walter Raleigh, dreaming of founding an American colony where English, Indians, and even blacks freed from Spanish slavery could live together amicably, sponsored a colony on **Roanoke** Island, off the modern North Carolina coast. An earlier attempt (1585–1586) had failed, in part because the colonists refused to grow their own food, expecting the Indians to feed them, and wore out their welcome. One hundred and ten colonists, many of them members of families, reached Roanoke in late summer 1587. Almost immediately the colony's leader, John White, returned to England for more supplies, leaving the settlers behind.

Roanoke Site of the first English attempt at New World colonization; it was a failure

Spain's attempt to crush England with the Great Armada in 1588 prevented White from returning to Roanoke until 1590. When he did, he found only rusty armor, moldy books, and the word CROATOAN (CROW-uh-tan) carved into a post. To this day, no one knows exactly what happened to the "Lost Colony," although they were probably living among the nearby Croatoan Indians. The miserable failure at Roanoke would postpone the establishment of English colonies for seventeen more years.

However, England's victory over the Spanish Armada in 1588 preserved English independence and confirmed its status as a major Atlantic power.

Failure and Success in Virginia, 1603–1625

Two events opened the way for English colonization: peace with Spain and the emergence of the joint-stock company. In the peace between England and Spain, concluded in 1604 by Elizabeth's successor, James I (ruled 1603–1625), the Spanish not only agreed to peace but also renounced their claims to Virginia, leaving England a free hand. At the same time, the development of joint-stock companies, which could amass money through sales of stock, created a way for potential colonizers to raise large sums of money with limited risk for the individual investor.

On April 10, 1606, James I granted charters to two separate joint-stock companies, one based in London and the other in Plymouth. The **Virginia Company of Plymouth** received a grant extending from modern Maine to the Potomac River; the **Virginia Company of London** received a grant from Cape Fear north to the Hudson River. The grants overlapped, with the land in question to go to the first successful colonizer. Both companies dispatched colonists in 1607.

The Virginia Company of Plymouth sent 120 men to Sagadahoc at the mouth of the Kennebec River in Maine. The following year, the colony disintegrated, the victim of Indian hostility (generally provoked) and the hard Maine winter. The company subsequently became dormant. The Virginia Company of London dispatched 105 settlers to a site on the James River near Chesapeake Bay that they named **Jamestown.** But the first colonists, who included many members of the gentry, hunted for gold and failed to plant crops. When relief ships arrived in January 1608, they found only thirty-eight survivors.

Near anarchy reigned at Jamestown until September 1608, when desperate councilors, representatives of the Virginia Company of London, turned to a brash soldier of fortune, Captain **John Smith.** Only twenty-eight, Smith found that his experiences fighting the Spanish and the Turks had prepared him well to assume control in Virginia. By instituting harsh discipline, organizing the settlers, and requiring them to build houses and plant food, he ensured Jamestown's survival. During the winter of 1608–1609, Smith lost just twelve men out of two hundred.

Smith also became the colony's best diplomat. After local Indians captured him late in 1607, Smith displayed such impressive courage that Powhatan (pow-uh-TAN), the leader of the nearby Powhatan Confederacy, arranged an elaborate ceremony in which Pocahontas, his daughter, "saved" Smith's life during a mock execution. This gesture was meant to remind the English that Powhatan's people were the stronger force and that reciprocity rather than force should govern their dealings with one another. Powhatan expected that the English would become his allies against local tribal enemies. Smith maintained satisfactory relations with the Powhatan Confederacy partly through his personality and partly through calculated demonstrations of English military strength.

When serious injuries forced Smith to return to England in 1609, discipline again crumbled. Expecting the Indians to furnish corn, the settlers did not store enough food for winter. One colonist reported that Jamestown residents ate dogs, cats, rats, and snakes in order to survive. He gruesomely added that "many besides fed on the corpses of dead men." Of the 500 residents at Jamestown in September 1609, only 100 lived to May 1610. An influx of new recruits and the imposition of military rule, however, enabled Virginia to win the First Anglo-Powhatan War (1610–1614) and, by 1611, to expand west to modern Richmond. The English population remained small—only 380 by 1616—and produced nothing of value for the stockholders.

Virginia Company of Plymouth Received charter to establish colonies from Chesapeake Bay northward

Virginia Company of London Received charter to establish colonies from Chesapeake Bay southward; founded Jamestown

Jamestown First successful English colony, established in 1607

John Smith Soldier of fortune who "saved" Jamestown by establishing order and maintaining good relations with Indians

John Rolfe Brought tobacco to Jamestown, thus ensuring its economic survival

Tobacco saved Virginia. **John Rolfe,** an Englishman who married Pocahontas, perfected a salable variety of tobacco for planting there, and by 1619 Virginia was exporting large, profitable amounts of the crop. Thereafter, the Virginia Company poured supplies and settlers into the colony.

To attract labor and capital, the company awarded fifty-acre land grants ("head-rights") to anyone paying his or her own passage or that of a laborer. By financing the passage of indentured servants, planters could accumulate large tracts of land. Thousands of single young men and a few hundred women became indentured servants, choosing the uncertainty of Virginia over poverty in England. In return for their passage, they worked a fixed term, usually four to seven years.

House of Burgesses First elected representative legislature in New World, in Virginia; first met in 1619

In 1619 the Virginia Company ended military rule and provided for an elected assembly, the **House of Burgesses.** Although the company could veto the assembly's actions, 1619 marked the beginning of representative government in North America. However, Virginia still faced three serious problems. First, local officials systematically defrauded shareholders, in the process sinking the company deeply into debt. Second, the colony's death rate soared. Malnutrition, salt poisoning, typhus, and dysentery (from drinking polluted river water) killed thousands of immigrants. Third, Indian relations worsened. After Powhatan's death in 1618, the new leader, Opechancanough (oh-peh-can-CUH-noo), worried about the relentless expansion of the English colony. In 1622 the Indians killed 347 of the 1,200 settlers in a surprise attack. With their livestock destroyed, spring planting impossible, and disease spreading through crowded stockades, hundreds more colonists died in the ensuing months.

The Virginia Company sent more men, and Governor Francis Wyatt took the offensive. Using tactics developed during the Irish war, Wyatt destroyed the Indians' food supplies, conducted winter campaigns to drive them from their homes when they would suffer most, and fought (according to John Smith) as if he had "just cause to destroy them by all means possible." By 1625 the English had won the Second Powhatan War, and the Indians had lost their best chance of forcing out the intruders.

But the struggle bankrupted the Virginia Company. After a report critical of its management, James I revoked its charter and made Virginia a royal colony in 1624. Only five hundred Old World settlers lived there, including a handful of Africans who had been brought in since 1619. With its combination of fabulous profits, unfree labor, and massive mortality, Virginia was truly a land of contradictions.

New England Begins, 1614–1625

After Virginia, the next permanent English settlements appeared in New England. Along the coast, a terrible epidemic in 1616–1618 had devastated the Indian population by about 90 percent. Later visitors found the ground littered with the "bones and skulls" of the unburied dead, along with acres of overgrown cornfields.

In 1620 the Virginia Company of London granted a patent for a settlement to a group of English merchants, who dispatched eighteen families (102 people) in a small, leaky ship, the *Mayflower*. The colonists promised to send back lumber, furs, and fish for seven years, after which they would own the tract.

The expedition's leaders, and half its members, belonged to a small religious community from the northern English town of Scrooby. Separatist Puritans, they had earlier fled to the Netherlands to practice their religion freely. Fearing that their children were adopting Dutch ways, they decided to immigrate to America.

In November 1620 the *Mayflower* landed at **Plymouth,** outside the bounds of Virginia. Because they had no legal right to be there, the leaders insisted that adult males in the group sign the **Mayflower Compact** before they landed. By this document they constituted themselves a "civil body politic"—a civil government—under James I's sovereignty and established Plymouth Plantation.

Weakened by their journey and unprepared for winter, half the Pilgrims, as they were later called, died within four months. Two Indians helped the others to survive: Squanto, a local Patuxet, and Samoset (SAM-oh-sett), an Abenaki (aah-beh-NAH-key) from Maine who had traded with the English. To stop the Pilgrims from stealing their food, the Indians taught the newcomers how to grow corn. Squanto and Samoset also arranged an alliance between the Pilgrims and the local Wampanoag (wahm-puh-NO-ag) Indians, who were headed by Chief Massasoit (MASS-uh-soyt).

Plymouth's relations with the Indians soon worsened. Learning of the Virginia massacre of 1622, the Pilgrims militarized their colony and threatened their Indian "allies" with their monopoly of firepower. Within a decade, Plymouth had attracted several hundred colonists and had become economically self-sufficient. After they abandoned communal farming for individually owned plots, prosperous farmers produced corn surpluses that they traded for furs. Prosperity allowed Plymouth's elite to buy out the colony's London backers.

Plymouth colony had three lasting influences. It constituted an outpost of Puritans dissenting from the Church of England, proved that a self-governing society could exist in New England, and foreshadowed the aggressive methods that would give Europeans mastery over the Indians. The Pilgrims became the vanguard of a massive migration of Puritans to New England in the 1630s (see Chapter 3).

Plymouth Colony established by Pilgrims in Massachusetts

Mayflower Compact Agreement signed by Pilgrims to govern themselves

A "New Netherland" on the Hudson, 1609–1625

The Dutch-speaking provinces of the Netherlands were among the most fervently Calvinist regions of Europe. Ruled by the Spanish during the sixteenth century and alienated by high taxes and religious intolerance, the Dutch rebelled in 1566. More than forty years later, in 1609, Spain and the Dutch Republic signed a truce. By then the Netherlands was a wealthy commercial power whose empire stretched from Brazil to South Africa to Taiwan. It would play a key role in colonizing North America.

In 1609 Henry Hudson sailed up the broad, deep river that today bears his name, and in the next year Dutch ships sailed up the Hudson to trade with Indians. In 1614 they began their New Netherland colony by establishing Fort Nassau at the site of modern Albany, New York, and in 1625 planted another fort on an island at the mouth of the Hudson. Within two years, Peter Minuit, director-general of the colony, bought the island from local Indians, named it Manhattan, and began a settlement christened **New Amsterdam.**

Furs, particularly beaver pelts, became the New Netherlanders' chief economic staple. The Mohawks, as well as the other nations of the Iroquois Confederacy, became the Dutch colonists' chief suppliers of furs and soon found themselves embroiled in competition with the French-supported Hurons.

New Amsterdam Dutch colony that would become New York

CHECKING IN

- Pushing northward from their New World empire, Spanish explorers roamed the American Southwest, and conquistadors conquered the Pueblo Indians.

- Early French colonies based on agriculture barely survived, but the French fur trade with Indians of the interior prospered.

- The first English colony, Roanoke, failed, but Jamestown and Plymouth survived despite hardship.

- The Dutch established New Amsterdam at the mouth of the Hudson River and relied on the fur trade.

Chapter Summary

What major changes were reshaping the African and European worlds in the fifteenth and sixteenth centuries? (page 17)

The fifteenth and sixteenth centuries were times of tumultuous change in both West Africa and Europe. In the West African savannah, powerful kingdoms such as Mali gave way to more fragmented political structures. In Europe, the Renaissance, the Reformation, a population boom, and the emergence of the market economy created new tensions as well as new opportunities. In England, the Reformation led to the rise of Puritanism, which found itself in a tense relationship with the monarchy.

What was the Atlantic world, and how did it emerge? (page 25)

The Atlantic world began to open as Portuguese explorers traveled along the African coast; one sad result of this was the brutal "new slavery," based primarily on race. Spanish explorers such as Columbus, Balboa, and Magellan opened the way for the creation of an empire that would encompass both the Aztecs and the Inca in the Americas. Plants, animals, drugs, and diseases crossed the Atlantic in both directions in the "Columbian exchange."

How did European exploration, conquest, and colonization of North America begin? (page 30)

The Spanish explored large parts of North America, conquered the Pueblo Indians of the Southwest, and incorporated them into their empire. Although France attempted to plant agricultural colonies, its primary success lay in establishing the fur trade with the Indians of the interior. After failure at Roanoke, Englishmen successfully planted colonies at Jamestown in Virginia and at Plymouth in Massachusetts. The Dutch established New Amsterdam.

KEY TERMS

savannah *(p. 17)*

Renaissance *(p. 19)*

enclosure *(p. 21)*

joint-stock company *(p. 22)*

Protestant Reformation *(p. 23)*

John Calvin *(p. 23)*

Puritans *(p. 24)*

Prince Henry "the Navigator" *(p. 25)*

"new slavery" *(p. 26)*

Treaty of Tordesillas *(p. 26)*

John Cabot *(p. 27)*

Hernán Cortés *(p. 29)*

"Columbian exchange" *(p. 30)*

Roanoke *(p. 34)*

Virginia Company of Plymouth *(p. 35)*

Virginia Company of London *(p. 35)*

Jamestown *(p. 35)*

John Smith *(p. 35)*

John Rolfe *(p. 36)*

House of Burgesses *(p. 36)*

Plymouth *(p. 37)*

Mayflower Compact *(p. 37)*

New Amsterdam *(p. 37)*

 CourseMate   Go to the CourseMate website at **www.cengagebrain.com** for additional study tools and review materials—including audio and video clips—for this chapter.

CHAPTER 3

The Emergence of Colonial Societies

1625–1700

Lord Baltimore, by Gerard Soest (1670)

CHAPTER PREVIEW

Chesapeake Society
How did tobacco shape the Chesapeake colonies?

Puritanism in New England
What was the "New England Way," and what challenges did it endure?

The Spread of Slavery: The Caribbean and Carolina
Why and how did plantation agriculture shape slavery in the Caribbean and Carolina?

The Middle Colonies
How did diversity distinguish the Middle Colonies?

Rivals for North America: France and Spain
How did the French and Spanish empires develop in the seventeenth century?

Courtesy of Enoch Pratt Free Library, Central Library/State Library Resource Center, Baltimore, MD

The seventeenth century witnessed a flood of English migration across the Atlantic. In 1600 no English person lived along the North American seacoast. By 1700, however, about 250,000 people of European birth or ancestry were dwelling in what would become the United States. In addition, nearly 30,000 enslaved Africans resided in North America in 1700, most of them in Chesapeake colonies and Carolina. Whereas English immigrants to America hoped to realize economic opportunity or religious freedom, Africans and their descendants were owned by others.

A devastating demographic upheaval, the depopulation and uprooting of Native Americans, made these two other migrations possible. Epidemic disease did much of the work of destroying the Indians, but warfare played an important role as well. About

1 million Indians had died as a result of contact with Europeans by 1700. European colonists built their farms, plantations, and cities not in wilderness but on lands long inhabited by Native Americans.

Indian depopulation and European and African immigration transformed North America in the seventeenth century. Europeans expanded their territorial domains and established colonial societies from the St. Lawrence River to the Rio Grande, increasing the continent's cultural diversity.

English immigrants, and English capital, ensured that England would dominate the East Coast as well as the Caribbean; by 1700 the English would force out the Dutch and leave France and Spain with lands less attractive to colonists. Four distinct regions emerged within England's mainland colonies: New England, the Chesapeake, Carolina, and the Middle Colonies, each shaped by its environment, the motives of white immigrants, and the concentrations of enslaved Africans.

CHESAPEAKE SOCIETY

How did tobacco shape the Chesapeake colonies?

Thanks to the tobacco boom of the 1620s, the English colonies on the Chesapeake Bay—Virginia and Maryland—were the first in North America to prosper. They shared similar economies, populations, and patterns of growth that gave them a distinct regional identity. Chesapeake society was highly unequal and unstable. Life for most colonists was short and living conditions poor. Not until English colonists seized large amounts of Native American land to grow tobacco and shifted from white indentured servants to black slaves did they finally achieve stability and at least minimal prosperity.

State and Church in Virginia

James I planned to rule Virginia through appointed officials, but Virginians petitioned repeatedly for the restoration of their elected assembly, the first in the New World.

View of Jamestown, 1625

As Virginia's tobacco production boomed, the capital expanded beyond the fort that had originally confined it.

Colonial National Historical Park

James I's successor, Charles I, grudgingly relented but only to induce the assembly to tax tobacco exports so as to transfer the cost of government from the crown to Virginia's taxpayers. After 1630, seeking more taxes, Virginia's royal governors called regular assemblies. During the 1650s the assembly split into two chambers, the elected House of Burgesses and the appointed Governor's Council.

Local government officials were appointed, rather than elected, during Virginia's first quarter-century. In 1634 Virginia adopted England's county-court system. Appointed by the royal governor, justices of the peace acted as judges, set local tax rates, paid county officials, and oversaw the construction and maintenance of roads, bridges, and public buildings. Thus, unelected county courts became the basic unit of local government south of New England.

Virginia had the Church of England as its established church. Anglican vestries governed each parish; elected vestrymen handled church finances, determined poor relief, and investigated complaints against the minister. Taxpayers were legally obliged to pay fixed rates to the Anglican church. Because of the large distances between settlements and churches, as well as a chronic shortage of clergymen, few Virginians regularly attended services. In 1662 Virginia had just ten ministers to serve its forty-five parishes.

State and Church in Maryland

Beginning in the 1630s, grants by the crown to reward English politicians replaced joint-stock companies as the primary mechanism of colonization. The first such grant, or proprietorship, went in 1632 to Lord Baltimore (Cecilius Calvert); he named the large tract east of Chesapeake Bay "Maryland" in honor of England's Queen Henrietta Maria. Lord Baltimore enjoyed broad power, lessened only by the stipulations that an elected assembly had to approve all laws and that the crown would control both war and trade.

Baltimore intended to make Maryland a refuge for England's Catholics, who could neither worship in public nor hold political office and who had to pay tithes to the Anglican church. To make Maryland a haven, Baltimore tried to install the old English manor system. In theory, a manor lord would employ a Catholic priest as chaplain and allow others to hear Mass and to receive the sacraments on the manor. In practice, this arrangement never worked, for relatively few Catholics settled in Maryland, which was overwhelmingly Protestant

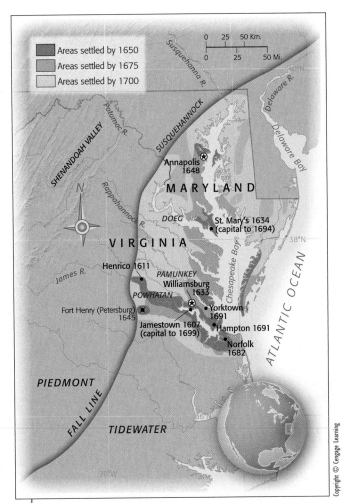

Map 3.1 Chesapeake Expansion, 1607–1700

The Chesapeake colonies expanded slowly before midcentury. By 1700, Anglo-Indian wars, a rising English population, and an influx of enslaved Africans permitted settlers to spread throughout the tidewater.

Interactive Map

from the beginning. Cheap land lured settlers who did not need to become tenants on the manors, and Baltimore's scheme fell apart. By 1675 all sixty of Maryland's nonproprietary manors had become plantations.

Religious tension gradually developed in Maryland society. Until 1642, Catholics and Protestants shared the chapel at St. Mary's, the capital, but they began to argue over its use. As antagonisms intensified, Baltimore drafted, and the assembly passed, the Act for Religious Toleration (1649).

Unfortunately, the Toleration Act did not secure religious peace. In 1654 the Protestant majority barred Catholics from voting; ousted Governor William Stone, a pro-tolerance Protestant; and repealed the Toleration Act. Stone raised an army, both Protestant and Catholic, in an attempt to regain the government but was defeated. The victors imprisoned Stone and hanged three Catholic leaders. Although Lord Baltimore was restored to control in 1658, Protestant resistance to Catholic political influence continued to cause problems in Maryland.

Chronology

1628	Massachusetts Bay colony founded
1630–1642	"Great migration" to North America
1633	First English settlements in Connecticut
1634	Lord Baltimore founds Maryland
1636	Roger Williams founds Providence, Rhode Island; Harvard College established
1637	Antinomian crisis in Massachusetts Bay; Pequot War in Connecticut
1638	New Sweden established
1642–1648	English Civil War
1644–1646	Third Anglo-Powhatan War in Virginia
1649	Maryland's Act for Religious Toleration; King Charles I beheaded
1655	New Netherland annexes New Sweden
1660	Restoration in England; Charles II becomes king
1661	Maryland defines slavery as a lifelong, inheritable racial status
1662	Half-Way Covenant adopted
1664	English conquer New Netherland; establish New York and New Jersey
1670	Charles Town, Carolina, established; Virginia defines slavery as a lifelong, inheritable racial status
1675–1676	King Philip's War in New England
1675–1676	Bacon's Rebellion in Virginia
1680	Pueblo Revolt begins in New Mexico
1681	William Penn founds Pennsylvania
1682	La Salle claims Louisiana for France
1691	Spain establishes Texas
1692–1693	Salem witchcraft trials
1692–1700	Spain "reconquers" New Mexico
1698	First French settlements in Louisiana

Death, Gender, and Kinship

So few women immigrated to the Chesapeake Bay that, before 1650, only one-third of male servants could find brides and then only after completing their indenture. Female scarcity gave women an advantage in negotiating favorable marriages. Some female indentured servants married prosperous planters who paid off their remaining time of service.

Death ravaged Chesapeake society and left domestic life exceptionally fragile. In 1650 malaria joined the killer diseases typhoid, dysentery, and salt poisoning, as the marshy lowlands of the tidewater Chesapeake became fertile breeding grounds for the mosquitoes that spread malaria. Life expectancy in the 1600s was twenty years lower in the Chesapeake than in New England. Servants died at appalling rates; 40 percent were dead within a decade of arrival and 70 percent before reaching age fifty.

Chesapeake widows often enjoyed substantial property rights. The region's men wrote wills giving their wives perpetual and complete control of their estate, so that their own children could inherit it. Although a widow in such circumstances had a degree of economic independence, she faced enormous pressure to remarry, particularly a man who could produce income by farming her fields.

The lopsided sex ratio and high death rates contributed to slow population growth in the Chesapeake. Although perhaps 100,000 English immigrated to the Chesapeake between 1630 and 1700, the white population was just 70,000 in 1700. In contrast, the benign disease environment and more balanced gender ratio of New England allowed that region's 28,000 white immigrants to burgeon to 91,000 during the same time period. Change came gradually as children acquired childhood immunities, life-spans lengthened, and the sex ratio evened out. By 1720 most Chesapeake residents were native born.

Tobacco Shapes a Region, 1630–1670

Chesapeake settlers were scattered across the landscape. A typical community included only twenty-four families in a twenty-five-square-mile area, a mere six people per square mile. (In contrast, New England often had five hundred people squeezed onto one square mile.) Most Chesapeake inhabitants lived in a world of few friendships and considerable isolation.

Isolated Chesapeake settlers shared a life governed by one overriding factor: the price of tobacco. After an initial boom, tobacco prices plunged 97 percent in 1629 before stabilizing at 10 percent of their original high. Tobacco was still profitable as long as it was grown on fertile soil near navigable water. As a result, 80 percent of Chesapeake homes were located along a riverbank. Wealthy planters built wharves that served as depots for tobacco exports and distribution centers for imported goods. Consequently, a merchant class was slow to materialize, and towns grew painfully slowly; by 1678 St. Mary's, Maryland's capital, had just thirty scattered houses.

Chesapeake society became increasingly unequal. A few planters used the headright system to build up large landholdings and to profit from their servants' labor. Wretchedly exploited—and poorly fed, clothed, and housed—servants faced a bleak future even when their indenture ended. Although some were able to claim fifty acres of land in Maryland, the majority who went to Virginia had no such prospects.

Indeed, in Virginia after 1650 most riverfront land was held by large planters and speculators, and upward mobility became virtually impossible.

In 1660 Chesapeake tobacco prices plunged 50 percent, setting off a depression that lasted fifty years. Despite losses, large planters earned some income from rents, interest on loans, and shopkeeping, and many landowners scrambled to sell corn and cattle in the West Indies. A typical family in this depression era lived in a small wooden shack, slept on rags, and ate mush or stew cooked in their single pot. Ex-servants in particular became a frustrated and embittered underclass that seemed destined to remain landless and poor. Having fled poverty in England for the promise of a better life, they found utter destitution in the Chesapeake.

| **Bacon's Rebellion, 1675–1676** | Virginia had been free of serious conflict with the Indians since the end of the Third Anglo-Powhatan War in 1646. By 1653 tribes encircled by English settlements had begun |

agreeing to remain within boundaries set by the government—in effect, on reservations. White settlement continued to expand northward to the Potomac River, and by 1675 whites outnumbered Indians by a ten-to-one ratio.

Tensions flared between Native Americans struggling to retain land and independence and settlers bent on expansion, especially white freedmen who often squatted illegally on tribal lands. The conflict also divided white society; Governor Berkeley, Lord Baltimore, and a few of their cronies held fur-trade monopolies that profited from friendly relations with some Indians. The monopolies alienated freedmen and wealthy planters. Colonists' resentment against Native Americans fused with resentment against the governor and the proprietor.

In June 1675 a dispute between some Doeg (Dohg) Indians and a Virginia farmer escalated. A force of Virginia and Maryland militia pursuing the Doegs murdered fourteen friendly Susquehannocks (suss-kweh-HAN-nocks) and later executed five of their chiefs. The violence was now unstoppable. Although Governor William Berkeley proposed defending the frontier with a costly system of forts, small farmers preferred the cheaper solution: a war of extermination against the Indians. Some three hundred settlers elected Nathaniel Bacon, a distant relative of Berkeley and a member of the Royal Council, to lead them against nearby Indians in April 1676. The expedition found only peaceful Indians but slaughtered them anyhow.

Returning to Jamestown in June 1676, Bacon asked for authority to wage war "against all Indians in general." The legislature voted for a program designed to appeal to both hard-pressed taxpayers and landless ex-servants. All Indians who had left their village without permission (even if fleeing Bacon) were declared enemies, and their lands were forfeited. Bacon's troops could seize any "enemy" property and enslave Indian prisoners.

However, Governor Berkeley soon had second thoughts about the slaughter and recalled Bacon and his thirteen hundred men. Forbidden to attack Indians, Bacon's forces turned against the government and burned Jamestown. The rebels offered freedom to any servants or slaves owned by Berkeley's allies who would join them, and then looted enemy plantations. What had begun as Indian warfare was now a social rebellion. Before the uprising could proceed further, however, Bacon died of dysentery in late 1676, and his followers dispersed.

Bacon's Rebellion revealed a society under deep internal stress. Begun as an effort to displace escalating tensions among whites onto the Indians, it became an excuse to plunder other whites. This rebellion was an outburst of pent-up frustrations by marginal taxpayers and ex-servants driven to desperation by the tobacco depression.

Bacon's Rebellion Uprising that showed deep stresses within the Virginia colony

From Servitude to Slavery

Race was fundamental in reshaping Chesapeake society. Whites drew racial boundaries between themselves and the region's growing African population and tried to avert class conflict by substituting black slaves for white servants.

Racial slavery developed in three stages. From 1619 to 1640, Anglo-Virginians carefully distinguished between whites and blacks in official documents but did not assume that every African sold was a slave for life. Some Africans gained their freedom, and a few even owned their own farms.

By 1640 blacks and some Indians were being treated as slaves, and their children inherited their status. Thus, their situation had become inferior to that of indentured white servants. In the final phase, after 1660, laws defined slavery as a lifelong, inheritable status based on color. By 1705 strict legal codes defined the place of slaves in society and set standards of racial etiquette.

Slavery was a system for blacks and Indians only. Whites never enslaved their white enemies; rather, they reserved the complete denial of human rights for nonwhites. To stabilize Chesapeake society and to defuse the resentment of poor whites, planter elites created a caste system based on race. This system simultaneously defined nonwhites as unfit for freedom and created a common, exclusive identity among whites.

Slavery grew slowly in the Chesapeake, with fewer than a thousand slaves in Virginia and Maryland as late as 1660. By 1680, however, the slave population had grown to twelve thousand; by 1700 slaves would make up nearly one-fourth of the Chesapeake population and much of the labor force.

The rise of a direct slave trade with Africa increased the growing gap between whites and blacks. Before 1690, most blacks in the Chesapeake, having spent long periods in West African ports or other American colonies, were familiar with English ways and spoke some English. They could carve out space for themselves as free landowners. After 1690, as slaves poured into the Chesapeake directly from the West African interior, language and culture became barriers rather than bridges, reinforcing increased racism among whites.

Racism was enforced by the changing composition of the white population, increasingly American-born and evenly distributed between male and female. Whites shared a sense of common racial identity vis-à-vis an increasingly fragmented and seemingly alien black population.

By 1700 the Chesapeake had been transformed; profits had fallen, but life expectancy had risen. As nonwhites' condition deteriorated, Virginia and Maryland expanded their territories, and their white colonists flourished.

CHECKING IN

- A cash-crop economy set the Chesapeake colonies apart from New England.
- Maryland was intended as a refuge for Catholics but became mainly Protestant.
- Tobacco shaped the economy and living conditions in Chesapeake colonies.
- Bacon's Rebellion began as an anti-Indian campaign but became a social and economic movement as well.
- Slavery developed in gradual stages in the Chesapeake colonies, eventually becoming a lifelong, inheritable status based on color.

Preparing a Slave Voyage
Africans weep as relatives or friends are taken to a slave vessel.

PURITANISM IN NEW ENGLAND

What was the "New England Way," and what challenges did it endure?

New England soon joined the Chesapeake as a prosperous colonial region. The Plymouth colony established in 1620 was dwarfed after 1630 as Puritans flooded into New England in the "Great Migration." By the time England's civil war halted the migration in 1642, about 21,000 newcomers had arrived. They established the colonies of Massachusetts Bay, Connecticut, New Haven (absorbed by Connecticut in 1662), and Rhode Island. New England's leaders endeavored to build colonies based on social and religious ideals. Even though the ideas ultimately weakened and then vanished, Puritanism shaped New England's distinctive regional identity.

In almost every way—the place of religion, economies, class structure, local communities, and living standards—New England contrasted sharply with the Chesapeake colonies. Both, however, shared English nationality and a determination to expand at Native Americans' expense.

A City upon a Hill, 1628–1632

Upon ascending the throne in 1625, Charles I scrapped James's policy of tolerance toward the Puritans and began a systematic campaign to eliminate Puritan influence within the Church of England. In response to continual harassment, in 1628 several Puritan merchants obtained a charter to settle north of the Separatist colony at Plymouth. Organized as the Massachusetts Bay Company, they moved the seat of their colony's government to New England, paving the way for Massachusetts to be self-governing.

In 1630 the company dispatched a "great fleet," eleven ships and seven hundred passengers, to New England. As the ships crossed the Atlantic, Governor John Winthrop delivered a lay sermon, "A Model of Christian Charity," in which he explained how and why the new colony would differ from England itself.

Winthrop boldly announced that "we shall be as **a city upon a hill,** the eyes of all people are upon us." The settlers would build a godly community whose compelling example would shame England. The English government would then truly reform the church, and a revival of piety would create a nation of saints. Denouncing economic jealousy, Winthrop explained that God intended "in all times some must be rich and some poor." The rich would practice charity and mercy, and the poor show their faith in God's will by practicing patience and fortitude. In a godly state, the government would prevent the greedy among the rich from exploiting the poor and the lazy among the poor from burdening their fellow citizens.

By 1631, thirteen hundred more settlers had arrived, and the colony was moving toward both economic and political stability. Most of the new colonists were land-owning farm families of modest means, who had neither indentured servants nor slaves. More than fifteen thousand colonists had settled in New England by 1642.

Massachusetts established a broad-based political system, permitting every adult male church member to vote; the widespread suffrage contrasted sharply with England itself, where property requirements restricted the vote to less than 30 percent of adult males. Within a few years of their arrival, the colonists had established a bicameral legislature, the General Court, with an appointed Governor's Council as the upper house and two delegates from each town as the lower house.

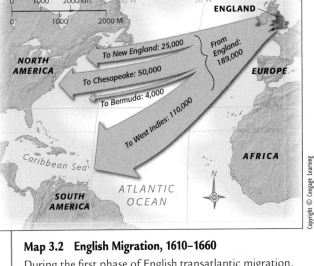

Map 3.2 English Migration, 1610–1660

During the first phase of English transatlantic migration, more than half of the colonists settled in the West Indies.

Interactive Map

a city upon a hill John Winthrop's vision of the Puritan settlement in New England as a model for the world

New England Ways

Self-governing Puritan congregations ignored the authority of Anglican bishops. Male "saints," as Puritans termed those who had been saved, ran each congregation. By majority vote they chose ministers, elected a board of elders to handle finances, and decided who were saints. Thus, control of New England churches was broadly based.

The clergy quickly asserted its power in New England's religious life. In England, Puritans had focused on their common opposition to Anglican practices. In America,

Copyright © Cengage Learning

the "New England Way"
Puritan orthodoxy that was supposed to govern the Massachusetts Bay colony

however, theological differences began to undermine the harmony that Winthrop had envisioned. Puritan ministers struggled to define orthodox practices—**the "New England Way"**—that strengthened their authority at the expense of the laypersons (nonclergy) within their congregations.

Education was a key means of establishing orthodoxy. Like most Protestants, Puritans insisted on familiarity with the Bible and, thus, literacy. They felt education should begin in childhood and be promoted by each colony.

Old Deluder Act Law requiring Puritan towns to establish and maintain schools; foundation of public education in New England

In 1647 the Massachusetts Bay colony passed the **Old Deluder Act** because "one chief project of that old deluder, Satan [is] to keep men from knowledge of the Scriptures." Every town of fifty or more households was to appoint one teacher from whom all children could receive instruction, and every town of one hundred households or more was to maintain a grammar school with a teacher capable of preparing students for university-level learning. This law, echoed by other Puritan colonies, was New England's first step toward public education, although attendance remained optional and boys were more likely to be taught reading and writing than girls.

An educated clergy was essential, so in 1636 Massachusetts founded Harvard College to produce learned ministers. In its first thirty-five years, the college turned out 201 graduates, 111 of them ministers. These alumni made New England the only American colony with a college-educated elite during the seventeenth century.

Although agreeing that the church must be free of state control, Winthrop and other Massachusetts Bay leaders insisted that a holy commonwealth required cooperation between church and state. Therefore, the colony required all adults to attend services and pay tithes to support their local church. Massachusetts thus had a state-sponsored or "established" religion. Some Puritans, however, dissented from their leaders' vision of social order and religious conformity. **Roger Williams,** who arrived in America in 1631, argued that civil government had to remain absolutely uninvolved with religious matters. Williams opposed compulsory church service and interference with private religious beliefs because he feared that the state would eventually corrupt the church and its saints.

Roger Williams Dissenter seen as a threat to the New England Way; ultimately banished; founded Rhode Island

Believing that the purpose of the colony was to protect true religion and to prevent heresy, political authorities declared Williams's opinions subversive and banished him in 1635. Williams went south to the edge of Narragansett Bay to a place that he later named Providence, which he purchased from the Indians. A steady stream of dissenters drifted to the group of settlements near Providence, forming Rhode Island in 1647. The only New England colony to practice religious toleration, Rhode Island grew to eight hundred settlers by 1650.

Anne Hutchinson Dissenter feared not only for her theology but also because she challenged gender roles; banished from Massachusetts

Anne Hutchinson presented the second major challenge to the New England Way. "A woman of haughty and fierce carriage, of a nimble wit and active spirit," Hutchinson maintained that her fellow Puritans were too certain that they could tell whether or not a person was a saint on the basis of his or her behavior. She reminded them that their creed stressed predestination, not good works, and argued that New England's ministers had gone astray.

Hutchinson's ideas directly attacked the clergy's authority to interpret and teach Scripture; critics charged that her beliefs would delude individuals into imagining that they were accountable only to themselves. Her followers were labeled "antinomians," meaning those opposed to the rule of law. Anne Hutchinson bore the additional liability of being a woman challenging traditional male roles in church and state. Her gender made her seem an especially dangerous foe. "You have stepped out of your places; you [would] rather have been a husband than a wife, a preacher than a hearer," one of her foes railed against her.

Massachusetts Bay split into pro- and anti-Hutchinson forces. Her opponents prevailed, bringing Hutchinson to trial for sedition in 1637 before the Massachusetts Bay legislature (the General Court) and then for heresy before a panel of ministers. Hutchinson's knowledge of Scripture was so superior to that of her inquisitors that she might well have been acquitted had she not claimed to communicate directly with the Holy Spirit. Because Puritans believed that God had ceased to make matters of faith known by personal revelation since New Testament times, Hutchinson was condemned by her own words. Banished from the colony along with other antinomians, Hutchinson settled in Rhode Island and then moved to New Netherland, where she was killed in that colony's war with Indians in 1643. Her banishment effectively ended the last challenge capable of splitting congregationalism and ensured the survival of the New England Way for two more generations.

New restrictions on women's independence and on equality within Puritan congregations followed antinomianism's defeat. Increasingly, women were prohibited from assuming the kind of public religious role claimed by Hutchinson and were even required to relate their conversion experiences in private to their minister rather than publicly before their congregation.

Towns, Families, and Farm Life

To ensure that colonists would settle in communities with congregations, all New England colonies provided for the establishment of towns by awarding a grant of land to several dozen landowning church members. These men laid out the settlement, organized its church, distributed land among themselves, and established a town meeting. At the center of each town was the meetinghouse, which served as both church and town hall.

Local administration lay in the hands of the town meeting, which resulted in a highly decentralized authority over political and economic decisions. Each town determined its own qualifications for voting and for holding office; most allowed all male taxpayers, including nonsaints, to participate.

Most towns attempted to maintain communities of tightly clustered settlers by distributing only as much land as was necessary for each family to support itself. The remaining land would be distributed to future generations as needed. Forcing residents to live close together was an attempt to foster social reciprocity. New England's generally compact system of settlement made people interact with each other and established an atmosphere of mutual watchfulness that promoted godly order.

Despite the restriction of their public roles after the antinomian crisis, women remained a social force in their communities. Remaining at home while husbands and older sons tended the families, fields, and business, women exchanged goods—a pound of butter for a section of spun wool, for example—advice, and news. Women confided in one another, creating a community of women that helped enforce morals and protect the poor and vulnerable.

Puritans defined matrimony as a contract, not a sacrament; they were thus married by justices of the peace rather than ministers. As a civil institution, marriage could be dissolved by the courts in cases of desertion, bigamy, adultery, or physical cruelty. However, New England courts saw divorce as a remedy only for extremely wronged spouses, such as the Plymouth woman who found that her husband also had wives in Boston, Barbados (bar-BAY-dose), and England.

New England wives enjoyed significant legal protections against spousal violence and nonsupport and had more freedom to escape a failed marriage than their English counterparts. However, they suffered the legal disabilities borne by all women under English law. A wife had no property rights independent of her husband except by premarital agreement. Only if there were no other heirs, or if a will so specified, would a widow receive control of household property, although law entitled her to lifetime use of one-third of the estate.

New England's families enjoyed greater stability and lived longer lives than their English counterparts. The region's cold climate limited the impact of disease, especially in winter when limited travel between towns slowed the spread of infection. Easy access to land contributed to a healthy diet, which strengthened resistance to disease and lowered death rates associated with childbirth. Life expectancy for Puritan men reached sixty-five, and women lived nearly that long. These life-spans were ten years or more longer than those in England. More than 80 percent of all infants survived long enough to marry. Because so many of the twenty thousand immigrants who arrived in New England between 1630 and 1642 came as members of families, an even sex ratio and a rapid natural increase of population followed.

Families were economically interdependent. Male heads of families managed the household's crops and livestock, conducted its business transactions, and represented it at town meetings. Wives bore and nurtured children, and performed or oversaw work in the house, garden, and barn. Sons depended on parents to provide them with acreage for a farm, and parents encouraged sons to stay at home and work in return for a bequest of land later on. Young males often tended their father's fields until their late twenties before receiving their own land. The average family, raising four sons to adulthood, could count on thirty to forty years of work if their sons delayed marriage until age twenty-six.

There were other benefits as well. Prolonged dependence for sons ensured that the family line and property would continue in the hands of capable, experienced men. Although daughters performed vital labor, they would marry into another family. Young women with many childbearing years ahead of them were the most valuable potential wives, and first-generation women tended to marry by the age of twenty-one.

Economic and Religious Tensions Saddled with a short growing season, rocky soil salted with gravel, and an inefficient system of land distribution that forced farmers to cultivate widely scattered strips, the colonists nevertheless managed to feed their families and to keep ahead of their debts. Few grew wealthy from farming. For wealth, New Englanders turned lumbering, shipbuilding, fishing, and rum distilling into major industries that employed perhaps one-fifth of all adults full time. As its economy diversified, New England prospered.

While most Puritans shared Winthrop's view of community, self-discipline, and mutual obligation, a large minority had come to America for prosperity and social mobility. The most visibly ambitious colonists were merchants, whose activities fueled New England's economy but whose way of life challenged its ideals.

Merchants fit uneasily into a religious society that equated financial shrewdness with greed. New England ministers attempted to curtail the acquisitive impulses transforming England itself. Merchants clashed with political leaders, who were trying to regulate prices so that consumers would not suffer from the chronic shortage of manufactured goods that afflicted New England. In 1635 the General Court forbade the sale of any item above 5 percent of its cost. Led by Robert Keayne, merchants protested that they needed to sell some goods at higher rates to offset losses incurred by shipwreck and inflation. In 1639 authorities fined Keayne for selling nails at 25 percent above cost and forced him to apologize in front of his congregation.

Keayne symbolized the fear that a headlong rush for prosperity would lead New Englanders to forget that they were their brothers' keepers. Controversies like these were part of a struggle for the New England soul. At stake was the Puritans' ability to insulate their city upon a hill from a market economy that threatened to strangle the spirit of community within a harsh world of frantic competition.

Other changes further undermined Winthrop's vision. After 1660 farmers voted themselves larger amounts of land and consolidated their scattered parcels of land. Farmers began to leave town centers to live on their outlying tracts. Friction grew between townspeople and "outlivers," whose distance from the town center limited their influence over town affairs. John Winthrop's vision of a society sustained by reciprocity was slowly giving way to the individualistic society that the original immigrants had fled in England.

As New England slowly prospered, old England fell into chaos and civil war. Alienated by years of religious harassment, Puritans gained control of the revolt, beheaded Charles I in 1649, and governed without a king for more than a decade. In 1660 a provisional English government recalled the Stuarts and restored Charles II to the throne.

The Stuart Restoration left American Puritans without a mission. Having conquered a wilderness and built their city upon a hill, they found that the eyes of the world were no longer fixed on them.

An internal crisis also gripped New England. First-generation Puritans had believed that they held a covenant, a holy contract, with God to establish a scripturally ordained church and to charge their descendants with its preservation. However, understandably reluctant to submit to a public review of their spirituality, relatively few second-generation Puritans were willing to join the elect by making the required conversion relation before the congregation. This generation also rejected the ritual of public conversion relation as an unnecessary source of division and bitterness that undermined Christian fellowship.

Because Puritan churches baptized only babies born to saints, first-generation Puritans faced the prospect that their own grandchildren would remain unbaptized unless the standards for church membership were lowered. They solved their dilemma in 1662 through a compromise known as the **Half-Way Covenant,** which permitted the children of all baptized members, including nonsaints, to be baptized. Church membership would pass down from generation to generation, but nonsaints would be "half-way" members, unable to take communion or to vote in church affairs. When forced to choose between a church system founded on a pure membership of

Half-Way Covenant Law to admit nonsaints to church membership; major blow to New England Way

the elect and one that embraced the entire community, New Englanders opted for worldly power over spiritual purity.

The Half-Way Covenant signaled the dilution of the New England Way. Most adults chose to remain in "half-way" status for life, and the saints became a shrinking minority in the third and fourth generations. By the 1700s there were more female than male saints in most congregations. But because women could not vote in church affairs, religious authority stayed in male hands.

Expansion and Native Americans

In contrast to the settlement of Virginia, the Puritan colonization of New England initially met little resistance from Native Americans, whose numbers had been drastically reduced by disease. Settlers brought new diseases such as diphtheria, measles, tuberculosis, and new outbreaks of smallpox to rage through the Indian population. Between 1616 and 1618 an epidemic killed 90 percent of New England's coastal Indians, and a second epidemic in 1633–1634 inflicted comparable casualties on Indians throughout the Northeast. By 1675, New England's Native American population had shrunk from 125,000 in 1600 to about 10,000. During the 1640s, Massachusetts Bay passed laws prohibiting Indians from practicing their own religion and encouraging missionaries to convert them to Christianity. The Massachusetts Indians surrendered much of their independence and moved into "praying towns," such as Natick, a reservation established by the colony.

The expansion of English settlement farther inland, however, aroused Indian resistance. As settlers moved into the Connecticut River Valley, beginning in 1633, friction developed with the Pequots, who controlled the trade in furs and wampum with New Netherland. After tensions escalated into violence, the English waged a ruthless campaign against the Pequots, using tactics similar to those devised to break Irish resistance (see Chapter 2). In a predawn attack, troops led by Captain John Mason surrounded and set fire to a Pequot village at Mystic, Connecticut, and then cut down all who tried to escape. Several hundred Pequots, mostly women and children, were killed. By late 1637, Pequot resistance was crushed, and English settlement of the new colonies of Connecticut and New Haven could proceed unimpeded.

Indians felt the English presence in many ways. The fur trade, initially beneficial to Native Americans of the interior, became a burden. Once Indians began hunting for trade instead of for their subsistence needs alone, they quickly depleted the supply of beavers and other fur-bearing animals. Because English traders advanced trade goods on credit before the hunting season began, many Indians fell into debt. Traders increasingly took Indian land as collateral and sold it to settlers.

English townspeople, eager to expand their agricultural output and provide for their sons, voted themselves much larger amounts of land after 1660. For example, Dedham, Massachusetts, had distributed only three thousand acres from 1636 to 1656; by 1668 it had allocated another fifteen thousand acres. Many farmers built homes on their outlying tracts, crowding closer to the Indians' settlements and hunting, fishing, and gathering areas.

Expansion put pressure on the natives and the land alike. By clearing trees for fields and for use as fuel and building material, the colonists were altering the entire ecosystem by the mid-1600s. Deer no longer grazed freely, and the wild plants on which the Indians depended for food and medicine could not grow. Clear-cutting trees not only dried the soil but also brought frequent flooding. Encroaching white settlers allowed their livestock to run wild, according to English custom. Pigs damaged Indian cornfields and shellfish-gathering sites. Cattle and horses devoured native grasses, which the settlers replaced with English varieties.

Powerless to reverse the alarming decline of population, land, and food supplies, many Indians became demoralized. Some turned to alcohol, which became increasingly available during the 1660s despite colonial attempts to suppress its sale to Native Americans. Interpreting the crisis as one of belief, other Indians converted to Christianity. By 1675 Puritan missionaries had established about thirty "praying towns." Although missionaries struggled to convert the Indians to "civilization"—English culture and ways of life—most Indians integrated the new faith with their native cultural identities, reinforcing the hostility of settlers who believed that all Indians were irrevocably "savage" and heathen.

Anglo-Indian conflict became acute in the 1670s because of pressure on the Indians to sell their land and to accept missionaries and the legal authority of English courts. Tension was especially high in the Plymouth colony, where Puritans had engulfed the Wampanoag tribe and forced a series of humiliating concessions from their leader, Metacom (MEH-tuh-comb), or "King Philip," the son of the Pilgrims' onetime ally, Massasoit.

In 1675 Plymouth hanged three Wampanoags for killing a Christian Indian. Then several other Wampanoags were shot while burglarizing a farmhouse, touching off the conflict known as **King Philip's War.** In response to the escalation of violence, Metacom organized two-thirds of the Native Americans, including a few praying Indians, into a military alliance. The war raged across New England. Metacom's forces, as well armed as the Puritans, devastated the countryside, wiping out twelve of New England's ninety towns and killing 2,500 colonists. The following year, 1676, saw the tide turn as Puritan militia destroyed their enemies' food supplies and sold hundreds of captives into slavery, including Metacom's wife and child. Perhaps five thousand Indians starved or died in battle, including Metacom himself.

King Philip's War Last major war between Indians and New England settlers; reduced Indian population by nearly 40 percent; ended Indian resistance

King Philip's War reduced southern New England's Indian population by almost 40 percent and eliminated open Indian resistance to white expansion. It also deepened whites' hostility toward all Native Americans, even the Christian Indians who had fought against King Philip. In 1677 ten praying towns were disbanded, and all Indians were restricted to the remaining four. Missionary work ceased.

Salem Witchcraft, 1691–1693

Nowhere in New England did the conflicts dividing white New Englanders converge more forcefully than in Salem, Massachusetts. Trade made Salem prosperous but destroyed the relatively equal society of the first generation. Such divisions were especially sharp in Salem Village, an economically stagnant district north of Salem Town; those who lived in the eastern section farmed richer soils and benefited from Salem Town's commercial expansion, whereas those in the less fertile western half did not share this prosperity and lost the political influence that they had once held.

In late 1691 several Salem Village girls encouraged an African slave woman, Tituba (TEE-too-bah), to tell fortunes and talk to them about sorcery. When the girls began behaving strangely, villagers assumed that they were victims of witchcraft. Pressed to identify their tormenters, they named two local white women and Tituba.

To this point the incident was not unusual; witchcraft beliefs remained strong in seventeenth-century Europe and its colonies. Generally, witches were women whose greed, pride, envy, or discontent supposedly drove them to sign pacts with the devil and use his supernatural power of evil to torment neighbors by causing illness, destroying property, or "possessing" their victims' minds and bodies. Witnesses also usually accused these women of unfeminine behavior. A disproportionate number of the accused witches in New England were women who had inherited or stood to inherit more property than the usual one-third of a husband's estate. In other words, most accused witches were assertive women who had or might have had more economic power and independence than many men. To New Englanders, who felt it necessary to limit both female independence and economic individualism, they were dangerous. In most earlier witchcraft accusations, there was only one defendant, and the case never went to trial. However, the **Salem witchcraft trials** would lead to a colonywide panic.

Salem witchcraft trials
Hysteria that delivered final blow to New England Way, revealing social divisions

By April 1692 the girls had denounced two prosperous farm wives long considered saints in the local church and identified the village's former minister as a wizard (male witch). Fear of witchcraft soon overrode doubts about the girls' credibility and led local judges to ignore legal bans on "spectral evidence," testimony that a spirit resembling the accused had been seen tormenting a victim. Thereafter, charges multiplied until the jails overflowed with 342 accused witches.

The pattern of hysteria and accusations reflected Salem Village's internal divisions. Most charges came from the western side of the village and were lodged against people from the eastern village and in Salem Town. Two-thirds of all accusers were girls aged eleven to twenty, and more than half of them had lost one or both parents in conflicts between Indians and settlers in Maine. They and other survivors had fled to Massachusetts, where most worked as servants in other families' households. They most frequently named as witches middle-aged wives and widows—women who had escaped the poverty and uncertainty that they themselves faced.

Those found guilty of witchcraft tried to stave off death by implicating others. As the pandemonium spread, fear dissolved ties of friendship and family. A minister was condemned by his granddaughter, a mother by her seven-year-old daughter, and a husband and father by his wife and daughter. Fifty saved themselves by confessing, but twenty were condemned and executed.

By late 1692, doubts about the charges were surfacing. Clergymen objected to the emphasis on spectral evidence, which was crucial to most convictions. By accepting such evidence in court, minister Increase Mather warned, the Puritans had fallen victim to a deadly game of "blind man's buffet" set up by Satan and were "hotly and madly mauling one another in the dark." In October, Governor William Phips forbade any further imprisonments for witchcraft. One hundred were still in jail, and two hundred more stood accused. In early 1693 Phips ended the terror by pardoning all those who were convicted or suspected of practicing witchcraft.

CHECKING IN

- John Winthrop proclaimed that Puritans would build "a city upon a hill" in the New World, a godly community that would be an example to the world.
- Threats to Puritan orthodoxy, the "New England Way," included religious dissenters Roger Williams and Anne Hutchinson and the growth of a market economy.
- White expansion steadily displaced New England's Native Americans; New Englanders celebrated the massacre of the Pequots, and later resistance, culminating in the bitter and costly King Philip's War, proved futile.
- The Half-Way Covenant relaxed standards for church membership and marked the beginning of the end of the New England Way.
- The Salem witchcraft hysteria delivered the final blow to the New England Way, revealing deep social divisions.

The witchcraft hysteria marked the end of Puritan New England. Colonists reaching maturity after 1692 would reject the ideals of earlier generations and become "Yankees" who shrewdly pursued material gain. True to their Puritan roots, they would retain their forceful convictions and self-discipline, giving New England a distinctive regional identity that would endure.

THE SPREAD OF SLAVERY: THE CARIBBEAN AND CAROLINA

Why and how did plantation agriculture shape slavery in the Caribbean and Carolina?

As European colonies expanded on the mainland, an even larger wave of settlement swept the West Indies. Between 1630 and 1642 nearly two-thirds of the English who emigrated to the Americas went to the Caribbean. Beginning in the 1640s both the French and the English followed the Spanish, Portuguese, and Dutch in using slave labor to produce sugar on large plantations. After 1670 large numbers of English islanders migrated to the Chesapeake and to Carolina; large-scale plantation slavery traveled with them.

Sugar and Slaves: The West Indies

Initially, the English West Indies developed along lines similar to Virginia, with tobacco the dominant crop. Because a single worker could tend only three acres of tobacco, tobacco farming demanded a large population. By 1640 more colonists lived on England's five West Indian islands than in all of Virginia.

Tobacco, requiring little equipment beyond a curing shed, was cheap to raise, and tobacco cultivation gave individuals with little money a chance at upward mobility. Through the 1630s the West Indies remained a society with a large percentage of independent landowners, an overwhelmingly white population, and no extreme inequality of wealth.

Sugar cane soon changed that, revolutionizing the islands' economy and society. Encouraged by Dutch merchants, wealthy English planters began to raise this enormously lucrative crop. The demand for labor soared because sugar required triple the labor force of tobacco. African slaves soon replaced indentured white servants in the fields. Most planters preferred black slaves to white servants because they could be driven harder and maintained more cheaply. Also, African slaves could better withstand the tropical diseases of the Caribbean, they had no rights under contract, and they toiled until they died. Although slaves initially cost two to four times more than indentured servants, they were an economical long-term investment. Some English immigrants to the Caribbean copied the example already set by the Spanish and enslaved both Indians and Africans.

By 1670 the sugar revolution had transformed the British West Indies into a predominantly black and slave society. In 1713 slaves outnumbered whites by four to one; the slave population leaped from 40,000 in 1670 to 130,000 in 1713, with the white population remaining stable at 33,000. Declining demand for white labor in the West Indies diverted the flow of England migration from the islands to mainland North America. Driven from the Indies by high land prices, thousands of English settlers went north to the mainland, settling in Carolina. By 1700 more than 30,000 left the islands.

Rice and Slaves: Carolina

In 1663 Charles II bestowed the swampy coast between Virginia and Spanish Florida on several English supporters, making it the first of several Restoration colonies. The proprietors named their colony Carolina in honor of Charles (*Carolus* in Latin).

Settlers from New England and the West Indies had established outposts along the northern Carolina coast in the 1650s; the proprietors organized them into a separate district with a bicameral legislature. In 1669 one of the proprietors, Anthony Ashley Cooper, accelerated settlement by offering immigrants fifty-acre headright grants for every family member, indentured servant, or slave they brought in. The next year, two hundred white Barbadians and their slaves began the settlement of

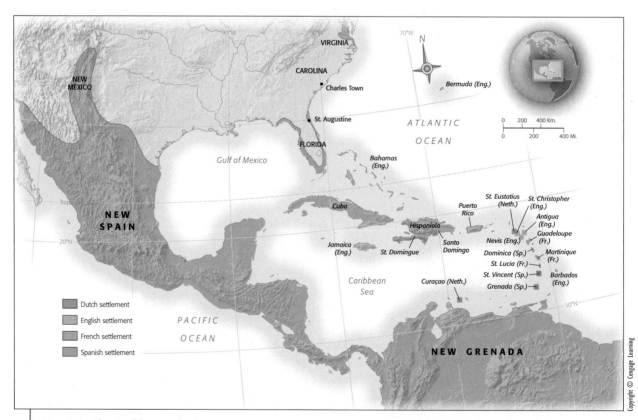

Copyright © Cengage Learning

Map 3.3   The Caribbean Colonies, 1670

By 1660, nearly every West Indian island had been colonized by Europeans and was producing sugar with slave labor. Ten years later English colonists from Barbados were settling the new mainland colony of Carolina.

Interactive Map

southern Carolina near modern Charleston, "in the very chops of the Spanish." In the settlement they called Charles Town, they formed the colony's nucleus, with a bicameral legislature distinct from that of the northern district.

Cooper and his secretary, John Locke, devised an intricate plan for Carolina's settlement and government. Their Fundamental Constitutions of Carolina attempted to ensure the colony's stability by decreeing that political power and social rank should accurately reflect settlers' landed wealth. Thus, they invented a three-tiered nobility that would hold two-fifths of all land, make laws through a council of nobles, and dispense justice through manorial courts.

In the early years, Carolina's population consisted mainly of small landowners who saw little reason to follow the complex system drawn up on the other side of the Atlantic. Southern Carolinians raised livestock, and colonists in northern Carolina exported tobacco, lumber, and pitch. In neither north nor south did the people realize enough profit to maintain slaves, so self-sufficient white families predominated. However, southern Carolinians eagerly sought a cash crop. In the early 1690s they found it—rice. Rice cultivation enriched the few settlers with enough capital to acquire the dikes, dams, and slaves necessary to grow it. By earning annual profits of 25 percent, successful rice planters within a generation became the only colonial mainland elite whose wealth rivaled that of the Caribbean sugar planters.

Treated inhumanely, white indentured servants did not survive in the humid rice paddies swarming with malaria-carrying mosquitoes. Thus, planters imported an ever-growing force of African slaves, who possessed two major advantages. First, some had cultivated rice in Africa and possessed expertise vital to teaching whites how to raise the unfamiliar crop. Second, many Africans were immune to malaria and yellow fever, which were endemic in coastal regions of West Africa, and which they carried to North America. (Tragically, the antibody against malaria also tended to produce the sickle-cell trait, an often-fatal genetic condition.) These two factors made commercial rice production possible in Carolina.

The typical rice planter, with 130 acres in cultivation, needed sixty-five slaves. Demand drove the proportion of slaves in southern Carolina's population from 17 percent in 1680 to 67 percent in 1720, when the region officially became South Carolina. By 1776 the colony, with at least 100,000 slaves, would have more bondsmen than any other mainland colony in the eighteenth century. It would be Britain's only eighteenth-century mainland colony with a black majority.

As the black majority increased, whites relied on force and fear to control their slaves. In 1696 Carolina adopted the galling restrictions and gruesome punishments of the Barbados slave code. Bondage in the mainland colony grew as cruel and harsh as in the West Indies.

White Carolinians' attitudes toward Native Americans likewise hardened. The most vicious result was the trade in Indian slaves. White Carolinians armed allied Indians, encouraged them to raid and capture unarmed Indians to the south and west, and sold the captives to the West Indies during the 1670s and 1680s. A recent study estimates that the Carolina traders enslaved tens of thousands of Indians. Once shipped to the West Indies, most Native Americans died because they lacked immunities to European and tropical diseases.

CHECKING IN

- The English Caribbean colonies became dependent on sugar, which required a large labor force.
- Plantations appeared in the Caribbean, and slavery spread.
- South Carolina became wedded to a cash crop (rice), plantations, and slavery.
- Northern Carolinians exported tobacco, lumber, and pitch.

THE MIDDLE COLONIES

How did diversity distinguish the Middle Colonies?

The Dutch and the Swedish established small commercial outposts between the Chesapeake and New England. The Dutch took over New Sweden, and in turn England seized New Netherland in 1664; by 1681 England had used this territory as the basis for New York, New Jersey, and Pennsylvania, creating a fourth colonial region, the Middle Colonies.

Precursors: New Netherland and New Sweden

New Netherland became North America's first multiethnic society. Barely half the settlers were Dutch; most of the rest comprised Germans, French, Scandinavians, and Africans, both free and slave. In 1643 the population included Protestants, Catholics, Jews, and Muslims, speaking eighteen European and African languages. Religion counted for little (in 1642 the colony had seventeen taverns but not a single place of worship). The trading company that had established the settlement struggled to control the settlers, whose get-rich-quick attitude sapped company profits as private individuals traded illegally in furs. Eventually, the company legalized the private trade.

Privatization rapidly increased the number of guns in the hands of New Netherland's Iroquois allies, giving them a distinct advantage over other tribes. As overhunting depleted local fur supplies and smallpox epidemics raged, the Iroquois encroached on Huron territory for pelts and captives (who were adopted into Iroquois families to replace the dead). After 1648 the Dutch-armed Iroquois attacked French settlements along the St. Lawrence.

Although the Dutch had allied with the inland Iroquois, relations with the nearer Indian neighbors were terrible. With greedy settlers and military weakness, New Netherland largely had itself to blame. In 1643 an all-out war erupted when Governor Willem Kiefft ordered the massacre of previously friendly Indians. By 1645 the Dutch had temporarily prevailed, but only by enlisting English help and inflicting atrocities. The fighting cut New Netherland's Indian population from sixteen hundred to seven hundred.

Another European challenger, Sweden, distracted the Dutch in their war with the Native Americans. In 1638 Sweden had planted a small fur-trading colony in the lower Delaware Valley that was diverting furs from New Netherland. In 1655 the Dutch colony's stern soldier-governor, Peter Stuyvesant (STY-vuh-sant), marched against New Sweden, whose four hundred residents peacefully accepted Dutch annexation. But New Netherland paid dearly for its victory.

Although tiny, the Dutch and Swedish colonies were significant. Above all, they bequeathed a religious and ethnic diversity that would continue in England's Middle Colonies.

English Conquests: New York and New Jersey

Like the Carolinas, New York and New Jersey originated with Restoration-era proprietors hoping to grow rich from rents collected from settlers within a hierarchical society. New York marginally achieved this dream, but New Jersey did not.

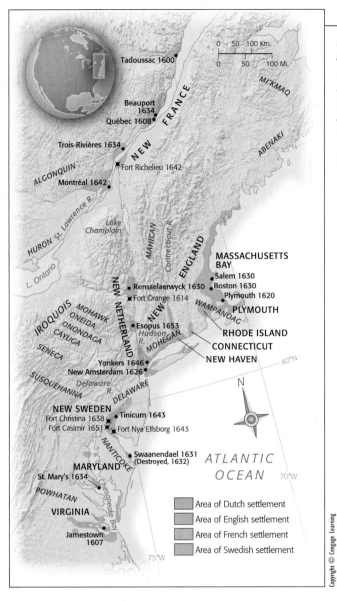

Copyright © Cengage Learning

Map 3.4 European Colonization in the Middle and North Atlantic, c. 1650

North of Spanish Florida, four European powers competed for territory and trade with Native Americans in the early seventeenth century. Swedish and Dutch colonization was the foundation upon which England's Middle Colonies were built.

 Interactive Map

In 1664, at war with the Dutch Republic, Charles II attacked the Dutch colony of New Netherland. Four hundred poorly armed Dutch civilians under Governor Peter Stuyvesant surrendered peacefully. Charles II made his brother James, Duke of York, proprietor of the new English colony and renamed it New York. With James's ascension to the throne in 1685, he converted New York into a royal colony. By 1700 immigration had swelled the population to twenty thousand, of whom just 44 percent were descended from the original Dutch settlers.

New York's governors rewarded their influential political supporters with large land grants. By 1703 five families held 1.75 million acres, which they carved into manors and rented to tenants. By 1750 the enormous income they earned from rents had made the New York estate owners a landed elite second in wealth only to the Carolina rice planters.

However, ambitious plans collided with American realities in New Jersey, which was also carved out of New Netherland. In 1664 the Duke of York awarded a group of supporters New Jersey, at the time inhabited by a few hundred Dutch and Swedes and several thousand Delaware Indians. Within a decade thousands of troublesome New England Puritans settled in New Jersey, and the proprietors sold the region to Quakers, who split the territory into East and West Jersey.

The Jerseys' Quakers, Anglicans, Puritans, Scottish Presbyterians, and Dutch Calvinists quarreled with one another and got along even worse with the proprietors. The governments collapsed between 1698 and 1701, and in 1702 the disillusioned proprietors surrendered their political powers to the crown, which then created the royal colony of New Jersey.

William Penn Quaker who tried to establish Pennsylvania as a "peaceable kingdom" that reflected Quaker ideals of tolerance

Quaker Pennsylvania

In 1681 Charles II paid off a huge debt by appointing a supporter's son, **William Penn,** as proprietor of the last unallocated tract of American territory at the king's disposal. Penn, a Quaker, thus founded the colony as a "holy experiment" based on the teachings of the English preacher George Fox. Penn also hoped for financial gain.

Quakers in late-seventeenth-century England stood well beyond the fringe of respectability. Challenging conventional foundations of social order, they appealed to those at the bottom of the economic ladder. But they also attracted some well-educated, well-to-do individuals disillusioned by the quarreling of rival religious faiths, including significant numbers of merchants. The members of this radical religious sect, which had been born in war-torn England during the 1640s and 1650s, called themselves the Society of Friends, but most others dubbed them Quakers.

At the heart of their founder George Fox's theology was the belief that the Holy Spirit, or "Inner Light," could inspire every soul. Mainstream Christians found this claim highly suspicious. In their religious services ("meetings"), Quakers sat silently until the Inner Light prompted one of them to speak. Quakers believed that the Inner Light could "speak in the female as well as the male," and they thus accorded women unprecedented equality.

Quaker behavior often seemed disrespectful to government and to the social elite, and thus aroused hostility. For example, Quakers refused to tip their hat to their social betters, insisting that spiritual state, not wealth or status, deserved recognition. Their refusal to bear arms appeared unpatriotic and cowardly, yet they faced persecution, imprisonment, and even death with courage.

Care and planning made the Quaker migration to Pennsylvania one of the most successful initial transplantations of Europeans in any North American colony. After sending an advance party, Penn arrived in 1682. He named his new capital Philadelphia, the "City of Brotherly Love." Within five years, eight thousand English Quakers had joined him. Quakers migrated in family groups, and their high birthrate led to rapid population growth. (Pennsylvania's religious toleration attracted not only Quakers but also many other religious groups: Presbyterians, Baptists, Anglicans, and Catholics from England, and Lutherans and radical sectarians from Germany.)

A victim of persecution, Penn hated intolerance and arbitrary governance. He offered Quakers the opportunity to make laws according to their ideals. His Frame of Government (constitution) featured a strong executive branch (a governor and governor's council) and a lower chamber (the assembly) with limited power. Friends, a majority in the colony, dominated the assembly, and Penn generally named Quakers to other positions. To prevent wrangling and to achieve an orderly disposition of property, Penn personally oversaw land sales. He also designed a grid plan for Philadelphia, reserving park areas to keep it a "greene country towne." Penn sought peace with Native Americans by reassuring the Indians that the Quakers wished "to live together as Neighbours and Friends" and by buying land from them fairly.

Pennsylvania seemed an ideal colony—intelligently organized, well financed, tolerant, open to all industrious settlers, and at peace with the Indians. Rich lands and a lengthy growing season produced bumper crops. West Indian demand for grain generated widespread prosperity. By 1700 Philadelphia had become a major port. In 1704 counties along the lower Delaware River, where Swedes and Dutch had settled long before Penn, gained the right to elect their own legislature and became the colony of Delaware.

However, by this time Penn's "peaceable kingdom" had bogged down in human bickering. In 1684 Penn returned to England, and during his fifteen-year absence the settlers quarreled incessantly. Struggles between pro- and anti-Penn forces deadlocked the government. Penn's return in 1699 restored some order, but before leaving again in 1701, he made the legislature unicameral (one chamber) and allowed it to initiate measures.

Despite Penn's hopes, conflict among Quakers shook Pennsylvania in the 1690s, prompting some Friends to join the Church of England. Their departure began a major decline in the Quaker share of Pennsylvania's population, which fell even further after 1710 as Quakers stopped migrating in large numbers.

The Middle Colonies demonstrated that English America could benefit by encouraging pluralism. New York and New Jersey successfully integrated Dutch and Swedish populations; Pennsylvania, New Jersey, and Delaware refused to require residents to support any official church. However, the virtual completion of English claim-staking along the Atlantic Coast set England on a collision course with France and Spain, which were also vying for American territory.

CHECKING IN

- The Dutch established New Netherland (later called New York) and took over Swedish colonies to the south.

- The Dutch colonies, seized by England in 1664, brought a tradition of religious and ethnic diversity and tolerance to the English empire.

- William Penn established the Pennsylvania colony as a refuge for Quakers, who suffered persecution.

- Penn tried to create a "peaceable kingdom" in Pennsylvania, encouraging good relations with Indians and religious tolerance.

RIVALS FOR NORTH AMERICA: FRANCE AND SPAIN

How did the French and Spanish empires develop in the seventeenth century?

Unlike England, with its compact seacoast colonial settlements in North America, France and Spain had cast enormous nets of widely separated trading posts and missions across the interior. The two Catholic nations had converted many Indians to Christianity and made them trading partners and allies. By 1720, scattered missionaries, fur traders, and merchants had spread French and Spanish influence across two-thirds of today's United States.

France Claims a Continent

After briefly losing Canada to England (1629–1632), France resumed and extended its colonization there. Initially a privately held company, the Company of New France issued extensive tracts to large landlords, who in turn imported indentured servants or rented out small tracts. Nonetheless, Canada's harsh winters and short growing season sharply limited their numbers.

More successful were the traders and missionaries who spread beyond the settlements and relied on stable relations with the Indians to succeed. The lucrative opportunities offered by trade converted many would-be farmers into traders.

Jesuit missionaries followed the traders into the interior, spreading French influence westward to the Great Lakes. Ursuline nuns ministered to Native American women and girls nearer Quebec, ensuring that Catholic piety and morality reached all members of Indian families.

Under King Louis XIV (personally reigned 1661–1715), France sought to subordinate its American colony to French interests, following the doctrine of *mercantilism*. According to this doctrine, colonies should serve as sources of raw materials and as markets for manufactured goods so that the colonial power did not have to depend on rival nations for trade. The French hoped that New France would increase the fur trade, provide agricultural surpluses to ship to France's West Indies colonies, and export timber for those colonies and for the French navy. To achieve this, the French government transformed New France into a royal colony, confronted and sought to stifle the Iroquois, and encouraged French immigration to Canada.

The Iroquois had long limited French colonial profits by intercepting convoys of fur pelts. In the 1660s Louis XIV dispatched French troops to New France, where the French army burned Mohawk villages. Sobered by the destruction, the Iroquois Confederacy made a peace that permitted New France's rapid expansion of fur exports.

The French crown energetically built up New France's population, primarily by sending indentured servants to New France; army members stationed there were encouraged to stay, become farmers, and marry the "king's girls," female orphans shipped over with dowries. After 1673, however, immigration dwindled. Colonists who returned to France—more than two-thirds of the immigrants—told horrifying tales of disease, Canada's hard winter, and "savage" Indians. Natural increase would replace immigration as the chief source of population growth, guaranteeing slow development for New France.

coureurs de bois French fur traders who spread throughout the French empire in North America

Even male immigrants who stayed did not always fulfill the French vision of sturdy farmers. Many of them struck out westward from the St. Lawrence Valley, becoming *coureurs de bois* (koo-RUHR duh BWAH), independent and sometimes disreputable fur traders. These French traders obtained furs from the Indians in exchange for European goods, including guns. The coureurs lived and married among the Indians, forging for France a precarious empire based on alliances with Canadian and Great Lakes Indians. Alarmed by the rapid expansion of England's colonies, France sought to contain the English colonies and prevent Spain from linking Florida with New Mexico by dominating the North American heartland.

As early as 1672, fur trader Louis Jolliet and Jesuit missionary Jacques Marquette became the first Europeans known to have reached the upper Mississippi; they later paddled twelve hundred miles downstream to the Mississippi's junction with the Arkansas. Ten years later, the Sieur de La Salle, an ambitious dreamer and adventurer, descended the entire Mississippi to the Gulf of Mexico, ultimately claiming the entire Mississippi basin—half the territory of the present-day United States—for Louis XIV.

Having asserted title to Louisiana, as La Salle christened this empire, the French began settling its southern gateway. The first colonizers arrived on the Gulf Coast in 1698; within a year, the French had erected a fort near modern Biloxi, Mississippi; in 1702 the French founded a trading post where De Soto had faltered and called it Mobile. But Louisiana's growth would be delayed for another decade.

New Mexico: The Pueblo Revolt

Lying at the northerly margin of Spain's empire, New Mexico and Florida remained small and weak through the seventeenth century. Their security depended on friendly relations with Native Americans, but Spanish policies made that nearly impossible.

The Spanish sought to rule New Mexico by subordinating the Pueblo Indians to their authority. Franciscan missionaries established churches in the native communities (pueblos) and tried to force the Indians to attend Mass and observe Catholic rituals and morality. Spanish landowners received *encomiendas* that allowed them to exploit Indian labor. Finally, the Spanish drove a wedge between the Pueblo Indians and their nonfarming trade partners, the Apaches (uh-PATCH-ees) and the Navajos (NAV-uh-hoes). Corn once used for trade was now claimed as tribute by the Spanish. In response, the Apaches raided both pueblos and Spanish settlements, driving most of the pueblo dwellers to stronger ties with the Spanish.

Spanish rule began to chafe, especially after 1660. Drought withered Pueblo crops, leaving populations vulnerable to disease and starvation. The Pueblo population plummeted from eighty thousand in 1600 to barely seventeen thousand by the 1670s. Compounding the misery, Apaches riding horses stolen from the Spanish raided and plundered the pueblos. Desperate Indians turned to traditional beliefs and ceremonies to restore the spiritual balance and bring rainfall and peace. Determined to suppress this "witchcraft," Franciscan missionaries entered sacred kivas, destroyed religious objects, and publicly whipped native religious leaders and their followers.

In 1675 Governor Juan Francisco Treviño ordered the kivas sacked and religious leaders arrested. Three leaders went to the gallows; a fourth hanged himself; forty-three others were jailed, whipped, and sentenced to be sold as slaves.

Indian resentment against the Spanish blazed, and Pueblo leaders began planning to overthrow the Spanish. At the head of the revolt was **Popé** (poe-PAY), who had been arrested in 1675. Other leaders included disillusioned Christian converts and individuals of mixed Pueblo-Spanish ancestry. Most had tried to reconcile Christianity and Spanish rule with their Indian identity, but the deteriorating conditions and Spanish intolerance turned them against Catholicism.

Popé Leader of the Pueblo Revolt against the Spanish in 1680

The Pueblo Revolt began in August 1680 as Popé and cohorts attacked Spanish colonists residing near Taos and killed sixty-eight of the seventy who lived there. Joined by Indians from neighboring pueblos, they laid siege to New Mexico's capital, Santa Fe. The rebels destroyed the churches and killed nearly four hundred colonists and missionaries. The Spanish fled, not to return for twelve years. They left behind them large numbers of livestock and horses, around which many Native Americans would build new ways of life.

New Mexico History Museum

Taos Pueblo, New Mexico
Although this photo was taken in 1880, Taos's appearance had changed little during the two centuries since the Pueblo Revolt.

CHECKING IN

- France created a New World empire that encompassed North America from the Appalachians to the Rockies.
- The French empire rested primarily on trade with Native Americans rather than on conquest and displacement.
- Spanish policies led to the Pueblo Revolt in 1680, but the Spanish reestablished control by 1700.
- The Spanish tried to establish frontiers in Texas and Florida, but their presence there was weak and scattered.

Led by a new governor, Diego de Vargas, the Spanish returned in 1692, using both violence and threats of violence to reestablish their rule. Spanish control of New Mexico remained limited as the Europeans abolished the *encomiendas* and reined in the Franciscans. Pueblo suspicion of the Spanish remained, but there were no more revolts. Instead, the Indians accepted the limited Spanish control and sustained their cultural identity within the boundaries of colonial rule.

Florida and Texas

The Spanish fared no better in Florida. Periodic rebellions swept the Spanish settlements; beginning in the 1680s, Indian slave raiders, allied with the English, killed or captured thousands of Florida natives and sold them to English slave traders. Even before a new round of warfare erupted in Europe at the turn of the century, Spain was ill prepared to defend its beleaguered North American empire.

English expansion threatened Florida, while the French establishment of Louisiana dashed Spanish hopes of linking Florida to New Mexico. To offset the French, Spanish authorities proclaimed the province of Tejas (Texas) in 1691, but no permanent Spanish settlements appeared there until 1716.

Chapter Summary

How did tobacco shape the Chesapeake colonies? (page 40)

Unlike New England with its diversified economy, the Chesapeake colonies relied on a single cash crop, tobacco. Tobacco shaped the Chesapeake region by leading to the plantation system and dependence on African slavery, which developed gradually in the seventeenth century.

What was the "New England Way," and what challenges did it endure? (page 46)

Puritans established "a city upon a hill" in Massachusetts Bay to serve as a model to the world. The "New England Way"—a society based on religion—was threatened by dissenters Roger Williams and Anne Hutchinson and by the rise of a market economy. White expansion steadily displaced New England's Native Americans, and from the Pequot War to the bitter and costly King Philip's War resistance was crushed. The Half-Way Covenant marked the beginning of the end for the New England Way by relaxing standards for church membership, and the Salem witchcraft hysteria delivered the final blow, revealing deep social divisions.

Why and how did plantation agriculture shape slavery in the Caribbean and Carolina? (page 55)

Dependent on sugar cane, the Caribbean colonies evolved a harsh form of plantation slavery, while rice created a similarly harsh system in southern Carolina, which became the only mainland colony with a black majority population. Carolinians also enslaved tens of thousands of Indians.

How did diversity distinguish the Middle Colonies? (page 58)

The Middle Colonies followed yet another path of development. The Dutch New Netherland colony, conquered and incorporated by the English, contributed a strong history of religious and ethnic diversity. William Penn's "holy experiment" in Pennsylvania flourished, although it gradually moved away from some of its founder's ideals. Nonetheless, it, too, maintained both religious and economic diversity.

KEY TERMS

Bacon's Rebellion *(p. 45)*
a city upon a hill *(p. 47)*
the "New England Way" *(p. 48)*
Old Deluder Act *(p. 48)*
Roger Williams *(p. 48)*
Anne Hutchinson *(p. 48)*
Half-Way Covenant *(p. 51)*
King Philip's War *(p. 53)*
Salem witchcraft trials *(p. 54)*
William Penn *(p. 60)*
coureurs de bois (p. 62)
Popé *(p. 63)*

How did the French and Spanish empires develop in the seventeenth century? (page 61)

In contrast to the fairly compact English settlements, the French empire became a far-flung web stretching from the Appalachians to the Rockies, dependent almost exclusively on trade and thus on good relations with Native Americans. After suppressing the Pueblo Revolt in the late seventeenth century, the Spanish tried to establish their imperial frontiers in Texas and Florida, but both remained only lightly settled.

Go to the CourseMate website at **www.cengagebrain.com** for additional study tools and review materials—including audio and video clips—for this chapter.

CHAPTER 4

The Bonds of Empire

1660–1750

Mrs. Harme Gansevoort (Magdalena Bouw),
by Pieter Vanderlyn, c. 1740

Courtesy, The Henry Francis du Pont Winterthur Museum

CHAPTER PREVIEW

Rebellion and War, 1660–1713
*How did the Glorious Revolution shape relations
between England and its North American colonies?*

Colonial Economies and Societies, 1660–1750
*What were the most important consequences
of British mercantilism for the mainland colonies?*

Competing for a Continent, 1713–1750
*What factors explain the relative success
of the British, French, and Spanish empires
in North America?*

Public Life in British America, 1689–1750
*How did politics, the Enlightenment, and religious
movements shape public life in the colonies?*

Two men, George Whitefield and Benjamin Franklin, exemplified the major cultural currents that swept across the Atlantic from Europe to the colonies in the mid-eighteenth century. The embodiment of the powerful revival of piety that reinvigorated Protestantism on both sides of the ocean, Whitefield also demonstrated and reinforced the close ties that bound England and the colonies. Franklin, considered the leading American scientist of his time, personified the faith in reason known as the Enlightenment.

Born on opposite sides of the Atlantic, both men moved easily in English and colonial society, leaving behind provincialism for careers that brought them renown on both sides of the Atlantic. Their lives illustrate the increasingly close ties between England and her mainland colonies, ties that strengthened as the political and economic bonds of the empire grew tighter.

67

This new imperial relationship enabled the Anglo-American colonies to achieve a level of growth and prosperity unequalled elsewhere in the Americas.

REBELLION AND WAR, 1660–1713

How did the Glorious Revolution shape relations between England and its North American colonies?

After the Restoration (1660), England undertook a concerted effort to expand overseas trade and to subordinate its colonies to English commercial interests and political authority. The fall of the Stuart dynasty in 1689 and a succession of international wars hindered but did not halt this effort. By the time peace was restored in 1713, the colonists had become closely tied to a new, powerful British empire.

Royal Centralization, 1660–1688

The sons of a king executed by Parliament, the last Stuart monarchs, Charles II and James II, disliked representative government. Beginning in the mid-1670s, they tried to rule England as much as possible without Parliament and eyed American colonial assemblies suspiciously.

As Duke of York during his brother Charles's rule, James showed his disdain for colonial assemblies almost as soon as he became the proprietor of New York. Calling elected assemblies "of dangerous consequence," he forbade legislatures to meet from 1664 to 1682. In Charles's twenty-five-year reign, more than 90 percent of the governors whom he appointed were army officers, a serious violation of the English tradition of holding the military accountable to civilian authority. When James became king, he continued the policy.

Ever resentful of outside meddling, New Englanders resisted such centralization of power. In 1661 the Massachusetts assembly declared its citizens exempt from all English laws and royal decrees except declarations of war.

Provoked, Charles moved to break the Puritan establishment's power. In 1679 he carved a new royal territory, New Hampshire, from Massachusetts. In 1684 he declared Massachusetts a royal colony and revoked its charter, the very foundation of the Puritan city upon a hill.

James II went further. In 1686 the new king merged five separate colonies—Massachusetts, New Hampshire, Connecticut, Rhode Island, and Plymouth—into the **Dominion of New England,** later adding New York and the Jerseys. Under the new system, these colonies' legislatures ceased to exist. Sir Edmund Andros, a former army officer, became governor of the new supercolony.

Andros's arbitrary actions ignited burning hatred in Massachusetts. He limited towns to one annual meeting and jailed prominent citizens to crush protests. He forced a Boston Puritan congregation to share its meetinghouse with an Anglican minister. Confronted by outraged colonists, he snapped "You have no more privileges left you than not to be sold for slaves."

Tensions also ran high in New York, where Catholics held high political and military posts under the Duke of York's rule. Anxious colonists feared that these

Dominion of New England
James II's attempt to tighten royal control of colonies by creating a new political entity

Chronology

1651–1733	England enacts the Navigation Acts
1660	Restoration of the English monarchy
1686–1689	Dominion of New England
1688–1689	Glorious Revolution in England
1689	Uprisings in Massachusetts, New York, and Maryland; royal authority established English Bill of Rights
1689–1697	King William's War (in Europe, War of the League of Augsburg)
1690	John Locke, *Essay Concerning Human Understanding*
1701	Iroquois Confederacy agrees to remain neutral in future wars between England and France
1702–1713	Queen Anne's War (in Europe, War of the Spanish Succession)
1715–1716	Yamasee War in Carolina
1716	San Antonio de Bexar founded
1718	New Orleans founded
1732	Georgia founded
1735	John Peter Zenger acquitted of seditious libel in New York; Jonathan Edwards leads revival in Northampton, Massachusetts
1739	Great Awakening begins with George Whitefield's arrival in British colonies; Stono Rebellion in South Carolina
1739–1740	Anglo-Spanish War
1739–1748	King George's War (in Europe, the War of the Austrian Succession)
1743	Benjamin Franklin founds American Philosophical Society
1750	Slavery legalized in Georgia

Catholic officials would betray the colony to France. When Andros's local deputy allowed harbor forts to deteriorate, New Yorkers suspected the worst.

The Glorious Revolution in England and America, 1688–1689

The Protestant majority in England also worriedly monitored Stuart displays of pro-Catholic sympathies. The Duke of York himself became a Catholic in 1676, and Charles II converted on his deathbed. Both rulers violated English law by allowing Catholics to hold high office and to worship openly.

In 1688 James's second wife bore a son, who would be raised—and perhaps would rule—as a Catholic. Aghast at the idea, English political leaders asked James's Protestant daughter Mary and her husband, William of Orange (the Dutch Republic's leader), to intervene. When William and Mary led a small army to England in November 1688, royal troops defected to them, and James II fled to France.

This nearly bloodless coup, the **"Glorious Revolution,"** created a "limited monarchy" as defined by England's **Bill of Rights** of 1689. The monarchs promised to summon Parliament annually, to sign its bills, and to respect civil liberties. Neither the English nor Anglo-Americans would ever forget this vindication of

"Glorious Revolution"
Overthrow of James II in favor of William and Mary

Bill of Rights Drastically limited kingly power; vindicated limited representative government

Courtesy of the City of New Rochelle

Jacob Leisler

Leisler led an ill-fated uprising in New York following the Glorious Revolution, and was executed for his efforts. Nevertheless, his followers remained politically forceful in New York for a generation after his death.

limited representative government. News of the Glorious Revolution electrified Massachusetts Puritans, who arrested Andros and his councilors. Acting in the name of William and Mary, the Massachusetts elite resumed its own government. The new monarchs allowed Connecticut and Rhode Island to resume election of their own governors and permitted Massachusetts to absorb the Plymouth colony. But Massachusetts enjoyed only a partial victory. The colony's new royal charter of 1691 reserved to the crown the appointment of the governor. Moreover, property ownership replaced church membership as the criterion for voting. Worst of all, the Puritan colony had to tolerate Anglicans and all other Protestants, who were proliferating in the port towns.

New York's counterpart to the anti-Stuart uprising was Leisler's Rebellion. In May 1689 the city militia, under Captain Jacob Leisler (LIES-luhr), seized the harbor's main fort and called elections for an assembly. In 1691 Leisler, still riding high, denied newly arrived English troops entry to key forts for fear that they were loyal to James II. But after a brief skirmish, Leisler was arrested and charged with treason. Elite New Yorkers, many of whom Leisler had arrested, packed the jury, and both he and his son-in-law were convicted and hanged.

Arbitrary government and fears of Catholic plots had also brought turmoil to Maryland by 1689, where the Protestant-dominated lower house and the Catholic upper chamber were feuding. When the Glorious Revolution toppled James II, Lord Baltimore, away in England, dispatched a courier to Maryland, commanding obedience to William and Mary. However, the courier died en route.

Protestant rebel John Coode organized the Protestant Association to secure Maryland for William and Mary. In July 1689 Coode and his coconspirators seized the capital, removed Catholics from office, and requested that the crown take over the colony. Maryland became a royal province in 1691 and made the Church of England its established religion in 1692. Catholics, making up less than one-fourth of the population, lost the right to vote and to worship in public. In 1715 the fourth Lord Baltimore joined the Church of England and regained his proprietorship.

The revolutionary events of 1688–1689 reestablished the colonies' legislative government and ensured Protestant religious freedom. William and Mary allowed colonial elites to reassert local control and encouraged Americans to identify their interests with England, laying the foundation for an empire based on voluntary allegiance, not raw force.

A Generation of War, 1689–1713

The Glorious Revolution ushered in a quarter-century of war that convulsed both England and the colonies. In 1689 England joined a European coalition against France's Louis XIV and plunged into the War of the League of Augsburg (which Anglo-Americans called **King William's War**).

In 1690 the war spread to North America, as New Yorkers and New Englanders launched an invasion of England's enemy, New France. The invasion deteriorated into cruel but inconclusive border raids by both sides. The Iroquois, allied to the English, bore the brunt of the war. French forces, enlisting the aid of virtually every other tribe from Maine to the Great Lakes, played havoc with Iroquois land and peoples. By 1700 one-fourth of the Iroquois warriors had been killed or taken prisoner, or had fled to Canada. The total Iroquois population declined 20 percent, to fewer than seven thousand. (By comparison, Europeans suffered about 1,300 casualties.) In 1701 the Iroquois agreed to let Canada's governor settle their disputes with other Indians and to remain neutral in future Anglo-French wars. Thereafter, playing French and English off against each other, the Iroquois maintained control of their lands, rebuilt their population, and held the balance of power along the Great Lakes.

In 1702 a new European war pitted England against France and Spain. During what the colonists called **Queen Anne's War,** Anglo-Americans became painfully aware of their own military weakness. French and Indian raiders from Canada destroyed New England towns, while the Spanish invaded southern Carolina and nearly took Charles Town in 1706. Colonial vessels fell to French and Spanish warships. English forces, however, gained control of the Hudson Bay region, Newfoundland, and Acadia (henceforth called Nova Scotia). The peace signed in 1713 allowed Britain to keep these lands but left the French and Indians in control of their interior.

These wars had a profound political consequence. Anglo-Americans, realizing how much they needed the protection of the Royal Navy and identifying with England's leadership in the Protestant cause, became more loyal than ever to the English crown.

King William's War European war that spilled over into North America (1689–1697)

Queen Anne's War European war that spilled over into North America

CHECKING IN

- After the Restoration, Britain attempted to tighten control over the colonies.
- The Glorious Revolution drove James II from the throne in 1688.
- The colonies regained their legislative rights.
- Protestant religious freedom was ensured.
- European wars from 1689 to 1713 played out in part in North America and strengthened colonial ties to England.

COLONIAL ECONOMIES AND SOCIETIES, 1660–1750

What were the most important consequences of British mercantilism for the mainland colonies?

The arrival of peace in 1713 shifted the competition among England, France, and Spain from the military to the economic. Britain and France sought to integrate their colonies into single colonial empires; Spain also attempted to do so but found its power north of Mexico and the Caribbean severely limited.

Mercantilist Empires in America

A set of political-economic assumptions known as **mercantilism** supplied the framework for the new imperial economies. The term refers to European policies aimed at guaranteeing prosperity by making the European country (England, France, or Spain) as self-sufficient as possible by eliminating its dependence on

mercantilism Political/economic theory that self-sufficiency was the way to national prosperity; tied colonial economies to the mother country

foreign suppliers, damaging its foreign competitors' commerce, and increasing the national stock of gold and silver by selling more goods abroad than it bought. Colonies would supply raw materials, but the home countries would do most of the manufacturing.

Navigation Acts Series of laws meant to make colonies conform to the ideas of mercantilism

A series of **Navigation Acts** governing commerce between Britain and its colonies embodied mercantilism. In 1651 the English Parliament passed the first Navigation Act to exclude the Dutch from English trade. During the Restoration, Parliament enacted the Navigation Acts of 1660 and 1663; they barred colonial merchants from exporting such commodities as sugar and tobacco to anywhere but England and from importing goods on non-English ships. Another major measure, the Molasses Act of 1733, sought to integrate Caribbean sugar growers into the imperial economy by slapping heavy import taxes on non-British imports and thus creating in effect a protective tariff.

By 1750 a long series of Navigation Acts was affecting the colonial economy in four major ways. First, the laws limited imperial trade to British-owned ships whose crews were three-quarters British (broadly defined to include all colonists, even slaves). This new shipping restriction helped Britain to become Europe's foremost shipping nation and laid the foundations for an American merchant marine. By the 1750s Americans owned one-third of all imperial vessels. The swift growth of the merchant marine diversified the colonial economy and made it more self-sufficient. The expansion of colonial shipping hastened urbanization. By 1770 New York, Philadelphia, Boston, and Charleston had become major ports.

Second, the Navigation Acts barred the colonies' export of "enumerated goods" unless they first passed through England or Scotland. Among these were tobacco, rice, furs, indigo, and naval stores (masts, hemp, tar, and turpentine). Parliament did not restrict grain, livestock, fish, lumber, or rum, which constituted 60 percent of colonial exports. To sweeten the deal, Parliament gave American tobacco a monopoly in British markets; it also eased the burden of customs duties on both tobacco and rice. Despite the restrictive laws, planters' profits dropped only 3 percent.

Third, the navigation system encouraged economic diversification. Parliament paid modest bounties to Americans producing silk, iron, dyes, hemp, lumber, and other products that Britain would otherwise have had to import from foreign countries. Parliament also erected protective tariffs against foreign goods. In addition, the trade laws forbade Anglo-Americans from competing with British manufacturing of certain products, especially clothing. There were no restrictions on the production of iron, and by the eve of the Revolution, 250 ironworks were in production.

Finally, the Navigation Acts made the colonies a protected market for low-priced consumer goods from Britain. As a result, the share of British exports bound for America rose from just 5 percent in 1700 to almost 40 percent by 1760. Mercantilism gave rise to a "consumer revolution" in British America.

Britain's fellow mercantilists in France and Spain enjoyed no such growth or prosperity. France's Canadian colonies had few materials other than furs to export, and they imported primarily wine and brandy. The French government actually lost money in the fur trade by sending sizable amounts of cloth, firearms, and other manufactured commodities to its Indian allies; the large army that France kept stationed in North America was also a drain on the French treasury. French Canada continued to lack the private investment, commercial infrastructure, consumer market, and manufacturing capacity that British North America was rapidly developing. The French did achieve some economic success in the West Indies, however, where sugar planters (in defiance of mercantilist principles) turned their cane into molasses and then sold much of the molasses to New England merchants. Louisiana remained unprofitable, a drain on French resources.

Spain's economic record was even more dismal. The revival of the Spanish and Latin American economies during the eighteenth century did not extend north of Mexico, where many Spanish colonists turned to smuggling goods to and from Spain's rivals as a source of income. These economic successes and failures mirrored what was happening in the European mother countries. In both France and Spain, most wealth was in the form of land held by the nobility and the Catholic Church; there was almost no liquidity. In contrast, England's economy was a commercial-mercantile one. More and more wealth was in the hands of merchants, who used it as capital to invest in commercial enterprises, trade, and manufacturing. Britain's navy protected that trade, while the Bank of England ensured a stable money supply. Great Britain was well on the way to becoming the world's first industrial nation, and its colonies benefited accordingly; indeed, the colonies' per capita income from 1650 to 1770 rose twice as fast as that of Britain.

Population Growth and Diversity

Demographic differences reinforced Britain's economic advantages. By 1750 the British North American colonies boasted more than 1.1 million inhabitants; the French colonies, 60,000; and the Spanish colonies, an almost negligible 19,000.

Potential Spanish immigrants generally chose the wealthier Latin American colonies as their destination. Spain saw its settlements north of Mexico primarily as a buffer against French or English expansion and consequently maintained a heavy military presence there.

Poverty kept most French people from immigrating, and tales of harsh Canadian winters and wretched Louisiana conditions often deterred those who might otherwise have tried their luck in the New World. French Canada's population growth was primarily the result of natural increase; to populate Louisiana, the French government dispatched paupers and criminals and encouraged the large-scale importation of slaves. By 1732 two-thirds of lower Louisiana's 5,800 people were slaves.

Unlike their French and Spanish rivals, the British colonies could offer potential immigrants ample farmland and a healthy imperial economy. Equally important, the British willingly accepted non-British immigrants—as long as they were not Catholics—including a handful of Jews. Thus, British North America had a much deeper pool of potential immigrants.

Natural increase fueled population growth. After 1700, when life expectancy and family size in the South rose to parallel those of the North, Anglo-America's growth far outpaced Britain's. In 1700 England's population outnumbered the colonies' by twenty to one; by 1775 the ratio would be only three to one. Nevertheless, continuing immigration contributed significantly to colonial population growth. In the forty years after Queen Anne's War, 350,000 newcomers had reached the colonies.

Between 1630 and 1700 approximately two thousand English settlers arrived in the colonies annually, constituting 90 percent of all European immigrants. After

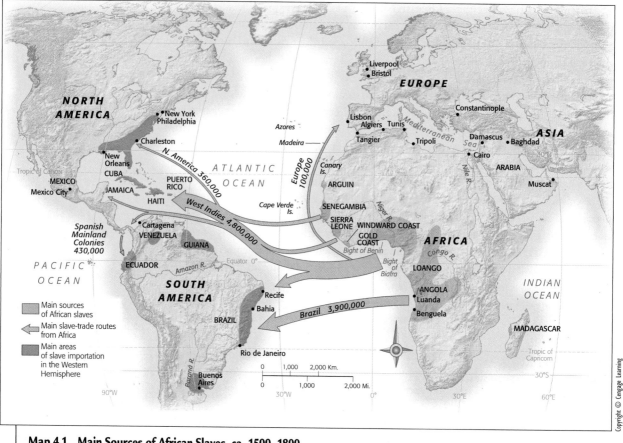

Map 4.1   Main Sources of African Slaves, ca. 1500–1800

The vast majority of enslaved Africans were taken to plantation colonies between Chesapeake Bay and the Brazilian coast.

Interactive Map

1713 the flood slowed to a trickle of five hundred English immigrants a year. Rising employment and wages in England made emigration less attractive, but economic hardships elsewhere in the British Isles and on the Continent guaranteed a steady stream of immigrants, greatly increasing ethnic diversity among white North Americans.

More than 100,000 newcomers in this era were from Ireland. Two-thirds of these were "Scots-Irish," the descendants of sixteenth-century Scottish Presbyterian settlers of northern Ireland. The Scots-Irish generally immigrated as complete families.

German-speaking lands in central Europe contributed some 125,000 settlers, the majority seeking escape from desperate poverty. One-third were "redemptioners" who had sold themselves or their children as indentured servants. Lutherans and Calvinists predominated, but a significant minority belonged to small, pacifist sects that desired above all to be left alone.

Indentured servants had to work one to four years for a master who might exploit them cruelly. Servants could be sold or rented out, beaten, kept from marrying, and sexually harassed; attempted escape usually meant an extension of service.

At the end of their term, most collected "freedom dues," which helped them to marry and acquire land.

The piedmont, a broad, rolling upland stretching along the eastern slope of the Appalachians, drew many immigrants seeking open land. Upper New York, Pennsylvania, and Maryland attracted large numbers of Germans and Scots-Irish. Charles Town became a popular gateway for immigrants who later moved westward to the Carolina piedmont to become small farmers. In 1713 few Anglo-Americans lived more than fifty miles from the Atlantic, but by 1750 one-third of the colonists resided in the piedmont.

Not all of the white immigrants came voluntarily. Between 1718 and 1783 some thirty thousand English convicts arrived in North America; some were murderers, but most were poor petty criminals. They were sold as servants. Relatively few committed crimes in the colonies, and some established themselves as successful backcountry farmers.

Benjamin Franklin reflected the attitude of many colonists when he asked, "Why should Pennsylvania, founded by the English, become a colony of aliens, who will shortly be so numerous as the Germanize us instead of us Anglicizing them, and will never adopt our language or customs any more than they can acquire our complexions?" Franklin also suggested that the colonists send rattlesnakes to Britain in exchange for its convict laborers.

There were no volunteers among the 140,000 enslaved Africans who constituted the largest single group of newcomers. Most were from Africa's west coast, and all had survived a sea crossing of sickening brutality known as the **Middle Passage.** Ship captains closely calculated how many slaves they could jam into their vessels. Kept below deck in near-darkness, surrounded by filth and stench, numbed by depression, the Africans frequently fell victim to disease. Slaves who refused to eat or otherwise defied shipboard authority were flogged. Open rebellions erupted on about 10 percent of the ships; shippers responded by hiring full-time guards and installing barricades to confine slaves even further.

By mid-century blacks constituted 20 percent of the North American colonies' population. Although slavery remained primarily a southern institution, 15 percent of all slaves lived north of Maryland; by 1750 one in seven New Yorkers was a slave.

West Indian and Brazilian slave buyers outbid Anglo-Americans, who of necessity not only bought a higher proportion of female slaves but also protected their investments by maintaining slaves' health. As a result, slaves in British mainland colonies, more often than their Caribbean or Brazilian

Map 4.2 Immigration and British Colonial Expansion, to 1755

Black majorities emerged in much of the Chesapeake tidewater and the Carolina-Georgia low country. Immigrants from Germany, Ireland, and Scotland predominated among the settlers in the Piedmont. A significant Jewish population emerged in the seaports.

Interactive Map

Middle Passage Brutal and often fatal slave journey from Africa to the Americas

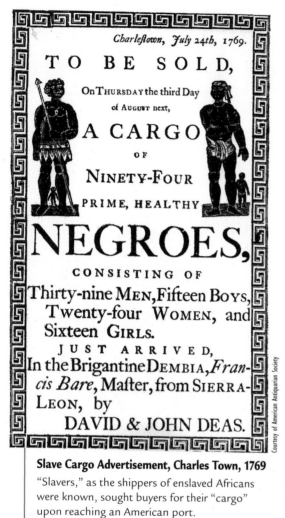

Slave Cargo Advertisement, Charles Town, 1769
"Slavers," as the shippers of enslaved Africans were known, sought buyers for their "cargo" upon reaching an American port.

counterparts, formed families and lived longer. Natural increase among African-Americans almost equaled that of whites, and in some places American-born slaves outnumbered those born in Africa.

Rural White Men and Women

Because the vast majority of colonial landowners had just enough acreage for a working farm, most could not provide land for their children when they married. Moreover, with longevity increasing, children often did not receive their inheritances until middle age or later, and because families were large, a farmer's wealth was typically divided into small portions. Under these circumstances, a young man typically worked from about age sixteen to age twenty-three as a field hand to save money just to buy farm equipment, and a young husband generally had to rent land until he reached his mid-thirties.

The payment of mortgages was slow. A farmer could expect to earn 6 percent cash income per year, which barely equaled mortgage interest. After making a down payment of one-third, a husband and wife generally paid the next third through their inheritances. The final third would be paid when the children reached their teens and helped to double the regular farm income. Most colonial parents found themselves free of debt only as they reached their late fifties.

Rural families depended somewhat on barter and much more on what wives and daughters manufactured: soap, preserved food, knitted goods, yarn, and the products of dairy, orchard, and garden. However, legal constraints bound colonial women. A woman's most independent decision was her choice of a husband. Once married, she lost control of any goods or money she brought into the marriage. Nevertheless, widows controlled substantial property—an estimated 8 to 10 percent of all property in eighteenth-century Anglo-America—and a few ran large estates or plantations.

Colonial Farmers and the Environment

As English settlement expanded, the environment east of the Appalachians changed rapidly. Eighteenth-century settlers cleared forest land to plant crops in its fertile soil. New England farmers also cleared from their land innumerable large rocks, debris from the last Ice Age. The felled trees provided timber to construct houses, barns, and fences and were burned as fuel for cooking and heating. Urban dwellers bought their firewood and construction timber from farmers and planters.

Removal of trees (**deforestation**) deprived large forest creatures, such as bears, panthers, and wild turkeys, of their habitat, while the planted land provided free

deforestation Removal of trees that had a devastating ecological impact

lunch for rabbits, mice, and possums. Deforestation removed protection from wind and sun, producing warmer summers and harsher winters, and, ironically, reinforcing the demand for firewood. By hastening the runoff of spring waters, deforestation led to heavier flooding and, where water could not escape, to larger swamps. Volatile temperatures and water levels rapidly reduced the number of fish in colonial streams and lakes.

Deforestation also dried and hardened the soil; colonial crops had even more drastic effects. Native Americans rotated their crops to protect against soil depletion, but many colonial farmers lacked enough land to do so—and many more were unwilling to sacrifice short-term profits for long-term benefits. Tobacco yields in the Chesapeake region declined in fields planted for only three or four consecutive years. As Chesapeake tobacco growers abandoned tidewater fields and moved to the piedmont, they hastened erosion. By 1750, to remain productive, many shifted from tobacco to wheat.

Well-to-do Europeans had already turned to conservation and "scientific farming." North American colonists, however, ignored such techniques. Some could not afford to implement them, and virtually all believed that America's vast lands, including those still held by Indians, would sustain them and future generations indefinitely.

Poor Farmer's House

Many poor Chesapeake farmers lived in a single room with a dirt floor, no interior walls, an unglazed window, and minimal furnishings.

The Urban Paradox

Cities were colonial America's economic paradox. Although they shipped the livestock, grain, and lumber that enriched the countryside, at the same time they were caught in a downward spiral of declining opportunity.

After 1740 many among the 4 percent of colonists in cities found economic success elusive. Philadelphia, New York, and Boston faced escalating poverty. The cities' poor rolls, moreover, always bulged with the survivors of mariners lost at sea; unskilled, landless men; and women (often widows) and children from the countryside. High population density and poor sanitation left colonial cities vulnerable to the rapid spread of contagious diseases. As a result, half of all city children died before age twenty-one, and urban adults averaged ten fewer years of life than rural residents.

Even the able-bodied found cities economically treacherous. Traditionally, artisans trained apprentices and employed them as journeymen until they could open their own shops. After 1750, however, more employers released their workers when business slowed. And from 1720 onward, recessions hit frequently, creating longer spells of unemployment.

After 1700 urban poverty became a major problem. In Boston, for example, the proportion of the population too poor to pay taxes climbed steadily. New York did not build its first poorhouse until 1736, but 4 percent of its population needed public assistance by 1772. The percentage of Philadelphia families listed as poor jumped from 3 percent in 1720 to 11 percent by 1760.

Wealth remained highly concentrated. New York's wealthiest 10 percent (mostly merchants) owned about 45 percent of the property throughout the eighteenth century; Boston and Philadelphia followed similar patterns.

In the South, most cities were little more than large towns, although Charles Town was North America's fourth-largest city. South Carolina's capital offered gracious living to wealthy planters during the months of heat and insect infestations on their plantations. But shanties on the city's outskirts sheltered a growing crowd of destitute whites. Like their counterparts in northern port cities, Charles Town's poor whites competed for work with urban slaves whose masters rented out their labor. Racial tensions simmered.

Middle-class urban women faced less manual drudgery than their rural counterparts. Nonetheless, they managed complex households, often including servants and other nonfamily members. Although they sewed, knitted, and raised poultry and vegetables, urban women generally purchased their cloth and most of their food. Household servants, usually young single women or widows, helped with cooking, cleaning, and laundering. Wives also worked in family businesses, usually located in the owner's home.

Widows and less affluent wives took in boarders and often spun and wove cloth for local merchants. As grim conditions in Boston forced many widows with children to look to the community for relief, more prosperous Bostonians scorned them. A leading minister lamented "thye swarms of children…that are continually strolling and playing about the streets of our metropolis, clothed in rags and brought up in idleness and ignorance." Another clergyman warned that charity for widows and their children was money "worse than lost."

Slavery

Masters could usually afford to keep slaves healthy, but they rarely made their human chattels comfortable. Slave upkeep generally cost 60 percent less than the maintenance of indentured servants. White servants ate two hundred pounds of beef or pork a year; slaves, fifty pounds. A master would spend as much providing beer and hard cider for a servant as food and clothing for a slave. Adult slaves received eight quarts of corn and one pound of pork weekly and were expected to grow vegetables and raise poultry.

Slaves worked for a longer portion of their lives than whites. Slave children worked part time from the age of seven and full time as early as eleven. African-American women performed hard work alongside men and tended tobacco and rice crops even when pregnant. Most slaves toiled until they died, although those in their sixties rarely did hard labor.

As the number of Creole (American-born) slaves grew, sharp differences between them and African-born blacks arose. Creoles enjoyed the advantage of knowing the English language, the local environment, and the ways of their masters. They often translated this advantage into greater autonomy. Wealthier planters in particular used African-born slaves as field hands while training Creoles to perform household duties, such as repairing and driving carriages, preparing and serving meals, sewing, and caring for their children.

Both Africans and Creoles maximized opportunities within this harsh system. House slaves demanded that guests tip them for shining shoes and stabling horses; they also expected gifts on holidays. In the Carolina and Georgia rice country, the task system gave slaves some control of their work. Under tasking, each slave spent half a day caring for one-quarter acre, after which his or her duties ended. Ambitious slaves used the rest of the day to keep hogs or to grow vegetables for sale in Charles Town.

The gang system used on tobacco plantations gave Chesapeake slaves less free time than their counterparts in Carolina. However, despite Carolina slaves' greater autonomy, racial tensions ran high, especially as blacks began to outnumber whites. For example, a law of 1735 imposed severe restrictions on slave clothing. Of far greater concern were large gatherings of blacks uncontrolled by whites. In 1721 Charles Town enacted a 9:00 p.m. curfew for blacks. Slaves responded with increased instances of arson, theft, flight, and violence.

By mid-century, slaves constituted 20 percent of New York City's population and formed a majority in Charles Town and Savannah. Skilled urban slaves hired themselves out and kept part of their wages. By 1770 one-tenth of Savannah's slaves were living in rented rooms away from their owners. Despite substantial personal freedom, they remained slaves.

Tensions erupted in 1739 when a slave uprising known as the **Stono Rebellion** jolted South Carolina. Stealing guns and ammunition from a store at the Stono River Bridge, one hundred slaves headed for Florida crying, "Liberty!" Along the way they burned seven plantations and killed twenty whites. Within a day, however, mounted militiamen surrounded the runaways, cut them down, and spiked a rebel head on every milepost back to Charles Town. Whites expressed their fears in a new slave code stipulating constant surveillance and discipline for slaves, and requiring legislative approval for manumission (the freeing of individual slaves). The Stono Rebellion thus accelerated South Carolina's emergence as a racist and fear-ridden society.

Stono Rebellion Failed South Carolina slave uprising

Racial tensions wracked cities as well as plantations. In 1712 rebellious slaves in New York City killed nine whites; as a result, thirteen slaves were hanged, one was starved to death, three were burned at the stake, one was broken on the wheel, and six committed suicide. In 1741 a wave of thefts and fires attributed to slaves in New York led to the torture and hanging of thirteen slaves, the burning of thirteen more, and the sale of seventy to the West Indies.

The Rise of the Colonial Elites

A few colonists benefited disproportionately from the growing wealth of Britain and its colonies. Most elite colonists derived their wealth the old-fashioned way, by birth and by marriage. Elite males were generally large planters or farmers, or attorneys, clergy, and other professionals who catered to fellow elites.

Before 1700 class structure in the colonies was relatively invisible; the rural elite spent its resources on land, servants, and slaves instead of on conspicuous luxuries.

CHECKING IN

- After 1713, competition for North America shifted from the military to the economic realm as Britain embraced mercantilism.

- Prosperity boomed in the English colonies.

- The English colonies saw rapid population growth, in part from immigration.

- The differences between rural and urban life sharpened, and the number of colonial elites rose.

- Slavery became more important both economically and socially.

A traveler visiting one of Virginia's richest planters noted that his host owned only "good beds but no curtains and instead of cane chairs…stools made of wood." After 1720, however, the display of wealth became more ostentatious. The greater gentry—the richest 2 percent of the population—built splendid estate homes. The lesser gentry, or the second-wealthiest 2 to 10 percent, lived in more modest field-stone or wood-frame houses, and middle-class farmers typically inhabited one-story wooden buildings with four small rooms.

The gentry also exhibited their wealth after 1720 by imitating European "refinements." They wore costly English fashions, drove carriages, and bought expensive china, books, and furniture. They pursued a gracious life by studying foreign languages, learning formal dances, and cultivating polite manners. Men were to be gentlemen: dignified, responsible, generous, kind to their dogs and horses, and community leaders. Wives were to be ladies: skillful household managers and refined, respectful hostesses.

COMPETING FOR A CONTINENT, 1713–1750

What factors explain the relative success of the British, French, and Spanish empires in North America?

Europeans transformed North America in the first half of the eighteenth century as they expanded their territorial claims, opened new areas for settlement, and engaged in more intensive trade and warfare with Native Americans. In turn, Native Americans often welcomed trade but resisted Europeans who tried to settle nearby.

France and the American Heartland

Louisiana became a principal focus of France's imperial efforts. New Orleans, established in 1718, became the colony's capital and port. France hoped to use the Choctaw Indians as allies, but by the 1730s the tribe had become bitterly divided between pro-English and pro-French factions.

Louisiana's sluggish export economy forced settlers and slaves to find other means of support. Like the Indians, they hunted, fished, gathered wild plants, and cultivated gardens. And Indian, white, and black Louisianans traded with one another. Indians provided corn, tallow, and, above all, deerskins to merchants in return for blankets, axes, chickens, guns, and alcohol. Indians from west of the Mississippi brought horses and cattle, usually stolen from Spanish ranches in Texas. West African slaves, familiar with cattle from their homelands, managed many of Louisiana's herds; some became rustlers and illicit traders of beef.

French settlements in Upper Louisiana, usually referred to as Illinois (but also including parts of Missouri), were somewhat better off. Wheat became Illinois's major export, a more stable and profitable crop than the plantation commodities grown farther south. However, the colony's remote location limited exports and attracted few whites. It continued to depend on Native American allies to defend it from Indian enemies.

French attention also turned to the Ohio Valley, which, thanks to Iroquois neutrality, had become a refuge for dislocated Native American tribes, such as the Kickapoos, Shawnees, and Delawares. To counter growing English influence and to secure commercial and diplomatic ties with the Indians, the French expanded their trade. Several French posts, including Detroit, ballooned into sizable villages of Indian, French, and mixed-ancestry residents. Although the French were generally more successful than the English among the Indians, they never won over the Carolina-backed Chickasaws, and waged brutal warfare against the Mesquakies at Detroit and the Natchez in Louisiana. The French sold captives seized in these wars as slaves in their mainland colonies and in the West Indies. By 1744 French traders had explored as far west as North Dakota and Colorado, buying beaver pelts and Indian slaves on the Great Plains. These traders and their competitors spread trade goods, including guns, to Native Americans throughout central Canada and the Plains. Meanwhile, Indians in the southern Plains and the Great Basin acquired horses from the thousands left behind by fleeing Spaniards after the Pueblo Revolt of 1680. Horses and guns enabled tribes such as the Lakota Sioux and the Comanche to move onto the Plains and build a new, highly mobile way of life based on the pursuit of the buffalo. By 1750, France claimed an immense territory but its domain was precariously dependent on relations with Native Americans.

Native Americans and British Expansion

The depopulation and dislocation of Native Americans made possible the colonies' rapid expansion. Epidemic diseases, environmental changes, war, and political pressure opened new land for Europeans. In Carolina, imperial wars and the trade in Indian slaves soon produced violence. Between 1711 and 1713, clashes between the Tuscaroras and white settlers led to the death or enslavement of about one-fifth of the tribe; most survivors migrated northward to upstate New York to become the sixth nation of the Iroquois Confederacy. Settler abuses against Indians continued, leading the Yamasees and several allied nations to attack English settlements in 1715 and 1716. Only by relying on the aid of the Cherokees and by arming four hundred slaves did the colony crush the uprising.

The defeat of the Yamasees in turn left their Catawba allies wedged uncomfortably between the English to the south and the Iroquois to the north. They turned to the English for help. In return for land and promises to defend the colony against other Indians, the Catawbas received guns, food, and clothing. Although this gave the Catawbas at least temporary security, the rapidly increasing white population and the competition for resources sharply limited Catawba autonomy.

To the north, the Iroquois tried to accommodate the English and consolidate their own power. Late in the seventeenth century, the Iroquois entered into a series of agreements, known as the **Covenant Chain,** to relocate Indians whose lands the colonists desired. These tribes were moved to areas of New York and Pennsylvania, on the periphery of the Iroquois homeland, where they served as buffers against English expansion. In that way, and by incorporating the Tuscaroras into their confederacy, the Iroquois created a center of Native American power distinct from, but cooperative with, the British.

▎**Covenant Chain** Treaties by which Iroquois agreed to relocate displaced tribes to the periphery of Iroquois lands

In similar fashion, Pennsylvania coerced the Delawares into selling more than fifty thousand acres between 1729 and 1734. Then the colony's leaders produced a fraudulent treaty, dated to 1686, that required the Delawares to cede twelve hundred square miles of land. The Iroquois forced the Delawares to move to the upper Ohio Valley while the proprietors made a huge profit by selling the Delawares' land. Indians elsewhere along the westward-moving frontier faced pressure from settlers on one side and the Iroquois on the other.

British Expansion in the South: Georgia

In 1732 Parliament chartered a new colony, Georgia. It was designed to be a refuge for debtors, whose settlement would buffer South Carolina against attacks from Spanish Florida. Further, the new English colony would export expensive commodities, such as wine and silk.

James Oglethorpe Founder of Georgia colony

James Oglethorpe, who dominated the provincial board of trustees, shaped Georgia's early years. He established the port of entry, Savannah, in 1733. By 1740

Map 4.3   European Occupation of North America, to 1750

Spanish and French occupation depended on ties with Native Americans. By contrast, British colonists had dispossessed Native peoples and densely settled the eastern seaboard.

Interactive Map

Copyright © Cengage Learning

nearly three thousand colonists resided in Georgia. Almost half were non-English immigrants from Germany, Switzerland, and Scotland, and most had their overseas passage paid by the government. A small number of Jews were among the early settlers. Thus, Georgia began as the last English colony.

Idealism and concerns about security led Oglethorpe to ban slavery from Georgia. Oglethorpe thought that slavery degraded blacks, made whites lazy, and presented a terrible risk. Parliament thus made Georgia the only colony where slavery was forbidden.

Oglethorpe's well-intentioned plans failed. Few debtors arrived because of Parliament's restrictions on their release from prison. Limitations that Oglethorpe had secured on settlers' rights to enlarge or sell their holdings discouraged immigrants, as did the ban on slavery. Georgia exported neither wine nor silk; only rice proved profitable. After a decade of struggle against economic reality, Oglethorpe yielded. In 1750 slavery became legal, and restrictions on landholdings ended. Within 10 years, 6,500 whites and 3,500 black slaves made Georgia even more prosperous.

Spain's Borderlands

While trying to maintain an empire in the face of Native American, French, and British adversaries, Spain spread its language and culture over much of North America, especially the Southwest. To repopulate New Mexico with settlers after the Pueblo Revolt (see Chapter 3), Spain handed out huge land grants and constructed fortifications, primarily for defense against, first, the Apaches and, later, the Comanches (cuh-MAN-cheese). Livestock-raising *ranchos* (ranches) monopolized vast amounts of land along the Rio Grande and blocked the establishment of further towns. On these ranchos, mounted herders of cattle and sheep (*vaqueros*) (vah-CARE-ohs) created the way of life later adopted by the American cowboy, featuring lariat and roping skills, cattle drives, and roundups.

By 1750 New Mexico's population numbered about 14,000, more than half of them Pueblos. Integrated into New Mexico society, most Pueblos practiced both Catholicism and their traditional religion and helped to defend the colony. Most Apaches had fled to Mexico or made peace with the Spanish to gain support against raids by Utes (yoots) and Comanches from the north.

To counter growing French influence among the Comanches and other Native Americans on the southern plains, Spain colonized Texas. In 1716 the Spanish established four missions. The most successful of the missions was at San Antonio de Bexar (day beh-HAR), where friars constructed a fortified building known as the Alamo. The Spanish presence in Texas remained light, however; by mid-century only 1,200 Spaniards lived there, and they were under constant threat of Indian raids.

Spain's position in Florida was only slightly less precarious. As early as 1700, when 3,800 English had settled in the Carolinas, only 1,500 Spanish were in Florida, a discrepancy that would continue to widen. To some extent, trade with the Creeks helped offset this numerical difference. But Florida's trade profits remained slim because it lacked cheap, desirable trade goods.

Florida gained more at English expense through its recruitment of escaped slaves from Carolina. In 1693 the Spanish monarch, Charles II, decreed that any

84   CHAPTER 4   THE BONDS OF EMPIRE, 1660–1750

English-owned slaves who reached Florida and became Catholic would be freed. Word of this spread back to the Carolinas, prompting more slaves to flee to Florida. Eventually the Spanish would recruit an all-black militia unit and build a fortified village for the former slaves and their families.

By 1750 the French and Spanish empires had reached their limits in North America. Spain controlled much of the Southeast and Southwest, and France claimed the Mississippi, Ohio, and Missouri river valleys. Spain also maintained a precarious hold on Florida. Both empires, spread thin, depended heavily on Indian goodwill. In contrast, British North America, compact and wealthy, was densely populated by whites and was generally antagonistic toward Native Americans.

CHECKING IN

- The French remained lightly scattered over their North American empire and dependent on maintaining good relations with the Indians.
- British expansion continued to push Indians westward.
- Spain extended its control in the Southwest and established a light presence in Texas.
- Early in the eighteenth century, continental European wars again spread to North America.

The Return of War, 1739–1748

From 1713 to 1739 peace and prosperity prevailed, but in 1739 war again erupted; Spanish authorities cut off the ear of Robert Jenkins, a British smuggler, and Britain launched the "War of Jenkins' Ear" against Spain. James Oglethorpe led a massive but unsuccessful assault on St. Augustine in 1740; Spanish troops and refugee slaves from South Carolina likewise failed in a counterattack on Georgia two years later. By then, the Anglo-Spanish War had merged with one in Europe, the War of the Austrian Succession (1739–1748), known as King George's War to the colonists. In this conflict, four thousand New Englanders besieged the French fortress at Louisbourg, at the mouth of the St. Lawrence, and captured it after seven intense weeks of fighting. The war was inconclusive, and in 1748 Britain returned Louisbourg to the French under terms of the peace treaty ending the conflict.

PUBLIC LIFE IN BRITISH AMERICA, 1689–1750

How did politics, the Enlightenment, and religious movements shape public life in the colonies?

During the early and middle eighteenth century, the ties linking Britain and its colonies extended far beyond the movement of goods and peoples. England's new Bill of Rights was the foundation of government and politics in the colonies. English thinkers inspired the Enlightenment, and English preacher George Whitefield (WHIT-field) sparked a generation of colonists to transform the practice of Protestantism in British America. Significantly, these developments involved many more colonists than before as active participants in politics, in intellectual discussions, and in new religious movements. This wider participation signaled the emergence of a broad Anglo-American "public."

Colonial Politics

The most important political development after 1700 was the rise of the assembly as the dominant force in colonial government. In most colonies, the crown or proprietors chose colonial governors, who in turn named a council, or upper legislative house. Only in the lower house, or assembly, could members of the gentry assert their interests. Until 1689 governors and councils drafted laws, and the assemblies generally followed passively. Thereafter, assemblies assumed a more central role in politics, as colonial leaders argued that their legislatures should exercise the same rights as Parliament's House of Commons, which represented the people, defended their rights, and enjoyed the exclusive right to originate money-raising measures. Parliament's victory in the Glorious Revolution convinced Americans that their governors should defer to the assemblies.

The lower houses refused to permit meddling in their procedures, took control over taxes and budgets, and kept a tight rein on the salaries of governors who received no salary from Britain and remained vulnerable to such financial pressure. This power of the purse often forced governors to sign laws opposed by the crown.

Moreover, Britain's lack of interest in colonial politics allowed the assemblies to take considerable power. The Board of Trade, established by Parliament in 1696 to monitor American affairs, did not have the staff, the energy, or the vision to maintain royal authority by supporting embattled governors. This political vacuum allowed the colonies to become self-governing in most respects except for regulating trade, printing money, and declaring war. Colonial autonomy, reinforced by self-assertive assemblies, would haunt British authorities when they attempted to exercise more direct rule after 1763 (see Chapter 5).

Elites, wealthy landowners, merchants, and attorneys dominated politics as well as society. Governors appointed members of the greater gentry to serve on councils and as judges in the highest courts. The upper gentry, along with militia majors and colonels, also dominated among the representatives elected to the legislatures' lower houses (the assemblies). Members of the lesser gentry sat less often in the legislatures, but they commonly served as justices of the peace in the county courts.

Outside New England, property restrictions barred 80 percent of white men from running for the assembly. In any case, few ordinary citizens could have afforded the high costs of elective office. Assemblymen received meager living expenses, which did not cover the cost of staying at the capital, much less make up for six to ten weeks of missed work. Consequently, political leadership fell to a small number of wealthy families with a tradition of public service.

The colonies generally set liberal qualifications for male voters, but all excluded women, blacks, and Indians from voting. In seven colonies, voters had to own land (usually forty to fifty acres), and in the others they had to have enough property to furnish a house and to work a farm. Most white males in Anglo-America could vote by age forty, whereas across the Atlantic, two-thirds of all Englishmen and 90 percent of Irishmen could never vote.

Rural voting participation was low, averaging 45 percent. Governors called elections randomly so that after years without an election, one could be called on short notice. Voters in isolated areas often did not know of an upcoming election. Voting took place at the county seat, and many voters did not risk traveling long distances over poor roads to reach the voting place. In many colonies voters stated their preference publicly, often face to face with the candidates, a practice that discouraged dissenters. There were no political parties to stimulate popular interest or to mobilize voters. Candidates nominated themselves and ran on their reputation, not on the issues.

In view of these factors, political indifference was widespread. For example, to avoid paying legislators' expenses, many Massachusetts towns refused to elect assemblymen. From 1731 to 1760, one-third of South Carolina's elected assemblymen neglected to take their seats. Apathy might have been even greater had candidates not plied voters with alcohol. For example, George Washington dispensed almost two quarts of liquor for each voter when he was first elected to Virginia's assembly in 1758.

Competitive politics first developed in the northern seaports. Wealthy colonists aligned themselves with or against royal and proprietary governors. To gain advantage over rivals, some factions courted artisans and small shopkeepers whose fortunes had stagnated or declined as the distribution of wealth favored the rich.

John Peter Zenger Central figure in a trial that opened the way for freedom of the press

In 1735 New York became the site of a celebrated trial. Newspaper printer **John Peter Zenger** was charged with seditiously libeling the colony's governor. Zenger's acquittal on the charge broadened political discussion and participation beyond a small circle of elites. It also established truth as a defense against the charge of libel, opening the way toward greater freedom of the press in the future.

The Enlightenment

If property and wealth were keys to political participation and office-holding, literacy and education enabled Anglo-Americans to participate in the transatlantic world of ideas and beliefs. Eighteenth-century Anglo-America was probably the world's most literate society. Ninety percent of New England's adult white males and 40 percent of its women could write well enough to sign documents. In other colonies the literacy rate varied from 35 to 50 percent. (In England it stood at just over 30 percent.) Nevertheless, ordinary Americans' reading encompassed only a few books: an almanac, a psalter, and the Bible.

Members of the gentry, well-to-do merchants, and educated ministers lived in a world of print culture. Although costly, books and writing paper opened eighteenth-century European civilization to men and women of these classes who could read. And a rich, exciting world it was. Great advances in natural science seemed to explain the laws of nature, human intelligence appeared poised to triumph over ignorance and prejudice, and life itself would surely become more pleasant. For those with time to read and think, an age of optimism and boundless progress had dawned: the **Enlightenment.**

Enlightenment Intellectual revolution that elevated reason, science, and logic

Enlightenment ideals combined confidence in reason with skepticism about beliefs not based on science or logic. Enlightenment thought drew on the work of the English physicist **Sir Isaac Newton** (1642–1727), who explained how gravitation ruled the universe. Newton's work demonstrated the harmony of natural laws and stimulated others to search for rational principles in medicine, law, psychology, and government.

Sir Isaac Newton British scientist whose ideas lay at the heart of the Enlightenment

Benjamin Franklin American who embodied Enlightenment ideas

No American more embodied the Enlightenment spirit than **Benjamin Franklin** (1706–1790). Born in Boston, Franklin migrated to Philadelphia at age seventeen, bringing considerable assets: skill as a printer, ambition, and insatiable curiosity. In 1732 Franklin began publishing *Poor Richard's Almanack,* a collection of maxims and proverbs that made him famous—and rich. By age forty-two he had saved enough money to retire from printing and devote himself to science and community service.

To Franklin, science and community service were intertwined; true science would make everyone's life more comfortable. For example, his experiments in flying a kite during a thunderstorm proved that lightning was electricity and led to the invention of the lightning rod. In 1743 Franklin organized the American Philosophical Society to encourage "all philosophical experiments that let light into the nature of things, tend to increase the power of man over matter, and multiply the conveniences and pleasures of life." By 1769 the society had blossomed into an intercolonial network of amateur scientists.

Although some plantation owners, among them Thomas Jefferson, championed the Enlightenment, it flourished primarily in the seaboard cities, where the latest ideas from Europe circulated and gentlemen and artisans met in small societies to investigate nature. To these individuals, the Royal Society in London, the foremost learned society in the English-speaking world, represented the ideal. The Enlightenment thus initially strengthened ties between British and colonial elites. Its adherents envisioned progress as gradual and proceeding from the top down. Just as Newton inspired the scientific bent of Enlightenment intellectuals, the *Essay Concerning Human Understanding* by English philosopher **John Locke** (1690) led many to embrace "reasonable" or "rational" religion. Locke contended that ideas are not inborn but are acquired by investigation of, and reflection on, experience. Enlightenment intellectuals believed that the study of the harmony and order of nature provided the best argument for God, a rational Creator. A handful insisted that where the Bible conflicted with reason, one should follow reason. Those—including Franklin and Jefferson—who took the argument furthest were called **Deists.** They concluded that God, having created a perfect universe, did not miraculously intervene in its workings but instead left it alone to operate according to natural law.

Benjamin Franklin
This earliest known portrait of Franklin dates to about 1740, when he was a rising leader in bustling Philadelphia.

Harvard University Art Museums, Fogg Art Museum, Bequest of Dr. John Collins Warren, 1856, H47 Photo: Imaging Department © President and Fellows of Harvard College

John Locke British philosopher who explained how reason functions

Deists Rationalists who insisted that the universe operates by natural law

Most colonists influenced by the Enlightenment considered themselves Christians but feared Christianity's excesses, particularly persecution in the name of religion and "enthusiasts" who emphasized emotion over reason. Mindful of Locke's caution that no human can be absolutely certain of anything but his or her own existence, they distrusted zealots and sectarians, and believed that religion's value lay in the encouragement of virtue and morality, not in theological hair splitting.

In 1750 the Enlightenment's greatest contributions to American life lay in the future, when Anglo-Americans would draw on the Enlightenment's revolutionary ideas as they declared independence and created a new nation. In the meantime, a series of religious revivals known as the Great Awakening would challenge the Enlightenment's most basic assumptions.

The Great Awakening

Rationalists viewed the world as orderly and predictable. Many Americans, however, did not enjoy orderly and predictable lives. The result was a spiritual longing that neither traditional religion nor Enlightenment philosophy could satisfy.

A quickening of religious fervor in scattered places in the 1730s became passionate revivalism throughout Anglo-America in 1739. This **"Great Awakening"** cut across lines of class, status, and education. Above all, the Great Awakening represented an unleashing among ordinary people of anxiety about sin and longing for assurances of salvation. Some revivalists were steeped in Enlightenment ideas; for all, however, religion was primarily a matter of emotional commitment.

In contrast to rationalists, who stressed the human potential for betterment, the ministers of the Great Awakening emphasized the corruption of human nature, the fury of divine wrath, and the need for immediate repentance. Congregationalist minister **Jonathan Edwards** of Northampton, Massachusetts, drove home this message with breathtaking clarity. During a 1735 revival Edwards preached his great sermon "Sinners in the Hands of an Angry God." "The God that holds you over the pit of Hell, much as one holds a spider or other loathsome insect over the fire, abhors you," Edwards intoned. "His wrath toward you burns like fire; He looks upon you as worthy of nothing else but to be cast into the fire."

Other colonial ministers—Presbyterian William Tennent and Dutch Reformed Theodore Frelinghuysen—had anticipated Edwards's themes. Pulling the diverse threads of revival together was the arrival in 1739 of the charismatic English cleric **George Whitefield.** A man of overpowering presence and a booming voice, Whitefield attracted some crowds exceeding 20,000. On a tour through the colonies, Whitefield inspired thousands, mainly young adults, to seek salvation.

Whitefield's powerful allure awed even his critics. However, divisions over the revivals developed in Whitefield's wake. For example, after leaving Boston in October 1740, Whitefield invited Gilbert Tennent (William's son) to follow "in order to blow up the divine flame lately kindled there." Denouncing Boston's established clergy as "dead Drones" and lashing out at elites, Tennent built a following among the poor and downtrodden.

Exposing colonial society's divisions, Tennent and other radicals corroded support for revivals among established ministers and officials. Increasingly, lines hardened between the revivalists, the "New Lights," and the rationalist clergymen, or "Old Lights," who dominated the Anglican, Presbyterian, and Congregational churches. In 1740 Gilbert Tennent hinted that most Presbyterian ministers lacked saving grace and were bound for hell, and he urged parishioners to abandon them for the New Lights. By sowing doubts about ministers, Tennent undermined one of the foundations of the social order: if people could not trust their ministers, whom *could* they trust? Old Light rationalists fired back. In 1742 Charles Chauncy, a Boston Congregationalist, condemned revivals as an epidemic of the "enthusiasm" that enlightened intellectuals so hated. Chauncy especially blasted enthusiasts who mistook the ravings of their overheated imagination for direct communications from God.

The Great Awakening thus split American Protestantism. In 1741 Old and New Light Presbyterians formed rival branches that reunited in 1758 when the revivalists emerged victorious. The Anglican church lost many members to New Light Presbyterians and Baptists. Congregationalists also splintered badly; by 1760 New Lights had seceded from one-third of all churches and formed separate parishes.

"Great Awakening" Protestant revival movement that emphasized each person's urgent need for salvation by God

Jonathan Edwards Revivalist preacher whose sermon "Sinners in the Hands of an Angry God" summarized Great Awakening beliefs

George Whitefield English preacher who toured the colonies and played a major role in the Great Awakening

The Great Awakening peaked in New England in 1742, but New Lights made steady gains into the 1770s, and the revival's long-term effects far exceeded its immediate impact. First, the revival started a decline in the influence of older sects, such as the Quakers, Anglicans, and Congregationalists. In turn, the number of Presbyterians and Baptists increased after 1740, and that of Methodists rose steadily after 1770. These churches have since dominated American Protestantism. Second, the Great Awakening stimulated the founding of new colleges unscarred by religious wars. The College of New Jersey (Princeton, 1746), King's College (Columbia, 1754), the College of Rhode Island (Brown, 1764), Queen's College (Rutgers, 1766), and Dartmouth (1769) trace their roots to this era. Third, the revival drew many African-Americans and Native Americans to Protestantism for the first time. Its oral and communal nature, and its emphasis on piety rather than learning, incorporated aspects of both groups' traditional cultures. The Great Awakening marked the emergence of black Protestantism as New Lights reached out to slaves. Meanwhile, a few New Light preachers, Indian as well as white, became missionaries to Indians. Still, nonwhites faced discrimination, even among New Lights.

The Great Awakening, moreover, gave women added prominence in colonial religion. For several decades, ministers had praised women—the majority of church members—as the embodiment of Christian piety. Now some New Light sects, mainly Baptist and Congregationalist, granted women the right to speak and vote in church meetings. Some women, like Anne Hutchinson a century earlier, presided over prayer meetings that included women, men, and sometimes even slaves. Although some of these women's activities were suppressed, none was prosecuted, as Hutchinson had been. The Great Awakening also fostered religious tolerance by blurring theological differences among New Lights. Indeed, revivalism's emphasis on inner experience, rather than on doctrinal fine points, emphasized Protestants' common experiences and promoted the coexistence of denominations.

Historians disagree about whether the Great Awakening had political effects. Although New Lights flayed the wealthy, they neither advocated a social revolution nor developed a political ideology. Yet, by empowering ordinary people to criticize those in authority, the revivals helped to lay the groundwork for political revolutionaries in this generation.

CHECKING IN

- Elected assemblies, dominated by colonial elites, became increasingly powerful.
- Political participation and competition were more evident in cities than in the countryside.
- The Enlightenment, with its optimism and strong emphasis on rationality, spread widely among colonial elites.
- At the same time, the Great Awakening expressed widespread religious longings, and new Protestant denominations challenged older ones.

Chapter Summary

How did the Glorious Revolution shape relations between England and its North American colonies? (page 68)

After the Restoration of the Stuart kings to England's throne, the British government attempted to tighten control over the colonies with measures such as the Navigation Acts and the Dominion of New England. When the Glorious Revolution drove James II from England, the colonies regained control of

KEY TERMS

Dominion of New England *(p. 68)*
"Glorious Revolution" *(p. 69)*
Bill of Rights *(p. 69)*

their own legislatures. England's wars on the continent of Europe spread to the New World, raising colonists' recognition of their own military weakness and strengthening their bonds to England.

What were the most important consequences of British mercantilism for the mainland colonies? (page 71)

The Navigation Acts, passed in response to a quickening sense of mercantilism in England, sought to control colonial trade. The primary effect was to increase colonial prosperity. Britain's colonies welcomed immigrants, and their population soared. Slavery became increasingly widespread, as did fears of slave rebellion. Population growth was a major factor in deforestation, which in turn stimulated westward movement away from depleted soils. Increased prosperity also contributed to the rise of colonial elites, but the poverty rate rose among ordinary city dwellers.

What factors explain the relative success of the British, French, and Spanish empires in North America? (page 80)

The first half of the eighteenth century saw renewed competition among the French, the British, and the Spanish for control of North America. France and Spain maintained sparse settlement and relied on good relations with Indians. English expansion created renewed problems for Native Americans.

How did politics, the Enlightenment, and religious movements shape public life in the colonies? (page 84)

The same time frame saw an explosion of colonial interest in politics and other elements of public life, such as intellectual discussion and new religious movements. Politics was far more an urban than a rural phenomenon; its chief feature was the rise of the colonial assembly. The Enlightenment brought the growth of rationalism and the religious movement known as Deism. At the same time, Protestant ministers, such as Jonathan Edwards, sought to restore religious enthusiasm. New denominations, such as Unitarians, Baptists, and Methodists, appeared. Women played a larger role in religion, and the questioning of authority was encouraged.

KEY TERMS continued

King William's War *(p. 71)*
Queen Anne's War *(p. 71)*
mercantilism *(p. 71)*
Navigation Acts *(p. 72)*
Middle Passage *(p. 75)*
deforestation *(p. 76)*
Stono Rebellion *(p. 79)*
Covenant Chain *(p. 81)*
James Oglethorpe *(p. 82)*
John Peter Zenger *(p. 86)*
Enlightenment *(p. 86)*
Sir Isaac Newton *(p. 86)*
Benjamin Franklin *(p. 86)*
John Locke *(p. 87)*
Deists *(p. 87)*
"Great Awakening" *(p. 88)*
Jonathan Edwards *(p. 88)*
George Whitefield *(p. 88)*

CourseMate

Go to the CourseMate website at **www.cengagebrain.com** for additional study tools and review materials—including audio and video clips—for this chapter.

CHAPTER 5

Roads to Revolution

1750–1776

The Boston Massacre, 1770, Engraving, by Paul Revere

Library of Congress

CHAPTER PREVIEW

Triumph and Tensions: The British Empire, 1750–1763
How did Britain and its colonies view their joint victory over France in the Seven Years' War?

Imperial Authority, Colonial Opposition, 1760–1766
What was imperial reorganization, and how did it change relations between Britain and the North American colonies?

Resistance Resumes, 1766–1770
In what ways did resistance to the Townshend duties differ from earlier colonial resistance efforts?

The Deepening Crisis, 1770–1774
In what ways did colonists' views of parliamentary authority change after 1770?

Toward Independence, 1774–1776
What led most colonists in 1776 to abandon their loyalty to Britain and choose national independence?

By 1763 Britain had defeated France, its chief competitor for preeminence in North America, and stood at the height of eighteenth-century imperial power. British rule ran undisputed from the Atlantic seacoast to the Mississippi River and from northernmost Canada to the Florida straits. Ironically, this greatest of British triumphs would turn into one of the greatest of British defeats.

The imperial reorganization that occurred after 1763 as a result of war and conquest radically altered Britain's relationship with its American colonies. Conflict arose between Britain and the colonies when Parliament, as it searched for ways to pay off the enormous debt accumulated during the war, attempted to tighten control over colonial affairs. The colonists, accustomed to legislating for themselves, resisted this effort to centralize decision making in London. American leaders interpreted Britain's clampdown as calculated antagonism, intended to deprive them of both prosperity and relative independence.

Conflict spilled out beyond constitutional issues. In port cities, crowds of poor and working people engaged in direct, often violent demonstrations against British authority. Settlers in the backcountry invoked the ideas of urban radicals when resisting large landowners and distant colonial governments dominated by elites. These movements reflected political and economic tensions within the colonies as well as growing defiance of elites by ordinary colonists. The growing participation of white women reflected impatience with restraints imposed by traditional gender norms. Nonwhites, both African-American and Native American, often perceived the colonists as greater threats to their liberty than the British. Within Britain itself many opposed the government's colonial policies.

Colonial resistance to British policies also reflected democratic stirrings in America and throughout the North Atlantic world. Among the products of this democratic surge were both the American Revolution, which erupted in 1776, and the French Revolution, which began in 1789 and sparked unrest over much of Europe and the Americas.

Despite their apprehension, colonial politicians expressed their opposition peacefully from 1763 to 1775 through legislative resolutions and commercial boycotts. Even after fighting erupted, the colonists agonized for more than a year about whether to sever their political relationship with Britain—which even native-born Americans sometimes referred to affectionately as "home." Of all the world's colonial peoples, none became rebels more reluctantly than Anglo-Americans did in 1776.

TRIUMPH AND TENSIONS: THE BRITISH EMPIRE, 1750–1763

How did Britain and its colonies view their joint victory over France in the Seven Years' War?

King George's War (see Chapter 4) did nothing to avert a showdown between Britain and France. The conflict resumed in 1756 and ended in 1763. Known as the **Seven Years' War,** it was a major turning point in both American and European history.

Seven Years' War Major French-British conflict known in North America as the French and Indian War

A Fragile Peace, 1750–1754

Because neither Britain nor France emerged from King George's War as the dominant power in North America, each prepared for another war. The Ohio Valley became the tinderbox for conflict. When France started building a chain of forts to regain control of the Virginia and Pennsylvania Indian trade, Virginia sent a twenty-one-year-old surveyor, George Washington, to demand that the French abandon their forts. In 1754 French troops drove the Virginians back to their homes.

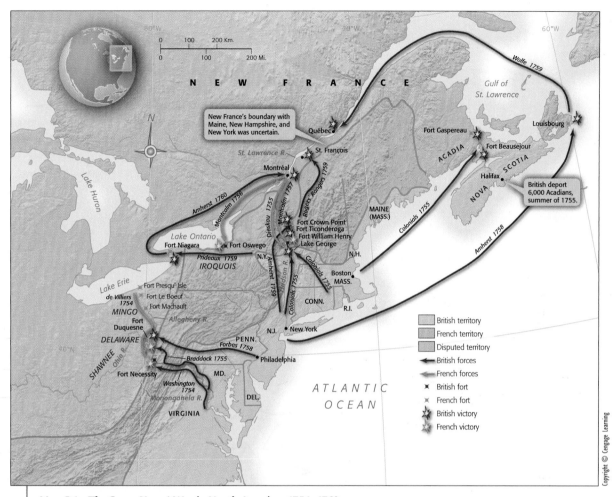

Map 5.1   The Seven Years' War in North America, 1754–1760

After experiencing major defeats early in the war, Anglo-American forces turned the tide against the French in 1758 by taking Fort Duquesne and Louisbourg. After Canada fell in 1760, the fighting shifted to Spain's Caribbean colonies.

🔲 Interactive Map

In mid-1754 seven colonies sent delegates to Albany, New York, to coordinate their mutual defense with British officials. The Albany Congress persuaded the wary Iroquois to support the British and endorsed a plan for a colonial confederation, the Albany Plan of Union, often seen as a predecessor to the federal system under the Constitution. However, the plan collapsed because no colonial legislature would surrender control over its powers of taxation.

The Seven Years' War in America, 1754–1760

Although France and Britain remained at peace in Europe until 1756, Washington's clash with the French had created a virtual state of war in North America. In 1754 Britain dispatched General Edward Braddock and one thousand regulars to take Fort Duquesne (doo-KAIN) at the headwaters of the Ohio River.

Chronology

1740–1748	King George's War
1754	Albany Congress
1756–1763	Seven Years' War
1760	George III becomes king of Great Britain; writ of assistance
1763	Proclamation of 1763; Treaty of Paris divides France's North American empire between Britain and Spain
1763	Pontiac leads Indian uprising in Ohio Valley and Great Lakes
1764	Sugar Act
1765	Stamp Act followed by colonial resistance; First Quartering Act
1766	Stamp Act repealed; Declaratory Act
1767	Revenue Act (Townshend duties); American Board of Customs Commissioners created
1768	Massachusetts circular letters; John Hancock's ship *Liberty* seized by Boston customs commissioner; St. George's Fields massacre in London; First Treaty of Fort Stanwix
1770	Townshend duties, except tea tax, repealed; Boston Massacre
1772	Somerset decision in Britain
1772–1774	Committees of correspondence formed
1773	Tea Act and Boston Tea Party
1774	Coercive Acts and Quebec Act (Intolerable Acts); First Continental Congress meets in Philadelphia and adopts Suffolk Resolves
1775	Battles of Lexington and Concord; Lord Dunmore offers freedom to Virginia slaves joining British forces; Olive Branch Petition; battles at Breed's Hill and Bunker Hill; King and Parliament declare colonies to be in rebellion
1776	Thomas Paine, *Common Sense*; Declaration of Independence

Scornful of colonial soldiers and friendly Native Americans, Braddock expected his disciplined regulars to make short work of the French. On July 9, 1755, about 850 French and Indians ambushed Braddock's 2,200 Britons and Virginians near Fort Duquesne. After three hours of steady fire, the British regulars broke and retreated, leaving Washington's Virginians to cover the withdrawal. Nine hundred regular soldiers and colonists died, including Braddock.

In 1756–1757 New France's daring commanding general, Louis Joseph de Montcalm, maintained the offensive. Anglo-Americans outnumbered Canadians twenty to one, but Montcalm benefited from large numbers of French regulars, Indian support, and full-scale mobilization of the Canadian population. The Anglo-American colonies supported the war grudgingly, providing few and usually poorly trained troops. French-armed Shawnees, Delawares, and Mingos struck hard at settlers in Western Pennsylvania, Maryland, and Virginia. These attacks halted British expansion and prevented the three colonies from joining the war against France for three years.

However, 1758 proved a turning point for the British. First, Indian support for the French evaporated. (Preferring competitive trade to warfare, most Indians hoped that neither European power would drive out the other.) Indian withdrawal enabled

Britain to capture Fort Duquesne and win control of the Ohio Valley. Second, British minister William Pitt took over Britain's military affairs. The imaginative and single-minded Pitt reinvigorated the military campaign, strengthened patriotism on both sides of the Atlantic, and became a popular hero in the colonies. Hard pressed in Europe by France and its allies (which after 1761 included Spain), Pitt believed that mobilizing colonial forces was the key to crushing New France. Keeping fewer than 4,000 British regulars in North America, he promised that Parliament would bear the cost of maintaining colonial troops.

Pitt's offer to free Americans from the war's financial burden generated unprecedented support. In 1758, and again in 1759, the colonies organized 40,000 troops. As a result, Britain took the offensive and captured Louisbourg and Fort Duquesne in 1758, followed by Quebec in September 1759. In 1760, with Montreal's surrender, French resistance in the New World ended.

The End of French North America, 1760–1763

In the **Treaty of Paris of 1763,** France ceded all its territories on the North American mainland. Several thousand French colonists, scattered from Quebec to Louisiana, became British or Spanish citizens. However, one group, the Acadians (uh-KAY-dee-uns) of Nova Scotia, suffered tremendous dislocation. The British deported the Acadians, nearly 5 percent of Canada's French population, to more southerly colonies, such as Pennsylvania and Maryland. Impoverished and facing intense anti-French, anti-Catholic prejudice, most fled to Louisiana, where they became known as the "Cajuns."

Treaty of Paris of 1763 Treaty by which France ceded virtually its entire North American empire to Britain and Spain

Under the Treaty of Paris, Britain received all French lands east of the Mississippi; Spain acquired the port of New Orleans and all French lands west of the Mississippi. Spain traded Florida to Britain in return for Cuba. Thus, Spain's New World empire actually increased in size, but France's virtually vanished, shrinking to a handful of islands. In contrast, Britain's North American empire quadrupled in size.

The effects of King George's War and the Seven Years' War were mixed. On one hand, shedding their blood in a common cause led British citizens and Americans to rely on each other as never before. However, the conclusion of both wars planted the seeds of mutual misunderstanding and suspicion.

Anglo-American Friction

During the war, British officers complained that colonial troops not only fought poorly but also tended to return home, even in the midst of campaigns, when their term was up or when their pay lagged. In turn, colonial soldiers complained that British officers treated their troops "little better than slaves."

Tensions flared as well between British officers and colonial civilians. Officers groused about colonial unwillingness to provide food or shelter, whereas colonists resented the officers' arrogance. Moreover, Pitt's promise to reimburse the colonies for their military expenses enraged Britons. Wartime spending had brought substantial profits to colonial farmers, artisans, and merchants. In addition, some merchants had continued their illicit trade with the French West Indies, simultaneously violating the Navigation Acts *and* trading with the enemy. Britain's national

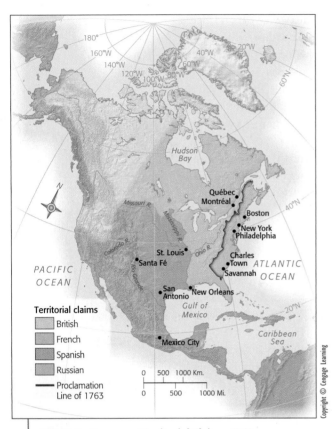

Map 5.2 European Territorial Claims, 1763

The treaties of San Ildefonso (1762) and Paris (1763) divided France's North American empire between Britain and Spain. In 1763 Britain established direct imperial authority west of the proclamation line.

Interactive Map

debt had nearly doubled during the war, to more than £132 million. In contrast, the total colonial debt amounted to less than £2 million. Staggering under debt and taxes, the British thought it outrageous to repay the Americans for defending themselves.

Colonists felt equally burdened. Wartime profits had gone to pay for British goods, accelerating the "consumer revolution" that had been under way for several decades (see Chapter 4). The wartime boom ended when peace returned. Now accustomed to a new middle-class lifestyle, colonists went into debt, and British creditors obliged by extending repayment terms from six months to a full year. Newly prosperous colonists began to suspect Britain of plotting to "enslave" the colonies to protect its own merchants and manufacturers.

The new revenue measures followed the ascension to the British throne of George III (reigned 1760–1820). The new king was determined to play a major role in government, but he proved ill suited to the task of building political coalitions or pursuing consistent policies. Until 1774, George III's frequent abrupt changes in government leadership destabilized politics in Britain and exacerbated relations with the colonies.

Frontier Tensions

Worse, Britain's victory over the French generated new Anglo-Indian conflicts that drove the British debt even higher. No longer able to play the two imperial powers off against each other, Indians feared the consequences. They were right. To cut costs after the war, the British stopped distributing food and ammunition to their Indian allies. Meanwhile, colonial squatters were moving onto Indian lands, raising both fears and tensions.

In early 1763 the Delaware Indian religious prophet Neolin called for Indians to repudiate European culture, goods, and alliances. **Pontiac,** an Ottawa Indian, and other leaders forged an anti-British coalition that sacked eight British forts and besieged British positions at Detroit and Pittsburgh. Short on food and ammunition, suffering a smallpox epidemic (deliberately spread by the British), and recognizing that the French would not return, the Indians surrendered in early fall.

However, the British victory was indecisive. Hoping to end the frontier fighting, George III issued the **Proclamation of 1763,** which asserted royal control of land transactions, settlements, and trade of non-Indians west of the Appalachians, and recognized existing Indian land titles everywhere west of the "proclamation line," which ran down the crest of the Appalachian Mountains. Although the policy

Pontiac Ottawa chief who created short-lived anti-British coalition among Native Americans

Proclamation of 1763 An attempt to end Indian problems by preventing westward movement by colonists

calmed Indian fears, it angered the colonies by subordinating their western land claims to imperial authority and slowing colonial expansion.

Pontiac's rebellion also led the British government to station ten thousand regular troops in North America to occupy the western lands that France had ceded and to intimidate the Indians. The cost of administering British North America reached almost £440,000 yearly. Britons believed it perfectly reasonable for the colonists to help offset this expense. The colonists, however, struggling with their own postwar economic recession, saw it as none of their responsibility.

Although partially offsetting the colonies' unfavorable balance of payments with Britain, these troops raised fears of a peacetime "standing army" that could threaten American liberty. With the French menace gone, increasing numbers of colonists viewed Indian lands to the west as the key to future prosperity. The British troops that enforced the Proclamation Act of 1763, rather than being protectors, became threats to that future.

CHECKING IN

- In 1754 the colonies considered and rejected the Albany Plan of Union.

- The European Seven Years' War pitted the French and their Indian allies against the British in North America.

- The Treaty of Paris of 1763 ended the French empire in North America and enormously enlarged Britain's North American holdings.

- Victory brought mixed consequences: closer ties between Britain and the colonies but also the seeds of friction.

IMPERIAL AUTHORITY, COLONIAL OPPOSITION, 1760–1766

What was imperial reorganization, and how did it change relations between Britain and the North American colonies?

Even as the Seven Years' War wound down, tensions developed between Britain and its colonies, largely as the result of Britain's plans to finance its greatly enlarged empire by a series of revenue measures whose enforcement bypassed local authorities and seemed a dangerous extension of Parliamentary powers. The success of protest and opposition movements after the Stamp Act revealed a widening gulf between British and colonial ideas about the proper relationship between the empire and its colonies.

The Writ of Assistance, 1760–1761

To halt American trade with the enemy in the French West Indies during the Seven Years' War, Britain cracked down on colonial smuggling. In 1760 the royal governor of Massachusetts authorized the use of the **writ of assistance** to seize illegally imported goods. A general search warrant, the writ permitted customs officials to enter any ship or building where smuggled goods might be hidden. Because it required no evidence of probable cause for suspicion, the writ was considered unconstitutional by most British legal authorities.

writ of assistance A general search warrant of dubious legality

The writ of assistance proved a powerful weapon against smuggling. Merchants in Boston, the colonies' smuggling capital, hired James Otis to challenge the device's constitutionality. The former prosecuting attorney for Boston's vice-admiralty court, Otis had resigned to protest the use of the writ. Before Massachusetts' highest court in 1761, he argued that "an act against the Constitution is void"—even an act of Parliament. But the court, noting the use of an identical writ of assistance in Britain, ruled against the merchants.

Despite losing his case, Otis had stated with clarity the colonial conception of Parliament's role under the British constitution. Most British politicians assumed that Parliament's laws themselves were part of the unwritten constitution and that Parliament could in effect alter the constitution at will. But, like most colonists, Otis believed that Parliament had no authority to violate the traditional "rights of Englishmen" by authorizing illegal searches and seizures in private homes.

Sugar Act Act passed by British Parliament that placed new taxes and restrictions on colonists' trade

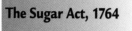
The Sugar Act, 1764

In 1764, three years after Otis's court challenge, Parliament passed the **Sugar Act** to offset part of Britain's North American military expenses. In ending the long-standing exemption of colonial trade from revenue-raising measures, the Sugar Act triggered new tension between Britain and the colonies. The Navigation Acts, in contrast, had been intended not to raise revenue but to benefit the imperial economy by controlling trade.

The Sugar Act amended the Molasses Act of 1733, which constituted a 6-pence-per-gallon tariff on French-produced molasses. Colonists commonly bribed customs inspectors 1½ pence per gallon to look the other way when they unloaded smuggled molasses. In designing the Sugar Act, British officials, well aware of the widespread bribery, wrongly assumed that the colonists would willingly pay a lower, 3-pence-per-gallon tax.

Colonists found other features of the Sugar Act equally objectionable. The act stipulated that the colonists had to export certain raw commodities *through Britain* instead of going directly to foreign ports, as they had been doing. It also complicated the requirements for shipping colonial goods. A captain had to fill out a confusing series of documents certifying the legality of his trade. The absence of any document left his cargo liable to seizure. The law's petty regulations made it virtually impossible for many colonial shippers to avoid committing technical violations of the act.

Finally, the Sugar Act discarded many traditional British protections for a fair trial. First, the law allowed customs officials to transfer smuggling cases from the colonial courts, in which juries decided the outcome, to vice-admiralty courts, in which a judge delivered the verdict. Because the act awarded vice-admiralty judges 5 percent of any confiscated cargo, it gave them a financial incentive to find defendants guilty. Second, until 1767 the law required all cases to be heard in the vice-admiralty court at Halifax, Nova Scotia. The law also reversed normal procedure by presuming the guilt of the accused and requiring the defendant to prove innocence.

The Sugar Act was no idle threat—the navy enforced it vigorously. A Boston resident complained that "no vessel hardly comes in or goes out but they find some pretence to seize and detain her."

Americans continued to smuggle molasses rather than pay the three-pence tax until 1766, when the British lowered the duty to a penny, making it cheaper to pay the tax than to smuggle. After that, the tax brought in about £30,000 a year.

Generally, opposition to the Sugar Act remained fragmented; the act provoked the most opposition in the most heavily affected colonies—Massachusetts, New York, and Pennsylvania. Other colonies that were unaffected protested very little. Although its immediate impact was slight, the Sugar Act heightened colonists' sensitivities to the new direction of imperial policies.

The Stamp Act Crisis, 1765–1766

Revenues raised by the Sugar Act did little to ease Britain's financial crisis. Britons groaned under the second-highest tax rates in Europe and looked resentfully at the lightly taxed colonists, who paid an average of one shilling per person compared to their twenty-six shillings per person.

In March 1765, to force colonists to shoulder a larger share of imperial expenses, Parliament passed the **Stamp Act.** The law obliged Americans to purchase and use specially marked or stamped paper for newspapers, customs documents, wills, contracts, and other public legal documents. Violators faced prosecution in vice-admiralty courts, without juries. Unlike the Sugar Act, which was an *external* tax levied on imports, the Stamp Act was an *internal* tax levied directly on property, goods, and services in the colonies. External taxes regulated trade and fell primarily on merchants and ship captains, but internal taxes were designed to raise revenue and affected most people, at least occasionally. William Pitt and others objected to such an internal tax, arguing that the colonies taxed themselves through their elected assemblies. But to Grenville and his supporters, the tax seemed a small price for the benefits of empire, especially because Britons had paid a similar tax since 1695. Grenville agreed with Stamp Act opponents that Parliament could not tax British subjects unless they enjoyed representation in that body. He contended, however, that the colonists, like many other British adult males who did not vote for members of Parliament, were *virtually* represented. According to the theory of virtual representation, every member of Parliament considered the welfare of *all* subjects, not just his constituents, in deciding issues. Whether or not they voted in parliamentary elections, all imperial subjects, including Americans, could depend on each member of Parliament to protect their well-being.

Grenville and his supporters also held that the colonial assemblies were local governments, with no powers other than those Parliament allowed them. This view clashed directly with the stance of the many colonists who had argued for decades that their assemblies exercised legislative power equivalent to that of Britain's House of Commons.

The Stamp Act caused many colonists to believe that they had to confront parliamentary taxation head on or surrender any claim to meaningful self-government. However much they admired Parliament, few Americans thought that it represented them. Although virtual representation might apply to Britain and Scotland, they argued, it certainly did not extend across the Atlantic. In the American view, unless a lawmaker shared his constituents' interests, he would have no personal stake in opposing bills contrary to their welfare. Thus, the colonists favored *actual,* rather than virtual, representation.

To the colonists, the Stamp Act demonstrated both Parliament's indifference to their interests and the shallowness of virtual representation. Nonetheless, they conceded that Parliament possessed limited powers of legislation, and they accepted the parliamentary regulation of imperial trade.

In a speech opposing the Sugar Act, James Otis expressed Americans' basic argument: "that by [the British] Constitution,

Stamp Act Revenue measure that provoked open opposition by colonists

Anti-Stamp Act Teapot

Some colonists signaled their opposition to the Stamp Act on the pots from which they drank tea (ironically, purchased from British merchants). Less than a decade later, they would protest a British tax on tea itself.

every man in the dominions is a free man; that no parts of His Majesty's dominions can be taxed without consent; that every part has a right to be represented in the supreme or some subordinate legislature." In essence, the colonists saw the empire as a loose federation (union) in which their legislatures possessed considerable autonomy.

Patrick Henry, a twenty-nine-year-old Virginia lawyer with a gift for fiery oratory, expressed the rising spirit of resistance in late May 1765. He persuaded Virginia's House of Burgesses to adopt four relatively mild resolutions denying Parliament's power to tax the colonies, but the House rejected three stronger ones. Garbled accounts of Henry's resolutions and speeches—he probably never said, "Give me liberty or give me death"—electrified other colonists.

Meanwhile, active resistance took shape outside elite political circles. In Boston by late summer, middle-class artisans and businessmen had created the Loyal Nine to fight the Stamp Act. They recognized that the stamp distributors, who alone could sell the specially watermarked paper, represented the law's weak link. If public pressure could force them to resign before the tax went into effect on November 1, the Stamp Act would not work.

Boston's preeminence in opposing Parliament was no accident. Bostonians lived primarily by trade and distilling, and in 1765 they were not living well. The heavy tax on molasses burdened rum producers, and the Sugar Act's trade restrictions dried up the wine import business and interfered with the direct export of New England products to profitable overseas markets. Moreover, its shipbuilding and fishing industries were declining; taxes, unemployment, and poverty had skyrocketed; and the city was recovering from a disastrous fire that had left every tenth family homeless.

This widespread economic distress produced an explosive situation. It was easy to blame British policy for hard times. Furthermore, poor and working-class Bostonians were accustomed to gathering in large crowds to express themselves politically. The morning of August 14, 1765, a likeness of Boston's stamp distributor, Andrew Oliver, was found swinging from a tree. Oliver did not take the hint to resign, so at dusk several hundred Bostonians demolished a new building of his at the dock. The mob then surged toward Oliver's house and vandalized it. Surveying his devastated home the next morning, Oliver announced his resignation.

Anger against the Stamp Act unleashed spontaneous, contagious violence. For example, in late August, rioting Bostonians demolished the elegant home of Lieutenant Governor and Chief Justice Thomas Hutchinson.

Sons of Liberty Groups formed to resist Stamp Act; formed by elites in an attempt to curb violence

At the same time, groups calling themselves **Sons of Liberty** were forming throughout the colonies. Elite leaders of these groups sought to curb violence, fearful that attacks on one set of elites could lead to attacks on all elites. The Sons of Liberty focused their actions against property and carefully left avenues of escape for their victims; they forbade their members to carry weapons in order to avoid harming royal soldiers or officials.

Stamp Act Congress Assembly where representatives from nine colonies met to discuss resistance to the Stamp Act

In October 1765 representatives from nine colonies met in New York City in the **Stamp Act Congress.** There the colonies agreed on, and boldly articulated, the principle that Parliament had no authority to levy taxes outside Britain or to deny any person a jury trial. The united front of the Stamp Act Congress was far more effective than the one earlier intercolonial meeting, the Albany Congress of 1754. Although they emboldened and unified the colonies, declarations of principle like the

Stamp Act Congress resolutions did little to sway Parliament. By late 1765 most stamp distributors had resigned or fled, and without the watermarked paper required by law, most customs officials and court officers refused to perform their duties. In response, legislators compelled them to resume operations by threatening to withhold their pay. At the same time, merchants obtained sailing clearances by insisting that they would sue if their cargoes spoiled while delayed in port. By late December the colonial courts and harbors were again functioning.

In these ways colonial elites assumed control of the public outcry against the Stamp Act. Respectable gentlemen kept an explosive situation under control by taking over leadership of local Sons of Liberty, by coordinating protest through the Stamp Act Congress, and by having colonial legislatures resume normal business. But the Stamp Act remained in effect. To force its repeal, New York's merchants agreed on October 31, 1765, to boycott all British goods. Others followed. Because the colonies purchased 40 percent of Britain's manufactures, this nonimportation strategy triggered panic within Britain's business community.

Parliamentary support for repeal gradually grew—the result of practicality, not principle. In March 1766 Parliament revoked the Stamp Act. Simultaneously, however, Parliament passed the **Declaratory Act,** affirming parliamentary power to legislate for the colonies "in all cases whatsoever."

Declaratory Act Parliamentary assertion of right to legislate for the colonies

Because Americans interpreted the Declaratory Act as merely a face-saving measure on Parliament's part, they ignored it. In truth, however, the House of Commons intended that the colonists take the Declaratory Act literally to mean that they were not exempt from *any* parliamentary statute, including a tax law. The Stamp Act crisis thus ended in a fundamental disagreement between Britain and America over the colonists' political rights.

Ideology, Religion, and Resistance

The Stamp Act crisis had revealed a chasm between the colonies and Great Britain. For the first time, some Anglo-Americans saw a sinister quality in the imperial relationship with Britain. To put their concerns into perspective, educated colonists turned to philosophers, historians, and political writers. Many more looked to religion.

Educated colonists were familiar with John Locke and other Enlightenment political thinkers. Locke argued that, in a state of nature, people enjoyed the "natural rights" of life, liberty, and property. To form governments to protect these rights, people entered into a "social contract." A government that encroached on natural rights broke its contract with the people. In such cases the people could resist their government. To many colonial readers, Locke's concept of natural rights justified opposition to Parliament's arbitrary legislation.

Colonists also read European writers who portrayed concentrations of executive power as threats to liberty. Some balanced Locke's emphasis on the rights of the individual with an emphasis on subordinating individual interests to the good of the people as a whole. Looking to the Greeks and Romans, these "republican" theorists admired the sense of civic duty of the Roman republic. Like the early Romans, they maintained that a free people had to practice "public virtue." An elected leader of a republic would command obedience "more by the virtue of the people than by the terror of his power."

The political writers read most widely in the colonies included a group known as the oppositionists. According to John Trenchard and Thomas Gordon, among others, Parliament—the freely elected representatives of the people—formed the foundation of Britain's unique political liberties and protected them against the inherent corruption and tyranny of executive power. Most members of Parliament, they held, no longer represented the true interests of their constituents; instead, they had sold their souls for financial gain and joined a "conspiracy against liberty."

Influenced by such ideas, a number of colonists believed they detected a diabolical conspiracy underlying British policy. Joseph Warren of Massachusetts observed that the Stamp Act "induced some to imagine that the minister designed by this to force the colonies into a rebellion, and from thence to take occasion to treat them with severity and, by military power, to reduce them to servitude."

Beginning with the Stamp Act crisis, many Protestant clergymen summoned their flock to stand up for God and liberty. Clergymen who exalted the cause of liberty exerted an enormous influence on popular opinion. Far more Americans heard or read sermons than had access to newspapers or pamphlets. A popular theme was how God sent the people woes only to strengthen and sustain them until victory. Moreover, protest leaders' calls to boycott British luxuries meshed neatly with ministers' traditional warnings against frivolity and wastefulness.

CHECKING IN

- The young British king George III was ill suited to the job.
- War and imperial expansion left Britain with staggering debt, and the British concluded that colonists should pay their fair share.
- Parliament passed a series of laws to rationalize control over the colonies, such as the Proclamation of 1763 and the Sugar Act, which colonists found distasteful.
- The Stamp Act, clearly intended to raise revenues, instead raised open resistance.
- Colonists welcomed repeal of the Stamp Act and unwisely ignored the Declaratory Act.

RESISTANCE RESUMES, 1766–1770

In what ways did resistance to the Townshend duties differ from earlier colonial resistance efforts?

Repeal of the Stamp Act temporarily quieted colonial protests, but Britain's search for new revenue soon revived them. Most colonists became convinced that the Stamp Act had been not an isolated mistake, but part of a deliberate design to undermine colonial self-government. Meanwhile growing numbers of British people likewise protested their government's policies.

Opposing the Quartering Act, 1766–1767

In August 1766 George III dismissed the government and summoned William Pitt, an opponent of taxing the colonies, to form a cabinet. However, Pitt's health collapsed in March 1767, and Charles Townshend, the chancellor of the exchequer (treasurer), became the effective leader.

Just as Townshend took office, a conflict arose with the New York legislature over the **Quartering Act** of 1765, which ordered colonial legislatures to pay for certain goods used by British soldiers stationed within their borders—candles, window-panes, mattress straw, and a small liquor ration. The law aroused resentment because it constituted an *indirect* tax. In other words, although it did not empower royal officials to collect money directly from the colonists, it obligated assemblies

Quartering Act Required colonial legislatures to provide supplies to British troops

to raise revenue by whatever means they considered appropriate. The act fell lightly on all the colonies except New York, where more soldiers were stationed than in any other province. New York refused to grant the supplies.

New York's resistance unleashed a torrent of anti-American feeling in Parliament, which was still bitter after revoking the Stamp Act. Townshend responded by drafting the New York Suspending Act, which threatened to nullify all laws passed by the colony after October 1, 1767, if it refused to provide the supplies. By the time George III signed the measure, New York had already appropriated the funds. Nonetheless, the conflict over the Quartering Act demonstrated that British leaders would not hesitate to defend Parliament's authority through the most drastic of all steps: interfering with American claims to self-government.

Crisis over the Townshend Duties, 1767–1770

This new wave of British resentment toward the colonies coincided with an outpouring of frustration over the government's failure to cut taxes from wartime levels. Townshend sought to tax the colonists by exploiting a loophole in their arguments against the Stamp Tax. Americans had emphasized their opposition to internal taxes but had said nothing about external taxes—Parliament's right to tax imports as they entered the colonies. Townshend interpreted this silence as evidence that the colonists accepted Britain's right to impose external taxes. Parliament passed Townshend's Revenue Act of 1767 (popularly called the **Townshend duties**) in the summer. The new law taxed glass, paint, lead, paper, and tea imported into the colonies.

Townshend duties More Parliamentary attempts to raise revenues from the colonies

Superficially, this measure seemed to adhere to colonial principles, but fundamentally the Townshend duties differed significantly from what Americans considered a legitimate way of regulating trade through taxation. To the colonists, charging a duty was a lawful way for British authorities to control trade only if it excluded foreign goods by making them prohibitively expensive. The Revenue Act of 1767, however, set moderate rates that did not price goods out of the colonial market; clearly, its purpose was to collect money for the treasury. Thus, from the colonial standpoint, Townshend's duties were taxes just like the Stamp Act duties.

The Revenue Act never yielded the income that Townshend had anticipated. Of all the items taxed, only tea produced any significant revenue—£20,000 of the £37,000 expected. And because the measure would serve its purpose only if the colonists could afford British tea, Townshend eliminated £60,000 in import fees paid on East Indian tea entering Britain before transshipment to America. On balance, the Revenue Act *worsened* the British treasury's deficit by £23,000. By 1767, Parliament had grown less concerned with raising revenues than with asserting its authority over the colonies.

The Colonists' Reaction, 1767–1769

Resistance to the Revenue Act remained weak until December 1767, when John Dickinson published *Letters from a Farmer in Pennsylvania*. These twelve essays stated that no tax designed to produce revenue could be considered constitutional unless a people's elected representatives voted for it. Dickinson's writings convinced Americans that their arguments against the Stamp Act also applied to the Revenue Act.

In early 1768 the Massachusetts assembly asked Samuel Adams, who had helped organize the Sons of Liberty in Boston, to draft a "circular letter" to other legislatures. Adams's circular letter denounced taxation without representation but acknowledged Parliament as the "supreme legislative Power over the whole Empire" and advocated no illegal activities.

Virginia's assembly warmly approved Adams's eloquent measure and sent out a more strongly worded letter of its own, urging all the colonies to oppose imperial policies that would "have an immediate tendency to enslave them." But most colonial legislatures reacted indifferently to these letters. In fact, resistance might have disintegrated had not the British government overreacted.

Parliamentary leaders saw even the mild Massachusetts letter as "little better than an incentive to Rebellion." Disorganized because of Townshend's sudden death in 1767, the king's Privy (PRIH-vee) Council (advisers) directed Lord Hillsborough, the first appointee to the new post of secretary of state for the colonies, to express the government's displeasure. Adopting a "no more Mr. Nice Guy" approach, Hillsborough ordered the Massachusetts assembly to disown its letter, forbade all overseas assemblies to endorse it, and commanded royal governors to dissolve any legislature that violated his instructions.

The tactic backfired. Protesting Hillsborough's bullying, many legislatures previously indifferent to the Massachusetts letter adopted it enthusiastically. Royal governors responded by dismissing legislatures in Massachusetts and elsewhere, playing into the hands of Samuel Adams and others who wished to ignite widespread opposition to the Townshend duties.

Increasingly outraged, the colonists still needed an effective means of pressuring Parliament for repeal. Nonimportation seemed especially promising because it offered an alternative to violence and would distress Britain's economy. Thus, in August 1768 Boston's merchants adopted a nonimportation agreement, and the tactic spread southward. "Save your money, and you save your country!" trumpeted the Sons of Liberty, who reorganized after two years of inactivity. However, not all colonists supported nonimportation. Many merchants continued to import British goods until early 1769. The boycott probably kept out about 40 percent of British imports, while encouraging colonists to resist British policies more actively.

In 1770 yet another new prime minister, Lord North, assumed office. At his urging, Parliament eliminated most of the Townshend duties—but kept the tea tax as a symbol of its authority. Colonial leaders faced a dilemma: It was intolerable that taxes remained on tea, but should they boycott all British goods or only tea? Ultimately the nonimportation movement collapsed, but colonists agreed not to drink British tea. Colonial resistance leaders derived little pleasure from forcing Parliament to compromise; the tea duty remained a galling reminder that Parliament refused to abandon its broad interpretation of the Declaratory Act.

Board of Customs Commissioners Officials sent to oversee the collection of taxes; their corruption was a target for colonial anger

Customs "Racketeering," 1767–1770

Townshend also sought to increase revenues by tightening enforcement of existing customs laws. In 1767 he induced Parliament to create the American **Board of Customs Commissioners** to strictly enforce the Navigation Acts.

The new law increased the number of port officials, funded a colonial coast guard to catch smugglers, and provided money for secret informers.

The act also included new provisions that awarded an informer one-third of the value of all goods and ships appropriated through a conviction of smuggling. The fact that fines could be tripled under certain circumstances provided an even greater incentive to seize illegal cargoes. Smuggling cases were heard in vice-admiralty courts where the probability of conviction was extremely high. However, the law quickly drew protests because of the ways it was enforced and because it reversed the traditional legal process by assuming the accused to be guilty until proven otherwise.

Revenue agents commonly perverted the law by filing charges for technical violations of the Sugar Act, even when no evidence existed of intent to conduct illegal trade. They most often exploited the provision that declared any cargo illegal unless it had been loaded or unloaded with a customs officer's written authorization.

Customs commissioners also fanned anger by invading sailors' traditional rights. Long-standing maritime custom allowed crews to supplement their income by making small sales between ports. Anything stored in a sailor's chest was considered private property, exempt from the Navigation Acts. But after 1767, revenue agents treated such belongings as cargo, thus establishing an excuse to seize the entire ship. Under this policy, crewmen saw arrogant inspectors break open their trunks and then lost trading stock worth several months' wages. In these ways the commissioners embarked on a program of "customs racketeering" that constituted legalized piracy. This program fed an upsurge in popular violence, as sailors waited for chances to get even. Above all, customs commissioners' use of informers provoked retaliation. The *Pennsylvania Journal* in 1769 scorned these agents as "dogs of prey, thirsting after the fortunes of worthy and wealthy men."

Nowhere were customs agents and informers more detested than in Boston, where citizens retaliated in June 1768. When customs agents seized colonial merchant John Hancock's sloop *Liberty* on a technicality, a crowd tried to prevent the towing of Hancock's ship and then began assaulting customs officials. Swelling to several hundred, the mob drove all revenue inspectors from the city. To appease angry colonists momentarily, British officials dropped the charges against Hancock. At the same time, to make it clear they conceded nothing to the colonists, they dispatched four thousand troops to Boston, a warning that they would not tolerate further violence in defiance of their authority.

Wilkes and Liberty, 1768–1770

By no means did all Britons support Parliament. Their protests became part of a larger movement in the 1760s against the policies of George III and a Parliament dominated by wealthy landowners. **John Wilkes,** a fiery London editor whose newspaper regularly and irreverently denounced the king, became both leader and focal point of the protest. A member of Parliament, Wilkes was tried for seditious libel and acquitted, to great popular acclaim. George III's government then shut down his newspaper and persuaded members of the House of Commons to deny Wilkes his seat. After publishing another slashing attack on the king, Wilkes fled to Paris.

John Wilkes British opponent of King George III who became a hero to American colonists

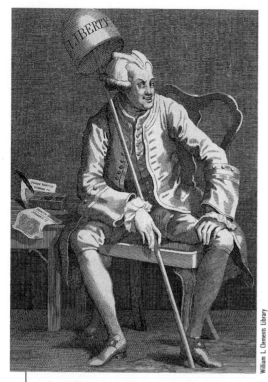

John Wilkes, by William Hogarth, 1763

Detesting Wilkes and all he stood for, Hogarth depicted the radical leader as menacing and untrustworthy.

William L. Clements Library

In 1768 Wilkes returned to Britain, defying an arrest warrant, and again ran for Parliament. By then, government policies, including the Townshend Acts, had unleashed a flood of protests against the "obnoxious" government ministers. Manufacturers, merchants, and artisans all rallied around the cry "Wilkes and Liberty."

When the newly elected Wilkes was once again arrested, twenty to forty thousand angry "Wilkesites" massed on St. George's Fields, outside the prison where he was being held. Soldiers and police opened fire on rock-throwing demonstrators, killing eleven. The "massacre of St. George's Fields" furnished martyrs to the protesters, and Wilkes received enormous outpourings of public support from the North American colonies as well as from Britain. From his prison cell, Wilkes maintained a regular correspondence with Boston's Sons of Liberty, and Bostonians cheered his release from prison in April 1770 with a massive celebration.

The Wilkes furor sharpened the political ideas of government opponents on both sides of the Atlantic. British voters sent petitions to Parliament proclaiming that its refusal to seat Wilkes was an affront to the electorate's will and calling "virtual representation" a sham. Emboldened by the "Wilkes and Liberty" movement, William Pitt and others forcefully denounced the government's colonial policies. The colonists themselves concluded that Parliament and the government represented a small but powerful minority whose authority they could legitimately question.

CHECKING IN

- The Quartering Act showed colonists that Parliament was willing to interfere with their self-government.
- The Townshend duties failed to raise revenues, but their intent to do so angered colonists even more.
- Colonial reaction to Parliament united in the protests of John Dickinson, the Massachusetts circular letter, and nonimportation agreements; women played an important public role in implementing nonimportation.
- The Board of Customs Commissioners sent to Boston to oversee collection of taxes were often corrupt and became a target for colonial anger.
- John Wilkes became a symbol of the dangers posed by a too-powerful government.

Women and Colonial Resistance

Colonial boycotts of British goods provided a unique opportunity for white women, whose participation in public affairs had been widening slowly for several decades, to join the resistance to British policies. By the 1760s, upper-class female patriots had played a part in defeating the Stamp Act, some by attending political rallies and many more through expressing their opposition in discussions and correspondence with family and friends.

In early 1770, urged on by American leaders convinced that women could exert a persuasive moral influence on public opinion, women calling themselves Daughters of Liberty assumed a more prominent role in protests against the tax on tea. In early 1770 more than three hundred "mistresses of families" in Boston denounced the consumption of the beverage. In some ways nonconsumption was more effective than nonimportation, for the colonists' refusal to consume imports would chill merchants' economic incentive to import British goods.

Nonconsumption agreements therefore became popular and were extended to include other goods, mainly clothes. Again, women played a vital role, because the boycott would fail unless the colonists replaced British imports with apparel of their own making. Responding to leaders' pleas for an expansion of domestic cloth production, women of all social ranks organized spinning bees. These attracted intense publicity as evidence of American determination to fight parliamentary taxation. Spinning bees not only helped to undermine the masculine prejudice that women had no place in public life, but also endowed spinning and weaving, previously considered routine tasks, with political virtue. Female activities such as spinning bees and tea boycotts dramatically demonstrated that American protests extended beyond a few male merchants and crowds of angry men, into the heart of American households and congregations. Women's participation showed that colonial protests reached into the heart of American households and were leading to broader popular participation in politics.

THE DEEPENING CRISIS, 1770–1774

In what ways did colonists' views of parliamentary authority change after 1770?

▌After 1770 the imperial crisis took on ominous new dimensions. Colonists and British troops clashed on the streets of Boston. Resistance leaders in the colonies developed ways to systematically coordinate their actions and policies. After the defiance manifested in the Boston Tea Party, Britain was determined to subordinate the colonies once and for all. Adding to the general tension were several violent conflicts that erupted in the western backcountry.

The Boston Massacre, 1770

British authorities responded to the violence directed at customs commissioners by dispatching four thousand British troops to Boston in 1768. However, the violence only escalated, intersecting with intracolonial tensions and extending the crisis beyond the port cities.

Crackling with tension, Boston took on the atmosphere of an occupied city. Armed soldiers and resentful civilians traded insults, and off-duty soldiers undercut local laborers by working for lower wages. Many of the soldiers were Irish Catholics, which was especially galling to the mainly Protestant Bostonians.

Bostonians' resentment of British authority boiled over on February 22, 1770, when a customs informer fired birdshot at several children throwing rocks at his house and killed an eleven-year-old boy. Samuel Adams organized a burial procession to maximize the horror over a child's death, relying on grief to unite the community in opposition to British policies. "My Eyes never beheld such a funeral," wrote his cousin John Adams. "A vast Number of Boys walked before the Coffin, a vast Number of Women and Men after it. . . . This Shows there are many more Lives to spend if wanted in the Service of their country."

Although the army had played no part in the shooting, it became a target for Bostonians' rage. A week after the funeral, tension erupted at the guard post protecting the customs office. When an officer tried to disperse a crowd led by Crispus Attucks, a seaman of African and Native American ancestry, the mob responded with a barrage of flying objects. One soldier, knocked down by a block of ice, fired, and then the others opened fire. Their volley killed five people, including Attucks.

Royal authorities moved quickly to defuse the crisis by isolating the army on a fortified island in the harbor and putting soldiers who had fired on trial. Patriot leader John Adams defended the accused British troops by claiming that they had been provoked by a "motley rabble," an accusation that resonated with Boston's "respectable" middle- and upper-class elites. Only two soldiers were found guilty; they received the relatively mild punishment of branding on their thumbs.

Boston Massacre
Confrontation between colonists and British troops in which five colonists were shot and killed

Burning hatred underlay the **Boston Massacre**—a name designed to invoke the St. George's Fields massacre two years earlier. For the first time colonists had to confront the stark possibility that a tyrannical British government was determined to coerce and suppress them through armed force.

The Committees of Correspondence, 1772–1773

In the fall of 1772 Lord North prepared to implement Townshend's goal of paying royal governors from customs revenues, freeing them from the control of the colonial assemblies. With representative government deeply threatened, Samuel Adams persuaded Boston's town meeting to request that every Massachusetts community appoint people to exchange information and coordinate measures to defend colonial rights. Within a year, most Massachusetts communities had established **committees of correspondence,** and the idea spread throughout New England.

committees of correspondence
Local committees established throughout colonies to coordinate anti-British actions

The committees of correspondence, the resistance leaders' first attempt to maintain close political cooperation over a wide area, allowed Samuel Adams to conduct a campaign of political education for all New England. He sent messages for each local committee to read at its town meeting, which debated the issues and adopted formal resolutions. The system made tens of thousands of citizens consider evidence that their rights were being endangered and committed them to take a stand. Adams's most successful venture in whipping up public alarm came in June 1773, when he published letters from the governor of Massachusetts, Thomas Hutchinson, obtained by Benjamin Franklin, advocating "an abridgement of what are called British liberties" and "a great restraint of natural liberty." The Hutchinson correspondence confirmed Americans' suspicions that a plot was afoot to destroy their basic freedoms.

Patrick Henry, Thomas Jefferson, and Richard Henry Lee had proposed in March 1773 that Virginia establish committees of correspondence, and by early 1774 a communications web linked leaders from all the colonies.

Conflicts in the Backcountry

Although most of the turbulence between 1763 and 1775 swirled through coastal seaports, rapid expansion led to violence in the West as well. There, numerous clashes involving Native Americans, colonists, and colonial governments flared in the Appalachian backcountry.

Tension then flared into violence in Pennsylvania's backcountry. Settlers in and around the town of Paxton blamed the Pennsylvania assembly, which was

The Granger Collection, NYC

Boys Expedition
Militia units organize in Philadelphia, ready to march against the Paxton Boys if necessary.

dominated by Quakers, for failing to provide military protection and for denying them equal representation in the assembly. The "Paxton Boys," as they were known, believed all Native Americans were their racial enemies. After laying waste to two villages of peaceful Conestoga Indians, killing and scalping men, women, and children, in February 1764 about 200 Paxton Boys headed for Philadelphia with plans to kill Christian Indian refugees there. A government delegation headed by Benjamin Franklin met the armed mob on the outskirts of the city and promised that the assembly would consider their grievances. Appeased, the Paxton Boys returned home.

Land pressures and the lack of adequate revenue from the colonies left the British government helpless to enforce the Proclamation of 1763. Speculators, squatters, hunters, and thieves trespassed on Native American lands, often leading Indians to respond violently, while the British withdrew troops that might have maintained order.

Under such pressures, Britain and the Iroquois, in the Treaty of Fort Stanwix (1768), turned land along the Ohio River that was occupied by the Shawnees, Delawares, and Cherokees over to the Virginia and Pennsylvania governments, resolving the two colonies' overlapping land claims in Ohio at the Indians' expense. The Shawnees assumed leadership among the Ohio Indians, who, with the Cherokees, were convinced that appeasement would not stop colonial expansion.

The treaty heightened rather than eased frontier tensions, especially in the Ohio country. Colonists moving westward into what they called Kentucky collided with Shawnee and Mingo Indians, and in 1774 Virginia launched Lord Dunmore's War.

After Virginia's victory at Point Pleasant, Virginia gained uncontested rights to all land south of the Ohio River in exchange for giving up all claims north of the river. Resentment continued to fester on both sides, and fighting would resume when war broke out between Britain and the colonies.

Other frontier disputes led to conflict among the colonists themselves. Settlers in western Massachusetts in the early 1760s, for example, found their titles challenged by New Yorker landlords. In 1766, threatened with eviction, the New Englanders staged an armed uprising. And in 1769 New Hampshire settlers calling themselves the Green Mountain Boys began guerrilla warfare against other New York landlords. The independent government they formed ultimately became that of Vermont.

Expansion also provoked conflict between frontier settlers and their own colonial governments. In North Carolina, westerners, who were underrepresented in the assembly, found themselves exploited by dishonest officeholders appointed by eastern politicians. Twenty-five hundred armed westerners, known as Regulators, clashed with thirteen hundred North Carolina militia on May 16, 1771, at the battle of Alamance Creek. Although the Regulators' uprising disintegrated, it crippled the colony's subsequent ability to resist British authority. A Regulator movement also arose in South Carolina, in this case to counter the government's unwillingness to prosecute bandits who terrorized the settlers. Fearful that the colony's slave population might revolt if the militia was dispatched, South Carolina's government yielded to the Regulators by establishing new courts and allowing jury trials in recently settled areas.

Although unrelated, these episodes reflected the tensions generated by a land-hungry white population willing to use violence against Native Americans, other colonists, and British officials.

The Tea Act, 1773

Smuggling and nonconsumption had taken a heavy toll on Britain's East India Company, the holder of the legal monopoly on importing tea into the British Empire. By 1773, as tons of tea rotted in warehouses, the East India Company was teetering on the brink of bankruptcy. But Lord North could not let the company fail because, by maintaining British authority in India at its own expense, the East India Company had become a vital component in the British imperial structure.

In May 1773, to save the beleaguered East India Company, Parliament passed the **Tea Act,** which eliminated all import duties on tea entering Britain and thus lowered the selling price to consumers. To reduce the price further, the Tea Act also permitted the company to sell tea directly to consumers rather than through wholesalers. These provisions reduced the cost of East India Company tea in the colonies to well below the price of smuggled tea. Parliament expected economic self-interest to overcome American scruples about buying taxed tea.

But the Tea Act alarmed many Americans, who recognized that the revenues raised by the law would place royal governors' purses beyond the reach of the colonial assemblies. The law also threatened to seduce Americans into accepting parliamentary taxation in return for a frivolous luxury. The committees of correspondence decided to resist the importation of tea by pressuring the East India Company's agents to refuse acceptance or by preventing the landing of East India Company cargoes.

Tea Act Attempt to bail out the East India Company that heightened tensions between Britain and colonists

In Boston on November 28, 1773, the first ship came under jurisdiction of the customhouse, to which duties would have to be paid within twenty days, or the cargo would be seized from the captain and the tea would be claimed by the company's agents and placed on sale. When Samuel Adams, John Hancock, and others asked customs officers to issue a special clearance for the ship's departure (to avoid the seizure and sale), Governor Hutchinson refused.

On the evening of December 16, 1773, Samuel Adams convened a meeting in the Old South Church, at which he told five thousand citizens about Hutchinson's insistence on landing the tea, warned them that the grace period would expire in a few hours, and proclaimed that "this meeting can do no more to save the country." About fifty young men disguised as Indians and armed with "tomahawks" headed for the wharf, followed by the crowd. Thousands lined the waterfront to watch them heave forty-five tons of tea overboard; for an hour the only sounds echoing through the crisp, moonlit night were the steady chop of hatchets breaking open wooden chests and the soft splash of tea on the water. Their work finished, the participants left quietly. The town lapsed into a profound hush—"never more still and calm," according to one observer.

CHECKING IN

- After the Boston Massacre, colonists confronted the possibility that Britain would use armed force against them.
- Lord North attempted partial conciliation by repealing most of the Townshend duties, but insisted on retaining the tax on tea.
- Under Sam Adams's leadership, the colonies formed committees of correspondence to coordinate inter-colonial actions.
- The Tea Act of 1773 was intended primarily to aid British imperialism in India but aroused colonial opposition.
- Colonists applauded the Boston Tea Party, but it fanned enormous anger in Britain.

▌ TOWARD INDEPENDENCE, 1774–1776

What led most colonists in 1776 to abandon their loyalty to Britain and choose national independence?

The calm that followed the Boston Tea Party was the calm before the storm. Furious at the colonists' actions, the British government became more determined than ever to quash colonial insubordination. Colonial leaders were equally determined to defend their self-government and liberty. The empire and its American colonies were on a collision course, but the colonists hesitated at a declaration of independence. In the meantime, African-Americans, both free and slave, pondered how to realize their own freedom.

Liberty for African-Americans

Throughout the imperial crisis, African-American slaves quickly responded to calls for liberty and equality. In 1772 a British court decision electrified much of the black population. A Massachusetts slave, James Somerset, whose master had taken him to Britain, sued for his freedom; Lord Chief Justice William Mansfield ruled that Parliament had never explicitly established slavery and that therefore no court could compel a slave to obey an order depriving him of his liberty.

Although the decision applied only in Britain, Massachusetts slaves petitioned the legislature to apply it in their colony as well. In the Chesapeake area, dozens of slaves ran away from their masters and sought passage on ships bound for Britain. As Anglo-American tensions mounted in 1774, many slaves began to anticipate the arrival of British troops as their path to liberation. White Chesapeake colonists began to fear that war would lead to slave rebellion.

Bearing out such fears in 1775, Virginia's royal governor, **Lord Dunmore,** promised freedom to any slave who enlisted in the cause of restoring royal authority. Nearly a thousand slaves responded to Dunmore's proclamation before angry colonists forced him to flee the colony. Perhaps more important, both whites and blacks began to see a clear link between British forces and slave liberation.

Lord Dunmore Royal governor of Virginia who promised freedom to slaves who fought to restore royal authority

The "Intolerable Acts"

Boston's "Tea Party" enraged the British, prompting them to once more adopt a "no more Mr. Nice Guy" policy. Only "New England fanatics" could imagine that cheap tea oppressed them, fumed Lord North. A Welsh member of Parliament declared that "the town of Boston ought to be knocked about by the ears, and destroy'd." The great orator Edmund Burke pled in vain for the one action that could end the crisis: "Leave America . . . to tax herself." But the British government swiftly asserted its authority through the passage of four Coercive Acts that, along with the Quebec Act, became known to many colonists as the **"Intolerable Acts."**

Intolerable Acts Laws intended to punish Massachusetts for the Boston Tea Party and strengthen royal authority

The first Coercive Act, the Boston Port Bill, was passed on April 1, 1774. It ordered the navy to close Boston Harbor unless the town arranged to pay for the ruined tea by June 1. The impossibly short deadline was meant to ensure the harbor's closing, which would plunge Boston into economic distress. The second Coercive Act, the Massachusetts Government Act, revoked the Massachusetts charter and made the colony's government less democratic. The upper house would be appointed for life by the crown, not elected annually by the assembly. The royal governor gained absolute control over the appointment of judges and sheriffs. Finally, the new charter limited town meetings to one a year. Although these changes brought Massachusetts government into line with that of other colonies, the colonists interpreted them as assaults on representative government.

The final two Coercive Acts—the Administration of Justice Act and a new Quartering Act—rubbed salt into the wounds. The first of these permitted any person charged with murder while enforcing royal authority in Massachusetts to be tried in Britain or in another colony. To colonists, this seemed like a declaration of open season upon them. The second went beyond the Quartering Act of 1765 by allowing the governor to requisition *empty* private buildings for quartering, or housing, troops. Americans learned of the unrelated Quebec Act at the same time as the Coercive Acts. Intended to cement loyalty to Britain among conquered French-Canadian Catholics, the law established Roman Catholicism as Quebec's official religion. Protestant Anglo-Americans, who associated Catholicism with arbitrary government, took alarm. Furthermore, the Quebec Act gave Canada's governor sweeping powers but established no legislature. The law extended Quebec's territorial claims south to the Ohio River and west to the Mississippi, a vast area populated by Indians and some French, and claimed by several colonies.

The Intolerable Acts, coupled with the appointment of General Thomas Gage, Britain's military commander in North America, convinced New Englanders that the crown planned to abolish traditional British liberties throughout North America.

Once the Coercive Acts destroyed these liberties in Massachusetts—many believed—the Quebec Act would serve as a blueprint for extinguishing representative government in other colonies. Parliament would replace all colonial governments with ones like Quebec's. Elected assemblies, freedom of religion for Protestants, and jury trials would vanish.

Intended only to punish Massachusetts, the Coercive Acts thus pushed most colonies to the brink of revolution. Repeal of these laws became the colonists' non-negotiable demand. The Declaration of Independence would refer to these laws six times in listing colonial grievances justifying the break with Britain.

The First Continental Congress

In response to the Intolerable Acts, the committees of correspondence of every colony but Georgia sent delegates to a **Continental Congress** in Philadelphia. The fifty-six delegates who assembled on September 5, 1774, included the colonies' most prominent politicians: Samuel and John Adams of Massachusetts; John Jay of New York; Joseph Galloway and John Dickinson of Pennsylvania; and Patrick Henry, Richard Henry Lee, and George Washington of Virginia.

Continental Congress Major step toward resistance to Britain and unity among colonies

The Continental Congress endorsed the Suffolk (SUFF-uk) Resolves, extreme statements of principle that proclaimed that the colonies owed no obedience to the Coercive Acts, advocated a provisional government until restoration of the Massachusetts charter, and vowed that defensive measures should follow any attack by royal troops. The Continental Congress also voted to boycott British goods after December 1, 1774, and to stop exporting goods to Britain and its West Indies possessions after September 1775. This agreement, called the Continental Association, would be enforced by locally elected committees of "observation" or "safety." But not all the delegates embraced such bold defiance. Jay, Dickinson, Galloway, and other moderates who dominated the contingent from the Middle Colonies feared that a confrontation with Britain would spawn internal colonial turmoil. They vainly opposed nonimportation and unsuccessfully sought support of a plan for an American legislature that would share with Parliament the authority to tax and govern the colonies.

Finally, the delegates summarized their principles and demands in a petition to George III. They conceded to Parliament the power to regulate colonial commerce but argued that parliamentary efforts to impose taxes, enforce laws through admiralty courts, suspend assemblies, and revoke charters were unconstitutional. By addressing the king rather than Parliament, Congress was imploring George III to end the crisis by dismissing the ministers responsible for passing the Coercive Acts.

From Resistance to Rebellion

Most Americans hoped that resistance would jolt Parliament into renouncing its claims of authority over the colonies. But tensions between American radicals and moderates ran high.

To solidify defiance, American resistance leaders used coercion against waverers and loyalists ("Tories"). Committees elected to enforce the Continental Association became vigilantes, compelling merchants to burn British imports, browbeating clergymen who preached pro-British sermons, and pressuring Americans to free themselves of dependence on British imports by adopting simpler diets and home-spun clothing. In colony after colony, moreover, the committees assumed governmental functions by organizing volunteer military companies and extralegal legislatures. By spring 1775 colonial patriots had established provincial "congresses" that paralleled existing royal governments.

In April 1775 armed conflict erupted in Massachusetts. Citizens had collected arms and organized militia units ("minutemen") to respond instantly in an emergency. The British government ordered Massachusetts's Governor Thomas Gage to quell the "rude rabble" and to arrest the patriot leaders. Aware that most of these had fled Boston, Gage, on April 19, 1775, sent seven hundred British soldiers to seize colonial military supplies stored at **Concord.** Two couriers, William Dawes and Paul Revere, alerted nearby towns of the British troop movements. At **Lexington** on the road to Concord, about seventy minutemen faced the British on the town green. After a confused skirmish in which eight minutemen died and a single redcoat was wounded, the British marched to Concord. They found few munitions but encountered a swarm of armed Yankees. When some minutemen mistakenly concluded that the town was being burned, they exchanged fire with British regulars and touched off a running battle that continued most of the sixteen miles back to Boston. By day's end the redcoats had lost 273 men. These engagements awakened the countryside. Within a day, some 20,000 New Englanders were besieging the British garrison in Boston.

Three weeks later, the Continental Congress reconvened in Philadelphia. Most delegates still opposed independence and agreed to send a "loyal message" to George III. The resulting Olive Branch Petition presented three demands: a cease-fire in Boston, repeal of the Coercive Acts, and negotiations to establish guarantees of American rights. Yet the same delegates who pleaded for peace voted to establish an "American continental army" and to appoint George Washington as commander, measures that the British could only see as rebellious.

The Olive Branch Petition reached London along with news of the Continental Army's formation and of the battles of Breed's Hill and Bunker Hill just outside Boston. Although the British dislodged the Americans in the clashes, they suffered 2,200 casualties, a 50 percent casualty rate, compared to colonial losses of only 311. After Bunker Hill the British public wanted retaliation, not reconciliation. In August, George III proclaimed New England to be in a state of rebellion; in December, Parliament declared all of the colonies rebellious, outlawing all British trade with them and subjecting their ships to seizure.

Concord Skirmish between colonists and British troops

Lexington One of the first armed conflicts between Britain and the colonists

Common Sense

Many Americans still clung to hopes of reconciliation. Even John Adams, who believed separation inevitable, said that he was "fond of reconciliation, if we could reasonably entertain Hopes of it on a constitutional basis." The majority of Americans who resisted independence blamed evil ministers, rather than the king, for unconstitutional measures and expected saner heads to rise to power in Britain. On both counts they were wrong.

Americans' sentimental attachment to the king, the last emotional barrier to independence, crumbled in January 1776 with the publication of Thomas Paine's

Common Sense. Paine had immigrated to the colonies from Britain in 1774 with a penchant for radical politics and a gift for plain and pungent prose. Paine told Americans what they had been unable to bring themselves to say: Monarchy was an institution rooted in superstition, dangerous to liberty, and inappropriate for Americans. The King himself was "the royal brute," a "hardened, sullen-tempered Pharoah." Further, America did not need its British connection. "The commerce by which she [America] hath enriched herself are the necessaries of life, and will always have a market while eating is the custom in Europe," Paine argued. And, he pointed out, the events of the preceding six months had made independence a reality. Finally, Paine linked America's awakening nationalism with a sense of religious mission: "We have it in our power to begin the world over again. A situation, similar to the present, hath not happened since the days of Noah until now." America, Paine wrote, would be a new *kind* of nation, a model republic free of oppressive European beliefs and corrupt institutions.

Common Sense, "a landflood that sweeps all before it," sold more than 100,000 copies in three months, one copy for every fourth or fifth adult male in the colonies. By spring 1776 Paine's pamphlet had dissolved lingering allegiance to George III and removed the last psychological barrier to independence.

Common Sense Brilliant pamphlet by Thomas Paine that summarized pro-independence arguments

Declaring Independence

Even as colonists absorbed Paine's views, the military conflict between Britain and the colonies escalated, further diminishing the prospects of reconciliation. In May 1775 colonial troops captured Fort Ticonderoga and Crown Point on the key route connecting New York and Canada. Six months later Washington ordered Colonel Henry Knox, in civilian life a book seller and in war the army's senior artillery officer, to bring the cannons captured at Ticonderoga to reinforce the siege of Boston. Using crude sleds, Knox and his men hauled fifty-nine cannons through dense forest and over snow-covered mountains, one of the Revolution's great feats of endurance. The Ticonderoga cannon forced the British to evacuate Boston on March 17, 1776.

Regrouping, the British planned an assault on New York to drive a wedge between New England and the other colonies. Washington countered by moving his forces there in April 1776. Other military moves quickened the drift toward all-out war. A two-pronged assault on Canada by the colonists failed, as did a British offensive in the southern colonies.

Stimulated by Paine's soaring rhetoric, local gatherings throughout the colonies, ranging from town meetings to militia musters, passed resolutions favoring American independence.

Thomas Paine
Having arrived in the colonies less than two years earlier, Paine became a best-selling author with the publication of *Common Sense* (1776).

Most of New England was already in rebellion, and Rhode Island declared itself independent in May 1776. The Middle Colonies hesitated to support revolution because they feared, correctly, that the war would largely be fought over control of Philadelphia and New York. The South began to press for separation. In April, North Carolina authorized its congressional delegates to vote for independence, and in June, Virginia followed suit. On July 2 the Continental Congress formally adopted the Virginia resolution and created the United States of America.

The drafting of a statement to justify the colonies' separation from Britain fell to Virginia's Thomas Jefferson. Congress made two important changes to Jefferson's first draft: It inserted the phrase "pursuit of happiness" instead of "property" in the document's most famous sentence, and it deleted a condemnation of George III for forcing the slave trade on unwilling colonists. Congress then approved Jefferson's manuscript on July 4, 1776. Even though parliamentary authority had been the focal point of dispute since 1765, the **Declaration of Independence** never mentioned Parliament by name because Congress was unwilling to imply that Parliament held any authority over America. Jefferson instead focused on George III, citing "repeated injuries and usurpations" against the colonies.

Declaration of Independence
Document drafted primarily by Thomas Jefferson presenting the American Revolution as a struggle for universal principles

Like Paine, Jefferson elevated colonial grievances to a struggle of universal dimensions. In the tradition of Enlightenment thought, Jefferson argued that Britain had violated its contract with the colonists, giving them the right to replace it with a government of their own. His emphasis on the equality of all individuals and their natural entitlement to justice, liberty, and self-fulfillment expressed the Enlightenment's deep longing for government that rested on neither legal privilege nor the exploitation of the majority by the few—and deliberately ignored the existence of slavery.

Jefferson addressed the Declaration of Independence as much to Americans uncertain about the wisdom of independence as to world opinion. Above all, he wanted to convince his fellow Americans that social and political progress was impossible within the British empire. However, the declaration did not address the status of blacks, poor white men, and women. All thirteen of the new states countenanced slavery, severely restricted the rights of free blacks, used property qualifications to determine voting rights, and relegated women to second-class status. Jefferson also put Indians beyond the pale when he accused the king of having unleashed "the merciless Indian savages" on innocent colonists.

Thus, the declaration expressed the sentiments of a minority of colonists at the same time that it set out the hopes of thousands upon thousands more. The struggle for independence from Britain had merged with a quest for equality and personal independence that would eventually transcend class, race, and gender. The declaration never claimed that perfect justice and equal opportunity existed; instead, it challenged the revolutionary generation and all who followed to bring this ideal closer to reality.

CHECKING IN

- The Coercive (or Intolerable) Acts pushed the colonies to the brink of war.
- Members of the First Continental Congress proclaimed that parliamentary taxation of the colonies was unconstitutional but stopped short of declaring independence.
- The battles of Lexington and Concord transformed colonial resistance from words into an armed struggle.
- Thomas Paine's *Common Sense* universalized American ideals and prodded colonies toward independence.
- In the Declaration of Independence, Thomas Jefferson proclaimed the colonies to be defending universal natural rights.

Chapter Summary

How did Britain and its colonies view their joint victory over France in the Seven Years' War? (page 92)

Great Britain emerged victorious in the Seven Years' War against France; in 1763 France ceded almost all of her North American empire to Britain, quadrupling the size of the British empire in North America. Ironically, this triumph would also provide the framework for friction between Britain and its colonies.

What was imperial reorganization, and how did it change relations between Britain and the North American colonies? (page 97)

Attempts at imperial reorganization in the early 1760s were intended to help defray the enormous costs of Britain's victory by increasing revenues from the colonies, but the attempts succeeded primarily in alienating the colonists. After open resistance boiled over in the Stamp Act crisis, Parliament backed down a bit but insisted that it had complete authority over the colonies.

In what ways did resistance to the Townshend duties differ from earlier colonial resistance efforts? (page 102)

Controversy between Britain and the colonies continued with measures such as the Quartering Act and the Townshend duties. Colonial protests found shape in the work of John Dickinson and a hero in the person of John Wilkes. In an attempt to increase tax revenues, Britain created a Board of Customs Commissioners, but many of the commissioners were corrupt, and the board became the target of colonial anger.

In what ways did colonists' views of parliamentary authority change after 1770? (page 107)

The Boston Massacre brought a temporary lull in conflict between Britain and the colonies, but Lord North's attempt to aid the East India Company led to the Boston Tea Party. Colonists defied Britain's continued revenue-raising measures.

KEY TERMS

Seven Years' War (p. 92)
Treaty of Paris of 1763 (p. 95)
Pontiac (p. 96)
Proclamation of 1763 (p. 96)
writ of assistance (p. 97)
Sugar Act (p. 98)
Stamp Act (p. 99)
Sons of Liberty (p. 100)
Stamp Act Congress (p. 100)
Declaratory Act (p. 101)
Quartering Act (p. 102)
Townshend duties (p. 103)
Board of Customs Commissioners (p. 104)
John Wilkes (p. 105)
Boston Massacre (p. 108)
committees of correspondence (p. 108)
Tea Act (p. 110)
Lord Dunmore (p. 112)
Intolerable Acts (p. 112)
Continental Congress (p. 113)
Concord (p. 114)
Lexington (p. 114)
Common Sense (p. 115)
Declaration of Independence (p. 116)

What led most colonists in 1776 to abandon their loyalty to Britain and choose national independence? (page 111)

In response to the Tea Party, Parliament passed a series of Coercive Acts—known to the colonists as the Intolerable Acts—which spawned the First Continental Congress and the beginning of fully coordinated colonial resistance. In 1775 the battles of Lexington and Concord transformed the friction between Britain and the colonies into armed conflict. Thomas Paine's *Common Sense* ridiculed the arguments against independence and portrayed the colonial struggle as one of universal principles on which Thomas Jefferson elaborated in the Declaration of Independence.

 **CourseMate**

Go to the CourseMate website at **www.cengagebrain.com** for additional study tools and review materials—including audio and video clips—for this chapter.

CHAPTER 6

Securing Independence, Defining Nationhood

Trumbull, "George Washington"

CHAPTER PREVIEW

The Prospects of War
What factors enabled the Americans to defeat the British in the American Revolution?

War and Peace, 1776–1783
How did the war unfold?

The Revolution and Social Change
How did the war affect relationships among Americans of different classes, races, and genders?

Forging New Governments, 1776–1787
What political concerns were reflected in the first state constitutions and Articles of Confederation?

Toward a New Constitution, 1786–1788
What were the principal issues dividing proponents and opponents of the new federal Constitution?

O n May 1, 1777, eighteen-year-old Agrippa Hull, a free African-American man from Stockbridge, Massa-chusetts, enlisted in the Continental Army. Like most black recruits, Hull enlisted for the duration of the Revolutionary War. He spent four years as an orderly for General Thaddeus Kósciuszko, a Polish republican and abolitionist who had volunteered for the American cause.

Upon discharge, Hull returned to Stockbridge, where he was welcomed as a hero and became a New England celebrity until his death at age eighty-nine. A gifted storyteller, Hull regaled locals and visitors with accounts of his wartime experiences—of horrors such as assist-ing surgeons in performing amputations, and of lighter moments such as Kósciuszko's finding him entertaining his black friends in the general's uniform. When Kósciuszko made a return visit to the United States in 1797, Hull and the Polish patriot reunited in New York to public acclaim.

For victorious patriots like Hull, military service strengthened a new national identity. In July 1776, the thirteen colonies had jointly declared their independence from Britain and formed a loosely knit confederation of states, later formalized with the adoption of the Articles of Confederation. Shaped by the collective hardships experienced during eight years of terrible fighting, the former colonists shifted from seeing themselves primarily as military allies to accepting one another as fellow citizens. But divisions remained, erupting in the national contest over replacing the Articles of Confederation. The ratification of the Constitution in 1787 marked a triumph for those favoring more centralization of power at the national level. It also left most of Agrippa Hull's fellow African-Americans in slavery.

THE PROSPECTS OF WAR

What factors enabled the Americans to defeat the British in the American Revolution?

The Revolution was both a collective struggle that pitted the independent states against Britain and a civil war among American peoples. American opponents of independence constituted one of several factors working in Britain's favor as war began. Others included Britain's larger population and its superior military resources and preparation. America, on the other hand, was located far from Britain and enjoyed the intense commitment to independence from patriots and the Continental Army.

Loyalists and Other British Sympathizers

Even after the Declaration of Independence, some Americans remained opposed to secession from Britain, including about 20 percent of all whites. Although these internal enemies of the Revolution called themselves **loyalists,** they were "Tories" to their patriot, or Whig, opponents.

loyalist Colonist who supported the British

Loyalists, like Whigs, typically opposed parliamentary taxation of the colonies. Many loyalists thus found themselves fighting for a cause with which they did not entirely agree; as a result, many switched sides during the war. But loyalists believed that separation was illegal and was not necessary to preserve the colonists' constitutional rights. Above all, they retained a profound reverence for the crown and believed that if they failed to defend their king, they would sacrifice their personal honor.

The mutual hatred between Whigs and Tories was intense. Each side saw its cause as sacred, and those who opposed it as traitors. The worst atrocities of the war were committed by Americans against each other.

The most important factor in determining loyalist strength in any area was the political power of local Whigs and their success in convincing their neighbors that Britain threatened their liberty. For several years, colonial resistance leaders in New England, Virginia, and South Carolina had vigorously pursued a program of political education and popular mobilization. As a result, probably no more than 5 percent of whites in these areas were committed loyalists in 1776. Loyalist strength was greatest in New York and New Jersey, where elites were especially reluctant to declare their allegiance to either side. Those two states eventually furnished about half of the twenty-one thousand Americans who fought as loyalists.

A second major factor in loyalist strength was the geographic distribution of recent British immigrants, who identified closely with their homeland. These newcomers included thousands of British veterans of the French and Indian War who had remained in the colonies, usually in New York. The 125,000 British immigrants who arrived between 1763 and 1775 formed major centers of loyalist sympathy. In New York, Georgia, and the Carolina piedmont, where these newcomers clustered, loyalists probably constituted 25 to 40 percent of the white population in 1776.

Quebec's religious and secular elites comprised another significant white minority with pro-British sympathies. When Continental forces invaded Quebec in 1775–1776, they found widespread support among non-elite French as well as British Canadians. After British forces repulsed the invasion, Britain's military, supported by local elites, retained control of Canada throughout the war.

Black slaves and Native Americans also widely supported the British. As in Virginia, hundreds of South Carolina slaves sought refuge on British ships before the outbreak of war. During the war itself, about twenty thousand slaves escaped their owners. Most were recaptured or died, especially from epidemics, but a small minority achieved freedom, often after serving as laborers or soldiers in the Royal Army. Meanwhile, about five thousand enslaved and free African-Americans, mostly from New England, calculated that supporting the rebels would hasten their own emancipation and equality.

Finally, most Indians, recognizing the threat that expansion-minded colonists posed, likewise supported the British. In the Ohio country, most Shawnees, Delawares, and other Indians continued to resent settlers' incursions, but a few communities initially supported the Americans. Most tribes of the Six Nations Iroquois confederacy followed the lead of the Mohawk chief **Joseph Brant** in supporting Britain. But the Oneidas (oh-NIE-duhs) and Tuscaroras (tuss-kuh-ROR-uhs), influenced by a New England missionary, actively sided with the rebels against other Iroquois. Meanwhile, Cherokee ranks were split between anti-American militants and those who thought that the Cherokees' best hope was to steer clear of the Anglo-American conflict.

Joseph Brant Mohawk chief (Thayendagea) and obstinate foe of American military and expansion

The Opposing Sides

Britain entered the war with two major advantages. First, Britain's 11 million people greatly outnumbered the 2.5 million colonists, one-third of whom were either slaves or loyalists. Second, Britain possessed the world's largest navy and one of its best armies. During the war, the army's size more than doubled, from 48,000 to 111,000 men. In addition, Britain hired 30,000 German mercenaries known as Hessians (HESH-uns) and enlisted 21,000 loyalists to supplement its own fighting force.

However, Britain's ability to crush the rebellion was weakened by the decline in its sea power, a result of budget cuts after 1763. Midway through the war, half of Britain's ships languished in dry dock awaiting major repairs. In addition, during the war U.S. Navy ships and privateers would capture more than 2,000 British merchant vessels and 16,000 crewmen. Seriously overextended, the navy barely kept the army supplied and never effectively blockaded American ports. Maintaining public support presented another serious problem for Britain. The war more than doubled the British national debt, adding to the burdens of a people already paying record taxes.

The United States faced different but equally severe problems. Besides the fact that many colonists, slaves, and Native Americans favored the British, the patriots faced a formidable military challenge. Although militias often performed well in hit-and-run guerrilla skirmishes, they were not trained to fight against professional armies like Britain's. Congress recognized that independence would never be secured if the new nation relied on guerrilla tactics, avoided major battles, and ceded its cities to the enemy. Moreover, potential European allies would recognize that dependence on guerrilla warfare meant the rebels could not drive out the British army.

The Continental Army would thus have to fight in European fashion, relying on precision movements of mass formations of troops and rapid maneuvers to crush an enemy's undefended flank or rear. After advancing within musket range, opposing troops would stand upright and fire at each other until one line weakened. Discipline, training, and nerve would be essential if soldiers were to hold their line as comrades fell around them.

In 1775, Britain possessed a well-trained army with a strong tradition of discipline and bravery under fire. In contrast, the Continental Army had neither an inspirational heritage nor experienced officers. Although the United States mobilized about 220,000 troops, compared to the 162,000 who served the British, most served short terms. Most whites and blacks who did sign up for longer terms were poor.

Chronology

1776	British force American troops from New York City
1777	Congress approves Articles of Confederation; American victory at Saratoga
1777–1778	British troops occupy Philadelphia; Continental Army winters at Valley Forge
1778	France formally recognizes the United States; declares war on Britain
1779	Spain declares war on Britain; John Sullivan leads American raids in Iroquois country
1780	British seize Charles Town Articles of Confederation ratified; Battle of Yorktown
1781	British General Cornwallis surrenders
1783	Treaty of Paris
1784	Spain closes New Orleans to American trade; economic depression begins in New England
1785	Ordinance of 1785; Treaty of Fort McIntosh
1786	Congress rejects Jay-Gardoqui Treaty
1786–1787	Shays's Rebellion in Massachusetts
1787	Northwest Ordinance; Philadelphia convention frames federal Constitution
1787–1788	Alexander Hamilton, James Madison, and John Jay, *The Federalist*
1788	Constitution ratified

Such men joined not out of patriotism but because, as one of them, a jailed debtor named Ezekiel Brown, put it, they had "little or nothing to lose."

The Americans experienced a succession of heartbreaking defeats in the war's early years. Yet, to win the war, the Continentals did not have to destroy the British army but only prolong the rebellion until Britain's taxpayers lost patience with the struggle. Until then, American victory would depend on the ability of one man to keep his army fighting. That man was George Washington.

After resigning his commission in 1758, Washington served in the Virginia House of Burgesses, where his influence grew, not because he thrust himself into every issue but because others respected him and sought his opinion. Having emerged as an early, though not outspoken, opponent of parliamentary taxation, he later sat in the Continental Congress. Washington was the logical choice to head the Continental Army.

The young Washington's mistakes and defeats in the Ohio Valley (see Chapter 5) taught him about the dangers of overconfidence and the need for determination in the face of defeat. He also learned that American soldiers fought best when led by example and treated with respect.

CHECKING IN

- At the war's start, the British enjoyed major advantages in population, economic development, and military preparedness.
- However, British supply lines were long and popular support for the war short-lived.
- Americans had no trained army when the war began.
- Americans did not have to defeat the British; they just had to prolong the rebellion.
- Washington kept his army fighting despite defeats; this experience taught him the need for determination and earned him enormous respect among Americans.

WAR AND PEACE, 1776–1783

How did the war unfold?

Each side initially won important victories in the North. West of the Appalachians, revolutionary forces prevailed over the British and their Indian allies. However, it was the American and French victory at Yorktown in 1781 that decided the war and gained British recognition of American independence.

Shifting Fortunes in the North, 1776–1778

During the second half of 1776, the two sides focused on New York. Under two brothers—General William Howe and Admiral Lord Richard Howe—130 British warships carrying 32,000 royal troops landed at New York in the summer of 1776. Defending the city were 18,000 poorly trained soldiers under George Washington. By the end of the year, William Howe's men had killed or captured one-quarter of Washington's troops and had forced the survivors to retreat from New York across New Jersey and the Delaware River into Pennsylvania.

With the British nearing Philadelphia, Washington decided to seize the offensive before the morale of his army and country collapsed completely. On Christmas night 1776, his troops returned to New Jersey and attacked a Hessian garrison at Trenton. At the **Battle of Trenton,** Washington captured 918 Germans and lost only four Continentals. Washington's men then attacked twelve hundred British at Princeton on January 3, 1777, and killed or captured one-third of them while sustaining only forty casualties.

The American victories at Trenton and Princeton boosted civilian and military morale and drove a wedge between New Jersey's five thousand loyalists and

Battle of Trenton New Jersey battle where Washington took more than 900 Hessian prisoners on Christmas Night, 1776; vital victory to improve national morale

the British army. Washington's victories forced the British to remove virtually all their New Jersey garrisons to New York early in 1777. Once the British were gone, New Jersey's militia disarmed known loyalists and jailed their leaders. Bowing to the inevitable, most remaining loyalists swore allegiance to the Continental Congress.

After the Battle of Princeton, the Marquis de Lafayette (mar-KEE deh lah-fay-ETT), a young French aristocrat, joined Washington's staff. Given Lafayette's close connections with the French court, his presence indicated that France might recognize American independence and declare war on Britain. Before recognizing the new nation, however, King Louis XVI wanted proof that the Americans could win a major battle.

Louis did not have to wait long. In the summer of 1777, the British planned a two-pronged assault intended to crush American resistance in New York State and thereby isolate New England. Pushing off from Montreal, a force under Lieutenant Colonel Barry St. Leger would invade central New York from the west. At the same time, General John Burgoyne would lead the main British force south from Quebec and link up with St. Leger near Albany (see Map 6.1).

However, nothing went according to British plans. St. Leger's force encountered a Continental force holding a chokepoint at Fort Stanwix. Unable to take the post after three weeks, St. Leger retreated in late August 1777. Burgoyne's campaign appeared more promising after his force of eighty-three hundred British and Hessians recaptured Fort Ticonderoga, but nearly seven thousand American troops under General Horatio Gates challenged him near Saratoga. In two battles in the fall, the British suffered twelve hundred casualties. Surrounded and hopelessly outnumbered, Burgoyne surrendered on October 17, 1777.

Battle of Saratoga American victory in 1777 that convinced the French to support the revolutionaries

The **Battle of Saratoga** would prove to be the war's turning point. The victory convinced France that the Americans could win the war. In February 1778, France formally recognized the United States. Four months later, it went to war with Britain. Spain and Holland ultimately joined the war as French allies.

In late August 1777, British General Howe landed eighteen thousand troops near Philadelphia. With Washington at their head and Lafayette at his side, sixteen thousand Continentals occupied the imperiled city. The two armies collided on September 11, 1777, at Brandywine Creek, Pennsylvania. After the Continentals crumbled in the face of superior British discipline, Congress fled Philadelphia, allowing Howe to occupy it. Howe again defeated Washington at Germantown on October 4. In one month's bloody fighting, 20 percent of the Continentals were killed, wounded, or captured.

While the British army wintered comfortably in Philadelphia, the Continentals huddled eighteen miles away in the bleak hills of Valley Forge. "The greatest part were not only shirtless and barefoot," wrote a seventeen-year-old Massachusetts recruit, "but destitute of all other clothing, especially blankets." Shortages of provisions, especially food, would continue to undermine morale and, on some occasions, discipline among American forces.

The army also lacked training. At Saratoga, the Americans' overwhelming numbers more than their skill had forced Burgoyne to surrender. Indeed, when Washington's men had met Howe's forces on equal terms, they lost badly. The Continental Army received a desperately needed boost in February 1778, when

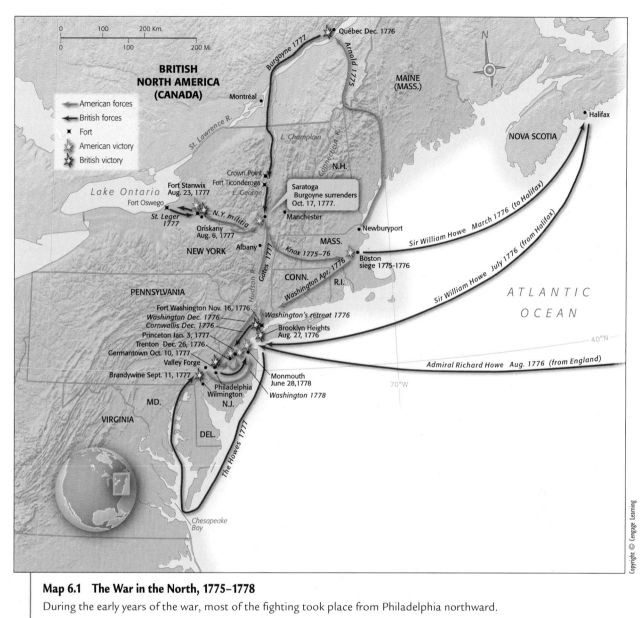

Map 6.1　The War in the North, 1775–1778

During the early years of the war, most of the fighting took place from Philadelphia northward.

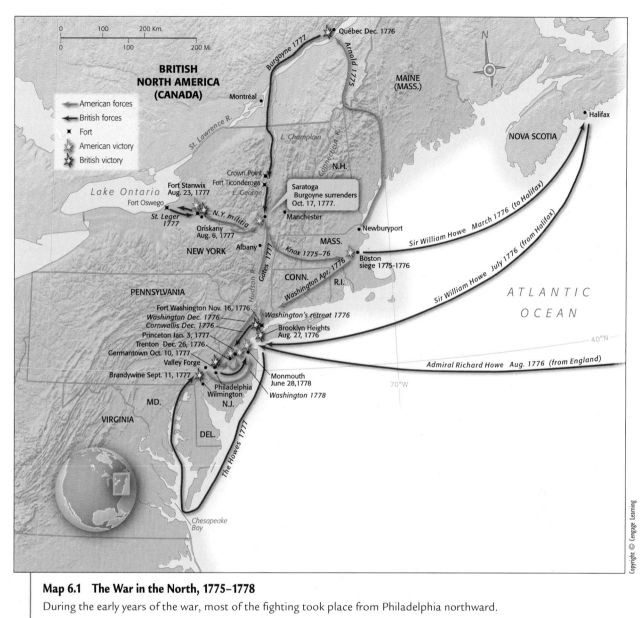 Interactive Map

a German soldier of fortune, Friedrich von Steuben, arrived at Valley Forge. This earthy German instinctively liked Americans and had a talent for motivating men (and for swearing forcefully in several languages). An administrative genius and immensely popular individual, Steuben almost single-handedly turned the army into a formidable fighting force in a mere four months.

The Continental Army got its first opportunity to demonstrate Steuben's training at Monmouth, New Jersey, on June 28, 1778, when it met a force led by General Henry Clinton, the new commander-in-chief in North America. The battle raged for six hours in one-hundred-degree heat, with the Continentals throwing back

Copyright © Cengage Learning

Britain's finest troops. The British finally broke off contact and slipped away under cover of darkness. Never again would they win easy victories against the Continental Army.

The Battle of Monmouth ended the contest for the North. Clinton occupied New York, which the Royal Navy made safe from attack. Washington kept his army on watch nearby, while Whig militia hunted down the last few Tory guerrillas.

The War in the West, 1776–1782

A different kind of war developed west of the Appalachians, consisting of small-scale skirmishes, often sparked by long-standing frontier tensions, rather than major battles involving thousands of troops. The war in the West erupted in 1776 when Cherokees began attacking settlers from North Carolina and nearby colonies who had encroached on their homelands (see Map 6.2). After suffering heavy losses, the

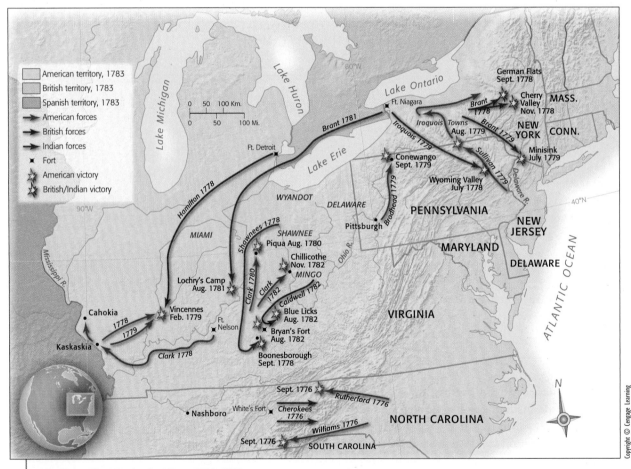

Map 6.2   The War in the West, 1776–1782

The war's western front was closely tied to Native Americans' defense of their homelands against expansionist settlers.

Interactive Map

Copyright © Cengage Learning

colonies recovered and organized retaliatory expeditions. Within a year, these expeditions had burned most Cherokee towns, forcing the Cherokees to sign treaties that ceded most of their land in the Carolinas and Tennessee.

The intense fighting lasted longer in the Northwest. Ohio Indians and white settlers fought for two years in Kentucky, with neither side gaining a clear advantage. But after British troops occupied French settlements in what is now Illinois and Indiana, Colonel George Rogers Clark led 175 Kentucky militiamen north of the Ohio River and took Vincennes by February 1779. Most Ohio Indians continued to resist the Americans until the war's end.

In the East, pro-British Iroquois under the gifted Mohawk leader Joseph Brant devastated the New York and Pennsylvania frontiers in 1778. General John Sullivan led a Continental force, with Tuscarora and Oneida allies, against the Iroquois. Victorious at what is now Elmira, New York, in 1779, Sullivan and his forces burned two dozen Iroquois villages and destroyed a million bushels of corn. The Iroquois fled north to Canada, and untold hundreds starved to death. Sullivan's campaign devastated the pro-British Iroquois.

Fighting continued in the West until 1782. Despite their intensity, the western campaigns did not determine the outcome of the war itself. Nevertheless, they would have a significant impact on the future shape of the United States.

American Victory in the South, 1778–1781

In 1778, the war's focus shifted to the South. By securing southern ports, Britain expected to acquire the flexibility needed to move its forces back and forth between the West Indies—where they faced French and Spanish opposition—and the mainland, as necessity dictated. In addition, the South looked like a relatively easy target. General Clinton expected to seize key southern ports and, with the aid of loyalist militiamen, move back toward the North, pacifying one region after another.

The plan unfolded smoothly at first. In the spring of 1778, British troops from East Florida took control of Georgia. After a two-year delay caused by political bickering at home, Clinton sailed from New York with nine thousand troops and forced the surrender of Charles Town, South Carolina. He left the mopping-up operation to **Lord Charles Cornwallis.** However, the British quickly found that there were fewer loyalists than they had expected.

Southern loyalism had suffered several serious blows since the war began. When the Cherokees had attacked the Carolina frontier in 1776, they killed whites indiscriminately. Numerous Tories joined the rebel militia to defend their homes. In addition, the arrival of British troops sparked a renewed exodus of enslaved Africans from their plantations. About one-third of Georgia's blacks and one-fourth of South Carolina's fled to British lines in the quest of freedom. The British made every effort to return them to their owners. Nonetheless, fear of slave rebellion caused many former loyalists to abandon their British ties and welcome the rebels' return to power.

Meanwhile, battles between British troops and Continental regulars led to a string of Continental defeats. America's worst loss of the entire war came at Camden, South Carolina, in August 1780. General Horatio Gates's combined force of professionals and militiamen faced Cornwallis's army. The militiamen fled after the first volley, and the badly outnumbered Continentals were overrun. Washington sent

Lord Charles Cornwallis
British general whose surrender at Yorktown in 1781 effectively ended the Revolutionary War

General Nathanael Greene to confront Cornwallis. Under Greene, the rebels lost three major battles in 1781 but won the campaign nonetheless by stretching British supply lines and inflicting heavy casualties. Greene's dogged resistance forced Cornwallis to abandon the Carolina backcountry and lead his battered troops into Virginia.

Cornwallis established a base at Yorktown, Virginia. Britain's undoing began on August 30, 1781, when a French fleet dropped anchor off the Virginia coast

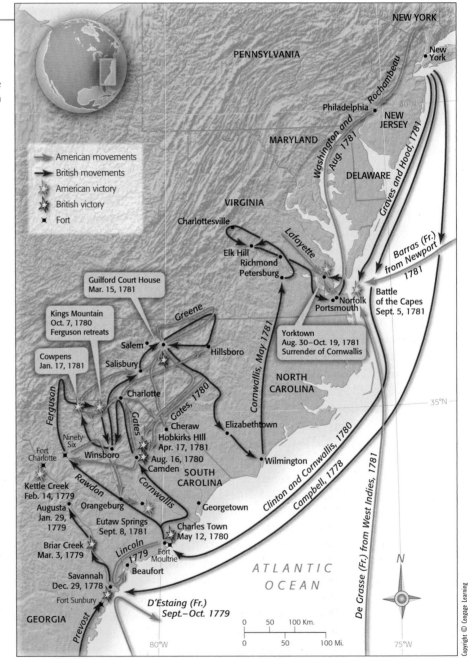

Map 6.3   The War in the South, 1778–1781

The South was the setting for the final, decisive phase of the war, culminating in the British surrender at Yorktown in October 1781.

Interactive Map

and landed troops near Yorktown. Lafayette and a small force of Continentals from nearby joined the French while Washington arrived with his army from New York. In the Battle of Yorktown, six thousand trapped British troops stood off eighty-eight hundred Americans and seventy-eight hundred French for three weeks before surrendering with military honors on October 19, 1781.

Peace at Last, 1782–1783

"Oh God!" Lord North exclaimed on hearing of Yorktown. "It's all over." Cornwallis's surrender had extinguished the will of Britain's overtaxed people to fight and forced the government to negotiate for peace. John Adams, Benjamin Franklin, and John Jay were America's principal delegates to the peace talks in Paris, which began in June 1782.

Military realities largely influenced the terms of the Treaty of Paris (1783). Britain recognized American independence and agreed to withdraw all royal troops from the new nation's soil. The British had little choice but to award the Confederation all lands east of the Mississippi. Twenty thousand Anglo-Americans now lived west of the Appalachians. Moreover, Clark's victories had given Americans control of the Northwest, while Spain had kept Britain out of the Southwest.

On the whole, the settlement was highly favorable to the United States, but it left some disputes unresolved. Under a separate treaty, Britain returned East and West Florida to Spain, but the boundaries designated by this treaty were ambiguous. Further, although the United States promised to urge state legislatures to compensate loyalists for property losses, several states would later refuse to comply. Completely left out of the treaty—and on their own—were the Native Americans who had supported the British. Indian leaders were outraged; many did not acknowledge the new nation's sovereignty over their territory.

Independence carried a heavy price. At least 5 percent of all free males between the ages of sixteen and forty-five—white, black, and Native American—died fighting the British. Furthermore, the war drove perhaps one of every six loyalists, several thousand slaves, and several thousand Native Americans into exile. And the peace left two important issues unsettled: what kind of society the United States would become and what sort of government it would possess.

CHECKING IN

- Initial rounds of the war were fought mainly in the North, with mixed results.
- The American victory at Saratoga represented a major turning point, because it drew the French into the war on the Americans' side.
- Success in the West allowed the revolutionaries to claim the Mississippi as their western boundary.
- In 1778 the focus of the war shifted to the South. Here, the British won inconclusive victories and were then forced to surrender at Yorktown.
- The Treaty of Paris of 1783 ended the war and confirmed the independence of the colonies.

THE REVOLUTION AND SOCIAL CHANGE

How did the war affect relationships among Americans of different classes, races, and genders?

Two forces shaped the Revolution's social effects: the principles articulated in the Declaration of Independence and the dislocations caused by the war. These factors combined to force questions of class, gender, and race into public discussion. Popular attitudes about the rights of non-elite white men and of white women, and the future of slavery, shifted somewhat. Although the resulting changes were not substantive, the discussions ensured that these issues would continue to be debated in the United States. For Native Americans, however, the Revolution was a step backward.

Egalitarianism Among White Men

Between 1700 and 1760 social relations between elites and common people had grown more formal, distant, and restrained. Members of the colonial gentry lived sumptuously to emphasize their position. By the late 1760s, however, many in the upper class were wearing homespun clothing in support of boycotts of British goods. When the Virginia planters organized militia companies in 1775, they put aside their expensive officers' uniforms and dressed in buckskin or homespun hunting shirts of a sort that even the poorest farmer could afford. Elites maintained the appearance, if not the substance, of equality.

The war accelerated the erosion of class differences by forcing gentry officers to respect ordinary men serving as privates. Indeed, the soldiers demanded to be treated with consideration, especially in light of the ringing statement of the Declaration of Independence that "all men are created equal."

After returning to civilian life, the soldiers retained their sense of self-esteem and insisted on respectful treatment by elites. As these feelings of personal pride gradually translated into political behavior and beliefs, many candidates took care not to scorn the common people. The war thus subtly democratized Americans' political assumptions.

Many elites who considered themselves republicans did not welcome the apparent trend toward democracy. These men continued to insist that each social class had its own particular virtues and that a chief virtue of the lower classes was deference to those possessing the wealth and education necessary to govern. "A popular government is the worse Curse," wrote John Adams in 1776, concluding that "despotism is better."

Nevertheless, most Americans from the Revolutionary War generation came to insist that virtue and sacrifice defined a citizen's worth independently of his wealth. Voters still elected the wealthy to office, but not if they flaunted their money or were condescending toward common people. The new emphasis on equality did not extend to males, women, and nonwhites without property, but it undermined the tendency to believe that wealth or distinguished family background conferred a special claim to public office.

Although many whites became more egalitarian in their attitudes, the Revolution left the actual distribution of wealth in the nation unchanged. The war had been directed at British imperial rule and not at the structure of American society. The exodus of loyalists did not affect the class structure because the 3 percent who fled the United States represented a cross-section of society. Overall, the American upper class seemed to own about as much of the national wealth in 1783 as it did in 1776.

White Women in Wartime

White women broadened their involvement in the anti-British cause, creating a wide range of activities during the war. Female "camp followers," many of them soldiers' wives, cooked, laundered, and nursed the wounded for both sides. A few women actually disguised themselves as men and joined the fighting. Women who remained at home managed families, households, farms, and businesses on their own. Despite—and because of—enormous struggles, women gained confidence in their ability to think and act on matters traditionally reserved for men. Although women's public roles and visibility increased during the Revolution, the question was to what extent the new nation would make these gains permanent.

As in all wars, women's public roles and visibility heightened during the Revolution. In 1779, a number of women, including Franklin's daughter Sally Franklin Bache, organized a campaign to raise money for the troops. They likened their role to Joan of Arc and other female heroes who had saved their people, and they proclaimed that American women were "born for liberty" and would never "bear the irons of a tyrannic government."

The most direct challenge to established gender relations came from **Abigail Adams.** "In the new Code of Laws…" she wrote to her husband John in 1776, "I desire that you would Remember the Ladies." Otherwise, she continued, "we are determined to foment a Rebellion and will not hold ourselves bound by any Laws in which we have no voice, or Representation." Abigail made it clear that women saw

Abigail Adams Wife of John Adams, who issued the most direct challenge to established gender relations

that the arguments against arbitrary British rule also applied to gender relations. Despite his high regard for his wife's intellect, John Adams dismissed her plea as an effort to extend rights and power to the unworthy. The assumption that women were naturally dependent continued to dominate discussions of the female role. For that reason, married women's property remained, in Abigail's bitter words, "subject to the control and disposal of our partners, to whom the law have given a sovereign authority."

The Library of Congress

A Revolution for Black Americans

The wartime condition of African-Americans contradicted the ideals of equality and justice for which Americans fought. About a half million blacks—20 percent of the total population—inhabited the United States in 1776, all but about twenty-five thousand of whom were enslaved. Free blacks could not vote, lived under curfews, and lacked the guarantees of equal justice afforded to even the poorest white criminal.

The war nevertheless presented new opportunities to African-Americans. Early fighting in New England drew several hundred blacks into the militia and Continental units. Some slaves ran off and posed as free persons. A 1775 ban on black soldiers was collapsing by 1777, when Washington agreed to Rhode Island's plea that it be allowed to raise a nonwhite

Phillis Wheatley, African-American Poet
Though a slave, Wheatley was the best-known poet in America at the time of the Revolution. Despite her fame, she died in poverty in 1784.

regiment. The regiment of African-Americans and Native Americans distinguished itself in several battles, including at Yorktown. Yet Washington was wary of arming slaves. When Congress urged Georgia and South Carolina to arm three thousand slaves against advancing British troops in 1779, Washington vetoed the plan.

Until the mid-eighteenth century, few Europeans and white Americans had criticized slavery at all. But in the decade before the Revolution, American opposition to slavery had swelled, especially as resistance leaders increasingly compared the colonies' relationship with Britain to that between slaves and a master. The earliest organized initiatives against slavery originated among Quakers. The yearly meeting of the New England Friends abolished slavery among its members in 1770. By 1779, Quaker slave owners had freed 80 percent of their slaves, and some activists were broadening their condemnations to include slavery everywhere.

antislavery movement
Opposition to slavery that began slowly during the revolutionary period

Discussions of liberty, equality, and natural rights, particularly in the Declaration of Independence, also spurred the beginnings of the **antislavery movement.** Between 1777 and 1784, Vermont, Pennsylvania, Massachusetts, Rhode Island, and Connecticut began phasing out slavery. New York did not do so until 1799, and New Jersey until 1804. Most state abolition laws provided for gradual emancipation, typically declaring all children born of a slave woman after a certain date—often July 4— free. In addition, most northern states granted some civil rights to free blacks after the Revolution. Many repealed or stopped enforcing curfews and other colonial laws restricting free African-Americans' freedom of movement and access to the courts.

No state south of Pennsylvania abolished slavery. Nevertheless, all states except South Carolina and Georgia ended slave imports and all but North Carolina passed laws making it easy for masters to manumit (set free) slaves. However, these "free persons of color" faced a future of destitution and second-class citizenship. Most had used up their cash savings to purchase their freedom and were past their physical prime. They found few whites willing to hire them. Most free blacks remained poor laborers or tenant farmers, although a few became landowners or skilled artisans. Phillis Wheatley, a slave in a Boston merchant family, gained her freedom in 1773, the same year her poems were published to acclaim in Britain. Several of these poems linked the liberty sought by white Americans with a plea for the liberty of slaves.

One of the most prominent free blacks to emerge during the Revolutionary War period was Prince Hall of Boston. After gaining his freedom in 1770, Hall took a leading role among Boston blacks protesting slavery. During the war he formed a separate black Masonic lodge, initiating a movement that spread to other northern communities. In 1786 he petitioned the Massachusetts legislature for support of a plan that would enable interested blacks "to return to Africa, our native country… where we shall live among our equals and be more comfortable and happy than we can be in our present situation." Later activists would echo his call for blacks to "return to Africa."

The Revolution neither ended slavery nor brought equality to free blacks. Most wartime opportunities for black men grew out of the army's need for personnel rather than a white commitment to equal justice. However, the war did begin a process by which slavery eventually might have been extinguished. In half the nation, the end of human bondage seemed to be in sight. Many white southerners viewed slavery as a necessary evil rather than as a positive good. Slavery had begun to crack, and free blacks had made some gains. However, events in the 1790s would reverse the tentative move toward egalitarianism (as discussed in Chapter 7).

Native Americans and the Revolution

Revolutionary ideology held out at least abstract hope for African-Americans and women, but it made no provisions for the many Indians who sought to maintain political and cultural independence. Moreover, in an overwhelmingly agrarian society, the Revolution's promise of equal economic opportunity for all set the stage for territorial expansion beyond settled areas, thereby threatening Indian lands. Even where Indians retained land, the influx of settlers posed dangers in the form of deadly diseases, farming practices hostile to Indian subsistence, and alcohol. Indians were all the more vulnerable because during the wars between 1754 and 1783, their population east of the Mississippi had fallen by about half, and many villages had been uprooted.

In the face of these uncertainties, Native Americans continued to incorporate aspects of European culture into their lives. From the early colonial period, they had adopted European-made goods of cloth, metal, and glass while retaining some of their traditional clothing, tools, and weapons. Indians also participated in the American economy by occasionally working for wages or selling food, craft items, and other products.

Thus, Native Americans did not hold stubbornly to traditional ways, but they did insist on retaining control of their communities and ways of life. In the Revolution's aftermath, it remained doubtful that the new nation would accommodate Native Americans on these terms.

CHECKING IN

- Egalitarianism among white males increased as a result of the war.

- The war offered free blacks some gains in opportunities and rights, but most still faced a future of uncertainty and second-class citizenship.

- Northern states provided for the eventual end of slavery, and an antislavery movement began.

- Women built on their contributions during the war to play a larger public role.

- Native Americans were left in an ambiguous and threatened position.

Forging New Governments, 1776–1787

What political concerns were reflected in the first state constitutions and Articles of Confederation?

In establishing new political institutions, revolutionary Americans endeavored to guarantee liberty at the state level by minimizing executive power and by subjecting all officeholders to frequent scrutiny by voters. In turn, the new national government was subordinate, under the Articles of Confederation, to the thirteen states. However, challenges facing the Confederation made clear to many elites the need for more centralized authority at the national level.

From Colonies to States

Before 1776, colonists had regarded their popularly elected assemblies as the bulwark of their liberties against encroachments by governors wielding executive power. Thereafter, the legislatures retained that role even when voters, rather than the British crown, chose governors.

In keeping with colonial practice, eleven states maintained bicameral (two-chamber) legislatures. Colonial legislatures had consisted of an elected lower house (or assembly) and an upper house (or council) appointed by the governor or chosen by the assembly. These two-part legislatures mirrored Parliament's division into the House of Commons and House of Lords, symbolizing the assumption that a government should have separate representation by the upper class and the common people. Likewise, few questioned the long-standing practice of setting property requirements for voters and elected officials. Property ownership, most people argued, enabled voters and officeholders to think and act independently. Nine of the thirteen states slightly reduced property requirements for voting, but none abolished such qualifications entirely.

Another colonial practice that persisted beyond independence was the equal (or nearly equal) division of legislative seats among all counties or towns, regardless of differences in population. As a result, a minority of voters usually elected a majority of assemblymen. Only the most radical constitution, Pennsylvania's, sought to avoid such outcomes by attempting to ensure that election districts would be roughly equal in population.

Despite the holdover of certain colonial-era practices, the state constitutions in other respects departed radically from the past. Above all, they were written documents that usually required popular ratification and could be amended only by the voters. In short, Americans jettisoned the British conception of a constitution as a body of customary arrangements and practices, insisting instead that constitutions were written compacts that defined and limited the powers of rulers and established the rights of citizens. By 1784, all state constitutions included explicit bills of rights that outlined certain freedoms that lay beyond the control of any government.

The earliest state constitutions strengthened legislatures at governors' expense. In most states, the governor became an elected official, and elections themselves occurred far more frequently. In most states, the power of appointments was transferred from the governor to the legislature. Legislatures usually appointed judges and could reduce their salaries, and legislatures could impeach both judges and governors (try them for wrongdoing). By relieving governors of most appointive powers, the constitutions gave governors little to do. Pennsylvania went further, simply eliminating the office of governor.

As the new state constitutions weakened the executive branch and vested more power in the legislatures, they also made the legislatures more responsive to the will of the voters. Nowhere could the governor appoint the upper chamber. Eight constitutions written before 1780 allowed voters to select both houses of the legislature. Pennsylvania and Georgia abolished the upper house altogether. States' weakening of the executive branch and enhancement of legislative and popular authority reflected Americans' fears of centralized authority, rooted in bitter memories of royal governors who had acted arbitrarily.

Despite their high regard for popularly elected legislatures, revolutionary leaders described themselves as republicans rather than democrats. These words had different connotations in the eighteenth century than they do today. To many elites, democracy suggested mob rule or, at least, the concentration of power in the hands of an uneducated multitude. In contrast, **republicanism** presumed that government would be entrusted to virtuous leaders elected for their superior talents and commitment to the public good. For most republicans, the ideal government would delicately balance the interests of different classes to prevent any one group from

republicanism Ideal of early revolutionaries that government should be entrusted to leaders chosen for wisdom

gaining absolute power. A few, including John Adams, thought that a republic could include a monarchy if needed to counterbalance democratic tendencies. But having rid themselves of one king, even most elites did not wish to enthrone another.

In the first flush of revolutionary enthusiasm, elites had to be content with state governments dominated by popularly elected legislatures. Gradually, however, wealthier landowners, bankers, merchants, and lawyers reasserted the prerogatives of wealth. In Massachusetts, an elite-dominated convention in 1780 pushed through a constitution largely authored by John Adams. The document stipulated stiff property qualifications for voting and holding office and a governor with considerable powers. The Massachusetts constitution signaled a general trend. Georgia and Pennsylvania substituted bicameral for unicameral legislatures by 1790. Other states raised property qualifications for members of the upper chamber in a bid to encourage the "senatorial element" and to make room for men of "Wisdom, remarkable integrity, or that Weight which arises from property."

Formalizing a Confederation, 1776–1781

Americans' first national government reflected their fears of centralized authority. In 1776, John Dickinson drafted a proposal for a national government, and in 1777, Congress sent a weakened version of this document, the **Articles of Confederation,** to the states for ratification. However, not until February 1781—six months before the American victory at Yorktown—did the last state, Maryland, agree to ratification.

> **Articles of Confederation**
> First American national government; all power held by states

The Articles of Confederation explicitly reserved to each state—and not to the national government—"its sovereignty, freedom and independence." The "United States of America" was no more than "a firm league of friendship" among sovereign states, much like today's European Union. As John Adams later explained, Congress never thought of "consolidating this vast Continent under one national Government" but instead erected "a Confederacy of States, each of which must have a separate government."

Under the Articles, the national government consisted of a single-chamber Congress, elected by the state legislatures, in which each state had one vote. Congress could request funds from the states but could not tax without every state's approval, nor could it regulate interstate or overseas commerce. The Articles provided for no executive branch. Rather, congressional committees oversaw financial, diplomatic, and military affairs. Nor was there a judicial system by which the national government could compel allegiance to its laws. The Articles did eliminate all barriers to interstate travel and trade, and guaranteed that all states would recognize one another's judicial decisions.

Finance, Trade, and the Economy, 1781–1786

Perhaps the greatest challenge facing the Confederation was putting the nation on a sound financial footing. Winning the war cost $160 million, far more than taxation could raise. The government borrowed from abroad and printed paper money, called continentals. But from 1776 to 1781 lack of public faith in the government destroyed 98 percent of the continentals' value, creating an inflationary disaster. Congress turned to Robert Morris, a wealthy Philadelphia merchant who became the nation's superintendent of finance in 1781. Morris proposed a national import duty of 5 percent to finance the congressional budget and to guarantee interest payments on the war debt, but the duty failed to pass because one state, Rhode Island, rejected it.

Meanwhile, seeing themselves as sovereign, most states had assumed some responsibility for the war debt and begun compensating veterans and creditors within their borders. But Morris and other nationally minded elites insisted that the United States needed sources of revenue independent of the states. Hoping to panic the country into seeing things their way, Morris and New York congressman Alexander Hamilton engineered a dangerous gamble known later as the **Newburgh Conspiracy.** In 1783, the two men secretly persuaded some army officers, encamped at Newburgh, New York, to threaten a coup d'état unless the treasury obtained the taxation authority necessary to raise funds for their pay, which was months late. George Washington forestalled the conspiracy by appealing to his officers' honor.

Newburgh Conspiracy
Threatened mutiny that showed how deeply some were concerned about the weakness of the national government

When peace came in 1783, Morris found it impossible to fund the government adequately. After New York blocked another congressional tax measure sent to the states, state contributions to Congress fell steadily. By the late 1780s the states lagged 80 percent behind in providing the funds that Congress requested.

Nor did the Confederation succeed in prying trade concessions from Britain. The continuation after the war of British trade prohibitions contributed to an economic depression that gripped New England beginning in 1784. A short growing season and poor soil kept yields so low, even in the best of times, that farmers barely produced enough grain for local consumption. New Englanders also faced high taxes to repay the money borrowed to finance the Revolution. Economic depression and overpopulation only aggravated the region's miseries.

Meanwhile, southern planters faced frustration at the failure of their principal crops, tobacco and rice, to return to prewar export levels. Whereas nearly two-thirds of American exports originated in the South in 1770, less than half were produced by southern states in 1790. As a result they were left with thousands of underemployed slave laborers. The mid-Atlantic states, on the other hand, were less dependent on British-controlled markets for their exports. As famine stalked Europe, farmers in Pennsylvania and New York prospered from climbing export prices. By 1788, the region had largely recovered from the Revolution's ravages.

The Confederation and the West, 1785–1787

The postwar settlement and administration of western lands posed another formidable challenge to the new government. Settlers and speculators were determined to possess these lands, and Native Americans were equally determined to keep them out. At the same time, Britain and Spain sought to contain the new nation's territorial expansion.

After the states surrendered claims to more than 160 million acres north of the Ohio River, Congress established procedures for surveying this land in the Ordinance of 1785. Subsequently, in the **Northwest Ordinance** (1787), Congress defined the steps for the creation and admission of new states. This law designated

Northwest Ordinance Law that provided for creating new states

the area north of the Ohio River as the Northwest Territory and provided for its later division into states. It forbade slavery while the region remained a territory, although the citizens could legalize the institution after statehood.

The Northwest Ordinance outlined three stages for admitting states into the Union. First, during the initial years of settlement, Congress would appoint a territorial governor and judges. Second, as soon as five thousand adult males lived in a territory, voters would approve a territorial constitution and elect a legislature. Third, when the total population reached sixty thousand, voters would ratify a state constitution, which Congress would have to approve before granting statehood.

The most significant achievements of the Confederation, the Ordinance of 1785 and Northwest Ordinance, had lasting effects. Besides laying out procedures for settling and establishing governments in the Northwest, they later served as models for organizing territories farther west. The Northwest Ordinance also established a significant precedent for banning slavery from certain territories.

The Northwest Territory seemed to offer enough land to guarantee property to American citizens for centuries. This fact satisfied republicans like Thomas Jefferson who feared that the rapidly growing white population would quickly exhaust available land east of the Appalachians and so create a large class of landless poor who could not vote.

However, the realization of these expansionist dreams was by no means inevitable. Most "available" territory from the Appalachians to the Mississippi River belonged to those peoples whom the Declaration of Independence had condemned as "merciless Indian savages." Divided into more than eighty tribes and numbering perhaps 150,000 people in 1789, Native Americans were struggling to preserve their own independence.

At postwar treaty negotiations, U.S. commissioners told Native Americans, "You are a subdued people. . . . We claim the country by conquest." Under threat of continued warfare, some Indian leaders initially yielded. Through treaties the Iroquois lost about half their land in New York and Pennsylvania, and the Delawares and Shawnees were obliged to recognize American sovereignty over their lands. But most Indians repudiated the treaties, denying that their negotiators had the authority to give up their nations' lands.

The Indians' resistance also stemmed from their confidence that the British would provide the arms necessary to defy the Americans. Britain had refused to abandon seven forts along the nation's northwestern frontier, ostensibly because Tories remained uncompensated for property losses. In April 1784 the British colonial office secretly ordered Canada's governor to hold onto the forts, hoping to reestablish Britain's claim to the Northwest Territory.

The Mohawk Joseph Brant initially sought to lead Indian resistance to white settlements. Courageous, skilled in

Fenimore Art Museum, Cooperstown, New York

Joseph Brant, by Gilbert Stuart, 1786
The youthful Mohawk leader was a staunch ally of the British during the Revolutionary War, and thereafter resisted U.S. expansion in the Northwest.

diplomacy, and well educated, he organized the northwestern Indians into a military alliance in 1786 to keep out white settlers. But Brant and his followers, who had relocated beyond American reach in Canada, could not win support from Native Americans on U.S. soil. Militia raids launched by Kentuckians and others gradually forced the Indian evacuation of southern Indiana and Ohio. In spring 1788, some fifty New Englanders sailed down the Ohio River in a bulletproof barge named the *Mayflower* to found the town of Marietta. A few months later a second group of latter-day pilgrims established a settlement on the Ohio at the site of modern Cincinnati.

The Confederation faced similar problems in the Southeast, where Spain and its Indian allies worked to block American encroachment on their land. The Spanish found an ally in the shrewd Creek leader **Alexander McGillivray,** who was determined to regain Creek territory held by Georgia. McGillivray negotiated a secret treaty with Spain that promised the Creeks weapons to protect themselves "from the Bears and other fierce Animals." In 1786, after Creeks expelled occupants of the disputed lands, Georgia quickly accepted McGillivray's offer of a cease-fire.

Spain also attempted to prevent American infiltration by denying western settlers permission to ship crops down the Mississippi River to New Orleans. In 1784, the Spanish closed New Orleans to American commerce. Spain and the United States negotiated the Jay-Gardoqui Treaty (1786), which opened Spanish markets to American merchants and renounced Spanish claims to disputed lands—at the cost, however, of postponing American exporters' access to New Orleans for another twenty years. Westerners and southerners charged that the treaty sacrificed their interests to benefit northern commerce, and Congress rejected it.

Unable to prevent American settlers from occupying territory it claimed in the Southeast, Spain sought to win the newcomers' allegiance through bribes and offers of citizenship. Some settlers began talking openly of secession. As young Andrew Jackson (the future president) concluded in 1789, making some arrangements with the Spanish seemed "the only immediate way to obtain peace with the Savage [Indians]."

Alexander McGillivray Creek leader determined to retain his people's territory

CHECKING IN

- Individual states, in drafting their state constitutions, served as workshops for the creation of new republican forms of government.

- Americans made their first national government under the Articles of Confederation deliberately weak, leaving most power to the states.

- National finances remained shaky, but prosperity returned quickly to the mid-Atlantic.

- The Ordinance of 1785 and Northwest Ordinance represented the new government's major accomplishments.

- Indian resistance and Spain's closing of the port of New Orleans hampered Americans' movement westward.

TOWARD A NEW CONSTITUTION, 1786–1788

What were the principal issues dividing proponents and opponents of the new federal Constitution?

Despite the United States' enormous strides in establishing itself as an independent nation, impatience with the national government's limitations continued to grow among those seeking to establish the republic on a more solid economic and military footing. Impatience became anxiety when protesting Massachusetts farmers defied local authorities and threatened to march on Boston. A national convention called to consider amendments to the Articles of Confederation instead created a radical new frame of government, the Constitution. In 1788, the states ratified the Constitution, setting a bold new course for America.

Shays's Rebellion, 1786–1787

The depression that had begun in 1784 persisted in New England, which had never recovered from the loss of its prime export market in the British West Indies. With farmers already squeezed financially, the state legislature, dominated by commercially minded elites, voted early in 1786 to pay off its Revolutionary War debt in three years. This ill-considered policy necessitated a huge tax hike. Meanwhile, the state's unfavorable balance of payments with Britain had produced a shortage of specie (gold and silver coin) because British creditors refused any other currency. Lowest in this cycle of debt were thousands of small family farmers.

The plight of small farmers was especially severe in western Massachusetts, where agriculture was least profitable. Facing demands that they pay their debts and taxes in hard currency, which few of them had, farmers held public meetings in which they denounced their own "tyrannical government." Farmers led by Daniel Shays in 1786 shut down the courts in five counties. Then in January 1787, they marched on a federal arsenal at Springfield, Massachusetts. But troops, funded by Boston elites to quell the uprising, reached the arsenal first and beat back the rebels. Thereafter, the troops scattered or routed bands of insurgents. Although the movement was defeated militarily, sympathizers of Shays won control of the Massachusetts legislature in elections later that year. They went on to cut taxes and secured a pardon for their leader.

Although **Shays's Rebellion** caused little bloodshed and never raised a serious threat of anarchy, critics of the Confederation painted it and similar, less radical movements elsewhere as a taste of the disorder to come under the weak national government. By threatening to seize weapons from a federal arsenal, the Shaysites unintentionally enabled nationalists to argue that the United States had become vulnerable to "mobocracy."

Instead of igniting an uprising from below, as Washington feared, Shays's Rebellion sparked elite nationalists into action from above. Shortly before the outbreak of the rebellion, delegates from five states had assembled at Annapolis, Maryland. They had intended to discuss means of promoting interstate commerce but instead called for a general convention to propose amendments to the Articles of Confederation. Accepting their suggestion, Congress asked the states to appoint delegations to meet in Philadelphia.

Shays's Rebellion Uprising by Massachusetts farmers that convinced many Americans their government was too weak

The Philadelphia Convention, 1787

In May 1787, fifty-five delegates, coming from every state but Rhode Island, began gathering at the Pennsylvania State House in Philadelphia, later known as Independence Hall. Among them were established figures like George Washington and Benjamin Franklin, as well as talented newcomers such as Alexander Hamilton and James Madison. Most were wealthy and in their thirties or forties, and nineteen owned slaves. More than half had legal training.

The convention immediately closed its sessions to the press and the public, kept no official journal, and even monitored the aged and talkative Franklin at dinner parties lest he disclose details of its discussions. Although these measures opened the convention to charges of being undemocratic, the delegates preferred secrecy to minimize public pressure on their debates.

Independence Hall, Philadelphia, 1776
While the Continental Congress deliberated inside on the grave issues of the day, city residents outside carried on with their everyday lives.

The delegates shared a "nationalist" perspective, instilled through their extended involvement with the national government. Thirty-nine had sat in Congress, where they had seen the Confederation's limitations firsthand. In the postwar years, they had become convinced that unless the national government was freed from the control of state legislatures, the country would disintegrate. Most were prepared to replace the Articles altogether with a new constitution that gave more power to the national government.

The first debate among the delegates concerned the conflicting interests of large and small states. James Madison's **Virginia Plan** boldly called for a national government rather than a confederation of states. It gave Congress virtually unrestricted powers to legislate, levy taxes, veto state laws, and authorize military force against the states. The Virginia Plan specified a bicameral legislature and made representation in both houses of Congress proportional to each state's population. The houses would jointly name the country's president and judges. But opposition to Madison's plan surfaced immediately, particularly to his call for proportional representation, which favored Virginia, the largest state. On June 15, William Paterson of New Jersey

Virginia Plan Madison's blueprint for a new national government; favored large states

offered a counterproposal, the **New Jersey Plan.** It featured a unicameral legislature in which each state had one vote, just as under the Articles.

New Jersey Plan Counter-proposal to Virginia Plan that favored small states

The two plans exposed the convention's great stumbling block: the question of representation. The Virginia Plan gave the four largest states—Virginia, Massachusetts, New York, and Pennsylvania—a majority in both houses. The New Jersey Plan allowed the seven smallest states, with only 25 percent of the U.S. population, to control Congress. By early July the convention was stalemated. To end the impasse, the delegates appointed a "grand committee" dedicated to compromise. This panel adopted a proposal by the Connecticut delegation: an equal vote for each state in the upper house and proportional representation in the lower house. The convention accepted the compromise on July 17 and in two months overcame the remaining hurdles.

As finally approved on September 17, 1787, the Constitution of the United States was an extraordinary document. In addition to reconciling the interests of large and small states, it balanced the delegates' desire for a strong national government against their fear of tyranny and interference with the states' sovereignty. It increased national authority in several ways. It vested in Congress the authority to levy and collect taxes, to regulate interstate commerce, and to conduct diplomacy. Under the Constitution, all acts and treaties of the United States would become "the supreme law of the land." State officials would have to uphold the Constitution, even against acts of their own state. The national government could use military force against any state.

The Constitution's Framers restrained the new national government in two key ways. First, they established a **separation of powers** among the three distinct branches within the government—the legislative, the executive, and the judicial. Second, they designed a system of checks and balances to prevent one branch from dominating the others. States' equal representation in the Senate offset proportional representation by population in the House, and each chamber could block measures passed by the other. Further, the president could veto acts of Congress, but to prevent capricious use of the presidential veto, a two-thirds majority in each house could override a veto. The president would conduct diplomacy, but only the Senate could ratify treaties. The president appointed his cabinet, but only with Senate approval. Congress could, by joint vote, remove the president and his appointees from office, but only for "high crimes," not for political disagreements.

separation of powers The establishment of three distinct branches of government

To further guarantee the independence of each branch, the Constitution provided that the members of one branch would not choose those of another, except judges, whose independence was protected by lifetime appointments. For example, the president was to be selected by electors, whom the states would select as their legislatures saw fit. The number of electors in each state would equal the number of its senators and representatives. State legislatures would also elect senators, whereas popular vote would determine delegates to the House of Representatives.

In addition to checks and balances, the Constitution embodied a form of federalism—a system of shared power and dual lawmaking by the state and national governments—to limit central authority. Not only did the state legislatures have a key role in electing the president and senators, but the Constitution could be amended by the votes of three-fourths of the state legislatures. Federalism assumed that the national government would limit its activities to foreign affairs, national defense, regulation of commerce, and coining of money. Most other political matters were left to the states. The states could otherwise act autonomously on purely internal matters, including slavery.

The dilemma confronting the Philadelphia convention centered not on whether slavery would be allowed but only on the much narrower question of whether slaves should be counted as persons when it came to determining a state's representation at the national level. For most legal purposes, slaves were regarded not as persons but rather as the chattel property of their owners. But southern states saw their large numbers of slaves as a means of augmenting their numbers in the House of Representatives and in the Electoral College. So strengthened, they hoped to prevent northerners from ever abolishing slavery.

"three-fifths clause" Provided that three-fifths of slaves were to be counted in determining congressional representation

Representing states that had begun ending slavery, northern delegates opposed giving southern states a political advantage. But after Georgia and South Carolina threatened to secede if their demands were not met, northerners agreed to the **"three-fifths clause,"** allowing three-fifths of all slaves to be counted for congressional representation and, thereby, in the Electoral College. The Constitution also reinforced slavery in other ways. It forbade citizens of any state, even those that had abolished slavery, to prevent the return of escaped slaves to another state. And it prohibited Congress from banning the importation of slaves until 1808. The Constitution limited slavery only in one respect—it maintained Congress's earlier ban on slavery in the Northwest Territory.

ratification Approval by state conventions of new federal Constitution

Although leaving much authority to the states, the Constitution established a national government clearly superior to the states in several spheres and abandoned the notion of a confederation of virtually independent states. Having thus strengthened national authority, the convention faced the issue of **ratification.** Two factors argued against submitting the Constitution to the state legislatures for ratification. First, the state legislatures would probably reject the Constitution, which shrank their power relative to that of the national government. Second, most of the Framers believed that the government had to rest on the consent of the American people themselves. The Constitution's opening words—"We the people of the United States"—embodied this view. In the end, the Philadelphia Convention provided for ratification by special state conventions composed of delegates elected by the people. Approval by nine such conventions would enable the new government to operate.

Under the Constitution, the Framers expected the nation's elites to continue exercising political leadership. Seeking to rein in the democratic currents set in motion by the Revolution, they curtailed what they considered the excessive power of popularly elected state legislatures. And while they located sovereignty in the people rather than in the states, they provided for an Electoral College that would actually elect the president. The Framers did provide for one crucial democratic element in the new government—the House of Representatives. Moreover, by making the Constitution amendable, and by dividing political power among competing branches of government, the Framers made it possible for the national government to be slowly democratized, in ways unforeseen in 1787.

The Struggle over Ratification, 1787–1788

At first the Constitution had little national support. Many Americans hesitated to accept the idea of a radically restructured government. To quiet fears of centralized national authority, the Constitution's supporters shrewdly dubbed themselves **Federalists,** a term implying that the Constitution successfully balanced the relationship between state and national governments.

The Constitution's opponents became known as Antifederalists. This negative-sounding title probably hurt them, for it did not convey the crux of their argument against the Constitution—that it was not "federalist" at all since it failed to balance the power of the national and state governments. By augmenting national authority, Antifederalists maintained, the Constitution would ultimately doom the states and the people's liberty.

Antifederalist arguments reflected the deep-seated Anglo-American suspicion of any concentration of power, a suspicion that had driven events from the Stamp Act Congress through the War of Independence and the early years of the new republic. Unquestionably, the Constitution gave the national government unprecedented authority in an age when most writers on politics agreed that the sole means of preventing despotism was restraining the power of government officials. Distant from the people, especially in an era when news traveled slowly, the national government would be far less responsive to the popular will than state governments would be. Furthermore, no one could be sure that the untried scheme of checks and balances would work. And the Constitution contained no guarantees that the new government would protect the liberties of individuals or the states. The absence of a bill of rights prompted Madison's nationalist ally and fellow Virginian George Mason, the author of the first state bill of rights in 1776, to oppose the Constitution.

The Antifederalists confronted several major disadvantages. While Antifederalist ranks included some prominent figures, none had the stature of George Washington or Benjamin Franklin. In addition, most newspapers were Federalist and did not hesitate to bias their reporting in favor of ratification. Finally, the Antifederalists, largely drawn from state and local leaders, lacked their opponents' contacts and experience at the national level. Ultimately, however, Federalist superiority in funds and political organizing proved decisive. The Antifederalists failed to create a sense of urgency among their supporters, assuming incorrectly that a large majority would rally to them. Only one-quarter of the voters turned out to elect delegates to the state ratifying conventions, and most had been mobilized by Federalists.

The Constitution became the law of the land when the ninth state, New Hampshire, ratified it on June 21, 1788. Federalist delegates prevailed in seven of the first nine state conventions by margins of at least two-thirds. Such lopsided votes reflected the Federalists' organizational skills rather than the degree of popular support for the Constitution. The Constitution's advocates rammed through approval in some states "before it can be digested or deliberately considered," in the words of a Pennsylvania Antifederalist.

However, unless the large states of Virginia and New York ratified, the new government would be unworkable. Antifederalism ran high in both states, especially among small farmers, who believed that the Constitution favored city dwellers and moneyed interests. Prominent Antifederalists included New York's Governor George Clinton and Virginia's Richard Henry Lee, George Mason, Patrick Henry, and future president James Monroe.

At Virginia's convention, Federalists won crucial support from the representatives of the western counties who wanted a strong national government capable

Federalists Name supporters of the new Constitution gave themselves during the ratification struggle

Map 6.4 Federalist and Antifederalist Strongholds, 1787–1790

Federalists drew their primary backing from densely populated areas, whereas Antifederalist support was strongest among small farmers in interior regions. However, some westerners advocated a strong central government that would push back Native Americans.

Interactive Map

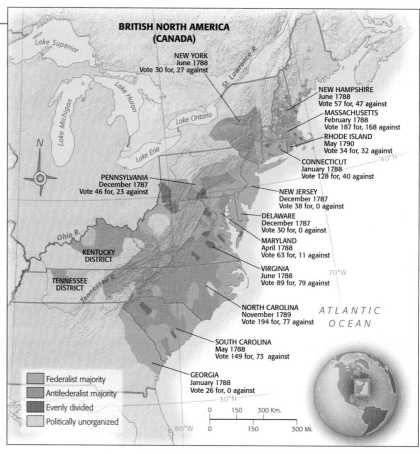

BRITISH NORTH AMERICA (CANADA)

NEW YORK
June 1788
Vote 30 for, 27 against

NEW HAMPSHIRE
June 1788
Vote 57 for, 47 against

MASSACHUSETTS
February 1788
Vote 187 for, 168 against

RHODE ISLAND
May 1790
Vote 34 for, 32 against

CONNECTICUT
January 1788
Vote 128 for, 40 against

PENNSYLVANIA
December 1787
Vote 46 for, 23 against

NEW JERSEY
December 1787
Vote 38 for, 0 against

DELAWARE
December 1787
Vote 30 for, 0 against

MARYLAND
April 1788
Vote 63 for, 11 against

KENTUCKY DISTRICT

TENNESSEE DISTRICT

VIRGINIA
June 1788
Vote 89 for, 79 against

NORTH CAROLINA
November 1789
Vote 194 for, 77 against

SOUTH CAROLINA
May 1788
Vote 149 for, 73 against

GEORGIA
January 1788
Vote 26 for, 0 against

ATLANTIC OCEAN

- Federalist majority
- Antifederalist majority
- Evenly divided
- Politically unorganized

0   150   300 Km.
0   150   300 Mi.

Copyright © Cengage Learning

CHECKING IN

- For many, Shays's Rebellion catalyzed fears that the national government was too weak.

- The delegates to the Philadelphia Convention struggled to balance the interests of the large and small states while creating a sufficiently strong national government.

- The Constitution created a new framework, federalism, allowing shared power between state and national governments, and embodied the separation of powers and checks and balances as ways to protect against tyranny.

- Ratification of the Constitution was won, but not automatically, with Antifederalists voicing loud opposition.

- The ratification struggle left an important legacy in *The Federalist* papers, which helped shape the American philosophy of government.

of ending Indian raids. Western Virginians' votes, combined with James Madison's leadership among tidewater planters, proved too much for Henry's spellbinding oratory. On June 25, the Virginia delegates ratified by a narrow 53 percent majority. The struggle was even hotter in New York. Antifederalists controlled the state convention and probably would have voted down the Constitution had not news arrived of New Hampshire's and Virginia's ratification. Federalist leaders Alexander Hamilton and John Jay spread rumors that if the convention failed to ratify, pro-Federalist New York City and adjacent counties would secede from the state and join the Union alone, leaving upstate New York a landlocked enclave. Alarmed, several Antifederalist delegates switched sides, and on July 26 New York ratified by a 30-to-27 vote.

In the end, the Antifederalists went down in defeat, and they did not survive as a political movement. Yet their influence was lasting. At their insistence, the Virginia, New York, and Massachusetts conventions approved the Constitution with the accompanying request that it be amended to include a bill of rights protecting Americans' basic freedoms.

Antifederalists' objections in New York also stimulated a response in the form of one of the great classics of political thought, **The Federalist,** a series of eighty-five newspaper essays penned by Alexander Hamilton, James Madison, and John Jay. Although *The Federalist* papers, as they are commonly termed, did little to influence the New York vote, they provided a glimpse of the Framers' intentions in designing the Constitution and thus powerfully shaped the American philosophy of government. The Constitution, insisted *The Federalist's* authors, had two main purposes: to defend minority rights against majority tyranny and to prevent a stubborn minority from blocking measures necessary for the national interest. In the most profound essay in the series, Federalist No. 10, Madison argued that the nation's size and diversity would neutralize the attempts of factions to steer unwise laws through Congress.

Madison's analysis was far too optimistic, however. The Constitution afforded enormous scope for special interests to influence government. The great challenge for Madison's generation would be maintaining a government that provided equal benefits to all, but special privileges to none.

> **The Federalist** Series of essays, known commonly as the Federalist Papers, designed to explain the new Constitution and convince people to support it

Chapter Summary

What factors enabled the Americans to defeat the British in the American Revolution? (page 120)

Although the British enjoyed huge advantages in military preparedness and manpower at the war's start, their supply lines were long and their population was tax-weary. The colonists eventually forged a professional army and defeated them. The most important key to American victory was George Washington's leadership, especially his determination to continue to fight.

How did the war unfold? (page 123)

Initially, the Continental Army suffered several defeats. Saratoga was the turning point of the war, because the colonial victory there convinced the French to support the Revolution with money, men, and ships. Once other nations joined the anti-British cause, making the Revolution an international war, the tide turned. Now fatally overextended, Britain was defeated by American-French forces at Yorktown and obliged to surrender.

How did the war affect relationships among Americans of different classes, races, and genders? (page 129)

Most wars bring major social changes; the Revolution was no exception. By war's end, white males enjoyed considerably more equality, slavery was clearly being rejected in the northern states, and women had played a significant public role. However, the war only worsened the position of Native Americans.

KEY TERMS

loyalist *(p. 120)*
Joseph Brant *(p. 121)*
Battle of Trenton *(p. 123)*
Battle of Saratoga *(p. 124)*
Lord Charles Cornwallis *(p. 127)*
Abigail Adams *(p. 131)*
antislavery movement *(p. 132)*
republicanism *(p. 134)*
Articles of Confederation *(p. 135)*
Newburgh Conspiracy *(p. 136)*
Northwest Ordinance *(p. 136)*
Alexander McGillivray *(p. 138)*
Shays's Rebellion *(p. 139)*
Virginia Plan *(p. 140)*
New Jersey Plan *(p. 141)*
separation of powers *(p. 141)*
"three-fifths clause" *(p. 142)*
ratification *(p. 142)*
Federalists *(p. 143)*
The Federalist (p. 145)

What political concerns were reflected in the first state constitutions and Articles of Confederation? (page 133)

In creating their constitutions, the new states served as workshops for experimenting with various forms of republican government. At the national level the Articles of Confederation created a weak government that almost immediately faced tremendous economic and diplomatic problems. Over time, elites favoring stronger executive power gained support for a plan to replace the Articles of Confederation with the new federal Constitution. A failed experiment in general, the Articles succeeded in formulating the Northwest Ordinance, a blueprint for future expansion.

What were the principal issues dividing proponents and opponents of the new federal Constitution? (page 138)

The new Constitution represented the triumph of nationalism and provided a strong central government, although its framework of federalism seemed to leave considerable power in the hands of the states. Its ratification was far from assured, but it enjoyed the support of respected men such as Franklin, Jefferson, and Washington; in the end, the Federalists achieved ratification. An important legacy of the struggle for ratification was *The Federalist* papers, which laid a foundation for an American philosophy of government.

 CourseMate

Go to the CourseMate website at **www.cengagebrain.com** for additional study tools and review materials—including audio and video clips—for this chapter.

CHAPTER 7

Launching the New Republic

1788–1800

Constitutional Government Takes Shape, 1788–1796
What role did George Washington play in translating the Constitution from words into government?

Hamilton's Domestic Policies, 1789–1794
Which points in Hamilton's economic program were most controversial and why?

The United States in a Wider World, 1789–1796
How did the new nation deal with France, Spain, and Britain?

Parties and Politics, 1793–1800
What principal issues divided Federalists and Republicans in the election of 1800?

Economic and Social Change
On what basis were some Americans denied full equality by 1800?

Judith Sargent Stevens (Murray) by John Singleton Copley, circa 1770

Terra Foundation for American Art, Chicago / Art Resource, NY

For most Americans, the 1790s was a decade marked by political and economic transformation. But Nancy Ward, a Cherokee Indian, had less reason to be optimistic. Born in about 1738, she became a "War Woman" in 1755 when, after attacking Creeks killed her husband, she picked up his gun and helped drive them off. As a War Woman, Ward not only participated in combat but conducted diplomacy and occasionally released war captives.

When the American Revolution broke out, the Cherokees were hopelessly divided. Ward and other leaders urged the Cherokees to avoid war and negotiate. Ward helped persuade the Americans not to take additional Cherokee land. But after the war ended,

147

U.S. treaty commissioners pressured the Cherokees in 1783 and 1785 to cede another eight thousand square miles. However, Ward continued to urge Cherokee resisters to make peace—not because she embraced the new republic, but because she recognized that resistance to its military power was futile.

Since the 1750s, the Cherokees had lost nearly half of their population and more than half of their land. During the same period, the former colonies had grown from just under 2 million people to over 5 million, 90 percent of whom lived and worked on the land. These farmers equated the ownership of land with liberty and political rights, and considered Native Americans like Ward an obstacle.

Besides holding common attitudes toward Native Americans, whites in 1789 successfully launched a new constitutional republic. But over the next decade, they became increasingly divided over the political and diplomatic course the United States should take. By 1798, voters had formed two parties, each viewing the other as a threat to liberty. Only when the election of 1800 had been settled—by the narrowest of margins—did it seem certain that the United States would endure.

CONSTITUTIONAL GOVERNMENT TAKES SHAPE, 1788–1796

What role did George Washington play in translating the Constitution from words into government?

Given the social and political divisions among Americans, compounded by their fears of centralized authority, success at implementing the new Constitution was anything but guaranteed. Would Americans accept the results of a national election? Would the three branches of the new government function effectively? Would a Bill of Rights, which several states had made a condition of ratification, amend the Constitution?

Implementing Government

The first order of business in putting the new government into practice was the election of a president and Congress. These first elections, in the fall of 1788, swept the Federalists into power with eighteen of twenty seats in the Senate and fifty-four of fifty-nine in the House. The Electoral College unanimously chose George Washington as the first president and John Adams as the vice president.

The choice of Washington was hardly a surprise. His leadership during the Revolutionary War and the Constitutional Convention had earned him a reputation as a national hero. Given his reputation, Washington was able to calm Americans' fears of presidential power.

Traveling slowly over the new nation's miserable roads, the men entrusted with launching the federal experiment assembled in New York, the new national capital, in March 1789. Washington did not arrive until April 23 and took his oath of office a week later.

The Constitution was vague about the executive departments, mentioning only in passing that the president must obtain the Senate's "advice and consent" to his nominees to head these bureaus. Otherwise, Congress was free to determine the organization and accountability of what became known as the cabinet, consisting of the secretaries of state, treasury, and war, as well as the attorney general and postmaster general. The Senate narrowly defeated a proposal to forbid the president from dismissing cabinet officers without its approval. This outcome strengthened the president's authority to make and carry out policy independently of congressional oversight, beyond what the Constitution required.

The Federal Judiciary and the Bill of Rights

The Constitution authorized Congress to establish federal courts below the level of the Supreme Court but provided no plan for their structure. In 1789 many citizens feared that federal courts would ride roughshod over local customs. In passing the **Judiciary Act** of 1789, Congress quieted popular apprehensions by establishing in each state a federal district court that operated according to local procedures. As the Constitution stipulated, the Supreme Court exercised final jurisdiction. Congress's compromise respected state traditions while offering wide access to federal justice.

Judiciary Act Established federal court system in 1789

The Constitution offered some protection of citizens' individual rights. It barred Congress from passing *ex post facto* laws (criminalizing previously legal actions) and bills of attainder (punishment without a trial). Nevertheless, the absence of a comprehensive bill of rights had prompted several delegates at Philadelphia to refuse to

Chronology

1788	First elections under the Constitution
1789	First Congress convenes in New York; George Washington sworn in as first president; Judiciary Act; French Revolution begins
1790	Alexander Hamilton submits his Reports on Public Credit and National Bank to Congress; Treaty of New York
1791	Bank of the United States granted a twenty-year charter; Bill of Rights ratified; slave uprising begins in French colony of Saint-Domingue
1792	Washington reelected president
1793	Fugitive Slave Law; France at war with Britain and Spain; Citizen Genêt arrives in the United States; first Democratic societies established
1794	Whiskey Rebellion; Battle of Fallen Timbers
1795	Treaty of Greenville; Jay's Treaty
1796	Treaty of San Lorenzo; Washington's Farewell Address; John Adams elected president
1798	XYZ Affair; Alien and Sedition Acts; Eleventh Amendment to the Constitution ratified
1798–1799	Virginia and Kentucky Resolutions
1798–1800	Quasi-War between United States and France
1800	Gabriel's rebellion in Virginia; Thomas Jefferson elected president

CHECKING IN

- Americans remained suspicious of executive power, and thus of the presidency.
- George Washington was unanimously chosen president by the first Electoral College.
- Although the Constitution did not spell out the organization of the executive branch, Washington named five department heads who formed his first cabinet.
- The Judiciary Act of 1789 helped allay state fears concerning federal courts.
- The Bill of Rights guaranteed personal liberties.

Bill of Rights First ten amendments to the Constitution; guaranteed personal liberties

Alexander Hamilton Washington's chief adviser; architect of major plans for American future

Reports on the Public Credit Hamilton's plan to ensure support for the new government by maintaining permanent debt

sign the Constitution. From the House of Representatives, James Madison led the drafting of the ten amendments that became known as the **Bill of Rights.**

The First Amendment safeguarded the most fundamental freedoms of expression—religion, speech, press, and political activity. The Second Amendment ensured that "a well-regulated militia" would preserve the nation's security by guaranteeing "the right of the people to bear arms." Like the Third Amendment, it sought to protect citizens from what Americans saw as the most sinister embodiment of tyranny: standing armies. The Fourth through Eighth Amendments limited the police powers of the states by guaranteeing individuals fair treatment in legal and judicial proceedings. The Ninth and Tenth Amendments reserved to the people or to the states powers not allocated to the federal government. In general, the Bill of Rights imposed no serious check on the Framers' nationalist objectives. The ten amendments were submitted to the states and ratified by December 1791.

HAMILTON'S DOMESTIC POLICIES, 1789–1794

Which points in Hamilton's economic program were most controversial and why?

Washington's reluctance to become involved with legislation enabled Secretary of the Treasury **Alexander Hamilton** to set domestic priorities. Hamilton emerged as an imaginative and dynamic statesman by formulating a sweeping program to strengthen the federal government and promote national economic development. While Hamilton succeeded in pushing his proposals through Congress, the controversies surrounding them undermined popular support for Federalist policies.

Establishing the Nation's Credit

In Hamilton's mind, the most immediate danger facing the United States concerned the possibility of war with Britain, Spain, or both. The republic could finance a major war only by borrowing heavily, but because Congress under the Confederation had not assumed responsibility for the Revolutionary War debt, the nation's credit was weakened abroad and at home.

Responding to a request from Congress, Hamilton in January 1790 issued the first of two **Reports on the Public Credit.** It outlined a plan to strengthen the country's credit, enable it to defer paying its debt, and entice wealthy investors to place their capital at its service. The report listed $54 million in U.S. debt, $42 million of which was owed to Americans, and the rest to Europeans.

Hamilton recommended first that the federal government "fund" the $54 million national debt by selling an equal sum in new government bonds. Purchasers of these securities would choose from several combinations of federal "stock" and western lands. Those who wished could retain their original bonds and earn 4 percent interest. His report also proposed that the federal government pay off the $25 million in state debts remaining from the Revolution in the same manner.

George Washington's Inaugural Journey Through Trenton, 1789
Washington received a warm welcome in Trenton, site of his first victory during the Revolutionary War.

Hamilton exhorted the government to use the money earned by selling federal lands in the West to pay off the $12 million owed to Europeans as quickly as possible. In his Second Report on the Public Credit, submitted to Congress in December 1790, he argued that the Treasury could accumulate the interest owed on the remaining $42 million by collecting customs duties on imports and an excise tax (a tax on products made, sold, or transported within a nation's borders) on whiskey. In addition, Hamilton urged that the government not attempt to repay the $42 million principal but instead keep paying interest to bondholders. Under Hamilton's plan, the government could uphold the national credit at minimal expense, without ever paying off the debt itself.

Hamilton advocated a perpetual debt as a lasting means of uniting the economic fortunes of the nation's creditors to the United States. In an age when financial investments were notoriously risky, the federal government would protect the savings of wealthy bondholders while offering an interest rate competitive with the Bank of England's. Few other investments would entail so little risk.

Hamilton's recommendations provoked immediate controversy. Although no one in Congress doubted that they would enhance the country's fiscal reputation, many objected that those least deserving of reward would gain the most. The original owners of more than three-fifths of the debt certificates issued by the Continental

Congress were Revolutionary War patriots of modest means who had long before sold their certificates for a fraction of their promised value, usually out of dire financial need. Foreseeing that the government would fund the debt, wealthy speculators had bought the certificates and now stood to reap huge gains at the expense of the original owners.

To Hamilton's surprise, Madison—his longtime ally—emerged as a leading opponent of funding. Facing opposition to the plan in his home state of Virginia, Madison tried but failed to obtain compensation for original owners who had sold their certificates. Opposition to Hamilton's proposal that the federal government assume states' war debts also ran high. Only Massachusetts, Connecticut, and South Carolina had failed to make effective provisions for satisfying their creditors. The issue stirred the fiercest indignation in the South, which except for South Carolina had already paid off 83 percent of its debt. Madison and others maintained that to allow residents of the laggard states to escape heavy taxes was to reward irresponsibility.

Southern hostility almost defeated assumption. In the end, however, Hamilton saved his proposal by enlisting Secretary of State Thomas Jefferson's help. Jefferson and other Virginians favored moving the capital to the Potomac River, hoping to preserve Virginia's position as the largest, most influential state. In return for the northern votes necessary to transfer the capital, Hamilton secured enough Virginians' support to win the battle for assumption. Despite this concession, the debate over state debts confirmed many southerners' suspicions that northern commercial interests would benefit from Hamilton's policies at southerners' expense.

Congressional enactment in 1790 of Hamilton's recommendations dramatically reversed the nation's fiscal standing. European investors grew so enthusiastic about U.S. bonds that by 1792 some securities were selling at 10 percent above face value.

Creating a National Bank

Having significantly expanded the stock of capital available for investment, Hamilton intended to direct that money toward projects that would diversify the national economy through a federally chartered bank. Accordingly, in December 1790 he presented Congress with the **Report on a National Bank.**

Report on a National Bank
Hamilton's proposal to create the Bank of the United States

The proposed Bank of the United States would raise $10 million through a public stock offering. Private investors could purchase shares by paying for three-quarters of their value in government bonds. In this way the bank would capture a substantial portion of the recently funded debt and make it available for loans; it would also receive steady interest payments from the treasury. Shareholders would profit handsomely.

Hamilton argued that the bank would cost taxpayers nothing and greatly benefit the nation. It would provide a safe place for federal deposits, make inexpensive loans to the government when taxes fell short, and relieve the scarcity of hard cash by issuing paper notes. Further, the bank would regulate the business of state banks and, above all, provide much-needed credit for economic expansion.

Hamilton's critics denounced the national bank as a dangerous scheme that gave a small elite special power to influence the government. These critics believed that the Bank of England had undermined the integrity of the government in Britain. Shareholders of the Bank of the United States could just as easily become tools of unscrupulous politicians. Members of Congress who owned bank stock would likely vote in support of the bank even at the cost of the national good.

Madison led the opposition to the bank in Congress, arguing that it was unconstitutional. Unless Congress closely followed the Constitution, he argued, the central government might oppress the states and trample on individual liberties, just as Parliament had done to the colonies. Strictly limiting federal power seemed the surest way of preventing the United States from degenerating into a corrupt despotism.

Congress approved the bank by only a thin margin. Dubious about its constitutionality, Washington asked Jefferson and Hamilton for advice. Like many southern planters whose investments in slaves left them short of capital and often in debt, Jefferson distrusted banking and did not want to extend government power beyond the letter of the Constitution. But Hamilton urged Washington to sign the bill. Because Article I, Section 8, of the Constitution specified that Congress could enact all measures "necessary and proper," Hamilton contended that the only unconstitutional activities were those *forbidden* to the national government. Washington accepted Hamilton's argument, and in February 1791 the Bank of the United States obtained a twenty-year charter. Washington's acceptance of a "loose interpretation" of the Constitution marked an important victory for advocates of an active, assertive national government. But the split between Jefferson and Hamilton, and Washington's siding with the latter, signaled a deepening political divide within the administration.

Emerging Partisanship

Hamilton built a political base by appealing to people's economic self-interest. His "rescue" of the national credit provided huge gains for speculators, merchants, and other urban "moneyed men" who by 1790 held most of the revolutionary debt. As holders of bank stock, these same groups had reason to use their prestige on behalf of national authority. Moreover, federal assumption of state debts liberated taxpayers from crushing burdens in New England, New Jersey, and South Carolina, while Hamilton's promotion of industry, commerce, and shipping won favor with the Northeast's budding entrepreneurs and hard-pressed artisans.

Opposition to Hamilton's program was strongest in sections of the country where it offered few benefits. Hamilton's plan offered little to the West and was especially detested in the South. Southern states had generally paid off their revolutionary debts, and few southerners still held revolutionary certificates. Moreover, the Bank of the United States had few southern stockholders. Resentment against eastern "moneyed men" and Yankees who refused to pay their debts united westerners, southerners, and some mid-Atlantic citizens into a political coalition. Challenging the Federalists, these opponents called for a return to true Republicanism.

With Hamilton presenting his measures as "Federalist," Jefferson, Madison, and their supporters began calling themselves "Republicans." They reached out to former Antifederalists whose ranks had been fatally weakened after the election of 1788. In 1791 they supported the establishment of an opposition newspaper, *The National Gazette.* The paper's editor, Philip Freneau, attacked Hamilton relentlessly, accusing him of trying to create an aristocracy and a monarchy in America.

Whiskey Rebellion, 1794
Rebels in Washington County, Pennsylvania, tar and feather a federal tax collector.

In response Hamilton, using pseudonyms, attacked Jefferson as an enemy of President Washington.

Although partisanship intensified as the election of 1792 approached, there was no organized political campaigning. Most voters saw organized factions, or parties, as inherently corrupt. The Constitution's Framers had neither wanted nor planned for political parties. In addition, Washington, by appearing to be above partisan disputes, remained supremely popular. Washington was unanimously chosen for a second term; by a fairly close margin, John Adams was again chosen vice president.

The Whiskey Rebellion

Whiskey Rebellion Tax protest by western farmers that gave Washington and Hamilton the opportunity to assert the power of national government

Hamilton's program not only sparked an angry congressional debate but also helped to ignite a civil insurrection in 1794 called the **Whiskey Rebellion.** Severely testing federal authority, this uprising posed the young republic's first serious crisis.

To augment national revenue, Hamilton had proposed an excise tax on domestically produced whiskey. He maintained that such a tax would not only distribute the expense of financing the national debt evenly but also improve morals by inducing Americans to drink less liquor. Although Congress passed Hamilton's program in March 1791, many doubted that Americans, who drank an average of six gallons of hard liquor per adult per year, would submit tamely to sobriety. James Jackson of Georgia, for example, warned the administration that his constituents "have long been in the habit of getting drunk and that they will get drunk in defiance of . . . all the excise duties which Congress might be weak or wicked enough to pass."

The validity of such doubts became apparent in September 1791 when a crowd tarred and feathered an excise tax agent near Pittsburgh. Western Pennsylvanians found the new tax especially burdensome. Unable to export crops through New Orleans, most local farmers distilled their rye or corn into alcohol, which could be carried across the Appalachians at a fraction of the price charged for bulkier grain.

Hamilton's excise tax equaled 25 percent of whiskey's retail value, enough to wipe out a farmer's profit.

The law also stipulated that trials for evading the tax would be conducted in federal courts. Any western Pennsylvanian indicted for noncompliance would have to travel three hundred miles to Philadelphia. Besides facing a jury of unsympathetic easterners, the accused would have to bear the cost of the long journey and lost earnings while at court, in addition to fines and other penalties if found guilty.

In a scene reminiscent of colonial protests against Britain, large-scale resistance erupted in July 1794. Roving bands torched buildings, assaulted tax collectors, and raised a flag symbolizing an independent country that they hoped to create from six western counties.

Echoing elites' denunciation of colonial protests, Hamilton blasted the rebellion as simple lawlessness. Washington concluded that a federal failure to respond strongly would encourage outbreaks in other frontier areas. The president accordingly mustered 12,900 militiamen to march west under his command, but opposition evaporated once the troops reached the Appalachians. The president left Hamilton in charge of making arrests. Of about 150 suspects seized, Hamilton sent twenty in irons to Philadelphia. Two men received death sentences, but Washington eventually pardoned them both.

The Whiskey Rebellion was a milestone in determining the limits of public opposition to federal policies. In the early 1790s, many Americans assumed that it was still legitimate to protest unpopular laws by using the methods that they had employed against British policies. By firmly suppressing the first major challenge to national authority, Washington served notice that citizens who resorted to violent means of political action would feel the full force of federal authority. In this way, he gave substance to elites' fears of "mobocracy," now resurfacing in reaction to the French Revolution.

CHECKING IN

- Alexander Hamilton proposed that the federal government assume and make permanent national and state debt from the revolutionary period.
- Hamilton proposed and achieved a national bank over the objections of Jefferson and Madison.
- Hamilton's opponents charged that his policies benefited eastern bankers and commercial interests at the expense of southern and western farmers.
- The Whiskey Rebellion gave Washington and Hamilton an opportunity to reinforce national authority.

THE UNITED STATES IN A WIDER WORLD, 1789–1796

How did the new nation deal with France, Spain, and Britain?

By 1793 disagreements over foreign affairs had become the primary source of friction in American public life. The division created by controversy over Hamilton's economic program hardened into ideologically oriented factions that disagreed vehemently over whether American foreign policy should favor industrial and mercantile interests or those of farmers, planters, and small businessmen. Complicating American policy making was the French Revolution, which had electrified all of Europe in 1789 and touched off a series of wars between France and its neighbors that would last until 1815.

As part of the Atlantic world, the United States could not avoid entanglement in these wars, despite the desire of most Americans to remain uninvolved. Thus, differences over foreign policy fused with differences over domestic affairs, further intensifying partisanship in American politics.

Spanish Power in Western North America

Spain enjoyed a brief resurgence of imperial success in the late eighteenth century. Stimulated by its acquisition of Louisiana, the Spanish built new presidios in northern Mexico, New Mexico, and Texas at which they stationed more troops and coordinated the actions of civilian and military authorities. By 1800 the Apaches, Navajos, and Comanches had agreed to cease their raids in New Mexico and Texas, but the success of the truce depended on Spain's ability to strengthen and broaden its imperial position in North America.

Spain's efforts in New Mexico and Texas were part of its larger effort to counter rivals for North American territory and influence. Russian fur traders had made substantial inroads along the Northwest Coast as early as the 1740s, and British and American traders followed in the 1780s. All three nations used American furs in the rapidly burgeoning and hugely profitable China trade, and their mounting influence threatened Spain's northwestern frontier.

"Alta California" Spanish colony on the Pacific coast, donated by missions

To counter these threats, Spain flung colonists and missionaries northward along the Pacific coast. However, efforts to encourage large-scale Mexican immigration to **"Alta California"** failed. The colony became a chain of religious missions, several presidios, and a few large ranches. Franciscan missionaries tried to convert coastal Indians to Catholicism and "civilize" them by imposing harsh discipline and putting them to work in vineyards and other enterprises. However, epidemic and venereal diseases carried by the Spanish raged among the native coastal tribes; between 1769 and 1830 the Indian population plummeted from about 72,000 to about 18,000.

Between New Mexico and California, Spain attempted to make alliances with Indians in the area later known as Arizona. In this way, Spain hoped to dominate North America between the Pacific and the Mississippi River. But resistance from the Hopi (HOE-pee), Yuma (YOU-muh), and other Native Americans thwarted these hopes.

Challenging American Expansion, 1789–1792

East of the Mississippi River, on the trans-Appalachian frontier, rivalries also multiplied. Spain, Britain, the United States, and Native Americans jockeyed for advantage in an area that all considered central to their interests.

Realizing that the United States was in no position to dictate developments immediately in the West, President Washington pursued a course of patient diplomacy that was intended "to preserve the country in peace if I can, and to be prepared for war if I cannot." The prospect of peace improved in 1789 when Spain unexpectedly opened New Orleans to American commerce. As a result, secessionist sentiment subsided.

In the 1790s the Spanish bribed many well-known political figures in Tennessee and Kentucky, including James Wilkinson, one of Washington's former generals. The admission of Vermont (1791), Kentucky (1792), and Tennessee (1796) as states was meant in part to strengthen their flickering loyalty to the Union.

Washington then moved to weaken Spanish influence in the West by neutralizing Spain's most important ally, the Creek Indians. The Creeks numbered more than twenty thousand, including perhaps five thousand warriors, and were fiercely hostile toward Georgian settlers, whom they called "the greedy people who want our lands." Under the terms of the 1790 Treaty of New York, American settlers could occupy the Georgia piedmont but not other Creek territory. Washington insisted that Georgia restore to the Chickasaws and Choctaws, Creek allies, a vast area along the Mississippi River that Georgia had already begun selling off to land speculators.

Washington adopted a harsher policy toward Native Americans who resisted efforts by American citizens to occupy the Ohio Valley. But two military campaigns, in 1790 and 1791, failed to force peace and cost the United States eleven hundred men. Matters worsened in 1792 when Spain persuaded the Creeks to renounce the Treaty of New York and resume hostilities. The damage done to U.S. prestige by these setbacks convinced many Americans that the combined strength of Britain, Spain, and the Native Americans could be counterbalanced only by an alliance with France.

France and Factional Politics, 1793

One of the most momentous events in history, the French Revolution, began in 1789. Many Americans watched sympathetically as the French abolished nobles' privileges, wrote a constitution, and repelled invading armies. In 1793, after becoming a republic, France proclaimed a war of all peoples against all kings and unleashed a "Reign of Terror," executing not only the king but also dissenting revolutionaries.

Americans were bitterly divided in their views of the French Revolution and how the United States should respond to it. Republicans such as Jefferson supported it as an assault on monarchy and tyranny. In contrast, Federalists like Hamilton denounced France as a "mobocracy" and supported Great Britain in resisting efforts to sow revolution abroad.

White southern slave owners were among France's fiercest supporters. In 1791 slaves in the French colony of Saint-Domingue (san doh-MIN-geh) rebelled against slavery and against French rule, a bloody uprising that took a heavy death toll among French planters and sent thousands fleeing to the United States. Fearful southern whites believed that the British had intentionally sparked the bloodshed and would do the same in the American South.

Many northerners, on the other hand, were more repelled by the bloodshed in revolutionary France. The revolution was "an open hell," thundered Massachusetts's Fisher Ames, "still smoking with sufferings and crimes." New England Protestants detested the French for worshiping Reason instead of God. Less religious Federalists condemned French leaders as evil radicals who incited the poor against the rich. Northern and southern reactions to the French Revolution also diverged for economic reasons. Merchants, shippers, and ordinary sailors in New England, Philadelphia, and New York feared that an alliance with France would provoke British retaliation against American commerce. They argued that the United States could win valuable concessions by demonstrating friendly intentions toward Britain.

Southerners had no such reasons to favor Britain. They perceived American reliance on British commerce as a menace to national self-determination, and they wished to divert most U.S. trade to France. Jefferson and Madison advocated reducing British imports through the imposition of steep duties. These recommendations threatened ties with Britain, which sold more manufactured goods to the

United States than to any other country. If Congress adopted trade retaliation, Hamilton predicted, "an open war between the United States and Great Britain" would result.

Pro-French feelings were also high in the western states, especially after France went to war against Spain and Great Britain in 1793. Westerners hoped that a French victory would remove Spanish and British roadblocks to expansion, put an end to Indian wars, and open the Mississippi for navigation.

After declaring war with Spain and Britain in 1793, France sought to embroil the United States in the conflict. France dispatched Edmond Genêt (zhe-NAY) as minister to the United States with orders to mobilize Republican sentiment in support of France and to enlist American mercenaries to conquer Spanish territories and attack British shipping. Much to France's disgust, President Washington issued a proclamation of neutrality on April 22, 1793.

Meanwhile, defying Washington's proclamation, **Citizen Genêt** (as he was known in French revolutionary style) recruited volunteers for his American Foreign Legion. Making generals of George Rogers Clark of Kentucky and Elisha Clarke, Genêt ordered them to seize Spanish garrisons at New Orleans and St. Augustine. Genêt also contracted with American privateers. By the summer of 1793, almost a thousand Americans were at sea in a dozen ships flying the French flag. These privateers seized more than eighty British vessels. Refusing Secretary of State Jefferson's patient requests that he desist, Genêt threatened to urge Americans to defy their own government.

> **Citizen Genêt** French minister to the United States who ignored U.S. neutrality and recruited Americans to fight the British and Spanish

Diplomacy and War, 1793–1796

Although Washington swiftly closed the nation's harbors to Genêt's buccaneers, the episode provoked an Anglo-American crisis. Britain decided that only a massive show of force would deter American aggression. Thus, on November 6, 1793, Britain's Privy Council issued orders confiscating foreign ships trading with the French islands in the Caribbean. The orders were kept secret until most U.S. ships carrying winter provisions to the Caribbean left port so that their captains would not know that they were sailing into a war zone. The Royal Navy ultimately seized more than 250 U.S. ships.

Meanwhile, the U.S. merchant marine suffered another galling indignity—the drafting of its crewmen into the Royal Navy. Thousands of British sailors had fled to American ships looking for an easier life than the tough, poorly paying British system. In late 1793 British naval officers began inspecting American crews for British subjects, whom they then impressed (forcibly enlisted) as the king's sailors. Overzealous commanders sometimes exceeded orders by taking U.S. citizens—and in any case Britain did not recognize its former subjects' right to adopt American citizenship. Impressment struck a raw nerve in most Americans.

The British, along with the Spanish and Native Americans, also challenged the United States for control of the West. In February 1794, Canada's governor denied U.S. claims north of the Ohio River and urged Indians to destroy every white settlement in the Northwest. Britain soon erected an eighth garrison on U.S. soil, Fort Miami, near present-day Toledo, Ohio. That same year, Spain encroached on U.S. territory by building Fort San Fernando at what is now Memphis, Tennessee.

Hoping to halt the drift toward war, Washington launched a desperate diplomatic initiative, sending Chief Justice John Jay to Great Britain and Thomas

Pinckney to Spain. The president also authorized General Anthony Wayne to negotiate a treaty with the Indians of the Ohio Valley.

The Indians scoffed at Washington's peace offer until "Mad Anthony" Wayne led three thousand regulars and militiamen deep into their homeland, ravaging every village in reach. On August 20, 1794, Wayne's troops routed four hundred Shawnees at the Battle of Fallen Timbers, two miles from Britain's Fort Miami. In August 1795 Wayne compelled twelve Ohio Valley tribes to sign the Treaty of Greenville, which opened most of modern-day Ohio and a portion of Indiana to white settlement and temporarily ended Indian hostilities.

Wayne's success allowed John Jay a major diplomatic victory in London: a British promise to withdraw troops from American soil. Jay also gained American access to West Indian markets, but only by bargaining away U.S. rights to load cargoes of sugar, molasses, and coffee from the Caribbean.

Aside from fellow Federalists, few Americans would interpret **Jay's Treaty** as preserving peace with honor. Jay's Treaty left Britain free to violate American neutrality and to restrict U.S. trade with France. Moreover, Jay did not succeed in ending impressment and failed to gain compensation for slaves taken by the British during the Revolution. After the Senate barely ratified the treaty in 1795, Jay nervously joked that he could find his way across the country at night by the fires of rallies burning him in effigy.

Despite its unpopularity, Jay's Treaty prevented war with Britain and finally ended British occupation of U.S. territory. The treaty also helped stimulate an expansion of American trade. Upon its ratification, Britain permitted Americans to trade with its West Indian colonies and with India. American exports to the British Empire shot up 300 percent.

On the heels of Jay's Treaty came an unqualified diplomatic triumph engineered by Thomas Pinckney. Ratified in 1796, the 1795 **Treaty of San Lorenzo** (also called Pinckney's Treaty) with Spain gave westerners unrestricted, duty-free access to world markets via the Mississippi River. Spain also promised to recognize the thirty-first parallel as the United States' southern boundary, to dismantle all fortifications on American soil, and to discourage Indian attacks against western settlers.

By 1796 the Washington administration had defended the nation's territorial integrity, restored peace to the frontier, opened the Mississippi for western exports, reopened British markets to U.S. shipping, and kept the nation out of a European war. However, as the outcry over Jay's Treaty showed, foreign policy had left Americans far more divided in 1796 than in 1789.

Jay's Treaty Agreement that opened some British markets to Americans but otherwise accomplished little

Treaty of San Lorenzo Agreement that gave Americans access to the Mississippi and to the Gulf of Mexico via New Orleans

CHECKING IN

- Spanish power enjoyed a brief resurgence in the 1790s, and Spain strengthened its position in the West and the Southeast.
- Washington countered Spanish expansion by neutralizing its Indian allies and making peace with other tribes.
- The French Revolution produced a deep split in American opinion.
- Citizen Genêt tried to embroil the United States in war against the British.
- Jay's Treaty stimulated American trade with the British Empire, and Pinckney's Treaty resolved many tensions with Spain.

PARTIES AND POLITICS, 1793–1800

What principal issues divided Federalists and Republicans in the election of 1800?

By the time of Washington's reelection, controversies over domestic and foreign policy had led to the formation of two distinct political factions. During the president's second term, these factions became formal political parties, Federalists and Republicans, which waged a bitter battle culminating in the election of 1800.

Ideological Confrontation, 1793–1794

Conflicting attitudes about events in France, federal power, and democracy accelerated the polarization of American politics. Linking the French Revolution and the Whiskey Rebellion, Federalists trembled at the thought of guillotines and "mob rule." Citizen Genêt had openly encouraged opposition to the Washington administration, and had found hundreds of Americans willing to fight for France. Federalists worried that all of this was just the tip of a revolutionary iceberg.

By the mid-1790s Federalists' worst fears of democracy seemed to have been confirmed. The people, they believed, were undependable and vulnerable to rabble rousers such as Genêt. Federalists saw democracy as "government by the passions of the multitude" and argued that personal merits, not policy, should decide elections. Elected officials, they maintained, should rule in the people's name but be independent of direct popular influence.

Republicans offered a very different perspective on government and politics. They stressed the corruption inherent in a powerful government dominated by a highly visible few, and insisted that liberty would be safe only if power were widely diffused among white male property owners.

It might at first glance seem contradictory for southern slave owners to support a radical ideology like Republicanism, with its emphasis on liberty and equality. A few southern Republicans advocated abolishing slavery gradually, but most did not trouble themselves over their ownership of human beings. The liberty and equality they advocated were intended for white men only.

Political ambition drove men like Jefferson and Madison to rouse ordinary citizens' concerns about civic affairs. The awe in which Washington was held precluded open criticism of him or his policies. However, Jefferson, Madison, and other Republicans hoped to hold the Federalists accountable to a public that could remove them from office for misguided or unpopular policies.

Jefferson's increasing frustration prompted him to resign from Washington's cabinet in 1793, widening the political split. Each side saw itself as the guardian of republican virtue and the other as an illegitimate "cabal" or "faction." In 1793–1794 opponents of Federalist policies began organizing Democratic societies. They drew into their ranks planters, small farmers and merchants, artisans, distillers, and sailors; conspicuously absent were big businessmen, the clergy, the poor, nonwhites, and women.

The Republican Party, 1794–1796

In 1794, party development reached a decisive stage after Washington openly identified himself with Federalist policies. Republicans attacked the Federalists' pro-British leanings in many local elections and won a slight majority in the House of Representatives. The election signaled the Republicans' transformation from a coalition of officeholders and local societies to a broad-based party capable of coordinating local political campaigns throughout the nation.

Federalists and Republicans alike used the press to mold public opinion. American journalism came of age in the 1790s as the number of newspapers multiplied from 92 to 242. By 1800, newspapers had about 140,000 paid subscribers (roughly one-fifth of the eligible voters), and their secondhand readership probably exceeded 300,000. Newspapers of both camps cheerfully engaged in fear mongering and character assassination. Federalists accused Republicans of plotting a reign of terror and of conspiring to turn the nation over to France. Republicans charged Federalists with favoring a royal dynasty that would form when John Adams's daughter married George III. Despite the extreme rhetoric, newspaper warfare stimulated citizens to become politically active.

Washington grew impatient with the nation's growing polarization into openly hostile parties, and he deeply resented Republican charges that he secretly supported alleged Federalist plots to establish a monarchy. Lonely and surrounded by mediocre advisers after Hamilton returned to private life, Washington decided in the spring of 1796 to retire after two terms. Washington recalled Hamilton to write his Farewell Address.

The heart of Washington's message was a vigorous condemnation of political parties. Partisan alignments, he insisted, endangered the republic's survival, especially if they became entangled in foreign policy disputes. Aside from fulfilling existing treaty obligations and maintaining foreign commerce, the United States had to avoid "political connection" with Europe and its wars. If the United States gathered its strength under "an efficient government," it could defy any foreign challenge; but if it was drawn into Europe's quarrels and corruption, the republican experiment would be doomed. Washington and Hamilton thus turned the central argument of Republicanism against their Republican critics. They also evoked a vision of a United States virtuously isolated from foreign intrigue and power politics, an ideal that would remain a potent inspiration for long thereafter.

Washington left the presidency in 1797 and died in 1799. Like many later presidents, he went out amid a barrage of partisan criticism.

The Election of 1796

As the election of 1796 approached, the Republicans cultivated a large, loyal body of voters, marking the first time since the Revolution that the political elite had effectively mobilized ordinary Americans to participate in politics. The Republican constituency included the Democratic societies, workingmen's clubs, and immigrant-aid associations.

Immigrants became a prime target for Republican recruiters. During the 1790s the United States absorbed twenty thousand French refugees from Saint-Domingue and sixty thousand Irish. Although few immigrants could vote, the Irish exerted critical influence in Pennsylvania and New York, where public opinion was so closely divided that a few hundred voters could tip the balance.

In 1796 the presidential candidates were Vice President John Adams, whom the Federalists supported, and the Republicans' Jefferson. Republican strength in the South offset Federalist strength in New England, leaving Pennsylvania and New York as crucial swing states where the Irish vote might tip the scales. In the end, the Republicans took Pennsylvania but not New York, so that Jefferson lost the presidency by just three electoral votes. As the second-highest vote-getter in the Electoral College, he became vice president. The Federalists narrowly regained control of the House and maintained their firm grip on the Senate.

Adams's intellect and devotion to principle have rarely been equaled among American presidents. But the new president was more comfortable with ideas than with people, especially non-elites. He inspired trust and often admiration but could not command personal loyalty or inspire the public. Adams's stubborn personality and disdain for ordinary people left him ill-suited to govern, and he ultimately proved unable to unify the country.

The French Crisis, 1798–1799

Even before the election, the French had recognized that Jay's Treaty was a Federalist-sponsored attempt to assist Britain in its war against France. On learning of Jefferson's defeat, France began seizing American ships carrying goods to British ports and within a year had plundered more than three hundred vessels. The French also directed that every American captured on a British naval ship (even those involuntarily impressed) should be hanged. Hoping to avoid war, Adams dispatched a peace commission to Paris. The French foreign minister, Charles de Talleyrand (sharl duh TAL-ee-rahn), refused to meet with the Americans, instead promising through three unnamed agents ("X, Y, and Z") that talks could begin after he received $250,000 and France obtained a $12 million loan. This barefaced demand for a bribe became known as the **XYZ Affair.** Outraged Americans adopted the battle cry "Millions for defense, not one cent for tribute."

XYZ Affair French demand for bribes from American negotiators; triggered great anger

The XYZ Affair discredited Republican foreign policy views. The party's leaders compounded the damage by refusing to condemn French aggression and opposing Adams's call for military preparedness. While Republicans tried to excuse French behavior, the Federalists rode a wave of militant patriotism to an enormous victory in the 1798 congressional elections.

Congress responded to the XYZ Affair by arming fifty-four ships to protect U.S. commerce. The new warships joined what became known as the Quasi (KWAH-zee)-War—an undeclared Franco-American naval conflict in the Caribbean from 1798 to 1800, during which U.S. forces seized ninety-three French privateers while losing just one ship. By early 1799 the French no longer posed a serious threat at sea.

Meanwhile, the Federalist-controlled Congress tripled the regular army to ten thousand men in 1798, with an automatic expansion of land forces to fifty thousand in case of war. But the risk of a land war with France was minimal. What Federalists actually wanted was a strong military force ready in case of a civil war, for the crisis had produced near-hysterical fears that French and Irish malcontents were hatching treasonous conspiracies.

The Alien and Sedition Acts, 1798

The Federalists insisted that the possibility of war with France demanded stringent legislation to protect national security. In 1798 the Federalist Congress passed four measures known collectively as the **Alien and Sedition Acts.** Although President Adams neither requested nor wanted the laws, he deferred to Congress and signed them.

Alien and Sedition Acts Federalist-supported measures to suppress Republican supporters of Jefferson

The least controversial of the four laws, the Alien Enemies Act, was designed to prevent wartime espionage or sabotage. It outlined procedures for determining

"Preparation for War to Defend Commerce" (1800) by William Birch
Birch's engraving depicts the building of the frigate *Philadelphia* during the Quasi-War.

The Library of Congress

whether a hostile country's citizens, when staying in America, posed a threat to the United States; if so, they would be deported or jailed. It also established principles to respect the rights of enemy citizens. This law would not be used until the War of 1812.

The second of the laws, the Alien Friends Act, authorized the president to expel foreign residents whose activities he considered dangerous. It required no proof of guilt. Republicans maintained that the law's real purpose was to deport immigrants critical of Federalist policies. Republicans also denounced the third law, the Naturalization Act. This measure increased the residency requirement for U.S. citizenship from five to fourteen years (the last five continuously in one state) to reduce Irish voting.

Finally came the Sedition Act, the only one of these measures enforceable against U.S. citizens. Although its alleged purpose was to punish attempts to encourage the violation of federal laws or to seed a revolution, the act defined criminal activity so broadly that it blurred distinctions between sedition and legitimate political discussion. Thus, it forbade an individual or a group "to oppose any measure or measures of the United States"—wording that could be interpreted to ban any criticism of the party in power. Another clause made it illegal to speak, write, or print any statement that would bring the president "into contempt or disrepute." A newspaper editor could therefore face imprisonment for criticizing Adams or his cabinet. However one regarded it, the Sedition Act interfered with free speech. The Federalists wrote the law to expire in 1801 so that it could not be used against them if they lost the next election.

A principal target of Federalist repression was the opposition press. Four of the five largest Republican newspapers were charged with sedition just as the election campaign of 1800 was getting under way. The attorney general used the Alien Friends Act to drive Irish journalists underground, and Scottish editor Thomas Callender went to prison for criticizing the president.

Federalist leaders never intended to fill the jails with Republican martyrs. Rather, they hoped to use a few highly visible prosecutions to silence Republican journalists and candidates during the election of 1800. The attorney general charged seventeen persons with sedition and won ten convictions. Among the victims was Republican congressman Matthew Lyon of Vermont, who spent four months in prison for publishing a blast against Adams.

In 1788, opponents of the Constitution had warned that giving the national government extensive powers would eventually endanger freedom. Ten years later, their prediction seemed to have come true. Shocked Republicans realized that because the Federalists controlled all three branches of the government, neither the Bill of Rights nor the system of checks and balances reliably protected individual liberties. In this context, they advanced the doctrine of states' rights as a means of preventing the national government from violating basic freedoms.

Virginia and Kentucky Resolutions Jefferson's and Madison's resolutions stressing states' rights and the power of nullification in response to the Alien and Sedition Acts

Recognizing that opponents of federal power would never prevail in the Supreme Court, which was still dominated by Federalists, Madison and Jefferson anonymously wrote manifestos on states' rights known as the **Virginia and Kentucky Resolutions,** adopted respectively by the legislatures of those states in 1798. Madison in the Virginia Resolutions declared that state legislatures retained both their right to judge the constitutionality of federal actions and an authority called *interposition,* which enabled them to protect the liberties of their citizens. Jefferson's resolution for Kentucky went further by declaring that states could "nullify"—declare invalid—objectionable federal laws. Although Kentucky's legislature deleted the term "nullify" before approving the resolution, the intention of both resolutions was to invalidate any federal law in a state that had deemed the law unconstitutional.

Although most states did not endorse the resolutions, their passage demonstrated the potential for disunion in the late 1790s. So did several near-violent confrontations between Federalist and Republican crowds in Philadelphia and New York City. National leaders acted as if a crisis were imminent. Vice President Jefferson hinted that events might push the southern states into secession from the Union; President Adams hid guns in his home. A tense atmosphere hung over the republic as the election of 1800 neared.

The Election of 1800

In the election campaign, the parties once again rallied around the Federalist Adams and the Republican Jefferson. Moderate leadership in both parties ensured that the nation would survive the tumultuous election. Jefferson and Madison discouraged radical activity, while Adams rejected demands by extreme "High Federalists" that he ensure victory by deliberately sparking an insurrection or asking Congress to declare war on France.

"Nothing but an open war can save us," declared a High (extreme) Federalist. But when the president discovered the French willing to seek peace in 1799, he proposed a special diplomatic mission. Adams obtained Senate approval for his envoys only by threatening to resign and thus making Jefferson president. Outraged High Federalists tried to dump Adams, but their ill-considered maneuver rallied most New Englanders around the stubborn, upright president.

Adams's negotiations with France did not achieve a settlement until 1801, but the expectation of normal relations prevented Federalists from exploiting charges of Republican sympathy for the enemy. With the immediate threat of war removed, voters grew resentful that, in just two years, taxes had soared 33 percent to support an army that had done virtually nothing. As the danger of war receded, voters gave Federalists less credit for standing up to France and more blame for adding $10 million to the national debt.

While High Federalists spitefully withheld the backing that Adams needed to win, Republicans redoubled their efforts to elect Jefferson. As a result of Republicans' mobilization of voters, popular interest in politics rose sharply. Voter turnout in 1800 leaped to more than double that of 1788, rising from about 15 percent to almost 40 percent; in hotly contested Pennsylvania and New York, more than half the eligible voters participated.

Adams lost the presidency by just eight electoral votes out of 138. But Adams's loss did not ensure Jefferson's election. Because all 73 Republican electors voted for both Jefferson and his running mate, New York's Aaron Burr, the Electoral College deadlocked in a tie between them. The choice of president devolved upon the House of Representatives, where thirty-five ballots over six days produced no result. Aware that Republican voters and electors wanted Jefferson to be president, the wily Burr cast about for Federalist support. But after Hamilton—Burr's bitter rival in New York politics—declared his preference for Jefferson as "by far not so dangerous a man," a Federalist representative abandoned Burr and gave Jefferson the presidency by history's narrowest margin.

CHECKING IN

- Federalists viewed the French Revolution with alarm, but Jefferson and his supporters initially viewed it optimistically.

- The XYZ Affair alienated many Americans and hardened party lines between Federalists and Republicans.

- Jefferson's supporters became the Republican Party by the mid-1790s; the election of 1796 was the first party-based election.

- In the Alien and Sedition Acts, the Federalists attempted to suppress the Republican Party.

- Jefferson's victory in the election of 1800 showed that the party system was firmly entrenched.

ECONOMIC AND SOCIAL CHANGE

On what basis were some Americans denied full equality by 1800?

During the nation's first twelve years under the Constitution, the spread of economic production for markets, even by family farms, transformed the lives of many Americans. These transformations marked the United States' first small steps toward industrial capitalism.

Meanwhile, some Americans rethought questions of gender and race in American society during the 1790s. Even so, legal and political barriers to gender and racial equality actually became more entrenched.

Producing for Markets

For centuries most economic production in European societies and their colonial offshoots took place in household settings. At the core of each household was a patriarchal nuclear family—the male head, his wife, and their unmarried children. Many households included additional people—relatives; boarders; apprentices and journeymen in artisan shops; servants and slaves in well-off urban households; and slaves, "hired hands," and tenant farmers in rural settings. Unlike in our modern world, before the nineteenth century most people except mariners worked at what was temporarily or permanently "home." The notion of "going to work" would have struck them as odd.

Although households varied greatly in the late eighteenth century, most were on small farms and consisted of only an owner and his family. By 1800, such farm families typically included seven children whose labor contributed to production. Husbands and older sons worked in the fields; wives and daughters maintained the barns and gardens; wives, of course, bore and reared the children as well. Most farm families produced food and other products largely for their own consumption.

After the American Revolution, this began to change in heavily settled regions of the Northeast. Prosperous farmers began to sell their surplus—produce, meat, and dairy products—to urban customers. Accordingly, men introduced clover into their pastures, expanded acreage devoted to hay, and built barns to shelter their cows in cold weather and to store the hay. Consequently, dairy production rose as mid-Atlantic farmwomen, or "dairymaids," by 1800 milked an average of six animals twice a day. Farmwomen turned much of the milk into butter for sale to urban consumers.

Poorer farmers found other ways to produce for commercial markets. Young men and young couples moved west, while unmarried daughters frequently remained at home and spun and wove cloth. Enterprising merchants began catering to an emerging urban market for cloth as well as selling to southerners who wanted the cheapest possible material for slave clothing. Merchants would supply raw flax (for linen), wool, and cotton to mothers and daughters in farm households, returning in a few weeks to pay the women cash for their handiwork. A similar system emerged in the shoe industry, where prosperous shoemakers began supplying leather to others and paying them for the finished product. Numerous other enterprises emerged, employing both men and women to satisfy needs, such as making nails, that self-contained households could not have met.

Behind the new industries was an ambitious class of risk-taking entrepreneurs. The country's first private banks were founded in the 1780s. Philadelphia merchants created the Pennsylvania Society for the Encouragement of Manufactures and the Useful Arts in 1787. This organization promoted the immigration of British artisans familiar with the latest industrial technology, including Samuel Slater, who helped establish a cotton-spinning mill at Pawtucket, Rhode Island, in 1790 (see Chapter 9). In 1791, investors from New York and Philadelphia started the Society for the Encouragement of Useful Manufactures, which attempted to demonstrate the potential of large-scale industrial enterprises by building a factory town at Paterson, New Jersey. That same year, the first formal association for trading government bonds appeared in New York; it ultimately became the New York Stock Exchange.

For many Americans, the choice between manufacturing and farming was moral as well as economic. Hamilton's support of industrialization was consistent with his larger vision for America and contradicted that of Jefferson. As outlined in his Report on the Subject of Manufactures (1791), Hamilton admired efficiently run factories in which a few managers supervised large numbers of workers. Manufacturing would provide employment opportunities, promote emigration, and expand the applications of technology. Jefferson, on the other hand, idealized white, landowning family farmers as bulwarks of republican liberty and virtue. "Those who labour in the earth are the chosen people," he wrote in 1784, whereas the dependency of European factory workers "begets subservience and venality." Hamilton embraced capital, technology, and managerial discipline; Jefferson envisioned land as the key to prosperity and liberty for all. The argument over these competing ideals would remain a constant in American politics until the twentieth century.

Advocating Women's Rights, 1792

In this illustration from an American magazine for women, the "Genius of the Ladies Magazine" and the "Genius of Emulation" present Liberty with a petition based on British feminist Mary Wollstonecraft's *Vindication of the Rights of Woman*.

White Women in the Republic

Along with the growing importance of women's economic roles, discussions of Republicanism raised larger questions of women's rights and equality. Neither the Revolution nor republican state constitutions had substantially altered the legal position of white women. Some states made it easier for women to obtain divorces, but only New Jersey allowed women to vote. In 1807, however, New Jersey disfranchised both women and free blacks.

Throughout American life, social change and republican ideology combined to challenge traditional attitudes toward women's rights. Americans increasingly recognized the right of a woman to choose her husband. In the Northeast, young women increasingly became pregnant as a way to force their father's consent to marriage. Pregnancy and marriage allowed young women to gain economic support in a region where the westward exodus of young men was increasingly leaving a growing number of women single.

White women also had fewer children than their mothers and grandmothers. Both declining farm sizes and urbanization contributed to the shrinkage; in one

Massachusetts town, for example, the average number of children a woman bore declined from nine per marriage in 1750 to six by 1800. Some women were clearly finding relief from the nearly endless cycle of pregnancy and nursing that had consumed their grandmothers.

As white women's roles expanded, so too did republican notions of male-female relations. "I object to the word 'obey' in the marriage-service," wrote a female author calling herself Matrimonial Republican. "The obedience between man and wife is, or ought to be mutual." Divorce petitions filed by women increasingly cited lack of mutuality as the cause for divorce. A few women also challenged the double standard that allowed men to engage in extramarital affairs while condemning their female partners. Writing in 1784, an author calling herself "Daphne" called on her "sister Americans" to "stand by and support the dignity of our own sex" by publicly condemning seducers rather than their victims.

Gradually, the subordination of women became the subject of debate. In "On the Equality of the Sexes" (1790), essayist and poet **Judith Sargent Murray** (see page 147) contended that the genders had equal intellectual ability and deserved equal education. Murray hoped that "sensible and informed" women would improve their minds rather than rush into marriage (as she had at eighteen).

Judith Sargent Murray Poet and foremost advocate of women's rights at the end of the eighteenth century

republican motherhood As virtuous wives and mothers, educated white women would strengthen the new nation

Like many of her contemporaries, Murray supported the idea of **republican motherhood.** Advocates of republican motherhood emphasized the importance of educating white women in the values of liberty and independence to strengthen virtue in the new nation. It was the republican duty of mothers to inculcate these values in their sons—the nation's future leaders—as well as their daughters. John Adams reminded his daughter that she would be "responsible for a great share of the duty and opportunity of educating a rising family, from whom much will be expected." Before the 1780s, only a few women had acquired an advanced education through private tutors. Thereafter, urban elites broadened such opportunities by founding numerous private schools, or academies, for girls; in 1789, Massachusetts forbade any town to exclude girls from its elementary schools.

Republican assertions of male and female moral and intellectual equality provoked scattered calls for political equality. However, the great struggle for women's political rights would begin only in the next century. Prohibitions against married women's ownership of property went virtually unchallenged. Women could indeed be virtuous wives and mothers, but the world outside their home offered them few opportunities to apply their education.

Land and Culture: Native Americans

Native Americans occupied the most tenuous position in American society. By 1800, Indians east of the Mississippi had suffered severe losses of population, territory, and political and cultural self-determination. Thousands of deaths had resulted from battle, famine, and disease during successive wars and from poverty, losses of land, and discrimination during peacetime (see Map 7.1). Settlers, liquor dealers, and criminals trespassed on Indian lands, often defrauding or inflicting violence on Native Americans and provoking them to retaliate. Indians who worked for whites were often paid in the unfamiliar medium of cash and then found little to spend it on in their isolated communities, except alcohol.

While employing military force against Native Americans who resisted U.S. authority, Washington recognized that American citizens' actions often contributed to Indians' resentment. Accordingly, they pursued a policy similar to Britain's under the Proclamation of 1763 (see Chapter 5) in which the federal government sought to regulate relations between Indians and non-Indians. Congress enacted the new policy gradually in a series of **Indian Trade and Intercourse Acts** (1790–1796). The acts prohibited transfers of tribal lands to outsiders except as authorized in formal treaties or by Congress. Other provisions regulated the conduct of non-Indians on lands still under tribal control. The legislation also authorized the federal government to establish programs that would "promote civilization" among Native Americans as a replacement for traditional culture. By "civilization," Knox and his supporters meant Anglo-American culture. But before 1800, the Indian Trade and Intercourse Acts went largely unenforced.

Indian Trade and Intercourse Acts Series of laws designed to promote better relations between Indians and whites

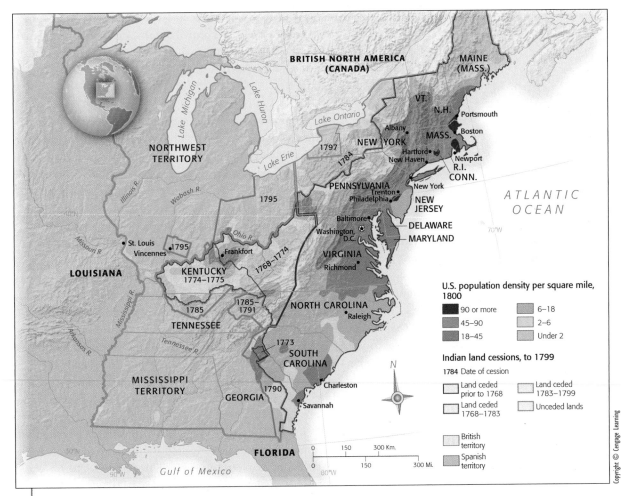

Map 7.1 Indian Land Cessions, 1768–1799

During the last third of the eighteenth century, Native Americans were forced to give up extensive homelands throughout the eastern backcountry and further west in the Ohio and Tennessee River valleys.

Interactive Map

Among the most devastated Native Americans in the 1790s were the Seneca Iroquois of western New York and Pennsylvania. Most surviving Iroquois had moved to Canada after the Revolution, and those like the Seneca who stayed behind were isolated from one another on tiny reservations. Unable to hunt, trade, or wage mourning wars, Seneca men frequently resorted to heavy drinking, often becoming violent.

In 1799, a Seneca prophet, Handsome Lake, emerged and led his people in a remarkable spiritual revival. Severely ill, alcoholic, and near death, he experienced a series of visions. Handsome Lake preached against alcoholism and sought to revive self-confidence among the Seneca. But whereas many Indian visionary prophets rejected all white ways, Handsome Lake welcomed civilization, as introduced by Quaker missionaries supported by federal aid. In particular, he urged a radical shift in gender roles, with Seneca men displacing women not only in farming but also as heads of their families. However, the most traditional Senecas rejected Handsome Lake's message that Native American men should work like white farmers. And women often resisted because they stood to lose their control of farming and their considerable political influence. After 1800, missionaries would expect Native Americans to convert to Christianity as well as adopt "civilization."

African-American Struggles   The republic's first years marked the high tide of African-Americans' revolutionary-era success in bettering their lot. Although racism persisted, Jefferson's eloquent words "all men are created equal" awakened many white consciences. In 1790, 8 percent of African-Americans enjoyed freedom. By 1800, 11 percent were free. State reforms, meanwhile, attempted to improve slaves' conditions. In 1791 the North Carolina legislature declared that the "distinction of criminality between the murder of a white person and one who is equally an human creature, but merely of a different complexion, is disgraceful to humanity" and authorized the execution of whites who murdered slaves. By 1794 most states had outlawed the Atlantic slave trade.

Hesitant measures to ensure free blacks' legal equality appeared in the 1780s and early 1790s. Most states dropped restrictions on their freedom of movement, protected their property, and allowed them to enroll in the militia. All but three states either permitted free blacks to vote or made no specific attempts to exclude them. But before the 1790s ended, the trend toward lessening the social and legal distances between the races ended. Abolitionist sentiment ebbed, slavery became more entrenched, and whites demonstrated reluctance to accept free blacks as fellow citizens.

Federal law led the way in restricting the rights of African-Americans. In 1790 congressional procedures for naturalizing aliens limited eligibility to foreign whites. The federal militia law of 1792 allowed states to exclude free blacks. The navy and marine corps forbade nonwhite enlistments in 1798. By 1807 Delaware, Maryland, Kentucky, and New Jersey had stripped free blacks of the vote. Although free blacks enjoyed rights in some areas, the number of places treating them as the political equals of whites dropped sharply in the early 1800s.

Some free blacks rose above these disadvantages, and a few of them gained recognition among whites. One of the best-known was Benjamin Banneker of Maryland, a self-taught mathematician and astronomer. Banneker was one of three surveyors who laid out the new national capital in Washington, DC, and after 1791 he published a series of widely read almanacs. Sending a copy of one to Thomas Jefferson, Banneker chided the future president for holding views of black inferiority that contradicted his ringing words in the Declaration of Independence.

Faced with growing constriction of their freedom and opportunities, free African-Americans turned to one another for support, especially through religious channels. During the 1780s Richard Allen and Absalom Jones formed the Free African Society of Philadelphia, whose members pooled their resources to aid one another and other blacks in need. When the white-dominated Methodist church they attended restricted black worshippers to the gallery, Allen and Jones and their followers formed their own congregation. Comparable developments in other northern communities would lead to the establishment of the African Methodist Episcopal Church (see Chapter 9).

In 1793 a yellow fever epidemic swept Philadelphia, leaving about four thousand dead. Most affluent whites fled the area. Allen and Jones organized a relief effort in which African-Americans tended to the sick and buried the dead of both races. Their only reward was a vicious publicity campaign wrongly accusing blacks of profiting at whites' expense.

An especially revealing symptom of changing attitudes occurred in 1793 when Congress passed the **Fugitive Slave Law.** The law required judges to award possession of a runaway slave on a formal request by a master or his representative. Accused runaways were denied jury trials and sometimes were refused permission to present evidence. Slaves' legal status as property disqualified them from claiming these constitutional privileges, but the Fugitive Slave Law denied even *free* blacks the legal protections guaranteed to them under the Bill of Rights. White Americans clearly found it easy to forget that the Constitution had not limited citizenship to their race.

The bloody slave revolt on Saint-Domingue (which victorious blacks would rename Haiti in 1802) undermined the trend toward abolition and reinforced the kinds of fears that spawned racism. Reports of the slaughter of French slaveholders made white Americans more reluctant to criticize slavery and helped to transform the image of blacks from that of victims of injustice to one of potential menaces. In August 1800 a planned insurrection of more than one thousand slaves in Richmond, Virginia, kindled smoldering white fears. The militia put down the conspiracy and executed thirty-five slaves, including the leader, Gabriel. **Gabriel's rebellion** fanned fears of future revolts. Isolated uprisings occurred in the United States for years after, and rumors persisted that a massive revolt was brewing. Antislavery sentiment diminished rapidly. The antislavery movement would not recover from the damage inflicted by the Saint-Domingue revolt until the early 1830s.

A technological development also strengthened slavery. During the 1790s, demand in the British textile industry stimulated the cultivation of cotton in coastal South Carolina and Georgia. Here the soil and climate were ideal for growing long-staple cotton, whose fibers could be separated easily from its seed. In the South's upland and interior regions, however, only short-staple cotton thrived. Its seed clung tenaciously to the fibers and defied cleaning. In 1793 a New Englander, Eli Whitney, invented a

Fugitive Slave Law Required return of runaway slaves; denied blacks any constitutional protections

Gabriel's rebellion Failed slave rebellion in Virginia

CHECKING IN

- By 1800 the market economy was beginning to challenge traditional household economies.

- White women gained educational but few other opportunities.

- The status of Native Americans continued to decline.

- The early republic moved slowly toward ending slavery, but the slave revolt on Saint-Domingue and Gabriel's rebellion in Virginia halted progress.

- The invention of the cotton gin in 1793 transformed southern agriculture and entrenched slavery firmly in the South.

cotton gin Invention that made cleaning of southern cotton fast and cheap

cotton gin that efficiently cleaned short-staple cotton. Improved by others, Whitney's machine removed a major obstacle to cotton cultivation, gave plantation slavery a new lease on life, and undermined the doubts of those who considered slavery economically outmoded.

By 1800, free blacks had suffered noticeable erosion of their post-Revolutionary War gains, and southern slaves were farther from freedom than a decade earlier. By arrangement with her late husband, Martha Washington freed the family's slaves a year after George died. But many of the freed blacks remained impoverished and dependent on the Washington estate because Virginia law prohibited the education of blacks. Meanwhile, across the Potomac, enslaved blacks were performing most of the labor on the new national capital that would bear the first president's name. African-Americans were manifestly losing ground.

Chapter Summary

What role did George Washington play in translating the Constitution from words into government? (page 148)

As president, Washington worked hard to lessen fears of the government by balancing his cabinet among competing sectional interests. He also established the precedent of serving only two terms. The Judiciary Act of 1789, which left room for state practice, and the Bill of Rights, which guaranteed personal liberties, underscored his commitment to the ideals of the Revolution.

Which points in Hamilton's economic program were most controversial and why? (page 150)

Alexander Hamilton, as Washington's treasury secretary, pushed through a series of controversial measures that strengthened federal and executive authority as well as northeastern commercial interests. Among other things, Hamilton advocated the assumption of revolutionary-era debt, establishment of a national bank, and strong support for industrial development. Jefferson, Madison, and others opposed these measures, arguing that they favored a few Americans at the expense of the rest and that they threatened liberty.

How did the new nation deal with France, Spain, and Britain? (page 155)

Spain attempted to expand its North American holdings, but Washington countered by neutralizing its Indian allies. The French Revolution proved a source of contention in the United States, especially with the arrival of Citizen Genêt and his scheme to enlist Americans to fight on France's behalf. To try to relieve tensions, Americans undertook diplomatic missions. Jay's Treaty solved few problems but stimulated the American economy by opening American trade with the British Empire. Pinckney's Treaty resolved tensions with Spain.

KEY TERMS

Judiciary Act (p. 149)

Bill of Rights (p. 150)

Alexander Hamilton (p. 150)

Reports on the Public Credit (p. 150)

Report on a National Bank (p. 152)

Whiskey Rebellion (p. 154)

"Alta California" (p. 156)

Citizen Genêt (p. 158)

Jay's Treaty (p. 159)

Treaty of San Lorenzo (p. 159)

XYZ Affair (p. 162)

Alien and Sedition Acts (p. 162)

Virginia and Kentucky Resolutions (p. 164)

Judith Sargent Murray (p. 168)

republican motherhood (p. 168)

Indian Trade and Intercourse Acts (p. 169)

Fugitive Slave Law (p. 171)

Gabriel's rebellion (p. 171)

cotton gin (p. 172)

What principal issues divided Federalists and Republicans in the election of 1800? (page 159)

During the mid-1790s, elites formed two rival political parties—the Federalists and the Republicans. The emergence of political parties clarified and intensified debate over the shape of the nation's future. Frightened by Jefferson's Republican supporters, the Federalists supported the Alien and Sedition Acts. The split over the French Revolution was only one of a series of major issues on which the two parties disagreed.

On what basis were some Americans denied full equality by 1800? (page 165)

The market economy began to transform society. While educated white women defined a public if subservient role for themselves as "republican mothers," Native Americans saw their condition continue to deteriorate. There were some moves toward ending slavery, especially in the northern states, but a series of events essentially put a halt to this—namely, the revolution in Saint-Domingue, Gabriel's rebellion in Virginia, and the invention of the cotton gin.

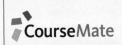

Go to the CourseMate website at **www.cengagebrain.com** for additional study tools and review materials—including audio and video clips—for this chapter.

CHAPTER 8

America at War and Peace

1801–1824

War of 1812 Scene

William L. Clements Library

CHAPTER REVIEW

The Age of Jefferson
How did Jefferson's philosophy shape policy toward public expenditures, the judiciary, and Louisiana?

The Gathering Storm
How did the United States slide into war with Great Britain?

The War of 1812
How did the War of 1812 influence American domestic politics?

The Awakening of American Nationalism
To what extent did Jefferson's legacy persist into the so-called Era of Good Feelings?

Jefferson's triumph in the election of 1800 left a bitter taste. Nevertheless, in his inaugural address, Jefferson struck a conciliatory note. He traced the political convulsions of the 1790s to different responses to the French Revolution, an external event whose fury had passed. What Americans needed to recognize was that they agreed on essentials, that "we are all republicans, we are all federalists."

However, foreign affairs continued to agitate American politics. A month before Jefferson's inauguration, Tripoli, an Islamic state in North Africa, declared war on the United States. Since 1785, the "Barbary pirates" from North Africa had been seizing American vessels and enslaving their crews. With its tiny navy, the United States had no choice but to pay exorbitant ransoms and bribes. Tripoli warred on the United States because its ruler wanted a bigger bribe. Instead, Jefferson authorized hostilities. The ensuing Tripolitan War (1801–1805) ended favorably for the United States.

American naval success also depended on European events over which it had no control. Starting in 1805, Britain renewed its seizure of American merchant ships bound for ports controlled by the French emperor Napoleon. Jefferson's answer was the Embargo Act of 1807, a self-blockade in which the United States sought to influence Britain and France by denying American trade to each. This policy of "peaceable coercion" failed, and in 1812 the United States went to war with Britain.

The treaty ending the War of 1812 did not guarantee neutral rights. But fortunately for the United States, the treaty coincided with Napoleon's decline. With peace in Europe, American trading ships enjoyed freedom of the seas for the next century. The American navy returned to the Mediterranean in 1815 and forced all the Barbary states to abandon forever their claims for tribute from the United States.

These developments fed American pride. However, the harmony for which Jefferson longed proved elusive. Between 1801 and 1824, the Federalist Party collapsed as a force in national politics. Yet the Federalists' decline opened the way to intensified factionalism within the Republican Party, especially during Jefferson's second term (1805–1809) and during the mistakenly named "Era of Good Feelings" (1817–1824). Most ominously, between 1819 and 1821, northern and southern Republicans split over the extension of slavery into Missouri.

THE AGE OF JEFFERSON

How did Jefferson's philosophy shape policy toward public expenditures, the judiciary, and Louisiana?

Narrowly elected, Jefferson saw his popularity rise in his first term as he scaled down seemingly unnecessary government expenditures. Increasingly confident of public support, he worked to loosen the Federalist grip on appointed offices, especially in the judiciary, and purchased Louisiana. Both political calculation and his philosophy of government, known as Jeffersonianism, guided his moves.

Jefferson and Jeffersonianism

A man of extraordinary attainments, Jefferson spoke fluent French, read Latin and Greek, and studied several Native American languages. For more than twenty years he was president of America's foremost scientific society, the American Philosophical Society. He designed Monticello (mon-te-CHELL-oh), his mountaintop mansion in Virginia, and spent forty years overseeing its construction. Fascinated by gadgets, he invented a device for duplicating his letters and a revolving book stand. His personal library of seven thousand books was the foundation of the Library of Congress. His public career was luminous: principal author of the Declaration of Independence, governor of Virginia, ambassador to France, secretary of state, vice president, and ultimately president.

Yet Jefferson was, and remains, a controversial figure. His critics, pointing to his doubts about some Christian doctrines and his early support for the French Revolution, portrayed him as an infidel and radical. In 1802 a former supporter, James Callender, wrote a newspaper account in which he named **Sally Hemings,** a house slave at Monticello, as Jefferson's mistress. Drawing on the DNA of Sally's male descendents and linking the timing of Jefferson's visits to Monticello with the

Sally Hemings Jefferson's slave rumored to be his mistress and mother of several of his children

start of Sally's pregnancies, most scholars now view it as very likely that Jefferson, a widower, was the father of at least one of her four surviving children.

Callender's story did little damage to Jefferson's reputation in Virginia. Jefferson acted according to the rules of white Virginia gentlemen by never acknowledging any of Sally's children as his own. Although he freed two of her children (the other two ran away), he never freed Sally, nor did he ever mention her in his correspondence. Yet the story of Sally fed the charge that Jefferson was a hypocrite, for throughout his career he condemned the "race mixing" that he seems to have practiced.

Jefferson did not believe that blacks and whites could live permanently side by side, and he greatly feared a race war so vicious that it could be suppressed only by a dictator. Only by colonizing blacks in Africa, he believed, could America avert revolution and chaos.

Jefferson worried that high taxes, standing armies, and corruption could destroy American liberty by turning government into the master rather than the servant of the people. To prevent tyranny, Jefferson advocated that state governments retain great authority because they were immediately responsive to popular will.

He also believed that popular liberty required popular virtue. For republican theorists like Jefferson, virtue consisted of a decision to place public good above private interest and to exercise vigilance in keeping government under control. To Jefferson, the most vigilant and virtuous people were educated farmers who were accustomed to acting and thinking with sturdy independence. Jefferson regarded cities as breeding grounds for mobs and as menaces to liberty. When the people "get piled upon one another in large cities, as in Europe," he wrote, "they will become corrupt as in Europe."

Jefferson's "Revolution"

Jefferson described his election as a revolution. However, the revolution he actually sought was to restore the liberty and tranquility that he thought the United States had enjoyed in its earliest years and to reverse what he saw as a drift into despotism. The $10 million growth in the national debt under the Federalists alarmed Jefferson and his secretary of the treasury, Albert Gallatin. They rejected Alexander Hamilton's argument that debt strengthened the government by giving creditors a stake in its health. Just paying interest on the debt would require taxes, which would suck money from industrious farmers, the backbone of the republic. Increased tax revenues might also tempt the government to establish a standing army, which was always a threat to liberty.

Jefferson and Gallatin secured the repeal of many taxes, and they slashed expenditures by closing some embassies overseas and reducing the army. A lull in the war between Britain and France persuaded Jefferson that minimal military preparedness was a sound policy. This may have been wishful thinking, but it rested on a sound economic calculation, for the vast territory of the United States could not be secured from attack without astronomical expense.

Jefferson and the Judiciary

Jefferson hoped to conciliate the moderate Federalists, but conflicts over the judiciary derailed this objective. Washington and Adams had appointed only Federalists to the bench, including the new chief justice, John Marshall. The Federalist-sponsored Judiciary Act of 1801 reduced the number of Supreme Court justices from six to five and created sixteen new federal judgeships, which outgoing president John Adams had filled by last-minute ("midnight") appointments of Federalists. To Jefferson, this was proof that the Federalists intended to use the judiciary as a stronghold from which "all the works of Republicanism are to be beaten down and erased." In 1802, he won congressional repeal of the Judiciary Act of 1801.

Jefferson's troubles with the judiciary were not over. On his last day in office, Adams had appointed a Federalist, William Marbury, as justice of the peace in the District of Columbia. When Jefferson's secretary of state, James Madison, refused to send him notice of the appointment, Marbury petitioned the Supreme Court to issue a writ compelling delivery. In *Marbury* v. *Madison* (1803), Chief Justice John Marshall ruled that he was under no legal obligation to do so because Congress had exceeded its constitutional authority in writing the Judiciary Act of 1789.

Marbury v. *Madison* Supreme Court decision that set the framework for judicial review

For the first time, the Supreme Court had asserted its authority to void an act of Congress on the grounds that it was "repugnant" to the Constitution—thus firmly establishing the doctrine of **judicial review.**

While the *Marbury* decision was brewing, the Republicans took the offensive against the judiciary by moving to impeach (charge with wrongdoing) two Federalist judges, John Pickering and Samuel Chase. Pickering, an insane alcoholic, was quickly removed from office, but Chase presented difficulties. He was a partisan Federalist notorious for jailing several Republican editors under the Sedition Act of 1798. Nonetheless, the Constitution specified that judges could be impeached only for treason, bribery, and "high Crimes and Misdemeanors." Was impeachment

judicial review Principle that Supreme Court can review and reject measures passed by Congress

Chronology

1801	Thomas Jefferson's inauguration; start of Tripolitan War (1801–1805)
1802	Repeal of the Judiciary Act of 1801; Yazoo land compromise
1803	*Marbury* v. *Madison*; conclusion of the Louisiana Purchase
1804	Aaron Burr kills Alexander Hamilton in a duel; Jefferson elected to a second term
1804–1806	Lewis and Clark expedition
1807	*Chesapeake* affair; Embargo Act passed
1808	James Madison elected president
1809	Non-Intercourse Act passed; Embargo Act repealed
1812	United States declares war on Britain; Madison reelected to a second term
1814	British burn Washington, DC; Hartford Convention; Treaty of Ghent signed
1815	Battle of New Orleans
1816	James Monroe elected president; Second Bank of the United States chartered
1818	British-American Convention of 1818 sets U.S.-Canada border in West; Andrew Jackson invades West Florida
1819	Adams-Onís (Transcontinental) Treaty; *Dartmouth College* v. *Woodward*; *McCulloch* v. *Maryland*
1820–1821	Missouri Compromise
1823	Monroe Doctrine

appropriate because a judge was excessively partisan? Moderate Republicans came to doubt it, and partly for that reason, the Senate narrowly failed to convict Chase.

Chase's acquittal ended Jefferson's skirmishes with the judiciary. Unlike his radical followers, Jefferson objected neither to judicial review nor to an appointed judiciary; he merely challenged Federalist use of judicial power for political goals. Federalists never tried to use their domination of the courts to undo Jefferson's "revolution" of 1800. The Marshall Court upheld the constitutionality of the repeal of the Judiciary Act of 1801. And for his part, Jefferson never proposed to impeach Marshall.

Extending the Land: The Louisiana Purchase, 1803

Jefferson's goal of avoiding foreign entanglements would remain beyond reach as long as European powers held large territories in North America. In the Treaty of San Ildefonso (san eel-duh-FON-soh) (1800), a weakened Spain returned the vast Louisiana Territory to France, which, under Napoleon Bonaparte, was emerging as Europe's strongest military power. Jefferson was appalled. The president had long imagined that the inevitable expansion of a free and

Burning of the *Philadelphia*

The American frigate *Philadelphia* ran aground in the shallow waters guarding Tripoli harbor. Both the ship and its crew were captured. To prevent the enemy from using it, on February 16, 1804, a small American force led by Lt. Stephen Decatur slipped into Tripoli harbor and boarded and burned the *Philadelphia*.

The Mariners' Museum, Newport News, Virginia

virtuous American people would create an "empire of liberty." Spain was no obstacle, but Jefferson knew that Bonaparte's capacity for mischief was boundless. Bonaparte dreamed of re-creating a French New World empire bordering the Caribbean and the Gulf of Mexico. The island of Saint-Domingue (modern Haiti and the Dominican Republic) would be the fulcrum of the empire, and Louisiana its breadbasket. Before this dream could become reality, however, the French would have to subdue Santo Domingo, where a bloody slave rebellion had led to the creation of a government under the black statesman Toussaint L'Ouverture (too-SAN loo-ver-TOOR). Napoleon accordingly dispatched an army to reassert French control and to reestablish slavery, but yellow fever and fierce resistance by the former slaves doomed the French forces.

In the short run, Jefferson worried most about New Orleans, the only port for the $3 million in annual produce of farmers along the Mississippi and Ohio river systems. Spain had temporarily granted Americans the right to park their produce there while awaiting transfer to seagoing vessels. But in 1802, the Spanish colonial administrator in New Orleans issued an order revoking this right. The order had originated in Spain, but most Americans assumed it had come from Bonaparte who, although he now owned Louisiana, had yet to take possession of it. "The day that France takes possession of N. Orleans," Jefferson wrote, "we must marry ourselves to the British fleet and nation."

The combination of France's failure to subdue Saint-Domingue and the termination of American rights to deposit produce in New Orleans led to the American purchase of Louisiana. Jefferson dispatched James Monroe and Robert R. Livingston to Paris to buy New Orleans from France. Meanwhile, Bonaparte concluded that his Caribbean empire was not worth the cost. In addition, he planned to resume war in Europe and needed cash. So he decided to sell *all* of Louisiana. The American commissioners and the French government settled on a price of $15 million. Thus, the United States gained an immense, uncharted territory between the Mississippi River and the Rocky Mountains (see Map 8.1). Although no one knew its exact size, the **Louisiana Purchase** virtually doubled the area of the United States at a cost, omitting interest, of thirteen and one-half cents an acre.

Louisiana Purchase
Jefferson's purchase of the interior of North America from France; virtually doubled the size of the United States

Jefferson found himself caught between ideals and reality. He believed in strict construction—the doctrine that the Constitution should be interpreted according to its letter—but recognized that doubling the size of the republic would guarantee land for American farmers, the backbone of the nation and the true guardians of liberty. Strict construction was not an end in itself but a means to promote republican liberty. If that end could be achieved in some way other than by strict construction, so be it. Political considerations also figured in Jefferson's calculations. Federalists generally opposed the Louisiana Purchase because it would decrease the relative importance of their strongholds on the eastern seaboard. As the leader of the Republican Party, the president saw no reason to hand the Federalists an issue by dallying over ratification of the treaty.

The Election of 1804

Jefferson's acquisition of Louisiana left the Federalists dispirited. As the election of 1804 approached, the main threat to Jefferson was not the Federalist Party but his

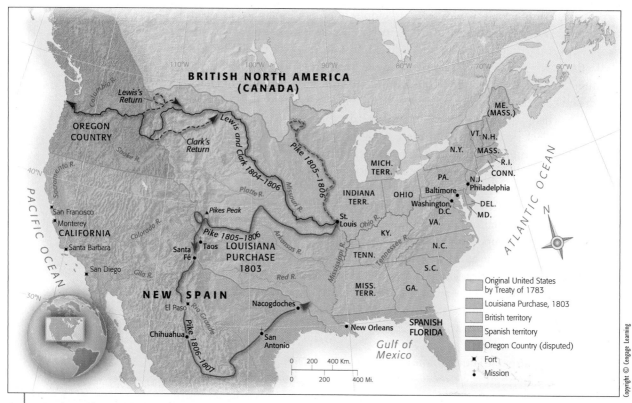

Map 8.1 The Louisiana Purchase and the Exploration of the West

The explorations of Lewis and Clark demonstrated the vast extent of the area purchased from France.

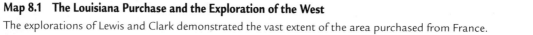 Interactive Map

own vice president, Aaron Burr. In 1800, Burr had tried to take advantage of a tie in the Electoral College to gain the presidency. The Twelfth Amendment had clarified the electoral process but had not eliminated Burr's conniving; he spent much of his vice presidency in intrigues with the Federalists. The Republicans dumped him from the ticket in 1804 in favor of George Clinton. In the election, the Federalist nominees Charles C. Pinckney and Rufus King carried only two states. Jefferson's overwhelming victory brought his first term to a fitting close. Between 1801 and 1804 the United States had doubled its territory and started to pay off its debt. President Jefferson basked in the sun of success.

Exploring the Land: The Lewis and Clark Expedition

Louisiana dazzled Jefferson's imagination. Americans knew virtually nothing about the immense territory, not even its western boundary. A case could be made for the Pacific Ocean, but Jefferson was content to claim that Louisiana extended at least to the mountains west of the Mississippi, mountains that few Americans had seen. Thus, the Louisiana Purchase was both a bargain and a surprise package.

Even before the purchase, Jefferson had planned an exploratory expedition; picked its leader, his personal secretary and fellow Virginian Lieutenant Meriwether

Lewis; and sent him to Philadelphia for a crash course in zoology, astronomy, and botany. Jefferson instructed Lewis to trace the Missouri River to its source, cross the western highlands, and follow the best water route to the Pacific. Although Jefferson stressed commercial possibilities in requesting congressional funding for the expedition, his instructions to Lewis cited the need to learn about Indian customs, climate, plants, birds, and insects. Above all, Jefferson hoped the **Lewis and Clark expedition** would find a water route across the continent.

Setting forth from St. Louis in May 1804, Lewis, his second-in-command, William Clark, and about fifty others followed the Missouri and then the Snake and Columbia rivers. In the Dakota Country they hired a French-Canadian fur trader, Toussaint Charbonneau (SHAR-bun-noh), as guide and interpreter. Slow-witted and inclined to panic in crises, Charbonneau proved to be a mixed blessing, but his wife, **Sacajawea** (sock-a-ja-WAYah) made up for his failings. A sixteen-year-old Shoshone (show-SHOW-nee), Sacajawea had been stolen by a rival tribe and then claimed by Charbonneau. When first encountered by Lewis and Clark, she had just given birth to a son; indeed, the infant's presence helped reassure Native American tribes of the expedition's peaceful intent.

Even with their peaceful intent established, Lewis and Clark faced obstacles. The expedition brought them into contact with numerous tribes, each with a history of warring on other tribes and carrying on its own internal feuds. Reliant on Indians for guides, packers, and interpreters, Lewis and Clark had to become instant diplomats. Jefferson had instructed them to assert American sovereignty over the Purchase. They distributed medals and uniforms to chiefs ready to support American authority and staged military parades and displays of their weapons, which included cannons. But no tribe had a single chief, and Lewis and Clark sometimes miscalculated, thinking a minor chief to be head of an entire tribe. Yet their diplomacy was generally successful, less because they were sophisticated ethnographers than because they avoided violence.

The group finally reached the Pacific Ocean in November 1805 and then returned to St. Louis, but not before collecting a mass of scientific information, including the disturbing fact that more than three hundred miles of mountains separated the Missouri from the Columbia. The expedition also produced a sprinkling of tall tales, many of which Jefferson believed, about gigantic Indians, soil too rich to grow trees, and a mountain composed of salt. Finally, the expedition's drawings of the geography of the region led to more accurate maps and heightened interest in the West.

Lewis and Clark expedition Two-year exploration of newly acquired territory; a scientific treasure trove

Sacajawea Shoshone Indian, wife of Charbonneau, who assisted Lewis and Clark on their expedition

CHECKING IN

- President Jefferson feared too strong a central government and saw educated farmers as the backbone of Republicanism.

- The Jefferson administration rejected the Hamiltonian idea of a permanent national debt and downplayed military preparedness.

- Despite qualms about its constitutionality, Jefferson eagerly carried out the Louisiana Purchase.

- With apparent success in both domestic and foreign policy, Jefferson easily won reelection in 1804.

- The Lewis and Clark expedition collected large amounts of scientific data and sparked interest in the West.

THE GATHERING STORM

How did the United States slide into war with Great Britain?

In gaining Louisiana, the United States benefited from the European powers' preoccupation with their own struggles. But between 1803 and 1814, the Napoleonic Wars turned the United States into a pawn in a chess game played by others and made Jefferson's second term far less successful than his first.

Europe was not Jefferson's only problem. He had to deal with a plot to dismantle the United States, hatched in the inventive and perverse mind of Aaron Burr, as well as face down challenges from within his own party.

Challenges on the Home Front

Aaron Burr suffered a string of reverses in 1804. After being denied re-nomination as vice president, he began to scheme with a faction of extreme (or "High") Federalists who were plotting to form a "Northern Confederacy" that would include Nova Scotia, New England, New York, and even Pennsylvania. To advance their plot, the Federalists helped Burr to gain the Federalist nomination for governor of New York. Alexander Hamilton, who had thwarted Burr's grab for the presidency in 1800 by supporting Jefferson, now foiled Burr a second time by allowing publication of his "despicable opinion" of Burr. After his defeat in the New York election, Burr challenged Hamilton to a duel and mortally wounded him at Weehawken, New Jersey, on July 11, 1804.

Indicted in two states for murdering Hamilton, Burr—still vice president—now hatched a scheme so audacious that not even his opponents could believe that he was capable of such treachery. Burr allied himself with General James Wilkinson, the unsavory military governor of the Louisiana Territory, who had been on Spain's payroll intermittently as a secret agent since the 1780s. Their plot had several dimensions: They would create an independent confederacy of western states, conquer Mexico, and invade West Florida. The scheming duo presented the plot imaginatively. To westerners they said that it had the covert support of the Jefferson administration; to the British, that it was a way to attack Spanish lands; and to the Spanish, that it would open the way to dividing up the United States.

In the fall of 1806, Burr and some sixty followers made their way down the Ohio and Mississippi rivers to join Wilkinson at Natchez (NATCH-ezz). In October, Jefferson denounced the conspiracy. Wilkinson abandoned the plot and proclaimed himself the most loyal of Jefferson's followers. Burr was captured and brought back to Richmond, where he was put on trial for treason. Chief Justice Marshall presided at the trial and instructed the jury that the prosecution had to prove actual treasonable acts—an impossible task because the conspiracy had never reached fruition. The jury returned a verdict of not proved, which Marshall entered as "not guilty." Still under indictment for his murder of Hamilton, Burr fled to Europe where he tried to interest Napoleon in making peace with Britain as a prelude to a proposed Anglo-French invasion of the United States and Mexico.

Besides the Burr conspiracy, Jefferson also faced a challenge from a group of Republicans led by fellow Virginian John Randolph, an eccentric man of acerbic wit. Randolph believed that governments always menaced popular liberty. Jefferson had originally shared this view, but he recognized it as an ideology of opposition, not power; once in office, he compromised. In contrast, Randolph remained frozen in the 1770s, denouncing every government action as decline and proclaiming that he would throw all politicians to the dogs except that he had too much respect for dogs.

Randolph turned on Jefferson, most notably, for backing a compromise in the Yazoo land scandal. In 1795, the Georgia legislature had sold the huge Yazoo tract

(35 million acres composing most of present-day Alabama and Mississippi) for a fraction of its value to land companies that had bribed virtually the entire legislature. The next legislature canceled the sale, but many investors had already bought land. In 1803, a federal commission compromised with an award of 5 million acres to the Yazoo investors. For Randolph, the compromise was further evidence of the decay of republican virtue.

The Suppression of American Trade and Impressment

Burr's acquittal and Randolph's taunts shattered the aura of invincibility that had surrounded Jefferson. Now foreign affairs posed even sharper challenges. As Britain and France resumed their war, the United States prospered at Britain's expense by carrying sugar and coffee from the French and Spanish Caribbean colonies to Europe. This trade not only provided Napoleon with supplies but also drove down the price of sugar and coffee from British colonies by adding to the glut of these commodities on the world market. The British concluded that their economic problems stemmed from American prosperity.

Fueling this boom was the re-export trade, which created conflicts with Britain. According to the British Rule of 1756, any trade closed during peacetime could not be opened during war. For example, France usually restricted the sugar trade to French ships during peacetime and thus could not open it to American ships during war. The U.S. response to the Rule of 1756 was the "broken voyage," by which U.S. ships would carry French sugar or coffee to American ports, unload it, pass it through customs, and then re-export it as *American* produce. Britain tolerated this dodge for nearly a decade but in 1805 initiated a policy of total war toward France, including the strangulation of French trade. In 1805, a British court declared broken voyages illegal.

Next came a series of British trade decrees ("Orders in Council"), through which Britain intended to blockade part of continental Europe and thus staunch the flow of any products that might aid the French war effort. French counter-decrees followed, proclaiming that ships obeying British regulations would be subject to seizure by France. In effect, this Anglo-French war of decrees outlawed virtually all U.S. trade; if an American ship complied with British regulations, it became a French target, and vice versa. In total war, however, there was no room for neutrality, so both Britain and France seized U.S. ships. British warships hovered just beyond the American coast, searching virtually every U.S. ship it encountered.

Although less damaging to the American economy than the seizure of ships, **impressments** were equally galling. Even American-born seamen, six thousand between 1803 and 1812, were impressed into the Royal Navy. British arrogance peaked in June 1807. A British warship, HMS *Leopard*, patrolling off Virginia, attacked an unsuspecting American frigate, USS *Chesapeake,* and forced it to surrender. The British then boarded the vessel and seized four supposed deserters. One, a genuine deserter, was later hanged; the other three, former Britons, had "deserted" only from impressments and were now American citizens. The so-called *Chesapeake-Leopard* Affair enraged the country. Jefferson remarked that he had not seen so belligerent a spirit in America since 1775.

impressment British practice of taking deserters and others from American ships for service in the Royal Navy

Boarding and Taking of the American Ship *Chesapeake*

The loss of the frigate *Chesapeake* to HMS *Leopard* in 1807 and the dying words of its commander, James Lawrence, inspired the motto "Don't Give Up the Ship," which was emblazoned on the battle flag of Captain Oliver Hazard Perry.

Embargo Act of 1807
Jefferson's attempt at "peaceable coercion" by suspending American trade with France and Britain

The Embargo Act of 1807

Yet while making some preparations for war, Jefferson adopted "peaceable coercion" by suspending trade with Britain and France to gain respect for neutral rights. By far the most controversial legislation of Jefferson's presidency, the **Embargo Act of 1807** prohibited vessels from leaving American harbors for foreign ports. Technically, it prohibited only exports, but its practical effect was to stop imports as well, for few foreign ships would venture into American ports if they had to leave without cargo. Amazed by the boldness of the act, a British newspaper described the embargo as "little short of an absolute secession from the rest of the civilized world."

The embargo did not have the intended effect. Although British sales to the United States dropped 50 percent between 1807 and 1808, the British quickly found new markets in South America. Furthermore, the Embargo Act contained some loopholes. For example, it allowed American ships blown off course to put in at European ports if necessary; suddenly, many captains were reporting that adverse winds had forced them across the Atlantic. Treating the embargo as a joke, Napoleon seized any

American ships he could lay hands on and then informed the United States that he was only helping to enforce the embargo.

The United States itself felt the harshest effects of the embargo. Some thirty thousand American seamen found themselves out of work. Hundreds of merchants went into bankruptcy, and jails swelled with debtors. Farmers were devastated. Unable to export their produce or sell it at a decent price to hard-pressed urban dwellers, many farmers could not pay their debts. New England suffered most; in Massachusetts, which accounted for a third of foreign trade, the embargo was a calamity.

The situation was not entirely bleak, however. The embargo forced a diversion of merchants' capital into manufacturing. Before 1808, the United States had only fifteen cotton textile mills; by the end of 1809, an additional eighty-seven mills had been constructed (see Chapter 9). But none of this comforted merchants who were already ruined or mariners driven to soup kitchens. Nor could New Englanders forget that the source of their misery was a policy initiated by one of the "Virginia lordlings," "Mad Tom" Jefferson, who knew little about New England and loathed cities, the very foundations of New England's prosperity.

James Madison and the Failure of Peaceable Coercion

With Jefferson's blessing, the Republicans nominated James Madison and George Clinton for the presidency and vice presidency in 1808. The Federalists re-nominated Charles C. Pinckney and Rufus King, the same ticket that had failed in 1804. In 1808 the Federalists staged a modest comeback, but Madison handily won the presidency, and the Republicans continued to control Congress.

The Federalists' revival, modest as it was, rested on two factors. First, the Embargo Act gave them the national issue that they had long lacked. Second, younger Federalists had abandoned their elders' gentlemanly disdain for campaigning and deliberately imitated such vote-winning techniques as barbecues and mass meetings, which had worked for the Republicans.

To some contemporaries, "Little Jemmy" Madison, five feet four inches tall, seemed a weak figure compared to Jefferson. In fact, Madison's intelligence and capacity for systematic thought equaled Jefferson's. He had the added advantage of being married to Dolley Madison. A striking figure in her turbans and colorful dresses, Dolley arranged receptions at the White House in which she charmed Republicans, and even some Federalists, into sympathy with her husband's policies.

Madison continued the embargo with minor changes. Like Jefferson, he reasoned that Britain was "more vulnerable in her commerce than in her armies." The American embargo, however, was coercing no one, and on March 1, 1809, Congress replaced the Embargo Act with the weaker, face-saving Non-Intercourse Act. This act opened trade to all nations except Britain and France and then authorized the president to restore trade with either of those nations if it stopped violating neutral rights. However, neither nation complied. In May 1810, Congress substituted a new measure, Macon's Bill No. 2, which opened trade with Britain and France and offered each a clumsy bribe: If either nation repealed its restrictions on neutral shipping, the United States would halt trade with the other.

None of these steps had the desired effect. While Jefferson and Madison lashed out at France and Britain as moral demons ("The one is a den of robbers and the other of pirates," snapped Jefferson), the belligerents saw the world as composed of a few great powers and many weak ones. When great powers went to war, there were no neutrals. Weak nations like the United States should stop babbling about moral ideals and seek the protection of a great power.

As peaceable coercion became a fiasco, Madison came under fire from militant Republicans, known as **"war hawks,"** who demanded more aggressive policies. Coming mainly from the South and West, regions where "honor" was a sacred word, the militants were infuriated by insults to the American flag. In addition, economic recession between 1808 and 1810 had convinced the firebrands that British policies were wrecking their regions' economies. The election of 1810 brought several war hawks to Congress. Led by Henry Clay of Kentucky, the war hawks included John C. Calhoun of South Carolina, Richard M. Johnson of Kentucky, and William King of North Carolina, all future vice presidents. Clay was elected Speaker of the House.

"war hawks" Members of Congress elected from western states in 1810 who wanted war with Britain

Tecumseh and the Prophet

More emotional and pugnaciously nationalistic than Jefferson or Madison, the war hawks called for the expulsion of the British from Canada and the Spanish from the Florida region. Their demands merged with westerners' fears that the British in Canada were recruiting Indians to halt the march of U.S. settlement. In reality, American policy, not British meddling, was the source of bloodshed on the frontier.

Jefferson believed that Indians and whites could live peacefully together if the Indians abandoned their hunting and nomadic ways and took up farming. If they farmed, they would need less land. However, the march of white settlement was steadily shrinking Indian hunting grounds, and some Indians were willing to sign away land in return for blankets, guns, and liquor.

No American was more eager to acquire Indian lands than William Henry Harrison, governor of the Indiana Territory. Harrison realized that Indiana would not become a state without more residents, and the best way to attract more residents was to offer them Indian land. Disregarding instructions from Washington, Harrison rounded up a delegation of half-starved Indians, none of whom lived on the rich lands along the Wabash (WAH-bash) River that he craved. By the Treaty of Fort Wayne in September 1809, these Indians ceded millions of acres along the Wabash at a price of two cents an acre.

This treaty outraged the numerous tribes that had not been party to it. Among the angriest were **Tecumseh** (tuh-CUM-suh), the Shawnee chief, and his brother Lalawéthica (la-la-WAY-thuh-kuh). In 1805, Lalawéthica had had a frightening dream, a vision of drunken Indians who were tormented for eternity. Overnight he was transformed from a drunken misfit into a preacher. He gave up liquor and began beseeching surrounding tribes to return to the old ways and avoid contact with whites. Now known as the Prophet, he took a new name, Tenskwatawa (tens-KWAH-tah-wah), the "open door" through which Indians could achieve salvation. Shawnees responded to his message.

Tecumseh Shawnee leader who tried to build a coalition of several western tribes; allied with British in War of 1812

In the meantime, Tecumseh had tried to build a coalition of several tribes to stem the tide of white settlement. He insisted that Indian lands belonged collectively

Cincinnati Museum Center

Tecumseh and William Henry Harrison at Vincennes, August 1810

This portrait of a personal duel between Tecumseh and Indiana governor William Henry Harrison is fanciful. But the confrontation between the two at Vincennes nearly erupted into violence. Tecumseh told Harrison that Indians could never trust whites because "when Jesus Christ came upon the earth you kill'd him and nail'd him on a cross."

to all the tribes and could not be sold by splinter groups. Failing to reach a settlement with Tecumseh or the Prophet, Harrison concluded that it was time to attack the Indians. His target was a Shawnee encampment near the mouth of the Tippecanoe (TIP-pee-cun-oo) River. With Tecumseh absent and recruiting more followers, the Prophet launched an attack on Harrison's forces in November 1811. Outnumbered two to one and short of ammunition, Tenskwatawa's force was beaten off after inflicting heavy casualties.

Although a small engagement, the Battle of Tippecanoe had far-reaching effects. Harrison became a national hero and ultimately rode his reputation to the White House. The Prophet was discredited, but his brother Tecumseh became recognized as a leader among the western tribes. Finally, Tecumseh concluded that an alliance with the British was the only way to stop the spread of American settlement.

Congress Votes for War

By spring 1812, President Madison had concluded that war was inevitable, and he sent a war message to Congress on June 1. Ironically, an economic slump prompted Britain to repeal its Orders in Council on June 23, but by then Congress had declared war. Neither the war hawks nor westerners held the key to the vote in favor of war; the votes of Republicans in states like Pennsylvania, Maryland, and Virginia were the decisive force in propelling the declaration of war through Congress. Opposition came mainly from Federalist strongholds in New England and New York.

Madison, in his war message, listed impressment, the presence of British ships in U.S. waters, and British violation of neutral rights as wrongs that justified war. None of these complaints fully explains why America declared war in 1812. Neither do continuing Indian problems (blamed on the British) along the frontier. A more important underlying cause for the war was the economic recession that affected the South and West after 1808. Finally, it was critical that Madison, rather than Jefferson, was president in 1812. Jefferson had believed that Britain was motivated primarily by its desire to defeat Napoleon, and that once the war in Europe ended, the provocations would stop. Madison held that Britain's real motive was to strangle American trade and thus to eliminate the United States as a trading rival.

CHECKING IN

- In his second term, Jefferson faced challenges from Aaron Burr and John Randolph.
- Impressment became a major issue between the United States and Great Britain.
- Jefferson tried "peaceable coercion" through the Embargo Act; however, it was a failure.
- "War hawks" from the southern and western states demanded more aggressive policies.
- James Madison ultimately asked Congress for a declaration of war because he saw Great Britain as a long-term threat to the United States.

THE WAR OF 1812

How did the War of 1812 influence American domestic politics?

Although American warships would win a few sensational duels with British men-of-war, the U.S. Navy simply could not challenge the Royal Navy on the high seas, or even prevent a British blockade of the American coast. Madison thus shifted his sights to Canada, whose small population made it seem an easy mark. Jefferson, for example, saw the conquest of Canada as "a mere matter of marching."

Little justified such optimism. Although the British remained preoccupied with the Napoleonic wars in Europe, they enlisted Native Americans as their allies—and used fear of these "uncontrollable savages" to force American surrenders. American militias were often Sunday soldiers who "hollered for water half the time, and whiskey the other." Few understood what the war was about, and fewer still cared.

On to Canada

From the summer of 1812 to the spring of 1814, the Americans launched a series of unsuccessful attacks on Canada (see Map 8.2). In July 1812, General William Hull led an American army from Detroit into Canada, quickly returned when Tecumseh cut his supply line, and surrendered Detroit and two thousand men to thirteen hundred British and Indian troops. In the fall of 1812, the British and their Mohawk allies crushed a force of American regulars at the Battle of Queenston, near Niagara Falls. A third American offensive in 1812, a projected attack on Montreal via Lake Champlain, fell apart when the militia again refused to advance into Canada.

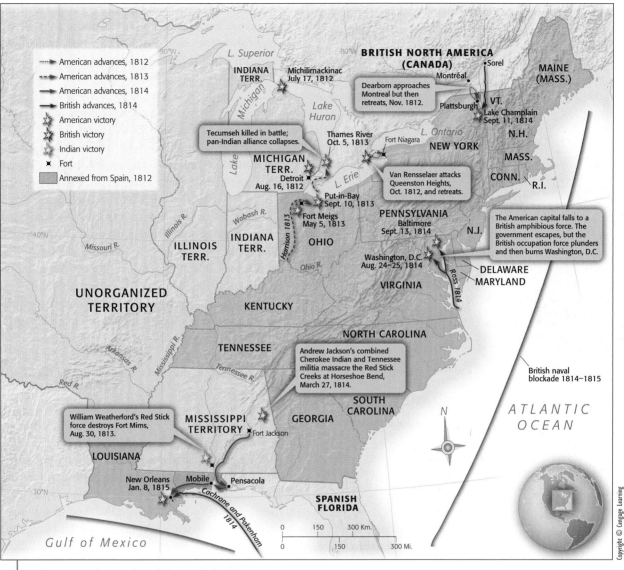

Map 8.2 Major Battles of the War of 1812

Most of the war's major engagements occurred on or near the United States' northern frontier, but the Royal Navy blockaded the entire Atlantic coast, and the British army penetrated as far south as Washington and New Orleans.

Interactive Map

Renewed U.S. offensives and subsequent reverses in 1813 convinced the Americans that they could not retake Detroit while the British controlled Lake Erie. During the winter of 1812–1813, U.S. captain Oliver Hazard Perry built ships and outfitted them with captured cannons, and on September 10, 1813, the homemade American fleet destroyed a British squadron at Put-in-Bay on the western end of Lake Erie. "We have met the enemy, and they are ours," Perry triumphantly reported. The British then pulled out of Detroit, but American forces under General William Henry Harrison overtook and defeated a combined British-Indian force at the Battle

Bettmann/CORBIS

First Lady Dolley Madison by Rembrandt Peale, c. 1809
Friendly, tactful, and blessed with an unfailing memory for names and events, First Lady Dolley Madison earned a reputation as an elegant hostess.

of the Thames (thaymes) on October 5. Tecumseh, a legend among whites, died in the battle. Perry's and Harrison's victories cheered Americans, but efforts to invade Canada continued to falter.

The British Offensive

With fresh reinforcements from Europe, where Napoleon had abdicated as emperor after his disastrous invasion of Russia, the British took the offensive in the summer of 1814. General Sir George Prevost led a force of ten thousand British veterans in an offensive meant to split New England from the rest of the country. The British advanced down Lake Champlain until meeting the well-entrenched American forces at Plattsburgh. After his fleet met defeat on September 11, Prevost abandoned the campaign.

Ironically, Britain's most spectacular success began as a diversion from Prevost's offensive. In 1814, a British army landed near Washington and met a larger American force, composed mainly of militia, at Bladensburg, Maryland, on August 24. The Battle of Bladensburg deteriorated into the "Bladensburg Races" as the American troops fled, almost without firing a shot. The British then descended on Washington. Madison, who had witnessed the Bladensburg fiasco, escaped into the Virginia hills. His wife, Dolley, loaded her carriage before joining her husband. British troops ate the supper prepared for the Madisons and then burned the presidential mansion and other public buildings in the capital. A few weeks later, the British attacked Baltimore, but after failing to crack its defenses, they broke off the operation.

The Treaty of Ghent, 1814

Napoleon's abdication made Britain's primary goal a lasting European peace, and thus the British had little to gain by prolonging a minor war in America. The **Treaty of Ghent,** signed on Christmas Eve, 1814, restored the *status quo ante bellum:*[*] The United States neither gained nor lost territory. The fixing of the Canadian-American border was referred to a joint commission for future settlement. Impressment was left hanging, but the end of the European war made neutral rights a dead issue.

Ironically, America's most dramatic victory came on January 8, 1815, two weeks after the treaty had been signed but before word of it reached America. A British force had descended on New Orleans. U.S. troops commanded by General Andrew ("Old Hickory") Jackson, legendary as a fierce Indian fighter, shredded the line of

Treaty of Ghent Treaty that ended War of 1812, restoring *status quo ante bellum*

---

[*] *Status quo ante bellum:* Latin for "the state of affairs before the war"

advancing redcoats, inflicting more than two thousand casualties while suffering only thirteen of their own.

The Hartford Convention

Although it meant nothing in terms of the war, the Battle of New Orleans had a devastating effect on the Federalist Party. The Federalist comeback had continued into the election of 1812, when their candidate, DeWitt Clinton, an antiwar Republican, carried all of New England except Vermont, along with New York and New Jersey. American military setbacks had intensified Federalist disdain for Madison. He seemed to epitomize a decade of Republican misrule at New England's expense. The Louisiana Purchase, while constitutionally dubious, had reduced the importance of New England, the Embargo Act had nearly destroyed the region's commerce, and "Mr. Madison's War" had brought fresh misery in the form of the British blockade. A few Federalists began to talk of New England's secession from the Union.

In late 1814, a special Federalist convention met in Hartford, Connecticut. Although some supported secession, moderates took control and passed a series of resolutions expressing New England's grievances. Convinced that New England was becoming a permanent minority in a nation dominated by southern Republicans who failed to understand the region's commercial interests, the **Hartford Convention** leaders proposed a series of constitutional amendments: to abolish the three-fifths clause, which allowed southerners to count slaves as a basis for representation; to require a two-thirds vote of Congress to declare war and to admit new states into the Union; to limit the president to a single term; to prohibit the election of two successive presidents from the same state; and to bar embargoes lasting more than sixty days.

These proposals were as bold as their timing was disastrous. News of the peace and of Jackson's victory at New Orleans dashed Federalist hopes of gaining popular support, while the states' rights emphasis of the convention smelled of treason to many delegates. The restoration of peace stripped the Federalists of their primary grievance. In the presidential election of 1816, James Monroe, Madison's hand-picked successor and another Virginia Republican, swept the nation over negligible Federalist opposition. He would win reelection in 1820 with only a single dissenting electoral vote. As a force in national politics, the Federalists were finished.

Hartford Convention
Federalist meeting that showed seeming disloyalty in time of war; began downfall of the party

CHECKING IN

- The United States failed in its attempts to invade Canada.
- When the war in Europe ended, Britain launched a major offensive in the United States, which included the ransacking of Washington, DC.
- The Treaty of Ghent ended the war with a restoration of the *status quo ante bellum*.
- At the Hartford Convention, dissatisfied Federalists toyed with the idea of secession, a move ultimately fatal to them as a political party.
- The war produced a hero in Andrew Jackson and a renewed sense of nationalism and confidence throughout the nation.

THE AWAKENING OF AMERICAN NATIONALISM

To what extent did Jefferson's legacy persist into the so-called Era of Good Feelings?

The United States emerged from the War of 1812 bruised but intact. In its first major war since independence, the American republic had demonstrated that it could fight on even terms against a major power and that republics could conduct wars without becoming despotisms. The war also produced several major symbols of American nationalism: the presidential mansion, whitewashed to hide smoke damage, became the White House; Britain's failed attack on Fort McHenry in Baltimore Harbor inspired Francis Scott Key's "Star-Spangled Banner"; and the Battle of New Orleans made Andrew Jackson a national hero and reinforced legends about the prowess of American frontier people and their marksmanship with a rifle. Much of the legend spun around the Battle of New Orleans was untrue, but Americans loved it nonetheless, especially because it confirmed their conviction that amateur soldiers and militiamen could outfight a professional army.

Madison's Nationalism and the "Era of Good Feelings," 1817–1824

The War of 1812 had three major political consequences. First, it eliminated the Federalists as a national political force. Second, it went far toward convincing the Republicans that the nation was strong and resilient, capable of fighting a war while maintaining liberty. Third, with political rivals removed, the Republicans began to embrace some Federalist ideas.

Both President Madison and Henry Clay became advocates of federal support for internal improvements, tariff protection for new industries, and the creation of a new national bank; Clay christened these ideas the American System and proclaimed that they would make the nation economically self-sufficient. In 1816 Congress chartered the Second Bank of the United States and enacted a moderate tariff, but federally supported internal improvements were more difficult. Madison vetoed an internal improvements bill in 1817, believing that a constitutional amendment was necessary to authorize such improvements.

"Era of Good Feelings"
Somewhat misleading label given to the period of one-party politics during the administration of James Monroe

As Republicans adopted positions they had once disdained, an **"Era of Good Feelings"** dawned on American politics. A Boston newspaper, impressed by the warm reception accorded President James Monroe while touring New England, coined the phrase in 1817. It has stuck as a description of Monroe's two administrations from 1817 to 1825.

However, the good feelings were paper-thin. Madison's 1817 veto of the internal-improvements bill revealed the persistence of disagreements about the federal government's role under the Constitution. Furthermore, the continuation of slavery was arousing sectional animosities that a journalist's phrase about good feelings could not dispel. Not surprisingly, the postwar consensus began to unravel almost as soon as Americans recognized its existence.

John Marshall and the Supreme Court

In 1819, Jefferson's old antagonist John Marshall, who was still chief justice, issued two opinions that stunned Republicans. The first case, *Dartmouth College* v. *Woodward,* focused on New Hampshire's attempt to transform a private corporation, Dartmouth College, into a state university. Marshall concluded that Dartmouth's original charter was a contract and thus was protected under the constitutional prohibition against state interference in contracts. Marshall's ruling had enormous implications. In effect, Marshall said that, once a state had chartered a college or business, that state surrendered its power to alter the charter and, in large measure, its authority to regulate the beneficiary.

A few weeks later, the chief justice handed down an even more momentous decision in **McCulloch v. Maryland.** At issue was whether the state of Maryland had the power to tax a national corporation—specifically, the Baltimore branch of the Second Bank of the United States. Marshall focused on two issues. First, did Congress have the power to charter a national bank? The Constitution, Marshall conceded, did not explicitly grant this power, but the broad sweep of enumerated powers implied the power to charter a bank. This was a clear enunciation of a broad, or "loose," construction (interpretation) of the Constitution. The second issue revolved around whether a state could tax an agency of the federal government that was located within its borders. Marshall argued that any power of the national government, enumerated or implied, was supreme within its sphere. States could not interfere with the exercise of federal power; thus, Maryland's attempt to tax the bank was plainly unconstitutional.

The *McCulloch* decision dismayed many Republicans. The bank, initially supported by Madison and Monroe, had triggered the Panic of 1819 by tightening credit. Distressed western farmers angrily blamed the bank for their dilemmas. And now Marshall's decision placed the hated bank beyond the reach of any state government. The Constitution, Marshall said, was the creation not of state governments but of the people of *all* the states and thus overrode state laws. The decision was as much an attack on state sovereignty as a defense of the bank itself.

Like Jefferson, most Republicans considered the Union a compact among states and saw state governments as the guarantors of popular liberty. In Republican eyes, the *Dartmouth* and *McCulloch* cases stripped state governments of the power to impose the will of their people on corporations and thus threatened liberty.

McCulloch v. Maryland Supreme Court decision that bolstered broad construction; restated national supremacy over states

The Missouri Compromise, 1820–1821

The controversy over statehood for Missouri highlighted the fragility of the so-called Era of Good Feelings. Carved from the Louisiana Purchase, Missouri had attracted many southerners who expected to use slaves to grow cotton and hemp. By 1819, slaves made up 16 percent of the territory's inhabitants.

In February 1819, the House of Representatives considered a bill to admit Missouri as a slave state. A New York Republican offered an amendment that prohibited the further introduction of slaves into Missouri and provided for the emancipation, at age twenty-five, of all slave offspring born after Missouri joined the Union. Following rancorous debate, the House accepted the amendment and the Senate rejected it. Both chambers voted along sectional lines.

Before 1819, slavery had not been a major source of the nation's sectional divisions, which tended to pit New England against the South and West. But the Missouri question, which Jefferson called "a fire bell in the night [which] awakened me and filled me with terror," thrust slavery into the center of long-standing sectional divisions.

Several factors drove the slavery issue to the forefront. In 1819, the Union had eleven free and eleven slave states. The admission of Missouri as a slave state would upset this balance to the advantage of the South. Equally important, Missouri was on the same latitude as the free states of Ohio, Indiana, and Illinois, and northerners worried that admitting Missouri as a slave state would set a precedent for the

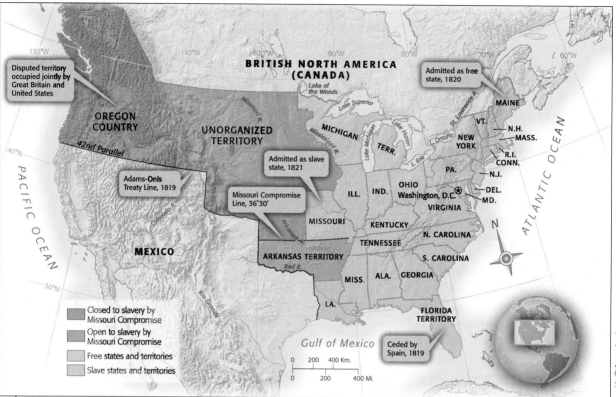

Map 8.3   The Missouri Compromise, 1820–1821

The Missouri Compromise temporarily quelled controversy over slavery by admitting Maine as a free state and Missouri as a slave state and by prohibiting slavery in the remainder of the Louisiana Purchase north of 36°30′.

Interactive Map

extension of slavery into the northern part of the Purchase. Finally, the disintegration of the Federalists as a national force reduced the need for unity among Republicans, and they increasingly heeded sectional pressures more than calls for party loyalty.

Virtually every issue that would wrack the Union in the next forty years was present in the Missouri controversy: southern charges that the North was conspiring to destroy the Union and to end slavery; northern accusations that southerners were conspiring to extend slavery. For a while, leaders doubted that the Union would survive the crisis; the words "disunion" and "civil war" were freely uttered, Henry Clay wrote.

A series of congressional agreements known collectively as the **Missouri Compromise** resolved the crisis. To balance the number of slave states and free states, Congress in 1820 admitted Maine as a free state and Missouri as a slave state; to forestall a further crisis, it also prohibited slavery in the remainder of the Louisiana Purchase north of 36°30′, Missouri's southern border.

The Missouri Compromise was widely viewed as a southern victory. The South had gained admission of Missouri, whose acceptance of slavery was controversial,

Missouri Compromise An attempt to end slavery controversy by bringing Missouri and Maine into the Union, drawing a line limiting slavery across the Louisiana Purchase while the North had merely gained Maine, whose rejection of slavery sparked no controversy. But at the same time, the South had allowed slavery to be banned from a vast territory north of 36°30′, an area that would not long remain a wilderness. The Missouri Compromise also reinforced the principle that Congress could prohibit slavery in some territories. Southerners had implicitly agreed that slaves were not like other forms of property that could be moved from place to place at will.

Foreign Policy Under Monroe

American foreign policy between 1816 and 1824 reflected more consensus than conflict. The end of the Napoleonic Wars and the signing of the Treaty of Ghent had removed most of the foreign-policy disagreements between Federalists and Republicans. Moreover, President Monroe had as his secretary of state an extraordinary diplomat, John Quincy Adams. The son of the last Federalist president, Adams had been the only Federalist in the Senate to support the Louisiana Purchase, and he later became an ardent Republican. Adams was a tough negotiator and a fervent nationalist.

Adams moved quickly to strengthen the peace with Great Britain. During his term the Rush-Bagot Treaty of 1817 demilitarized the Great Lakes, and the British-American Convention of 1818 fixed the Canadian-American boundary and restored U.S. fishing rights off Newfoundland. With its northern border secure, the United States could turn its attention southward and westward.

The nation now turned its attention to dealing with Spain, who still owned East Florida and claimed West Florida. It had never been clear whether the Louisiana Purchase included West Florida. Acting as if it did, the United States in 1812 simply added a slice of West Florida to the state of Louisiana and another piece to the Mississippi Territory. Using the pretext that it was a base for Seminole Indian raids and a refuge for fugitive slaves, Andrew Jackson, now a military commander in the South, invaded West Florida in 1818, hanged two British subjects, and captured Spanish forts. Although Jackson had acted without explicit orders, Adams supported the raid, guessing correctly that it would panic the Spanish into further concessions. In 1819, Spain agreed to the **Adams-Onís (Transcontinental) Treaty,** ceding East Florida to the United States, renouncing all claims to West Florida, and agreeing to a southern border of the United States west of the Mississippi, while Spain agreed to a northern limit to its claims to the West Coast (see Map 8.3). It thereby left the United States free to pursue its interests in Oregon.

Adams-Onís (Transcontinental) Treaty An 1819 treaty by which Spain conceded Florida to the United States; established boundary lines in the West

The Monroe Doctrine, 1823

John Quincy Adams believed that God and nature had ordained that the United States would eventually span the entire continent of North America. While negotiating the purchase of Florida, he made it clear to Spain that the United States might seize what it could not purchase—including Texas and Mexico. Besides, Spain was concerned with larger issues than American encroachment. Its primary objective was to suppress the revolutions against Spanish rule that had broken out in South America. Britain's foreign minister, George Canning, proposed a joint U.S.-British statement opposing European interference in South America and pledging that neither nation would annex any part of Spain's empire in the New World.

Monroe Doctrine Statement that proclaimed U.S. primacy in the New World

While sharing Canning's opposition to European intervention in the New World, Adams preferred that the United States make a declaration of policy on its own rather than "come in as a cock-boat in the wake of the British man-of-war." Adams flatly rejected Canning's insistence on a joint pledge never to annex Spain's former territories, for Adams wanted the freedom to annex Texas or Cuba.

This was the background of the **Monroe Doctrine,** as President Monroe's message to Congress on December 2, 1823, later came to be called. Written largely by Adams, the message announced three key principles: that U.S. policy was to avoid European wars unless American interests were involved; that the "American continents" were not "subjects for future colonization by any European power"; and that the United States would construe any attempt at European colonization in the New World as an "unfriendly act."

Europeans widely derided the Monroe Doctrine as an empty pronouncement. With hindsight, however, the Europeans might have taken the doctrine more seriously, for it had important implications. First, by pledging itself not to interfere in European wars, the United States was excluding the possibility that it would support revolutionary movements in Europe. Second, by keeping open its options to annex territory in the Americas, the United States was using the Monroe Doctrine to claim a preeminent position in the New World.

CHECKING IN

- As the Federalist Party faded as a national force, Monroe's years in the White House became known as the Era of Good Feelings.
- John Marshall's Supreme Court strengthened the power of the central government with critical rulings on the use of implied powers and the limits of state power.
- The Missouri Compromise showed how dangerous the issue of slavery was.
- Through a series of treaties, the United States consolidated its northern and southern borders.
- Although derided by other nations, the Monroe Doctrine represented a major step toward American domination of the Western Hemisphere.

Chapter Summary

How did Jefferson's philosophy shape policy toward public expenditures, the judiciary, and Louisiana? (page 175)

Jefferson brought with him to the White House a well-defined set of ideas about the necessity for tightly controlled central government, payment of the national debt, and downsizing the American military. Nonetheless, when offered the chance to buy Louisiana, an action not specified in the Constitution, Jefferson eagerly jumped at the chance to rid the New World of France. His sponsorship of the Lewis and Clark expedition exemplified his interest in science and his hope for practical results from science.

How did the United States slide into war with Great Britain? (page 181)

Despite the success of his first term, Jefferson struggled throughout his second term. He faced challenges from within his own party, notably from the mischief of Aaron Burr and from old Republicans like John Randolph, who charged that Jefferson was abandoning pure Republican doctrines. Relations with Great Britain steadily worsened. His attempts at "peaceable coercion" were fruitless, and "war hawks" from the western states became increasingly vocal

KEY TERMS

Sally Hemings (p. 175)
Marbury v. Madison (p. 177)
judicial review (p. 177)
Louisiana Purchase (p. 179)
Lewis and Clark expedition (p. 181)
Sacajawea (p. 181)
impressment (p. 183)
Embargo Act of 1807 (p. 184)
"war hawks" (p. 186)
Tecumseh (p. 186)
Treaty of Ghent (p. 190)
Hartford Convention (p. 191)
"Era of Good Feelings" (p. 192)
McCulloch v. Maryland (p. 193)

and powerful. James Madison, Jefferson's successor, saw Britain as a continuing threat to the United States; his declaration of war was based much more on that long-term fear than on short-term problems such as impressment.

KEY TERMS continued

Missouri Compromise *(p. 194)*

Adams-Onís (Transcontinental) Treaty *(p. 195)*

Monroe Doctrine *(p. 196)*

How did the War of 1812 influence American domestic politics? (page 188)

The War of 1812 saw few American successes, but in the Treaty of Ghent, Great Britain essentially restored the *status quo ante bellum*. Nonetheless, the war destroyed the Federalists, who committed political suicide at the Hartford Convention. It also produced at least one major hero, Andrew Jackson, and spawned a renewed sense of confidence and nationalism. With the Federalist Party evaporating as a political force, the nation entered what one observer dubbed an Era of Good Feelings. But despite the appearance of harmony, conflict was never far below the surface. In the absence of Federalist opposition, Republicans began to fragment into sectional factions.

To what extent did Jefferson's legacy persist into the so-called Era of Good Feelings? (page 191)

During the Monroe administration, the United States consolidated its northern and southern borders, saw a broad interpretation of the Constitution put in place by the Marshall court, and confronted and then dodged the issue of slavery with the Missouri Compromise. Finally, the Monroe Doctrine represented a major step toward American domination of the Western Hemisphere.

 Go to the CourseMate website at **www.cengagebrain.com** for additional study tools and review materials—including audio and video clips—for this chapter.

CHAPTER 9

The Transformation of American Society

1815–1840

Middlesex Company, Woolen Mills,
Lowell, Massachusetts, c. 1840

American Textile History Museum

CHAPTER PREVIEW

Westward Expansion
What caused the surge of westward migration after the War of 1812?

The Growth of the Market Economy
What changes were linked to the rise of the market economy?

Industrial Beginnings
What caused the rise of industrialization?

Equality and Inequality
What caused urban poverty in this period?

The Revolution in Social Relationships
How did the rise of the market economy and industrialization change relationships within families and communities?

The life of Harriet Jane Hanson Robinson (1825–1911) intersected several developments that left a distinct imprint on America between 1820 and the Civil War. She directly experienced early industrialization as one of the "operatives" in the Lowell, Massachusetts, textile mills. Harriet entered factory work at the age of ten but managed to acquire an education in a public high school. Her literary refinement, along with her handsome features and lively wit, attracted her future husband, William Stevens Robinson. Like William, Harriet supported the antislavery movement and the Whig political party. Later, she embraced women's suffrage.

Harriet's experiences serve as a window on her times. By 1820, New England's small, rock-strewn farms could no longer support its rural population. Many of its young men moved west, while young women sought work in the new textile mills. In 1830, more than 70 percent of the female workers in Lowell were between the ages of fifteen and nineteen. When she was eleven, Harriet led her young coworkers in a "turn-out" (strike) to protest a reduction in wages. But native-born, Protestant girls like Harriet did not see themselves as part of a permanent working class—most left factory work when they married.

Rather, the mill girls sought "betterment." Between 1839 and 1845, the girls edited their own literary monthly, the *Lowell Offering*, which gained international repute. These upwardly mobile farm girls became part of the "middling classes" in antebellum America. They came to see themselves as individuals who could control their lives and bodies. Harriet's maternal grandfather had sired fifteen children; Harriet gave birth to only four.

The world Harriet knew in the mills was passing by the time of her marriage in 1848. A new generation of mill workers, many of them Irish immigrants, was forming a permanent factory working class. Founded as a pastoral "mill village," Lowell was turning into a city with sharpening tensions between the native-born and the Irish, Protestants and Catholics, rich and poor. As such, it was becoming a mirror of a changing America.

WESTWARD EXPANSION

What caused the surge of westward migration after the War of 1812?

In 1790, the vast majority of the non-Indian population of the United States lived east of the Appalachian Mountains; by 1840, one-third were living between the Appalachians and the Mississippi River, defined as the West. These Americans rapidly developed a distinctive western culture.

Most Americans came west dreaming of a better version of the life they had known in the East. Several factors fed this dream: the growing power of the federal government; its often-ruthless removal of Indians from the path of white settlements; and a boom in the prices of agricultural commodities.

The Sweep West

This westward movement occurred in several thrusts. Americans leapfrogged the Appalachians after 1791 to bring four new states into the Union by 1803: Vermont, Kentucky, Tennessee, and Ohio. From 1816 to 1821, momentum carried settlers farther west, even across the Mississippi River, and six more states entered: Indiana, Mississippi, Illinois, Alabama, Maine, and Missouri. Ohio's population jumped from 45,000 in 1800 to 1,519,000 by 1840; Michigan's rose from 5,000 in 1810 to 212,000 by 1840.

Seeking security, pioneers usually migrated as families. To reach markets with their produce, most settlers clustered near the navigable rivers of the West, especially the magnificent water system created by the Ohio and Mississippi rivers. Only with the spread of canals in the 1820s and 1830s, and later of railroads, did westerners feel free to venture far from rivers.

Western Society and Customs

Migrants to the West brought with them values and customs peculiar to the regions they had left behind. For example, migrants who hailed from New England or upstate New York settled the northern areas of Ohio, Indiana, and Illinois, where they primarily grew wheat, supplemented by dairying and fruit orchards. Emigrants from the Upland South settled the southern parts of Ohio, Indiana, and Illinois, where they raised corn and hogs.

Regardless of their origins, most westerners craved sociability. Rural families joined their neighbors for sports and festivities. Men met for games that tested strength and agility: wrestling, lifting weights, pole jumping (for distance, not height), and hammer throwing. Women usually combined work and play in quilting and sewing bees, carpet tackings, and even goose and chicken pluckings. At "hoe-downs" and "frolics," the settlers danced to a fiddler's tune.

The West developed a character of its own. Eastern elegance yielded to western lack of refinement, making westerners easy targets for easterners' contemptuous jibes. Westerners responded that at least they were honest democrats, not soft would-be aristocrats. Pretension got short shrift. A sojourner at a tavern who hung a blanket to cover his bed from public gaze might find it ripped down. A politician who rode to a public meeting in a buggy instead of on horseback lost votes.

Chronology

1790	Samuel Slater opens his first Rhode Island mill
1793	Eli Whitney invents the cotton gin
1807	Robert R. Livingston and Robert Fulton introduce the steamboat *Clermont* on the Hudson River
1811	Construction of the National Road begins at Cumberland, Maryland
1813	Establishment of the Boston Manufacturing Company
1816	Second Bank of the United States chartered
1817	Construction of the Erie Canal started; Mississippi enters the Union
1819	Economic panic, ushering in four-year depression; Alabama enters the Union
1820s	Expansion of New England textile mills
1824	*Gibbons v. Ogden*
1828	Baltimore and Ohio Railroad chartered
1830	Indian Removal Act passed by Congress
1831	*Cherokee Nation v. Georgia*
1832	*Worcester v. Georgia*
1834	First strike at the Lowell mills
1835–1838	Trail of Tears
1837	Economic panic begins a depression that lasts until 1843
1840	System of production by interchangeable parts perfected

The Far West

Exploration carried some Americans even farther west. Zebulon Pike explored the Spanish Southwest in 1806. By 1811, in the wake of Lewis and Clark, the New York merchant John Jacob Astor founded a fur-trading post at the mouth of the Columbia River in the Oregon Country. At first, whites relied on the Native Americans for furs, but in the 1820s such "mountain men" as Kit Carson and Jedediah Smith penetrated deep beyond the Rockies.

Jedediah Smith was representative of these men. Born in the Susquehanna Valley of New York in 1799, Smith moved west with his family to Pennsylvania and Illinois and signed on with an expedition bound for the upper Missouri River in 1822. In the course of this and subsequent explorations, he was almost killed by a grizzly bear in South Dakota, learned from the Native Americans to trap beaver and kill buffalo, explored California's San Joaquin Valley, and hiked back across the Sierras to the Great Salt Lake, a forbidding trip. The exploits of Smith and the other mountain men were popularized in biographies, and they became legends in their own day.

The Federal Government and the West

The federal government's growing strength spurred westward expansion. Under the Articles of Confederation, several states had ceded western lands to the national government, creating a bountiful public domain. The Louisiana Purchase brought the entire Mississippi River under American control. Six million acres of public land had been promised to volunteers during the War of 1812. The **National Road,** a highway begun in 1811 in Cumberland, Maryland, stretched farther westward, reaching Wheeling, Virginia, in 1818 and Vandalia, Illinois, by 1838. Soon settlers thronged the road.

National Road Federally sponsored highway that crossed the Appalachians and opened the way for families to move west

The same government strength that aided whites brought misery to the Indians. Virtually all the foreign-policy successes during the Jefferson, Madison, and Monroe administrations worked to Native Americans' disadvantage. In the wake of the Louisiana Purchase, Lewis and Clark bluntly told the Indians that they must "shut their ears to the counsels of bad birds" and listen henceforth only to the "Great Father" in Washington. The outcome of the War of 1812 also worked against the Native Americans. Early in the negotiations leading to the Treaty of Ghent, the British had insisted on the creation of an Indian buffer state in the Old Northwest. But the British eventually dropped the demand and essentially abandoned the Indians to the Americans.

The Removal of the Indians

Westward-moving white settlers found sizable numbers of Native Americans in their paths, particularly in the South, home to the so-called **"Five Civilized Tribes":** the Cherokees, Choctaws, Creeks, Chickasaws, and Seminoles. Years of commercial dealings and intermarriage with whites had created in these tribes an influential minority of mixed-bloods who embraced Christianity, practiced agriculture, built gristmills, and even owned slaves. Cherokees had a written form of their language and their own bilingual newspaper, the *Cherokee Phoenix.*

"Five Civilized Tribes" Once-powerful southeastern Indians "removed" in the 1830s to make way for white settlement

The "civilization" of the southern Indians impressed New England missionaries more than southern whites, who viewed the Civilized Tribes with contempt and their land with envy. A handful of tribes had sold their lands to the federal government and accepted removal west of the Mississippi River by 1830, but most clung to their land and customs. When the Creek mixed-blood chief William McIntosh sold all Creek lands in Georgia and two-thirds of Creek lands in Alabama to the government in 1825, the tribal council executed him.

In the 1820s, white squatters moved onto tribal lands; southern legislatures, loath to restrain white settlers, moved to expropriate Indian lands. State laws extended state jurisdiction over the tribes and excluded Indians from serving as witnesses in court cases involving whites, which effectively made it virtually impossible for Indians to collect debts owed them by whites.

These measures delighted President Andrew Jackson. Himself a frontiersman contemptuous of Native Americans, Jackson believed it was ridiculous to treat the

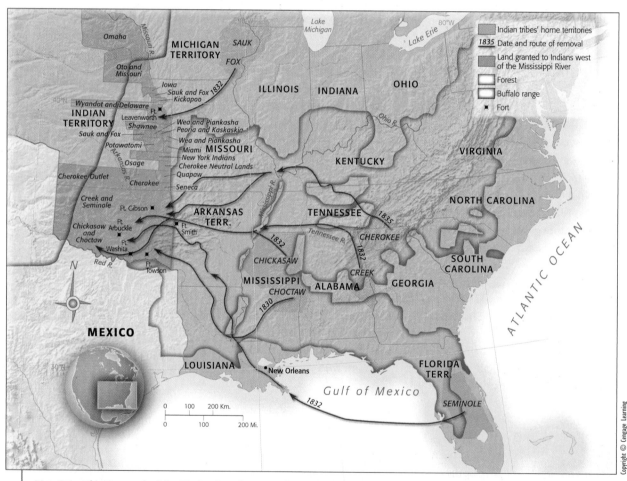

Map 9.1   The Removal of the Native Americans to the West, 1820–1840

The so-called Trail of Tears, followed by the Cherokees, was one of several routes along which various tribes migrated on their forced removal to reservations west of the Mississippi.

Interactive Map

Indians as independent nations; rather, he felt they should be subject to the laws of the states where they lived. This position spelled doom for the Indians, who could not vote or hold state office. In 1834, Cherokee chief John Ross got a taste of what state jurisdiction meant: Georgia, without consulting him, put his house up as a prize in the state lottery.

In 1830, President Jackson secured passage of the Indian Removal Act, which authorized him to exchange public lands in the West for Indian territories in the East. During Jackson's eight years in office, the federal government forced Indians to exchange 100 million acres of their lands for 32 million acres of public lands. The Choctaws, Creeks, and Chickasaws began their "voluntary" migration in the late 1820s. In 1836, Creeks who clung to their homes were forcibly removed, many in chains. Most Seminoles were removed from Florida, but only after a bitter war between 1835 and 1842 that cost the federal government $20 million (see Map 9.1).

Ironically, the Cherokees, often considered the "most civilized" tribe, suffered the worst fate. Pursuing their claims before the Supreme Court, they won two favorable decisions from Chief Justice John Marshall. In *Cherokee Nation* v. *Georgia* (1831), Marshall recognized the Cherokees as a "domestic dependent nation" with a legitimate claim to their lands in Georgia. A year later, in *Worcester* v. *Georgia,* Marshall declared them a "distinct" political community entitled to federal protection from Georgia's claims.

President Andrew Jackson reportedly sneered, "John Marshall has made his decision; now let him enforce it" and ignored the ruling. Next, federal agents persuaded some minor Cherokee chiefs to sign the Treaty of New Echota (1835), which ceded all Cherokee lands in the United States for $5.6 million and free passage west. Congress ratified this treaty, but the vast majority of Cherokees denounced it. In 1839, a Cherokee party took revenge by murdering its three principal signers.

The end of the story was simple and tragic. In 1838, the Cherokees were forcibly removed to the new Indian Territory along what became known as the **Trail of Tears.** Perhaps as many as eight thousand Cherokees, more than one-third of the entire nation, died during and just after the removal.

Indians in the Northwest Territory fared no better after they signed land-cession treaties. Two uprisings marked their westward removal. The first was quickly crushed, but the second, led by a Sac and Fox chief, Black Hawk, raged along the Illinois

Cherokee Nation v. Georgia Supreme Court decision recognizing Cherokees' claim to their lands; ignored by President Jackson

Worcester v. Georgia Court decision declaring that Cherokees were entitled to federal protection; ignored by President Jackson

Trail of Tears The death of one-third or more of the Cherokee tribe upon their "removal" to the West

"Trail of Tears" by Robert Lindneux. Woolaroc Museum, Bartlesville, OK

Trail of Tears, by Robert Lindneux

Forced by Andrew Jackson's removal policy to give up their lands east of the Mississippi and migrate to an area in present-day Oklahoma, the Cherokee people suffered disease, hunger, and exhaustion on what they remembered as the "Trail of Tears."

frontier until federal troops and state militiamen virtually annihilated the Indians in 1832. Black Hawk's downfall persuaded the other Old Northwest tribes to cede their lands. Between 1832 and 1837, the United States acquired nearly 190 million acres of Indian land in the Northwest for $70 million.

CHECKING IN

- The War of 1812 opened the way for several thrusts of westward migration that carried the American population across the Mississippi River.
- Western society evolved its own set of values and prided itself on its democratic nature.
- Expansion multiplied the problems of Native Americans, culminating in the "removal" of tribes in the Southeast and the Old Northwest.
- An agricultural boom fueled the drive west.
- In the South, the cotton gin combined with rich western lands to create a huge surge in cotton production and export.

Working the Land: The Agricultural Boom

After the War of 1812, the rising prices of agricultural commodities sharpened white land hunger. Several factors accounted for rising farm prices. With the conclusion of the Napoleonic Wars, American farmers found brisk demand for their wheat and corn in Britain and France. In addition, demand within the United States for western farm commodities intensified after 1815 with the quickening pace of industrialization and urbanization in the East. Finally, the West's splendid river systems made it possible for farmers to ship wheat and corn downriver to New Orleans. Just as government policies made farming in the West possible, high prices for foodstuffs made it attractive.

Cotton, and Eli Whitney's cotton gin, provided the impetus for settlement of the Old Southwest, especially Alabama and Mississippi. Indeed, the explosive westward thrust of southern farmers and planters after the War of 1812 resembled a gold rush. By 1817, "Alabama fever" gripped the South; settlers bid the price of good land up to thirty to fifty dollars an acre. Accounting for less than a quarter of all American exports between 1802 and 1807, cotton comprised nearly two-thirds by 1836.

THE GROWTH OF THE MARKET ECONOMY

What changes were linked to the rise of the market economy?

The high prices of agricultural commodities, such as wheat and cotton, tempted a growing number of farmers to add a cash crop, thus venturing into commercial agriculture or the **market economy.** In the South, the sale of slaves from older states to the new Cotton Belt accelerated rapidly after 1815. However, farmers often launched into the market economy without weighing the risks. The new commercial farmers encountered wildly fluctuating markets and long intervals between harvest and the sale of crops, sending many deeply into debt. Meanwhile, the federal government struggled to devise an effective policy for transferring the public domain directly into the hands of small farmers.

market economy Newly developing commercial economy that depended on goods and crops produced for sale rather than consumption

Federal Land Policy

Partisan and sectional pressures buffeted federal land policy like a kite in a March wind. The result was a succession of land laws passed between 1796 and 1820, each of which sought to undo the damage caused by its predecessors.

At the root of early federal land policy lay a preference for the orderly settlement of the public domain. To this end, the Ordinance of 1785 divided public lands into sections of 640 acres. Ordinary farmers could not afford such large purchases, but it was assumed that they would pool their money to buy sections. Federalists, with their political base in the East, were reluctant to encourage western settlement but were eager to sell land to raise revenue for the government. They reconciled their conflicting goals by encouraging the sale of huge tracts of land to speculators who waited for its value to rise and then sold off parcels to farmers.

Sure that the small farmer was the backbone of the republic, Jefferson and the Republicans took a different tactic. The land law of 1800 dropped the minimum purchase to 320 acres and allowed up to four years for full payment. By 1832, the minimum purchase had shrunk to 40 acres.

Although Congress steadily liberalized land policy, speculators always remained one step ahead. With agricultural prices soaring, speculators were willing to bid high on new land, which they resold to farmers at hefty profits. The growing availability of credit after the War of 1812 fed speculation. The chartering of the Second Bank of the United States in 1816 increased the amount of money in circulation and stimulated the growth of state banks. Between 1812 and 1817, bank notes in circulation soared from $45 million to $100 million. The result was an orgy of speculation; by 1819, the dollar value of sales of public lands was more than 1,000 percent greater than the average from 1800 to 1814.

The Speculator and the Squatter

Despite these problems, most of the public domain found its way into the hands of small farmers. The desire to recoup investments led speculators to sell quickly, as did the proliferation of squatters.

Squatters had long helped themselves to western land. George Washington himself had been unable to drive squatters off lands he owned in the West. Proud and independent, they hated land speculators and pressured Congress to allow "preemption" rights—that is, the right to purchase at the minimum price the land that they already lived on and had improved. After passing a series of limited preemption laws, Congress acknowledged a general right of preemption in 1841.

Preemption laws were of no use to farmers who arrived after speculators had already bought up land. These settlers had to buy land from speculators on credit at interest rates that were as high as 40 percent. Many western farmers, drowning in debt and forced to raise cash crops in a hurry, worked their acreage to exhaustion and thus had to keep moving in search of new land. The phrase "the moving frontier" refers not only to the obvious fact that the line of settlement shifted farther west with each passing decade, but also to the fact that the same people kept moving, chasing their elusive dreams. Typical was Abraham Lincoln's family, who migrated from the East through several farms in Kentucky and then on to Indiana.

The Panic of 1819

In 1819, the land boom collapsed, the victim of a financial panic caused in large part by state banks that issued their own bank notes, which were little more than a promise to pay the bearer a certain amount of specie (gold and silver coin) on demand. These plentiful notes had helped fuel the land boom after 1815. Farmers also borrowed to buy more land and plant more crops. But even as they did so, bumper crops in Europe combined with an economic slump in Britain to trim foreign demand for U.S. crops.

The result was a cascade of economic catastrophes. In the summer of 1819, the Bank of the United States, holding large amounts of state bank paper, began to insist that the state banks redeem this paper in specie. To pay these debts, state banks demanded that farmers and land speculators repay their loans. Credit contracted sharply throughout the nation, particularly in the West. Prices for commodities like wheat, corn, cotton, and tobacco sank by 50 percent or more. Hard-pressed farmers could not pay their debts, speculators could not collect their money, and land values collapsed from nearly $70 an acre to barely $2.

The Panic left a bitter taste about banks, particularly the Bank of the United States, which was widely blamed for the hard times. The Panic also demonstrated how dependent farmers had become on distant markets. This in turn accelerated the search for better, cheaper ways to get crops to market.

The Transportation Revolution: Steamboats, Canals, and Railroads

The transportation system linking Americans in 1820 had severe weaknesses. The great rivers west of the Appalachians flowed north to south and hence could not by themselves connect western farmers to eastern markets. Roads were expensive to maintain, and horse-drawn wagons had limited capacity. After 1820 investment shifted to improving transportation on waterways, thus initiating the **transportation revolution.**

transportation revolution
Rapid expansion of canals, steamships, and railroads

Clermont First of the steamboats that revolutionized river travel

In 1807, Robert R. Livingston and Robert Fulton introduced the steamboat *Clermont* on the Hudson River. They soon gained a monopoly from the New York legislature to run a New York–New Jersey ferry service. Competitors filed suit to break the Livingston-Fulton monopoly. After a long court battle, the Supreme Court decided against the monopoly in 1824 in the famous case of *Gibbons* v. *Ogden.* Chief Justice John Marshall ruled that Congress's constitutional power to regulate interstate commerce prevailed over New York's power to license the Livingston-Fulton monopoly. In the aftermath of this decision, other state-granted monopolies collapsed, and steamboat traffic increased rapidly. The number of steamboats operating on western rivers jumped from seventeen in 1817 to 727 by 1855.

Steamboats assumed a vital role along the Mississippi-Ohio river system. It took a keelboat (a covered flatboat pushed by oars or poles) three or four months to complete the 1,350-mile voyage from New Orleans to Louisville; in 1817, a steamboat could make the trip in twenty-five days. The development of long, shallow hulls permitted navigation of the Mississippi-Ohio river system even when hot, dry summers lowered the river level. Steamboats became more ornate as well as more practical, offering luxurious cabins and lounges, called saloons. The saloon of the *Eclipse*, a Mississippi River steamboat, was the length of a football field and featured skylights, chandeliers, a ceiling crisscrossed with Gothic arches, and velvet upholstered mahogany furniture.

While steamboats proved their value, canals replaced roads and turnpikes as the focus of popular enthusiasm and financial speculation. Although the cost of canal construction was mind-boggling—Jefferson dismissed the idea of canals as "little short of madness"—canals offered the possibility of connecting the Mississippi-Ohio river system with the Great Lakes and even the East Coast.

A canal boom followed the completion in 1825 of the **Erie Canal,** which stretched 363 miles from Buffalo to Albany. Ohio built a network of canals that enabled farmers to ship wheat by water to Lake Erie; the wheat was then shipped to Rochester for milling and finally traveled via the Erie Canal and the Hudson River to New York City. Shipping costs via the canal network were 10 percent of costs via road (see Map 9.2).

Erie Canal Major canal that linked the Great Lakes to New York City, opening the upper Midwest to wider development

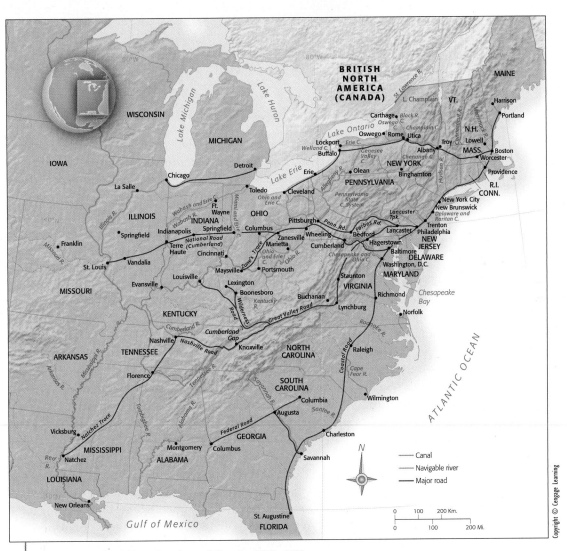

Map 9.2 Major Rivers, Roads, and Canals, 1825–1860

Railroads and canals increasingly tied the economy of the Midwest to that of the Northeast.

Interactive Map

Erie Canal, **by John William Hill, 1831**
Construction of the Erie Canal was a remarkable feat, all the more so because the United States did not have any engineering school at the time. The project's heroes were lawyers and merchants who taught themselves engineering and brawny workmen, often Irish immigrants, who hacked a waterway through the forests and valleys of New York.

Collection of the New-York Historical Society

When another economic depression hit in the late 1830s, states found themselves overcommitted to costly canal projects and ultimately scrapped many. As the canal boom was ending, the railroad, an entirely new form of transportation, was being introduced. In 1825, the world's first commercial railroad began operation in Britain, and by 1840 some three thousand miles of track had been laid in America, about the same as the total canal mileage.

Since they were cheaper to build, faster, and able to reach more places, railroads had obvious advantages over canals. But railroads' potential was only slowly realized. Most early railroads ran between cities in the East, rather than from east to west, and carried more passengers than freight. Not until 1849 did freight revenues exceed passenger revenues, and not until 1850 was the East Coast connected by rail to the Great Lakes.

There were two main reasons for this slow pace of development. First, unlike canals, most railroads were built by private companies that tended to skimp on costs, and as a result they produced lines requiring constant repair. In contrast, canals needed little maintenance. Second, shipping bulky commodities, such as iron, coal, and grain, was cheaper by canal than by rail.

CHECKING IN

- For farmers, the market economy was alluring but risky.
- Federal land policy was aimed at small farmers but helped feed a speculative boom.
- When the speculative bubble burst, the Panic of 1819 created economic havoc and intensified the American distrust of banks.
- The transportation revolution—steamboats, canals, and railroads—played a major role in westward expansion.
- Western cities mushroomed, first along rivers and then on the Great Lakes.

The Growth of the Cities

The transportation revolution accelerated the growth of towns and cities. Indeed, the forty years before the Civil War, 1820 to 1860, saw the most rapid urbanization in U.S. history. By 1860, New York City's population had rocketed from 124,000 to 800,000. Even more spectacular was the transformation of sleepy villages into bustling towns.

City and town growth was particularly fast in the West. The War of 1812 stimulated manufacturing and transformed villages into towns, as did the agricultural boom and the introduction of steamboats after 1815. Virtually all the major western cities were river ports. Of these, Pittsburgh, Cincinnati, Louisville, and New Orleans were the most prominent. Pittsburgh was a manufacturing center, but the others were commercial hubs flooded by people eager to make money.

What the transportation revolution gave, it could also take away. The completion of the Erie Canal shifted the center of western economic activity toward the Great Lakes. The result was a gradual decline in the importance of river cities and a rise in the importance of lake cities such as Buffalo, Cleveland, Detroit, Chicago, and Milwaukee. In 1830, nearly 75 percent of all western city-dwellers lived in the river ports of New Orleans, Louisville, Cincinnati, and Pittsburgh; by 1840 the proportion had dropped to 20 percent.

INDUSTRIAL BEGINNINGS

What caused the rise of industrialization?

Industrialization gave an added boost to the growth of cities and towns. In any way possible, Americans sought to counter Britain's full-generation lead in building factories; Britain in turn banned the emigration of its skilled mechanics. However, one of those mechanics, **Samuel Slater,** was able to reach the United States in 1789. He helped design and build the first cotton mill in the United States the following year. The mill's work force mushroomed from nine to one hundred, and his mills multiplied. The pace of industrialization quickened in the 1810s and 1820s, especially in cotton textiles and shoes.

Samuel Slater British "mechanic" who carried plans for a textile mill to the United States; began the American textile industry

Industrialization was uneven. There was little in the South, where planters preferred to invest in land and slaves, and much in New England, where poor soil made agriculture an even poorer investment. Generally, industrialization involved three steps: the subdivision of tasks, the gathering of workers in large factories, and the use of high-speed machines to replace handwork.

Industrialization changed lives. Many benefited from industrialization as former luxury goods became cheaper. And while cheap machine-made goods brought luxuries within the reach of working people, they also undermined skilled artisans. Most early factory workers were recruited from farms, where they had set their own pace and took breaks as tasks were completed. In contrast, machines and the clock dictated the factory worker's pace. Finally, industrialization led to specialization; farmers could now concentrate on farming and buy clothes, shoes, and other products they had previously made.

Causes of Industrialization

A host of factors stimulated industrialization. Merchants barred from foreign trade by the Embargo Act of 1807 redirected their capital into factories. After the War of 1812, acceptance of tariffs was widespread. Protected from foreign competition, New England's textile output rose from 4 million yards in 1817 to 323 million yards by 1840. New England's farm families were deserting worn-out soils for full-time manufacturing. And the transportation revolution gave manufacturers easier access to markets in the South and West.

Technology played a major role. Lacking craft organizations that tied artisans to a single trade, Americans could freely experiment with machines outside their own craft. Americans also improved on foreign ideas and techniques. For example, in 1798 Eli Whitney, inventor of the cotton gin, gained a government contract to produce ten thousand muskets within a two-year period by using interchangeable parts, an idea originally developed in France. Although Whitney missed his deadline by more than a decade, his idea captured the imagination of many American leaders and foreshadowed the rise of a full-scale industrial economy.

Textile Towns in New England

New England became America's first industrial region. The trade wars leading up to the War of 1812 had devastated the Northeast's traditional economy and stimulated capital investment in manufacturing. New England's many swift-flowing rivers were ideal sources of waterpower for mills. The westward migration of New England's young men, unable to wrest a living from rocky soil, left a surplus of young women who supplied cheap industrial labor. The establishment of the Boston Manufacturing Company in 1813 opened a new chapter in U.S. manufacturing. Backed by ample capital, the Boston Company built textile mills in the Massachusetts towns of **Lowell** and **Waltham;** by 1836 the company employed more than six thousand workers.

Unlike Slater's mills, the Waltham and Lowell factories turned out more finished products, thus elbowing aside Slater's cottage industry. Slater had tried to preserve tradition by hiring entire families to work at his mills—the men to raise crops, the women and children to toil in the mills. In contrast, 80 percent of the workers in the Lowell and Waltham mills were unmarried women who were fifteen to thirty years old. Hired managers and company regulations, rather than families, provided discipline. Workers had to live in company boarding houses or approved private homes, attend Sabbath services, observe a 10:00 p.m. curfew, and accept the company's "moral police." These regulations were designed to give mills a good reputation so that families would continue to send their daughters to work there.

Conditions in the mills were dreadful. To provide the humidity necessary to keep the threads from snapping, overseers nailed factory windows shut and sprayed the air with water. Operatives also had to contend with flying dust and the deafening roar of the machines. Keener competition and a worsening economy in the late 1830s led mill owners to reduce wages and speed up work schedules.

Owners rarely visited factories; their agents, all men, gave orders to the workers, mainly women. In 1834 and again in 1836, women at the Lowell mills quit work to

Lowell, Waltham
Massachusetts towns where two large textile mills were established as early experiments in factory manufacturing

Jack Naylor Collection/Picture Research Consultants & Archives

Mill Girl Around 1850
This girl most likely worked in a Massachusetts textile mill, at either Lowell or Waltham. Her swollen and rough hands suggest that she was a "warper," one of the jobs usually given to children. Warpers were responsible for constantly straightening out the strands of cotton or wool as they entered the loom.

protest low wages. The largest strikes in American history to that point, they not only pitted workers against management but also women against men.

The Waltham and Lowell mills were much larger than most factories; as late as 1860, the average industrial establishment employed only eight workers. Outside of textiles, many industries continued to depend on industrial "outwork." For example, before the introduction of the sewing machine led to the concentration of all aspects of shoe manufacture in large factories in the 1850s, women often sewed parts of shoes at home and sent the piecework to factories for finishing.

Artisans and Workers in Mid-Atlantic Cities

The skilled artisans of New York City and Philadelphia tried to protect their interests by forming trade unions and "workingmen's" political parties. Initially, they sought to restore privileges and working conditions that artisans had once enjoyed, but gradually they joined forces with unskilled workers. When coal heavers in Philadelphia struck for a ten-hour day in 1835, carpenters, cigar makers, leather workers, and other artisans joined in what became the first general strike in the United States. The emergence of organized worker protests underscored the mixed blessings of economic development. Whereas some people prospered, others found their economic position deteriorating. By 1830 many Americans were questioning whether their nation was truly a land of equality.

CHECKING IN

- Multiple factors stimulated industrialization, including protective tariffs, available capital, and advances in technology.
- Textile mills made New England America's first industrial region.
- Mills like those at Waltham and Lowell relied heavily on the labor of young women.
- "Outwork" dominated early industrialization outside the textile industry.
- Industrialization brought mixed results; as many workers' economic position deteriorated, new questions arose about equality in the United States.

EQUALITY AND INEQUALITY

What caused urban poverty in this period?

The idea that one (white) man was as good as another became the national creed in antebellum America. For example, servants insisted on being viewed as neighbors invited to assist in running the household rather than as permanent subordinates. Politicians never lost an opportunity to celebrate artisans and farmers as the equal of lawyers and bankers. A French visitor observed that the wealthiest Americans pretended to respect equality by riding in public in ordinary rather than luxurious carriages.

The market and transportation revolutions, however, were placing new pressure on the ideal of equality between 1815 and 1840. At the same time that improved transportation enabled some eastern farmers to migrate to the richer soils of the West, it became difficult for those left behind to compete with the cheaper grain carried east by canals and railroads. Many eastern farmers now had to move to cities to take whatever work they could find, often as casual day laborers on the docks or in small workshops.

Urban Inequality: The Rich and the Poor

The gap between rich and poor widened in the first half of the nineteenth century. In cities, a small fraction of the people owned a huge share of the wealth. For example, in New York City, the richest 4 percent owned nearly half the wealth in 1828 and more than two-thirds by 1845. Splendid residences and social clubs set the rich apart. In

1828, over half of the five hundred wealthiest families in New York City lived on just eight of its more than 250 streets. By the late 1820s, the city had a club so exclusive that it was called simply The Club.

Although commentators celebrated the self-made man and his rise "from rags to riches," few actually fit this pattern. Less than 5 percent of the wealthy had started life poor; almost 90 percent of well-off people had been born rich. Clearly, the old-fashioned way to wealth was to inherit it, to marry more of it, and to invest it wisely. Occasional rags-to-riches stories like that of John Jacob Astor and his fur-trading empire sustained the myth, but it was mainly a myth.

At the opposite end of the social ladder were the poor. By today's standards, most antebellum Americans were poor. They lived close to the edge of misery and depended heavily on their children's labor to meet expenses. But when antebellum Americans spoke of poverty, they were referring to "pauperism," a state of dependency or inability to fend for oneself. Epidemics of yellow fever and cholera could devastate families. A frozen canal, river, or harbor spelled unemployment for boatmen and dock workers. The absence of health insurance and old-age pensions condemned many infirm and aged people to pauperism.

Contemporaries usually classified all such people as the "deserving" poor and contrasted them with the "undeserving" poor, such as indolent loafers and drunkards whose poverty was seen as self-willed. Most moralists assumed that since pauperism resulted either from circumstances beyond anyone's control, or from voluntary decisions to squander money on liquor, it would not pass from generation to generation.

This assumption was comforting but also misleading. A class of people who could not escape poverty was emerging in the major cities during the first half of the nineteenth century. One source was immigration. As early as 1801, a New York newspaper called attention to the arrival of boatloads of immigrants with large families, without money or health, and "expiring from the want of sustenance."

The poorest white immigrants were from Ireland, where British landlords had evicted peasants from the land and converted it to commercial use. Severed from the land, the Irish increasingly became a nation of wanderers. By the early 1830s, the great majority of canal workers in the North were Irish immigrants. Without their backbreaking labor, the Erie Canal would never have been built. Other Irish congregated in New York's infamous Five Points district.

The Irish were not only poor but were also Catholics, a faith despised by the Protestant majority in the United States. But even the Protestant poor came in for rough treatment in the years between 1815 and 1840. The more that Americans convinced themselves that success was within everyone's grasp, the more they were inclined to hold the poor responsible for their own misery. Ironically, even as many Americans blamed the poor for being poor, they practiced discrimination that kept some groups mired in enduring poverty. Nowhere was this more true than in the case of northern free blacks.

Free Blacks in the North   Prejudice against blacks was deeply ingrained in white society throughout the nation. Although slavery had largely disappeared in the North by 1820, discriminatory laws remained. The voting rights of African-Americans were severely restricted; for example, New York eliminated property requirements for whites but kept them for blacks. There were attempts to bar free blacks from migrating. And segregation prevailed in northern schools, jails, and hospitals. By 1850, blacks could vote on equal terms with whites in only one city, Boston.

Of all restrictions on free blacks, the most damaging was the social pressure that forced them into the least-skilled and lowest-paying occupations. Although a few free blacks accumulated moderate wealth, free blacks in general were only half as likely as other city-dwellers to own real estate.

One important response of African-Americans to discrimination was the establishment of their own churches. When a group of free blacks was ejected from a Philadelphia church, they ultimately established the first black-run Protestant denomination, the **African Methodist Episcopal Church,** in 1816. The A.M.E. rapidly expanded to encompass a territory bounded by Washington, DC, Pittsburgh, and New York City. Its members campaigned against slavery, provided education for black children, and formed mutual-aid societies.

African Methodist Episcopal Church First American denomination established by and for African-Americans

Just as northern African-Americans left white churches to form their own, free blacks gradually acquired some control over the education of their children. Northern city governments made little provision for the education of free persons of color, at first leaving northern blacks dependent on the philanthropy of sympathetic whites to educate their children. But the 1820s and 1830s witnessed an explosion of black self-hope societies devoted to encouraging black education and run by graduates of the African Free School.

The "Middling Classes"

Most antebellum Americans were neither fabulously rich nor grindingly poor, but instead were part of the **"middling classes."** Even though the wealthy owned an increasing proportion of wealth, per capita income grew at 1.5 percent annually between 1840 and 1860, and the standard of living generally rose after 1800.

"middling classes" Americans who were neither fabulously rich nor grindingly poor

Americans applied the term "middling classes" to families headed by professionals, small merchants, landowning farmers, and self-employed artisans. Commentators portrayed these people as living stable and secure lives. In reality, life in the middle often was unpredictable. The economy of antebellum America created greater opportunities for success and for failure. An enterprising import merchant, Allan Melville, the father of novelist Herman Melville, did well until the late 1820s, when his business sagged. By 1830, he was "destitute of resources and without a shilling." In 1832 he died, broken in spirit and nearly insane.

Artisans shared the perils of life in the middling classes. During the colonial period, many had attained the ideal of self-employment, owning their tools, taking orders, making their products, and training their children and apprentices in the craft. By 1840, in contrast, artisans had entered a new world of economic relationships. Some carpenters and shoemakers, usually those with access to capital, became contractors and small manufacturers. In effect, the old class of artisans was splitting into two new groupings. On one side were artisans who had become entrepreneurs; on the other, journeymen with little prospect of self-employment.

CHECKING IN

- The gap between rich and poor widened, especially in cities.
- Americans generally blamed the poor for being poor.
- Free blacks saw their rights and economic position erode even further.
- The "middling classes" increased, but many did not achieve stability.
- More than ever, transience characterized American society.

An additional characteristic of the middling classes, one they shared with the poor, was a high degree of transience, or spatial mobility. The transportation revolution made it easier for Americans to purchase services as well as goods and spurred many young men to abandon farming for the professions. The itinerant clergyman riding an old nag to conduct revivals became a familiar figure in newly settled areas. Even well-established lawyers and judges spent part of each year riding from one county courthouse to another.

Transience affected the lives of most Americans. Farmers exhausted their land by intensive cultivation of cash crops and then moved on. City-dwellers moved frequently as they changed jobs—public transportation lagged far behind the spread of the cities. A survey on September 6, 1851, found that on that day 41,729 entered the city of Boston while 42,313 left. Most of these were searching for work, a frequent necessity for the middling classes as well as the poor.

THE REVOLUTION IN SOCIAL RELATIONSHIPS

How did the rise of the market economy and industrialization change relationships within families and communities?

Following the War of 1812, the growth of interregional trade, commercial agriculture, and manufacturing disrupted traditional social relationships and forged new ones. Two broad changes took place. First, Americans began to question traditional forms of authority and to embrace individualism; once the term had meant nothing more than selfishness, but now it connoted positive qualities such as self-reliance and the ability of each person to judge his or her own best interests. Wealth, education, and social position no longer received automatic deference. Second, Americans created new foundations for authority. For example, women developed the idea that they possessed a "separate sphere" of authority in the home, and individuals formed voluntary associations to influence the direction of society.

The Attack on the Professions

Intense criticism of lawyers, physicians, and ministers exemplified the assault on, and erosion of, traditional authority. Between 1800 and 1840, the wave of religious revivals known as the Second Great Awakening (see Chapter 10) sparked fierce attacks on the professions. Revivalists blasted the clergy for creating complex theologies, drinking expensive wines, and fleecing the people. One revivalist accused physicians of inventing fancy Latin and Greek names for diseases to disguise their inability to cure them.

These jabs at the learned professions peaked between 1820 and 1850. Samuel Thomson led a successful movement to eliminate all barriers to entry into the medical profession, including educational requirements. By 1845, every state had repealed laws requiring licenses or education to practice medicine. In religion, ministers found little job security as finicky congregations dismissed clergymen whose theology displeased them. In turn, ministers became more ambitious and more inclined to leave poor, small churches for large, wealthy ones.

The increasing commercialization of the economy led to both more professionals and more attacks on them. In 1765, America had one medical school; by 1860 there were sixty-five. The newly minted doctors and lawyers had neither deep roots in the towns where they practiced nor convincing claims to social superiority. "Men dropped down into their places as from clouds," one critic wrote. "Nobody knew who or what they were, except as they claimed."

This questioning of authority was particularly sharp on the frontier. Easterners sneered that every man in the West claimed to be a "judge," "general," "colonel," or "squire." Where neither law nor custom sanctioned claims of superiority, would-be gentlemen substituted an exaggerated sense of personal honor. Obsessed with their fragile status, many reacted testily to the slightest insult. Dueling became a widespread frontier practice. At a Kentucky militia parade in 1819, for example, an officer's dog jogged onto the field and sat at his master's knee. Enraged by this breach of military decorum, another officer ran the dog through with his sword. A week later, the two men met with pistols at ten paces. One was killed, the other maimed for life.

The Challenge to Family Authority

Meanwhile, children quietly questioned parental authority. The era's economic change forced many young people to choose between staying at home to help their parents and venturing out on their own. This desire for independence fueled westward migration as well. Restless single men led the way. Two young men from Virginia put it succinctly: "All the promise of life now seemed to us to be at the other end of the rainbow—somewhere else—anywhere else but on the farm."

As young antebellum Americans tried to escape close parental supervision, courtship and marriage patterns also changed. No longer dependent on parents for land, young people wanted to choose their own mate. Romantic love, rather than parental preference, increasingly determined marital decisions.

Courtesy Childs Gallery, Boston

The Country Parson Disturbed at Breakfast

This young couple's decision to wed seems to have been made on the spur of the moment. As young men and women became more independent of parental control, they gave their impulses freer play.

One sign of young people's growing control over courtship and marriage was the declining likelihood that the young women of a family would marry in their birth order. Traditionally, fathers wanted their daughters to marry in the order of their birth to avoid any suspicion that there was something wrong with one or more of them. By the end of the eighteenth century, daughters were making their own decisions about marriage, and the custom of birth order vanished. Another mark of the times was the growing popularity of long engagements; young women were reluctant to tie the knot, fearing that marriage would snuff out their independence. Equally striking was the increasing number of young women who chose not to marry.

Thus, young people lived more and more in a world of their own. Moralists reacted with alarm and flooded the country with books of advice to youth, which stressed the same message: newly independent young people should develop self-control and "character." The self-made adult began with the self-made youth.

Wives and Husbands

Another class of advice books counseled wives and husbands about their rights and duties. These books were a sign that relations between spouses were also changing. Young men and women accustomed to making their own decisions would understandably approach marriage as a compact among equals. Although inequalities within marriage remained—especially the legal tradition that married women could not own property—the trend was toward a form of equality.

One source of this change was the rise of the doctrine of **separate spheres.** Traditionally, women had been viewed as subordinate to men in all spheres of life. Now middle-class men and women developed a kind of separate-but-equal doctrine that portrayed men as superior in making money and governing the world, and women as superior for their moral influence on family members.

Most important was the shift of responsibility for child rearing from fathers to mothers. During the eighteenth century, church sermons reminded fathers of their duty to govern the family; by the 1830s, child-rearing manuals were addressed to mothers rather than fathers. Advice books instructed mothers to discipline children by withdrawing love rather than using corporal punishment. A whipped child might obey but would remain sullen and bitter; gentler methods would penetrate the child's heart, making the child want to do the right thing.

The idea of a separate women's sphere blended with the image of family and home as secluded refuges from a disorderly society. Popular culture painted an alluring portrait of the pleasures of home in such sentimental songs as "Home, Sweet Home" and such poems as "A Visit from St. Nicholas." Even the physical appearance of houses changed. The prominent architect Andrew Jackson Downing published plans for peaceful single-family homes to offset the hurly-burly of daily life. "There must be nooks about it," he wrote, "where one would love to linger; windows, where one can enjoy the quiet landscape at his leisure; cozy rooms, where all fireside joys are invited to dwell."

But reality diverged far from this ideal. Ownership of a quiet single-family home lay beyond the reach of most Americans, even much of the middle class. Farm homes, far from tranquil, were beehives of activity, and city-dwellers often had to sacrifice privacy by taking in boarders to supplement family income.

separate spheres Popular doctrine that emphasized women's morality and authoritative role within the home

The decline of cottage industry and the growing number of men (merchants, lawyers, brokers) who worked outside the home gave women more time to lavish attention on children. Married women found these ideals sources of power. A subtle implication of the doctrine of separate spheres was that women should control not only the discipline of children but also the number they would bear.

In 1800, the United States had one of the highest birthrates ever recorded. The average American woman bore 7.04 children. Children were valuable for the labor they provided and for the relief from the burdens of survival that they could bring to aging parents. The more children, the better, most couples assumed. However, the growth of the market economy raised questions about children's economic value. Unlike a farmer, a merchant or lawyer could not send his children to work at the age of seven or eight. The average woman was bearing only 5.02 children by 1850, and 3.98 by 1900. The birthrate remained high among blacks and many immigrant groups, but it fell drastically among native-born whites, particularly in towns and cities.

Abstinence, *coitus interruptus* (the withdrawal of the penis before ejaculation), and abortion were common birth-control methods. Remedies for "female irregularity"—unwanted pregnancy—were widely advertised. The rubber condom and the vaginal diaphragm were familiar to many Americans by 1865. Whatever the method, husbands and wives jointly decided to limit family size. Husbands could note that the economic value of children was declining; wives, meanwhile, noted that having fewer children would give them more time to nurture each one and thereby to carry out their domestic duties.

Supporters of the ideal of separate spheres did not advocate full legal equality for women. Indeed, the ideal of separate spheres was an explicit alternative to legal equality. But the concept enhanced women's power within marriage by giving them influence in such vital issues as child rearing and the frequency of pregnancies.

Horizontal Allegiances and the Rise of Voluntary Associations

As some forms of authority weakened, Americans devised new ways by which individuals could extend their influence over others. The antebellum era witnessed the widespread substitution of *horizontal* allegiances for *vertical* allegiances. In vertical allegiances, authority flowed from the top down. Subordinates identified their interests with those of superiors rather than with others in the same subordinate roles. The traditional patriarchal family was an example of vertical allegiance, as was the traditional apprentice system.

Although vertical relationships did not disappear, they became less important in people's lives. Increasingly, relationships were more likely to be marked by horizontal allegiances that linked those in a similar position. For example, in large textile mills, operatives discovered they had more in common with one another than with their managers and overseers. Similarly, married women formed maternal associations to exchange advice about child rearing, and young men developed associations with other young men. Maternal and debating societies exemplified the American zeal for **voluntary associations**—associations that arose apart

voluntary association
Horizontal allegiance (as opposed to superior-subordinate relationship) of individuals with similar interests or circumstances

CHECKING IN

- As the market economy took hold, American society placed greater emphasis on individualism.

- As part of a general questioning of authority, most Americans viewed professions such as law and medicine with increasing skepticism.

- Young people increasingly rebelled against family authority.

- The doctrine of "separate spheres" appeared as part of a transformation of ideas about gender roles.

- Voluntary associations flourished.

Alexis de Tocqueville Young Frenchman whose *Democracy in America* provides rich insight into the United States in the 1830s

from government and sought to accomplish some goal of value to their members. **Alexis de Tocqueville,** a brilliant French observer, described them as "public associations in civil life."

Voluntary associations encouraged sociability as transients and newcomers came together, usually in associations based on gender or race. These associations served as vehicles for members to assert their influence. Temperance societies fought to abolish alcohol, while moral-reform societies combated prostitution. Just as strikes in Lowell in the 1830s were a form of collective action by working women, moral-reform societies represented collective action by middle-class women to increase their influence in society.

Chapter Summary

What caused the surge of westward migration after the War of 1812? *(page 199)*

An agricultural boom lured people west, as did the swelling demand for cotton created by the cotton gin. Westward movement carried the American population across the Mississippi River by 1820, raising both hopes and problems. A new society was rising in the West, one that viewed itself as more democratic and more egalitarian than the East. Native Americans were ruthlessly pushed aside or "relocated" to make room for white settlers.

What changes were linked to the rise of the market economy? *(page 204)*

Western farmers soon entered the market economy, which was both lucrative and volatile. They began to plant cash crops and to purchase manufactures. Although federal land policy was meant to sell parcels to small farmers, speculators snapped up much of the land. The speculative boom collapsed in the Panic of 1819, but the movement westward continued, with the transportation revolution opening the way for settlers and products. And cities mushroomed, especially in the Great Lakes area.

What caused the rise of industrialization? *(page 209)*

Protective tariffs, technology, and the ready availability of capital stimulated industrial development, especially in New England, where the textile industry led the way. Young women formed the primary work force at many New England mills, but elsewhere a piecemeal system of work predominated. Results of this early industrialization were uneven, particularly in terms of equality and inequality.

What caused urban poverty in this period? *(page 211)*

In America's cities, the gap between rich and poor widened; most people held the poor responsible for their poverty. While the "middling classes" increased, free blacks saw even more of their rights slip away.

KEY TERMS

National Road *(p. 201)*
"Five Civilized Tribes" *(p. 201)*
Cherokee Nation v. *Georgia (p. 203)*
Worcester v. *Georgia (p. 203)*
Trail of Tears *(p. 203)*
market economy *(p. 204)*
transportation revolution *(p. 206)*
Clermont (p. 206)
Erie Canal *(p. 207)*
Samuel Slater *(p. 209)*
Lowell, Waltham *(p. 210)*
African Methodist Episcopal Church *(p. 213)*
"middling classes" *(p. 213)*
separate spheres *(p. 216)*
voluntary association *(p. 217)*
Alexis de Tocqueville *(p. 218)*

How did the rise of the market economy and industrialization change relationships within families and communities? (page 214)

Individualism increasingly characterized American society, while most Americans questioned authority in general and viewed the professions with skepticism. Young people more and more defied or ignored familial authority. Women both benefited from and were harmed by the doctrine of "separate spheres." Voluntary, horizontal organizations thrived.

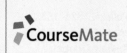
CourseMate

Go to the CourseMate website at **www.cengagebrain.com** for additional study tools and review materials—including audio and video clips—for this chapter.

Democratic Politics, Religious Revival, and Reform

CHAPTER 10

1824–1840

First State Election in Michigan

CHAPTER PREVIEW

The Rise of Democratic Politics, 1824–1832
How did the democratization of American politics contribute to the rise of Andrew Jackson?

The Bank Controversy and the Second Party System, 1833–1840
What were the major factors in the rise of the second party system?

The Rise of Popular Religion
What new assumptions about human nature lay behind the religious movements of the period?

The Age of Reform
Did the reform movements aim primarily at making Americans more free or more orderly?

One cold Sunday in March 1841, schoolteacher Dorothea Dix was teaching a religious class for women prisoners in the House of Corrections at East Cambridge, Massachusetts. After class, she was shocked to discover a number of insane inmates shivering in unheated cells. When she confronted the jailer, he explained that providing stoves for "lunatics" was not only dangerous but unnecessary, because they did not suffer from cold. The outraged Dix went to court and successfully petitioned to have stoves provided for the jail's insane inmates.

For two years, Dix traveled the state documenting the conditions of the mentally ill. In 1843, she presented to the legislature a report or "memorial" describing the insane confined "in cages, closets, cellars, stalls, pens! Chained, naked, beaten with rods, and lashed into obedience." The Massachusetts legislature responded by funding an expansion of the state's

Detroit Institute of Arts, USA / Gift of Mrs Samuel T. Carson / The Bridgeman Art Library

mental hospital. Encouraged by her success, Dix spent the next fifteen years traveling throughout the nation, documenting abuses and presenting her memorials. By the time of the Civil War, twenty-eight states, four cities, and the federal government had constructed public mental institutions.

What drove this sickly woman to endure dangerous travel, confront the terrible living conditions of the mentally ill, and endure the ridicule of those who found her crusade "unladylike"? Dorothea Dix's reform impulse drew from a deep well of religious conviction. She embraced theological perfectionism: the belief in the innate moral capacities of all men and women and their ability to strive toward spiritual perfection. Even the raving lunatic, in Dix's eyes, carried a spark of inner divinity that should be nurtured.

Dorothea Dix's perfectionist faith was shared by other reformers who regarded asylums—such as penitentiaries, almshouses, and orphan homes—as the solution for many of society's ills. If humankind was fundamentally good, they reasoned, then poor environments must be at fault when people went wrong. The solution was to place deviants in specially designed environments that imposed strict order on their disorderly lives and minds.

Spread primarily by the wave of religious revivals known as the Second Great Awakening, theological perfectionism shaped a host of reforms that swept the United States after 1820, including temperance, antislavery, education, women's rights, and utopian communitarianism. Most of these movements, like Dix's crusade for the mentally ill, raised fundamental questions about the proper balance of order and freedom in the new American democracy. Such questions also lay at the heart of the new two-party system that would reshape American political life during the presidential terms of Andrew Jackson.

THE RISE OF DEMOCRATIC POLITICS, 1824–1832

How did the democratization of American politics contribute to the rise of Andrew Jackson?

In 1824, Andrew Jackson and John Quincy Adams were both members of Jefferson's Republican Party; by 1834, Jackson was a Democrat and Adams, a Whig. Tensions spawned by industrialization, the rise of the Cotton South, and westward expansion split Jefferson's old party. Generally, supporters of states' rights joined the **Democrats,** and advocates of national support for economic development became **Whigs.**

Democrat or Whig, leaders had to adapt to the rising notion that politics should be an expression of the will of the common people rather than an activity that gentlemen conducted on the people's behalf. Americans still looked up to their leaders, but the leaders could no longer look down on the people.

Democrats Members of the political party that emerged from Jefferson's Republican Party; one of two dominant parties in the second party system

Whigs Initially called National Republicans; members of the other dominant party

Democratic Ferment

Political democratization took several forms. One of the most common was the abolition of the requirement that voters own property; no western states had such a requirement, and eastern states gradually liberalized their laws. Moreover, written

Chronology

1824	John Quincy Adams elected president by the House of Representatives
1826	American Temperance Society organized
1828	Andrew Jackson elected president; "Tariff of Abominations"; John Calhoun anonymously writes *South Carolina Exposition and Protest*
1830	Jackson's Maysville Road Bill veto; Indian Removal Act
1830–1831	Charles G. Finney's Rochester revival
1831	William Lloyd Garrison starts *The Liberator*
1832	Jackson vetoes recharter of the Bank of the United States; Jackson reelected president; South Carolina Nullification Proclamation
1833	Force Bill; Compromise Tariff; American Anti-Slavery Society founded; South Carolina nullifies the Force Bill
1834	Whig party organized
1836	Specie Circular; Martin Van Buren elected president
1837	Elijah Lovejoy murdered by proslavery mob; Grimké sisters set out on lecture tour of New England
1838	Sarah Grimké's *Letters on the Condition of Women and the Equality of the Sexes* released
1840	Independent Treasury Act passed; William Henry Harrison elected president; first Washington Temperance Society started
1841	Dorothea Dix begins exposé of prison conditions
1844	Brook Farm community founded; Joseph Smith murdered by anti-Mormon mob
1848	Seneca Falls Convention

ballots replaced the custom of voting aloud, which had enabled elites to influence their subordinates at the polls. Appointive offices became elective. Though the Electoral College survived, the choice of presidential electors by state legislatures gave way to direct election by the voters. By 1832, only South Carolina followed the old custom.

The fierce tug of war between Republicans and Federalists that began in the 1790s had taught both parties to court voters. At grand party-run barbecues in the North and South, potential voters washed down free clams and oysters with free beer and whiskey.

Political democratization had its limitations. The parties were still run from the top down as late as 1820, with candidates nominated by caucus (a conference of party members in the legislature). And political democracy did not extend to allowing either women or free blacks the right to vote.

The Election of 1824 and the Adams Presidency

In 1824, sectional tensions ended the Era of Good Feelings when five Republican candidates vied for the presidency. John Quincy Adams emerged as New England's favorite. John C. Calhoun and William Crawford fought for southern support. Out of the West marched the ambitious Henry Clay of Kentucky, confident that his American System of protective tariffs and internal improvements would win votes from both eastern manufacturing interests and western

TABLE 10.1   THE ELECTION OF 1824

CANDIDATE	PARTY	ELECTORAL VOTE	POPULAR VOTE	PERCENTAGE OF POPULAR VOTE
John Quincy Adams	Democratic-Republican	84	108,740	30.5
Andrew Jackson	Democratic-Republican	99	153,544	43.1
William H. Crawford	Democratic-Republican	41	46,618	13.1
Henry Clay	Democratic-Republican	37	47,136	13.2

agriculturalists. Opposing Henry Clay was the popular war hero, Andrew Jackson of Tennessee.

A paralyzing stroke soon removed Crawford from the race. Calhoun assessed Jackson's support and prudently decided to run unopposed for the vice presidency. In the election, Jackson won more popular and electoral votes than any other candidate but failed to gain the majority required by the Constitution. Therefore, the election was thrown into the House of Representatives. Clay threw his support to New Englander John Quincy Adams, who won the election. When the new president appointed Clay his secretary of state, Jackson's supporters accused Adams of stealing victory by entering a "corrupt bargain" with Clay, an allegation that formed a dark cloud over Adams's presidency.

The guiding principle of the Adams presidency was social improvement. In his First Annual Message to Congress, he laid out his plans to improve public education, expand commerce, and fund internal improvements. But Adams's ambitions met with growing political opposition. Strict constructionists opposed internal improvements on constitutional grounds. Southerners protested Adams's plan to participate in a pan-American conference because it required association with regimes that had abolished slavery, including the black republic of Haiti. Instead of building new bases of support, Adams clung to the increasingly obsolete view of the president as custodian of the public good, aloof from partisan politics. Idealistic though his view was, it guaranteed him a single-term presidency.

The Rise of Andrew Jackson and the Election of 1828

As President Adams's popularity declined, Andrew Jackson's rose. While seasoned politicians distrusted his notoriously hot temper and his penchant for duels, Jackson was still a popular hero for his victory over the British in the Battle of New Orleans. And because he had fought in the American Revolution as a boy, Jackson seemed to many Americans a living link to a more virtuous past.

The presidential campaign of 1828 began almost as soon as Adams was inaugurated. Jackson's supporters began to put together a modern political machine based on local committees, partisan newspapers, and public rallies. By 1826, towns and villages across the country buzzed with political activity. Because supporters of Jackson, Adams, and Clay all still called themselves Republicans, few realized that a new political system was being born. The man most alert to the new currents was Martin Van Buren, who would be Jackson's vice president and then president.

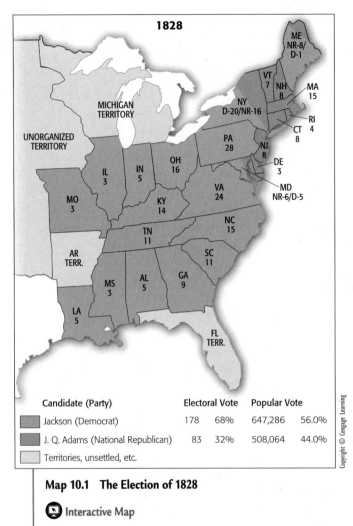

1828

Candidate (Party) | Electoral Vote | | Popular Vote |
--- | --- | --- | --- | ---
Jackson (Democrat) | 178 | 68% | 647,286 | 56.0%
J. Q. Adams (National Republican) | 83 | 32% | 508,064 | 44.0%
Territories, unsettled, etc. | | | |

Map 10.1   The Election of 1828

Interactive Map

Van Buren exemplified a new breed of politician. A tavern keeper's son, he had worked his way up through New York politics and created a powerful statewide machine, the Albany Regency, composed of men like himself from the middling and lower ranks. His archrival, DeWitt Clinton, was everything Van Buren was not—tall, handsome, and aristocratic. But Van Buren's geniality put ordinary people at ease.

The election of 1824 had convinced Van Buren of the need for two-party competition. Without the discipline imposed by party competition, the Republicans had splintered into sectional factions. The country would be better served, he thought, by reducing the shades of opinion in the country to just two so that parties could clash and a clear winner would emerge. Jackson was the logical leader, and the presidential nominee, of one new party, which would become known as the Democratic Party; its opponents, calling themselves National Republicans, nominated Adams. The second American party system was taking shape.

The 1828 campaign was a vicious, mudslinging affair. The National Republicans called Jackson a murderer for killing several men in duels and military executions. They charged him with adultery for living with Rachel Robards when she was still married to another man. Jackson's supporters responded by accusing Adams of wearing silk underwear, spending public funds on a billiard table for the White House, and offering a beautiful American prostitute to the Russian tsar.

Although both sides slung mud, Jackson's men had better aim. Charges by Adams's supporters that Jackson was an illiterate backwoodsman backfired, increasing his popularity by casting him as a common man. Jackson's supporters presented him as the common man incarnate—his mind unclouded by learning, his morals simple and true, his will fierce and resolute. Adams, in contrast, was an aristocrat, a scholar whose learning obscured the truth, a writer rather than a fighter.

The election swept Jackson into office with twice Adams's electoral votes. The popular vote, which was much closer, reflected the strong sectional bases of the new parties. Adams doubled Jackson's vote in New England, while Jackson doubled Adams's vote in the South and nearly tripled it in the Southwest.

Jackson in Office

Jackson rode to the presidency on a wave of opposition to corruption and privilege. One of his first moves was to institute "rotation in office"—the removal of officeholders of the rival party. Nearly half of the higher-ranking civil servants were summarily fired. Although his opponents called it the **"spoils system,"** Jackson defended rotation in office on the basis of democracy: The duties of most officeholders were so simple that as many plain people as possible should have the chance to work for the government.

"spoils system" Practice of rewarding political supporters with public office

Jackson's positions on internal improvements and tariffs sparked even more intense controversy. He did not oppose all federal aid for internal improvements. However, Jackson suspected that public officials used such aid to win political support by handing out favors. To end such corruption, he flatly rejected federal support for roads within states. In 1830, when a bill came before him that would have provided federal money for a road between Maysville and Lexington, Kentucky, Jackson vetoed it.

The tariff issue tested Jackson's support even in the South, where the Indian Removal Act of 1830 (see Chapter 9) enhanced his popularity. In 1828, while Adams was still president, some of Jackson's supporters in Congress had helped pass a high protective tariff favorable to western agriculture and New England manufacturing. Jackson's supporters had calculated that southerners would blame the Adams administration for this **"Tariff of Abominations."** Instead, they leveled their fury at Jackson.

"Tariff of Abominations" Protective tariff of 1828 that infuriated southerners; spawned the Nullification Crisis

Nullification

The 1828 tariff opened a major rift between Jackson and his vice president, John C. Calhoun. Although he had entered Congress as a "war hawk" and had championed nationalism early in his career, Calhoun had gradually become a states' rights sectionalist. He had supported the tariff of 1816 but would fiercely oppose that of 1828.

Calhoun also burned with ambition to be president. Since Jackson had stated that he would serve only one term, Calhoun, as vice president, assumed that he would succeed Jackson. To do so, he needed to maintain the support of the South, which was increasingly taking an antitariff stance. Calhoun's own state, South Carolina, had suffered economic decline throughout the 1820s; its citizens blamed protective tariffs. Tariffs, according to Calhoun's constituents, not only drove up the price of manufactured goods; they also threatened to damage the American market for British textiles and thus reduce British demand for southern cotton.

Calhoun also opposed the tariff on constitutional grounds. He embraced the view, set forth in the Virginia and Kentucky Resolutions of 1798–1799, that the Union was a compact by which the states had conferred limited and specified powers on the federal government. He insisted that the only constitutional tariff was one that raised money for

Memphis Brooks Museum of Art, Memphis, TN, Memphis Park Commission Purchase

***Andrew Jackson,* by Ralph Earl**
Jackson during the Nullification Crisis, looking serene in the uniform of a major-general and determined to face down the greatest challenge to his presidency.

National Portrait Gallery, Smithsonian Institution/Art Resource, NY

John C. Calhoun, **by Charles Bird King, c. 1825**

The magnetic Calhoun, Jackson's vice president, broke with Jackson over nullification and the Peggy Eaton affair, and resigned the vice presidency in 1832.

Nullification Crisis
Controversy over nullification that pitted Jackson against Calhoun and led to talk of secession by southerners

the common national defense. Calhoun expressed these views anonymously in the widely circulated *South Carolina Exposition and Protest* (1828), which argued that aggrieved states had the right to nullify that tariff within their borders.

Like Calhoun, Jackson was strong-willed and proud. Unlike Calhoun, he already was president and the leader of a national party that included supporters of the tariff. To retain key northern support while soothing the South, Jackson devised two policies. First, he distributed surplus federal revenue, derived largely from the tariff duties, to the states, hoping to remove the taint of sectional injustice from the tariff. Second, he tried to ease tariffs down from the sky-high 1828 rates, and Congress passed slight reductions in 1832. But these measures did little to satisfy Calhoun and the South Carolinians.

Meanwhile, two personal issues further damaged relations between Calhoun and Jackson. In 1829, Jackson's secretary of war, John H. Eaton, married the widowed daughter of a Washington tavern keeper. The newlyweds were snubbed socially by Calhoun's wife and his friends in the cabinet. To make matters worse, in 1830 Jackson received conclusive evidence supporting his long-time suspicion that in 1818, then-secretary of war Calhoun had urged that Jackson be punished for his unauthorized raid into Spanish Florida. This confirmation combined with the Eaton affair to convince Jackson that he had to "destroy [Calhoun] regardless of what injury it might do me or my administration." At a Jefferson Day dinner in April 1830, when Jackson proposed the toast, "Our Union: It must be preserved," Calhoun pointedly responded, "The Union next to Liberty the most dear. May we always remember that it can only be preserved by distributing equally the benefits and burdens of the Union."

The stage was set for the **Nullification Crisis.** In November 1832, a South Carolina convention, citing Calhoun's states' rights doctrine, nullified the tariffs of 1828 and 1832 and forbade the collection of customs duties within the state. Jacksons reacted quickly. He labeled nullification an "abominable doctrine" that would reduce the government to anarchy, and denounced the nullifiers as "unprincipled men who would rather rule in hell, than be subordinate in heaven." He sent arms to Unionists in South Carolina and issued a proclamation that lambasted nullification as unconstitutional. The Constitution, he emphasized, had established "a single nation," not a league of states.

The crisis eased in March 1833 when Jackson signed into law two measures, called by one historian "the olive branch and the sword." The olive branch was the Compromise Tariff of 1833, which provided for a gradual reduction of duties between 1833 and 1842. The sword was the Force Bill, authorizing the president to use arms to collect customs duties in South Carolina. Although South Carolina promptly nullified the Force Bill, it construed the Compromise Tariff as a concession and rescinded its nullification of the tariffs of 1828 and 1832.

This so-called Compromise of 1833 mixed partisanship with statesmanship. Its chief architect was Henry Clay of Kentucky, who had long favored high tariffs. Clay supported tariff reduction because he feared that without some concessions to South Carolina, the Force Bill would produce civil war. Clay preferred to take responsibility for lowering tariffs himself, rather than pass the responsibility to the Jacksonians. The nullifiers, recognizing that no other states had supported them, preferred that Clay, not Jackson, be the hero of the hour. So they supported Clay's Compromise Tariff. Everywhere Americans hailed Clay as the Great Compromiser. Even Martin Van Buren acknowledged that Clay had "saved the country."

The Bank Veto and the Election of 1832

Jackson recognized that the gap between rich and poor was widening. Although he did not object to wealth earned by hard work, he believed that the wealthy too often enjoyed privileges granted by corrupt legislatures. Additionally, disastrous speculation early in his life had led him to distrust all banks, paper money, and monopolies. The **Bank of the United States** was guilty on all counts.

The Second Bank of the United States had received a twenty-year charter from Congress in 1816. As a creditor to state banks, with the option of demanding repayment in specie (gold or silver coinage), the Bank of the United States held the power to restrain the state banks from excessive printing and lending of money. Such power provoked hostility. Many Americans blamed the bank for precipitating the Panic of 1819. Further, as the official depository for federal revenue, the bank's capital of $35 million was more than double the annual expenditures of the federal government. Yet this powerful institution was only distantly controlled by the government. Its stockholders were private citizens and its directors enjoyed considerable independence. Its president, the aristocratic Nicholas Biddle, viewed himself as a public servant, duty-bound to keep the bank above politics.

Encouraged by Henry Clay, who hoped that supporting the bank would help carry him to the White House in 1832, Biddle secured congressional passage of a bill to recharter the bank. Jackson vetoed it, denouncing the bank as a private and privileged monopoly that drained the West of specie, eluded state taxation, and made "the rich richer and the potent more powerful."

By 1832, Jackson had made his views on major issues clear. He was simultaneously a strong defender of states' rights *and* a staunch Unionist. Although he cherished the Union, Jackson believed the states were far too diverse to accept strong direction from the federal government. Throwing aside earlier promises to retire, Jackson ran for the presidency again in 1832, with Martin Van Buren as his running mate. Henry Clay ran on the National Republican ticket, stressing his American System of protective tariffs, national banking, and federal support for internal improvements. Jackson won. Secure in office for another four years, he was ready to finish dismantling the Bank of the United States.

Bank of the United States
National Bank created by Alexander Hamilton

CHECKING IN

- During the 1820s politics became increasingly democratic, and voter participation increased dramatically.
- Andrew Jackson emerged as "the common man."
- As president, Jackson opposed the use of federal funds for internal improvements.
- The Nullification Crisis of 1828–1833 exposed deep divisions between the North and the South.
- Jackson saw his veto of the charter of the Bank of the United States as a victory for the common man.

THE BANK CONTROVERSY AND THE SECOND PARTY SYSTEM, 1833–1840

What were the major factors in the rise of the second party system?

Jackson's bank veto ignited a searing controversy that threatened to engulf all banks. One major problem was that the United States had no paper currency of its own. Instead, private bankers issued paper notes, which they promised to redeem in specie. These IOUs fueled economic development by making credit easy. But if a bank note depreciated, wage earners paid in paper would suffer. Further, paper money encouraged speculation, which multiplied both profit and risk. For example, farmers could now buy land on credit in the belief that its value would rise; if it did, they could sell the land at a profit, but if its value fell, the farmers became mired in debt. Would the United States embrace swift economic development at the price of allowing some people to get rich quickly while others languished? Or would the nation undergo more modest growth in traditional molds, anchored by "honest" manual work and frugality?

The War on the Bank

Jackson could have allowed the bank to die quietly when its charter ran out in 1836. But Jackson and some of his followers feared the bank's power too much to wait. When Biddle, anticipating further attacks, began to call in the bank's loans and contract credit during the winter of 1832–1833, Jacksonians saw their darkest fears confirmed. The bank, Jackson assured Van Buren, "is trying to kill me, but I will kill it." Jackson then began to remove federal deposits from the Bank of the United States and place them in state banks, called "pet banks" by their critics because they were usually selected for loyalty to the Democratic Party.

However, Jackson's redistribution of federal deposits backfired. He himself opposed paper money and easy credit. But as state banks became depositories for federal revenue, they were able to print more paper money and extend more loans to farmers and speculators eager to buy public lands in the West. Government land sales rose from $6 million in 1834 to $25 million in 1836. Jackson's policy was producing exactly the kind of economy he wanted to suppress.

Jackson was caught between crosswinds. Western Democrats resented the Bank of the United States because it periodically contracted credit and restricted lending by state banks. Advocating "soft" or paper money, these Democrats in 1836 pressured a reluctant Jackson to sign the Deposit Act, which increased the number of deposit banks and loosened federal control over them. But Jackson continued to believe that paper money sapped "public virtue" and "robbed honest labour of its earnings to make knaves rich, powerful and dangerous." Seeking to reverse the damaging effects of the Deposit Act, Jackson issued a proclamation in 1836 called the Specie Circular, which provided that only specie could be accepted in payment for public lands.

Meanwhile, the hard-money (specie) view was advocated within Jackson's inner circle and by a faction of the New York Democratic Party called the Locofocos.

The Locofocos grew out of several different "workingmen's" parties that called for free public education, the abolition of imprisonment for debt, and a ten-hour workday.

The Rise of Whig Opposition

During Jackson's second term, the opposition National Republican Party gave way to the new Whig party. Jackson's magnetic personality had swept him to victory in 1828 and 1832. As Jackson's policies became clearer and sharper, the opposition attracted people alienated by his positions.

For example, Jackson's crushing of nullification led some southerners to the Whigs, as did his war against the bank and opposition to federal aid for internal improvements. Although most of the South remained Democratic, the Whigs made substantial inroads. And supporters of Henry Clay's American System joined advocates of public education and temperance in seeking a more activist, interventionist national government.

Northern social reformers were attracted to the Whigs. Just as Clay hoped to use government to promote economic development, these reformers wanted government to improve American society by ending slavery and liquor consumption, improving public education, and elevating public morality. The reformers, overwhelmingly Protestant, distrusted immigrants, especially Irish Catholics, who viewed drinking as a normal recreation and opposed public schools because they promoted Protestantism. The reform agitation and its association with the Whigs drove the Irish into the Democratic Party. In turn, many native-born Protestant workers, contemptuous of the Irish, turned Whig.

The most remarkable source of Whig strength was Anti-Masonry. Freemasonry had long provided prominent men, including George Washington, with fellowship and exotic rituals. The spark that ignited the Anti-Masonic crusade was the abduction and disappearance in 1826 of William Morgan, a Mason who had threatened to expose the order's secrets. Efforts to solve the mystery of Morgan's disappearance failed because local officials were themselves Masons, seemingly determined to thwart the investigation. Rumors spread that Masonry was a powerful anti-Christian conspiracy of the rich in order to suppress popular liberty and an exclusive retreat for drunkards. Anti-Masonry brought many northeastern small farmers and artisans into the Whig party.

By 1836, the Whigs had become a national party with widespread appeal. Whigs everywhere assailed Andrew Jackson as an imperious dictator, "King Andrew I," and the name "Whigs" evoked memories of the American patriots who had opposed King George III in 1776.

The Election of 1836

Andrew Jackson was a hard act to follow. Democrats nominated Martin Van Buren, proclaiming that he and the Democratic Party were Jackson's heirs, the perfect embodiment of the popular will. The Whigs ran three candidates from different sections of the country. The Democrats accused the Whigs of attempting to split the vote and throw the election into the House, where they could wheel and deal as in 1824. In reality, the Whigs were simply divided, and Van Buren won a clear majority.

But there were signs of trouble ahead for the Democrats. The popular vote was close. In the South, where four years earlier the Democrats had won two-thirds of the votes, they now won barely half.

The Panic of 1837

Jackson left office in 1837 in a burst of glory. Yet he bequeathed to his successor a severe depression.

In the speculative boom of 1835 and 1836, born of Jackson's policy of placing federal funds in state banks, the total number of banks doubled, the value of bank notes in circulation nearly tripled, and both commodity and land prices soared skyward. But the overheated economy began to cool rapidly in May 1837. Prices tumbled as bank after bank suspended specie payments.

The ensuing depression had multiple roots. Domestically, Jackson's Specie Circular of July 1836—declaring that only specie, not paper money, could be used to purchase public lands—dried up credit. Global events played a major role as well. In the 1820s, Americans had used freshly mined silver imported from Mexico to buy tea, silks, and other goods in China. By the early 1830s, the Chinese were using increasing amounts of this silver to pay for opium grown in India and peddled by British merchants. In turn, large amounts of silver flowed out of British coffers to invest in canals and other American projects. Worried that British investors were overextended, in 1836 the Bank of England drastically raised interest rates.

Making a bad situation much worse, the price paid for American cotton by British merchants plummeted in the late 1830s because of bumper cotton harvests in the United States. But crop prices remained high; to pay for imported foodstuffs, the Bank of England raised money by raising interest rates again. This dried up the source of investment in American canals, leaving the American landscape littered with half-finished canals to nowhere.

The depression was far more severe and prolonged than the Panic of 1819. Wages fell by one-third between 1836 and 1842. In despair, many workers turned to the teachings of William Miller, a New England religious enthusiast convinced that the end of the world was imminent. Miller's followers roamed urban sidewalks and rural villages in search of converts. Many sold their possessions and purchased white robes to ascend into heaven on October 22, 1843, the day the world was supposed to end.

"Little Magician" Martin Van Buren needed all his political skills to confront the depression that was damaging not only ordinary citizens but the Democratic Party itself. To seize the initiative, Van Buren called for the creation of an independent Treasury. The idea was simple: The federal government, instead of depositing its money in banks, which would use it as the basis for speculative loans, would hold onto its revenues and keep them from the grasp of corporations. When Van Buren finally signed the Independent Treasury Bill into law on July 4, 1840, his supporters hailed it as a second Declaration of Independence.

The Whigs, who blamed the depression on Jackson's Specie Circular rather than on the banks, continued to encourage bank charters as a way to spur economic development. But the independent Treasury reflected the deep Jacksonian suspicion of an alliance between government and banking. In Louisiana and Arkansas, Democrats prohibited banks altogether, and elsewhere they imposed severe restrictions—banning, for example, the issuing of paper money in small denominations. After 1837, the Democrats became an antibank, hard-money party.

Log Cabins, Hard Cider, and a Maturing Second Party System

Despite the depression, the Democrats renominated Van Buren. Avoiding the mistake of 1836, the Whigs nominated a single candidate, Ohio's William Henry Harrison, and ran John Tyler of Virginia for vice president.

Early in the campaign the Democrats made a fatal mistake, ridiculing Harrison as "Old Granny," who desired only to spend his declining years in a **log cabin** sipping cider. In so doing, they handed the Whigs the most famous campaign symbol in American history. The Whigs saluted Harrison as a rugged frontiersman, the hero of the Battle of Tippecanoe (tip-pee-cuh-NOO), and a defender of all those people who lived in log cabins. Disdaining a platform, the Whigs ran a "hurrah" campaign using log cabins for headquarters, singing log cabin songs, and ladling out log cabin cider. Instead of a platform, they trumpeted, "Tippecanoe and Tyler, too!" and attacked Van Buren as an aristocrat who lived in "regal splendor."

Harrison was elected in a clear victory. The depression would have made it difficult for any Democrat to win, but many of Van Buren's problems stemmed from his style of campaign. While the Whigs ran a rousing race aimed directly at the "common man," Van Buren quietly wrote letters of encouragement to key supporters. Ironically, the Whigs beat the master politician at his own game.

The strong contrasts between the two parties and the sharp choices they presented jolted the American electorate. Nearly 2.4 million people voted in 1840, up an astonishing 60 percent from 1836. Prior to 1840 the proportion of white males who voted had ranged from 55 to 58 percent; in 1840 it rose to 80 percent.

Both the depression and the frenzied log cabin campaign brought voters to the polls in 1840, but voter turnouts stayed high even after prosperity returned. The second party system reached a high plateau in 1840 and remained there for over a decade. The gradual hardening of the line between the two parties stimulated popular interest in politics. Another major current feeding partisan political passion in American life was reform. Yet the social and moral reform movements that burst onto the national scene in the 1830s originated not in politics, but in religion.

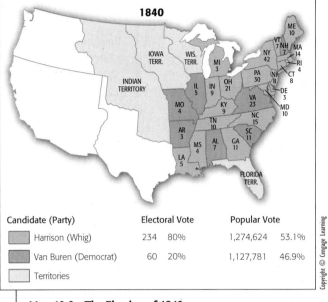

1840

Candidate (Party)	Electoral Vote		Popular Vote	
Harrison (Whig)	234	80%	1,274,624	53.1%
Van Buren (Democrat)	60	20%	1,127,781	46.9%
Territories				

Copyright © Cengage Learning

Map 10.2   The Election of 1840

Interactive Map

log cabin Symbol of the Whig party in the 1840 "hurrah" campaign for the presidency

CHECKING IN

- Jackson's "war" on the bank intensified the differences between the Democrats and the Whigs.

- The new Whig party included reformers and opponents of Jackson.

- The Panic of 1837 exploded during the administration of Martin Van Buren and greatly strengthened the Whigs.

- The election of 1840, the first real "hurrah" campaign, gave the Whigs the White House for the first time.

- After 1840 the second party system was firmly in place.

THE RISE OF POPULAR RELIGION

What new assumptions about human nature lay behind the religious movements of the period?

In *Democracy in America,* Alexis de Tocqueville called religion "the foremost of the political institutions" in the United States. Tocqueville was referring to the way religious impulses reinforced democracy and liberty. Just as Americans demanded that politics be accessible to average people, they insisted that ministers preach doctrines that appealed to ordinary men and women. Successful ministers used plain language to move the heart, not theological complexity to dazzle the intellect. Increasingly, Americans put individuals in charge of their own religious destiny, thrusting aside Calvinist predestination in favor of the belief that anyone could attain heaven. A series of religious revivals known as the Second Great Awakening contributed to the growing harmony between religion and politics and to the growing conviction that heaven itself was democratic.

Second Great Awakening
Religious revival that swept the country and fed into reform movements

The Second Great Awakening

The **Second Great Awakening** ignited in Connecticut during the 1790s. At first, educated Congregationalists and Presbyterians such as Yale president Timothy Dwight dominated the revivals. But as they spread to frontier states like Tennessee and Kentucky, revivals underwent striking changes that were typified by the rise of camp meetings. These were gigantic, prolonged revivals in which members of several denominations gathered into sprawling open-air camps to hear revivalists proclaim that the time for repentance was now.

The most famous camp meeting occurred at Cane Ridge, Kentucky, in August 1801, when a huge crowd assembled to hear thunderous sermons, sing hymns, and experience the influx of divine grace. Among the more extreme features of frontier revivals was the "exercises" in which men and women rolled around like logs, jerked their heads furiously, and barked like dogs. The most successful revivalists were not college graduates but ordinary farmers and artisans who had themselves experienced powerful religious conversions and regarded learned ministers with contempt for their dry expositions of orthodox theology.

Methodists Arose out of revivalism to become the largest American Protestant denomination

No religious denomination proved more successful on the frontier than the **Methodists.** The Methodists became America's largest Protestant denomination by 1844, claiming over a million members. In contrast to New England Congregationalists and Presbyterians, Methodists emphasized that religion was primarily a matter of the heart rather than the head. The frontier Methodists disdained "settled" ministers tied to fixed parishes. They preferred itinerant circuit riders—young, often unmarried men who traveled from place to place on horseback and preached in houses, open fields, and wherever listeners gathered.

Although the frontier revivals disrupted religious custom, they also promoted social and moral order on the frontier. After Methodist circuit riders left an area, their converts formed weekly "classes" that served as the grassroots structure for Methodist churches. The classes established a Methodist code of behavior, called the Discipline, which reinforced family and community values amidst the social disorder of frontier life. Class members reprimanded one another for drunkenness, fighting, fornication, gossiping, and even sharp business practices.

Eastern Revivals

By the 1820s, the Second Great Awakening had begun to shift back to the East. The hottest revival fires blazed in an area of western New York known as the Burned-Over District. No longer a frontier, western New York teemed with people drawn by the hope of wealth after the completion of the Erie Canal. It was a fertile field of high expectations and bitter discontent. The man who harnessed these anxieties to religion was **Charles Grandison Finney,** a lawyer-turned-Presbyterian minister. His greatest "harvest" came in the thriving canal city of Rochester in 1830–1831.

Charles Grandison Finney One of the most important revivalists; stressed individual responsibility

Finney's innovations at the Rochester revival justified his reputation as the "father of modern revivalism." First, it was a citywide revival in which all denominations participated. Finney was a pioneer of cooperation among Protestant denominations. Second, in Rochester and elsewhere, Finney introduced new devices for speeding conversions, such as the "anxious seat," where those ready for conversion were led so they could be made objects of special prayer, and the "protracted meeting," which went on nightly for up to a week.

Although a Presbyterian, Finney rejected the Calvinist doctrine of total depravity, humankind's irresistible inclination to sin. Instead, he proclaimed, sin was a voluntary act, and those who willed themselves to sin could just as readily will themselves not to sin. In theory, men and women could live perfect lives, free of sin. Those converted by Finney or other evangelists (ee-VAN-juh-lists) believed that they were cleansed of past guilt and were beginning a new life. "I have been born again," a young convert wrote. "I am three days old when I write this letter."

Originally controversial, Finney's ideas came to dominate "evangelical" (eh-van-JELL-ih-cull) Protestantism, which focused on the need for an emotional religious conversion. He succeeded because he told people what they wanted to hear: that their destiny was in their own hands. A society that celebrated the self-made individual embraced Finney's assertion that, even in religion, people could make of themselves what they chose. Finney multiplied his success by emphasizing the role of women, who outnumbered male converts nearly two to one. Finney encouraged women to give public testimonials of their conversion, and he often converted men by first winning over their wives and daughters.

Critics of Revivals: The Unitarians

Although some praised revivals for saving souls, others doubted their lasting effects. The **Unitarians** were a small, but influential group of critics. Although their basic doctrine—that Jesus Christ was less than fully divine—gained acceptance among religious liberals in the eighteenth century, Unitarianism became a formal denomination only in the early nineteenth century. Unitarians won few converts outside New England, but their tendency to attract the wealthy and educated gave them influence beyond their numbers.

Unitarians Denomination of generally educated, wealthy New Englanders upset by the emotionalism of revivals

Unitarians criticized revivals as uncouth emotional exhibitions and argued that "character building" was more effective than sudden emotional conversion. Yet they and the revivalists agreed in rejecting the Calvinist emphasis on human wickedness. Christianity had only one purpose, a Unitarian leader proclaimed: "the perfection of human nature, the elevation of men into nobler beings."

The Rise of Mormonism

Far more controversial than the Unitarians were the Mormons and their church, another new denomination of the 1820s named the Church of Jesus Christ of Latter-day Saints. **Joseph Smith,** its founder, grew up in the heart of the Burned-Over District. Conflict among the various religious denominations that thrived in the region—Methodists, Presbyterians, Baptists—left Smith confused. He wondered who was right and who was wrong or whether they were "all wrong together."

Smith's religious perplexity was common in the Burned-Over District, but his path to resolving the confusion was unique. An angel named Moroni, he reported, led him to a buried book of revelation and special seer stones to help with its translation, which he completed in 1827. The Book of Mormon tells the story of an ancient Hebrew prophet, Lehi, whose descendants migrated to America and created a prosperous civilization. Jesus had appeared and performed miracles in the New World, but Lehi's descendants had departed from the Lord's ways and quarreled among themselves. God had cursed some of these defectors with dark skin; these were the American Indians, who had long since forgotten their history.

Smith quickly gathered followers. For some believers, the Book of Mormon resolved the turmoil created by conflicting Protestant interpretations of the Bible. But Smith's claim to a new revelation guaranteed a hostile response from many American Protestants, who believed he had undermined the authority of their Scripture. To escape persecution, and move closer to the Indians whose conversion was one of their goals, Smith and his followers began relocating west from New York. In Illinois, they built a model city called Nauvoo and a magnificent temple supported by thirty huge pillars. However, in 1844 a group of dissident Mormons accused Smith and his inner circle of practicing plural marriage. When Smith destroyed the group's newspaper press, militias moved in to restore law and order. They arrested Smith and his brother Hirum and threw them into jail in Carthage, Illinois, where a lynch mob killed them both.

Joseph Smith had once hoped that Americans would fully embrace Mormonism. But ongoing persecution had gradually convinced the Mormons' prophet that their survival lay in separation from American society. In removing from the larger society of "Gentiles," the Mormons mirrored the efforts of many other religious communities during the 1830s and 1840s. One in particular, the Shakers, has held an enduring fascination for Americans.

Joseph Smith Founder of the Mormon Church, the first major denomination founded in the United States

The Shakers

The founder of the **Shakers** (who derived their name from a convulsive religious dance that was part of their ceremony) was Mother Ann Lee, the illiterate daughter of an British blacksmith. Lee and her followers established a series of tightly knit agricultural-artisan communities in America after her arrival in 1774. Shaker artisanship, particularly in furniture, quickly gained renown for its simple lines,

Shakers Sect that stressed withdrawal from society; known for craftsmanship beauty, and strength. Shaker advances in the development of new farm tools and seed varieties were a boon to the growing market economy.

For all their achievements as artisans, the Shakers were fundamentally otherworldly. Mother Ann, who had lost four infant children, had a religious vision in which God expelled Adam and Eve from the Garden of Eden for their sin of sexual intercourse. Shaker communities practiced celibacy and carefully separated the sleeping and working quarters of men and women to discourage contact between them. To maintain their membership, Shakers relied on new converts and the adoption of orphans. As part of their pursuit of religious perfection, they practiced a form of Christian socialism, pooling their land and implements to create remarkably prosperous villages.

While the Shakers chose to separate themselves from the competitive individualism of the larger society, the message of most evangelical Protestants, including Charles G. Finney, was that religion and economic self-advancement were compatible. Most revivalists taught that the pursuit of wealth was acceptable as long as people were honest, temperate, and bound by conscience. But many of them recognized that the world was in serious need of improvement, and they believed that converts had a religious responsibility to pursue moral and social reform.

CHECKING IN

- The "democratization" process reached religion as well as politics.
- The Second Great Awakening emphasized the emotional aspects of religion.
- Methodism emerged as a major Protestant denomination.
- The Mormon Church and the Shakers were born amid the fever of revivalism, but their members lived apart from society.
- Despite such new sects, revivalists generally encouraged involvement in society and were a powerful stimulus to reform movements.

THE AGE OF REFORM

Did the reform movements aim primarily at making Americans more free or more orderly?

At the heart of religious revival was the democratic belief that individual men and women could take charge of their own spiritual destinies and strive toward perfection. For many converts, similar expectations applied to the society around them. Saved souls, they believed, could band together to stamp out the many evils that plagued the American republic. The abolition of slavery, the rights of women, temperance, the humane treatment of criminals and the insane, and public education were high on reformers' agendas. Carrying the moralism of revival into their reform activities, they tended to view all social problems as clashes between good and evil.

Not all reformers were converts of revivalism. Many school reformers and women's rights advocates were either hostile or indifferent to revivals. Abolitionists openly criticized the churches for condoning slavery. However, by portraying slaveholding as a sin that called for immediate repentance, even religiously liberal abolitionists borrowed their language and their psychological appeal from revivalism. Whatever a reformer's personal relationship to the revivals of the Second Great Awakening, the Age of Reform drew much of its fuel from that evangelical movement.

The War on Liquor

Early nineteenth-century Americans were very heavy drinkers. In 1825, the average adult male drank about seven gallons of alcohol annually, in contrast to less than two gallons in our own time. One reason for this heavy consumption was the state of western agriculture. Before the transportation revolution, western farmers could not make a profit by shipping grain in bulk to eastern markets. But they could profit by condensing their corn and rye into whiskey. Drunkenness pervaded all social classes and occupations.

temperance Abstinence from alcohol; name of the movement against alcohol

Before 1825, **temperance** (TEM-per-enss) reformers advocated moderation in consuming alcohol. But in that year, Connecticut revivalist Lyman Beecher delivered six widely acclaimed lectures that condemned all use of alcoholic beverages. A year later, evangelical Protestants created the American Temperance Society, the first national temperance organization. By 1834, some five thousand state and local temperance societies were affiliated with it.

The primary strategy of the American Temperance Society was to use "moral suasion" to persuade people to "take the pledge"—the promise never to consume any alcoholic beverage. Among the main targets of evangelical temperance reformers were the laboring classes. In the small workshops of the pre-industrial era, passing the jug every few hours throughout the workday was a time-honored practice. But early factories demanded a more disciplined, sober work force, so industrial employers were quick to embrace temperance reform. Industrial employers in Rochester, New York, invited Charles G. Finney to preach up a revival in their city as part of an effort to convince their workers to abstain from alcohol.

Workers themselves initially showed little interest in temperance. But after the Panic of 1837, some grew convinced that their economic survival depended on a commitment to sobriety. In 1840, in Baltimore, they formed the Washington Temperance Society. Many members were themselves reformed drunkards. Take care of temperance, one Washingtonian assured his Baltimore audience, and the Lord will take care of the economy. The Washington Societies spread farther and faster than any other antebellum temperance organization.

As the temperance movement won new supporters, some crusaders began to demand legal prohibition—the banning of liquor traffic at the local and state level. In 1838, Massachusetts prohibited the sale of distilled spirits in amounts less than fifteen gallons. In 1851, Maine banned the manufacture and sale of all intoxicating beverages. Taken together, the two central strategies of the temperance movement—moral suasion and legal prohibition—scored remarkable success. Per capita consumption of distilled spirits began to fall during the 1830s. By the 1840s, consumption had dropped to less than half its peak rate in the 1820s.

Public-School Reform

Like temperance crusaders, school reformers worked to encourage orderliness and thrift in the common people. Rural "district" schools were a main target. Here students ranging in age from three to twenty crowded into a single room and learned to read and count, but little more.

District schools enjoyed considerable support from rural parents. However, reformers insisted that schools had to equip children for the emerging competitive and industrial economy. In 1837, **Horace Mann** of Massachusetts became the first secretary of his state's newly created board of education. He presided over sweeping reforms to transform schools from loose organizations into highly structured institutions that occupied most of a child's time and energy. Mann's goals included

Horace Mann Important public-school reformer

shifting financial support of schools from parents to the state, compelling attendance, extending the school term, introducing standardized textbooks, and dividing students into grades based on their age and achievements.

School reformers sought to spread industrial values as well as combat ignorance. Requiring students to arrive on time would teach punctuality, and matching children against their peers would stimulate competitiveness. The McGuffey readers, which sold 50 million copies between 1836 and 1870, preached industry, honesty, sobriety, and patriotism.

Success did not come easily. Educational reformers faced challenges from farmers who were satisfied with the district school, from Catholics objecting to anti-Catholic and anti-Irish barbs in the textbooks, and from the working poor, who widely saw compulsory education as a menace to families dependent on children's wages. Mann and other school reformers prevailed in part because their opponents could not cooperate with one another and in part because the reformers attracted influential allies, including urban workers, manufacturers, and women. Reformers predicted that school reform would make teaching a suitable profession for women, and they were right. By 1900, about 70 percent of the nation's schoolteachers were women.

School reform also appealed to native-born Americans alarmed by the influx of immigrant foreigners. The public school was coming to be seen as the best mechanism for creating a common American culture out of an increasingly diverse society. As one reformer observed, "We must decompose and cleanse the impurities which rush into our midst" through the "one infallible filter—the SCHOOL." Very few educational reformers, however, called for the integration of black and white children. When black children did enter public schools, they encountered open hostility and sometimes violence.

Abolition

Antislavery sentiment had flourished among whites during the revolutionary era but faded in the early nineteenth century. The American Colonization Society, founded in 1817, was the main antislavery organization of this period. It proposed gradual emancipation, compensation for slave owners when slaves became free, and the shipment to Africa of freed blacks. Although these proposals attracted some support from slave owners in the Upper South, they were unrealizable. The growing cotton economy had made slavery more attractive than ever to most southerners, and few owners were unwilling to free their slaves, even if compensated. Between 1820 and 1830—a period when the slave population nearly doubled in size—only 1,400 blacks migrated to Liberia, and most of them were already free blacks.

Most African-Americans opposed colonization. As native-born Americans, they asked, how could they be sent back to a continent they had never known? "We are natives of this country," one black pastor proclaimed. "We only ask that we be treated as well as foreigners." In opposition to colonization, blacks formed their own abolition societies. One free black, David Walker of Boston, urged slaves to rise up and murder their masters if slavery were not abolished.

In 1821, Benjamin Lundy, a white Quaker, began a newspaper, the *Genius of Universal Emancipation,* that trumpeted repeal of the Constitution's three-fifths

William Lloyd Garrison Outspoken radical opponent of slavery

clause, the outlawing of the internal slave trade, and the abolition of slavery in U.S. territories. Seven years later Lundy hired a young New Englander, **William Lloyd Garrison,** as an editorial assistant. The prematurely bald, bespectacled Garrison would become a potent force in the antislavery movement.

In 1831, Garrison launched a newspaper, *The Liberator,* to spread his radical antislavery message. "I am in earnest," he wrote. "I will not equivocate—I will not excuse—I will not retreat a single inch—AND I WILL BE HEARD." His battle cry was "immediate emancipation"; his demand, civil and legal equality for African-Americans. However, even Garrison did not believe that all slaves could be freed overnight. People first had to realize that slavery was sinful and its continued existence intolerable.

Frederick Douglass Escaped slave who became a major figure in the antislavery movement

Black abolitionists supported Garrison; in its early years three-fourths of *The Liberator's* subscribers were African-American. Other blacks were also emerging as powerful writers and speakers. **Frederick Douglass,** an escaped slave, could rivet an audience with an opening line: "I appear before the immense assembly this evening as a thief and a robber. I stole this head, these limbs, this body from my master, and ran off with them."

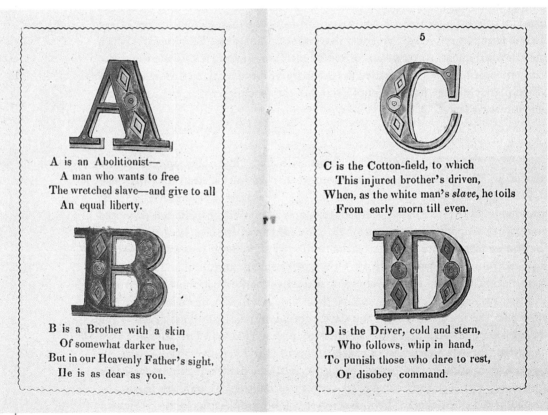

A is an Abolitionist—
A man who wants to free
The wretched slave—and give to all
An equal liberty.

B is a Brother with a skin
Of somewhat darker hue,
But in our Heavenly Father's sight,
He is as dear as you.

C is the Cotton-field, to which
This injured brother's driven,
When, as the white man's *slave,* he toils
From early morn till even.

D is the Driver, cold and stern,
Who follows, whip in hand,
To punish those who dare to rest,
Or disobey command.

Boston Athenaeum

The Alphabet
Viewing children as morally pure and hence as natural opponents of slavery, abolitionists produced antislavery toys, games, and, as we see here, alphabet books.

Relations between white and black abolitionists were not always harmonious. Many white abolitionists called for legal, but not civil and social, racial equality; preferred light-skinned to dark-skinned blacks; and hesitated to admit African-Americans to antislavery societies. And widespread white prejudice made the life of any abolitionist precarious. Mobs attacked abolitionists often. In 1837, a mob in Alton, Illinois, destroyed the printing press of antislavery editor Elijah P. Lovejoy, then shot him dead and dragged his mutilated corpse through the streets.

Furthermore, Protestant churches did not rally solidly behind abolition. Lyman Beecher roared against the evils of strong drink but merely whispered about those of slavery.

Even as the obstacles mounted, issues of strategy and tactics divided abolitionists during the 1830s. Some believed that the legal and political arena presented the best opportunities for ending slavery. But Garrison and his followers were beginning to reject all participation not only in party politics, but in government itself. In 1838, they founded the New England Non-Resistance Society, based on Garrison's radical new doctrine of nonresistance. According to that doctrine, the fundamental evil of slavery was its reliance on force, the opposite of Christian love. And just like slavery, government itself ultimately rested on coercion. True Christians, Garrison concluded, should refuse to vote, hold office, or have anything to do with government.

Another major issue dividing abolitionists was the role of women in the movement. In 1837, **Angelina and Sarah Grimké** (GRIM-kee), the daughters of a South Carolina slaveholder, made an antislavery lecture tour of New England. The Grimké sisters were controversial because they spoke to audiences of both men and women at a time when it was thought indelicate for women to address male audiences. Clergymen chastised the Grimké sisters for lecturing men rather than obeying them.

The Grimkés responded in 1838 by writing two classics of American feminism: Sarah Grimké's *Letters on the Condition of Women and the Equality of the Sexes,* and Angelina Grimké's *Letters to Catharine E. Beecher* (who opposed female equality). Some abolitionists dismissed their efforts: Women's grievances, said poet John Greenleaf Whittier, were "paltry" compared to the injustices of slavery. Garrison, welcoming the controversy, promptly espoused women's rights and urged equal treatment for women in the American Anti-Slavery Society. In 1840, the election of Abby Kelley to a previously all-male committee split the society, with many profeminists splintering off to form their own groups.

However, the break-up of the American Anti-Slavery Society did not significantly damage the larger movement. By 1840, there were more than fifteen hundred local antislavery societies circulating abolitionist tracts, newspapers, and even chocolates wrapped in antislavery messages. Local societies pursued a grassroots campaign to flood Congress with petitions calling for an end to slavery in the District of Columbia. When exasperated southerners in 1836 adopted a "gag rule" automatically tabling these petitions without discussion, they triggered a debate that shifted public attention from abolitionism to the constitutional rights of free expression—a debate that further served the antislavery cause. The less secure southerners felt, the more they blundered into clumsy overreactions like the gag rule.

Angelina and Sarah Grimké Sisters who were powerful antislavery speakers; later leaders of women's rights movement

Women's Rights

When Sarah and Angelina Grimké took up the cause of women's rights in 1838, they were not merely defending their right to participate in the antislavery movement. They were responding to perceived similarities between the conditions of slaves and women. Early issues of *The Liberator* contained a "Ladies' Department" illustrated with a kneeling slave woman imploring, "Am I Not a Woman and a Sister?" When abolitionists such as Lucretia (loo-CREE-shuh) Mott, Lucy Stone, and Abby Kelley embraced women's rights, they were acknowledging a sisterhood in oppression with female slaves.

Women occupied a paradoxical position in the 1830s. They could not vote and, if married, had no right to own property or to keep their own wages. Divorced women could not gain custody of their children; domestic violence went virtually unchallenged. At the same time, reform movements gave women unprecedented opportunities to work in public without openly defying the dictate that their proper sphere was the home. When women left their homes to distribute religious tracts, battle intemperance, or work for peace, they could claim they were transforming wretched homes into nurseries of happiness.

The argument that women were natural guardians of family life was double-edged. It justified reform activities on behalf of the family but undercut women's demands for legal equality. However, the experiences acquired in a range of reform activities provided invaluable skills for women to take up the cause of their own rights. And the women's rights movement, at its most radical, openly challenged gender-based double standards. "Men and women," Sarah Grimké wrote, "are CREATED EQUAL! They are both moral and accountable beings, and whatever is right for man to do, is right for woman."

Although feminism first emerged within abolitionism, the discrimination encountered by women in the antislavery movement drove them to make women's rights a separate cause. In the 1840s, Lucy Stone became the first abolitionist to give a lecture devoted entirely to women's rights. When Lucretia Mott arrived at the World's Anti-Slavery Convention in London in 1840, and was seated in a screened-off section for women, her own allegiance to women's rights was sealed. The incident made a deep impression on Mott and Elizabeth Cady Stanton. In 1848, Mott and Stanton together organized the Seneca Falls Convention for women's rights at **Seneca** (SEN-ih-cuh) **Falls, New York.** That convention's Declaration of Sentiments, modeled on the Declaration of Independence, began with the assertion that "all men and women are created equal." The participants

| **Seneca Falls, New York** Site of first women's rights convention in 1848

Miriam and Ira D. Wallach Division of Art, Prints and Photographs, The New York Public Library, Astor, Lenox and Tilden Foundations

Sojourner Truth, 1864

Born into slavery in New York, the woman who named herself Sojourner Truth became a religious perfectionist, a powerful evangelical preacher, and one of the most influential abolitionists and feminists of her time.

passed a series of resolutions, including a call for the right of women to vote, which would become the centerpiece of women's rights activity after the Civil War.

Women's rights advocates won a few notable victories. In 1860, Stanton's lobbying helped secure passage of a New York law allowing married women to own property. But women's rights had less impact than many other reforms, including temperance, school reform, and abolitionism. Women would not secure the national right to vote until 1920, fifty-five years after the Thirteenth Amendment abolished slavery. Nineteenth-century feminists had to content themselves with piecemeal gains.

Penitentiaries and Asylums

Beginning in the 1820s, reformers began to combat poverty, crime, and insanity by establishing new model institutions based on innovative theories about the roots of deviancy. As urban poverty and crime grew increasingly visible, investigators concluded that such problems arose not from innate sinfulness, but from poor home environments. Both religious and secular reformers believed that human nature could be improved through placement in the proper moral environment. For paupers, criminals, and the mentally ill, that place was the asylum, an institution that would remove deviants from corrupting influences and provide them with moral supervision and disciplined work.

The colonial jail had been merely a temporary holding cell for offenders awaiting trial; early American criminals were punished by flogging, branding, or hanging rather than extended prison terms. By contrast, the nineteenth-century penitentiary (pen-ih-TEN-char-ee) was an asylum designed to lead criminals to "penitential" reformation by isolating them and encouraging them to contemplate their guilt. Two different models for the penitentiary emerged in the antebellum era. New York's "Auburn (AW-burn) system" forbade prisoners to speak to one another and confined them in individual, windowless cells by night. Under the more extreme "Pennsylvania" or "separate system," each prisoner was confined day and night in a single cell with a walled courtyard for exercise, deprived of human contact within the prison, and permitted visits from the outside.

Antebellum reformers also designed special asylums for the poor and the mentally ill. The prevailing colonial practice of poor relief was "outdoor relief," supporting the poor by placing them in other people's households. The new "indoor relief" confined the infirm poor in almshouses (AHMS-houses) and the able-bodied poor in workhouses. A parallel movement shaped new approaches to treating the mentally ill, as illuminated in the work of humanitarian reformer **Dorothea Dix.** Instead of imprisoning the insane in jails and sheds, she argued, society should house them in orderly hospitals where they should receive proper medical and moral care.

Dorothea Dix Leader of the crusade to improve conditions for the insane

Penitentiaries, almshouses and workhouses, and insane asylums all reflected the same optimistic belief that the solution for deviancy lay in proper moral environments. From one point of view, such efforts were humanitarian. But from another point of view, the asylum reformers were practicing extreme forms of social control. Convinced that criminals, the poor, and the insane required regimentation, they confined them in prison-like conditions, policed their social interaction, and controlled their every move.

Utopian Communities

The reformist belief in the possibility of human perfection assumed purest expression in the utopian (yoo-TOH-pee-ehn) communities that first began to surface in the 1820s. Most of these, founded by intellectuals, were meant to be alternatives to the prevailing competitive economy and models whose success would inspire others.

In 1825, British industrialist Robert Owen founded the **New Harmony** community in Indiana. As a mill owner, Owen had improved his workers' living conditions and educational opportunities; he was convinced that the problems of the early industrial age were social, not political. Vice and misery would vanish if social arrangements were perfected, he thought. The key was the creation of small, planned communities—"Villages of Unity and Mutual Cooperation"—with a perfect balance of occupational, religious, and social groups.

Upon founding New Harmony, Owen confidently predicted that northerners would embrace its principles within two years. Instead, the community became a magnet for idlers and fanatics, and failed within two years. Nonetheless, Owen's ideas survived the wreckage of New Harmony. His insistence that human character was formed by environment and that cooperation was superior to competition had an enduring impact on urban workers, who took up his cause of educational reform in the years to come.

Experimental communities multiplied rapidly during the economic crises of the late 1830s and 1840s. Brook Farm, near Boston, was the creation of a group of religious philosophers called **transcendentalists** (tran-sen-DEN-tuh-lists), who sought to revitalize Christianity by proclaiming the infinite spiritual capacities of ordinary men and women. Convinced that the competitive commercial life of the cities was unnatural, Brook Farmers spent their days milking cows and mowing hay, and their evenings contemplating philosophy. This utopian community attracted several renowned writers, including Ralph Waldo Emerson and Nathaniel Hawthorne, and its literary magazine, *The Dial,* became an important forum for transcendentalist ideas (as discussed further in Chapter 11). But its life-span was brief.

The most controversial utopian experiment was the Oneida (oh-NYE-duh) Community, established in 1848 in New York by John Humphrey Noyes (noise). A convert of Charles Finney, Noyes also became a theological perfectionist. At Oneida, he advocated a form of Christian communism. The Oneidans renounced private property, put men to work in kitchens, and adopted the radical new bloomer costume for women. But what most upset their critics was the application of communism to marriage. Noyes advocated "complex marriage," in which every member of the community was married to every other member of the other sex. Oneida did not promote sexual free-for-all, however: Couplings were arranged through an intermediary, in part to track paternity.

Contemporaries dismissed Noyes as a licentious crackpot. Yet Oneida achieved considerable economic prosperity and was attracting new members long after other, less radical utopias had failed. Despite the ridicule of many of their contemporaries, utopian communities exemplified the idealism and hopefulness that permeated nearly all reform movements in the antebellum period.

New Harmony One of the most important utopian communities, founded in Indiana by Robert Owen

transcendentalists American religious philosophers who believed in the capacity of the human spirit; included many renowned writers

CHECKING IN

- Reform movements, invigorated by revivalism, swept over the North and West, but had little impact in the South.
- The temperance movement targeted workers and enjoyed considerable success.
- Educational reform aimed both to prepare children for life in an industrializing economy and to reinforce Protestant American culture; reformers also established new institutions to deal with the poor, criminals, and the insane.
- The antislavery movement gained momentum but was split by disagreements.
- The struggle for women's rights emerged from women's participation in the antislavery movement and other reform efforts.
- Reformers established a variety of utopian communities (usually unsuccessful), which sought to create a model for ideal society.

Chapter Summary

How did the democratization of American politics contribute to the rise of Andrew Jackson? (page 221)

Starting in the 1820s, restrictions on voting for white males dwindled, and politics became increasingly inclusive. Andrew Jackson, seen as the incarnation of democratic politics, won the White House for two terms and fought for what he saw as the causes of the common man, especially in his crusade against the Bank of the United States. However, the Nullification Crisis revealed sharp differences between North and South.

What were the major factors in the rise of the second party system? (page 228)

In waging his "war" against the bank, Jackson intensified differences between the Democrats and the Whigs. This war helped to solidify the second party system but led to the Panic of 1837. The resulting depression engulfed and destroyed the presidency of Martin Van Buren and handed the White House to the Whigs in 1840, putting the second party system firmly in place. New styles of campaigning emerged with the "log cabin" campaign of 1840, and voter participation soared.

What new assumptions about human nature lay behind the religious movements of the period? (page 232)

Revivalism dominated religion for many Americans during the Second Great Awakening, bringing changes of both style (emotionalism) and substance (an emphasis on personal responsibility and a growing belief in the capacity of all people to achieve moral and spiritual perfection). The Mormon Church, the first American-born religion, rose amid the fervor of revivalism. Revivalists generally emphasized the need for involvement in society and thus became a powerful stimulus to reform movements.

KEY TERMS

Democrats *(p. 221)*

Whigs *(p. 221)*

"spoils system" *(p. 225)*

"Tariff of Abominations" *(p. 225)*

Nullification Crisis *(p. 226)*

Bank of the United States *(p. 227)*

log cabin *(p. 231)*

Second Great Awakening *(p. 232)*

Methodists *(p. 232)*

Charles Grandison Finney *(p. 233)*

Unitarians *(p. 233)*

Joseph Smith *(p. 234)*

Shakers *(p. 234)*

temperance *(p. 236)*

Horace Mann *(p. 236)*

William Lloyd Garrison *(p. 238)*

Frederick Douglass *(p. 238)*

Angelina and Sarah Grimké *(p. 239)*

Seneca Falls, New York *(p. 240)*

Dorothea Dix *(p. 241)*

New Harmony *(p. 242)*

transcendentalists *(p. 242)*

Did the reform movements aim primarily at making Americans more free or more orderly? (page 235)

Reform movements targeted a wide range of social issues, including alcohol consumption, education, the treatment of the mentally ill, prisons, slavery, and women's rights. Reformers sought the radical improvement of human nature through a combination of individual and institutional efforts. Yet for all their optimism, many reformers proved willing to coerce people into change by such measures as prohibiting liquor sales, requiring school attendance, and placing prisoners in solitary confinement. One movement frequently led to another, as antislavery spawned the drive for women's rights. Utopian communities appeared; most collapsed. But the search for social and political alternatives continued.

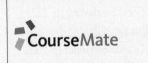

Go to the CourseMate website at **www.cengagebrain.com** for additional study tools and review materials—including audio and video clips—for this chapter.

CHAPTER 11

Technology, Culture, and Everyday Life

1840–1860

Steam Locomotive Crossing the Niagara
Railway Suspension Bridge

William B. Becker Collection/American Museum of Photography

CHAPTER PREVIEW

Technology and Economic Growth
What technological improvements brought about American economic growth between 1840 and 1860?

The Quality of Life
In what ways did technology transform the lives of ordinary Americans?

Democratic Pastimes
In what new ways did Americans pass their free time during this period?

The Quest for Nationality in Literature and Art
How did the work of American writers and artists become distinctly American?

In 1850, Isaac M. Singer's life was not going well. Thirty-nine and often penniless, he had been an unsuccessful actor, carpenter, and inventor. His early inventions had been clever, but not commercially successful. Having deserted his wife and children, he lured Mary Ann Sponslor into living with him by promising marriage. Sponslor nursed him when he was sick, but instead of marrying her, Singer beat her and had affairs with other women. But in 1850, Singer made significant improvements on a sewing machine similar to one patented in 1846 by Elias Howe, Jr., and within ten years, he was a wealthy man.

Here was a machine everyone wanted. Contemporaries could not praise sewing machines enough. The *New York Tribune* predicted that, with the spread of sewing machines, people "will dress better, change oftener, and altogether grow better looking." This optimistic

245

technology The practical application of science to improving life

response to technological change was typical of the 1850s. Many Americans believed that **technology** was God's chosen instrument of progress. For New Englander Edward Everett in 1852, the locomotive was "a miracle of science, art, and capital, a magic power."

Yet progress had a darker side. Ralph Waldo Emerson said bluntly, "Machinery is dangerous. The weaver becomes the web, the machinist the machine. If you do not use the tools, they use you." The newly invented revolver was useless for hunting, but excellent for violently settling private scores. Philosophers and artists began to worry about the despoliation of the landscape by the factories that made guns and sewing machines, and conservationists launched efforts to preserve natural enclaves as retreats from the evils of progress.

TECHNOLOGY AND ECONOMIC GROWTH

What technological improvements brought about American economic growth between 1840 and 1860?

Widely hailed as democratic, technology drew praise from all sides. Conservative statesman Daniel Webster, for example, praised machines for doing the work of people without consuming food or clothing.

The technological improvements that transformed life in antebellum America included the steam engine, the cotton gin, the reaper, the sewing machine, and the telegraph. Some of these originated in Europe, but Americans had a flair for investing in others' inventions and perfecting their own. Sadly, these advances did not benefit everyone. The cotton gin, for example, riveted slavery firmly in place by intensifying southern dependence on cotton. Nonetheless, the improved transportation and increased productivity that technology made possible raised the living standard of many free Americans between 1840 and 1860.

Agricultural Advancement

After 1830, American settlers were edging westward from the woodlands of Ohio and Kentucky into parts of Indiana, Michigan, Illinois, and Missouri, where the flat grasslands of the prairie alternated with forests. Prairie soil, though richly fertile, was root-matted and difficult to break. But in 1837, **John Deere** invented a steel-tipped plow that cut in half the labor required to till for planting. Timber for houses and fencing was available in nearby woods, and settlements spread rapidly.

John Deere Inventor of the steel plow

Wheat became to midwestern farmers what cotton was to the South. Technological advances sped the harvesting as well as the planting of wheat. The traditional hand sickle consumed huge amounts of time and labor, and the cut wheat also had to be picked up and bound by hand. But in 1834, **Cyrus McCormick** of Virginia patented a horse-drawn mechanical reaper that harvested grain seven times faster with half the work force. In 1847, he opened a factory in Chicago, and by 1860 he had sold 80,000 reapers. The mechanical reaper guaranteed that wheat would dominate the midwestern prairies.

Cyrus McCormick Inventor of the mechanical reaper

Ironically, just as Connecticut Yankee Eli Whitney's cotton gin had created the Old South's economy, an invention by Cyrus McCormick, a pro-slavery Democrat,

Chronology

1823	Philadelphia completes the first urban water-supply system; James Fenimore Cooper, *The Pioneers*
1826	Cooper, *The Last of the Mohicans*
1833	The *New York Sun,* the first penny newspaper, is established
1834	Cyrus McCormick patents the mechanical reaper
1835	James Gordon Bennett establishes the *New York Herald*
1837	Ralph Waldo Emerson, "The American Scholar"
1839	Edgar Allen Poe, "The Fall of the House of Usher"
1841	P. T. Barnum opens the American Museum
1844	Samuel F. B. Morse patents the telegraph; Poe, "The Raven"
1846	William T. G. Morton successfully uses anesthesia; Elias Howe, Jr., patents the sewing machine
1849	Second major cholera epidemic
1850	Nathaniel Hawthorne, *The Scarlet Letter*
1851	Hawthorne, *The House of the Seven Gables;* Herman Melville, *Moby-Dick;* Erie Railroad completes its line to the West
1853	Ten small railroads are consolidated into the New York Central Railroad
1854	Henry David Thoreau, *Walden*
1855	Walt Whitman, *Leaves of Grass*
1856	Illinois Central completed between Chicago and Cairo, Illinois
1858	Frederick Law Olmsted is appointed architect-in-chief for Central Park

would help the Union win the Civil War. Northern agriculture took advantage of his reaper and copies of it to raise agricultural production; southerners, reliant on slave labor, had little reason to mechanize. The reaper would keep northern agricultural production high despite the mobilization of hundreds of thousands of northern men.

Although Americans generally remained wasteful farmers—abundant cheap land made it more "practical" to move west than to try to improve played-out soil— a movement for more efficient cultivation developed before the Civil War, primarily in the East. By feeding their cows better and improving dairy processing, New York dairy farmers produced a superior butter that commanded more than double the price of ordinary butter. Other eastern farmers turned to soil improvement. By fertilizing their fields with plaster left over from canal construction, Virginia wheat growers raised their average yield from six bushels per acre in 1800 to fifteen bushels by the 1850s. American cotton planters in the Southeast began to import guano (sea bird droppings) from Peru to fertilize their fields in an effort to compete successfully with the fertile soil of the Old Southwest.

Technology and Industrial Progress

Industrial advances between 1840 and 1860 owed an immense debt to the development of effective machine tools. By the 1840s, machine tools had greatly reduced the need to hand file parts to make them fit, and they were applied to the manufacture of firearms, clocks, and sewing machines. After mid-century, Europeans began to call this system of manufacturing **interchangeable parts** the "American System of Manufacturing." After touring American factories in 1854, a British engineer concluded that Americans "universally and willingly" resorted to machines as a substitute for manual labor.

The American manufacturing system had several distinct advantages. Traditionally, damage to any part of a mechanical contrivance had rendered the whole thing useless, because no new part would fit. The perfection of interchangeable parts made replacement parts possible. In addition, improved machine tools enabled entrepreneurs to push inventions into mass production with a speed that attracted investors. Sophisticated machine tools, according to one manufacturer, increased production "by confining a worker to one particular limb of a pistol until he had made two thousand."

After Samuel F. B. Morse transmitted the first telegraph message, Americans eagerly seized on the telegraph's promise to eliminate the constraints of time and place. They formed telegraph companies and strung lines with stunning speed. By 1852, more than fifteen thousand miles of line connected cities as distant as Quebec, New Orleans, and St. Louis. The first transcontinental line was completed in 1860. A later historian would christen the telegraph the "Victorian Internet" because of the ways it changed business and personal communication.

The Railroad Boom

Even more than the telegraph, the railroad dramatized technology's democratic promise. In 1790, even European royalty could travel no faster than fourteen miles an hour and then only with frequent changes of horses. By 1850, an ordinary American could travel three times as fast—by train.

Americans loved railroads, reported one Frenchman, "as a lover loves his mistress." Their love of early railroad travel had a great deal to overcome. Sparks from locomotives showered passengers riding in open cars, and discouraged passengers in closed coaches from opening the windows. In the absence of brakes, passengers on trains often had to get off to help stop them. Trains rarely ran at night because they lacked lights. Before the introduction of standard time zones in 1883, scheduling was a nightmare and delays were frequent. Individual railroads used different gauge track, making frequent train changes necessary; even in the 1850s, a journey from Charleston to Philadelphia required eight transfers.

Yet nothing slowed the advance of railroads or cured Americans' mania for them. In 1851, the editor of the *American Railroad Journal* wrote that in the previous twenty years, the locomotive had become "the great agent of civilization and progress, the most powerful instrument for good the world has yet reached." Between 1840 and 1860, the size of the rail network and the power and convenience of trains underwent a stunning transformation. Railroads extended track mileage from three thousand to thirty thousand miles; closed coaches replaced open cars; kerosene lamps made night travel possible; and increasingly powerful engines enabled trains to climb steep hills. By 1860, the United States had more track than all the rest of the world combined.

Railroads represented the second major phase of the transportation revolution. Canals remained in use—the Erie Canal did not reach its peak volume until

interchangeable parts
Identical components made by machine tools, speeding the manufacturing process; pioneered by Eli Whitney

1880—but the railroads gradually overtook them, first in passengers and then in freight. By 1860, the value of goods transported by railroads greatly surpassed that carried by canals.

By 1860, railroads had spread like vast spider webs east of the Mississippi River (see Map 11.1). They transformed southern cities like Atlanta and Chattanooga into thriving commercial hubs. Most important, the railroads linked the East and the Midwest. New York City was joined with Buffalo while Philadelphia was linked to Pittsburgh. Intense construction in Ohio, Indiana, and Illinois created trunk lines that tied these routes to cities farther west.

Chicago's growth illustrates the impact of these rail links. In 1849, it was a village of a few hundred people with virtually no rail service. By 1860, it had become a metropolis of 100,000, served by eleven railroads. Farmers in the upper Midwest no longer had to send their grain, livestock, and dairy products down the Mississippi to New Orleans; they could now ship their products directly east. Chicago supplanted New Orleans as the interior's main commercial hub.

Rail lines stimulated the settlement of the Midwest. By 1860, Illinois, Indiana, and Wisconsin had replaced Ohio, Pennsylvania, and New York as the leading wheat-growing states. Railroads increased the value of farmland and promoted additional settlement. In turn, population growth stimulated industrial development in cities such as Chicago and Minneapolis, for the new settlers needed lumber for fences and houses, as well as mills to grind wheat into flour.

Railroads also spurred the growth of small towns along their routes. The Illinois Central Railroad,

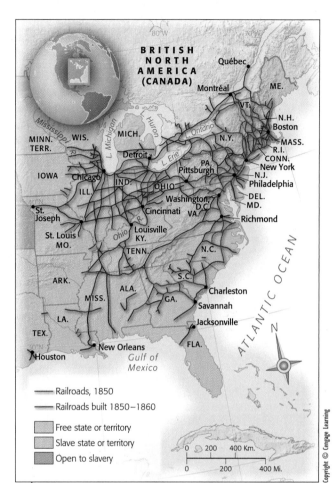

Map 11.1 Railroad Growth, 1850–1860
Rail ties between the East and the Midwest greatly increased during the railroad boom of the 1850s.

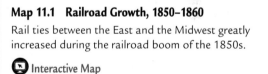 Interactive Map

which had more track than any other railroad in 1855, made money not only from its traffic but from real estate speculation. Purchasing land along its path, the Illinois Central laid out entire towns around its stations. The railroad used a template for all such towns, laying them out on a grid with east-west streets named after trees and north-south streets numbered. By the Civil War, few thought of the railroad-linked Midwest as a frontier region.

As the nation's first big business, the railroads transformed the way business was conducted. During the early 1830s railroads, like canals, depended on state funding. With the onset of a financial depression in the late 1830s, however, state governments scrapped many railroad projects. Convinced that railroads burdened them with high taxes and blasted hopes, voters in several states amended their constitutions to bar state funding for railroads and canals. Federal aid would not become widely available until the Civil War. However, the large railroads of the 1850s needed more capital than small investors alone could generate.

Gradually, the center of railroad financing shifted to New York City, where the railroad boom of the 1850s helped make Wall Street the nation's greatest capital market. The securities of all the leading railroads were traded on the floor of the New York Stock Exchange. Investment firms evaluated the securities of railroads and found purchasers for these securities in New York and Philadelphia, Paris and London, and Hamburg. Investment bankers soon began to exert influence over the railroads' internal affairs. A Wall Street analyst noted that railroad men seeking financing "must remember that money is power, and that the [financier] can dictate to a great extent his own terms."

Rising Prosperity

Technology also improved life by lowering prices. Clocks that cost $50 to make by hand in 1800 could be made by machine for 50¢ by 1850. Widespread use of steam power led to a 25 percent rise in the average worker's real income (purchasing power) between 1840 and 1860; unlike water wheels, steam engines could run in all seasons, so workers did not have to face long winter layoffs. Although cotton textile workers saw little gain in hourly wages, their average annual wages rose from $160 to $201 between 1830 and 1859.

The growth of towns and cities also contributed to the upward trend in average annual wages. In contrast to rural farming areas, with their heavily seasonal labor, urban settings offered jobs year-round. Towns and cities also provided women and children—who seldom were paid for farm labor—new opportunities for paid work. Children's wages played an important role in family finances for working-class families. An average New York or Philadelphia working-class family spent $500 to $600 per year on food, rent, clothing, and fuel. However, an average male head of household earned $300 a year. Clearly, the survival of many families depended on the wages of children and wives.

The average urban worker was marginally better off than the average rural worker, primarily because of seasonal fluctuations in agricultural work. Most antebellum Americans continued to see farming as the ideal occupation, but comparatively few could raise the $500 or so in cash necessary to purchase, clear, and stock a farm and then wait three to five years for any reward. The economic advantages of urban living help explain why so many Americans were moving to cities. During the 1840s and 1850s, American cities provided their residents with an unprecedented range of comforts and conveniences.

CHECKING IN

- Technology, such as the steel plow, the mechanical reaper, and the cotton gin, revolutionized American agriculture.
- The American system of manufacturing, based on interchangeable parts, grew rapidly.
- The amount of railroad track multiplied tenfold, linking major cities and transforming villages into cities.
- Railroads, America's first big business, revolutionized not only transportation but also financial systems.
- Prices fell and prosperity increased for most white Americans.

THE QUALITY OF LIFE

In what ways did technology transform the lives of ordinary Americans?

"Think of the numberless contrivances and inventions for our comfort and luxury," exclaimed poet Walt Whitman, "and you will bless your star that Fate has cast your lot in the year of Our Lord 1857." Improvements in the quality of life affected such mundane activities as eating, drinking, and washing. Machine-made furniture began to transform the interiors of houses. Stoves revolutionized heating and cooking.

However, change occurred unevenly. Technology made it possible for the middle class to enjoy luxuries formerly reserved for the rich, yet it widened the gulf between middle class and poor. As middle-class homes became increasingly lavish, the urban poor crowded into cramped tenements. And some critical elements—medicine, for example—lagged far behind in the technological explosion.

Dwellings

During the early 1800s, the randomly sited wood frame houses that had dotted colonial cities began to yield to more orderly brick row houses. Row houses, which were practical responses to rising land values (as much as 750 percent in Manhattan between 1785 and 1815), drew criticism for their "extreme uniformity." But they were not all alike. Middle-class row houses were larger and more elaborate than working-class row houses and less likely to be subdivided for occupancy by several families. The worst of the subdivided row houses, called tenements, were often inhabited by Irish immigrants and free blacks.

Home furnishings also revealed the widening gap between the prosperous and the poor. Middle- and upper-class families decorated their houses with fine furniture in the ornate, rococo style, along with wool carpeting, wallpaper, pianos, pictures, and gilt-framed mirrors. The mass-production of furniture reduced prices and tended to level taste between the middle and upper classes, while still setting those classes off from everyone else.

In rural areas, the quality of housing depended largely on the age of the settlement. In new settlements, the standard dwelling was a rude log cabin with planked floors, clay chimneys, and windows covered by oiled paper or cloth. As rural communities matured, log cabins gave way to insulated balloon-frame houses of two or more rooms. The balloon-frame—built with a skeleton of two-by-fours spaced at eighteen-inch intervals—was lighter and stronger than the older post-and-beam method. The simplicity and cheapness of such houses endeared them to western builders.

Conveniences and Inconveniences

By today's standards, everyday life in the 1840s and 1850s was primitive. But contemporaries were struck by how much better it was becoming. Stoves made it possible to cook several dishes at once, and railroads brought fresh vegetables to the city, an unobtainable luxury in the 1830s. Urban waterworks carried fresh water from rivers and reservoirs to hydrants. In 1823, Philadelphia completed the first urban water-supply system; by 1860, sixty-eight public water systems were operating in the United States.

Despite these improvements, home comforts remained limited. Coal burned longer and hotter than wood, but left a dirty residue that polluted the air. Only the rich could afford fruit out of season, since they alone could afford the sugar to preserve it. Home iceboxes were rare before 1860, so salt remained the most widely used preservative. (One reason antebellum Americans ate more pork than beef was that salt pork didn't taste quite as bad as salt beef.) Although public waterworks were engineering marvels, their impact is easily exaggerated. Only a fraction of the urban population lived near water hydrants, so most houses still had no running water. Taking a bath still required heating the water, pot by pot, on a stove. A New England physician reported that not one in five of his patients took even one bath a year.

Infrequent bathing added pungent body odors to the many strong smells of urban life. In the absence of municipal sanitation, street cleaning was done by private contractors with a reputation for slack performance. Hogs were allowed to roam freely and scavenge. Mounds of stable manure and outdoor privies added to the stench. Flush toilets were rare, and sewer systems lagged behind water-supply systems. Boston—which boasted more flush toilets than most other cities—had only five thousand for a population of 178,000 in 1860. Conveniences like running water and flush toilets became one more way for progress to set off the upper and middle classes from the poor. Conveniences also sharpened gender differences. Freed from making articles for home consumption, women were now expected to achieve fulfillment by obsessively making every house a "glorious temple" of spotless floors and gleaming furniture.

Disease and Health

epidemic diseases Diseases, such as cholera and yellow fever, that spread rapidly and were difficult to control

Despite the slowly rising living standard, Americans remained vulnerable to disease. **Epidemic diseases** swept through antebellum American cities and felled thousands. Yellow fever and cholera (CAH-luh-rah) killed one-fifth of New Orleans's population in 1832–1833, and cholera alone carried off 10 percent of St. Louis's population in 1849.

The transportation revolution increased the danger of epidemic diseases. The cholera epidemic of 1832, which was the first truly national epidemic, followed transportation networks out of New York City: one disease route ran up the Hudson River across the Erie Canal to Ohio and down the Ohio and Mississippi rivers to New Orleans; the other route followed shipping lines up and down the East Coast.

The failure of physicians to explain epidemic diseases reinforced hostility toward their profession. No one understood that bacteria caused cholera and yellow fever. Physicians clashed over whether epidemic diseases were spread by human touch or by "miasmas" (MY-az-muz), gases arising from rotten vegetation or dead animals. Neither theory worked. Quarantines failed to prevent the spread of epidemics (an argument against the contagion theory), and many residents of swampy areas contracted neither yellow fever nor cholera (a refutation of the miasma theory). Understandably, municipal leaders declined to delegate more than advisory powers to boards of health, which were dominated by physicians.

Although epidemic diseases baffled antebellum physicians, the discovery of anesthesia opened the way for advances in surgery. Laughing gas (nitrous oxide) had long provided partygoers who inhaled it with enjoyable sensations of giddiness and painlessness, but it was difficult to handle. Then in 1842, Crawford Long, a Georgia physician who had attended laughing gas frolics in his youth, employed sulfuric ether (a liquid with the same properties as nitrous oxide) during surgery. Dr. Long did not follow up his discovery, but four years later William T. G. Morton, a dentist, successfully employed sulfuric ether during an operation at Massachusetts General Hospital. Within a few years, ether came into wide surgical use.

The discovery of anesthesia improved the public image of surgeons, long viewed as brutes who tortured their patients. It also permitted longer and thus more careful operations. However, the failure of most surgeons to recognize the importance of clean hands and sterilized instruments partially offset the value of anesthesia. As early as 1843, Oliver Wendell Holmes, Sr., a poet and physician, published a paper on how unclean hands spread puerperal (poo-ER-puh-rul) fever among women giving birth, but disinfection was accepted only gradually. Operations remained as dangerous as the conditions they tried to heal. The mortality rate for amputations hovered around 40 percent.

Popular Health Movements

Suspicious of orthodox medicine, antebellum Americans turned to various alternative therapies that promised longer and healthier lives. Hydropathy (high-DRAW-puh-thee), the "water cure," offered "an abundance of water of dewy softness and crystal transparency, to cleanse, renovate, and rejuvenate the disease-worn and dilapidated system." The water cure held a special attraction for women: hydropathy promised to relieve the pain associated with childbirth and menstruation, and sanatoriums proved to be congenial gathering places for middle-class women.

In contrast to the relatively expensive water cure, Sylvester Graham, a former temperance reformer, propounded a health system that anyone could afford. In response to the 1832 cholera epidemic, Graham urged Americans to eat vegetables, fruits, and whole-grain bread (called Graham bread), and abstain from meat, spices, coffee, and tea as well as alcohol. Soon he added to his list of forbidden indulgences "sexual excess"—which for married couples meant having intercourse more than once a month. Just as temperance reformers blamed the craving for alcohol and abolitionists blamed the craving for illicit power, Graham blamed the craving for meat, stimulants, and sex.

Graham was dismissed by Ralph Waldo Emerson as "the prophet of bran bread and pumpkins." But Graham's doctrines attracted a broad audience. Boarding houses began to set Grahamite tables in their dining rooms. Graham's books sold well, and his public lectures were thronged. His regime

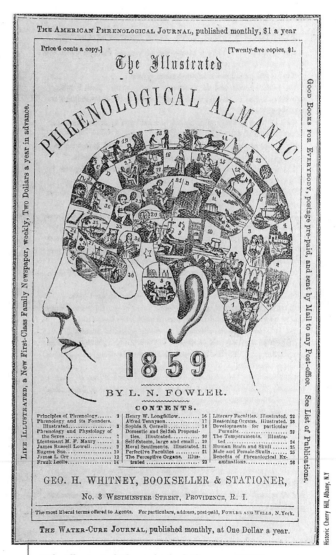

"The Illustrated Phrenological Almanac, 1859"
By dividing the brain into a large number of "faculties," phrenologists like Lorenzo Fowler, editor of the *Phrenological Almanac* for 1859, made the point that each person, regardless of whether born high or low, had an abundance of improvable talents.

Historic, Cherry Hill, Albany, N.Y.

addressed the popular desire for better health at a time when orthodox medicine seemed to do more damage than good.

Phrenology

The belief that each person was master of his or her own destiny underlay not only evangelical religion and health movements but also the most popular of the antebellum scientific fads: **phrenology** (free-NAHL-uh-jee). Phrenology rested on the idea that the human mind comprised thirty-seven distinct faculties, or "organs," each localized in a different part of the brain. Phrenologists thought that the degree of each organ's development determined skull shape, so that they could accurately analyze an individual's character by examining the bumps and depressions of the skull.

In the United States two brothers, Orson and Lorenzo Fowler, became the chief promoters of phrenology in the 1840s. Orson opened a publishing house in New York City (Fowlers and Wells) that marketed phrenology books on the subject. The Fowlers met criticisms that phrenology was godless by pointing out a huge organ called "Veneration" to prove that people were naturally religious, and they answered charges that phrenology was pessimistic by claiming that exercise could improve every desirable mental organ. Lorenzo proudly reported that several of his own skull bumps had been grown.

Americans were drawn to the practicality of phrenology. In a mobile, individualistic society, it promised a quick assessment of others. Some merchants used phrenological charts to pick suitable clerks, and some women asked their fiancés to undergo phrenological analysis before the wedding. Easily understood and practiced, and filled with the promise of universal improvement, phrenology was ideal for antebellum Americans. Just as they had invented machines to better their lives, they invented "sciences" that promised personal improvement.

phrenology Belief that one can read a person's character by examining bumps on the skull

CHECKING IN

- Housing generally improved in the mid-nineteenth century, but class distinctions became more pronounced.
- Improvements in urban living conditions, such as stoves and water systems, were somewhat offset by increased pollution.
- Epidemic diseases still flourished, but anesthesia came into use, and interest in antisepsis stirred.
- Health fads like hydropathy proliferated.
- Phrenology became a popular phenomenon.

DEMOCRATIC PASTIMES

In what new ways did Americans pass their free time during this period?

Between 1830 and 1860, technology transformed leisure by making Americans more dependent on recreation methods that were manufactured and sold. People purchased entertainment in the form of cheap newspapers and novels as well as affordable tickets to plays, museums, and lectures. Men like James Gordon Bennett, one of the founders of the **penny press** in America, and P. T. Barnum, the greatest showman of the nineteenth century, amassed fortunes by making the public want whatever they had to sell.

penny press Cheap newspapers developed by James Gordon Bennett

Technology also began the process by which individuals became spectators rather than creators of their own amusements. Americans had also found ways to enjoy themselves—even the gloomiest Puritans had enjoyed games and sports. After 1830, however, the provision of entertainment began to shift from individuals to the entrepreneurs who supplied ways to entertain the public. Commercial entertainment encouraged the passivity of those who consumed it.

Newspapers

In 1830, the typical American newspaper was four pages long, with the front and back pages filled almost completely with advertisements. The interior pages contained editorials, details of ship arrivals and cargoes, reprints of political speeches, and notices of political events. Such papers relied financially not on circulation, but on subsidies from the political groups with which they allied. In this way, they could profit without offering the exciting news stories and eye-catching illustrations that later generations of newspaper readers would take for granted.

The 1830s witnessed the beginnings of a stunning transformation in the American newspaper. Cheaper paper and steam-driven presses drastically lowered production costs, and enterprising journalists, among them James Gordon Bennett, saw the implications: slash prices, boost circulation, and reap vast profits. In 1833, New York's eleven daily newspapers had a combined daily circulation of only 26,500. Two years later, the combined circulation of the three largest "penny" newspapers had soared to 44,000. From 1830 to 1840, the combined daily circulation of American newspapers rose from roughly 78,000 to 300,000, and the number of weekly newspapers more than doubled.

The penny press also revolutionized the marketing and format of newspapers. Newsboys hawked the penny papers on busy street corners, and reporters filled the papers with gripping news stories designed to attract readers. The penny papers subordinated political and commercial coverage to human-interest stories of robberies, murders, rapes, and abandoned children. They dispatched reporters to police courts and printed transcripts of sensational trials. Charles Dickens parodied such coverage by naming one fictional American newspaper the *New York Stabber.*

But despite such limitations, as sociologist Michael Schudson observes, "The penny press invented the modern concept of 'news.'" Penny newspapers also invented modern news reporting, employing their own correspondents and using the telegraph to speed the communications process. The best penny papers, such as Bennett's *New York Herald* and Horace Greeley's *New York Tribune,* pioneered modern financial and political reporting. The *Herald* featured a daily "money article" that analyzed and interpreted financial events. "The spirit, pith, and philosophy of commercial affairs is what men of business want," Bennett wrote.

The Theater

Like newspapers, theaters increasingly appealed to a mass audience. Antebellum theaters were large and crowded; cheap seats drew a democratic throng of lawyers, merchants, and their wives; artisans and clerks; sailors and noisy boys; and a sizable body of prostitutes.

The presence of prostitutes in the audience was only one of many factors that made theaters vaguely disreputable. Theater audiences were notoriously ill-behaved: they stamped their feet, hooted at villains, and threw potatoes and garbage at the stage when they disliked the characters or the acting. Contributing to such rowdiness was the animosity between the fan bases of different theatrical stars. In 1849, a long-running feud between the leading American actor Edwin Forrest and popular British actor William Macready culminated in the Astor Place riot in New York City, which left twenty-two people dead.

The most popular plays were emotionally charged melodramas in which virtue was rewarded, vice punished, and the hero won the beautiful heroine. Melodramas offered sensational features such as volcanic eruptions, staged battles, even live horses on stage. Yet the single most popular dramatist was William Shakespeare. In 1835, Philadelphia audiences witnessed sixty-five performances of his plays. However, Shakespeare might not have recognized some of these performances, adapted as they were for popular audiences. Theatrical managers highlighted sword fights and assassinations, cut long speeches, and occasionally substituted happy endings for sad ones. And they entertained audiences between acts with jugglers and acrobats, impersonations of Tecumseh or Aaron Burr, or the exhibition of a three-year-old child who weighed one hundred pounds.

minstrel show Blackface show of "Negro" song and dance

National Portrait Gallery, Smithsonian Institution/Art Resource, NY

P. T. Barnum and Tom Thumb

When P. T. Barnum posed with his protégée—whose real name was Charles Sherwood Stratton—sometime around 1850, the twelve-year-old "human curiosity" stood a little over two feet in height. Barnum and Stratton enjoyed a long partnership which brought considerable wealth to both of them.

Minstrel Shows

The popular **minstrel shows** of the 1840s and 1850s forged enduring racial stereotypes that buttressed white Americans' sense of superiority by diminishing black Americans.

Minstrel shows featured white performers in burnt-cork blackface who entertained their audiences with songs, dances, and humorous sketches that pretended to mimic black culture. But while minstrelsy did borrow a few elements of African-American culture, most of its contents were white inventions. The shows' images of African-Americans both expressed and reinforced the prejudices of the working-class whites who dominated the audience. Minstrel troupes depicted blacks as stupid, clumsy, and absurdly musical, and parodied Africanness by naming their performances the "Nubian Jungle Dance" and the "African Fling." Minstrel shows used stock characters to capture white expectations about black behavior. These included Uncle Ned, the tattered and docile slave, and Zip Coon, the arrogant urban freeman who paraded around in high hat and long-tailed coat and lived off his girlfriends.

By the 1850s, major cities from New York to San Francisco had several minstrel theaters. Touring professionals and local amateurs brought minstrelsy to small towns and villages. Author Mark Twain recalled how minstrelsy had burst upon Hannibal, Missouri, in the early 1840s as "a glad and stunning surprise." Minstrel troupes even entertained a succession of presidents in the antebellum White House.

P. T. Barnum

No one understood better than **P. T. Barnum** how to turn the public's craving for entertainment into a profitable business. He was simultaneously a hustler who cheated his customers before they could cheat him, and an idealist who founded a newspaper to attack wrongdoing and who thought of himself as a public benefactor.

After moving to New York City in 1834, Barnum launched his career as an entertainment entrepreneur. He got his start exhibiting a black woman named Joice Heth, whom he billed as the 169-year-old former slave nurse of George Washington. In fact, she was probably around eighty, but Barnum neither knew nor cared, so long as people paid to see her. He was playing a game with the public, and the public played right back.

In 1841 Barnum purchased a run-down museum in New York City, rechristened it the American Museum, and opened a new chapter in the history of popular entertainment. Avoiding the educational slant of other museums, Barnum concentrated on curiosities and faked exhibits; he wanted to interest people, not to educate them. The American Museum included ventriloquists, magicians, albinos, a twenty-five-inch-tall five-year-old whom Barnum named General Tom Thumb, and the "Feejee Mermaid," billed by Barnum as "positively asserted by its owner to have been taken alive in the Feejee Islands." By 1850, the American Museum had become the best-known museum in the nation.

Blessed with a genius for publicity, Barnum recognized that newspapers could invent as well as report news. One of his favorite tactics was to puff his own exhibits by writing letters to newspapers (under various names) hinting that the scientific world was agog over some astonishing curiosity that the public could soon view at the American Museum. At a time when each year brought new technological marvels, Americans would believe in anything, even the Feejee Mermaid. But Barnum did not rely solely on curiosities and clever marketing. To secure that his museum had a reputation for providing safe family entertainment, he provided regular lectures on the evils of alcohol and the benefits of Christian religion—thus wrapping the exotic and sensational in a sheen of respectability.

P. T. Barnum Showman who exhibited "natural wonders," real and otherwise

CHECKING IN

- Between 1830 and 1860, entrepreneurs found new business opportunities with popular entertainment.
- James Gordon Bennett revolutionized the newspaper world with the penny press.
- Theater became a major source of entertainment for diverse and often rowdy audiences.
- Blackface minstrel shows provided popular entertainment while reinforcing negative stereotypes of African-Americans.
- P. T. Barnum introduced Americans to the wonders of the Feejee Mermaid and other oddities.

THE QUEST FOR NATIONALITY IN LITERATURE AND ART

How did the work of American writers and artists become distinctly American?

Europeans paid no attention to American poetry or fiction before the 1820s. Although Americans could point with pride to Washington Irving's tales of Sleepy Hollow and Rip Van Winkle, they also had to admit that Irving had done most of his work while living in Britain.

After 1820, the United States experienced a literary flowering known as the **American Renaissance.** Leading figures of this burst of creativity included James Fenimore Cooper, Ralph Waldo Emerson, Henry David Thoreau (theh-ROW), Margaret Fuller, Walt Whitman, Nathaniel Hawthorne, Herman Melville, and

American Renaissance Literary movement that flourished after 1820

Edgar Allan Poe. In 1830, 40 percent of books published in the United States were written by Americans; by 1850, this number had increased to 75 percent.

American writers often sought to depict the national features of the United States—its land and its people—in their work. The quest for a distinctively American literature shaped the writings of Cooper, Emerson, and Whitman. It also revealed itself in the majestic paintings of the Hudson River School, the first home-grown movement in art, and in the landscape architecture of Frederick Law Olmsted.

Roots of the American Renaissance

Two broad movements, one economic and the other philosophical, contributed to this development. First, the transportation revolution created a national market for books, especially fiction. First to benefit from this new market was Sir Walter Scott, a British author whose historical novels became wildly popular in the United States and showed that there was a huge market for fiction. Scott became a model for many American authors, including James Fenimore Cooper.

Second, a new philosophical movement, romanticism, saturated the American Renaissance. Romantics emphasized emotion and inner feelings, focusing on the individual and his or her unique response to nature and emotion. This new emphasis on emotion created a more democratic literature, accessible to virtually everyone (unlike earlier classicism, which demanded knowledge of ancient history and mythology). Women entered the fiction market in large numbers; although barred from higher education and the classics, they could easily access their emotions and tweak the emotions of their readers. Harriet Beecher Stowe's massive bestseller, *Uncle Tom's Cabin,* illustrates how successful women authors were in tugging at their readers' heartstrings. Novels also possessed a subversive quality, a freedom of plot and character not available to the essayist. Authors could create unconventional characters, situations, and outcomes, and left more room for interpretation by the reader, who was far more likely to focus on plot and characters than moral sentiments.

Cooper, Emerson, Thoreau, Fuller, and Whitman

James Fenimore Cooper was a trailblazer in the development of a national literature with distinctively American themes. In his frontiersman Natty Bumppo, "Leatherstocking," Cooper created an American archetype. Natty first appears in *The Pioneers* (1823) as an old man, a former hunter, who blames the farmers for wantonly destroying upstate New York's game and turning the silent and majestic forests into deserts of tree stumps. As a spokesman for nature against the march of civilization, Natty became a highly popular figure, and his life unfolded in several other enormously popular novels, such as *The Last of the Mohicans* (1826), *The Pathfinder* (1840), and *The Deerslayer* (1841).

During the 1830s, Ralph Waldo Emerson emerged as the most influential spokesman for those who sought a national literature and art. Emerson, who served briefly as a Unitarian minister and then became a popular lecturer, voiced American intellectual ambitions in his 1837 address "The American Scholar," which called on American writers to break free of European standards.

As the leader of transcendentalism, the American offshoot of romanticism, Emerson contended that ideas of God and freedom were innate, not the result of reason. Knowledge was like sight—an instantaneous and direct perception of truth. Anyone, whether a learned university professor or a common farmer, could glimpse truth by following the promptings of his heart. Thus, the United States, young and democratic, could produce as noble a literature and art as any tradition-bound European nation. "Our day of independence, our long apprenticeship to the learning of other lands draws to a close," he proclaimed. Let "the single man plant himself indomitably on his instincts and . . . the huge world will come around to him."

Although he admired Cooper's fiction, Emerson expressed his own version of literary nationalism in essays characterized by a homely reliance on the individual as well as an interest in broad philosophical questions. The true scholar, he stressed, must be independent. Emerson did not present systematic arguments backed by evidence to prove his point. Rather, he relied on a sequence of vivid if unconnected assertions whose truth the reader was supposed to see instantly. (One reader complained that she might have understood Emerson better if she had stood on her head.)

Emerson had a magnetic attraction for young intellectuals who were ill at ease in conventional society. Henry David Thoreau, born in 1817, typified the younger Emersonians. Unlike Emerson, whose adventurousness was largely intellectual, Thoreau was both a thinker and a doer. At one point he went to jail rather than pay poll taxes that would support the Mexican War, a conflict that he saw as part of a southern conspiracy to extend slavery. The experience of jail led Thoreau to write *Civil Disobedience* (1849), in which he defended disobedience of unjust laws.

On July 4, 1845, in a personal declaration of independence, Thoreau moved a few miles from Concord Center to the woods near Walden Pond. He spent two years there living in a small cabin he constructed on land owned by Emerson and providing for his own wants as simply as possible. His purpose in retreating to Walden was to write an account of a canoe trip he took with his brother in 1839. But he wrote a more important book, *Walden* (1854), which was filled with day-to-day descriptions of hawks and the pond, his invention of raisin bread, and his trapping of the woodchucks that ravaged his vegetable garden. But Walden had a larger transcendentalist message. Thoreau's retreat taught him that anyone could satisfy his material wants with only a few weeks' work each year and preserve the remainder of his time for examining life's purpose. The problem with Americans, he said, was that they turned themselves into "mere machines" to acquire pointless wealth.

One of the most remarkable figures in Emerson's circle was Margaret Fuller, an intellectual whose status distanced her from conventional society. Her father, although disappointed that she was not a boy, gave her the sort of education a young man might have received at Harvard; she read Latin and Greek, the modern German romantics, and the British literary classics. Transcendentalism, with its emphasis on the free life of the spirit and the need for each person to discover truth on his or her own, opened a new world for Fuller. For five years she supported herself by presiding over "conversations" by Boston's elite men and women. Transcendentalism also reinforced her feminist ideas; in *Women in the Nineteenth Century* (1845) she cast aside the doctrine of "separate spheres" and contended that no woman could achieve

Margaret Fuller

In 1846, Margaret Fuller was sent by Horace Greeley to Europe as the *Tribune's* foreign correspondent. There she met artists and writers, observed the Revolutions of 1848, and married an Italian nobleman. On her return to America in 1850, she, her husband, and her infant son died in a shipwreck off Long Island.

Walt Whitman Protégé of Emerson and author of daringly original poetry

personal fulfillment without developing her intellectual abilities and overcoming her fear of being called masculine.

One of Emerson's qualities was an ability to sympathize with such dissimilar people as the prickly Thoreau, the scholarly Fuller, and the outgoing and earthy **Walt Whitman.** The self-educated Whitman had left school at age eleven and worked his way up from printer's apprentice to journalist and then newspaper editor. A familiar figure at Democratic Party functions, he marched in party parades and put his pen to the service of its antislavery wing.

Leaves of Grass shattered existing poetic conventions. Whitman composed in free verse, and his blunt, often lusty words assailed "delicacy." He wrote of "the scent of these armpits finer than prayer" and "winds whose soft-tickling genitals rub against me."

To some contemporary critics, *Leaves of Grass* seemed the work of an escaped lunatic. One derided it as a "heterogeneous mass of bombast, egotism, vulgarity, and nonsense." Emerson and a few others, however, reacted enthusiastically. Emerson had long awaited the appearance of "the poet of America" and knew immediately that Whitman was that poet.

Hawthorne, Melville, and Poe

Three major writers of the 1840s and 1850s strayed far from Emerson's ideals. Nathaniel Hawthorne, Herman Melville, and Edgar Allan Poe wrote fiction that paid little heed to Emerson's call for a literature treating the everyday experiences of ordinary Americans. Hawthorne, for example, set *The Scarlet Letter* (1850) in New England's Puritan past, *The House of the Seven Gables* (1851) in a mansion haunted by memories of the past, and *The Marble Faun* (1859) in Rome. Poe set several of his short stories in Europe; and Melville's novels *Typee* (1846), *Omoo* (1847), and *Mardi* (1849) took place in the exotic South Seas, whereas his masterpiece, *Moby-Dick* (1851), was set aboard a whaler. If the only surviving documents from the 1840s and 1850s were its major novels, historians would face an impossible task in trying to understand daily life in antebellum America.

In part, these three writers felt that American life lacked the materials for great fiction. Hawthorne bemoaned the difficulty of writing about a country "where there is no shadow, no antiquity, no mystery, no picturesque and gloomy wrong, nor anything but a commonplace prosperity in broad and simple daylight." Psychology, not society, fascinated these writers. Each probed the depths of the human mind rather than the intricacies of social relationships. Their work displayed an underlying pessimism about the human condition and the fundamental irrationality of human nature.

Pessimism led these authors to create characters obsessed by pride, guilt, a desire for revenge, or a quest for perfection and then to set their stories along the byways of society, where they could explore the complexities of human motivation without the jarring intrusions of everyday life. For example, in *The Scarlet Letter* Hawthorne returned to the Puritan era to examine the psychological and moral consequences of the adultery committed by Hester Prynne (prin) and the minister Arthur Dimmesdale, although he devoted little attention to depicting the Puritan village in which the action takes place. Melville, in *Moby-Dick,* created the frightening Captain Ahab (AY-hab), whose relentless pursuit of a white whale fails to fill the chasm in his soul and brings death to all his crew except the narrator. Poe, in his short story "The Fall of the House of Usher" (1839), interwove the symbol of a crumbling mansion to convey the moral agony of a decaying, incestuous family.

Although these three authors ignored Emerson's call to write about the ordinary life of their fellow Americans, they fashioned a distinctively American fiction. Their works, preoccupied with analysis of moral dilemmas and psychological states, fulfilled Tocqueville's prediction that writers in democratic nations, while rejecting traditional sources of fiction, would explore the abstract and universal questions of human nature.

Literature in the Marketplace

The suspicion that commercialism would corrupt art did not entirely vanish in nineteenth-century America, but it certainly withered. The brilliant poet Emily Dickinson made little or no attempt to publish her work at all. But other authors, hard strapped for cash, entered the marketplace. Poe, for example, scratched out a meager living writing short stories for popular magazines. Thoreau craved recognition and tried to market his poems in New York City; failing that, he turned to detailed narratives of nature that sold very well.

Emerson, too, wanted to reach a broader public. After abandoning his first vocation as a Unitarian minister, he reached for a new sort of audience and a new source of income: the lyceum. Lyceums—local organizations for sponsoring lectures—spread throughout the northern tier of states after the late 1820s to meet popular demands for entertainment and self-improvement. Thanks to newly built railroads and the cheap newspapers that publicized lyceum programs, other speakers followed in Emerson's path. As Herman Melville pledged, "If they will pay my expenses and give a reasonable fee, I am ready to lecture in Labrador or on the Isle of Desolation off Patagonia."

The age offered women few opportunities for public speaking, and most lyceum lecturers were men. But women were tapping into the growing market for literature. Fiction-writing became the most lucrative occupation open to women before the Civil War. Novelist Susan Warner's *The Wide, Wide World,* published in 1850, went through fourteen editions by 1852. Harriet Beecher Stowe's *Uncle Tom's Cabin,* published in 1852, exceeded all previous sales by selling 100,000 copies in just five months. Nathaniel Hawthorne, whose own works sold modestly, bitterly condemned what he called the "d—d mob of scribbling women" who were outselling and outearning him.

The most popular form of fiction in the 1840s and 1850s was the sentimental or domestic novel, written mostly by women for women. In a typical novel, a female orphan or a spoiled rich girl was thrown into hard times by a drunken father and learned to prevail. The moral was clear: Women could overcome trials and improve their lives. Another popular genre in the antebellum reading market was sensationalist fiction, which drew on such dark romantic themes as criminality, mystery, and horror.

Therefore, authors such as Hawthorne, Poe, and Melville had to compete with the popular culture of the story newspapers, sentimental fiction, and sensationalism. The philosopher Emerson shared the lecture circuit with the showman P. T. Barnum. By and large, however, the major writers of the American Renaissance were successful. But the writers most likely to achieve commercial success were those who best met certain popular expectations, such as moral and spiritual uplift, horror and mystery, or love stories and happy endings.

Wadsworth Athenaeum Museum of Art/Art Resource, NY

Thomas Cole, The Last of the Mohicans, Cora Kneeling at the Feet of Tamenund, 1827
One year after James Fenimore Cooper's novel *The Last of the Mohicans* was published, Thomas Cole painted the white captive Cora pleading with Tamenund, Chief of the Delaware, not to be forced into marriage with an evil Indian warrior. In Cole's painting, this human drama is dwarfed by the sublime beauty of the American wilderness.

American Landscape Painting

At the same time as American writers were trying to create a distinctly American literature, American painters were searching for a national style in art. Lacking a mythic past of gods and goddesses, they subordinated historical and figure painting to landscape painting. The American landscape, though barren of the "poetry of decay" that Europe's ruined castles and crumbling temples provided, was fresh and relatively unencumbered by the human imprint. These conditions posed a challenge to the painters of the **Hudson River School,** which flourished from the 1820s to the 1870s. Its best-known representatives—Thomas Cole, Asher Durand, and Frederic Church—painted scenes of the unspoiled region around the Hudson River.

Although all three men compared the majesty of the Hudson to that of the Rhine, none was exclusively a landscapist. Some of Cole's most popular paintings were allegories, such as *The Course of Empire,* a sequence of five canvases depicting the rise and fall of an ancient city; it implied that luxury doomed republican virtue.

The works of Washington Irving and the opening of the Erie Canal had piqued interest in the Hudson during the 1820s. Then, after 1830, Emerson and Thoreau lauded primitive nature; "in wildness is the preservation of the world," Thoreau wrote. By this time, much of the original American forest had already fallen to pioneer axes, and one writer urgently concluded that "it behooves our artists to rescue from [civilization's] grasp the little that is left before it is too late."

The Hudson River painters did more than preserve a passing wilderness; they also emphasized emotional effect. Cole's rich colors; billowing clouds; massive, gnarled trees; towering peaks; and deep chasms so heightened the dramatic impact of his paintings that poet William Cullen Bryant compared them to "acts of religion." Similar motifs marked Frederick Church's paintings of the Andes Mountains, which used erupting volcanoes and thunderstorms to evoke dread and a sense of majesty. In powerful, evocative canvases, American artists aimed to capture the natural grandeur of their land.

Like Cole, George Catlin tried to preserve a vanishing America through his art. His goal was to paint as many Native Americans as possible in their pure and "savage" state. By 1837, he had created 437 oil paintings and thousands of sketches of faces and customs from nearly fifty tribes. Catlin's romantic view of the Indians as noble savages was a double-edged sword. His admirers delighted in his dignified portrayals of Indians but shared his foreboding that the march of progress had already doomed these noble creatures to oblivion.

Landscape architects tried to create small enclaves of nature to provide spiritual refreshment to harried city-dwellers. "Rural" cemeteries with pastoral names like Harmony Grove, placed near major cities, became tourist attractions, designed as much for the living as for the dead. On a grander scale **Frederick Law Olmsted** and Calvert Vaux (voh) designed New York City's Central Park to look like undisturbed countryside. Drainage pipes carried water to man-made lakes, and trees screened out the surrounding buildings. Central Park became an idealized version of nature, meant to remind visitors of landscapes that they had seen in pictures. Thus, nature was made to mirror art.

Hudson River School
Landscape painting that emphasized grandeur, emotion

Frederick Law Olmsted
Prominent landscape architect and co-designer, with Calvert Vaux, of New York City's Central Park

CHECKING IN

- Romanticism combined with the technological revolution to produce an American Renaissance.
- American literature took on nationalistic themes with James Fenimore Cooper and his tales of the frontier.
- Ralph Waldo Emerson was the center of the transcendentalist movement, which included Henry David Thoreau and Margaret Fuller.
- American writers such as Poe, Hawthorne, and Melville plumbed the depths of the human psyche.
- The Hudson River School of painting romanticized the American landscape and drenched it in emotion.

Chapter Summary

What technological improvements brought about American economic growth between 1840 and 1860? (page 246)

Rapid technological growth revolutionized agriculture and greatly increased productivity in the manufacturing sector as well. Railroads played a vital role, linking cities, spawning new cities, creating markets, and providing a new business model. Prices fell, and prosperity rose.

In what ways did technology transform the lives of ordinary Americans? (page 250)

As cities grew, housing and living conditions improved for better-off residents, but squalor and pollution persisted, and class distinctions sharpened. The inability to control epidemic disease fed such popular fads as hydropathy and phrenology.

In what new ways did Americans pass their free time during this period? (page 254)

Popular entertainment became the realm of entrepreneurs such as James Bennett Gordon with his "penny press" and P. T. Barnum with his stable of wonders. Theater flourished, drawing diverse and rowdy audiences, and black-face minstrel shows reinforced negative stereotypes.

How did the work of American writers and artists become distinctly American? (page 257)

The disappearing frontier elicited a distinctly American literature from James Fenimore Cooper. An American Renaissance produced such democratic writers as Whitman and Emerson, as well as those fascinated by the darker side of human nature, such as Poe, Hawthorne, and Melville. The Hudson River School emphasized the grandeur and emotion of the American landscape.

KEY TERMS

technology *(p. 246)*
John Deere *(p. 246)*
Cyrus McCormick *(p. 246)*
interchangeable parts *(p. 248)*
epidemic diseases *(p. 252)*
phrenology *(p. 254)*
penny press *(p. 254)*
minstrel show *(p. 256)*
P. T. Barnum *(p. 257)*
American Renaissance *(p. 257)*
Walt Whitman *(p. 260)*
Hudson River School *(p. 263)*
Frederick Law Olmsted *(p. 263)*

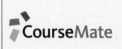
CourseMate

Go to the CourseMate website at **www.cengagebrain.com** for additional study tools and review materials—including audio and video clips—for this chapter.

CHAPTER PREVIEW

King Cotton
How did the rise of cotton cultivation affect the South?

The Social Groups of the White South
What major social divisions segmented the white South?

Social Relations in the White South
How did slavery affect social relations in the South?

Life Under Slavery
How did slaves and free blacks respond to their circumstances?

The Emergence of African-American Culture
What were the distinctive features of African-American society and culture in the South?

Courtesy of George Eastman House, International Museum of Photography and Film

Family Group
The African-American woman shown here probably was a slave mammy who substituted for the absent mother of the children.

Nat Turner Leader of the largest slave rebellion in U.S. history

Slipping through the swampy woodlands of Southampton County, Virginia, in the early morning of August 22, 1831, a band of slaves led by **Nat Turner** embarked on a grisly campaign of liberation. As the death count rose, so did the number of slaves following Turner; by noon more than sixty slaves had taken up axes, hatchets, and muskets, and more than sixty whites had been shot, clubbed, or hacked to death.

Despite Southampton County's isolation, word of the slave uprising soon reached the capital, Richmond, and neighboring North Carolina counties, and thousands of militia and vigilantes poured into the area. Shocking destruction greeted them; dismembered bodies and fresh blood testified to the rage unleashed by the rebels. In turn, the slaves would fall victim to white rage, as scores of blacks were killed, whether or not they had actually been involved. Most of Turner's followers were either shot on sight or jailed, tried, and hanged. Turner himself eluded capture until late October; after a trial he, too, was hanged.

The Granger Collection, New York

Nat Turner

By noon Turner's army, which had grown to sixty or seventy followers, had murdered about sixty whites. As word of trouble spread, militia and vigilantes, thousands strong, poured into Southampton from across the border in North Carolina and from other countries in Virginia.

Revenge was one thing, but understanding was another. In his subsequently published "Confessions" (recorded by his court-appointed lawyer), Turner did not claim that he had been mistreated by his owners. What they did reveal was an intelligent and deeply religious man who had somehow learned to read and write as a boy, and who claimed to have seen heavenly visions of white and black spirits fighting each other. Christianity was supposed to make slaves more docile, but Nat Turner's ability to read had enabled him to find passages in the Bible that threatened death to him who "stealeth" a man, a fair description of slavery. Asked by his lawyer if he now found himself mistaken, Turner replied, "Was not Christ crucified?" Small wonder that a niece of George Washington concluded that she and all other white Virginians were now living on a "smothered volcano."

In the wake of Turner's insurrection, many Virginians, especially nonslaveholding whites in the western part of the state, urged that Virginia follow the lead of northern states and emancipate its slaves. During the winter of 1831–1832, the Virginia legislature wrangled over emancipation proposals. The narrow defeat of these proposals marked a turning point; thereafter, opposition to slavery steadily weakened not only in Virginia but throughout the region known to history as the Old South.

As late as the Revolution, *south* referred more to a direction than to a place. But as one northern state after another embraced emancipation, slavery became the "peculiar institution" that distinguished the Old South from other sections.

A rift of sorts split the Old South into the **Upper South** and the **Lower (Deep) South.** With its diversified economy, the Upper South relied far less than the Lower South on slavery and cotton, and in 1861 it approached secession more reluctantly than its sister states. Yet in the final analysis, slavery forged a single Old South where it scarred all social relationships. Without slavery, there never would have been an Old South.

Upper South Virginia, North Carolina, Tennessee, and Arkansas; a more economically diverse region

Lower (Deep) South South Carolina, Georgia, Florida, Alabama, Mississippi, Louisiana, and Texas

KING COTTON

How did the rise of cotton cultivation affect the South?

In 1790, the South was essentially stagnant. Tobacco, its primary cash crop, had lost its economic vitality even as it had depleted the once-rich southern soils, and neither rice nor cotton could replace tobacco's economic importance. Three out of four southerners still lived along the Atlantic seaboard, specifically in the Chesapeake and the Carolinas. One of three resided in Virginia alone.

Chronology

1790s	Methodists and Baptists start to make major strides in converting slaves to Christianity
1800	Gabriel Prosser plans a slave rebellion in Virginia
1808	Congress prohibits external slave trade
1816–1819	Boom in cotton prices stimulates settlement of the Southwest
1820–1821	Missouri Compromise
1822	Denmark Vesey's conspiracy is uncovered in South Carolina
1831	Nat Turner leads a slave rebellion in Virginia
1832	Virginia legislature narrowly defeats a proposal for gradual emancipation
1844–1845	Methodist and Baptist churches split over slavery into northern and southern wings
1849	Sugar production in Louisiana reaches its peak
1849–1860	Period of high cotton prices

The contrast between that South and the dynamic South of 1850 was stunning. By 1850, southerners had moved south and west—now only one out of seven southerners lived in Virginia—and cotton reigned as king, shaping this new South. The growth of the British textile industry had created a huge demand for cotton, while Indian removal had made way for southern expansion into the "Cotton Kingdom," a broad swath of land that stretched from South Carolina, Georgia, and northern Florida in the East through Alabama, Mississippi, central and western Tennessee, and Louisiana, and from there on to Arkansas and Texas.

The Lure of Cotton

Southerners extolled **King Cotton.** A warm climate, wet springs and summers, and relatively dry autumns made the Lower South the ideal location for cultivating cotton. A cotton farmer did not need slaves, cotton gins, or the capital required for sugar cultivation. Perhaps 50 percent of farmers in the "Cotton Belt" owned no slaves, and to process their harvest they could turn to the widely available commercial gins. Cotton promised to make poor men prosperous and rich men kings.

Yet large-scale cotton cultivation and slavery grew together as the southern slave population nearly doubled between 1810 and 1830 (Figures 12.1 and 12.2).

King Cotton Term expressing the southern belief that U.S. and British economies depended on cotton

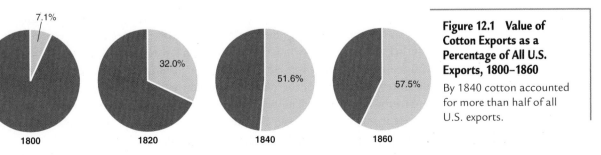

7.1% — 1800
32.0% — 1820
51.6% — 1840
57.5% — 1860

Figure 12.1 Value of Cotton Exports as a Percentage of All U.S. Exports, 1800–1860

By 1840 cotton accounted for more than half of all U.S. exports.

Figure 12.2   Growth of Cotton Production and the Slave Population, 1790–1860

Cotton and slavery rose together in the Old South.

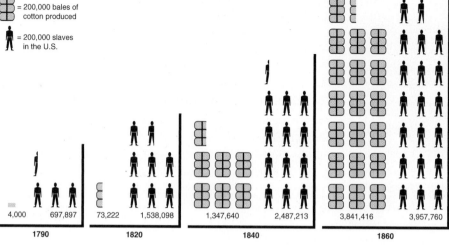

= 200,000 bales of cotton produced

= 200,000 slaves in the U.S.

4,000	697,897
73,222	1,538,098
1,347,640	2,487,213
3,841,416	3,957,760

1790   1820   1840   1860

Three-fourths of all southern slaves worked in the cotton economy in 1830. Owning slaves enabled a planter to harvest vast fields of cotton speedily, a crucial advantage because a sudden rainstorm at harvest time could pelt cotton to the ground and soil it.

Cotton was also compatible with corn production. Corn could be planted either earlier or later than cotton and harvested before or after. Because the cost of owning a slave remained the same regardless of whether he or she was working, corn production allowed slaveholders to shift slave labor between corn and cotton. By 1860 the acreage devoted to corn in the Old South actually *exceeded* that devoted to cotton. Economically, corn and cotton gave the South the best of two worlds. Intense demand in Britain and New England kept cotton prices high and money flowing into the South. Because of southern self-sufficiency in growing corn and raising hogs that thrived on the corn, money did not drain away to pay for food. In 1860 the twelve wealthiest counties in the United States were all in the South.

Ties Between the Lower and Upper South

Two giant cash crops, sugar and cotton, dominated agriculture in the Lower South. The Upper South, a region of tobacco, vegetable, hemp, and wheat growers, depended far less on the great cash crops. Nevertheless, a common dependence on slavery unified the Upper and the Lower South, and made the Upper South identify more with the Lower South than with the nation's free states.

A range of social, political, and psychological factors promoted this unity. First, many settlers in the Lower South had come from the Upper South. Second, all white southerners benefited from the Constitution's three-fifths clause, which let them count slaves as a basis for congressional representation. Third, abolitionist attacks on slavery stung all southerners and bound them together. Fourth, economic ties linked the two Souths. The profitability of cotton and sugar increased the value of slaves throughout the South. The sale of slaves from the declining **plantation** states of the Upper South to the booming Lower South was a huge business.

plantation Large landholding devoted to a cash crop, such as cotton or tobacco

The North and South Diverge

However, the changes responsible for the dynamic growth of the South widened the distance between it and the North. The South remained predominantly rural, whereas the North became more and more urban.

Lack of industry kept the South rural; by 1860, it had one-third of the U.S. population but accounted for only one-tenth of the nation's manufacturing. The industrial output of the entire South in 1850 was less than one-third that of Massachusetts alone.

A few southerners advocated industrialization to reduce the South's dependency on northern manufactured products. After touring northern textile mills, South Carolina's William Gregg established a company town for textiles at Graniteville in 1845. By 1860, Richmond boasted the nation's fourth-largest producer of iron products, the Tredegar (TREH-du-gur) Iron Works. But these were exceptions.

Compared to factories in the North, most southern factories were small, produced for nearby markets, and were closely tied to agriculture. The leading northern factories turned hides into tanned leather and leather into shoes, or cotton into threads and threads into suits. In contrast, southern factories turned grain into flour, corn into meal, and logs into lumber.

Slavery posed a major obstacle to southern industrialization, but not because slaves were unfit for factories; the Tredegar Iron Works, for example, was among many factories that employed slaves. However, industrial slavery troubled slaveholders. Away from the strict discipline and supervision possible on a plantation, slaves sometimes behaved as if they were free, shifting jobs, working overtime, and even negotiating better working conditions. But the chief brake on southern industrialization was money, not labor. To raise the capital needed to build factories, planters would have had to sell their slaves. They had little incentive to do so. Cash crops like cotton and sugar were proven winners, whereas the benefits of industrialization were remote and doubtful. As long as southerners believed that an economy founded on cash crops would remain profitable, they had little reason to leap into the uncertainties of industrialization.

As in industry, the South lagged behind the North in education. Whereas northerners recognized the benefits of an educated work force for their growing manufacturing economy, agriculturally oriented southerners rejected compulsory education and were reluctant to tax property to support schools. They abhorred the thought of educating slaves, and southern lawmakers made it a crime to teach slaves to read. For most whites, the only available schools were private. White illiteracy thus remained high in the South as it declined in the North. Before the Civil War, for example, nearly 60 percent of North Carolinians who enlisted in the U.S. Army were illiterate, compared to 30 percent for northern enlistees.

Agricultural, self-sufficient, and independent, the middling and poor whites of the South remained unconvinced of the need for public education. They had little dependence on the printed word, few complex commercial transactions, and infrequent dealings with urban people. Planters did not need an orderly and disciplined white work force; they already had a black one that they were determined to keep illiterate lest it acquire ideas about freedom.

Because the South diverged so sharply from the North, outsiders often dismissed it as backward. A northern journalist wrote of white southerners in the 1850s,

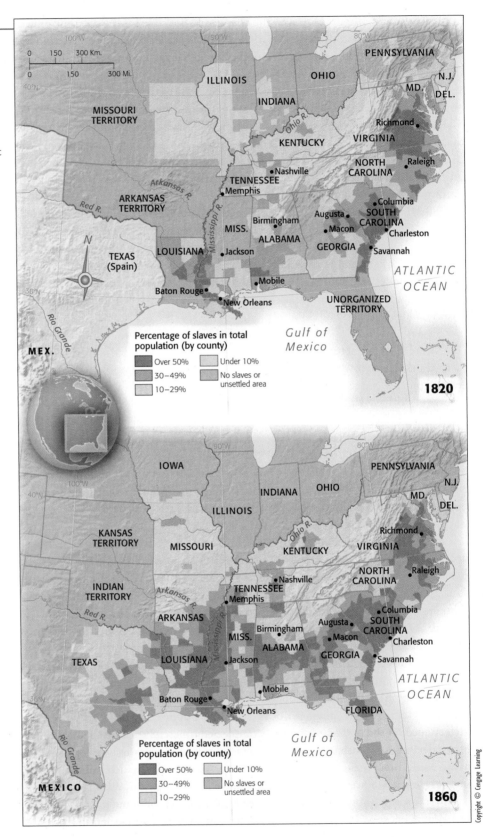

Map 12.1 Distribution of Slaves, 1820 and 1860

In 1790 the majority of slaves resided along the southeastern seaboard. By 1860, however, slavery had spread throughout the South, and slaves were most heavily concentrated in the Deep South states.

(Ordeal by Fire: The Civil War and Reconstruction *by James M. McPherson. Copyright 1982 by Alfred A. Knopf, Inc.*)

Interactive Map

Percentage of slaves in total population (by county)

Over 50%   Under 10%
30–49%   No slaves or
10–29%   unsettled area

1820

Percentage of slaves in total population (by county)

Over 50%   Under 10%
30–49%   No slaves or
10–29%   unsettled area

1860

Copyright © Cengage Learning

"They work little, and that little, badly; they earn little, they sell little; they buy little, and have little—very little—of the common comforts and consolations of civilized life."

Yet the South did not lack progressive features. By 1860, white per capita income in the South exceeded the national average. Like northerners, white southerners were restless, eager to make money, and skillful at managing complex commercial enterprises. Thus, the white South was not economically backward—it was merely different. Cotton was a wonderful crop, and southerners could hardly be blamed for making it their ruler. As a southern senator wrote in 1858, "You dare not make war upon cotton; no power on earth dares to make war upon it. Cotton is king."

CHECKING IN

- By 1830, the cotton economy dominated the South.
- Although cotton production flourished primarily in the Lower South, the Upper South benefited as well.
- "King Cotton" brought great prosperity to the South, but it also made slavery seem ever more vital to white southerners.
- The South nevertheless lagged far behind the North in industrialization and education.

THE SOCIAL GROUPS OF THE WHITE SOUTH

What major social divisions segmented the white South?

There was wide diversity within and between the South's slaveholding and non-slaveholding classes. Although some planters owned hundreds of slaves and lived lavishly, most lived more modestly. In 1860 one-fourth of all white families in the South owned slaves; nearly half of those owned fewer than five slaves, and three-fourths had fewer than ten slaves. Only 12 percent owned twenty or more slaves, and only 1 percent owned a hundred or more. Nonslaveholders were equally diverse. Most owned farms and drew on the labor of family members, but other whites squatted on land in the pine barrens or piney woods and scratched out a living by raising livestock, hunting, fishing, and planting a few acres of corn, oats, or sweet potatoes.

Planters, small slaveholders, family farmers, and pine-barrens folk composed the South's four main white groups. Lawyers, physicians, merchants, and artisans did not fall into any of these groups, but they tended to identify their interests with one or another of the agricultural groups.

Planters and Plantation Mistresses The plantation, with its porticoed mansion and fields teeming with slaves, stands at the center of the popular image of the Old South. This romanticized view, reinforced by novels and movies like *Gone with the Wind,* is not entirely false, for the South did contain plantations that travelers found "superb beyond description." Abundant slaves, the division of labor they afforded, and plentiful land allowed large plantations to generate incomes of $20,000 or more a year, an immense sum in those years.

In the eighteenth century during the initial flush of settlement in the piedmont and trans-Appalachian South, even well-off planters generally had lived in humble log cabins. After 1810, however, elite planters vied with one another to build stately mansions. Yet most planters counted their wealth not in grand mansions and elegant furnishings but in the value of their slaves. A field hand was worth as much as $1,700 in the 1850s, and few planters sold their slaves to buy furniture and silver plates.

In their constant worry about profit, planters enjoyed neither repose nor security. High fixed costs—housing and feeding slaves, maintaining cotton gins, hiring overseers—led them to search for more and better land, higher efficiency, and greater self-sufficiency. Because cotton prices tended to fluctuate seasonally, planters often assigned their cotton to commercial agents in cities who held the cotton until the price was right. The agents extended credit so that the planters could pay their bills before the cotton was sold. Indebtedness became part of the plantation economy and intensified the planters' quest for profitability. Psychological strains compounded economic worries. Frequent moves disrupted circles of friends and relatives, particularly as migration to the Southwest (Alabama and Mississippi) carried families into less settled, more desolate areas. Until 1850, this area was still the frontier (see Map 12.1).

Migration to the Southwest often deeply unsettled plantation women. They suddenly found themselves in frontier conditions surrounded by slaves and without friends, neighbors, or relatives nearby. Frequent absences by husbands, regardless if they were looking for new land, supervising outlying plantations, or conducting business in the city, intensified wives' loneliness.

Planters and their wives found various ways of coping with their isolation. Employing overseers to run the plantation, some lived in cities; in 1850 half the planters in the Mississippi Delta lived in New Orleans or Natchez. Most planters acted as their own overseers, however, and dealt with harsh living conditions by opening their home to visitors. The responsibility for such hospitality fell heavily on wives, who might have to entertain as many as fifteen people for breakfast and attend to the needs of visitors who stayed for days. Plantation wives also bore the burdens of raising their children, supervising house slaves, making clothing and carpets, looking after smokehouses and dairies, planting gardens, and, often, keeping the plantation accounts.

Among the heaviest sorrows of some plantation mistresses was the presence of mulatto (moo-LOT-oh) children, who stood as daily reminders of their husbands' infidelities. Mary Boykin Chesnut, an astute Charleston woman and famous diarist, commented, "Any lady is ready to tell you who is the father of all the mulatto children in everybody's household but her own. These, she seems to think, drop from clouds." Insisting on sexual purity for white women, southern men followed a looser standard for themselves. Richard M. Johnson of Kentucky was elected vice president of the United States in 1836 despite having lived openly for years with his black mistress.

The Small Slaveholders

In 1860, 88 percent of all slaveholders owned fewer than twenty slaves, and most possessed fewer than ten. One out of every five slaveholders worked outside of agriculture, as a lawyer, physician, merchant, or artisan.

Small slaveholders experienced conflicting loyalties and ambitions. In upland regions they absorbed the outlook of the more numerous **yeomen** (YO-men), who owned only a few slaves and rarely aspired to become large planters. In contrast, in the plantation-dominated low country and delta regions, small slaveholders often aspired to planter status. There someone with ten slaves could realistically look forward to owning thirty. And ambitious, acquisitive individuals equated success with owning more slaves. The logic of slavery remained the same: The only way to justify

yeoman Independent small farmer, usually nonslaveholding the investment in slaves was to set them to work on profitable crops. Such crops demanded more and better land, and both the planters and the small slaveholders of the deltas were restless and footloose.

The social structure of the deltas was fluid. In the early antebellum period, large planters had been reluctant to risk transporting their hundreds of valuable slaves in a still-turbulent region. It was small slaveholders who led the initial westward push into the Cotton Belt in the 1810s and 1820s. Gradually, large planters, too, moved westward, buying up the land that the small slave owners had developed and turning the region from Vicksburg to Natchez into large plantations. Small slave owners took the profits from selling their land, bought more slaves, and moved on. They gradually transformed the region from Vicksburg to Tuscaloosa (tusk-uh-LOO-suh), Alabama, into a belt of medium-sized farms with a dozen or so slaves on each.

The Yeomen

Nonslaveholding family farmers, or yeomen, composed the largest single group of southern whites. Most owned land, and many hired slaves to help at harvest. In areas of poor soil, such as eastern Tennessee, yeomen were typically subsistence farmers, although most yeomen grew some cash crops. Their landholdings were comparatively small, ranging from fifty to two hundred acres. Yeomen generally inhabited uplands, such as the piedmont of the East or the hilly upcountry of the Southwest, far from the rich coastal plains and deltas.

Above all, the yeomen valued self-sufficiency. Unlike planters, who were driven to acquire more land and to plant more cash crops, the yeomen devoted much of their acreage to subsistence crops, such as corn, sweet potatoes, and oats. The planter's ideal was profit with modest self-sufficiency; in contrast, the yeoman's goal was self-sufficiency with modest profit.

Yeomen living in planter-dominated regions were often dismissed as "poor white trash." However, in the upland regions that they dominated, the yeomen were highly respected. Upland slaveholders tended to own only a few slaves; like the yeomen, they were essentially family farmers.

Unlike southern planters, yeomen marketed their cash crops locally, trading cotton, wheat, and tobacco for goods and services from nearby artisans and merchants. In some areas yeomen sold their surplus corn to drovers and herdsmen who specialized in raising hogs. Along the French Broad River in eastern Tennessee, for example, twenty thousand to thirty thousand hogs a year were fattened for market. At peak season a traveler would see one thousand hogs a mile. The hogs were penned at night in huge stock stands—veritable hog hotels—and fed with corn supplied by the local yeomen.

The People of the Pine Barrens

Independent whites of the wooded "pine barrens" were among the most controversial groups in the Old South. Making up about 10 percent of southern whites, they usually squatted on the land; put up crude cabins; cleared some acreage, where they planted corn between tree

CHECKING IN

- The white South consisted of four main social groups: plantation owners, small slaveholders, yeomen, and the people of the pine barrens.
- Plantation owners, who owned most of the slaves, were at the top of the social structure.
- Small slaveholders, including professionals as well as farmers, most often owned fewer than ten slaves.
- Yeomen farmers, who generally owned no slaves, were the largest segment of the white population.
- The fiercely proud and independent people of the pine barrens composed 10 percent of the white population.

stumps; and grazed hogs and cattle in the woods. They neither raised cash crops nor engaged in the daily routine of orderly work that characterized family farmers. With their ramshackle houses and handfuls of stump-strewn acres, they appeared lazy and shiftless.

Abolitionists cited the pine-barrens people as proof that slavery degraded whites, but southerners responded that, although the pine-barrens folk were poor, they could at least feed themselves, unlike the paupers of northern cities. In general, the people of the pine barrens were both self-sufficient and fiercely independent. Pine-barrens men were reluctant to hire themselves out as laborers to do "slave" tasks, and the women refused to become servants.

SOCIAL RELATIONS IN THE WHITE SOUTH

How did slavery affect social relations in the South?

Northerners often charged that slavery twisted the entire social structure of the South out of shape. The enslavement of blacks, they alleged, robbed lower-class whites of the incentive to work, reduced them to shiftless misery, and rendered the South a throwback in an otherwise progressive age. The behavior of individual southerners also struck northerners as running to extremes. One minute, southerners were hospitable and gracious; the next, savagely violent. The practice of dueling intensified in the Old South at a time when it was dying in the North.

In reality, a curious mix of aristocratic and democratic, premodern and modern features marked social relations in the white South. Although it contained considerable class inequality, property ownership was widespread. Rich planters occupied seats in state legislatures out of proportion to their numbers in the population, but they did not necessarily get their way, nor did their political agenda always differ from that of other whites.

Conflict and Consensus in the White South

Planters tangled with yeomen on several issues. With extensive economic dealings and the need for credit, planters inclined toward the Whig party, which generally supported economic development. The independent yeomen, cherishing their self-sufficiency, tended to be Democrats.

Yet few conflicts arose between these groups. An underlying political unity reigned in the South. Geography was in part responsible: Planters, small slaveholders, yeomen, and pine-barrens folk tended to cluster in different regions, each independent of the others. There was somewhat more geographical intermingling of groups in the Upper South. With widespread land ownership and few factories, the Old South was not a place where whites worked for other whites, and this tended to minimize friction.

The white South's political structure was sufficiently democratic to prevent any one group from gaining exclusive control over politics. Planters dominated state legislatures, but they owed their election to the popular vote. And the democratic currents that swept northern politics between 1815 and 1860 affected the South as well; newer southern states entered the Union with democratic constitutions that included universal white manhood suffrage—the right of all adult white males to vote.

Although yeomen often voted for planters, the nonslaveholders did not give their elected representatives a blank check to govern as they pleased. During the 1830s and 1840s, Whig planters who favored banks faced intense and often successful opposition from Democratic yeomen. The nonslaveholders got their way often enough to nurture their belief that they, not the slaveholders, controlled politics.

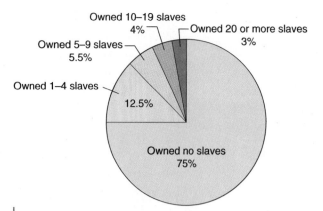

Figure 12.3   Slave Ownership, 1860

In combination with the impact of Hinton R. Helper's *The Impending Crisis of the South* (1857), which called on nonslaveholders to abolish the institution of slavery in their own interest, this decline left slaveholders worried about the loyalty of nonslaveholders to slavery.

Conflict over Slavery

Nevertheless, considerable *potential* existed for conflict between slaveholders and nonslaveholders. The southern white carpenter who complained in 1849 that "unjust, oppressive, and degrading" competition from slave labor depressed his wages surely had a point. Between 1830 and 1860 the slaveholding class shrank in size in relation to the total white population, but its share of total wealth increased. As a Louisiana editor wrote in 1858, "The present tendency of supply and demand is to concentrate all the slaves in the hands of the few, and thus excite the envy rather than cultivate the sympathy of the people."

Yet although pockets of opposition dotted the South, slavery did not create profound or lasting divisions between slaveholders and nonslaveholders (Figure 12.3). For example, antagonism to slavery flourished in parts of Virginia up to 1860, but proposals for emancipating the slaves dropped from the state's political agenda after 1832. Kentucky had a history of antislavery activity dating back to the 1790s, but after calls for emancipation suffered a crushing defeat in an 1849 referendum, slavery ceased to be a political issue there.

The rise and fall of pro-emancipation sentiment in the South raises a key question: As most white southerners were nonslaveholders, why didn't they attack slavery more consistently? To look ahead, why were so many southerners willing to fight ferociously and to die bravely during the Civil War in defense of an institution in which they apparently had no real stake? There are several reasons. First, some nonslaveholders hoped to become slaveholders. Second, most southerners accepted the racist assumptions on which slavery rested; they dreaded the likelihood that emancipation would encourage "impudent" blacks to entertain ideas of social equality with whites. Third, no one knew where the slaves, if freed, would go or what they would do. Colonizing freed blacks in Africa was unrealistic, southerners concluded, but they also believed that, without colonization, emancipation would lead to a race war.

The Proslavery Argument

Between 1830 and 1860, southerners constructed a defense of slavery as a **positive good** rather than a necessary evil. St. Paul's injunction that servants obey their

positive good Southern argument that slavery benefited both black and white

THE NEGRO IN HIS OWN COUNTRY.

THE NEGRO IN AMERICA.

Chicago Historical Society

Chicago Historical Society

The Negro in His Own Country and the Negro in America
Proslavery propagandists contrasted what they believed to be the black's African savagery with the blessings of civilization on an American plantation.

masters became a biblical justification for some. Others looked to the classical past to argue that slavery was both an ancient and a classical institution; the slave society of Athens, they said, had produced Aristotle (AIR-iss-taht-ul) and Plato (PLAY-toh), and Roman slaveholders had laid the foundations of Western civilization. George Fitzhugh of Virginia contrasted the plight of the northern "wage slaves," callously discarded when they became too ill or too old to work, with the lot of southern slaves, cared for by masters who attended to their health, their clothing, and their discipline.

At the same time, southerners increasingly suppressed any open discussion of slavery within the South. Proslavery writers warned that abolitionists wanted to destroy the family as well as slavery by undermining the "natural" submission of children to parents, wives to husbands, and slaves to masters. In the 1830s, proslavery southerners seized abolitionist literature from the southern mail and burned it. Although Kentucky abolitionist Cassius Marcellus Clay protected his press with two cannons, in 1845 a mob dismantled it anyway.

The rise of the proslavery argument coincided with a shift in southern churches' position on slavery. During the 1790s and early 1800s, some Protestant ministers had assailed slavery as immoral, but by the 1830s, most clergymen had convinced themselves that slavery was both compatible with Christianity and necessary for the proper exercise of Christian religion. Slavery, they proclaimed, displayed Christian responsibility toward one's inferiors, and it helped African-Americans to develop Christian virtues, such as humility and self-control. Southerners increasingly attacked antislavery evangelicals in the North for disrupting the "superior" social arrangement of the South. In 1837, southerners and conservative northerners had combined forces to drive antislavery New School Presbyterians out of that denomination's main body; in 1844, the Methodist Episcopal Church split into northern and southern wings; and in 1845, Baptists formed a separate Southern Convention.

In effect, southern evangelicals seceded from national church organizations long before the South seceded from the Union.

Violence, Honor, and Dueling in the Old South

Throughout the colonial and antebellum periods, violence deeply colored the daily lives of white southerners. In the 1760s, a minister described backcountry Virginians "biting one anothers Lips and Noses off, and gowging one another—that is, thrusting out anothers Eyes, and kicking one another on the Cods [genitals], to the great damage of many a Poor Woman." Gouging out eyes became a specialty of sorts among poor southern whites. On one occasion a South Carolina judge entered his court to find a plaintiff, a juror, and two witnesses all missing one eye. Stories of eye gougings and ear bitings became part of Old South folklore. Mike Fink, a legendary southern fighter and hunter, boasted that he was so mean in infancy that he refused his mother's milk and howled for whiskey. Yet beneath the folklore lay the reality of violence that gave the Old South a murder rate as much as ten times higher than that of the North.

At the root of most violence in the white South lay intensified feelings of personal pride that reflected the inescapable presence of slaves. White southerners saw slaves degraded, insulted, and powerless to resist. In turn, whites reacted violently to even trivial insults to demonstrate that they had nothing in common with slaves.

Among gentlemen this exaggerated pride took the form of a code of honor, with honor defined as an extraordinary sensitivity to one's reputation. Northern moralists celebrated a rival idea—character—the quality that enabled an individual to behave in steady fashion regardless of how others acted toward him or her. In the honor culture of the Old South, however, even the slightest insult, as long as it was perceived as intentional, could become the basis for a duel.

Formalized by French and British officers during the Revolutionary War, **dueling** gained a secure niche in the Old South as a means by which gentlemen dealt with affronts to their honor. Seemingly trivial incidents—a harmless brushing against the side of someone at a public event, a hostile glance—could trigger a duel. Yet dueling did not necessarily lead to violence. Gentlemen viewed dueling as a refined alternative to the random violence of lower-class life. Instead of leaping at his antagonist's throat, a gentleman remained cool, settled on a weapon with his opponent, and agreed to a meeting place. In the interval, friends of the parties negotiated to clear up the "misunderstanding" that had provoked the challenge. Most confrontations ended peaceably rather than on the field of honor at dawn.

dueling Formal man-to-man fight over a matter of honor

Nonetheless, many ended violently. Many southerners saw recourse to the law as a way to settle personal disputes involving honor as cowardly and shameless. Andrew Jackson's mother told the future president, "The law affords no remedy that can satisfy the feelings of a true man."

Dueling rested on the assumption that gentlemen could recognize each other and know when to respond to a challenge. Nothing in the code of honor compelled a person to duel with someone who was not a gentleman, for such a person's opinion hardly mattered. An insolent porter who insulted a gentleman might get a whipping but did not merit a duel. Yet it was often difficult to determine who was a gentleman. Indeed, the Old South teemed with would-be gentlemen.

The Southern Evangelicals and White Values

With its emphasis on the personal redress of grievances and its inclination toward violence, the ideal of honor conflicted with the values preached by the southern evangelical churches, notably the Baptists, Methodists, and Presbyterians. These denominations stressed humility and self-restraint, virtues that sharply contrasted with the culture of display that buttressed the extravagance and violence of the Old South.

By the 1830s, however, southern evangelicals had begun to change. They no longer made an effort to reach out to women, blacks, and the poor; instead, women were now expected to remain silent in church, while urban blacks increasingly formed their own churches. Both Methodists and Baptists began to attract the well-to-do, a tendency that increased with the opening of colleges such as Randolph-Macon and Wake Forest. More and more, southern gentry and evangelicals shared values, including a prickly regard for their honor and reputation. By the 1860s the South counted many gentlemen like the Bible-quoting Presbyterian general Thomas J. "Stonewall" Jackson, fierce in a righteous war but a sworn opponent of strong drink, gambling, and dueling.

CHECKING IN

- Southern politics became more democratic.
- White southerners, even those who owned no slaves, united in support of slavery.
- The defense of slavery as a "positive good" emerged after 1830.
- White "gentlemen" had an exaggerated sense of honor, which often led to duels.
- Southern evangelicals became supporters of existing systems, including slavery.

LIFE UNDER SLAVERY

How did slaves and free blacks respond to their circumstances?

Slavery, the institution at the root of the code of honor and other distinctive features of the Old South, has long inspired controversy among historians. Some have seen slavery as a benevolent institution in which African-Americans lived contentedly under kindly masters; others, as a brutal system that drove slaves into constant rebellion. Neither view is accurate, but both contain a germ of truth. There were kind masters, and some slaves developed genuine affection for their owners. Yet slavery inherently oppressed its African-American victims by forcibly appropriating their life and labor. Even kind masters exploited blacks in order to earn profits. And kindness was a double-edged sword; the benevolent master expected grateful affection from his slaves and interpreted that affection as loyalty to slavery itself. When northern troops descended on the plantations during the Civil War, masters were genuinely surprised and dismayed to find many of their most trusted slaves deserting to Union lines.

The kindness or cruelty of masters was important, but three other factors primarily determined slaves' experience: the kind of agriculture in which they worked, whether they resided in rural or urban areas, and what century they lived in. The experiences of slaves working on cotton plantations in the 1830s differed radically from those of slaves in 1700, for reasons unrelated to the kindness or brutality of masters.

The Maturing of the Plantation System

Slavery changed significantly between 1700 and 1830. In 1700, the typical slave was a man in his twenties, recently arrived from Africa or the Caribbean, who worked on an isolated small farm. Drawn from different regions of Africa, few slaves spoke the same language. Because slave ships carried twice as many men as women, and because slaves were widely scattered, blacks had difficulties finding partners and creating a semblance of family life. Severe malnutrition sharply limited the number of children slave women bore. Without continuing importations, the number of slaves in North America would have declined between 1710 and 1730.

In contrast, by 1830 the typical North American slave was as likely to be female as male, had been born in America, spoke English, and worked beside numerous other slaves on a plantation. The rise of plantation agriculture in the eighteenth century was at the heart of the change. Plantation slaves found mates more easily than slaves on scattered farms. The ratio

Collection of the New-York Historical Society

Black Women and Men on a Trek Home, South Carolina
Here African-American women loaded down with cotton join their men on the march home after a day in the fields.

between slave men and women fell into balance, and marriage between slaves on the same or nearby plantations increased. The native-born slave population soared after 1750. The importation of African slaves declined, and in 1808 Congress banned it.

<table>
<tr><td>

Work and Discipline of Plantation Slaves

</td><td>

In 1850, the typical slave worked on a large farm or plantation with at least ten fellow bond servants. Almost three-quarters of all slaves that year were owned by masters with

</td></tr>
</table>

ten or more slaves, and slightly over one-half lived in units of twenty or more slaves. In smaller units, slaves usually worked under the task system. Each slave had a daily or weekly quota of tasks to complete. On large cotton and sugar plantations, slaves would occasionally work under the task system; however, more closely supervised and regimented gang labor prevailed.

An hour before sunrise, a horn or bell awakened the slaves. After a sparse breakfast, they marched to the fields, where slave men and women worked side by side. Those female slaves who did not labor in the fields remained busy. A former slave, John Curry, described how his mother milked cows, cared for children whose mothers worked in the fields, cooked for field hands, washed and ironed for her master's household, and looked after her own seven children. Plantations never lacked tasks for slaves of either gender, and in any season the slave's day stretched from dawn to dusk. When darkness made fieldwork impossible, slaves toted cotton bales to the ginhouse, gathered wood for supper fires, and fed the mules. Weary from their labors, they slept in log cabins on wooden planks.

Although virtually all antebellum Americans worked long hours, no others experienced the combination of long hours and harsh discipline that slave field hands endured. Northern factory workers did not live in fear of drivers walking among them with a whip. Repulsive brutality pervaded American slavery. For example, pregnant slave women were sometimes forced to lie in depressions in the ground and endure whipping on their backs, a practice that supposedly protected the fetus while abusing the mother. Masters often delegated discipline and punishment to white overseers and black drivers. The barbaric discipline meted out by others twinged the conscience of many masters, but most justified it as their Christian duty to ensure the slaves' proper "submissiveness."

Despite the system's brutality, some slaves advanced—not to freedom but to semiskilled or skilled indoor work. Some became blacksmiths, carpenters, or gin operators, and others served as cooks, butlers, and dining room attendants. These house slaves became legendary for their disdain of field hands and poor whites. Slave artisans and house slaves generally enjoyed higher status than the field hands.

The Slave Family

Masters thought of slaves as naturally promiscuous and flattered themselves into thinking that they alone held slave marriages together. Masters had powerful incentives to encourage slave marriages: bringing new slaves into the world and discouraging slaves from running away. Some masters baked wedding cakes for slaves and even arbitrated marital disputes. Still, the keenest challenge to the slave family came not from the slaves themselves but from slavery. The law did not recognize or protect slave families. Although some slaveholders were reluctant to break apart slave marriages by sale, economic hardships might force their hand. The reality, one historian calculated, was that in a lifetime, on average, a slave would witness the sale of eleven family members.

Inevitably, the commonplace buying and selling of slaves disrupted attempts to create a stable family life. Poignant testimony to the effects of sale on slave families appeared in advertisements for runaway slaves. An 1851 North Carolina advertisement said that a particular fugitive was probably "lurking in the neighborhood of E. D. Walker's, at Moore's Creek, who owns most of his relatives, or Nathan Bonham's who owns his mother; or perhaps, near Fletcher Bell's, at Long Creek, who owns his father." Small wonder that a slave preacher pronounced a couple married "until death or *distance* do you part."

Other factors disrupted slave marriages. The marriage of a slave woman did not protect her against the sexual demands of her master or, indeed, of any white person. Slave children of white masters sometimes became targets for the wrath of white mistresses. Field work kept slave mothers from their children, who were cared for by the elderly or by the mothers of other children.

Despite these enormous obstacles, relationships within slave families were often intimate and, where possible, long lasting. Lacking legal protection, slaves developed their own standards of family morality. A southern white woman observed that slaves "did not consider it wrong for a girl to have a child before she married, but afterwards were extremely severe upon anything like infidelity on her part." Given the opportunity, slaves solemnized their marriages before members of the clergy. White clergymen who accompanied Union armies into Mississippi and Louisiana

Map 12.2 Internal Slave Trade, 1810–1860

An internal slave trade developed after the slave trade with Africa ended in 1808. With the growth of cotton production, farmers in the Upper South found it profitable to sell their slaves to planters in the Lower South.

 Interactive Map

during the Civil War conducted thousands of marriage rites for slaves who had long viewed themselves as married and desired a formal ceremony and registration.

On balance, slave families differed profoundly from white families. Many planters divided their holdings into several farms and distributed slaves among them without regard to marriage ties. Conditions on small farms and new plantations discouraged the formation of families. Spouses were always vulnerable to being sold.

Broad kinship patterns—close ties between children and grandparents, aunts, and uncles, as well as parents—had marked West African cultures, and they were reinforced by the separation of children and parents that routinely occurred under slavery. Frederick Douglass never knew his father and saw his mother rarely, but he vividly remembered his grandmother. In addition, slaves often created "fictive" kin networks, naming friends as their uncles, aunts, brothers, or sisters. In this way they helped to protect themselves against the disruption of family ties and established a broader community of obligation. When plantation slaves greeted each other as "brother," they were making a statement not about actual kinship, but about obligations to each other.

The Longevity, Health, and Diet of Slaves

Of the 10 million to 12 million Africans imported to the New World between the fifteenth and nineteenth centuries, North America received only 550,000 of them (about 5 percent), whereas Brazil received 3.5 million (nearly 33 percent). Yet by 1825, 36 percent of all slaves in the Western Hemisphere lived in the United States, and only 31 percent in Brazil. The reason for this difference is that slaves in the United States reproduced faster and lived longer than those in Brazil and elsewhere in the Western Hemisphere.

Several factors account for U.S. slaves' longer lives and higher rates of reproduction. First, with the gender ratio among slaves equalizing more rapidly in North America, slaves there married earlier and had more children. Second, because raising corn and livestock was compatible with growing cotton, the Old South produced plentiful food. Slaves generally received a peck of cornmeal and three to four pounds of fatty pork a week, which they often supplemented with vegetables grown on small plots and with catfish and game.

Slaves enjoyed greater immunity from malaria and yellow fever than whites but suffered more from cholera, dysentery, and diarrhea. Lacking privies, slaves usually relieved themselves behind bushes; consequently, urine and feces contaminated the sources of their drinking water. Slave remedies for stomach ailments, although commonly ridiculed by whites, often worked. For example, slaves ate white clay to cure dysentery and diarrhea. We now know that white clay contains kaolin, a remedy for these disorders.

Nonetheless, slaves suffered a higher mortality rate than whites. The very young suffered most; infant mortality among slaves was double that among whites, and one in three African-American children died before age ten. Plantations in the disease-ridden lowlands had the worst overall mortality rates, but even in healthier areas overworked field hands often miscarried or bore weakened infants.

Away from the Plantation: Slaves in Town and Free Blacks

Greater freedom from supervision and greater opportunities awaited slaves who worked off plantations in towns and cities. Most southern whites succumbed to the lure of cotton and established small farms; the resulting shortage of white labor created a steady demand for slaves outside the plantation economy. Driving wagons, working as stevedores on the docks, manning river barges, and toiling in mining and lumbering gave slaves an opportunity to work somewhere other than the cotton fields. Other African-Americans served as engineers for sawmills or artisans for ironworks. African-American women and children constituted the main labor force for the South's fledgling textile industry.

The draining of potential white laborers from southern cities also provided the opportunity for slaves to become skilled artisans. Slave or free, blacks found it easier to pursue skilled occupations in southern cities than in northern ones, where immigrant laborers competed with blacks for work.

Despite slavery's stranglehold, urban African-Americans in the South enjoyed opportunities denied to their counterparts in the North. Generally, slaves who worked in factories, mining, or lumbering were hired out by their masters rather than owned by their employers. If working conditions for hired-out slaves deteriorated badly, masters would refuse to provide employers with more slaves. Consequently, working conditions for slaves off the plantation generally stayed at a tolerable level.

Even more likely than southern blacks in general to live in cities were free blacks. In 1860, one-third of the free blacks in the Upper South and more than half in the

Lower South were urban. The relatively specialized economies of the cities provided free people of color with opportunities to become carpenters, barrel makers, barbers, and even small traders. Most of the meat, fish, and produce in an antebellum southern market was prepared for sale by free blacks. Urban free blacks formed their own fraternal orders and churches; in New Orleans free blacks also had their own opera and literary journals. In Natchez, a free black barber, William Tiler Johnson, invested the profits of his shop in real estate, rented it out, bought slaves and a plantation, and hired a white overseer.

As Johnson's career suggests, some free blacks were highly successful. They continued to increase in absolute numbers (a little more than 250,000 free people of color lived in the South in 1860), but the rate of growth of the free black population slowed radically after 1810. Fewer masters freed their slaves after that time, and following the Nat Turner rebellion in 1831, states legally restricted the liberties of free blacks. By the mid-1830s most southern states made it a felony to teach blacks to read and write. Every southern state forbade free blacks to enter, and in 1859, Arkansas ordered all free blacks to leave.

Although a free-black culture flourished in certain cities, that culture did not reflect the conditions under which the majority of blacks lived. Most free blacks dwelled in rural areas, where whites lumped them together with slaves, and a much higher percentage of blacks were free in the Upper South than in the Lower South.

Many free blacks were mulattos, the product of white masters and black women, and looked down on "darky" field hands and laborers. But as discrimination against free people of color intensified during the late antebellum period, many free blacks realized that whatever future they had was as blacks, not whites. Feelings of racial solidarity increased during the 1850s, and after the Civil War, the leaders of the ex-slaves were usually blacks who had been free before the war.

Slave Resistance

Ever-present fears of slave insurrection haunted the Old South. In the delta areas of the Lower South where blacks outnumbered whites, slaves experienced continuous forced labor on plantations. In the cities, free blacks could have provided leadership for rebellions. Rumors of slave conspiracies flew within the southern white community, and all whites knew of the massive black revolt that had destroyed French rule in Saint-Domingue.

Yet Nat Turner's revolt remained the only slave rebellion that actually resulted in white deaths. Most slave rebellions were conspiracies that never materialized. For example, in 1800 a Virginia slave named Gabriel Prosser plotted an uprising but was betrayed by other slaves and executed. In 1822, **Denmark Vesey** (VEE-see) and his followers planned to attack Charleston, South Carolina, and seize the city's arms and ammunition, but other slaves informed the authorities, and the conspirators were executed.

Denmark Vesey Free black who planned a slave uprising in 1822; conspiracy was thwarted and Vesey executed

The Old South experienced far fewer rebellions than the Caribbean region or South America. Several factors explain this apparent tranquility. First, although slaves formed a majority in South Carolina and a few other areas, they did not constitute a *large* majority in any state. Second, unlike Caribbean slave owners, most southern masters lived on their plantations; they possessed armed force and were willing to use it. Third, family ties among U.S. slaves made them reluctant to risk death and thereby to orphan their children. Finally, slaves who ran away or plotted rebellion had no allies. Southern Indians routinely captured runaway slaves and claimed rewards for them; some Indians even owned slaves.

Unable to rebel, many slaves tried to escape to freedom in the North. Some light mulattos who passed as whites succeeded. More often, however, slaves borrowed, stole, or forged passes from plantations or obtained papers describing them as free. For example, Frederick Douglass borrowed a sailor's papers to make his escape from Baltimore to New York City. Some former slaves, including Harriet Tubman and Josiah Henson, returned to the South to help others escape. Despite legends of an "underground railroad" of abolitionists helping slaves to freedom, fugitive slaves owed little to abolitionists. The "safe houses" of white sympathizers in border states were better known to slave catchers than to runaways.

Escape to freedom was a dream rather than a realistic alternative for most blacks. Out of millions of slaves, probably fewer than a thousand actually escaped to the North. Often, slaves ran away from masters not to escape to freedom but to visit spouses or avoid punishment. Most runaways remained in the South; some sought only to return to kinder former masters. During the eighteenth century, African slaves had often run away in groups and tried to create the sort of villages they had known in Africa. But the American acquisition of Florida deprived potential runaways of their major haven, leaving them few uninhabited places to which they could flee.

Despite poor prospects for permanent escape, slaves could disappear for prolonged periods into the free-black communities of southern cities. Slaves enjoyed a fair degree of practical freedom to drive wagons to market and to come and go when they were off plantations. Slaves sent to a city might overstay their leave and pass themselves off as free. This kind of practical freedom did not change slavery's underlying oppressiveness, but it did give slaves a sense of having certain rights, and it helped to channel slave resistance into activities that were furtive and relatively harmless, rather than open and violent. Theft, for example, was so common that planters kept tools, smokehouses, and closets under lock and key. Overworked field hands might leave tools out to rust, feign illness, or simply refuse to work. Slaves could not be fired for such malingering or negligence. And Frederick Law Olmsted even found masters afraid to punish a slave "lest [he or she] should abscond, or take a sulky fit and not work, or poison some of the family, or set fire to the dwelling, or have recourse to any other mode of avenging himself."

Olmsted's reference to arson and poisoning is a reminder that not all furtive resistance was peaceful. Arson and poisoning, both common forms of vengeance in African culture, flourished in the Old South. So did fear. Masters afflicted by dysentery never knew for sure that they had not been poisoned.

Arson, poisoning, theft, work stoppage, and negligence acted as alternatives to violent rebellion, but their goal was not freedom. Their object was merely to make slavery bearable. Most slaves would have preferred freedom but settled for less. "White folks do as they please," an ex-slave said, "and the darkies do as they can."

CHECKING IN

- Plantation field hands often labored under brutal conditions, whereas "house slaves" fared better.
- Nuclear slave families were precarious, but the slave culture of extended families offset this to some extent.
- Although slaves in the United States generally lived longer than slaves elsewhere in the Western Hemisphere, the mortality rate of slave children under the age of ten was 35 percent.
- Free blacks had opportunities but also faced stifling restrictions.
- Although the Nat Turner rebellion was a notable exception, slave resistance generally was subtle, furtive, and widespread.

THE EMERGENCE OF AFRICAN-AMERICAN CULTURE

What were the distinctive features of African-American society and culture in the South?

Enslaved blacks combined elements of African and American cultures to create a distinctive culture of their own, giving a distinctive twist to both the African and American components of slave culture.

The Language of Slaves

Before slaves could develop a common culture, they needed a common language. During the colonial period, African-born slaves, speaking a variety of languages, had developed a **"pidgin"** (PID-jin)—that is, a language that has no native speakers but in which people with different native languages can communicate. Many African-born slaves spoke English pidgin poorly, but their American-born descendants used it as their primary language.

Like all pidgins, English pidgin was a simplified language. Slaves often dropped the verb *to be* (which had no equivalent in African tongues) and ignored or confused genders. Instead of saying "Mary is in the cabin," they typically said, "Mary, he in cabin." They substituted *no* for *not,* as in "He no wicked." Some African words, among them *banjo,* moved from pidgin to standard English, and others, such as *goober* ("peanut"), entered southern white slang. Although many whites ridiculed pidgin and black house servants struggled to speak standard English, pidgin proved indispensable for communication among slaves.

"pidgin" Common language spoken by slaves who spoke many different tongues

African-American Religion

Religion played an equally important role in forging an African-American culture. Africa contained rich and diverse religious customs and beliefs. Despite the presence of a few Muslims and Christians in the early slave population, most of the slaves brought from Africa followed one of many native African religions. Most of these religions drew little distinction between the spiritual and natural worlds—storms, illnesses, and earthquakes were all assumed to stem from supernatural forces.

For these reasons, African religions did not unify blacks in America. Yet remnants of African religion remained. Dimly remembered African beliefs such as the reverence for water may have predisposed slaves to accept Christianity when they were finally urged to do so, because water has a symbolic significance for Christians, too, in the sacrament of baptism. Evangelical Christianity also resembled African religions in that it also drew few distinctions between the sacred and the secular. Just as Africans believed that droughts and plagues resulted from supernatural forces, the early revivalists knew in their hearts that every drunkard who fell off his horse and every Sabbath-breaker struck by lightning had experienced a deliberate and direct punishment from God.

By the 1790s, African-Americans formed about one-quarter of the membership of the Methodist and Baptist denominations. The fact that converted slaves played significant roles in the South's three slave rebellions reinforced whites' fears that a

Christian slave would be a rebellious slave. These slave uprisings, especially the Nat Turner rebellion, spurred Protestant
missionaries to intensify their efforts among slaves. They
pointed to the self-taught Turner as proof that slaves could
learn about Christianity and claimed that only organized
efforts at conversion would ensure that the slaves were taught
correct versions of Christianity.

The experiences of Christianized blacks in the Old South
illustrate the contradictions of life under slavery. Urban
blacks often had their own churches, but rural blacks and
slaves worshipped in the same churches as whites. Although
African-Americans sat in segregated sections, they heard the
same service as whites. Churches became the most interracial
institutions in the Old South, and biracial churches sometimes disciplined whites for abusing black Christian members. But Christianity was not a route to black liberation.
Ministers went out of their way to remind slaves that spiritual
equality was not the same as civil equality.

However, slaves listening to the same sermons as whites
often came to different conclusions. For example, slaves
drew parallels between their captivity and that of the Jews,
the Chosen People. Like the Jews, slaves concluded, they were
"de people of de Lord." If they kept the faith, they would reach
the Promised Land.

A listener could interpret a phrase like "the Promised
Land" in several ways; it could refer to Israel, to heaven, or to
freedom. From the perspective of whites, the only permissible
interpretations were Israel and heaven, but some blacks, like
Denmark Vesey, thought of freedom as well. Many plantations had black preachers, slaves trained by white ministers to
spread Christianity among blacks. In the presence of masters
or ministers, African-American preachers repeated the famil-
iar biblical command "Obey your master." Often, however, slaves met for services
apart from whites, and then the message changed.

Some slaves privately interpreted Christianity as a religion of liberation, but
most recognized that their prospects for freedom were slight. Generally, Christianity
neither turned blacks into revolutionaries nor made them model slaves. It did, however, provide slaves with a view of slavery different from their masters' outlook.
Masters argued that slavery was a benign and divinely ordained institution, but
Christianity told slaves that the institution was an affliction, a terrible and unjust
system that God had allowed in order to test their faith. For having endured slavery,
he would reward slaves. For having created it, he would punish masters.

Slave Handicraft
These two musical instruments, a banjo and a
gourd fiddle, were made by slaves in Virginia.

Collection of the Blue Ridge Institute & Museums/Ferrum College

Black Music and Dance

African-American culture expressed blacks' feelings. Long
after white rituals had grown sober and sedate, the congregation in African-American religious services shouted

"Amen" and let their body movements reflect their feelings. Slaves also expressed their emotions in music and dance. Southern law forbade them to own "drums, horns, or other loud instruments, which may call together or give sign or notice to one another of their wicked designs and intentions." Instead, slaves made rhythmic clapping, called "patting juba" (JOO-buh), an indispensable accompaniment to dancing. Slaves also played an African instrument, the banjo, and beat tin buckets as substitutes for drums. Slave music was tied to bodily movement; slaves expressed themselves in a dance that was African in origin, emphasizing shuffling steps and bodily contortions rather than quick footwork and erect backs as in whites' dances.

Whether at work or prayer, slaves liked to sing. Work songs usually consisted of a leader's chant and a choral response. Masters encouraged such songs, believing that singing induced slaves to work harder and that the innocent content of work songs proved that slaves were happy. However, Frederick Douglass, recalling his own past, observed that "slaves sing most when they are most unhappy. The songs of the slave represent the sorrows of his heart; and he is relieved by them, only as an aching heart is relieved by its tears."

Blacks also sang religious songs, later known as **spirituals,** which reflected the powerful emphasis that slave religion placed on deliverance from earthly travails. Whites took a dim view of spirituals and tried to make slaves sing "good psalms and hymns" instead of "the extravagant and nonsensical chants, and catches, and hallelujah songs of their own composing." But enslaved blacks clung to their spirituals, drawing hope from them that "we will soon be free, when the Lord will call us home," as one spiritual promised.

spiritual Slave religious song that stressed liberation from difficult situations

CHECKING IN

- Slaves developed "pidgin" as a way of communicating.
- After 1800 most slaves were Christian.
- Masters tried to use Christianity to encourage submissiveness, but slaves saw it as a faith that promised rewards for them and punishment for their masters.
- Slave music and dance incorporated many African elements.
- Spirituals reflected the slaves' desire for deliverance.

Chapter Summary

How did the rise of cotton cultivation affect the South? *(page 266)*

By the 1830s cotton production dominated the South, and southerners spoke proudly of "King Cotton." Although it brought great prosperity, the cotton economy also slowed down the development of industry and education. And it made slavery seem more vital than ever.

What major social divisions segmented the white South? *(page 271)*

Geography and economics divided white southerners into four distinct groups: plantation owners, small slave owners, yeomen, and the people of the pine barrens. Yeomen, the largest group, generally owned no slaves, nor did the people of the pine barrens.

KEY TERMS

Nat Turner *(p. 265)*
Upper South *(p. 266)*
Lower (Deep) South *(p. 266)*
King Cotton *(p. 267)*
plantation *(p. 268)*
yeoman *(p. 272)*
positive good *(p. 275)*
dueling *(p. 277)*
Denmark Vesey *(p. 283)*
"pidgin" *(p. 285)*
spiritual *(p. 287)*

How did slavery affect social relations in the South? (page 274)

Whites, although divided politically, were united in defense of slavery, which gave all whites an automatically superior position. They defended slavery as a "positive good," and southern churches became supporters and defenders of slavery as well.

How did slaves and free blacks respond to their circumstances? (page 278)

Field hands labored under harsh conditions. Nuclear families were always threatened, but the tradition of extended families somewhat offset this. Free blacks faced a life bounded by severe restrictions. Rebellion against slavery, despite the spectacular example of Nat Turner, was usually subtle, emerging in the form of pretended illness, carelessness, or feigned stupidity.

What were the distinctive features of African-American society and culture in the South? (page 285)

Whites tried to use Christianity to preach submission and obedience, but slaves saw it as a faith of hope and liberation. Slave music and dance frequently incorporated African elements, and spirituals expressed the slave desire for deliverance.

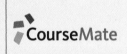

Go to the CourseMate website at **www.cengagebrain.com** for additional study tools and review materials—including audio and video clips—for this chapter.

CHAPTER 13

Immigration, Expansion, and Sectional Conflict

1840–1848

Gold Miners

Unknown maker, American. Gold Miners with Sluice, ca 1850 Nelson-Atkins Museum of Art, Kansas City, Missouri. Gift of Hallmark Cards, Inc., 2005.27.116

Tejano A native Texan of Mexican descent

CHAPTER PREVIEW

Newcomers and Natives
How did immigration in the 1840s influence the balance of power between the Whig and Democratic parties?

The West and Beyond
What economic and political forces fed westward expansion during the 1840s?

The Politics of Expansion, 1840–1846
How did "Manifest Destiny" influence American politics?

The Mexican-American War and Its Aftermath, 1846–1848
How did the outcome of the Mexican-American War intensify intersectional conflict?

Visitors to Texas will find a thoroughfare named after José Antonio Navarro in his native San Antonio, an official Navarro Day, and Navarro County. As one of the two native Texans to have signed the state of Coahuila-Texas's Declaration of Independence from Mexico in 1836, and later a member of the Congress of the independent Republic of Texas, Navarro is justly remembered as a founder of Texas.

However, Navarro's **Tejano** identity placed him uncomfortably between two nations vying for control over Texas. Captured by Mexican troops and jailed in 1841, he was offered freedom and wealth if he would renounce his allegiance to Texas. "I will never forsake Texas and her cause," Navarro replied. "I am her son."

Navarro escaped and returned to San Antonio, only to find that the now-dominant Anglos were forsaking people like him.

"The continuation of greasers [Mexicans] among us," a resolution drafted by Anglos in Goliad proclaimed, "is an intolerable nuisance." Navarro was starting to realize that the Texas he knew, a place where Anglos and Tejanos lived in harmony, was being swallowed by the relentless expansion of the United States. Navarro never held public office again.

"Americans regard this continent as their birthright," thundered Sam Houston, the first president of the Republic of Texas, in 1847. Indians and Mexicans had to make way for "our mighty march." This was not idle talk. In barely a thousand days during James K. Polk's administration (1845–1849), the United States expanded by 50 percent. It annexed Texas, gained half of the vast Oregon territory through negotiations with Britain, and claimed California and New Mexico after deliberately provoking war. At the same time, Brigham Young led the main body of Mormons on a trek from Illinois to the Great Salt Lake Valley, in search of a better life beyond the constraints of eastern settlements. And immigrants poured into the United States, largely from Europe.

Immigration and territorial expansion were linked, with most immigrants gravitating to the expansionist Democratic Party. The immigrant vote helped tip the election of 1844 to Polk, an ardent expansionist. But tensions flared between immigrants and the native-born. Influential Democrats concluded that the best solution to intensifying class and ethnic conflicts lay in expanding the national boundaries, bringing more land under cultivation, and recapturing the ideal of America as a nation of self-sufficient farmers.

Democrats also saw expansion as a way to reduce strife between the sections. Oregon would gratify the North; Texas, the South; and California, everyone. In reality, expansion brought sectional antagonisms to the boiling point, split the Democratic Party in the late 1840s, and set the nation on the path to Civil War.

NEWCOMERS AND NATIVES

How did immigration in the 1840s influence the balance of power between the Whig and Democratic parties?

Between 1815 and 1860, 5 million European immigrants reached the United States. Of these, 4.2 million arrived between 1840 and 1860, and 3 million crowded in from 1845 to 1854 alone, the largest immigration relative to population in U.S. history. The Irish and the Germans dominated this wave of newcomers; by 1860 three-fourths of foreign-born Americans were Irish or German (see Figure 13.1).

Expectations and Realities

Although a desire for religious freedom drew some immigrants to U.S. shores, hopes of economic betterment lured the majority. Travelers' accounts and relatives' letters assured Europeans that America was an ideal world, a utopia. Yet, typically, immigrants faced hard times.

Their problems began at ports of embarkation. Because ships sailed irregularly, many spent precious savings in waterfront slums while awaiting departure. Squalid

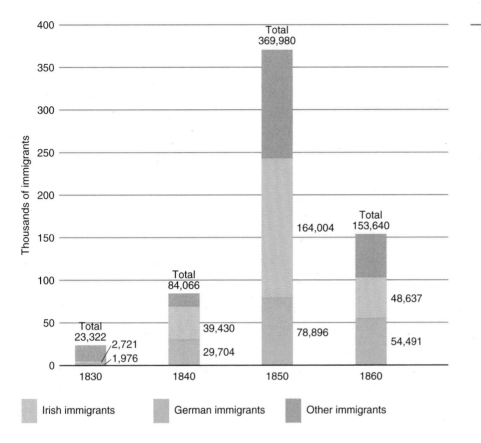

Figure 13.1 German, Irish, and Total Immigration, 1830–1860

Irish and German immigrants led the more than tenfold growth of immigration between 1830 and 1860.

Source: U.S. Bureau of the Census, Historical Statistics of the United States, Colonial Times to 1970, Bicentennial Edition I (Washington, DC, 1975)

cargo ships carried most of the emigrants, who endured quarters almost as crowded as on slave ships.

For many, the greatest shock came after landing. Immigrants quickly discovered that farming in America was a perilous prospect, radically different from what they had known in Europe. Unlike the compact farming communities of Europe, American agricultural areas featured scattered farms, and Americans' individualism led them to speculate in land and to move frequently.

Clear patterns emerged amid the shocks and dislocations of immigration. For example, most Irish immigrants lacked the capital to purchase land and consequently crowded into urban areas of New England, New York, New Jersey, and Pennsylvania, where they could find jobs. German immigrants often arrived at southern ports, but slavery, climate, and lack of economic opportunity gradually drove them north to settle in Illinois, Ohio, Wisconsin, and Missouri.

Cities, rather than farms, attracted most antebellum immigrants. By 1860, **German and Irish immigrants** formed more than 60 percent of the population of St. Louis and nearly half the population of New York City, Chicago, Cincinnati, Milwaukee, Detroit, and San Francisco. These fast-growing cities needed people with strong backs who were willing to work for low wages. In addition to jobs, cities provided immigrants with the community life lacking in farming areas.

German and Irish immigrants
Largest contingents of migrants seeking opportunity in the United States before 1860

Chronology

1822	Stephen F. Austin founds the first American community in Texas
1830	Mexico closes Texas to further American immigration
1835	Santa Anna invades Texas
1836	Texas declares its independence from Mexico; fall of the Alamo; Goliad massacre; Battle of San Jacinto
1840	William Henry Harrison elected president
1841	Harrison dies; John Tyler becomes president
1842	Webster-Ashburton Treaty
1844	James K. Polk elected president
1845	Congress votes by joint resolution to annex Texas; Mexico rejects Slidell mission
1846	The United States declares war on Mexico; John C. Frémont proclaims the Bear Flag Republic in California; Congress votes to accept a settlement of the Oregon boundary issue with Britain; Tariff of 1846; Wilmot Proviso introduced
1847	Mexico City falls to Scott; Lewis Cass's principle of "squatter sovereignty"
1848	Gold discovered in California; Treaty of Guadalupe-Hidalgo signed; Zachary Taylor elected president

The Germans

In 1860, there was no German nation, only a collection of principalities and small kingdoms. Immigrants from this area thought of themselves as Bavarians, Westphalians, or Saxons, rather than Germans.

German immigrants spanned a wide spectrum of class and occupation. Most were farmers, but professionals, artisans, and tradespeople made up a sizable minority. For example, Levi Strauss, a Jewish tailor from Bavaria, reached the United States in 1847. When gold was discovered in California the next year, Strauss gathered rolls of cloth and sailed for San Francisco. There he fashioned tough work overalls from canvas. Demand soared, and Strauss opened a factory to produce his cheap overalls, later known as blue jeans or Levi's.

A common language transcended the differences among German immigrants and bound them together. They clustered in the same neighborhoods, formed their own militia and fire companies, and established German-language parochial schools and newspapers. The diversity of the German-speaking population further fostered solidarity. Because Germans supplied their own lawyers, doctors, teachers, and merchants from their midst, they had no need to go outside their neighborhoods. Native-born Americans simultaneously admired German industriousness and resented German self-sufficiency, which they interpreted as clannishness. The Germans responded by becoming even more clannish. Their separateness made it difficult for the Germans to be as politically influential as the Irish immigrants.

The Irish

There were three waves of Irish immigration. Between 1815 and the mid-1820s, most Irish immigrants were Protestants, small landowners, and tradespeople drawn by enthusiastic veterans of the War of 1812 who reported that America was a paradise where "all a man needed was a gun and sufficient ammunition to be able to live like a prince." From the mid-1820s to the mid-1840s, Irish immigration became both more Catholic and poorer, comprised primarily of tenant farmers evicted by Protestant landlords. Rich or poor, Protestant or Catholic, nearly a million Irish crossed the Atlantic to the United States between 1815 and 1845.

Then, between 1845 and the early 1850s, the character of Irish immigration changed dramatically. In Ireland, blight destroyed harvest after harvest of potatoes, virtually the only food of the peasantry, and triggered one of the most gruesome famines in history. The Great Famine killed a million people. Those who survived, a landlord wrote, were "famished and ghastly skeletons." To escape suffering and death, 1.8 million Irish emigrated to the United States in the decade after 1845.

Overwhelmingly poor and Catholic, these newest Irish immigrants entered the work force at the bottom. While Irish men dug streets, canals, and railroads, Irish women worked as maids and textile workers. Poverty drove women to work at early ages, and the outdoor, all-season labor performed by their husbands turned many of them into working widows. Because the Irish usually married late, almost half the Irish immigrants were single adult women, many of whom never married.

It sometimes seemed that, no matter what the Irish did, they clashed with other Americans. The poorer Irish who dug canals, took in laundry, or worked as domestics competed with equally poor free blacks. This competition stirred up Irish animosity toward blacks and a hatred of abolitionists. At the same time, the Irish who secured skilled or semiskilled jobs clashed with native-born white workers.

Anti-Catholicism, Nativism, and Labor Protest

The surge of Irish immigration revived anti-Catholic fever, long a latent impulse among American Protestants. A groundswell of anti-Catholic publications climaxed in 1836 with Maria Monk's best-selling *Awful Disclosures of the Hotel Dieu Nunnery in Montreal,* which vividly described wild sexual relations between nuns and priests. Although she claimed to be a former nun, Maria Monk was actually a former prostitute.

The surge of Catholic immigration in the 1840s also had political ramifications fueled by **nativism.** Protestants formed anti-immigrant societies with names like the American Republicans and the United Order of Americans. One such secret society, the Order of the Star-Spangled Banner, would become the **"Know-Nothing" party,** or American Party, which was a major political force in the 1850s. In the 1840s, nativist parties prospered during flare-ups over local issues, such as whether the Protestant or Catholic version of the Bible should be used in predominantly Catholic schools. In 1844, for example, the "Bible Riots" in Philadelphia, spurred on by the electoral success of American Republican Party candidates, led to the deaths of sixteen people and the destruction of thirty buildings at the hands of Protestant mobs.

Nativism fed on an explosive mixture of fears and discontents. Protestants thought that their doctrine that each individual could interpret the Bible was more democratic than Catholicism, which made doctrine the province of the pope and bishops. In addition, at a time when the wages of native-born artisans and journeymen were depressed in the aftermath of the Panic of 1837 (see Chapter 10),

nativism Reaction against immigrants of different ethnic and/or religious backgrounds

"Know-Nothing" party Also "Order of the Star-Spangled Banner" or American Party; expression of nativism

many Protestant workers concluded that poor Catholic immigrants were threats to their jobs.

Many Irish immigrants, refugees from an agricultural society, believed that they could gain more through unions and strikes than through farming. Even women workers organized unions in these years; the leader of a seamstresses' union proclaimed, "Too long have we been bound down by tyrant employers."

Probably the most important development for workers in the 1840s was a state court decision. In *Commonwealth v. Hunt* (1842), the Massachusetts Supreme Court ruled that labor unions were not illegal monopolies that restrained trade. However, because less than 1 percent of the work force at that time belonged to a union, their impact was sharply limited. Thus, Massachusetts employers easily brushed aside the *Commonwealth* decision, firing union agitators and replacing them with cheap immigrant labor.

Ethnic and religious tensions also split the antebellum working class during the 1830s and 1840s. Friction between native-born and immigrant workers inevitably became intertwined with the political divisions of the second party system.

Immigrant Politics

Few immigrants had voted before reaching America, and even fewer had fled political persecution. Political upheavals had erupted in Austria and some German states in the turbulent year of 1848, but among the million German immigrants to the United States, only about 10,000 were political refugees, or "Forty-Eighters."

Once settled in the United States, however, many immigrants became politically active. They discovered that urban political organizations could help them find housing and jobs—in return for votes. Both the Irish and the Germans identified overwhelmingly with the Democratic Party. By 1820, the Irish controlled Tammany Hall, the New York City Democratic organization; Germans became staunch Democrats in cities like Milwaukee and St. Louis.

Immigrants' fears about jobs partly explained their widespread Democratic support. Former president Andrew Jackson had given the Democratic Party an anti-aristocratic coloration, making the Democrats seem more sympathetic than the Whigs to the common people. In addition, antislavery was linked to the Whig party, and the Irish loathed abolitionism because they feared that freed slaves would become their economic competitors. Moreover, the Whigs' moral and religious values seemed to threaten those of the Irish and Germans. Hearty-drinking Irish and German immigrants shunned temperance-crusading Whigs, many of whom were also rabid anti-Catholics. Even public-school reform, championed by the Whigs, was perceived as a menace to the Catholicism of Irish children and as a threat to the integrity of German language and culture.

Although liquor regulations and school laws were city or state concerns rather than federal responsibilities, the Democratic Party schooled immigrants in broad, national principles. It taught them to venerate George Washington and Thomas Jefferson, and to view "monied capitalists" as parasites who would tremble when the people spoke. It introduced immigrants to Democratic newspapers, Democratic picnics, and Democratic parades. The Democrats helped give immigrants a sense of themselves as Americans.

CHECKING IN

- Immigrants often found American realities far less attractive than their utopian dreams.
- German immigrants tended to cluster together, cutting off their access to political power.
- Irish immigrants, poor and usually Catholic, triggered an ethnic and religious backlash known as nativism.
- Immigrants often spearheaded early union movements.
- German and Irish immigrants generally became Democrats; most nativists were Whigs.

By the same token, the Democratic Party introduced immigrants to national issues. It redirected political loyalties that often had been forged on local issues into the arena of national politics. During the 1830s, the party had persuaded immigrants that national measures that were seemingly remote from their daily lives, like banking reform and the tariff, were vital to them. Now, in the 1840s, the Democrats would try to convince immigrants that national expansion likewise advanced their interests.

THE WEST AND BEYOND

What economic and political forces fed westward expansion during the 1840s?

As late as 1840, the American West meant the area between the Appalachian Mountains and the Mississippi River or just beyond. West of that lay the inhospitable Great Plains. A semiarid, treeless plateau, the Plains sustained huge buffalo herds and the nomadic Indians who lived off the buffalo. Because the Great Plains presented would-be farmers with formidable obstacles, public interest shifted toward the Far West, the fertile region beyond the Rockies.

The Far West

By the Transcontinental (or Adams-Onís) Treaty of 1819, the United States had relinquished to Spain its claims to Texas west of the Sabine River, and in return Spain renounced its claims to the Oregon country north of California. Two years later, the Mexican Revolution brought Mexico independence from Spain and possession of all North American territory claimed by Spain—Texas, California, and the southwest quadrant of the continent. In 1824 and 1825, Russia yielded its claims to Oregon south of Alaska. In 1827, the United States and Great Britain revived an earlier agreement for the joint occupation of the Oregon Territory. Texas, New Mexico, California, and Oregon stretched over an area larger than Britain, France, and Germany combined. Although this vast region should have tempted them, in the 1820s Mexico, the United States, and Britain all viewed the Far West as a remote and shadowy frontier. The American line of settlement reached only to Missouri, a 2,000-mile trek (allowing for mountains) from the West Coast.

Far Western Trade

After sailing around South America and up the Pacific coastline, early merchants established American and British outposts on the West Coast. Between the late 1790s and the 1820s, for example, Boston merchants built a thriving trade, exchanging goods from the eastern United States for western sea-otter fur, cattle, hides, and tallow (rendered from cattle fat and used for making candles and soap). The British Hudson's Bay Company developed a similar trade in Oregon and northern California. The California trade generated little friction with Mexico. Californians were as eager to buy as the traders were to sell. Traders who settled in California, like the Swiss-born John Sutter, learned to speak Spanish and became assimilated into Mexican culture.

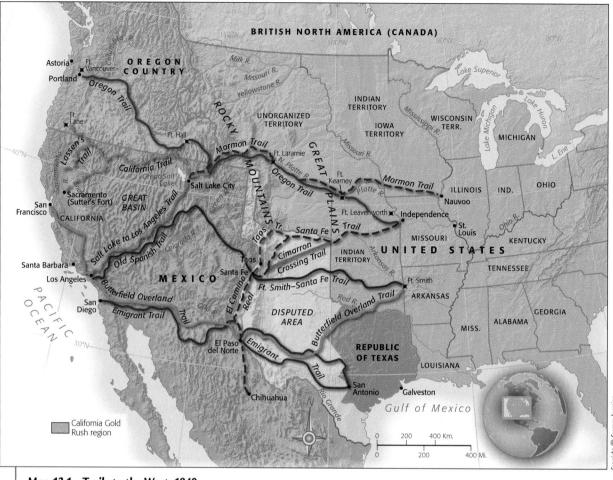

Map 13.1   Trails to the West, 1840

By 1840 several trails carried pioneers from Missouri and Illinois to the West.

Interactive Map

Also during the 1820s, trading links developed between St. Louis and Santa Fe. Each spring, midwesterners loaded wagon trains with tools, clothing, and household sundries and rumbled westward to Santa Fe, where they traded their goods for mules and silver (see Map 13.1). Mexico welcomed this trade. By the 1830s, more than half the goods trucked west along the Santa Fe Trail trickled into the mineral-rich Mexican provinces of Chihuahua and Sonora, and were exchanged for Mexican silver pesos, which became the principal medium of exchange in Missouri.

Some Americans ventured north from Santa Fe to trap beaver in what is today western Colorado and eastern Utah. Americans from St. Louis soon found themselves competing with both the Santa Fe traders and the agents of the Hudson's Bay Company for lucrative beaver pelts. Gradually, the St. Louis traders wrested the beaver trade from their Santa Fe competitors. Although silk hats were overtaking beaver ones in popularity by 1854, more than half a million beaver pelts were auctioned off in London that year.

Although the relations between Mexicans and Americans were mutually beneficial during the 1820s, the potential for conflict was always present. Spanish-speaking,

Roman Catholic, and accustomed to a more hierarchical society, the Mexicans formed a striking contrast to the largely Protestant, individualistic Americans. Further, American traders returned with glowing reports of the climate and fertility of Mexico's northern provinces. By the 1820s, American settlers were already moving into eastern Texas. At the same time, the ties that bound the central government of Mexico to its northern frontier provinces were starting to fray.

Mexican Government in the Far West

Spain, and later Mexico, recognized that the key to controlling the frontier provinces lay in promoting their settlement by civilized Hispanic people—Spaniards, Mexicans, and Indians who had embraced Catholicism and agriculture. The key instruments of Spain's expansion on the frontier had long been the Spanish missions. Protected by forts, or presidios, the Franciscan priests who staffed the missions endeavored to convert Native Americans and settle them as farmers on mission lands. San Francisco was the site of a mission and a presidio founded in 1776, and did not develop as a town until the 1830s.

Dealt a blow by the successful struggle for Mexican independence, Spain's system of missions began to decline in the late 1820s. The Mexican government gradually "secularized" the missions by distributing their lands to ambitious government officials and private ranchers who turned the mission Indians into forced laborers. As many Native Americans fled the missions and returned to their nomadic ways, lawlessness surged on the Mexican frontier.

To bring in settlers and to gain protection against Indian attacks, in 1824 the Mexican government began to encourage Americans to settle in the eastern part of the Mexican state known as Coahuila-Texas (koh-uh-WHEEL-uh TAY-has) by bestowing generous land grants on agents known as *empresarios* (em-pre-SAR-ee-ohs) to recruit American settlers. Initially, most Americans, like the *empresario* **Stephen F. Austin,** were content to live in Texas as naturalized Mexican citizens. But trouble brewed quickly. Most of the American settlers were southern farmers, often slaveholders. Having emancipated its own slaves in 1829, Mexico closed Texas to further American immigration in 1830 and forbade the introduction of more slaves. But the Americans, white and black, kept coming, and in 1834 Austin secured repeal of the 1830 prohibition on American immigration. By 1836, Texas contained some thirty thousand white Americans, five thousand black slaves, and four thousand Mexicans.

Stephen F. Austin *Empresario* who led first Americans into Texas

As American immigration swelled, Mexican politics (which Austin compared to the country's volcanic geology) grew increasingly unstable. In 1834, Mexican president Antonio López de **Santa Anna** instituted a policy of restricting the powers of the regimes in Coahuila-Texas and other Mexican states. His actions ignited a series of rebellions in those regions, the most important of which became known as the Texas Revolution.

Santa Anna Mexican dictator who helped provoke Texas Revolution

The Texas Revolution, 1836

Santa Anna's brutality in crushing most of the rebellions alarmed the initially moderate Austin and others. When Santa Anna invaded Texas in the fall of 1835, Austin cast his lot with the more radical Americans who wanted independence.

Alamo Site of the famed defeat of Texans during the Texas Revolution

Sam Houston Military and political leader of Texas during and after the Texas Revolution

Santa Anna's army initially met with success. In February 1836, four thousand of his men laid siege to San Antonio, where two hundred rebels had retreated into an abandoned mission, the **Alamo.** On March 6—four days after Texas had declared its independence, although they did not know about it—the defenders of the Alamo were overwhelmed by Mexican troops. Under Santa Anna's orders, the Mexican army killed all the Alamo's defenders, including the wounded. A few weeks later, Mexican troops massacred some 350 prisoners taken from an American settlement at Goliad (GO-lee-add).

Meanwhile, the Texans formed an army, with **Sam Houston** at its head. A giant man who wore leopard-skin vests, Houston retreated east to pick up recruits (mostly Americans who crossed the border to fight Santa Anna). Once reinforced, Houston turned and surprised the complacent Mexicans at San Jacinto (juh-SIN-toh), just east of what is now the city of Houston. Shouting "Remember the Alamo!" Houston's army of eight hundred tore through the Mexican lines, killing nearly half of Santa Anna's men in fifteen minutes and taking Santa Anna himself prisoner. Houston then forced Santa Anna to sign a treaty (which the Mexican government never ratified) recognizing the independence of Texas (see Map 13.2).

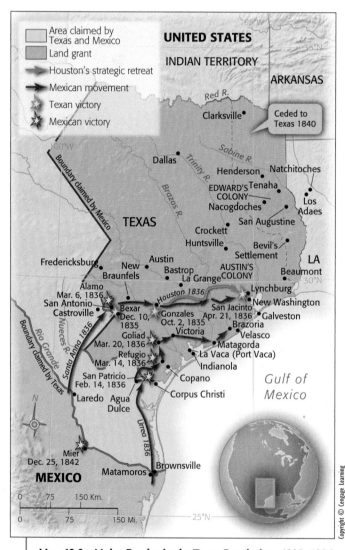

Map 13.2 Major Battles in the Texas Revolution, 1835–1836
Sam Houston's victory at San Jacinto was the decisive action of the war and avenged the massacres at the Alamo and Goliad.

Interactive Map

American Settlements in California, New Mexico, and Oregon

Before 1840, California and New Mexico, which were both less accessible than Texas, exerted no more than a mild attraction for American settlers. Only a few hundred Americans resided in New Mexico in 1840 and perhaps four hundred lived in California. A contemporary observed that the Americans living in California and New Mexico "are scattered throughout the whole Mexican population, and most of them have Spanish wives. . . . They live in every respect like the Spanish."

Yet the beginnings of change were evident. During the 1840s, Americans streamed into the Sacramento Valley, lured by favorable reports of the region and welcomed by the Hispanic population as a way to encourage economic development. To the north, Oregon's abundant farmland beckoned settlers from the Mississippi Valley. By 1840, some five hundred Americans had settled there, in what was described as a "pioneer's paradise" where "the pigs are running around under the great acorn trees, round and fat and already cooked, with knives and forks sticking in them so that you can cut off a slice whenever you are hungry."

The Huntington Library & Art Collections, San Marino, California

Crossing the River Platte
In the absence of bridges, pioneers had to bet on shallow river bottoms to cross rivers.

The Overland Trails   Whether bound for California or Oregon, Americans faced a four-month ordeal crossing terrain little known in reality but vividly depicted in fiction as an Indian killing ground. Cautious pioneers stocked up on enough guns to equip an army in jump-off towns such as Independence and St. Joseph, Missouri. In fact, they were more likely to shoot one another than to be shot by the usually cooperative Indians, and much more likely to be scalped by the inflated prices charged by merchants in Independence or "St. Joe."

Once embarked, the emigrants faced new hardships and hazards: kicks from mules, oxen that collapsed from thirst, and overloaded wagons that broke down. Trails were difficult to follow—at least until they became littered by the debris of broken wagons and by the bleached bones of oxen. Guidebooks were more like guessbooks. The Donner party lost so much time following the advice of one such book that its members became snowbound in the High Sierras and reached California only after its survivors had turned to cannibalism. Emigrants met the challenges of the **overland trails** by close cooperation with one another, traveling in huge wagon trains rather than alone. Men yoked and unyoked the oxen, drove the wagons and stock, and hunted. Women packed, cooked, and assisted in childbirths.

Between 1840 and 1848, an estimated 11,500 pioneers followed an overland trail to Oregon, and some 2,700 reached California. Such small numbers made a difference, for the British did not settle Oregon at all, and the Mexican population of California was small and scattered. By 1845, California was clinging to Mexico by the thinnest of threads. The territory's Hispanic population, the *californios*, felt little allegiance to Mexico, which they contemptuously called "the other shore." Some of them wanted

overland trails Routes westward to Oregon and California followed by thousands of Americans

CHECKING IN

- By the 1820s Americans were deeply involved in trade along Mexico's northern frontiers.

- In the 1820s the Mexican government invited Americans to settle in Texas as a buffer against Indians; within a decade more than thirty thousand Americans lived in Texas.

- Texans rebelled against Mexico in 1836 and won their independence.

- In the 1840s, Americans began streaming into Oregon and California.

- More than fourteen thousand Americans followed the overland trails west.

independence from Mexico, whereas others contemplated British or French rule. But these *californios,* with their tenuous allegiances, faced a growing number of American settlers with definite political sympathies.

THE POLITICS OF EXPANSION, 1840–1846

How did "Manifest Destiny" influence American politics?

Westward expansion raised the question of whether the United States should annex the independent Texas republic. In the mid-1840s, the Texas-annexation issue sparked political passions and became entangled with equally unsettling issues relating to California, New Mexico, and Oregon. Between 1846 and 1848, a war with Mexico and a dramatic confrontation with Britain settled all these questions on terms favorable to the United States.

At the start of the 1840s, western issues received little attention in a nation concerned primarily with issues relating to economic recovery—tariffs, banking, and internal improvements. Only after politicians failed to address the economic problems coherently did opportunistic leaders thrust expansion-related issues to the top of the political agenda.

The Whig Ascendancy

The election of 1840 brought Whig candidate William Henry Harrison to the presidency and installed Whig majorities in both houses of Congress. The Whigs proposed to replace Van Buren's Independent Treasury (see Chapter 10) with some sort of national fiscal agency, like the defunct Bank of the United States. The Whig party also favored a revised tariff that would increase government revenues but remain low enough to permit the importation of foreign goods. According to the Whig plan, the states would then receive tariff-generated revenues for internal improvements.

The Whig agenda might have breezed into law, but Harrison died after only one month in office. His successor, Vice President John Tyler, an upper-crust Virginian put on the ticket in 1840 for his southern appeal, then assumed the presidency. A former Democrat and a supporter of states' rights, he repeatedly vetoed Whig proposals, including a bill to create a new national bank.

Tyler also played havoc with the Whig tariff policy. The Compromise Tariff of 1833 had provided for a gradual scaling down of tariff duties to 20 percent. Amid the depression of the early 1840s, however, the tariff appeared too low to generate the revenue Whigs needed to distribute among the states for internal improvements. In response, Whigs passed two bills in the summer of 1842 that simultaneously postponed the final reduction of tariffs to 20 percent and ordered distribution to the states to proceed. Tyler promptly vetoed both bills, infuriating Whig leadership. Some Whigs spoke of impeachment. Finally, in August, Tyler signed a new bill that maintained some tariffs above 20 percent but abandoned distribution to the states.

Tyler's erratic course confounded and disrupted his party. By maintaining some tariffs above 20 percent, the tariff of 1842 satisfied northern manufacturers, but by abandoning distribution, it infuriated many southerners and westerners. In the congressional elections of 1842, the Whigs paid a heavy price for failing to enact their program. Although retaining a slim majority in the Senate, they lost control of the House to the Democrats. Now the nation had one party in control of the Senate, its rival in control of the House, and a president who appeared to belong to neither party.

Tyler and the Annexation of Texas

Although disowned by his party, Tyler ardently desired a second term as president. Domestic issues offered him little hope of building a popular following, but foreign policy was another matter. In 1842, Tyler's secretary of state, Daniel Webster, concluded the Webster-Ashburton Treaty with Great Britain, settling a long-festering dispute over the Maine-Canada border. Tyler reasoned that if he could follow the treaty, which was highly popular in the North, with the annexation of Texas, he could build a national following.

The issue of slavery, however, clouded every discussion of Texas. Antislavery northerners saw proposals to annex Texas as part of a southern conspiracy to extend slavery, because Texas would certainly enter the Union as a slave state. In fact, some southerners dreamed of creating four or five slave states from Texas's vast area.

Nevertheless, in summer 1843, Tyler launched a propaganda campaign for Texas annexation. He alleged that Britain had designs on Texas, which Americans would be prudent to forestall. In spring 1844, Tyler and John C. Calhoun, who became secretary of state in 1844, submitted to the Senate a treaty annexing Texas. Accompanying the treaty was a letter from Calhoun to the British minister in Washington, defending slavery as beneficial to African-Americans, the only way to protect them from "vice and pauperism." Abolitionists now had evidence that the annexation of Texas was linked to a conspiracy to extend slavery. Consequently, both Whig and Democratic leaders came out in opposition to the annexation of Texas, and the treaty went down to crushing defeat in the Senate. However, this vote only postponed the final decision on annexation to the upcoming election of 1844.

The Election of 1844

Tyler's ineptitude turned the presidential campaign into a free-for-all. Unable to gather support as an independent, he dropped out of the race. Henry Clay had a secure grip on the Whig nomination, but Martin Van Buren's apparently clear path to the head of the Democratic ticket vanished as the issue of annexation split his party. A deadlocked Democratic Party finally turned to James K. Polk of Tennessee, the first "dark horse" nominee in American history and a supporter of immediate annexation.

Jeering "Who is James K. Polk?" the Whigs derided the nomination. Polk was little known outside the South. Yet he persuaded many northerners that annexation of Texas would benefit them. Conjuring an imaginative scenario, Polk and his supporters argued that if Britain succeeded in abolishing slavery in Texas, slavery would not be able to move westward; racial tensions in existing slave states would intensify; and the chances of a race war would increase. However far-fetched, this argument played effectively on northern racial phobias and helped Polk detach annexation from Calhoun's narrow, prosouthern defense of it.

In contrast to the Democrats, whose position was clear, Clay kept muddying the waters. After several shifts, Clay finally came out against annexation, but not until September. His wavering alienated his southern supporters and prompted some of his northern supporters to bolt the Whigs for the antislavery Liberty party, formed in 1840. The Whigs also infuriated Catholic immigrant voters by nominating Theodore Frelinghuysen (fray-ling-HIGH-zun) for the vice presidency. A supporter of temperance and an assortment of other causes, Frelinghuysen confirmed fears that the Whigs were the orthodox Protestant party. Catholic immigrants turned out in large numbers to vote for the Democrats.

On the eve of the election in New York City, so many Irish marched to the court-house to be qualified for voting that the windows had to be opened to allow people to enter and leave. Polk won the electoral vote 170 to 105, but his margin in the popular vote was only 38,000 out of 2.6 million votes cast. A shift of 6,000 votes in New York, where the immigrant vote and Whig defections to the Liberty party had hurt Clay, would have given Clay the state and the presidency.

Manifest Destiny, 1845

The election of 1844 demonstrated the strength of national support for the annexation of Texas. The surging popular sentiment for expansion reflected a growing conviction that America's natural destiny was to expand into Texas and all the way to the Pacific Ocean.

Expansionists emphasized extending the "area of freedom" and talked of "repelling the contaminating proximity of monarchies upon the soil that we have consecrated to the rights of man." Americans needed only a phrase to capture this ebullient spirit. In 1845, John L. O'Sullivan, a New York Democratic journalist, supplied that phrase when he wrote of "our manifest destiny to overspread and to possess the whole of the continent which Providence has given us for the development of the great experiment of liberty and federated self-government entrusted to us."

Manifest Destiny Phrase coined to describe beliefs of ardent expansionists

Advocates of **Manifest Destiny** used lofty language and invoked God and Nature to sanction expansion. Northern Whigs frequently dismissed Manifest Destiny as a smoke screen aimed at concealing the evil intent of expanding slavery. In reality, many expansionists were neither supporters of slavery nor zealous annexationists. Most had their eyes not on Texas but on Oregon and California. Blaming the post-1837 depression on the failure of Americans to find markets for their agricultural surplus, they saw California and Oregon as solutions. An Alabama Democrat praised California's "safe and capacious harbors," which "invite to their bosoms the rich commerce of the East."

However, more than trade was at stake. At the heart of their thinking lay an impulse to preserve the predominantly agricultural character of the American people and thereby to safeguard democracy. Fundamentally Jeffersonian, expansionists equated industrialization and urbanization with social stratification and class strife. To avoid the "bloated wealth" and "terrible misery" that afflicted Britain, the United States *had* to expand.

Democrats saw expansion as a logical complement to their support of low tariffs and their opposition to centralized banking. High tariffs and banks tended to "favor and foster the factory system," but expansion would provide farmers with land as well as access to foreign markets. Americans would continue to be farmers, and the foundations of the republic would remain secure.

This message, trumpeted by the penny press, made sense to the working poor, many of them Irish immigrants. Expansion would open economic opportunity for the common people and thwart British plans to free American slaves, whom the poor viewed as potential competition for already-scarce jobs.

Expansionism drew on the ideas of Thomas Jefferson, John Quincy Adams, and other leaders of the early republic who had proclaimed the American people's right to displace any people, uncivilized or European, from their westward path. Early expansionists had feared that overexpansion might create an ungovernable empire, but their successors had no such qualms. Although they pointed with alarm to the negative effects of industrialization, the expansionists also relied on the technology of industrialization. The railroad and the telegraph, they said, had annihilated the problem of distance and made expansion safe.

James K. Polk Memorial Association, Columbia, Tennessee

James K. Polk

Lacking charm, Polk bored even his friends, but few presidents could match his record of acquiring land for the United States.

Polk and Oregon

The growing spirit of Manifest Destiny intensified the Oregon issue. To soften northern criticism of the pending annexation of Texas, the Democrats included in their 1844 platform the assertion that American title "to the whole of the Territory of Oregon is clear and unquestionable." Taken literally, this statement, which Polk later repeated, pressed an American claim to the entire Oregon Territory between California and 54°40', the southern boundary of Alaska, a claim never before advanced.

Polk's objectives in Oregon were more subtle than his language. He knew that the United States could never obtain all of Oregon without a war with Britain, and he wanted to avoid that. He hoped the belligerent language would persuade the British to accept what they had previously rejected, a division of Oregon at the forty-ninth parallel. This settlement would give the United States the superb deep-water harbor of Puget Sound and the southern tip of Vancouver Island. The British had long held out for a division along the Columbia River, which entered the Pacific Ocean far south of the forty-ninth parallel.

CHECKING IN

- The death of William Henry Harrison threw Whig control of the national government into turmoil.

- Attempts to bring Texas into the Union raised the volatile issue of slavery.

- Dark horse candidate and expansionist James K. Polk won the 1844 election.

- "Manifest Destiny" became the slogan of expansionists.

- Polk won a treaty dividing the Oregon Territory with Great Britain, giving the United States its first Pacific boundary.

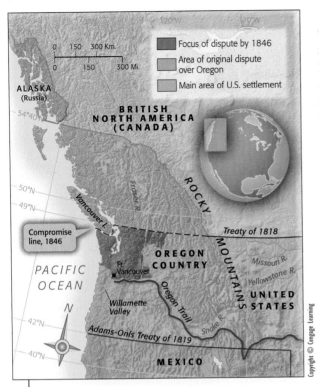

Map 13.3   Oregon Boundary Dispute

Although demanding that Britain cede the entire Oregon Territory south of 54°40', the United States settled for a compromise at the forty-ninth parallel.

Interactive Map

Polk's position roused furious interest in acquisition of the entire territory. Mass meetings adopted such resolutions as "The Whole or None!" and "Fifty-four Forty or Fight!" Each year brought new American settlers into Oregon. John Quincy Adams, although no supporter of the annexation of Texas or the 54°40' boundary for Oregon, believed that American settlements gave the United States a stronger claim than discovery and exploration had given the British. The United States, Adams preached, was the nation bound "to make the wilderness blossom as the rose, to establish laws, to increase, multiply, and subdue the earth," all "at the first behest of God Almighty."

In April 1846, Polk forced the issue by notifying Britain that the United States was terminating the joint British-American occupation of Oregon. In effect, this message was that the British could either go to war over the American claims to 54°40'—or negotiate. Britain chose to negotiate. Although the British raged against "that ill-regulated, overbearing, and aggressive spirit of American democracy," they had too many other problems to wage war over "a few miles of pine swamp." The ensuing treaty divided Oregon at the forty-ninth parallel, although Britain retained all of Vancouver Island and temporary navigation rights on the Columbia River (see Map 13.3). On June 15, 1846, the Senate ratified the treaty.

THE MEXICAN-AMERICAN WAR AND ITS AFTERMATH, 1846–1848

How did the outcome of the Mexican-American War intensify intersectional conflict?

Between 1846 and 1848, the United States successfully fought a war that cost Mexico its claims to Texas and the provinces of New Mexico and California. Many Americans rejoiced in the stunning victory. But some recognized that deep divisions over the status of slavery in New Mexico and California boded ill for their nation's future.

The Origins of the Mexican-American War

While Polk was challenging Britain over Oregon, the United States and Mexico moved toward war. The impending conflict had both remote and immediate causes. One long-standing grievance lay in the Mexican government's failure to pay some $2 million in debts owed to American citizens. Bitter memories of the Alamo and the Goliad massacre reinforced American loathing of Mexico. Above all, the issue of Texas poisoned relations between the two nations. Beset by internal strife—Mexico's presidency changed hands twenty times between 1829 and 1844—Mexico feared that, once in control of Texas, the "Colossus of the North" might seize other provinces, perhaps even Mexico itself, and treat Mexicans much as it treated its slaves.

Polk's election increased the strength of the pro-annexationists, as his campaign had persuaded many northerners that Texas's annexation would bring national benefits. In February 1845, both houses of Congress responded to popular sentiment by passing a resolution annexing Texas. However, Texans balked, in part because some feared that union with the United States would provoke a Mexican invasion and war on Texas soil.

Polk moved rapidly. To sweeten the pot for Texans, he supported their claim that the Rio Grande (REE-oh GRAN-day) constituted Texas's southern border, despite Mexico's contention that the Nueces (NOO-ay-sess) River, one hundred miles farther north, bounded Texas. Because the Rio Grande meandered west and north nearly two thousand miles, it encompassed a huge territory, including part of modern New Mexico. The Texas that Polk proposed to annex was thus far larger than the Texas that had gained independence from Mexico. On July 4, 1845, reassured by Polk's support, Texas voted to accept annexation. Under Polk's orders, American troops under General Zachary Taylor deployed at Corpus Christi, south of the Nueces River, in territory still claimed by Mexico.

California and its fine harbors influenced Polk's actions, for he had entered the White House with the firm intention of extending American control over that province, too. If Mexico went to war with the United States over Texas, Polk's supporters claimed, "the road to California will be open to us." Reports from American agents convinced Polk that the way lay open for California to join the United States as Texas would—by revolution and then annexation.

Continued turmoil in Mexican politics further complicated this complex situation. In early 1845, a new Mexican government agreed to negotiate with the United States, and Polk decided to give negotiations a chance. In November 1845, he dispatched John Slidell to Mexico City with instructions to gain Mexican recognition of the annexation of Texas with the Rio Grande border. In exchange, the U.S. government would assume the debt owed by Mexico to American citizens. Polk also authorized Slidell to offer up to $25 million for California and New Mexico. However, by the time Slidell reached Mexico City, the government there had become too weak to make concessions and refused to negotiate. Polk then ordered Taylor to move southward to the Rio Grande, hoping to provoke a Mexican attack and unite the American people behind war.

The Mexican government dawdled. Polk was about to send a war message to Congress when word finally arrived that Mexican forces had crossed the Rio Grande and attacked the U.S. army. *"American blood has been shed on American soil!"* one of Polk's followers jubilantly proclaimed. On May 11, 1846, Polk informed Congress that war "exists by the act of Mexico herself" and called for $10 million to fight the war.

Polk's disarming assertion that the United States was already at war provoked furious opposition in Congress. For one thing, the Mexican attack on Taylor's troops had taken place on land never before claimed by the United States. By announcing that war already existed, moreover, Polk seemed to be undercutting Congress's power to declare war and using a mere border incident as a pretext to acquire more slave territory. But Polk had maneuvered the Whigs into a corner. They could not afford to appear unpatriotic—they remembered vividly what opposition to the War of 1812 had cost the Federalists—so they swallowed their outrage and supported war.

Polk's single-minded pursuit of his goals had prevailed. As a humorless, austere man who banned dancing and liquor from the White House, he inspired little personal warmth. But he triumphed over all opposition, in part because of his opponents' fragmentation, in part because of expansion's popular appeal, and in part because of his foreign antagonists' weakness. Reluctant to fight over Oregon, Britain had negotiated. Too weak to negotiate, Mexico chose to fight over territory that it had already lost (Texas) and where its hold was feeble (California and New Mexico).

The Mexican-American War

Most European observers expected Mexico to win the war. Its army was four times the size of the American forces, and it was fighting on home ground. Having botched its one previous attempt to invade a neighbor, Canada, in 1812, the United States now had to sustain offensive operations in an area remote from American settlements. American expansionists, however, hardly expected the Mexicans to fight at all. Racism and arrogance convinced many Americans that the Mexican people, degraded by their mixed Spanish and Indian population, were "as sure to melt away at the approach of [American] energy and enterprise as snow before a southern sun."

In fact, the Mexicans fought bravely and stubbornly, although unsuccessfully. In May 1846, Taylor, "Old Rough and Ready," routed the Mexican army in Texas and pursued it across the Rio Grande, eventually capturing the major city of Monterrey (mon-ter-RAY). War enthusiasm surged in the United States. Recruiting posters blared, "Here's to old Zach! Glorious Times! Roast Beef, Ice Cream, and Three Months' advance." Taylor's conspicuously ordinary manner—he went into battle wearing a straw hat and a plain brown coat—endeared him to the public, which kicked up its heels in celebration to the "Rough and Ready Polka" and the "General Taylor Quick Step."

After taking Monterrey, Taylor, starved for supplies, halted and granted Mexico an eight-week armistice. Eager to undercut Taylor's popularity—the Whigs were already touting him as a presidential candidate—Polk stripped him of half his forces and reassigned them to General Winfield Scott. Scott was to mount an amphibious attack on Vera Cruz (VEHR-uh-krooz) and proceed to Mexico City, following the path of Cortés and his conquistadors. Events outstripped Polk's scheme, however, when Taylor defeated a far larger Mexican army at the Battle of Buena Vista (BWAY-nuh VEES-tuh), on February 22–23, 1847.

Farther north, American forces took advantage of the shakiness of Mexican rule to strip away New Mexico and California. In spring 1846, Colonel Stephen Kearny led an army from Fort Leavenworth, Kansas, toward Santa Fe. Reaching New Mexico, Kearny took the territory by a combination of bluff, bluster, and perhaps bribery, all without firing a shot. The Mexican governor, following his own advice that "it is better to be thought brave than to be so," fled at Kearny's approach. Once he had suppressed a brief rebellion by Mexicans and Indians, Kearny controlled New Mexico securely enough that he could dispatch part of his army south into Mexico to support Taylor at Buena Vista.

California also fell easily into American hands. In 1845, Polk had ordered the Pacific Squadron under Commodore John D. Sloat to occupy California's ports in the event of war. The president had also dispatched a courier overland with secret orders for the colorful **John C. Frémont**. A Georgia-born adventurer, Frémont took advantage of his marriage to the daughter of a powerful senator to have accounts of his explorations in the Northwest published as official government documents, and then basked in glory as "the Great Pathfinder." Polk's courier caught up with Frémont in Oregon. Instructed to proceed to California and "watch over the interests of the United States," Frémont interpreted his orders liberally. In June 1846, he rounded up some American insurgents, seized the town of Sonoma (suh-NOH-muh), and proclaimed the independent "Bear Flag Republic." The combined efforts of Frémont, Sloat, and Kearny (who arrived in California after capturing New Mexico) established U.S. control over California.

John C. Frémont Adventurer who played a role in California rebellion against Mexico; later a force in national politics

The final and most important campaign of the war saw the conquest of Mexico City itself. In March 1847, Winfield Scott landed near Vera Cruz and quickly pounded that city into submission. Moving inland, Scott encountered Santa Anna at the seemingly impregnable pass of Cerro Gordo (SERR-oh GORD-oh), but a young captain in Scott's command, Robert E. Lee, helped find a trail that led around the Mexican flank to a small peak overlooking the pass. There Scott planted howitzers and, on April 18, stormed the pass and routed the Mexicans. Scott now moved directly on Mexico City. Taking the key fortresses of Churubusco and Chapultepec (where another young captain, Ulysses S. Grant, was cited for bravery), Scott took the city on September 13, 1847 (see Map 13.4).

Although the Mexican army outnumbered the Americans in virtually every battle, they could not match the superior artillery or the logistics and organization of the "barbarians of the North." The Americans died like flies from yellow fever, and they carried into battle the agonies of venereal disease, which they picked up (and left) in many of the Mexican towns they took. But the Americans benefited from the unprecedented quality of their weapons, supplies, and organization.

By the **Treaty of Guadalupe-Hidalgo** (gwah-duh-LOO-pay ee-DOLL-go) (February 2, 1848), Mexico ceded Texas with the Rio Grande boundary, New Mexico, and California to the United States; from the Mexican cession would come the states of New Mexico, California, Nevada, and Utah, most of Arizona, and parts of Colorado and Wyoming. In turn, the United States assumed the claims of U.S. citizens against the Mexican government and paid Mexico $15 million. Although some rabid expansionists denounced the treaty because it failed to include all of Mexico, Polk, like most Americans, was satisfied. Empty territory was fine, but few Americans wanted to annex the mixed Spanish and Indian population of Mexico itself and incorporate into the United States "ignorant and indolent half-civilized Indians," in one writer's words. The virulent racism of American leaders allowed the Mexicans to retain part of their nation. On March 10, 1848, the Senate ratified the treaty by a vote of 38 to 10.

Treaty of Guadalupe Hidalgo Agreement ending the Mexican-American War; ceded vast amounts of land to the United States

The War's Effects on Sectional Conflict

Despite wartime patriotic enthusiasm, sectional conflict sharpened between 1846 and 1848. Territorial expansion sparked the Polk administration's major battles. To Polk, it mattered little whether new territories were slave or free. Expansion would serve the

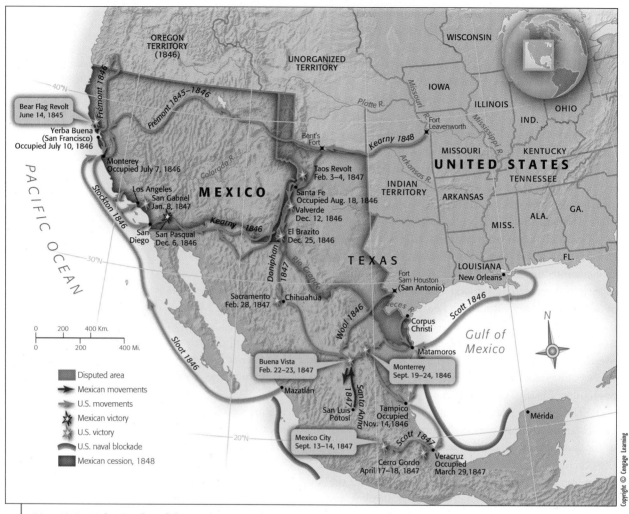

Map 13.4   Major Battles of the Mexican-American War

The Mexican-American War's decisive campaign began with General Winfield Scott's capture of Vera Cruz and ended with his conquest of Mexico City.

Interactive Map

nation's interests by dispersing population and retaining its agricultural and democratic character. Focusing attention on slavery in the territories struck him as "not only unwise but wicked." The Missouri Compromise, prohibiting slavery north of 36°30′, impressed him as a simple and permanent solution to the problem of territorial slavery.

However, many northerners were coming to see slavery in the territories as a profoundly disruptive issue that neither could nor should be solved simply by extending the 36°30′ line westward. Amounting to a small minority, abolitionists, who opposed any extension of slavery on moral grounds, posed a minor threat to Polk. More important were northern Democrats who feared that expansion of slavery into California and New Mexico (parts of each lay south of 36°30′) would deter free laborers from settling those territories. These Democrats argued that competition with slaves degraded free labor, that the westward extension of slavery would check the westward migration of free labor, and that such a barrier would aggravate the social problems already beginning to plague the East: class strife, social stratification, and labor protest.

The Wilmot Proviso

A young Democratic congressman from Pennsylvania, David Wilmot, became the spokesman for these disaffected northern Democrats. In August 1846, he introduced an amendment to an appropriations bill. This amendment, which became known as the **Wilmot Proviso,** stipulated that slavery must be prohibited in any territory acquired by the war with Mexico. Neither an abolitionist nor a critic of Polk on tariff policy, Wilmot spoke for those loyal Democrats who had supported the annexation of Texas on the assumption that Texas would be the last slave state. Wilmot's intention was not to split his party along sectional lines but instead to hold Polk to what Wilmot and other northern Democrats took as an implicit understanding: Texas for the slaveholders, California and New Mexico for free labor.

| **Wilmot Proviso** Attempt to ban slavery from any territory acquired from Mexico

With strong northern support, the proviso passed in the House but stalled in the Senate. Polk refused to endorse it, and most southern Democrats opposed any barrier to the expansion of slavery south of the Missouri Compromise line. They believed that the westward extension of slavery would reduce the concentration of slaves in the older regions of the South and thus lessen the chances of a slave revolt.

The proviso raised unsettling constitutional questions. Calhoun and other southerners contended that, because slaves were property, the Constitution protected slaveholders' right to carry their slaves wherever they chose. This position led to the conclusion that the Missouri Compromise was unconstitutional. On the other side, many northerners cited the Northwest Ordinance of 1787, the Missouri Compromise, and the Constitution itself, which gave Congress the power to "make all needful rules and regulations respecting the territory or other property belonging to the United States," as justification for congressional legislation over slavery in the territories. With the election of 1848 approaching, politicians of both sides, eager to hold their parties together and avert civil war, frantically searched for a middle ground.

The Election of 1848

The Whigs watched in dismay as prosperity returned under Polk's program of an independent treasury and low tariffs. Never before had Henry Clay's American System of national banking and high tariffs seemed so irrelevant. But the Wilmot Proviso gave the Whigs a political windfall; originating in the Democratic Party, it allowed the Whigs to portray themselves as the South's only dependable friends.

These considerations inclined the majority of Whigs toward Zachary Taylor. As a Louisiana slaveholder, he had obvious appeal to the South. As a political newcomer, he had no loyalty to a discredited American System. And as a war hero, he had broad national appeal. Nominating Taylor as their presidential candidate in 1848, the Whigs presented him as an ideal man "without regard to creeds or principles" and ran him without any platform.

The Democrats faced a greater challenge because David Wilmot was one of their own. They could not ignore the issue of slavery in the territories, but if they embraced the positions of either Wilmot or Calhoun, the party would split along sectional lines. When Polk declined to run for reelection, the Democrats nominated Lewis Cass of Michigan, who had formulated the doctrine of "squatter sovereignty," or **popular sovereignty,** as it was later called. Cass argued that Congress should let the question of slavery in the territories be decided by the people who settled there. Squatter sovereignty appealed to many because of its arresting simplicity and vagueness; it neatly dodged the explosive question of whether Congress actually possessed the power to prohibit territorial slavery.

popular sovereignty Proposal that settlers in new territories should decide the issue of slavery for themselves

In the campaign, both parties tried to avoid the issue of slavery in the territories, but neither succeeded. A pro-Wilmot faction of the Democratic Party linked up with the abolitionist Liberty party and antislavery "Conscience" Whigs to form the Free-Soil party. Declaring their dedication to "Free Trade, Free Labor, Free Speech, and Free Men," the Free-Soilers nominated Martin Van Buren on a platform opposing any extension of slavery.

Zachary Taylor benefited from the opposition's alienation of key northern states over the tariff issue, from Democratic disunity over the Wilmot Proviso, and from his war-hero stature. He captured a majority of electoral votes in both the North and the South. Although it failed to carry any state, the Free-Soil party ran well enough in the North to demonstrate the grassroots popularity of opposition to the extension of slavery. By showing that opposition to the spread of slavery had far more appeal than outright abolitionism, the Free-Soilers sent both Whigs and Democrats a message that they would be unable to ignore in future elections.

The California Gold Rush

When Wilmot introduced his proviso, the issue of slavery in the West was more abstract than immediate, for Mexico had not yet ceded any territory. The picture quickly changed when an American carpenter discovered gold while building a sawmill in the foothills of California's Sierra Nevada only nine days before the Treaty of Guadalupe-Hidalgo was signed. A frantic gold rush erupted. A San Francisco paper complained that all California "resounds with the sordid cry to *GOLD, GOLD, GOLD!* while the field is left half-planted, the house half-built, and every thing neglected but the manufacture of shovels and pickaxes."

By December 1848, pamphlets with titles like *The Emigrant's Guide to the Gold Mines* hit the streets of New York City, and the gold rush was on. Overland emigrants to California increased from 400 in 1848 to 44,000 in 1850. Arriving by land as well as by sea, gold-rushers swelled California's population from 15,000 in the summer of 1848 to 250,000 by 1852. They came from every corner of the world; one journalist reported that, when she walked through a miners' camp, she heard English,

"Union" Woodcut by Thomas W. Strong, 1848
This 1848 campaign poster for Zachary Taylor reminded Americans of his military victories, unmilitary bearing (note the civilian dress and straw hat), and deliberately vague promises.

Library of Congress

Italian, French, Spanish, German, and Hawaiian. Clashes between Anglo-Americans and Hispanics were frequent. Anglo-Americans particularly resented the Chinese who flooded into California in the 1850s as contract laborers. Rampant prejudice did not stop Americans from hiring Chinese workers, however.

Within a decade, the gold rush turned the sleepy Hispanic town of Yerba Buena (YAIR-buh BWAY-nah), with 150 people in 1846, into "a pandemonium of a city" of 50,000 known as San Francisco. No other American city boasted people from more parts of the world. The ethnic and racial tensions of the gold fields spilled over into the city. In 1851, San Francisco's merchants organized the first of several Committees of Vigilance, which patrolled the streets, deported undesirables, and tried and hanged alleged thieves and murderers.

The gold rush made the issue of slavery in the West an immediate, practical concern. The newcomers to California included free blacks and slaves brought by planters from the South. White prospectors loathed the idea of competing with these groups and wanted to drive them from the gold fields. Violence mounted, and demands grew for a strong civilian government to replace the ineffective military government left over from the war. Polk began to fear that without a satisfactory congressional solution to the slavery issue, Californians might organize a government independent of the United States. The gold rush guaranteed that the question of slavery in the Mexican cession would be the first item on the agenda for Polk's successor and the nation.

CHECKING IN

- The United States entered into the Mexican-American War by choice rather than by necessity.
- After losing the war, Mexico ceded to the United States the Southwest quadrant of the present United States and recognized Texas's independence.
- Victory in the war again raised the question of the expansion of slavery.
- The election of 1848 revealed the growing strength of opposition to the expansion of slavery.
- The discovery of gold in California guaranteed that, despite politicians' wishes to sidestep the issue, the expansion of slavery would rise to the top of the national agenda.

Chapter Summary

How did immigration in the 1840s influence the balance of power between the Whig and Democratic parties? (page 290)

The massive immigration of the 1840s changed the face of American politics. Angered by Whig nativism and anti-Catholicism, the new German and Irish immigrants swelled the ranks of the Democratic Party. Meanwhile, the Whigs were unraveling. The untimely death of President Harrison brought John Tyler, a Democrat in Whig's clothing, to the White House. Tyler's vetoes of key Whig measures left the Whig party in disarray.

What economic and political forces fed westward expansion during the 1840s? (page 295)

Americans had begun trading along Mexico's northern frontiers early in the nineteenth century. In the 1820s, Mexico invited Americans to settle in Texas as a buffer against hostile Native Americans. But Texans rebelled against Mexico in 1836 and won their independence. In the following decade, thousands of people followed the overland trails to California and Oregon.

KEY TERMS

Tejano (p. 289)
German and Irish immigrants (p. 291)
nativism (p. 293)
"Know-Nothing" party (p. 293)
Stephen F. Austin (p. 297)
Santa Anna (p. 297)
Alamo (p. 298)
Sam Houston (p. 298)
overland trails (p. 299)
Manifest Destiny (p. 302)
John C. Frémont (p. 307)
Treaty of Guadalupe Hidalgo (p. 307)
Wilmot Proviso (p. 309)
popular sovereignty (p. 310)

How did "Manifest Destiny" influence American politics? (page 300)

The issue of annexation of Texas stalled because it raised the vexatious issue of the expansion of slavery. But the pro-expansion sentiment known as Manifest Destiny helped bring ardent expansionist James K. Polk to the White House in 1844 and fueled support for Texas annexation despite the slavery question. Polk and his followers ingeniously argued that national expansion was in the interests of northern working-class voters, many of them immigrants.

How did the outcome of the Mexican-American War intensify intersectional conflict? (page 304)

In the Treaty of Guadalupe-Hidalgo, the United States gained one-fourth of its present territory, and Mexico recognized Texas's independence. However, once again the question of the expansion of slavery came to the forefront of American politics. The Wilmot Proviso exposed deep sectional divisions that had only been papered over by the ideal of Manifest Destiny. Victorious over Mexico and enriched by the discovery of gold in California, Americans counted the blessings of expansion but began to fear its costs.

Go to the CourseMate website at **www.cengagebrain.com** for additional study tools and review materials—including audio and video clips—for this chapter.

CHAPTER 14

From Compromise to Secession

1850–1861

Kansas State Historical Society

Southern Rights Flag
Proslavery forces carried this flag while attacking the antislavery stronghold of Lawrence in the Kansas Territory.

CHAPTER PREVIEW

The Compromise of 1850
How did the Fugitive Slave Act lead to the undoing of the Compromise of 1850?

The Collapse of the Second Party System, 1853–1856
Why did the Whig party disintegrate, and what were the consequences?

The Crisis of the Union, 1857–1860
What major issues dominated American politics from 1857 to 1860?

The Collapse of the Union, 1860–1861
Why did southerners conclude that the North was bent on extinguishing slavery in southern states?

On April 12, 1861, Edmund Ruffin, a sixty-seven-year-old agricultural reformer and political pundit who had joined the Palmetto Guards, a volunteer military company, stood by a cannon on Morris Island in the bay of Charleston, South Carolina. With flowing white hair that dropped below his shoulders, he cut a striking figure among the Guards. Although young enough to be his grandchildren, many of the volunteers knew him as a champion of secession. The only way to save the South's civilization, he had argued for decades, was for the southern states to leave the United States and start a new nation.

Led by South Carolina, seven states in the Lower South had already done so, and in February 1861, they had formed the Confederate States of America. Now, the question became who would commit the first hostile act, Union or Confederacy? President Abraham Lincoln had vowed to defend federal property in the seceding states, including Fort Sumter in Charleston Bay. Impatient Confederate leaders demanded its immediate surrender; the fort's commander refused. At 4:30 A.M., Ruffin pulled the cannon's lanyard and commenced the bombardment that compelled the fort's surrender the next day. Lincoln responded by calling for 75,000 volunteers to suppress the rebellion. The Civil War had begun.

Just over four years later and back in his native Virginia, Ruffin breakfasted with his family and then went to his room to compose a farewell message: "I hereby declare my unmitigated hatred to Yankee rule—to all political, social, and business connections with Yankees—& to the Yankee race. Would that I could impress these thoughts on every living southerner, & bequeath them to everyone yet to be born!" Putting his pen down, Ruffin then put the muzzle of a rifle inside his mouth and used a forked stick to pull the trigger.

Irony marked Ruffin's dramatic suicide in the name of the "South." Before 1860, few listened to his ranting. The Republican Party, formed in the 1850s, dedicated itself to stopping the extension of slavery into the territories, but the party's leaders insisted that they lacked constitutional authority to interfere with slavery in the southern states. Most white southerners trusted their influence in national institutions, especially the Democratic Party, to secure slavery.

John Brown Self-appointed agent of God sent to destroy slavery; responsible for the Pottawatomie Massacre as well as the Harpers Ferry raid

However, sectional conflicts over slavery extension during the 1850s eroded the appeal of national parties. Then, in October 1859, a fanatical abolitionist named **John Brown** led a small band in seizing the federal arsenal at Harpers Ferry, Virginia, in the hope of igniting a slave insurrection. An abject failure, Brown's raid nevertheless brought to the surface all the white South's doubts about the "real" intentions of the North. Ruffin, long the prophet without honor in his own country, became the man of the hour and secession became a bright star on the horizon.

THE COMPROMISE OF 1850

How did the Fugitive Slave Act lead to the undoing of the Compromise of 1850?

Ralph Waldo Emerson's grim prediction that a U.S. victory in the Mexican War would be like swallowing arsenic proved disturbingly accurate. When the war ended in 1848, the United States contained an equal number (fifteen each) of free and slave states, but the vast territory gained by the war threatened to upset this balance. Any solution to the question of slavery in the Mexican cession—a free-soil policy, extension of the Missouri Compromise line, or popular sovereignty—ensured controversy. The prospect of free soil angered southerners, whereas extension of the Missouri Compromise line antagonized free-soil northerners as well as southern extremists who proclaimed that Congress could not bar slavery's expansion. Popular sovereignty offered the greatest hope for compromise by taking the question of slavery out of national politics and handing it to each territory, but this notion pleased neither free-soil nor proslavery extremists.

As the rhetoric escalated, events plunged the nation into crisis. Utah and then California, both acquired from Mexico, sought admission to the Union as free states. Texas, admitted to the Union as a slave state in 1845, aggravated matters by claiming the eastern half of New Mexico, thus potentially opening the door to slavery's extension into other newly acquired territory.

Chronology

1848	Zachary Taylor elected president
1849	California seeks admission to the Union as a free state
1850	Nashville convention assembles to discuss the South's grievances; Compromise of 1850
1852	Harriet Beecher Stowe, *Uncle Tom's Cabin*; Franklin Pierce elected president
1853	Gadsden Purchase
1854	Ostend Manifesto; Kansas-Nebraska Act
1854–1855	Know-Nothing and Republican parties rise
1855	Proslavery forces steal the election for a territorial legislature in Kansas, establish a government in Lecompton; free-soil government established in Topeka, Kansas
1856	The "sack" of Lawrence, Kansas; John Brown's Pottawatomie Massacre; James Buchanan elected president
1857	*Dred Scott* decision; President Buchanan endorses the Lecompton constitution in Kansas
1858	Congress refuses to admit Kansas to the Union under the Lecompton constitution; Lincoln-Douglas debates
1859	John Brown's raid on Harpers Ferry
1860	Abraham Lincoln elected president; South Carolina secedes from the Union
1861	The remaining Lower South states secede; Confederate States of America established; Crittenden compromise plan collapses; Lincoln takes office; firing on Fort Sumter; Civil War begins; Upper South secedes

By 1850 other issues had become intertwined with territorial questions. Northerners had grown increasingly unhappy with slavery in the District of Columbia, within the shadow of the Capitol; southerners, meanwhile, complained about lax enforcement of the Fugitive Slave Act of 1793. Any broad compromise would have to take both matters into account.

Zachary Taylor's Strategy

President Zachary Taylor believed that the South must not kindle the issue of slavery in the territories, because neither New Mexico nor California was suited for slavery. Taylor's position differed significantly from the thinking behind the still-controversial Wilmot Proviso, which proposed that Congress bar slavery in the territories ceded by Mexico. Taylor's plan, in contrast, left the decision to the states. He prompted California to apply for admission as a free state, bypassing the territorial stage, and hinted that he expected New Mexico (where the Mexican government had abolished slavery) to do the same. This strategy appeared to offer a quick, practical solution to the problem of extending slavery. The North would gain two new free states, and the South would gain acceptance of each individual state's right to bar or permit slavery as it chose.

But southerners rejected Taylor's plan. Not only would it yield the Wilmot Proviso's goal—the banning of slavery from the lands acquired from Mexico—but it rested on the shaky assumption that slavery could never take root in California or New Mexico. Southerners also protested the addition of two new free states. "If we are to be reduced to a mere handful . . . wo, wo, I say to this Union," John C. Calhoun warned. Disillusioned with Taylor, a slaveholder from whom they had expected better, nine southern states agreed to send delegates to a convention to meet in Nashville in June 1850.

Henry Clay Proposes a Compromise

Had Taylor held a stronger position in the Whig party, he might have blunted mounting southern opposition. But many leading Whigs had never accepted this political novice, and in early 1850 Kentucky senator Henry Clay challenged Taylor's leadership by forging a compromise bill to resolve the whole range of contentious issues. Clay proposed (1) the admission of California as a free state; (2) the division of the remainder of the Mexican cession into two territories, New Mexico and Utah, without federal restrictions on slavery; (3) the settlement of the Texas–New Mexico boundary dispute on terms favorable to New Mexico; (4) as an incentive for Texas, an agreement that the federal government would assume the state's large public debt; (5) continuation of slavery in the District of Columbia but abolition of the slave trade there; and (6) a more effective fugitive slave law.

Clay rolled all these proposals into a single "omnibus" bill. The debates over the compromise bill during late winter and early spring 1850 marked the last major appearance on the public stage of Clay, Calhoun, and Webster—the trio of distinguished senators whose lives had mirrored every public event of note since the War of 1812. Clay, ever the conciliator, warned the South against the evils of secession and assured the North that nature would check the spread of slavery. Gaunt and gloomy, the dying Calhoun listened as another senator read Calhoun's address for him, a repetition of his warnings that only if the North treated the South as an equal could the Union survive. Webster spoke vividly in favor of compromise, "not as a Massachusetts man, nor as a Northern man, but as an American," and chided the North for trying to "reenact the will of God" by excluding slavery from the Mexican cession.

However eloquent, the conciliatory voices of Clay and Webster made few converts. Strident voices countered these attempts at conciliation. The antislavery Whig William Seward (SOO-urd) of New York enraged southerners by talking of a "higher law than the Constitution"—namely, the will of God—against the extension of slavery. Clay's compromise faltered as Clay broke with President Taylor, who attacked Clay as a glory-hunter.

As the Union faced its worst crisis since 1789, events in the summer of 1850 eased the way toward resolution. When the Nashville convention met in June, only nine of the fifteen slave states, primarily in the Lower South, sent delegates. Despite the reckless pronouncements of the "fire-eaters" (extreme advocates of "southern rights"), moderates dominated. Then Zachary Taylor celebrated too extravagantly on July 4 and died five days later of a stomach ailment. His successor, Millard Fillmore of New York, supported Clay's compromise. Finally, Senator Stephen A. Douglas of Illinois took over stewardship of the compromise. He broke the omnibus into a series of individual measures; to secure Democratic support, Douglas proposed that popular sovereignty settle the slavery issue in New Mexico and Utah. These

Map 14.1   The Compromise of 1850

The Compromise of 1850 admitted California as a free state. Utah and New Mexico were left open to slavery or freedom according to the principle of popular sovereignty.

◉ Interactive Map

tactics worked. By summer's end the **Compromise of 1850** had become reality (see Map 14.1).

Compromise of 1850
Last-ditch attempt to paper over the issue of slavery expansion; ultimately a failure

Assessing the Compromise
Although President Fillmore hailed the compromise as a final settlement of sectional issues, it failed to bridge the underlying differences between the North and the South. Southerners had voted against the admission of California and northerners against the Fugitive Slave Act.

Each section both gained and lost from the Compromise of 1850. The North won California as a free state, New Mexico and Utah as likely future free states, a favorable settlement of the Texas–New Mexico boundary, and the abolition of the slave trade in the District of Columbia. The South's benefits were cloudier. By stipulating popular sovereignty for New Mexico and Utah, the compromise, to most southerners' relief, had buried the Wilmot Proviso's insistence that Congress formally prohibit slavery in these territories. But to southerners' dismay, the compromise left open the question of whether Congress could prohibit slavery in territories outside of the Mexican cession.

The one clear advantage gained by the South, a more stringent fugitive slave law, quickly proved a mixed blessing. Because few slaves had been taken into the Mexican cession, the question of slavery there had a hypothetical quality. However, the new fugitive slave law authorized real southerners to pursue real fugitives on northern soil. Here was a concrete issue to which the average northerner, who may never have seen a slave and who cared little about slavery a thousand miles away, would respond with fury.

Fugitive Slave Act Harsh measure allowing recapture of escaped slaves; part of the Compromise of 1850; alienated northerners and southerners alike

Enforcement of the Fugitive Slave Act

Northern moderates accepted the **Fugitive Slave Act** of 1850 as the price of saving the Union, but the law outraged antislavery northerners. It denied alleged fugitives the right of trial by jury, forbade them to testify at their own trials, permitted their return to slavery merely on the testimony of a claimant, and enabled court-appointed commissioners to collect ten dollars if they ruled for the slaveholder but only five if they ruled for the fugitive. As one commentator noted, the law threatened to turn the North into "one vast hunting ground." It targeted *all* runaways, putting at risk even fugitives who had lived as free blacks for thirty years or more. Above all, the law brought home to northerners the uncomfortable truth of their own complicity in slavery's continuation. By legalizing the activities of slave-catchers on northern soil, the law reminded northerners that slavery was a national problem, not merely a southern institution.

Efforts to catch and return runaways inflamed emotions in both the North and the South. In 1854, a Boston mob, aroused by antislavery speeches, killed a courthouse guard in an abortive effort to rescue fugitive slave Anthony Burns. Determined to enforce the law, President Franklin Pierce sent federal troops to escort Burns to the harbor, where a ship carried him back to slavery. As five platoons of troops marched Burns to the ship, fifty thousand people lined the streets. The Burns incident shattered the complacency of conservative supporters of the Compromise of 1850. "We went to bed one night old fashioned conservative Compromise Union Whigs," textile manufacturer Amos A. Lawrence wrote, "and waked up stark mad Abolitionists."

Northerners devised ways to interfere with the enforcement of the Fugitive Slave Act. "Vigilance" committees spirited endangered blacks to Canada, lawyers dragged out hearings to raise slave-catchers' expenses, and "personal liberty laws" hindered state officials' enforcement of the law. These obstructionist tactics convinced southerners that the "victory" represented by the passage of the Fugitive Slave Act was increasingly illusory.

Uncle Tom's Cabin Harriet Beecher Stowe's classic novel about slavery; had enormous political impact

Uncle Tom's Cabin

Harriet Beecher Stowe's novel *Uncle Tom's Cabin* (1852) drummed up wide northern support for fugitive slaves. Stowe, the daughter of famed evangelical Lyman Beecher, greeted the Fugitive Slave Act with horror. In one of the novel's most memorable scenes, she depicted the slave Eliza, clutching her infant son, bounding to freedom across ice floes on the Ohio River. Slavery itself was Stowe's main target. Much of her novel's power derived from its view that good intentions mean little in the face of so

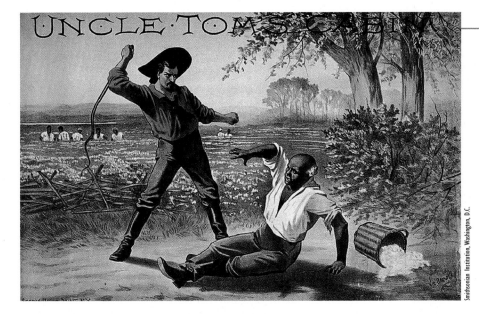

Uncle Tom's Cabin Theater Poster

With its vivid imagery of slavery, Harriet Beecher Stowe's *Uncle Tom's Cabin* translated well to the stage. Scenes of Eliza crossing the ice of the Ohio River with bloodhounds in pursuit and the evil Simon Legree whipping Uncle Tom outraged northern audiences and turned many against slavery. Southerners, however, damned Mrs. Stowe as a "vile wretch in petticoats."

evil an institution. The good intentions of a kindly slave owner die with him, and Uncle Tom is sold to the vicious Yankee Simon Legree, who whips Tom to death.

Three hundred thousand copies of *Uncle Tom's Cabin* were sold in 1852, and 1.2 million by summer 1853. Stage dramatizations reached perhaps fifty times more people than the novel did. As a play, *Uncle Tom's Cabin* enthralled working-class audiences who were normally indifferent or hostile to abolitionism. A reviewer of one stage performance observed that the gallery was filled with men "in red woollen shirts." Astonished by the silence that fell over these men at the point when Eliza escapes across the river, the reviewer turned to discover that many of them were in tears.

Although *Uncle Tom's Cabin* hardly lived up to a proslavery lawyer's prediction that it would convert 2 million people to abolitionism, it did push many waverers to an aggressive antislavery stance. Indeed, fear of its effect inspired a host of southerners to pen anti-*Uncle Tom* novels. As historian David Potter concluded, the northern attitude toward slavery "was never quite the same after *Uncle Tom's Cabin*."

Sojourner Truth

Sojourner Truth was born into slavery in upstate New York and named Isabella by her Dutch owner. She was illiterate and a mystic given to hearing messages from God, including one in 1843 that told her to change her name to Sojourner Truth. By then she had joined William Lloyd Garrison's band of abolitionists. In the 1840s and 1850s she traveled from New England to Indiana preaching against slavery. In one notable instance, when hecklers questioned her femininity, she bared her breasts to silence them.

CHECKING IN

- The Compromise of 1850 brought California into the Union and attempted to postpone any further dealing with the expansion of slavery.

- The compromise was passed by a series of coalitions, not a united Congress.

- The compromise did not resolve deep divisions, and the new, stringent Fugitive Slave Act worsened North-South relations.

- *Uncle Tom's Cabin* had an enormous impact on northern popular opinion against slavery.

- The Whig party fragmented over the compromise and lost the election of 1852 by a wide margin.

The Election of 1852

The Fugitive Slave Act fragmented the Whig party. Northern Whigs took the lead in defying the law, and southern Whigs had a difficult time explaining away the power of vocal free-soil Whigs.

In 1852, the Whigs' nomination of Mexican-American War hero General Winfield Scott as their presidential candidate widened the sectional split in the party. Although a Virginian, Scott owed his nomination to the northern free-soil Whigs. His single, feeble statement endorsing the Compromise of 1850 undercut southern Whigs who were trying to portray the Democrats as the party of disunion and themselves as the party of both slavery and the Union.

The Democrats bridged their own sectional division by nominating Franklin Pierce of New Hampshire, a dark-horse candidate whose chief attraction was that no faction of the party strongly opposed him. Northern and southern Democrats alike rallied behind the Compromise of 1850 and behind the ideal of popular sovereignty, and Pierce won a smashing victory. In the most one-sided election since 1820, he carried twenty-seven of the thirty-one states and collected 254 of 296 electoral votes. The Whigs were devastated in the South; one Whig stalwart lamented "the decisive breaking-up of our party."

THE COLLAPSE OF THE SECOND PARTY SYSTEM, 1853–1856

Why did the Whig party disintegrate, and what were the consequences?

Franklin Pierce was the last presidential candidate to carry the popular and electoral vote in both the North and the South until Franklin D. Roosevelt swept into office in 1932. Pierce also became the last president to hold office under the second party system—Whigs against Democrats. Within four years of Pierce's election, the Whig party would disintegrate, to be replaced by two newcomers: the American (Know-Nothing) party and the **Republican Party.**

> **Republican Party** Party, opposed to slavery expansion, that emerged after the Whig party's disintegration; strong in the North, nonexistent in the South

Unlike the Whigs, the Republican Party was a purely sectional, northern party, drawing its support from both former Whigs and discontented Democrats. The Democrats survived as a national party, but with a base so shrunken in the North that the newborn Republican Party captured two-thirds of the free states in 1856.

For decades the second party system had kept the conflict over slavery in check by providing Americans with other issues to argue about—banking, internal improvements, tariffs, and temperance. By the 1850s the debate over slavery extension overshadowed such issues and exposed raw divisions in each party. Whigs, with their larger, more aggressive free-soil wing, were much more vulnerable to disruption than the Democrats. Thus, when Stephen A. Douglas put forth a proposal in 1854 to organize the vast Nebraska Territory with no restrictions on slavery, he ignited a firestorm that consumed the Whig party.

The Kansas-Nebraska Act

Signed in late May 1854, the **Kansas-Nebraska Act** shattered the already weakened second party system and triggered renewed sectional strife. The bill's roots lay in the seemingly uncontroversial desire of farmers to organize the large territory west of Iowa and Missouri. Railroad enthusiasts who dreamed of a rail line linking the Midwest to the Pacific also wanted the territory organized.

In January 1854, Democratic senator Stephen A. Douglas of Illinois proposed a bill to organize Nebraska as a territory. Douglas believed that a railroad to the Pacific would bring national benefits, including a continuous line of settlement, and he thought that a railroad-based western expansion would unite the splintering Democratic factions.

Two sources of potential conflict loomed. First, some southerners advocated a southern-based Pacific route rather than a midwestern one. Second, Nebraska lay north of the Missouri Compromise line in the Louisiana Purchase, a region closed to slavery. Under Douglas's bill, the South would lose the Pacific rail route *and* face the possibility of more free territory in the Union. To placate southerners and win their votes, Douglas made two concessions. He stated publicly that the Nebraska bill "superseded" the Missouri Compromise and rendered it "void." Next, he agreed to a division of Nebraska into two territories: Nebraska to the west of Iowa, and Kansas to the west of Missouri. Because Missouri was a slave state, most congressmen assumed that the division aimed to secure Kansas for slavery and Nebraska for free soil.

These modifications to Douglas's original bill set off a storm of protest. Despite Douglas's belief that national expansion was the critical issue, most attention focused on the extension of slavery. Antislavery northerners assailed the bill as "an atrocious plot" to violate the "sacred pledge" of the Missouri Compromise and to turn Kansas into a "dreary region of despotism, inhabited by masters and slaves." Their anger provoked an equal response among southerners and added the issue of sectional pride to the already-volatile mix of expansion and slavery.

Despite the uproar, Douglas successfully guided the Kansas-Nebraska bill through the Senate. In the House, where the bill passed by little more than a whisker, 113 to 100, the true dimensions of the conflict became apparent. Not a single northern Whig representative in the House voted for the bill, whereas the northern Democrats split evenly.

Kansas-Nebraska Act
Attempt to allow popular sovereignty in newly organizing territories

The Surge of Free Soil

Amid the clamor over his bill, Douglas ruefully observed that he could now travel to Chicago by the light of his own burning effigies. Neither a fool nor a political novice, he was the victim of a political bombshell—**free soil**—that exploded under his feet.

Support for free soil united many who agreed on little else. Many free-soilers were racists who opposed allowing any African-Americans, slave or free, into the West. Others repudiated slavery on moral grounds and rejected blatantly racist legislation. Although split over the morality of slavery, most free-soilers agreed that slavery impeded whites' progress. Because a slave worked for nothing, free-soilers claimed, no free laborer could compete with a slave. If slavery secured a toehold in Kansas, free-soilers warned, Minnesota would fall to slavery as well.

free soil Movement opposed to any expansion of slavery

To free-soilers, the Kansas-Nebraska Act, with its erasure of the Missouri Compromise, was the last straw, for it revealed, one wrote, "a continuous movement by slaveholders to spread slavery over the entire North." Free-soilers saw southern planters, southern politicians, and their northern dupes, such as Stephen A. Douglas, entangled in a gigantic conspiracy to extend slavery.

The Ebbing of Manifest Destiny

The uproar over the Kansas-Nebraska Act embarrassed the Pierce administration. It also doomed Manifest Destiny, the one issue that had held the Democrats together in the 1840s.

Franklin Pierce had come to office championing Manifest Destiny, but increasing sectional rivalries sidetracked his efforts. In 1853 his emissary, James Gadsden, negotiated the purchase of a strip of land south of the Gila River (now southern Arizona and part of southern New Mexico), an acquisition favored by advocates of a southern railroad route to the Pacific. Fierce opposition to the Gadsden Purchase revealed mounting free-soilers' suspicions of expansion, and the Senate approved the treaty only after slashing nine thousand square miles from the purchase. The sectional rivalries beginning to engulf the Nebraska bill clearly threatened any proposal to gain new territory.

Cuba provided even more vivid proof of the change in public attitudes toward expansion. In 1854 a former Mississippi governor, John A. Quitman, planned a filibuster (an unofficial military expedition) to seize Cuba from Spain. Pierce wanted to acquire Cuba and may first have encouraged Quitman's plans, but the president backed down in the face of northern opposition. Northerners saw the filibuster as another manifestation of the Slave Power—the conspiracy of slaveholders and their northern dupes to grab more territory for slavery.

Events, however, slipped out of Pierce's control. In October 1854, the American ambassadors to Great Britain, France, and Spain, two of them southerners, met in Belgium and issued the unofficial Ostend Manifesto, calling on the United States to acquire Cuba by any means, including force.

Despite the Pierce administration's disavowal of the Ostend Manifesto, the idea of expansion into the Caribbean continued to attract southerners, including the Tennessee-born adventurer William Walker. Between 1853 and 1860, the year a firing squad in Honduras (hahn-DURE-uss) executed him, Walker led a succession of filibustering expeditions into Mexico and Nicaragua (nee-ka-RAH-gwa). Taking advantage of civil chaos in Nicaragua, he made himself the chief political force there, reinstituted slavery, and talked of making Nicaragua a U.S. colony.

Although some southerners were against expansion—among them the Louisiana sugar planters who opposed acquiring Cuba because Cuban sugar would compete with their product—southern expansionists stirred up enough commotion to worry antislavery northerners that the South aspired to establish a Caribbean slave empire. Like a card in a poker game, the threat of expansion southward was all the more menacing for not being played. As long as the debate on the extension of slavery focused on the continental United States, prospects for expansion were limited. However, adding the wild card of Caribbean territory changed all calculations.

The Whigs Disintegrate, 1854–1855

While straining Democratic unity, the Kansas-Nebraska Act wrecked the Whig party. Although Democrats lost ground in the 1854 congressional elections, the Whigs failed to benefit. No matter how furious the free-soil Democrats were at Douglas for introducing the act, they could not forget that southern Whigs had supported him. Northern Whigs split into two camps: anti-slavery "Conscience" Whigs, led by Senator William Seward of New York, and conservatives, led by former president Millard Fillmore. The conservatives believed that the Whig party had to adhere to the Compromise of 1850 to maintain itself as a national party.

This deep division within the Whig party repelled antislavery Democrats and prompted antislavery Whigs to look for an alternative party. By 1856 the new Republican Party would become home for these antislavery refugees; however, in 1854 and 1855 the American, or Know-Nothing, party emerged as the principal alternative to the faltering established parties.

The Rise and Fall of the Know-Nothings, 1853–1856

One of a number of nativist societies that mushroomed in opposition to the massive immigration of the 1840s, the **Know-Nothings** originated in the secret Order of the Star-Spangled Banner. The party's popular name derived from the standard response of its members to inquiries about its activities: "I know nothing." The Know-Nothings' core purpose was to rid the United States of immigrant and Catholic political influence. To this end, they pressured the existing parties to elevate only native-born Protestants to office and advocated an extension of the naturalization period before immigrants could vote.

Know-Nothings Nativist party that enjoyed a brief surge of power in the early 1850s

Throughout the 1840s, nativists usually voted Whig, but their allegiance to the Whigs started to buckle during Winfield Scott's campaign for the presidency in 1852. In an attempt to revitalize his party, Scott had courted the traditionally Democratic Catholic vote. But Scott's tactic backfired. Most Catholics voted for Franklin Pierce, while many nativists bailed out of the Whig party. The Kansas-Nebraska Act cemented nativist allegiance to the Know-Nothings. The Know-Nothings, unified by an obsessive fear of conspiracies, simultaneously denounced a papal conspiracy against the American republic and a Slave Power conspiracy reaching its tentacles throughout the United States. The Know-Nothings' surge was truly stunning. In 1854, they captured the governorship, all the congressional seats, and almost all the seats in the state legislature in Massachusetts.

After rising spectacularly between 1853 and 1855, the star of Know-Nothingism plummeted and gradually disappeared below the horizon after 1856. The Know-Nothings proved as vulnerable as the Whigs to sectional conflicts over slavery. Although primarily a force in the North, the Know-Nothings had a southern wing, comprised mainly of former Whigs who loathed both the antislavery northerners who were abandoning the Whig party and the southern Democrats, whom they viewed as disunionist firebrands. In 1855, these southern Know-Nothings combined with northern conservatives to make acceptance of the Kansas-Nebraska Act part of the Know-Nothing platform. Thus, they blurred the attraction of Know-Nothingism to those northern voters who were more antislavery than anti-Catholic.

One Whig refugee, Illinois congressman Abraham Lincoln, asked pointedly, "How can anyone who abhors the oppression of negroes be in favor of degrading classes of white people?" "We began by declaring," Lincoln continued, "that 'all men are created equal.' We now practically read it 'all men are created equal except negroes.' When the Know-Nothings get control, it will read 'all men are created equal, except Negroes and Foreigners and Catholics.'" Even most Know-Nothings concluded that "neither the Pope nor the foreigners ever can govern the country or endanger its liberties, but the slavebreeders and slavetraders do govern it, and threaten to put an end to all government but theirs." Consequently, the Know-Nothings proved vulnerable to the challenge posed by the emerging Republican Party, which did not officially embrace nativism and had no southern wing to placate.

The Republican Party and the Crisis in Kansas, 1855–1856

Born in the chaotic aftermath of the Kansas-Nebraska Act, the Republican Party would become the main opposition to the Democratic Party by 1856 and would win each presidential election from 1860 until 1884. In 1855, however, few would have predicted such a bright future. While united by opposition to the Kansas-Nebraska Act, the Republicans held various shades of opinion in uneasy balance. At one extreme were conservatives who merely wanted to restore the Missouri Compromise; at the other was a small faction of former Liberty Party abolitionists; and the middle held a sizable body of free-soilers.

Faced with these diverse constituencies, Republican leaders became political jugglers. To maintain internal harmony, the party's leaders avoided potentially divisive national issues such as the tariff and banking. Even so, Republican leaders recognized that they and the Know-Nothings were competing for many of the same voters. Republicans had clearer antislavery credentials than the Know-Nothings, but this fact alone did not guarantee that voters would respond more to antislavery than to anti-Catholicism or temperance. The Republicans needed a development that would make voters worry more about the Slave Power than about rum or Catholicism. Violence in Kansas united the party around its free-soil center and boosted Republican fortunes.

In the wake of the Kansas-Nebraska Act, Boston-based abolitionists sent antislavery settlers into Kansas. The abolitionists' aim was to stifle efforts to turn Kansas into a slave state. But the bulk of the territory's early settlers came from Missouri or elsewhere in the Midwest. Very few of these early settlers opposed slavery on moral grounds. Some, in fact, favored slavery; others simply wanted to keep all blacks, whether slave or free, out of Kansas.

Despite most settlers' racist leanings and utter hatred of abolitionists, Kansas became a battleground between proslavery and antislavery forces. In March 1855, thousands of proslavery Missourian "border ruffians," led by Senator David R. Atchison, crossed into Kansas to vote illegally in the first election for a territorial legislature. By stealing the election, the proslavery forces committed a grave tactical blunder. A cloud of fraudulence thereafter hung over the proslavery legislature subsequently established at Lecompton, Kansas. This legislature then further darkened its image by passing a succession of outrageous laws, limiting officeholding to individuals who would swear allegiance to slavery, punishing the harboring of fugitive

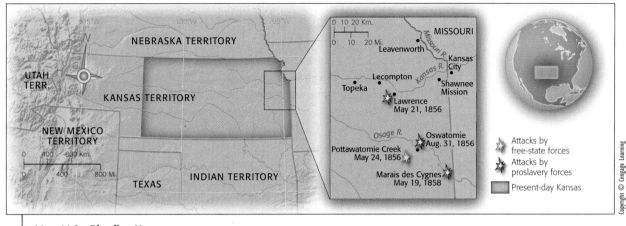

Map 14.2 Bleeding Kansas

Kansas became a battleground between free-state and slave-state factions in the 1850s.

 Interactive Map

slaves by ten years' imprisonment, and making the circulation of abolitionist literature a capital offense.

The territorial legislature's actions set off a chain reaction. Free-staters organized a rival government at Topeka in the summer and fall of 1855. In response, the Lecompton government in May 1856 dispatched a posse to Lawrence, where free-staters had taken up arms. Bearing banners emblazoned with slogans such as "Southern Rights" and "Let Yankees Tremble and Abolitionists Fall," the proslavery posse tore through Lawrence, burning several buildings and destroying two free-state presses. There were no deaths, but Republicans immediately dubbed the incident "the sack of Lawrence."

The next move was made by John Brown. The sack of Lawrence convinced Brown that God now beckoned him "to break the jaws of the wicked." In late May, Brown led seven men, including his four sons and his son-in-law, toward the Pottawatomie (pot-uh-WATT-uh-mee) Creek near Lawrence. Setting upon five men associated with the Lecompton government, they shot one to death and hacked the others to pieces with broadswords. Brown's "Pottawatomie Massacre" struck terror into the hearts of southerners and completed the transformation of Bleeding Kansas into a battleground between the South and the North (see Map 14.2).

Popular sovereignty had failed in Kansas. Instead of resolving the issue of slavery extension, popular sovereignty merely institutionalized the division over slavery by creating rival governments in Lecompton and Topeka. The Pierce administration then shot itself in the foot by denouncing the Topeka government and recognizing only its Lecompton rival. Pierce had forced northern Democrats into the awkward position of appearing to ally with the South in support of the "Bogus Legislature" at Lecompton.

Nor did popular sovereignty keep the slavery issue out of national politics. On the day before the sack of Lawrence, Republican senator Charles Sumner of Massachusetts delivered a bombastic and wrathful speech, "The Crime Against

Kansas." Sumner singled out Senator Andrew Butler of South Carolina for making "the harlot, slavery" his mistress and for the "loose expectoration" of his speech (a nasty reference to the aging Butler's tendency to drool). Two days later, a relative of Butler, Democratic representative Preston Brooks of South Carolina, strode into the Senate chamber, found Sumner at his desk, and struck him repeatedly with a cane. The hollow cane broke after five or six blows, but Sumner required stitches, experienced shock, and did not return to the Senate for three years. Brooks became an instant hero in the South, and the fragments of his weapon were "begged as sacred relics." A new cane, presented to Brooks by the city of Charleston, bore the inscription "Hit him again."

Now Bleeding Kansas and Bleeding Sumner united the North. The sack of Lawrence, Pierce's recognition of the proslavery Lecompton government, and Brooks's actions seemed to clinch the Republican argument that an aggressive "slaveocracy" held white northerners in contempt. Abolitionists remained unpopular in northern opinion, but southerners were becoming even less popular. By denouncing the Slave Power more than slavery itself, Republican propagandists sidestepped the issue of slavery's morality, which divided their followers, and focused on portraying southern planters as arrogant aristocrats and the natural enemies of the laboring people of the North.

The Election of 1856

The presidential race of 1856 revealed the scope of the political realignment of the preceding few years. The Republicans, in their first presidential contest, nominated John C. Frémont, the "pathfinder" of California "Bear State" fame. Northern Know-Nothings also endorsed Frémont, while southern Know-Nothings nominated Millard Fillmore, the last Whig president. The Democrats dumped the battered Pierce for James Buchanan (byoo-CAN-un) of Pennsylvania, who had had the luck to be out of the country (as minister to Great Britain) during the Kansas-Nebraska furor. A signer of the Ostend Manifesto, Buchanan was popular in the South; virtually all of his close friends in Washington were southerners.

The campaign became two separate races: Frémont versus Buchanan in the free states and Fillmore versus Buchanan in the slave states. Buchanan was in effect the only national candidate. Although Frémont attracted wide support in the North and Fillmore equal support in the South, Buchanan carried enough votes in both the North and South to win the presidency.

The election yielded three clear conclusions. First, the American party was finished as a major national force. Having worked for the Republican Frémont, most northern Know-Nothings joined that party. Fillmore's dismal showing in the South convinced southern Know-Nothings to abandon their party and seek a new political affiliation. Second, although in existence for barely a year, lacking any base in the South, and running a political novice, the Republican Party did very well. A purely sectional party had nearly captured the presidency. Third, as long as the Democrats could unite behind a single national candidate, they would be hard to defeat. To achieve unity, however, the Democrats would have to find more James Buchanans— "doughface" moderates acceptable to southerners and northerners alike.

CHECKING IN

- The Kansas-Nebraska Act set off a firestorm of controversy.

- The free-soil movement strengthened as the Whigs splintered over the act.

- The Know-Nothings briefly flourished as an alternative to the Whigs.

- "Bleeding Kansas" boosted the sectional Republican Party, which was emerging in the North with former free-soilers, Whigs, and Know-Nothings.

- The election of 1856 showed that the Whigs had vanished as a political force and that the Republicans were on the rise.

THE CRISIS OF THE UNION, 1857–1860

What major issues dominated American politics from 1857 to 1860?

No one ever accused James Buchanan of impulsiveness or fanaticism. Although a moderate who wished to avoid controversy, Buchanan would preside over one of the most controversy-ridden administrations in American history. A Supreme Court decision concerning Dred Scott, a Missouri slave who had resided in free territory for several years; the creation of the proslavery Lecompton constitution in Kansas; the raid by John Brown on Harpers Ferry, Virginia; and secession itself would wrack Buchanan's administration. The forces driving the nation apart were spinning out of control by 1856, and Buchanan could not stop them. By his inauguration, southerners saw creeping abolitionism in the guise of free soil, and northerners detected an ever more insatiable Slave Power. Once these potent images took hold in the minds of the American people, politicians could do little to erase them.

The *Dred Scott* Case, 1857

Pledged to congressional "noninterference" with slavery in the territories, Buchanan looked to the courts for resolution of the vexatious issue of slavery's extension. A case that appeared to promise a solution had been winding its way through the courts for years; on March 6, 1857, two days after Buchanan's inauguration, the Supreme Court handed down its decision in *Dred Scott v. Sandford.*

During the 1830s, Dred Scott, a slave, had been taken by his master from the slave state of Missouri into Illinois and the Wisconsin Territory, which were both closed to slavery. After his master's death, Scott sued for his freedom on the grounds of his residence in free territory.

The Court faced two key questions. Did Scott's residence in free territory during the 1830s make him free? Did Scott, again enslaved in Missouri, have the right to sue in the federal courts? The Supreme Court could have neatly sidestepped controversy by ruling that Scott had no right to sue, but it chose not to do so.

Instead, Chief Justice Roger B. Taney, a seventy-nine-year-old Marylander, handed down a sweeping decision that touched off another firestorm. First, Taney wrote, Scott, a slave, could not sue for his freedom. Further, no black, whether a slave or a free descendant of slaves, could become a U.S. citizen. Continuing his incendiary opinion, Taney ruled that even had Scott been entitled to sue, his residence in free territory did not make him free, because the Missouri Compromise, whose provisions prohibited slavery in the Wisconsin Territory, was itself unconstitutional. The compromise, declared Taney, violated the Fifth Amendment's protection of property (including slaves).

The ***Dred Scott* decision,** instead of settling the issue of the expansion of slavery, touched off another blast of controversy. The antislavery press flayed it as "willful perversion" filled with "gross historical falsehoods." Republicans saw the decision as further evidence that the fiendish Slave Power gripped the nation. Five of the six justices in the majority were from slave states.

Like Stephen A. Douglas after the Kansas-Nebraska Act, James Buchanan now appeared as another northern dupe of the "slaveocracy." Republicans restrained

***Dred Scott* decision** Judicial decision that threw out the Missouri Compromise, creating political turmoil

themselves from open defiance of the decision only by insisting that it did not bind the nation; Taney's comments on the constitutionality of the Missouri Compromise, they contended, were opinions unnecessary to settling the case and therefore technically not binding.

Reactions to the decision provided more proof that no "judicious" or nonpartisan solution to slavery extension was possible. Anyone who still doubted this needed only to read the fast-breaking news from Kansas.

The Lecompton Constitution, 1857

In Kansas, the free-state government at Topeka and the officially recognized proslavery government at Lecompton regarded each other with profound distrust. Buchanan's plan for Kansas looked simple: An elected territorial convention would draw up a constitution that would either prohibit or permit slavery; Buchanan would submit the constitution to Congress; Congress would then admit Kansas as a state.

Unfortunately, the plan exploded in Buchanan's face. Popular sovereignty, the essence of the plan, demanded fair play, a scarce commodity in Kansas. The territory's history of fraudulent elections left both sides reluctant to commit their fortunes to the polls. In June 1857, an election for a constitutional convention took place, but free-staters, by now a majority in Kansas, boycotted the election on grounds that the proslavery forces would rig it. A constitutional convention dominated by proslavery delegates then met and drew up the **Lecompton constitution,** which protected the rights of slaveholders already residing in Kansas and provided for a referendum to decide whether to allow more slaves into the territory.

Lecompton constitution
Advanced by proslavery advocates in Kansas; would have protected rights of slaveholders; endorsed by Buchanan

Buchanan faced a dilemma. As a supporter of popular sovereignty, he had favored letting Kansas voters decide the slavery issue. But now he confronted a constitution drawn up by a convention chosen by less than 10 percent of the eligible voters. However, there were compelling reasons to accept the Lecompton constitution. The South, which had provided Buchanan's winning margin in the 1856 election, supported it. To Buchanan, the wrangling over slavery in Kansas was a case of extremists' turning minor issues into major ones, especially because only about two hundred slaves resided in Kansas and because prospects for slavery in the remaining territories were slight. The admission of Kansas to the Union as free or slave seemed the quickest way to end the commotion. Therefore, in December 1857, Buchanan endorsed the Lecompton constitution.

Stephen A. Douglas and other northern Democrats broke with Buchanan. To them, the Lecompton constitution, in allowing voters to decide only whether more slaves could enter Kansas, violated the spirit of popular sovereignty. "I care not whether [slavery] is voted down or voted up," Douglas declared. However, he felt that refusing to allow a vote on the constitution itself, with its protection of existing slave property, smacked of a "system of trickery and jugglery to defeat the fair expression of the will of the people."

Meanwhile, in Kansas, the newly elected territorial legislature called for a referendum on the Lecompton constitution and thus on slavery itself. Two elections followed. In December 1857, the referendum called by the constitutional convention took place. Free-staters boycotted it, and the Lecompton constitution passed overwhelmingly. Two weeks later, the election called by the territorial legislature took place. This time proslavery forces boycotted, and the constitution went down to crushing defeat. Buchanan tried to ignore this second election, but when he attempted to bring Kansas into the Union under the Lecompton constitution, Congress blocked him and forced yet another referendum. This time, Kansas could accept or reject the entire constitution, with the proviso that rejection would delay statehood. Despite the proviso, Kansans voted down the Lecompton constitution.

Buchanan had simultaneously failed to tranquilize Kansas and alienated northerners in his own party, who now more than ever believed that the southern Slave Power pulled all the important strings in the Democratic Party. Douglas emerged as a hero for northern Democrats but saw his cherished formula of popular sovereignty become a prescription for strife rather than harmony.

The Lincoln-Douglas Debates, 1858   Despite the acclaim that he received for his stand against the Lecompton constitution, Douglas faced a stiff challenge in the 1858 Illinois senatorial election. Of his Republican opponent, Abraham Lincoln, Douglas remarked, "I shall have my hands full. He is the strong man of his party—full of wit, facts, and dates—and the best stump speaker with his droll ways and dry jokes, in the West."

Physically and ideologically, the two candidates presented a striking contrast. Tall (6'4") and gangling, Lincoln possessed energy, ambition, and a passion for self-education that had carried him from the Kentucky log cabin where he was born into law and politics in his adopted Illinois. First elected as a Whig, he joined the Republican Party in 1856. The New England–born Douglas stood a foot shorter than Lincoln, but to the small farmers of southern origin who populated the Illinois flatlands, he was the "little giant," the personification of the Democratic Party in the West. The campaign quickly became more than just another Senate race, for it pitted the Republican Party's rising star against the Senate's leading Democrat, and, thanks to the railroad and the telegraph, it received unprecedented national attention.

Opening his campaign with his famous "House Divided" speech ("this government cannot endure permanently half *slave* and half *free*"), Lincoln stressed the gulf between his free-soil position and Douglas's popular sovereignty. Douglas dismissed the house-divided doctrine as an invitation to secession. What mattered to him was not slavery but the continued expansion of white settlement. Douglas believed popular sovereignty was the surest way to attain this goal without disrupting the Union.

The high point of the campaign came in a series of seven debates held from August to October 1858. Douglas used the debates to portray Lincoln as a virtual abolitionist and advocate of racial equality. Lincoln replied that Congress had no constitutional authority to abolish slavery in the South. He also asserted that "I am not, nor ever have been in favor of bringing about the social and political equality of the white and black man."

In the debate at Freeport, Illinois, Lincoln tried to make Douglas squirm by asking how popular sovereignty could be reconciled with the *Dred Scott* decision. Lincoln maintained that if Congress had no authority to exclude slavery from a territory, then it seemingly followed that a territorial legislature created by Congress also lacked the power to do so. Douglas responded that, although the Supreme Court

National Portrait Gallery, Smithsonian Institution, Washington, DC, U.S.A./Art Resource, Inc.

Stephen A. Douglas

Douglas's politics were founded on his unflinching conviction that most Americans favored national expansion and would support popular sovereignty as the fastest and least controversial way to achieve it. However, Douglas's self-assurance blinded him to rising northern sentiment for free soil.

Library of Congress

Abraham Lincoln

Clean-shaven at the time of his famous debates with Douglas, Lincoln would soon grow a beard to give himself a more distinguished appearance.

had ruled that Congress could not exclude slavery from the territories, the voters in a territory could do so by refusing to enact laws that gave legal protection to slave property. This "Freeport doctrine" salvaged popular sovereignty but did nothing for Douglas's reputation among southerners, who preferred the guarantees of *Dred Scott* to the uncertainties of popular sovereignty. Trying to move beyond debates on free soil and popular sovereignty, Lincoln shifted in the closing debates to attacks on slavery as "a moral, social, and political evil." He argued that Douglas's view of slavery as merely an eccentric and unsavory southern custom would dull the nation's conscience and facilitate the legalization of slavery everywhere. At the same time, however, Lincoln compromised his own position by rejecting both abolition and equality for blacks.

Neither man scored a clear victory in the debates, and the senatorial election, which Douglas won, settled no major issues. Nonetheless, the candidates' contest was crucial. It solidified the sectional split in the Democratic Party and made Lincoln famous in the North—and infamous in the South.

The Legacy of Harpers Ferry

Although Lincoln explicitly rejected abolitionism, he called free soil a step toward the "ultimate extinction" of slavery. Many southerners ignored the differences between free soil and abolitionism and saw the entire North locked in the grip of demented leaders bent on civil war.

Nothing did more to freeze this southern image of the North than the evidence of northern complicity in John Brown's raid on the federal arsenal at **Harpers Ferry,** Virginia, on October 16, 1859. Brown and his followers were quickly overpowered; Brown himself was tried, convicted, and hanged. Lincoln and Seward condemned the raid, but some northerners turned Brown into a martyr; Ralph Waldo Emerson exulted that Brown's execution would "make the gallows as glorious as the cross." Further, captured correspondence disclosed that Brown had received financial support from northern abolitionists. His objective, to inspire an armed slave insurrection, rekindled the deepest fears of white southerners.

Harpers Ferry Federal arsenal in Virginia; site of John Brown's abortive attempt to fuel a slave uprising in the South

In the wake of Brown's raid, rumors flew around the South, and vigilantes turned out to battle conspiracies that existed only in their minds. Volunteers, for example, mobilized to defend northeastern Texas against thousands of abolitionists supposedly on their way to pillage Dallas and its environs. Elsewhere, vigilantes rounded up thousands of slaves, tortured some into confessing to nonexistent plots, and then lynched them. The hysteria generated by such rumors played into the hands of the extremists known as fire-eaters, who encouraged the witch-hunts in order to gain political support.

More and more southerners concluded that the Republican Party itself directed abolitionism and deserved blame for John Brown's raid. After all, had not influential Republicans assailed slavery, unconstitutionally tried to ban it, and spoken of an "irrepressible conflict" between slavery and freedom?

The South Contemplates Secession

A pamphlet published in 1860 embodied a growing southern conviction: *The South Alone Should Govern the South.* Most southerners, however, reached this conclusion gradually and reluctantly. In 1850, insulated from the main tide of immigration, southerners thought themselves the most American of Americans. The events of the 1850s led growing numbers of southerners to conclude that the North had deserted the principles of the Union and had virtually declared war on the South by using such headline-grabbing phrases as "irrepressible conflict" and "a higher law." To southerners, the North, not slavery, was the problem.

Viewed as a practical tactic to secure concrete goals, secession did not make a great deal of sense. Some southerners contended that secession would make it easier

CHECKING IN

- In the *Dred Scott* decision, which nullified the Missouri Compromise, the Supreme Court tossed a bombshell into American politics.
- Turmoil and bloodshed continued in Kansas.
- Although he lost the 1858 senatorial election in Illinois, his campaign debates with Stephen Douglas made Abraham Lincoln a national figure.
- John Brown's raid on Harpers Ferry intensified the deep divisions between North and South.
- By 1860 many southerners seriously contemplated secession.

for the South to acquire more territory for slavery in the Caribbean; yet the South was scarcely united in desiring additional slave territory in Mexico, Cuba, or Central America. Furthermore, if the South were to secede, the remaining continental territories would belong exclusively to the North. Nor would secession stop future John Browns from infiltrating the South to provoke slave insurrections.

Yet to dwell on the impracticality of secession as a choice for the South is to miss the point. Talk of secession was less a tactic with clear goals than an expression of the South's outrage at the Republicans. Southerners believed that the North was treating the South as its inferior, as no more than a slave. They bitterly dismissed Republican portrayals of the South as a region of arrogant planters and degraded white common folk. Submission to the Republicans, declared Democratic senator Jefferson Davis of Mississippi, "would be intolerable to a proud people."

THE COLLAPSE OF THE UNION, 1860–1861

Why did southerners conclude that the North was bent on extinguishing slavery in southern states?

As long as the pliant James Buchanan occupied the White House, southerners only talked of secession. However, once Buchanan declined to seek reelection, they anxiously awaited the next presidential election. By 1860, voters were deciding not just an election but also the fate of the Union. Lincoln's election began the parade out of the Union by southern states. Initially only the Lower South seceded, encouraging moderates to search frantically for a compromise to save the Union. But the time for compromise had passed.

The Election of 1860

As a single-issue, free-soil party, the Republicans had done well in the election of 1856. To win in 1860, however, they would have to broaden their appeal. Republican leaders needed an economic program to complement their advocacy of free soil. A severe economic slump following the Panic of 1857 provided them an opening. The depression shattered a decade of prosperity and thrust economic concerns to the fore. In response, the Republicans developed an economic program based on support for a protective tariff, federal aid for internal improvements, and grants to settlers of free 160-acre homesteads carved from public lands.

To broaden their appeal, the Republicans chose Abraham Lincoln as their presidential candidate over the better-known William H. Seward. Lincoln offered a stronger possibility of carrying such key states as Pennsylvania and his home state of Illinois, and projected a more moderate image than Seward, whose penchant for phrases like "irrepressible conflict" and "higher law" made him appear radical. In contrast, Lincoln had repeatedly said that Congress had no constitutional right to interfere with slavery in the South and had rejected the "higher law" doctrine.

The Democrats, still clinging to national party status, had to bridge their own sectional divisions. The *Dred Scott* decision and the conflict over the Lecompton constitution had weakened northern Democrats and strengthened southern Democrats. While Douglas still desperately defended popular sovereignty, southern Democrats stretched *Dred Scott* to conclude that Congress now had to protect slavery in the territories.

The Democratic Party's internal turmoil boiled over at its Charleston convention in the spring of 1860. Failing to win a platform guaranteeing the federal protection of slavery in the territories, delegates from the Lower South stormed out. The convention adjourned to Baltimore, where a new fight erupted over whether to seat the pro-Douglas delegates hastily chosen to replace the absent delegates from the Lower South. When the convention voted to seat these new delegates, representatives from Virginia and the Upper South walked out. What remained of the original Democratic convention nominated Douglas, but the seceders marched off to yet another hall in Baltimore and nominated Buchanan's vice president, John C. Breckinridge of Kentucky, on a platform calling for the congressional protection of slavery in the territories. The spectacle of two different Democratic candidates for the presidency signaled the complete disruption of the party.

The South still contained a sizable number of moderates, often former Whigs. In 1860, these southern moderates joined former northern Whigs in the new Constitutional Union party. They nominated John Bell of Tennessee, a slaveholder who had opposed the Kansas-Nebraska Act and the Lecompton constitution. Calling for the Union's preservation, the new party took no stand on slavery's extension.

The four candidates presented a relatively clear choice. At one end of the spectrum, Lincoln conceded that the South had the constitutional right to preserve slavery, but he demanded that Congress prohibit its extension. At the other end, Breckinridge insisted that Congress had to protect slavery anywhere it existed. In the middle were Bell and Douglas, the latter still trying to salvage popular sovereignty. In the end, Lincoln won 180 electoral votes; his three opponents, only 123. However, Lincoln's popular votes, 39 percent of the total, came almost completely from the North. Douglas, the only candidate to run in both sections, ran second in the popular vote but carried only Missouri. Bell won most of the Upper South, and Breckinridge took Maryland and the Lower South.

The Movement for Secession

Lincoln's election struck most of the white South as a calculated northern insult. The North, a South Carolina planter told a visitor from Britain, "has got so far toward being abolitionized as to elect a man avowedly hostile to our institutions."

Few southerners believed that Lincoln would fulfill his promise to protect slavery in the South; most feared that he would act as a mere front man for more John Browns. "Now that the black radical Republicans have the power I suppose they will Brown us all," a South Carolinian lamented.

Some southerners had threatened secession at the prospect of Lincoln's election, and now the moment of decision had arrived. On December 20, 1860, a South Carolina convention voted unanimously for secession; in short order Alabama,

Map 14.3　Secession

Four key states—Virginia, Arkansas, Tennessee, and North Carolina—did not secede until after the fall of Fort Sumter. The border slave states of Maryland, Delaware, Kentucky, and Missouri stayed in the Union.

Interactive Map

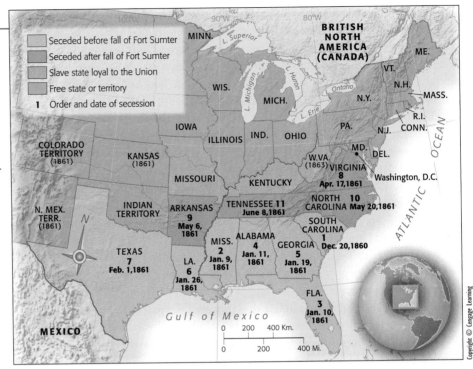

Mississippi, Florida, Georgia, Louisiana, and Texas followed. On February 4, 1861, delegates from these seven states met in Montgomery, Alabama, and established the Confederate States of America. But uncertainty colored the secession movement. Many southerners, even in the Deep South, had resisted the fire-eaters' call to leave the Union. Jefferson Davis, inaugurated in February 1861 as president of the Confederacy, was a reluctant secessionist who had remained in the Senate two weeks after his own state of Mississippi had seceded.

At first, the Upper South rejected secession completely. More economically dependent on the North, it had proportionately fewer slaves and more nonslaveholders, whose loyalty in case of secession was dubious. Finally, if secession precipitated a war, the Upper South was the likely battleground. Consequently, the secession movement that South Carolina had begun so boldly in December 1860 seemed to be falling apart by March 1861.

The Search for Compromise

The lack of southern unity confirmed the view of most Republicans that the secessionists were more bluster than substance. Seward described secession as the work of "a relatively few hotheads," and Lincoln believed that the loyal majority of southerners would soon wrest control from the fire-eating minority.

This perception stiffened Republican resolve to resist compromise. Moderate John J. Crittenden of Kentucky suggested compensation for owners of runaway slaves, repeal of northern personal-liberty laws, a constitutional amendment to prohibit the federal government from interfering with slavery in southern states, and another amendment to restore the Missouri Compromise line. But in the face of adamant Republican opposition, the **Crittenden plan** collapsed.

Lincoln's faith in a "loyal majority" of southerners exaggerated both their numbers and their dedication to the Union. Many southern opponents of the fire-eating secessionists sat on the fence, waiting for major concessions from the North; their allegiance to the Union was conditional. But compromise would have meant the abandonment of free soil, a basic principle of the Republican Party, and Lincoln, who misread southern opinion, resisted.

Beyond the issue of compromise, the precipitous secession of the Lower South had changed the question that Lincoln faced. The issue no longer revolved around slavery's extension but around secession. The Lower South had left the Union in the face of losing a fair election. For Lincoln to cave in to such pressure would violate majority rule, the sacred principle on which the nation had been founded.

Crittenden plan Attempt to find a compromise that would prevent the Union from splitting

The Coming of War

By the time Lincoln took office in March 1861, only a spark was needed to set off a war. Lincoln had pledged in his inaugural address to "hold, occupy, and possess" federal property in the states that had seceded, a statement that committed him to the defense of Fort Pickens in Florida and **Fort Sumter** in the harbor of Charleston, South Carolina. Accordingly, the president informed South Carolina's governor of his intention to supply Fort Sumter with provisions but neither reinforcements nor ammunition. Shortly before dawn on April 12, 1861, Confederate shore batteries bombarded the fort, which surrendered the next day.

Proclaiming an insurrection in the Lower South, Lincoln called for 75,000 volunteers to suppress the rebellion. The outbreak of hostilities ended fence-sitting in the Upper South. "I am a Union man," one southerner wrote, "but when they [the Lincoln administration] send men south it will change my notions. I can do nothing against my own people." In quick succession Virginia, North Carolina, Arkansas, and Tennessee joined the Confederacy. Acknowledging that "I am one of those dull creatures that cannot see the good of secession," Robert E. Lee resigned from the U.S. Army rather than lead troops against his native Virginia.

The North, too, was ready for a fight, less to abolish slavery than to punish secession. Stephen Douglas, exhausted by his efforts to find a peaceable solution to the issue of slavery extension, assaulted "the new system of resistance by the sword and bayonet to the results of the ballot-box" and affirmed, "I deprecate war, but if it must come I am with my country, under all circumstances, and in every contingency."

Fort Sumter Federal fort in Charleston, South Carolina, harbor, where the first shots of the Civil War were fired when the Union attempted to resupply troops

CHECKING IN

- Lincoln's victory in the 1860 presidential election brought matters to a head.

- Fearing they were now at the mercy of abolitionists, states in the Lower South began to secede.

- Moderates sought a compromise, but Republicans resisted.

- An attempt to resupply Fort Sumter, a federal fort in Charleston harbor in South Carolina, met with armed resistance.

- When President Lincoln called for militia to suppress an insurrection, the states of the Upper South seceded.

Chapter Summary

How did the Fugitive Slave Act lead to the undoing of the Compromise of 1850? (page 314)

Unlike the Compromise of 1820, the Compromise of 1850 was a medley of different bills supported by shifting coalitions. It temporarily averted disunion, but it failed to resolve underlying divisions between the North and the South. In particular, the new Fugitive Slave Act alienated the North because of its harshness and the South because of northern resistance.

Why did the Whig party disintegrate, and what were the consequences? (page 320)

The surprising strength of the Know-Nothings and the free-soil movement both undercut the Whigs, who were already battered into sectional fragments by the Compromise of 1850; the Kansas-Nebraska Act delivered the final blow. Temporarily the Democrats were the only major political party, and when the Republicans emerged as a counterpart, they were a sectional rather than a national party.

What major issues dominated American politics from 1857 to 1860? (page 327)

The last years of the 1850s saw several tumultuous political issues emerge: the *Dred Scott* decision, Bleeding Kansas, and John Brown's raid on Harpers Ferry. Each one dramatized the failures of popular sovereignty, frayed the political fabric of the nation a bit further, and galvanized northern opposition to the southern "slavocracy."

Why did southerners conclude that the North was bent on extinguishing slavery in southern states? (page 332)

Southerners, already feeling besieged, did not believe Abraham Lincoln's promise to leave slavery untouched in the South. They saw his election as a sign that they had lost all influence at the national level. Lower South states seceded quickly, but the Upper South remained in the Union until Lincoln ordered the resupplying of Fort Sumter, a federal fort in the harbor of Charleston, South Carolina, and shooting erupted. Emotion, as much as reason, dictated these moves.

KEY TERMS

John Brown *(p. 314)*

Compromise of 1850 *(p. 317)*

Fugitive Slave Act *(p. 318)*

Uncle Tom's Cabin (p. 318)

Republican Party *(p. 320)*

Kansas-Nebraska Act *(p. 321)*

free soil *(p. 321)*

Know-Nothings *(p. 323)*

Dred Scott decision *(p. 327)*

Lecompton constitution *(p. 328)*

Harpers Ferry *(p. 331)*

Crittenden plan *(p. 335)*

Fort Sumter *(p. 335)*

CourseMate

Go to the CourseMate website at **www.cengagebrain.com** for additional study tools and review materials—including audio and video clips—for this chapter.

CHAPTER 15

Crucible of Freedom: Civil War

1861–1865

Union Soldiers

National Library of Medicine

CHAPTER PREVIEW

Mobilizing for War
What major advantages did each side possess at the start of the Civil War?

In Battle, 1861–1862
How was the war fought in its early years?

Emancipation Transforms the War, 1863
How did the issue of emancipation transform the war?

War and Society, North and South
In what ways did the Civil War affect the two sides?

The Union Victorious, 1864–1865
How did the Union finally win the war?

"Events transcending in importance anything that has ever happened within the recollection of any living person in our country, have occurred since I have written last in my journal," wrote Georgia matron Gertrude Clanton Thomas in July 1861. "War has been declared."

At her marriage in 1852, Gertrude Thomas had become mistress of a small estate, Belmont, about six miles south of Augusta, Georgia. Slavery was the basis of Gertrude Thomas's wealth and social position; she disliked it not because it oppressed the enslaved but because it posed problems for the slave-owning elite. When war began, Gertrude fervently supported the newborn Confederacy. Her husband, Jefferson Thomas, enlisted in a cavalry company and served until 1862. "We claim nothing of the North but—to be let alone."

As war raged on, Gertrude Thomas longed for its end. But the Civil War's end brought hardship to the Thomas family, which lost fifteen thousand dollars in Confederate bonds and ninety slaves. One by one, the former slaves left the Belmont estate, never to return. "As to the emancipated Negroes," Gertrude Thomas told her journal in May 1865, "while there is of course a natural dislike to the loss of so much property, in my inmost soul, I cannot regret it."

In their determination, militance, and false expectations, the Thomases were not alone. Few volunteers or even politicians anticipated a protracted war. Most northern estimates ranged from one month to a year; rebels, too, counted on a speedy victory. Neither side anticipated the carnage that war would bring; one out of every five soldiers who fought in the Civil War died in it. Once it became clear that war would extend beyond a few battles, leaders on both sides considered strategies once unpalatable or even unthinkable. By the war's end, the Confederacy was ready to arm its slaves in an ironically desperate effort to save a society founded on slavery. The North, which began the war with the limited objective of overcoming secession and explicitly disclaimed any intention of interfering with slavery, found that in order to win, it had to shred the fabric of southern society by destroying slavery.

MOBILIZING FOR WAR

What major advantages did each side possess at the start of the Civil War?

Neither the North nor the South was prepared for war. In April 1861, most of the Union's small army, a scant sixteen thousand men, was scattered across the West. One-third of its officers had resigned to join the Confederacy. The nation had not had a strong president since James K. Polk in the 1840s, and many viewed the new president, Abraham Lincoln, as a yokel. It seemed doubtful that such a government could marshal its people for war. The Confederacy was even less prepared. It had no tax structure, no navy, only two tiny gunpowder factories, and poorly equipped, unconnected railroad lines.

During the first two years of war, both sides would have to overcome these deficiencies, raise and supply large armies, and finance the war. In each region, mobilization would expand the powers of the central government to a degree that few had anticipated.

Recruitment and Conscription

The Civil War armies were the largest organizations ever created in America; by the end of the war, more than 2 million men had served in the Union army and 800,000 in the Confederate army.

At first the raising of armies was a local, rather than a national or state, effort. Regiments usually consisted of volunteers from the same locale. Southern cavalrymen provided their own horses, and uniforms were left to local option. In both armies the troops themselves elected officers up to the rank of colonel. This informal, democratic way of raising and organizing soldiers reflected the nation's political traditions but could not long withstand the stresses of the Civil War. As early as July 1861, the Union began examinations for officers. With casualties mounting, moreover, military demand exceeded the supply of volunteers. The Confederacy felt the pinch first and in April 1862 enacted the first **conscription** law in American history, requiring all able-bodied white men aged eighteen to thirty-five to serve in the military. (By war's end the limits would be seventeen and fifty.) The Confederacy's Conscription Act aroused little enthusiasm. A later amendment exempting owners or overseers of twenty or more slaves evoked complaints about "a rich man's war but a poor man's fight."

conscription Drafting men to serve in the army

Despite opposition, the Confederate draft became increasingly difficult to evade; this fact stimulated volunteering. Seventy to eighty percent of eligible white southerners served in the Confederate army. Only one soldier in five was a draftee. The requirement that soldiers serve for at least three years ensured that a high proportion of Confederate soldiers would be battle-hardened veterans.

Once the Confederacy raised the army, it needed supplies. At first, the South imported arms and ammunition from Europe to supplement weapons taken from federal arsenals and guns captured on the battlefield. Gradually, the Confederacy assigned contracts to privately owned factories, such as the Tredegar Iron Works in Richmond; provided loans to establish new plants; and created government-owned industries, such as the giant Augusta Powder Works in Georgia. The South lost few, if any, battles for want of munitions.

Supplying troops with clothing and food proved more difficult. When the South invaded Maryland in 1862, thousands of Confederate soldiers remained behind because they could not march barefoot on Maryland's gravel-surfaced roads. Late in the war, Robert E. Lee's Army of Northern Virginia ran out of food but never out of ammunition. Supply problems had several sources: railroads that fell into disrepair or were captured, an economy that grew more cotton and tobacco than food, and Union capture of the livestock and grain-raising districts of central Tennessee and Virginia. Close to desperation, the Confederate Congress in 1863 passed the Impressment Act, authorizing army officers to take food from reluctant farmers at prescribed prices and to impress slaves into labor for the army.

The industrial North had fewer supply problems, but recruitment was another matter. When the initial tide of enthusiasm for enlistment ebbed, Congress followed the Confederacy's example and turned to conscription with the Enrollment Act of March 1863. Every able-bodied white male citizen aged twenty to forty-five faced the draft.

Like the Confederate conscription law of 1862, the Enrollment Act provided some exemptions and offered two ways of escaping the draft: substitution, or paying another man to serve; and commutation, or paying a $300 fee to the government. Democrats denounced conscription as a violation of individual liberties and states' rights, and ordinary citizens resented the substitution and commutation privileges, leveling their own "poor man's fight" charges. Nevertheless, as in the Confederacy, the law stimulated volunteering. Only 8 percent of all Union soldiers were draftees or substitutes.

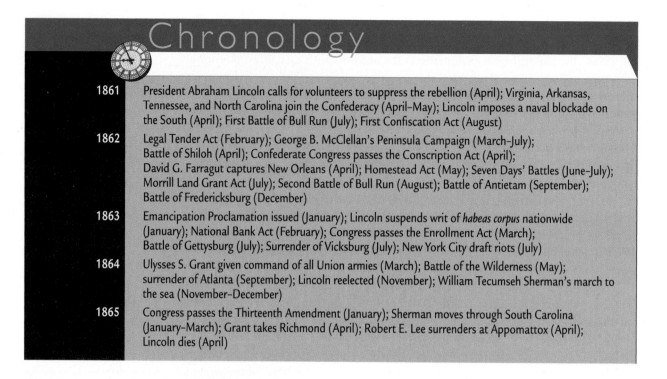

Chronology

1861	President Abraham Lincoln calls for volunteers to suppress the rebellion (April); Virginia, Arkansas, Tennessee, and North Carolina join the Confederacy (April–May); Lincoln imposes a naval blockade on the South (April); First Battle of Bull Run (July); First Confiscation Act (August)
1862	Legal Tender Act (February); George B. McClellan's Peninsula Campaign (March–July); Battle of Shiloh (April); Confederate Congress passes the Conscription Act (April); David G. Farragut captures New Orleans (April); Homestead Act (May); Seven Days' Battles (June–July); Morrill Land Grant Act (July); Second Battle of Bull Run (August); Battle of Antietam (September); Battle of Fredericksburg (December)
1863	Emancipation Proclamation issued (January); Lincoln suspends writ of *habeas corpus* nationwide (January); National Bank Act (February); Congress passes the Enrollment Act (March); Battle of Gettysburg (July); Surrender of Vicksburg (July); New York City draft riots (July)
1864	Ulysses S. Grant given command of all Union armies (March); Battle of the Wilderness (May); surrender of Atlanta (September); Lincoln reelected (November); William Tecumseh Sherman's march to the sea (November–December)
1865	Congress passes the Thirteenth Amendment (January); Sherman moves through South Carolina (January–March); Grant takes Richmond (April); Robert E. Lee surrenders at Appomattox (April); Lincoln dies (April)

Financing the War

The recruitment and supply of huge armies lay far beyond the capacity of American public finance at the start of the war. During the 1840s and 1850s, the federal government met its meager revenue needs from tariff duties and income from the sale of public lands. During the war, however, annual federal expenditures gradually rose, and the need for new sources of revenue became urgent. Yet neither Union nor Confederacy initially wished to impose taxes, to which Americans were unaccustomed.

Both sides therefore turned to war bonds; that is, to loans from citizens to be repaid by future generations. However, many hoarded their gold rather than spend it on bonds. Grasping the limits of taxes and of bond issues, both sides began to print paper money. Early in 1862, President Lincoln signed into law the Legal Tender Act, authorizing the issue of $150 million in paper **"greenbacks."** Although the North's financial officials distrusted paper money, they came around to the idea as funds dwindled. However, unlike gold and silver, which had established market values, the value of paper money depended on the public's confidence in the government that issued it. To bolster that confidence, Union officials made the greenbacks legal tender (that is, acceptable in payment of most public and private debts).

In contrast, the Confederacy never made its paper money legal tender; suspicions arose that the southern government lacked confidence in it. To compound the problem, the Confederacy raised less than 5 percent of its wartime revenue from taxes (compared to 21 percent in the North). The Confederacy did enact a comprehensive tax measure in 1863, but Union invasions and poor internal transportation made tax collection a hit-or-miss proposition.

Confidence in the Confederacy's paper money quickly evaporated, and the value of paper money in relation to gold plunged. The Confederate response—printing

"greenbacks" Paper money used by the Union to help finance war

more paper money, a billion dollars by 1865—merely accelerated inflation. Whereas prices in the North rose about 80 percent during the war, the Confederacy suffered an inflation rate of over 9,000 percent.

By raising taxes, floating bonds, and printing paper money, both the North and the South broke with the hard-money, minimal-government traditions of American public finance. In the North, Republicans took advantage of the departure of southern Democrats to push through Congress a measure that they and their Whig predecessors had long advocated: a national banking system. Passed in February 1863, the National Bank Act allowed banks to obtain federal charters and to issue national bank notes (backed by the federal government). The North's ability to revolutionize its system of public finance reflected both its long experience with complex financial transactions and its political cohesion.

Abraham Lincoln
A portrait of Lincoln made in the Washington, DC, studio of photographer Alexander Gardner in November 1863, eleven days before the president gave the Gettysburg Address.

Political Leadership in Wartime

The Civil War pitted rival political systems as well as armies and economies against each other. The South entered the war with several apparent political advantages. Lincoln's call for militiamen to suppress the rebellion had transformed southern waverers into tenacious secessionists. Southerners also had a strong leader in Jefferson Davis, the president of the Confederacy, who possessed experience, honesty, courage, and what one officer called "a jaw sawed in *steel*."

In contrast, the Union's list of political liabilities appeared lengthy. Loyal but contentious northern Democrats disliked conscription, the National Bank Act, and the abolition of slavery. Among Republicans, Lincoln, with little national experience, had trouble commanding respect. A small but vocal group of Republicans known as the Radicals—including Secretary of the Treasury Salmon P. Chase, Senator Charles Sumner of Massachusetts, and Representative Thaddeus Stevens of Pennsylvania—vigorously criticized Lincoln. They assailed him early in the war for failing to make emancipation a war goal and later for being too eager to readmit the conquered rebel states into the Union.

Lincoln's style of leadership both encouraged and disarmed opposition among Republicans. Self-contained until ready to act, he met criticism with homespun anecdotes that threw his opponents off guard. Caught between Radicals and conservatives, Lincoln used his cautious reserve to maintain open communications with both wings of the party and to fragment his opposition. He also co-opted some members of the opposition, including Chase, by bringing them into his cabinet.

In contrast, Jefferson Davis had a knack for making enemies. A West Pointer, he would rather have led the army than the government. Davis's cabinet suffered frequent resignations; the Confederacy had five secretaries of war in four years. Relations between Davis and his vice president, Alexander Stephens of Georgia, verged on disastrous. Leaving Richmond, the Confederate capital, in 1862, Stephens spent most of the war in Georgia, where he sniped at Davis as "weak and vacillating, timid, petulant, peevish, obstinate."

The clash between Davis and Stephens involved not just personalities but also the ideological divisions that lay at the heart of the Confederacy. The Confederate Constitution explicitly guaranteed the sovereignty of the Confederate states and prohibited the government from enacting protective tariffs or supporting internal improvements. For Stephens and other influential Confederate leaders, the Confederacy existed to protect slavery and to enshrine states' rights. In contrast, Davis's main objective was to secure the independence of the South from the North, even at the expense of states' rights, if necessary.

This difference between Davis and Stephens somewhat resembled the discord between Lincoln and the northern Democrats. Like Davis, Lincoln believed that victory demanded a strong central government; like Stephens, northern Democrats resisted centralization. But Lincoln could control his opponents more effectively than Davis controlled his. By temperament Lincoln was more suited to reconciliation than Davis was, and the different nature of party politics in the two sections favored him as well.

In the South, the Democrats and the remaining Whigs agreed to suspend party politics for the war's duration. Although intended to encourage unity, this decision led to discord. As southern politics disintegrated along personal and factional lines, Davis found himself without organized political support. In contrast, in the Union, northern Democrats' opposition to Lincoln tended to unify the Republicans. After Democrats won control of five states in the election of 1862, Republicans swallowed a bitter lesson: No matter how much they disdained Lincoln, they had to rally behind him or risk being driven from office. Ultimately, the Union developed more political cohesion than the Confederacy, not because it had fewer divisions but because it managed those divisions more effectively.

Securing the Union's Borders

Even before large-scale fighting began, Lincoln moved to safeguard Washington, which was bordered by two slave states (Virginia and Maryland) and filled with Confederate sympathizers. A week after Fort Sumter's fall, a Baltimore mob attacked a Massachusetts regiment bound for Washington, but enough troops slipped through to protect the capital. Lincoln then dispatched federal troops to Maryland and suspended the writ of *habeas corpus** (HAY-bee-uss CORE-puss); federal troops could now arrest prosecession Marylanders without formally charging them with specific offenses. Both Maryland and Delaware, another border slave state, voted down secession.

Next, Lincoln authorized the arming of Union sympathizers in Kentucky, a slave state with a Unionist legislature, a secessionist governor, and a thin chance of staying

---

*Habeas corpus: a court order requiring that the detainer of a prisoner bring the person in custody to court and show cause for his or her detention.

neutral. Lincoln also stationed troops just across the Ohio River from Kentucky, in Illinois; when a Confederate army invaded Kentucky early in 1862, those troops drove it out. Officially, at least, Kentucky became the third slave state to declare for the Union. Four years of murderous fighting ravaged the fourth, Missouri, as Union and Confederate armies and bands of guerrillas clashed. Despite the savage fighting and the divided loyalties of its people, Missouri stayed in the Union. West Virginia was formed in 1861 when thirty-five counties in the primarily nonslaveholding regions west of the Shenandoah Valley refused to secede; it became a state in 1863.

By holding the border slave states in the Union, Lincoln kept open his lines to the free states and gained access to the river systems in Kentucky and Missouri that led into the heart of the Confederacy. Lincoln's firmness, particularly in the case of Maryland, scotched charges that he was weak-willed. The crisis also forced the president to exercise long-dormant powers. In *Ex parte Merryman* (1861), Chief Justice Roger B. Taney ruled that Lincoln had exceeded his authority in suspending the writ of *habeas corpus* in Maryland. Lincoln, citing the Constitution's authorization of the writ's suspension in "Cases of Rebellion" (Article I, Section 9), insisted that he would determine whether a rebellion existed, and simply ignored Taney's ruling.

CHECKING IN

- The North enjoyed enormous manpower and industrial advantages.
- Both sides resorted to conscription, although most soldiers were volunteers.
- The Union was far more successful than the Confederacy in raising money to finance the war.
- The Union could rely on established political, military, and economic systems; the Confederacy suffered from political divisions and conflicting views of the Confederate government's role.
- Abraham Lincoln proved to be a far better leader than Jefferson Davis.

IN BATTLE, 1861–1862

How was the war fought in its early years?

The Civil War was the first war in which both sides relied extensively on railroads, the telegraph, mass-produced weapons, joint army-navy tactics, iron-plated warships, rifled guns and artillery, and trench warfare. Thus, there is some justification for its description as the first modern war. But to its participants slogging through muddy swamps and weighed down with equipment, the war hardly seemed modern.

Armies, Weapons, and Strategies

The Confederacy had 9 million people, one-third of them slaves, in 1861. By comparison, the Union had 22 million people at that time. The North also enjoyed 3.5 times as many white men of military age, 90 percent of all U.S. industrial capacity, and two-thirds of its railroad track (see Figure 15.1). Nonetheless, the North faced a daunting challenge: to force the South back into the Union. The South, in contrast, fought only for independence. To subdue the Confederacy, the North would have to sustain offensive operations over a vast area.

Measured against this challenge, the North's advantages in population and technology shrank. The North had more men but needed them to defend long supply lines and to occupy captured areas. Consequently, a smaller proportion of its overall force was available to commit to combat. The South, relying on slaves for labor, could assign a higher proportion of its white male population to combat. And

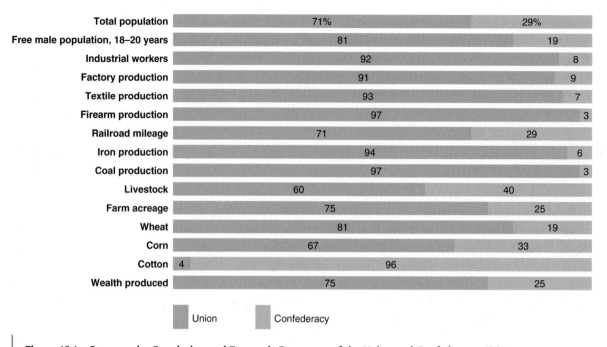

Figure 15.1   Comparative Population and Economic Resources of the Union and Confederacy, 1861

At the start of the war, the Union enjoyed huge advantages in population, industry, railroad mileage, and wealth, and—as it would soon prove—a superior ability to mobilize its vast resources. The Confederacy, however, enjoyed the many advantages of fighting a defensive war.

although the Union had superior railroads, it had to move its troops and supplies huge distances, whereas the Confederacy could shift its troops relatively short distances within its defense area without railroads. Finally, southerners had an edge in morale, for Confederate troops usually fought on home ground.

The Civil War witnessed experiments with a variety of new weapons, including the submarine, the repeating rifle, and the multibarreled Gatling gun, the predecessor of the machine gun. Whereas smooth-bore muskets had an effective range of 80 yards, the Springfield or Enfield rifles widely in use by 1863 were accurate at 400 yards. However, the rifle's development posed a challenge to long-accepted military tactics, which stressed the mass infantry charge. Armed with muskets, defenders could fire only a round or two before being overwhelmed. Armed with rifles, however, defenders could fire several rounds before closing with the enemy. Attackers would have far greater difficulty getting close enough to thrust bayonets; fewer than 1 percent of the casualties in the Civil War resulted from bayonet wounds.

As the fighting wore on, both sides recognized the value of trenches, which offered defenders protection against withering rifle fire. In addition, the rifle forced generals to depend less on cavalry. Traditionally, cavalry had been among the most prestigious components of an army, in part because cavalry charges were often devastatingly effective and in part because the cavalry helped to maintain class distinctions within the army. More accurate rifles reduced cavalry effectiveness by increasing the firepower of foot soldiers. Thus, both sides relegated cavalry to reconnaissance (reh-CAHN-nuh-sense) missions and raids on supply trains.

Still, the introduction of the rifle did not totally invalidate traditional tactics. An attacking army still had a good chance of success if it surprised its enemy, and the lush forests of the South offered abundant opportunities for surprise. In contrast, lack of the element of surprise could doom an attacking army. At the Battle of Fredericksburg in December 1862, Confederate forces virtually annihilated Union forces charging uphill over open terrain. Likewise, at Gettysburg in July 1863, Union riflemen and artillery shredded charging southerners.

Much like previous wars, the Civil War was basically fought in a succession of battles during which exposed infantry traded volleys, charged, and countercharged. The side that withdrew first from the battlefield was considered the loser, even though it frequently sustained lighter casualties than the supposed victor. The defeated army usually moved back a few miles to lick its wounds; the winners stayed in place to lick theirs. Politicians on both sides berated generals for not pursuing a beaten foe, but it was almost impossible for a mangled victor to gather horses, mules, supply trains, and exhausted soldiers for a new attack. Not surprisingly, for much of the war, generals on both sides concluded that the best defense was a good offense.

"Scott's Great Snake," 1861
General Winfield Scott's scheme to surround the South and await a seizure of power by southern Unionists drew scorn from critics who called it the Anaconda plan. In this lithograph, the "great snake" prepares to push down the Mississippi, seal off the Confederacy, and crush it.

Library of Congress

What passed for long-range Union strategy in 1861 was the **Anaconda plan,** which called for the Union to blockade the southern coast and to thrust, like a huge snake, down the Mississippi River. In theory, sealing off and severing the Confederacy would make the South recognize the futility of secession and end the war quickly. However, the lack of adequate ships and men to seize the Mississippi in 1861 prevented the implementation of this ambitious plan.

Anaconda plan Early Union strategy to split the Confederacy down the Mississippi and force its surrender

Early in the war, the need to secure the border slave states, especially Kentucky and Missouri, dictated Union strategy in the West, sending northern armies plunging southward from Kentucky into Tennessee. The Appalachian Mountains tended to separate this western theater from the eastern theater, where major clashes took place in 1861.

Stalemate in the East

The Confederacy's decision in May 1861 to move its capital from Montgomery, Alabama, to Richmond, Virginia, shaped Union strategy. "Forward to Richmond!" became the Union's first war cry. But before Union troops could reach Richmond, one hundred miles southwest of Washington, they would have to dislodge a Confederate army brazenly encamped at Manassas (muh-NASS-suss) Junction, Virginia, only twenty-five miles from the Union capital. Lincoln ordered General Irvin McDowell

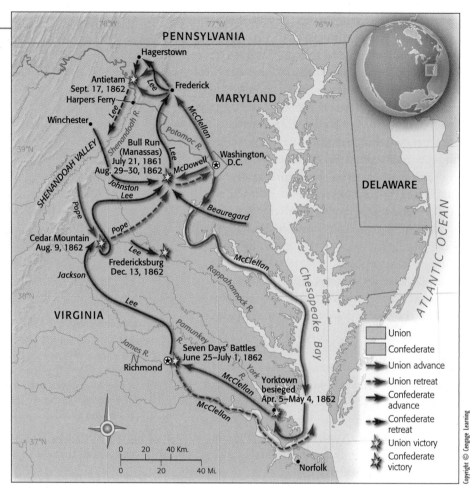

Map 15.1   The War in the East, 1861–1862

Union advances on Richmond were turned back at Fredericksburg and the Seven Days' Battles, and the Confederacy's invasion of Union territory was stopped at Antietam.

Interactive Map

First Battle of Bull Run The war's first full battle, also called First Manassas; fiasco that showed war would be longer and harder than first thought

George B. McClellan Union general who was very popular with troops; Lincoln thought he had the "slows" and replaced him

to attack the rebel force. In the resulting **First Battle of Bull Run** (or First Manassas), amateur armies clashed in bloody chaos under a blistering July sun. Well-dressed, picnicking Washington dignitaries witnessed the carnage, as the Confederates routed the larger Union army.

After Bull Run, Lincoln appointed General **George B. McClellan** to replace McDowell as commander of the Army of the Potomac, the Union's main fighting force in the east. McClellan, a master of administration and training, transformed a ragtag mob into a disciplined fighting force. His soldiers adored him, but Lincoln became disenchanted. To the president, the key to victory lay in launching simultaneous attacks on several fronts so that the North could exploit its advantages in manpower and communications. McClellan, a proslavery Democrat, hoped for a relatively bloodless southern defeat, followed by readmission of the Confederate states with slavery intact.

In the spring of 1862, McClellan got a chance to demonstrate the value of his strategy. After Bull Run, the Confederates pulled back behind the Rappahannock River to block a Union march toward Richmond. McClellan decided to go around the southerners by transporting his troops down the Chesapeake Bay to the tip of the peninsula formed by the York and James rivers and then to attack Richmond from the rear.

At first, McClellan's Peninsula Campaign unfolded smoothly. By late May, McClellan was within five miles of Richmond. But then he hesitated. Overestimating Confederate strength, he refused to launch a final attack without further reinforcements, which were turned back by Confederate general Thomas "Stonewall" Jackson in the Shenandoah Valley. As McClellan delayed, General **Robert E. Lee** assumed command of the Confederacy's Army of Northern Virginia. A foe of secession and so courteous that at times he seemed too gentle, Lee possessed the qualities that McClellan most lacked: boldness and a willingness to accept casualties.

Robert E. Lee Bold and resourceful commander of the Army of Northern Virginia

Seizing the initiative, Lee attacked McClellan in late June 1862. The ensuing Seven Days' Battles, fought in the forests east of Richmond, cost the South nearly twice as many men as the North and ended in a virtual slaughter of Confederates. Unnerved by mounting casualties, McClellan sent increasingly panicky reports to Washington. Lincoln, who cared little for McClellan's Peninsula Campaign, ordered McClellan to call off the campaign and return to Washington.

With McClellan out of the picture, Lee and his lieutenant, Stonewall Jackson, pushed north, routing a Union army at the Second Battle of Bull Run (Second Manassas) in August 1862. Lee's next stroke was even bolder. Crossing the Potomac River in early September 1862, he invaded western Maryland, where the forthcoming harvest could feed his troops. Lee could now threaten Washington, indirectly relieve pressure on Richmond, improve the prospects of peace candidates in the North's fall elections, and possibly induce Britain and France to recognize Confederate independence. But McClellan met Lee at the Battle of **Antietam** (or Sharpsburg) on September 17. A tactical draw, Antietam proved a strategic victory for the North: Lee subsequently canceled his invasion and retreated south of the Potomac.

Antietam Union victory in August 1862 that gave Lincoln the opportunity to announce the Emancipation Proclamation

Heartened by the success of Union forces, Lincoln then issued the **Emancipation Proclamation,** a war measure that freed all slaves under rebel control. Lincoln complained that McClellan had "the slows" and faulted him for not pursuing Lee after Antietam. McClellan's replacement, General Ambrose Burnside, thought himself unfit for high command. He was right. In December 1862, he led 122,000 federal troops against 78,500 Confederates at the Battle of Fredericksburg (Virginia). Burnside captured the town but then sacrificed his army in futile charges up the heights west of the town. Even Lee shuddered at the carnage. "It is well that war is so terrible, or we should grow too fond of it," he told an aide during the battle. Richmond remained, in the words of a southern song, "a hard road to travel." The war in the East had become a stalemate.

Emancipation Proclamation Declaration that freed all slaves in Confederate-held territory; changed the nature of the Civil War

The War in the West

The Union fared better in the West. There, the war ranged over a vast terrain that provided access to rivers leading directly into the South. The West also spawned new leadership in the person of an obscure Union general, **Ulysses S. Grant.** A West Point graduate with a reputation for heavy drinking, and a failed farmer and businessman, Grant soon proved to be one of the Union's best leaders.

Ulysses S. Grant Lincoln-appointed head of the Army of the Potomac; ultimately defeated Lee

In 1861–1862, Grant stabilized control of Missouri and Kentucky and then moved south to attack Corinth (CORE-inth), Mississippi, a major rail junction.

Antietam National Battlefield, Sharpsburg, MD

Library of Congress

Scenes of Antietam

A painting of the Antietam battlefield by James Pope, a Union soldier of the Second Vermont Infantry, shows three brigades of Union troops advancing under Confederate fire. In the photograph of Antietam, dead rebel gunners lie next to the wreckage of their battery. The building in both the painting and photograph, a church, was the scene of furious fighting.

In early April 1862, Confederate forces staged a surprise attack on Grant's army, encamped at Shiloh (SHY-loe) Church in southern Tennessee. Driven back on the first day, Union forces counterattacked on the second day and drove the Confederate army from the field. Of 77,000 men who fought at Shiloh, 23,000 were killed or wounded. Defeated at Shiloh, the Confederates evacuated Corinth.

To attack Grant at Shiloh, the Confederacy had stripped the defenses of its largest city, New Orleans. A combined Union land-sea force under General Benjamin Butler and Admiral David G. Farragut (FAIR-uh-gut) seized the opportunity. Farragut took New Orleans in late April and soon conquered Baton Rouge and Natchez as well. When a Union flotilla moved down the river in June and took Memphis, the North controlled the great river except for a 200-mile stretch between Port Hudson, Louisiana, and Vicksburg, Mississippi.

Union and Confederate forces also clashed in 1862 in the trans-Mississippi West. On the banks of the Rio Grande, Union volunteers and Mexican-American companies drove a Confederate army from Texas out of New Mexico. A thousand miles to the east, opposing armies battled for control of the crucial Missouri River. In Pea Ridge, Arkansas, in March 1862, northern troops scattered a Confederate force of 16,000.

These Union victories changed the trans-Mississippi war. As the rebel threat faded, western volunteers who had mobilized to crush Confederates turned to fighting Indians. After 1865, federal troops moved west to complete the rout of the Indians that had begun during the Civil War.

The Soldiers' War

Civil War soldiers were typically volunteers from farms and small towns who joined companies of recruits from their area. Local loyalties spurred enrollment, especially in the South, as did ideals of honor and valor. Soldiers on both sides saw military life as a transforming experience in which citizens became warriors and boys became men. Exultant after a victory, an Alabama volunteer told his father, "With your first shot you become a new man."

Recruits were meshed into regiments and then sent to training camps. Training was meager, and much of army life was tedious and uncomfortable. Union troops ate beans, bacon, salt pork, pickled beef, and hardtack—biscuits that were almost impossible to crack. Confederate forces ate bacon and cornmeal, and they often ran out of food, blankets, shoes, socks, and clothes. Both sides suffered from a multitude of lice, fleas, ticks, flies, and rats, as well as from the diseases they carried.

Dreams of military glory faded swiftly. Soldiers quickly learned to inure themselves to the stench of death. "Soldier," a Confederate chaplain told his troops in 1863, "your business is to die." The deadly cost of battle fell most heavily on the

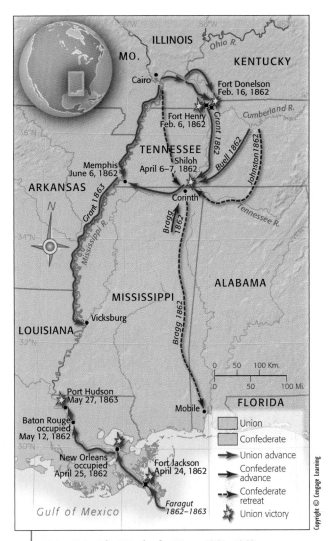

Map 15.2 The War in the West, 1861–1862
By the end of 1862 the North held New Orleans and the entire Mississippi River except for the stretch between Vicksburg and Port Hudson.

Interactive Map

infantry, in which at least three out of four soldiers served. A combination of inexperience, inadequate training, and barriers of terrain curbed their impact. Large masses of soldiers faced one another at close range for long periods of time, exchanging fire until one side or the other gave up and fell back. Armies gained in efficiency in battle through experience, and only late in the war.

In their voluminous letters home (Civil War armies were the most literate armies that had ever existed), volunteers discussed their motives as soldiers. Some Confederates joined to defend slavery, which they paired with liberty. As the war ground on, more and more Union soldiers came to see emancipation as their goal, sometimes for humanitarian reasons. "Since I am down here I have learned and seen more of what the horrors of slavery was than I ever knew before," an Ohio officer wrote from Louisiana. Others had more practical goals. By the summer of 1862, Union soldiers in the South had become agents of liberation. Many who had once damned the "abolitionist war" now endorsed emancipation as part of the war effort. As an Indiana soldier said, "Every negro we get strengthens us and weakens the rebels."

Ironclads and Cruisers: The Naval War

By plunging the navy into the Confederacy like a dagger, the Union exploited a clear-cut advantage. The North began the war with more than forty active warships—the South had none—and by 1865 northern industrial advantages had given the United States the largest navy in the world. Steamships could penetrate the South's river systems from any direction.

Yet the Union navy faced an extraordinary challenge in its efforts to blockade the South's 3,500 miles of coastline. Sleek Confederate blockade runners darted in and out of southern harbors with little chance of capture early in the war. Their chances of success gradually diminished, however, as the North tightened the blockade and began to capture key southern ports. In 1861, almost 90 percent of blockade runners made it through; by 1865, the rate had sunk to 50 percent. Union seizure of rebel ports and coastal areas shrank the South's foreign trade even more. In daring amphibious assaults in 1861 and 1862, the Union captured the excellent harbor of Port Royal, South Carolina; the coastal islands off South Carolina; and most of North Carolina's river outlets. Naval patrols and amphibious operations shrank the South's ocean trade to one-third its prewar level.

Despite meager resources, the South made impressive efforts to offset the North's naval advantage. Early in the war the Confederates raised a scuttled Union frigate, the *Merrimac*; sheathed its sides in iron; rechristened it the *Virginia*; and deployed it to attack wooden Union ships at Hampton Roads, Virginia. The *Virginia* met its match on March 9, 1862, when it tangled with the hastily built Union ironclad *Monitor*. This battle, the first ever fought between ironclads, ended in a draw.

The South constructed other ironclads and even the first submarine, which dragged a mine through the water to sink a Union ship off Charleston in 1864. Unfortunately, the "fish" failed to surface and went down with its prey. However, the South never built enough ironclads to overcome northern supremacy in home waters. Nor did Confederate success on the high seas—where wooden, steam-driven raiders wreaked havoc on the Union's merchant marine—tip the balance of war in the South's favor: the North, unlike its foe, did not depend on imports for war materials. The South would go on to lose the naval war.

The Diplomatic War

While armies and navies clashed in 1861–1862, conflict developed on a third front: diplomacy. At the war's start southerners had confidently opened a campaign to gain swift diplomatic recognition for the Confederacy. They were sure of the support of Britain's and France's upper classes and even more certain that Britain, dependent on the South for four-fifths of its cotton, would have to break the Union blockade.

In 1861, Confederate diplomats James Mason and John Slidell sailed for Europe to lobby for recognition of an independent South, but their ship, the *Trent*, fell into Union hands. When the pair ended up as prisoners in Boston, British tempers exploded. Considering one war at a time quite enough, President Lincoln ordered Mason and Slidell released.

Settling the *Trent* affair did not eliminate friction between the United States and Britain, however. Union diplomats protested the construction in British shipyards of the Confederate commerce raiders *Alabama* and *Florida*. In 1863, the U.S. minister to London, Charles Francis Adams (son of President John Quincy Adams and grandson of President John Adams), threatened war if two British-built ironclads commissioned by the Confederacy were turned over to the South. Britain capitulated to Adams's protests and purchased the ships for its own navy.

The South fell far short of its diplomatic objectives. Neither Britain nor France ever recognized the Confederacy as a nation. Southerners overestimated the power of its vaunted "cotton diplomacy." Forces beyond southern control had weakened British demand. Bumper cotton crops in the late 1850s had glutted the British market by the start of the war and Britain had found new suppliers in Egypt and India. Gradually, too, the North's tightened blockade restricted southern exports. The South's share of the British cotton market slumped from 77 percent in 1860 to only 10 percent in 1865.

The South had also exaggerated Britain's stake in helping the Confederacy. As a naval power that had frequently blockaded its own enemies, Britain's diplomatic interest lay in supporting the Union blockade in principle; from Britain's standpoint, to help the South break the blockade would set a precedent that could easily boomerang. Finally, although France and Britain often considered recognizing the Confederacy, the timing never seemed quite right. Union success at Antietam in 1862 and Lincoln's subsequent issuance of the Emancipation Proclamation dampened Europe's enthusiasm for recognition at a crucial juncture. The Emancipation Proclamation stirred pro-Union feelings in antislavery Britain. The proclamation, declared Henry Adams (diplomat Charles Francis Adams's son) from London, "has done more for us here than all of our former victories and all our diplomacy."

CHECKING IN

- Despite new weapons, such as the rifle, the Civil War was basically fought as a traditional war, with mass infantry charges and large battles.

- In the early years of the conflict, the war in the East was a stalemate.

- The South found a brilliant leader in Robert E. Lee, but Lincoln continued to search fruitlessly for a comparable Union general.

- Union forces established superiority west of the Mississippi early in the war.

- Despite hopes based on the British textile industry's need for cotton, the Confederacy never succeeded in enlisting Great Britain and France as allies.

EMANCIPATION TRANSFORMS THE WAR, 1863

How did the issue of emancipation transform the war?

"I hear old John Brown knocking on the lid of his coffin and shouting 'Let me out! Let me out!'" abolitionist Henry Stanton wrote to his wife after the fall of Fort Sumter. "The Doom of Slavery is at hand." In 1861, this prediction seemed wildly premature. In his inaugural address Lincoln had stated bluntly, "I have no purpose, directly or indirectly, to interfere with the institution of slavery in the states where it exists." Yet within two years both necessity and ideology made emancipation a primary northern goal.

The rise of emancipation as a war goal reflected the changing character of the conflict itself. As the fighting raged on, demands for the prosecution of a "total war" intensified in the North, and many people who were unconcerned about the morality of slavery started to recognize the military value of emancipation as a tactic to cripple the South.

From Confiscation to Emancipation
The Union's policy on emancipation developed in several stages. As soon as northern troops invaded the South, questions arose about captured rebel property, including slaves. Generally, slaves who fled behind Union lines were considered "contraband"—enemy property liable to seizure—and were put to work for the Union army. In August 1861, Congress passed the first Confiscation Act, which authorized the seizure of all property, including slaves, used in military aid of the rebellion. However, nothing in the act actually freed these individuals, nor did the law apply to fugitive slaves who had not worked for the Confederate military.

Several factors underlay the Union's cautious approach. Officially maintaining that the South could not legally secede, Lincoln argued that southerners were still entitled to the Constitution's protection of property. The president also had practical reasons to walk softly. He did not want to alienate slaveholders in the border states or proslavery Democrats in the North. Aware of such fears, Lincoln assured Congress in December 1861 that the war would not become a "remorseless revolutionary struggle."

From the start of the war, however, Radical Republicans pushed Lincoln to adopt a policy of emancipation. Radicals agreed with black abolitionist Frederick Douglass that "to fight against slaveholders without fighting against slavery, is but a half-hearted business." Each Union defeat, moreover, reminded northerners that the Confederacy, with a slave labor force in place, could commit a higher proportion of its white men to battle. The idea of emancipation as a military measure thus gained increasing favor in the North, and in July 1862 Congress passed the second Confiscation Act. This law authorized the seizure of the property of all persons in rebellion and stipulated that slaves who came within Union lines "shall be forever free." The law also authorized the president to employ blacks as soldiers.

Nevertheless, Lincoln continued to stall. "My paramount object in this struggle is to save the Union, and is not either to save or destroy slavery," Lincoln averred. "If I could save the Union without freeing *any* slave, I would do it, and if I could save it by freeing *all* the slaves, I would do it; and if I could save it by freeing some and leaving others alone, I would also do that." Yet Lincoln had always loathed slavery, and by the spring of 1862, he had accepted the Radical position that the war must lead to its abolition. Reluctant to push the issue while Union armies reeled in defeat, he drafted a proclamation of emancipation and waited for the right moment to announce it. After the Union victory at Antietam, Lincoln issued the Preliminary Emancipation Proclamation (September 1862), which declared all slaves under rebel control free as of January 1, 1863. The final Emancipation Proclamation, issued on January 1, 1863, declared "forever free" all slaves in areas in rebellion.

The proclamation had limited practical impact, however. It applied only to areas in which it could not be enforced, those still in rebellion, and did not touch slavery in the border states. But the Emancipation Proclamation was a brilliant political stroke. By making it a military measure, Lincoln pacified northern conservatives, and by issuing the proclamation himself, he stole the initiative from the Radicals in Congress. Through the proclamation, moreover, Lincoln mobilized support for the Union among European liberals, pushed the border states toward emancipation (both Missouri and Maryland abolished slavery before the war's end), and increased slaves' incentives to escape as Union troops neared.

The Emancipation Proclamation did not end slavery everywhere or free "*all* the slaves," but it changed the war. From 1863 on, the war for the Union was also a war against slavery.

Crossing Union Lines The attacks and counterattacks of the opposing armies turned many slaves into pawns of the war: free when Union troops overran their area, slaves again if the Confederates regained control. One North Carolina slave celebrated his liberation twelve different times. By 1865, about half a million former slaves were in Union hands.

Although in the first year of the war masters could retrieve slaves from Union armies, after 1862 slaves who crossed Union lines were considered free. Many freed slaves served in army camps as cooks, teamsters, and laborers. Some worked for pay on abandoned plantations or were leased out to planters who swore allegiance to the Union. Whether in camps or on plantations, freedmen questioned the value of liberation. Deductions for clothing and food ate up most of their earnings, and labor contracts bound them for long periods of time. Moreover, the freedmen encountered fierce prejudice among Yankee soldiers, who widely feared that emancipation would propel blacks northward after the war. The best solution to the widespread "question of what to do with the darkies," wrote one Union soldier, "would be to shoot them."

But this was not the whole story. Fugitive slaves who aided the Union as spies and scouts helped to break down bigotry. "The sooner we get rid of our foolish prejudice the better for us," a Massachusetts soldier wrote home. In March 1865, Congress established the Freedmen's Bureau to provide relief, education, and work for the former slaves. The same law also provided that forty acres of abandoned or confiscated land could be leased to each freedman or southern Unionist, with an option to buy after three years. This was the first and only time that Congress provided for the redistribution of confiscated Confederate property.

Black Soldiers in the Union Army

During the first year of the war, the Union had rejected African-American soldiers. Only after the Emancipation Proclamation did the large-scale enlistment of blacks begin. Prominent African-Americans, including Frederick Douglass, worked as recruiting agents in northern cities. Douglass clearly saw the link between military service and citizenship. "Once let the black man get upon his person the brass letters, U.S.; let him get an eagle on his button, and a musket on his shoulder and bullets in his pocket, and there is no power on earth which can deny that he has earned the right to citizenship." By the war's end, 186,000 African-Americans had served in the Union army, making up one-tenth of all Union soldiers. Half of them came from the Confederate states.

White Union soldiers commonly objected to the new recruits on racial grounds. But some, including Colonel Thomas Wentworth Higginson, a liberal minister and former John Brown supporter who led a black regiment, welcomed the black soldiers. "There is a fierce energy about them [in battle]," he exulted, "beyond anything of which I have ever read, except it be the French Zouaves [(zoo-AHVZ), troops in North Africa]." Even Union soldiers who held blacks in contempt came to approve of "anything that will kill a rebel." All blacks served in segregated regiments under white officers. Colonel Robert Gould Shaw of the 54th Massachusetts Infantry, an elite black regiment, died in combat—as did half his troops—in an attack on Fort Wagner in Charleston harbor in July 1863.

Black soldiers suffered a far higher mortality rate than whites. Seldom committed to combat, they were far more likely to die of disease in bacteria-ridden garrisons. The Confederacy refused to treat captured black Union soldiers as prisoners of war; instead, they were sent back to the states from which they had come to be re-enslaved or executed. In an especially gruesome incident, when Confederate troops under General Nathan Bedford Forrest captured Fort Pillow, Tennessee, in 1864, they massacred 262 blacks—an act that provoked outcries but no retaliation from the North.

Black soldiers also faced inequities in pay. Not until June 1864 did Congress belatedly equalize the earnings of black and white soldiers. Although fraught with inequities and hardships, military service symbolized citizenship for blacks. It proved that "black men can give blows as well as take them," Frederick Douglass declared. "Liberty won by white men would lose half its luster." Above all, the use of black soldiers, especially former slaves, struck a telling blow against the Confederacy. "They will make good soldiers," General Grant wrote to Lincoln in 1863, "and taking them from the enemy weakens him in the same proportion they strengthen us."

Slavery in Wartime

Anxious white southerners on the home front felt as if they were perched on a volcano. "We should be practically helpless should the negroes rise," declared a Louisiana planter's daughter, "since there are so few men left at home." To control 3 million slaves, they tightened slave patrols, spread scare stories among slaves, and sometimes even moved entire plantations to relative safety in Texas.

Some slaves remained faithful to their owners, hiding treasured belongings from marauding Union soldiers. Others wavered between loyalty and hunger for freedom: one slave accompanied his master to war, rescued him when he was wounded, and then escaped on his master's horse. Slaves who were given the chance to flee to Union lines usually did.

Most slaves, however, lacked the means of escape and remained under their owners' nominal control. Despite the fears of southern whites, no general slave uprising occurred, and the Confederate war effort continued to utilize slave labor. Thousands of slaves worked in war plants, toiled as teamsters and cooks in army camps, and served as nurses in field hospitals.

But even slaves with no chance of flight were alert to the opportunity that war provided and swiftly tested the limits of enforced labor. Moreover, wartime conditions reduced the slaves' productivity. With most of the white men off at war, the master-slave relationship weakened and the women and boys who remained on plantations complained of difficulty in controlling slaves. Many refused to work, did their work inefficiently, or destroyed property.

Whether slaves fled to freedom or merely stopped working, they effectively undermined the plantation system. Slavery disintegrated even as the Confederacy fought to preserve it. By 1864, a desperate Confederate Congress considered impressing slaves into the army in exchange for their freedom at the war's end. Although Robert E. Lee himself favored making slaves into soldiers, others were adamantly opposed. "If slaves will make good soldiers," a Georgia general argued, "our whole theory of slavery is wrong." In March 1865, however, the Confederate Congress passed a bill to arm 300,000 slave soldiers, although it omitted any mention of emancipation. Since the war ended a few weeks later, however, the plan was never put into effect.

Although the Confederacy's decision to arm the slaves came too late to affect the war, the debate over arming them hurt southern morale. By then, the South's military position had started to deteriorate.

The Turning Point of 1863

In summer and fall 1863, Union fortunes improved dramatically in every theater of the war. Yet the year began badly, as General Joseph "Fighting Joe" Hooker, a windbag fond of issuing pompous proclamations to his troops, suffered a crushing defeat at Chancellorsville, Virginia, in May 1863. Although Chancellorsville cost the South dearly—Stonewall Jackson was accidentally killed by his own troops—it humiliated the North, whose forces had outnumbered the Confederate troops two to one. Reports from the West brought no better news: Grant was still unable to take Vicksburg, and the rebels clung to a vital two-hundred-mile stretch of the Mississippi.

Union fortunes rose after Chancellorsville when Lee decided to invade the North. Lee needed supplies that war-racked Virginia could no longer provide; he also hoped that Lincoln would move troops from Vicksburg back into the eastern theater. Lee envisioned a major Confederate victory on northern soil that would increase the sway of pro-peace Democrats and gain European recognition of the Confederacy. Lee led his 75,000 men into Maryland and then pressed forward into southern Pennsylvania. Lincoln, rejecting Hooker's plan to attack a virtually unprotected Richmond, replaced him with the more reliable General George G. Meade.

Early in July 1863, Lee's offensive ground to a halt at a Pennsylvania road junction, **Gettysburg.** Confederates foraging for shoes in the town stumbled into Union cavalry, and both sides called for reinforcements. Thus began the war's greatest

Gettysburg Union victory that halted the Confederate invasion of Pennsylvania; turning point in the war in the East

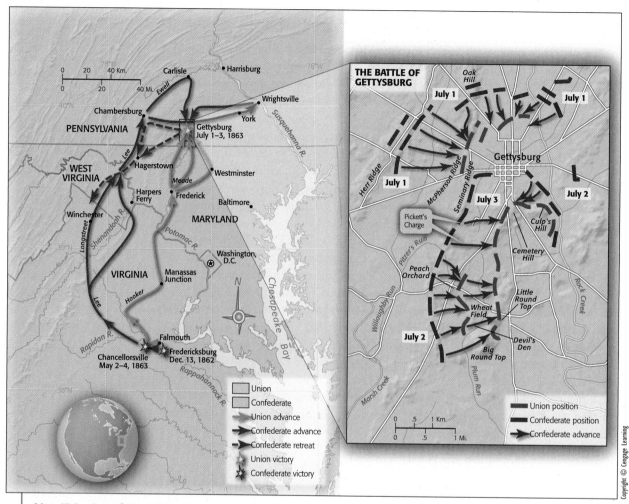

Map 15.3   Gettysburg, 1863

The failure of Pickett's charge against the Union center on July 3 was the decisive action in the war's greatest battle.

Interactive Map

battle. The Union fielded 90,000 troops against Lee's 75,000, and the struggle raged for the first three days of July. On July 2, Lee rejected advice to plant his army in a defensive position between Meade's force and Washington and instead attacked the Union flanks. But because Confederate assaults were uncoordinated, and some southern generals disregarded orders and struck where they chose, the Union was able to move in reinforcements and regain its earlier losses.

On the afternoon of the third day, Lee ordered a direct frontal assault on the Union lines, and 15,000 men under General George E. Pickett charged across the open field, flags bright in the brilliant sunshine. Union rifles poured volley after volley into the onrushing Confederates, whose line wavered and then broke. More than half of Pickett's force lay dead, wounded, or captured. When Lee withdrew to Virginia on July 4, he had lost seventeen generals and more than one-third of his army. Total Union and Confederate casualties numbered 50,000. Although Meade failed to pursue the retreating rebels, he had halted Lee's foray into the North; the Union rejoiced.

Almost simultaneously, the North won a strategically vital battle in the West, at **Vicksburg.** After arduous maneuvering, Grant had besieged Vicksburg, the key to the Mississippi. After a six-week siege, during which southern soldiers and civilians alike survived by eating mules and even rats, the Confederate commander surrendered his 30,000-man garrison to Grant on July 4, the day that Lee began his withdrawal from Pennsylvania. Port Hudson, the last Confederate stronghold on the Mississippi, soon surrendered. "The Father of Waters flows unvexed to the sea," Lincoln proclaimed.

A second crucial Union victory in the West soon followed, as Union reinforcements broke a Confederate siege on the forces of General William S. Rosecrans, who had been bottled up in Chattanooga, Tennessee. With Chattanooga secure, the way lay open for a Union strike into Georgia.

Union successes in the second half of 1863 stiffened the North's will to continue fighting and plunged some Confederate leaders into despair. Hearing of Vicksburg's fall, Confederate ordnance chief Josiah Gorgas lamented, "Yesterday we rode the pinnacle of success—today absolute ruin seems our portion. The Confederacy totters to its destruction."

Totter it might, but the South was far from beaten. Lee defended Virginia and Richmond. Although the loss of Vicksburg had cut the Confederacy in half, southern states west of the Mississippi could still provide soldiers. And the heart of the Confederacy—the Carolinas, Georgia, Florida, Mississippi, and Virginia—remained in southern hands. Few thought the fate of the Confederacy was sealed.

Vicksburg Union victory that gave the North complete control of the Mississippi River

CHECKING IN

- The Emancipation Proclamation made the war a conflict about slavery, but it only freed slaves in rebel-held territory.
- The proclamation kept Britain and France from recognizing the Confederacy.
- Confederate slaves posed a refugee problem for Union armies; the refugees suffered discrimination but performed valuable tasks for the federal troops.
- Despite early reluctance to enlist black soldiers, 186,000 African-Americans served in Union armies; the South ultimately authorized the use of black troops, but too late to take effect.
- Union victories at Gettysburg and Vicksburg in early July 1863 were the turning point of the war.

WAR AND SOCIETY, NORTH AND SOUTH

In what ways did the Civil War affect the two sides?

The Civil War, engulfing two economies and societies, extended far beyond the battlefields. By 1863, the contrasts between North and South were stark. Superior resources enabled the Union to meet wartime demand as the imperiled Confederacy could not. But both sides confronted similar problems: labor shortages, inflation, and disunity and dissent. Families were disrupted and dislocated, especially in the South. Women on both sides took on new roles at home, in the workplace, and in relief efforts.

The War's Economic Impact: The North

War affected the Union's economy unevenly. Some industries fared poorly; for example, the cotton-textile industry, deprived of raw cotton, went into a tailspin. But northern industries directly related to the war effort, such as the manufacture of arms and uniforms, benefited from huge government contracts. Railroads flourished. Some privately owned lines, which had overbuilt before the war, doubled their volume of traffic.

Pacific Railroad Act
Legislation that gave cash and land subsidies to those building the transcontinental railroad

Republicans in Congress, now a big majority, actively promoted business growth. Congress hiked the tariff in 1862 and again in 1864 to protect domestic industries. In July 1862, it passed the **Pacific Railroad Act** to build a transcontinental railroad. With the South out of the picture and unable to demand a southern route, Congress chose a northern route from Omaha to San Francisco. The government chartered the Union Pacific and Central Pacific corporations and gave each large land grants and generous loans: more than 60 million acres and $20 million. Issuance of greenbacks and the creation of a national banking system brought a measure of uniformity to the nation's financial system.

Homestead Act Measure that provided free land on the Great Plains to those willing to live there and develop it

Morrill Land Grant Act Law that established funding for agricultural and mechanical colleges, not traditional liberal arts colleges

Republicans designed these measures to help all social classes, and partially succeeded. The **Homestead Act,** passed in May 1862, embodied the party's ideal of "free soil, free labor, free men." It granted 160 acres of public land to settlers after five years of residence on the land. By 1865, twenty thousand homesteaders occupied new land in the West under the Homestead Act. Republicans also sponsored the **Morrill Land Grant Act** of 1862, which gave states proceeds from public land sales to establish universities emphasizing "such branches of learning as are related to agriculture and mechanic arts [engineering]." The law spurred the growth of large state universities, mainly in the Midwest and West, including Michigan State, Iowa State, and Purdue, among many others.

In general, however, the war benefited wealthy citizens more than others. Corrupt contractors grew rich by selling the government substandard merchandise, such as the notorious "shoddy" clothing made from compressed rags, which quickly disintegrated. Speculators made millions in the gold market, profiting more from Union defeats than from Union victories. Dealers with access to scarce commodities reaped astonishing profits. Manpower shortages in agricultural areas stimulated demand for Cyrus McCormick's mechanical reaper. McCormick redoubled his profits by investing in pig iron and watching as wartime demand almost doubled its price.

However, ordinary Americans suffered. Higher protective tariffs, wartime excise taxes, and inflation bloated the price of finished goods, while wages lagged 20 percent or more behind cost increases. As boys and women poured into government offices and factories to replace men serving in the army, they drew lower pay, and the threat that employers could hire more youths and females undercut the bargaining power of the men who remained in the labor force.

Many workers decried low wages, and some, such as cigar makers and locomotive engineers, formed national unions. Employers denounced worker complaints as unpatriotic hindrances to the war effort, and in 1864, the government diverted troops from combat to put down protests in war industries.

The War's Economic Impact: The South

The war shattered the South's economy. In fact, if both regions are considered together, the war retarded *American* economic growth. For example, American commodity output, which had increased 51 percent and 62 percent in the 1840s and 1850s, respectively, rose only 22 percent during the 1860s. Even this modest gain depended wholly on the North, for during that same decade commodity output in the South *declined* 39 percent.

Multiple factors offset the South's substantial wartime industrial growth. War destroyed the South's railroads. Cotton production plunged from 4 million bales in 1861 to 300,000 in 1865. Southern food production also declined because of Union occupation and a shortage of manpower. In areas under Confederate control, the yields per acre of crops like wheat and corn contracted; scarcities abounded. Agricultural shortages compounded the South's already severe inflation. By 1860, salt selling for $1.25 a sack in New York City cost $60 in the South, and food riots erupted in Mobile, Atlanta, and Richmond.

Part of the blame for the South's food shortage rested with planters. Despite government pleas to grow more food, many planters continued to raise cotton. To feed its hungry armies, the Confederacy impressed food from civilians. Farms and plantations run by the wives of active soldiers provided the easiest targets for food-impressment agents, and the women sent desperate pleas to their husbands to return home. By late 1864, half the Confederacy's soldiers were absent from their units.

The manpower drain that hampered food production reshaped the lives of southern white women. With three of every four white men in the military during the war, southern women faced new challenges and chronic shortages. With manufactured goods in short supply, women wove cloth and improvised replacements for unavailable goods, such as ink, dye, coffee, shoes, and candles. The war made refugees of many women; Texas became an appealing haven for those who sought to preserve their slave property.

In one respect, the persistence of cotton growing aided the South, as cotton became the basis for the Confederacy's flourishing trade with the enemy. In July 1861, the U.S. Congress virtually legalized this trade by allowing northern commerce with southerners loyal to the Union. In practice, it proved impossible to tell loyalists from rebels, and northern traders happily swapped bacon, salt, blankets, and other products for southern cotton. By 1864, traffic through the lines provided enough food for Lee's Army of Northern Virginia. A northern congressman lamented that it seemed the Union's policy was "to feed an army and fight it at the same time."

Dealing with Dissent

Both wartime governments faced mounting dissent and disloyalty. Within the Confederacy, dissent assumed two basic forms. First, a vocal group of states' rights supporters persistently attacked Jefferson Davis's government as despotic. Second, pro-Union sentiment flourished among the nonslaveholding small farmers who lived in the Appalachian region. To these people, the Confederate rebellion was a slave-owners' conspiracy. An Alabama farmer complained of the planters, "All they want is to get you pupt up and to fight for their infurnal negroes and after you do there fighting you may kiss there hine parts for o they care." On the whole, the South responded mildly to such popular disaffection. In 1862, the Confederate Congress gave President Davis the power to suspend the writ of *habeas corpus,* but he used it sparingly.

Lincoln faced similar challenges in the North, where the Democratic minority opposed both emancipation and the wartime growth of centralized power. One faction, the "Peace Democrats" (called **Copperheads** by their opponents, to suggest a resemblance to a species of easily concealed poisonous snakes), demanded a truce

Copperheads Northern "Peace Democrats" who opposed war

and a peace conference. They charged that the administration's war policy would "exterminate the South," make reconciliation impossible, and spark "terrible social change and revolution."

Strongest in the border states, the Midwest, and northeastern cities, the Democrats mobilized farmers of southern background and the urban working class, especially recent immigrants, who feared losing their jobs to free blacks. In 1863, this volatile mix of political, ethnic, racial, and class antagonisms exploded into anti-draft protests in several cities. By far the most violent eruption occurred in July 1863 in New York City, where mobs of Irish working-class men and women roamed the streets for four days until federal troops suppressed them. The Irish loathed the idea of being drafted to fight a war on behalf of slaves who, once freed, might compete with them for jobs. They also bitterly resented the provision of the draft law that allowed the rich to purchase substitutes. The rioters lynched at least a dozen blacks, injured hundreds more, and burned draft offices, the homes of wealthy Republicans, and the Colored Orphan Asylum.

President Lincoln's dispatch of federal troops to quash these riots typified his forceful response to dissent. Lincoln imposed martial law with far less hesitancy than Davis; he suspended the writ of *habeas corpus* nationwide in 1863 and authorized the arrest of rebels, draft resisters, and anyone engaged in "any disloyal practice." The responses of Davis and Lincoln to dissent underscored the differences between the two regions' wartime political systems. Davis lacked the institutionalization of dissent provided by party conflict and had to tread warily, lest his foes brand him a despot. In contrast, Lincoln and other Republicans used dissent to rally patriotic fervor against the Democrats.

Yet Lincoln did not unleash a reign of terror against dissent. In general, the North preserved freedom of the press, speech, and assembly. Of some fifteen thousand civilians arrested during the war, most were quickly released. A few cases aroused concern, however. In 1864, a military commission sentenced an Indiana man to be hanged for an alleged plot to free Confederate prisoners. The Supreme Court reversed his conviction two years later; it ruled that civilians could not be tried by military courts when the civil courts were open (*Ex parte Milligan,* 1866). Of more concern were arrests of politicians, notably Clement L. Vallandigham, an Ohio Peace Democrat, who in 1863 was sentenced to jail by a military commission. When Ohio Democrats nominated him for governor, Lincoln banished him from the country.

The Medical War

U.S. Sanitary Commission
Major source of medical aid for soldiers

Wartime patriotism impelled civilians in both the North and the South, especially women, to work tirelessly to aid soldiers. The **U.S. Sanitary Commission,** organized in June 1861 to assist the Union's medical bureau, depended on women volunteers. The commission raised funds, bought and distributed supplies, and ran special kitchens to supplement army rations. The legendary "Mother" Mary Ann Bickerdyke served sick and wounded Union soldiers as both nurse and surrogate mother. When a doctor asked her by what authority she demanded supplies for the wounded, she shot back, "From the Lord God Almighty. Do you have anything that ranks higher than that?"

Women also reached out to aid the battlefront through the nursing corps. Some 3,200 women nurses served the Union and the Confederacy. Dorothea Dix, famed for her campaigns on behalf of the insane, became head of the Union's nursing corps. **Clara Barton,** an obscure clerk in the Patent Office, found ingenious ways of channeling medicine to the sick and wounded. Learning of Union movements before Antietam, she showed up at the battlefield on the eve of the clash with a wagonload of supplies. When army surgeons ran out of bandages and started to dress wounds with corn husks, she raced forward with lint and bandages. In 1881, she founded the American Red Cross.

Clara Barton Nurse who worked for the Sanitary Commission; later founded the Red Cross

The Confederacy, too, had legendary nurses. Belle Boyd, both a nurse and a spy, once dashed through a field to give Stonewall Jackson information. However, danger stalked nurses even in hospitals far from the front. Louisa May Alcott, a nurse at the Union Hotel Hospital in Washington, DC, contracted typhoid. Wherever they worked, nurses witnessed haunting, nightmarish scenes. "About the amputating table," one wrote, "lay large piles of human flesh—legs, arms, feet, and hands . . . the stiffened membranes seemed to be clutching oftentimes at our clothing."

Pioneered by British reformer Florence Nightingale in the 1850s, nursing was a new vocation for women and, to critics, a brazen departure from women's proper sphere. Male doctors were unsure about how to react to women in the wards. Some saw a potential for mischief in women's presence in male hospital wards. Other physicians, however, viewed nursing and sanitary work as useful. The miasm theory of disease (see Chapter 11) won wide respect among physicians and stimulated valuable sanitary measures. In partial consequence, the ratio of disease to battle deaths was much lower in the Civil War than in the Mexican-American War. Nonetheless, for every soldier killed during the Civil War, two died of disease. The germ theory of disease was unknown, and arm and leg wounds often led to gangrene (GAN-green) or tetanus (TET-uh-nuss). Typhoid, malaria, diarrhea, and dysentery raged through army camps.

Prison camps posed a special problem. The two sides had far more prisoners than they could handle, and prisoners on both sides suffered gravely. The worst conditions plagued the southern camps. Squalor and insufficient rations turned the Confederate prison camp at Andersonville, Georgia, into a virtual death camp; 3,000 prisoners a month (out of a total of 32,000) were dying there by August 1864. After the war an outraged northern public demanded, and got, the execution of Andersonville's commandant.

The War and Women's Rights

Nurses and Sanitary Commission workers were not the only women to serve society in wartime. In the North and South alike, thousands of women took over jobs vacated by men. In rural areas, where manpower shortages were most acute, women often plowed, planted, and harvested.

Northern women's rights advocates hoped that the war would yield equality for women as well as freedom for slaves. A grateful North, they contended, should reward women for their wartime service and recognize the link between black rights and women's rights. In 1863, feminists Elizabeth Cady Stanton and Susan B. Anthony organized the National Woman's Loyal League. The league gathered four hundred thousand

CHECKING IN

- During the war, northern Republicans pushed several economic development measures through Congress—tariffs, railroad subsidies, national banking, and homestead legislation—and industrialization thrived.
- The Confederate economy, in contrast, crumpled under wartime pressure, and civilians suffered shortages and hardship.
- Lincoln was much quicker than Davis to suppress dissent.
- The war stimulated the use of women as nurses and led to advances in anesthesia and sanitary conditions.
- Women like Elizabeth Cady Stanton pointed to women's wartime service to promote women's rights; however, in the end, the war did not bring acceptance of women's political or economic equality.

signatures on a petition calling for a constitutional amendment to abolish slavery, but Stanton and Anthony used the organization to promote woman suffrage as well.

Despite high expectations, the war did not bring women significantly closer to economic or political equality. Nor did it much change the prevailing definition of women's sphere. Men continued to dominate the medical profession, and for the rest of the century the census classified nurses as domestic help. The keenest disappointment of women's rights advocates lay in their failure to capitalize on rising abolitionist sentiment to secure the vote for women. Northern politicians saw little value in woman suffrage. The *New York Herald,* which supported the Loyal League's attack on slavery, dismissed its call for woman suffrage as "nonsense and tomfoolery." Stanton wrote bitterly, a few years later, "Women's cause is in deep water."

THE UNION VICTORIOUS, 1864–1865

How did the Union finally win the war?

Successes at Gettysburg and Vicksburg in 1863 notwithstanding, the Union stood no closer to taking Richmond at the start of 1864 than in 1861, and most of the Lower South remained under Confederate control. The North's persistent inability to destroy the main Confederate armies eroded the Union's will to attack. War weariness strengthened the Democrats and jeopardized Lincoln's reelection in 1864.

The year 1864 was crucial for the North. A Union army under General William Tecumseh Sherman captured Atlanta in September, boosting northern morale and helping to reelect Lincoln. Sherman then marched unimpeded across Georgia and into South Carolina and devastated the states. In Virginia, Grant backed Lee into trenches around Petersburg and Richmond and forced the evacuation of both cities—and ultimately the Confederacy's collapse.

The Eastern Theater in 1864

Early in 1864, Lincoln made Grant the commander of all Union armies and promoted him to lieutenant general. At first glance, the stony-faced, cigar-puffing Grant seemed an unlikely candidate for so exalted a rank, held previously only by George Washington. Grant's only distinguishing characteristics were his ever-present cigar and a penchant for whittling sticks into chips. "There is no glitter, no parade about him," a contemporary noted. But Grant's successes in the West had made him the Union's most popular general. He moved his headquarters to the Army of the Potomac in the East and mapped a strategy for final victory.

Grant shared Lincoln's belief that the Union had to coordinate its attacks on all fronts to exploit its numerical advantage. He planned a sustained offensive against Lee in the East while ordering Sherman to attack the rebel army in Georgia. Sherman's mission was "to break it [the Confederate army] up, and to get into the interior of the enemy's country . . . inflicting all the damage you can."

The war's pace quickened dramatically. In early May 1864, Grant led 118,000 men against Lee's 64,000 in a forested area near Fredericksburg, Virginia, called the Wilderness. The Union army fought the Army of Northern Virginia in a series of bloody engagements in May and June. These battles ranked among the war's fiercest; at Cold Harbor, Grant lost 7,000 men in one hour. Instead of recoiling from such an immense "butcher's bill," Grant pressed on, forcing Lee to pull back to trenches guarding Petersburg and Richmond.

Once entrenched, Lee could not threaten the Union rear with rapid moves, as he had done for three years. Lee sent General Jubal A. Early on raids down the Shenandoah (sheh-nan-DOH-uh) Valley, which served the Confederacy as a granary as well as an indirect way to menace Washington. Grant countered by ordering General Philip Sheridan to march down the valley from the north and "lay it waste." By September 1864, Sheridan controlled the Shenandoah Valley.

While Grant and Lee grappled in the Wilderness, Sherman led 98,000 men into Georgia. Opposing him with 53,000 men (later reinforced to 65,000), General Joseph Johnston slowly retreated toward Atlanta, conserving his strength for a defense of the city and forcing Sherman to elongate his supply lines. Dismayed by this defensive strategy, President Davis replaced Johnston with the adventurous John B. Hood. He gave Davis what he wanted, a series of attacks on Sherman, but Sherman pressed relentlessly forward against Hood's increasingly depleted army. Unable to defend Atlanta, Hood evacuated the city, which fell to Sherman on September 2, 1864.

The Election of 1864

Atlanta's fall came at a timely moment for Lincoln, who was in the thick of a tough campaign for reelection. Radical Republicans opposed his re-nomination, largely because of his desire to restore occupied parts of the Confederacy to the Union, and rallied around Secretary of the Treasury Salmon P. Chase. The Democrats, meanwhile, had not forgiven Lincoln for making emancipation a war goal, and now the Copperheads demanded an immediate armistice followed by negotiations.

Lincoln, however, benefited from his own resourcefulness and his foes' problems. Chase's challenge failed, and by the time of the Republican convention, Lincoln's managers controlled the nomination. To isolate the Peace Democrats, the Republicans formed a temporary organization, the National Union party, and chose a southern Unionist, Democratic senator Andrew Johnson of Tennessee, for the vice presidency. The Democrats nominated George B. McClellan, former commander of the Army of the Potomac, who advocated military victory and tried to distance himself from the Democratic platform, which called for peace without victory.

Lincoln doubted that he would be reelected and even arranged furloughs so that Union soldiers, most of whom supported him, would be able to vote in states lacking absentee ballots. The fall of Atlanta provided an enormous boost and saved Lincoln's presidency. With 55 percent of the popular vote and 212 out of 233 electoral votes, he swept to victory.

The convention that nominated Lincoln also endorsed a constitutional amendment to abolish slavery, which Congress passed early in 1865. The **Thirteenth Amendment** would be ratified by the end of the year.

Thirteenth Amendment
Ended slavery in all U.S. territory

Map 15.4 The Final Virginia Campaign, 1864–1865

Refusing to abandon his campaign in the face of enormous casualties, Grant finally pushed Lee (below) into defensive fortifications around Petersburg, whose fall doomed Richmond. When Lee tried to escape to the west, Grant cut him off and forced his surrender.

Interactive Map

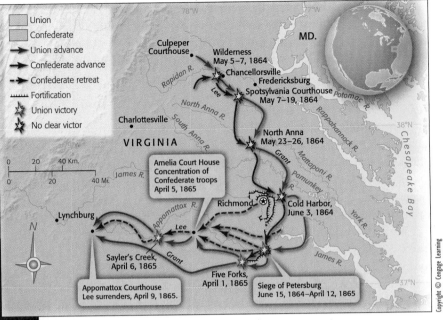

Sherman's March Through Georgia

Meanwhile, Sherman gave the South a lesson in total war. Refusing to chase Hood back into Tennessee, he decided to abandon his own supply lines, to march his army across Georgia to Savannah (suh-VAN-uh), and to live off the countryside. He would break the South's will to fight, terrify its people, and "make war so terrible . . . that generations would pass before they could appeal again to it."

Sherman began by burning much of Atlanta and forcing the evacuation of its civilian population. This harsh measure freed him of the need to feed and garrison the city. Then he led the bulk of his army, 62,000 men, out of Atlanta toward Savannah. Four columns of infantry, augmented by cavalry squads and followed by thousands of jubilant slaves, moved on a front sixty miles wide and at a pace of ten miles a day, destroying everything that could aid the Confederacy—arsenals, railroads, munitions plants, cotton gins, crops, and livestock. This ruin far exceeded Sherman's orders. Although told not to destroy civilian property, foragers ransacked and demolished homes. Indeed, havoc seemed a vital part of Sherman's strategy. By the time he occupied Savannah, he estimated that his army had destroyed $100 million worth of property.

After taking Savannah in December 1864, Sherman's army wheeled north toward South Carolina, the first state to secede and, in his view, one "that deserves all that seems in store for her." Sherman's columns advanced unimpeded to Columbia, where fires set by looters, slaves, soldiers of both sides, and liberated Union prisoners razed the city. Sherman then headed for North Carolina. By spring 1865, his army had left behind four hundred miles of ruin. Other Union armies controlled the entire Confederacy, except Texas and Florida, and destroyed its wealth. "War is cruelty and you cannot refine it," Sherman wrote. "Those who brought war into our country deserve all the curses and maledictions a people can pour out."

Toward Appomattox   While Sherman headed north, Grant renewed his assault on the entrenched Army of Northern Virginia. His main objective was Petersburg, a railroad hub south of Richmond. The fall of Atlanta and the devastation wrought by Sherman's army took a heavy toll on Confederate morale. Desertions reached epidemic proportions. Late in March 1865, Grant, reinforced by Sheridan, swung his army around the western flank of the Petersburg defenders. Lee could not stop him. On April 2, a courier brought the grim news to Jefferson Davis, attending church in Richmond: "General Lee telegraphs that he can hold his position no longer."

Davis left his pew, gathered his government, and fled. On the morning of April 3, Union troops entered Richmond, pulled down the Confederate flag, and raised the Stars and Stripes over the capital. Explosions set by retreating Confederates left the city "a sea of flames." Union troops liberated the jail, which held slaves awaiting sale, and its rejoicing inmates poured into the streets. On April 4, Lincoln toured the city and for a few minutes sat at Davis's desk with a dreamy expression on his face.

Lee led a last-ditch effort to escape westward to Lynchburg and its rail connections. But Grant and Sheridan choked off the route, and on April 9 Lee bowed to the inevitable. He asked for terms of surrender and met Grant in a private home in the village of **Appomattox** (app-oh-MAT-tux) **Courthouse,** east of Lynchburg. As stunned troops gathered outside, Lee appeared in full dress uniform, complete with sword. Grant entered in his customary disarray, smoking a cigar. The final surrender came four days later, as Lee's troops laid down their arms between federal ranks. "On our part," wrote a Union officer, "not a sound of trumpet . . . nor roll of drum; not a cheer . . . but an awed stillness rather." Grant paroled Lee's 26,000 men and sent them home with the horses and mules "to work their little farms." Within a month the remnants of Confederate resistance collapsed. Johnston surrendered to Sherman on April 18, and Davis was captured in Georgia on May 10.

Grant headed back to a jubilant Washington. On April 14, he turned down a theater date with the Lincolns; his wife found Mrs. Lincoln overbearing. That night at Ford's Theater an unemployed pro-Confederate actor, John Wilkes Booth, entered Lincoln's box and shot him in the head. Shouting the

Appomattox Courthouse Site of Lee's surrender to Grant

National Archives

Grant in 1864
Exuding determination and competence, General Ulysses S. Grant posed in front of his tent in 1864. Within a year, Grant's final assault on Petersburg and the Union army's triumphant march into Richmond would bring the war to an end.

Virginia state motto, *"Sic Semper Tyrannis"* ("Such is always the fate of tyrants"), Booth leaped onto the stage and fled. Assassination attempts on the secretary of state and vice president failed, and Booth escaped. Within two weeks Union troops hunted him down and shot him to death. Four accused accomplices were hanged, and four more were imprisoned. On April 15, Lincoln died, and Andrew Johnson became president. Six days later, Lincoln's funeral train left Washington on its mournful journey to Springfield, Illinois. Crowds of thousands gathered at stations to weep as the black-draped train passed.

The Impact of the War

The Civil War took a larger human toll than any other war in American history. More than 620,000 soldiers died during the tragic four years of war, nearly equal the number of American soldiers killed in all the nation's earlier and later wars. The death count stood at 360,000 Union soldiers and 260,000 Confederates. Most families in the nation suffered losses. Vivid reminders remained well into the twentieth century. For many years, armless and legless veterans gathered at regimental reunions, and thousands of communities built monuments to the dead.

The war's costs were staggering, but only the southern economy was destroyed. By war's end the North had most of the nation's wealth and industrial capacity. Spurring economic modernization, the war provided opportunities for industrial development and capital investment. No longer the largest slave-owning power in the world, the United States would become a major industrial nation.

The war had political ramifications as well. States never regained their antebellum range of powers. The national banking system gradually supplanted state banks, and greenbacks provided a national currency. The war also promoted large-scale organization in both the business world and public life.

Finally, the Civil War fulfilled abolitionists' prophecies as well as Union goals, producing the very sort of radical upheaval within southern society that Lincoln had tried to avoid. Beaten Confederates wondered whether blacks and Yankees would permanently take over the South. "Hello, massa," an African-American Union soldier called out when he spotted his former owner among Confederate prisoners whom he was guarding. "Bottom rail top dis time." The nation now shifted its attention to the reconstruction of the conquered South and the fate of 3.5 million newly freed slaves.

CHECKING IN

- Lincoln finally found the general he needed in Ulysses S. Grant, who realized that the South could not withstand the enormous casualties of relentless combat.

- Sherman brought total war to the South with his march through Georgia and the Carolinas.

- Lincoln's triumph in the 1864 election reflected increasing Union confidence in victory.

- Forced to leave Richmond undefended, Lee surrendered in April 1865, effectively ending major combat.

- In the final months of the war, Congress passed the Thirteenth Amendment, abolishing slavery, but the assassination of Lincoln left the postwar future in limbo.

Chapter Summary

| *What major advantages did each side possess at the start of the Civil War? (page 338)*

The Union had enormous manpower advantages, as well as a strong industrial base. However, to sustain Confederate independence, the South had to fight a defensive war, whereas the northern armies had to invade and occupy a vast region. As war dragged on, both regions faced political and economic problems. The North weathered these problems somewhat better than the South, where political rifts appeared over the role of national government in the Confederacy. Lincoln was a far better political leader than Davis.

| *How was the war fought in its early years? (page 343)*

Although new weapons, such as the rifle, appeared, the Civil War was basically fought as a traditional war, with mass infantry charges and large battles. The war in the East quickly became a stalemate, but the Union established supremacy west of the Mississippi early in the war. Many Confederate leaders assumed that the British textile industry's need for southern cotton would force Britain to become an ally, but the British remained aloof.

| *How did the issue of emancipation transform the war? (page 352)*

The Emancipation Proclamation transformed the Civil War from a conflict over secession into a war about slavery, and it effectively prevented Great Britain from openly supporting the Confederacy. Whenever possible, slaves strove to escape from slavery. Slave refugees posed problems for Union armies but also performed valuable tasks for federal troops. Nearly 190,000 African-Americans fought in Union armies, and manpower shortages drove the Confederacy to authorize the use of black troops as well.

| *In what ways did the Civil War affect the two sides? (page 357)*

During the war, the federal Congress passed major bills promoting economic development: tariffs, railroad subsidies, national banking laws, and legislation to encourage homesteading. However, the war devastated the South's economy, with resulting shortages and hardships for civilians. Women assumed new roles as nurses and hoped that their service would advance the cause of women's rights.

KEY TERMS

conscription (p. 339)

"greenbacks" (p. 340)

Anaconda plan (p. 345)

First Battle of Bull Run (p. 346)

George B. McClellan (p. 346)

Robert E. Lee (p. 347)

Antietam (p. 347)

Emancipation Proclamation (p. 347)

Ulysses S. Grant (p. 347)

Gettysburg (p. 355)

Vicksburg (p. 357)

Pacific Railroad Act (p. 358)

Homestead Act (p. 358)

Morrill Land Grant Act (p. 358)

Copperheads (p. 359)

U.S. Sanitary Commission (p. 360)

Clara Barton (p. 361)

Thirteenth Amendment (p. 363)

Appomattox Courthouse (p. 365)

How did the Union finally win the war? (page 362)

Lincoln found the general he had been searching for in Ulysses S. Grant, who was willing to absorb enormous casualties to inflict the losses he knew the South could not afford. Sherman's capture of Atlanta guaranteed Lincoln's reelection in 1864 and boosted northern determination. By April 1865, Lee was forced to abandon the defense of Richmond and surrendered at Appomattox Courthouse. The Thirteenth Amendment, passed in the final months of the war, ended slavery. However, Lincoln's assassination left the postwar future in limbo.

 **CourseMate**

Go to the CourseMate website at **www.cengagebrain.com** for additional study tools and review materials—including audio and video clips—for this chapter.

CHAPTER 16

The Crisis of Reconstruction

1865–1877

CHAPTER PREVIEW

Reconstruction Politics, 1865–1868
How did Radical Republicans gain control of Reconstruction politics?

Reconstruction Governments
What impact did federal Reconstruction policy have on the former Confederacy and ex-Confederates?

The Impact of Emancipation
How did the newly freed slaves reshape their lives after emancipation?

New Concerns in the North, 1868–1876
Why did northern concern about Reconstruction begin to wane?

Reconstruction Abandoned, 1876–1877
What factors contributed to the end of Reconstruction in 1877?

The Devastated South

Louisiana and Lower Mississippi Valley Collection, (-)LSU Libraries, Louisiana State University

"I never forget de day we was set free," former slave Katie Rowe recalled. "Dat morning we all go to de cotton field early. After a while de old horn blow up at de overseer's house, and we all stop and listen, 'cause it de wrong time of day for de horn." Later that day, after several more blasts of the horn, a stranger, apparently a Yankee, addressed the slaves. "'Today you is free, just lak I is,' de man say," Katie Rowe declared. "'You is your own bosses now.'" The date was June 4, 1865. Rowe called it the day "that I begins to live."

Emancipation in June 1865 brought an era of transition for the former slaves. "None of us know whar to go," Katie Rowe remembered. The plantation overseer charged the former slaves "half de crop for de quarter and all de mules and tools and grub." His replacement offered better arrangements: "[W]e all got something left over after dat first go-out." But new changes occurred. The next year the former owner's heirs sold the plantation, "and we scatter off." Katie eventually married a Cherokee man and moved to Oklahoma.

For the nation, as for Katie Rowe, the end of the Civil War was an instant of uncharted possibilities and a time of unresolved conflicts. While former slaves exulted over their freedom, their former owners were often as grim as the wasted southern landscape. Several thousand fled to Brazil, Mexico, or Europe, but most remained.

In most armed conflicts, the morale of the vanquished rarely concerns the victors. However, the Civil War was a special case, for the Union had sought not merely military triumph but the return of national unity. Therefore, the federal government in 1865 faced unprecedented questions. How could the Union be restored and the South reintegrated? Who would control the process—Congress or the president? Should Confederate leaders be tried for treason? Most important, what would happen to the 3.5 million former slaves? The freedmen's future was *the* crucial issue of the postwar era, for emancipation had set in motion a profound upheaval. Before the war, slavery had determined the South's social, economic, and political structure. What would replace it? The end of the Civil War, in short, posed two huge challenges that had to be solved simultaneously: how to readmit the South to the Union and how to define the status of free blacks in American society.

Between 1865 and 1877, the nation met these challenges, but not without discord and turmoil. Conflict prevailed in the halls of Congress, in the former Confederacy, and in the industrializing postwar North. The crises of Reconstruction—the restoration of the former Confederate states and the fate of the former slaves—reshaped the legacy of the Civil War.

RECONSTRUCTION POLITICS, 1865–1868

How did Radical Republicans gain control of Reconstruction politics?

The end of the Civil War offered multiple possibilities for chaos and vengeance. The federal government could have imprisoned or executed Confederate leaders, demobilized Confederate soldiers might have continued armed resistance, and freed slaves might have taken revenge on former masters. However, none of this occurred. Instead, intense *political* conflict dominated the immediate postwar period. National politics produced new constitutional amendments, a presidential impeachment, and some of the most ambitious domestic legislation ever enacted by Congress: the Reconstruction Acts of 1867–1868. It culminated in something that few expected: the enfranchisement of African-American men.

In 1865 only a handful of **Radical Republicans** advocated African-American suffrage. But in the complex political battles of Reconstruction, the Radicals won broad support for their program, including African-American male enfranchisement. Just as the Civil War had led to emancipation, Reconstruction led to African-American suffrage.

Radical Republicans Faction in Congress, led by Thaddeus Stevens and Charles Sumner, that called for full civil rights for freedmen without compromise

Lincoln's Plan

Conflict over Reconstruction began even before the war ended. In December 1863, President Abraham Lincoln issued the Proclamation of Amnesty and Reconstruction, which enabled southern states to rejoin the Union if at least 10 percent of those who had voted in the 1860 elections swore an oath of allegiance to the Union and accepted emancipation. This plan excluded most Confederate officials and military officers, who would have had to apply for presidential pardons, as well as African-Americans, who had not voted in 1860. Through these requirements, Lincoln hoped both to undermine the Confederacy and to build a southern Republican Party.

Radical Republicans in Congress, however, envisioned a slower readmission process that would bar even more ex-Confederates from political life. The Wade-Davis Bill, passed by Congress in July 1864, provided that a military governor would rule each former Confederate state; after at least half the eligible voters took an oath of allegiance to the Union, delegates could be elected to a state convention that would repeal secession and abolish slavery. To qualify as a voter or a delegate, a southerner would have to take a second, "ironclad" oath, swearing that he had never voluntarily supported the Confederacy. The Wade-Davis Bill would have delayed readmission of southern states almost indefinitely.

Chronology

1863	Abraham Lincoln issues the Proclamation of Amnesty and Reconstruction
1864	Wade-Davis Bill passed by Congress and pocket-vetoed by Lincoln
1865	Freedmen's Bureau established; Civil War ends; Lincoln assassinated; Andrew Johnson becomes president; Johnson issues his Proclamation of Amnesty and Reconstruction; ex-Confederate states hold constitutional conventions; Thirteenth Amendment added to the Constitution
1866	Civil Rights Act of 1866 and the Supplementary Freedmen's Bureau Act passed over Johnson's vetoes; Ku Klux Klan founded in Tennessee; race riots occur in southern cities; Republicans win congressional elections
1867	Reconstruction Act of 1867; William Seward negotiates the purchase of Alaska; constitutional conventions meet in the ex-Confederate states
1868	Andrew Johnson impeached, tried, and acquitted; Fourteenth Amendment added to the Constitution; Ulysses S. Grant elected president
1869	Transcontinental railroad completed
1870	Congress readmits the four remaining southern states to the Union; Fifteenth Amendment added to the Constitution; Enforcement Act of 1870
1871	Second Enforcement Act; Ku Klux Klan Act
1872	Liberal Republican party formed; Amnesty Act; *Alabama* claims settled; Grant reelected president
1873	Panic of 1873 begins, setting off five-year depression
1874	Democrats gain control of the House of Representatives
1875	Civil Rights Act of 1875; Specie Resumption Act
1876	Disputed presidential election: Rutherford B. Hayes versus Samuel J. Tilden
1877	Electoral commission decides election in favor of Hayes; the last Republican-controlled state governments fall
1879	"Exodus" movement spreads through several southern states

Lincoln pocket-vetoed* the Wade-Davis Bill, and an impasse followed. Arkansas, Louisiana, Tennessee, and parts of Virginia moved toward readmission under variants of Lincoln's plan, but Congress refused to seat their delegates. What Lincoln's ultimate policy would have been remains unknown. But after his assassination, on April 14, 1865, Radical Republicans turned with hope toward his successor, Andrew Johnson of Tennessee.

Andrew Johnson Former slave owner and senator from Tennessee; as Lincoln's successor and seventeenth president, he lost control over Reconstruction policy and barely survived impeachment in 1868

Presidential Reconstruction Under Johnson

At first glance, **Andrew Johnson** seemed a likely ally for the Radicals. The only southern senator to remain in Congress when his state seceded, Andrew Johnson served as military governor of Tennessee from 1862 to 1864. Defying the Confederate stand, he declared that "treason is a crime and must be made odious." Self-educated, of humble origins, a foe of the planter class, a supporter of emancipation—Johnson carried impeccable credentials. However, as a lifelong Democrat he had his own political agenda, which was sharply different from that of the Radicals. He neither adopted abolitionist ideals nor challenged racist sentiments. He hoped mainly that the fall of slavery would cripple southern aristocrats.

In May 1865, with Congress out of session, Johnson shocked Republicans by announcing his own program, A Proclamation of Amnesty and Reconstruction, to bring back into the Union the seven southern states still without Reconstruction governments—Alabama, Florida, Georgia, Mississippi, North Carolina, South Carolina, and Texas. Almost all southerners who took an oath of allegiance would receive a pardon and amnesty; all their property except slaves would be restored. Oath takers could elect delegates to state conventions, which would call regular elections, proclaim secession illegal, repudiate debts incurred under the Confederacy, and ratify the Thirteenth Amendment, which abolished slavery. As under Lincoln's plan, Confederate civil and military officers would still be disqualified, as would well-off ex-Confederates (those with taxable property worth $20,000 or more). This purge of the plantation aristocracy, Johnson said, would benefit "humble men, the peasantry of the South, who have been decoyed . . . into rebellion." Poorer whites would now be in control.

Presidential Reconstruction

Andrew Johnson's plan to pardon ex-Confederate leaders and readmit former Confederate states to the union on lenient terms

Presidential Reconstruction began in the summer of 1865, but developed unforeseen consequences. Johnson handed out pardons liberally (some thirteen thousand) and dropped his plans to punish treason. By the end of 1865 all seven states had created new civil governments that in effect restored the status quo from before the war. Confederate officers and large planters resumed state offices. Former Confederate congressmen and officials—including Alexander Stephens of Georgia, the former Confederate vice president—won election to Congress. Some states even refused to ratify the Thirteenth Amendment or to repudiate their Confederate debts.

"black codes" Laws passed by southern states to limit the rights of freedmen

Most infuriating to the Radicals, all seven states passed **"black codes"** intended to ensure a landless, dependent black labor force. These codes, which replaced earlier slave codes, guaranteed the freedmen some basic rights—to marry, own property, make contracts, and testify in court against other blacks—but also harshly restricted freedmen's behavior. Some states established segregation; most prohibited racial

---

*Pocket-vetoed: failed to sign the bill within ten days of Congress's adjournment.

intermarriage, jury service by blacks, and court testimony by blacks against whites. All codes included provisions that effectively barred former slaves from leaving the plantations, usually through labor contracts stipulating that anyone who had not signed a labor contract was a vagrant and subject to arrest.

As a result of the black codes, freedmen were no longer slaves but not really liberated either. In practice, many clauses in the codes never took effect: the Freedmen's Bureau suspended the enforcement of the racially discriminatory provisions of the new laws. Nonetheless, the black codes revealed white southern intentions and showed what "home rule" would have been like without federal intervention.

Many northerners denounced what they saw as southern defiance. When Congress convened in December 1865, it refused to seat delegates of ex-Confederate states and prepared to dismantle the black codes and to lock ex-Confederates out of power.

Congress Versus Johnson

Southern blacks' status became the major issue in Congress. With Congress split into four blocs—Radical, moderate, and conservative Republicans, as well as Democrats—a politically adroit president could have protected his program. Ineptly, Johnson alienated a majority of the moderates and pushed them into the Radicals' arms.

In late 1865 Congress voted to extend the life of the Freedmen's Bureau for three more years. This federal agency, headed by former Union general O. O. Howard and staffed mainly by army officers, provided relief, rations, and medical care; built schools for freed blacks; put them to work on abandoned or confiscated lands; and tried to protect their rights as laborers. To strengthen the bureau, Congress gave it new power to run special military courts, to settle labor disputes, and to invalidate labor contracts forced on freedmen by the black codes. In February 1866, Johnson vetoed the bill. The Constitution, he declared, did not sanction military trials of civilians in peacetime, nor did it support a system to care for "indigent persons." Then in March 1866 Congress passed the **Civil Rights Act of 1866,** which made African-Americans U.S. citizens with the same civil rights as other citizens and authorized federal intervention to ensure black rights in court. Johnson vetoed this measure as well, arguing that it would "operate in favor of the colored and against the white race." In April Congress overrode his veto, and in July it enacted the Supplementary Freedmen's Bureau Act over another presidential veto.

Civil Rights Act of 1866 Made blacks U.S. citizens; first major law ever passed over a presidential veto

These vetoes puzzled many Republicans because the new laws did not undercut presidential Reconstruction. Although the vetoes gained support for Johnson among northern Democrats, they cost him dearly among moderate Republicans, who now joined Radicals to oppose him. Was Johnson a political incompetent, or was he merely trying, unsuccessfully, to forge a centrist coalition? Whatever the case, he drove moderate and Radical Republicans together toward their next step: the passage of a constitutional amendment to protect the new Civil Rights Act.

The Fourteenth Amendment, 1866

In April 1866, Congress adopted the **Fourteenth Amendment,** its most ambitious attempt to deal with the problems of Reconstruction. In the first clause, the

Fourteenth Amendment Defined citizenship and guaranteed equal protection under the law

amendment proclaimed that all persons born or naturalized in the United States were citizens and that no state could abridge their rights without due process of law or deny them equal protection under the law. This section nullified the *Dred Scott* decision of 1857, which had declared that blacks were not citizens. Second, the amendment guaranteed that, if a state denied suffrage to any male citizen, its representation in Congress would be proportionally reduced. Third, the amendment disqualified from state and national offices *all* prewar officeholders who had supported the Confederacy. In so providing, Congress intended to invalidate most of the pardons that President Johnson had ladled out. Finally, the amendment repudiated the Confederate debt and maintained the validity of the federal debt.

The amendment's passage created a firestorm. Abolitionists decried it as a "swindle" because it did not explicitly ensure black suffrage, southerners blasted it as vengeful, and President Johnson denounced it. His defiance solidified the new alliance between moderate and Radical Republicans, and transformed the congressional elections of 1866 into a referendum on the Fourteenth Amendment.

Over the summer, Johnson set off on a whistle-stop train tour from Washington to St. Louis and Chicago and back. But this innovative campaign tactic—the "swing around the circle," as Johnson called it—failed. Humorless and defensive, the president made fresh enemies and doomed his hope of sinking the Fourteenth Amendment, which moderate and Radical Republicans defended.

Republicans carried the congressional elections of 1866 in a landslide, winning almost two-thirds of the House and four-fifths of the Senate. They had secured a mandate for the Fourteenth Amendment and their own Reconstruction program.

Congressional Reconstruction, 1866–1867

Congressional debate over reconstructing the South began in December 1866 and lasted three months. Radical leaders called for black suffrage, federal support for public schools, confiscation of Confederate estates, and extended military occupation of the South. Moderate Republicans accepted parts of this plan. In February 1867, after complex legislative maneuvers, Congress passed the Reconstruction Act of 1867. Johnson vetoed the law, and on March 2, Congress passed it over his veto. Three more Reconstruction acts—passed in 1867 and 1868 over presidential vetoes—refined and enforced the first act.

Reconstruction Act of 1867
Imposed military rule on ten southern states and required them to ratify the Fourteenth Amendment

The **Reconstruction Act of 1867** invalidated the state governments formed under the Lincoln and Johnson plans. Only Tennessee, which had already ratified the Fourteenth Amendment and had been readmitted to the Union, escaped further Reconstruction. The new law divided the other ten former Confederate states into five temporary military districts, each run by a Union general (see Map 16.1). Voters—all black men, plus whites not disqualified by the Fourteenth Amendment—could elect delegates to a state convention that would write a new state constitution granting black suffrage. Once Congress approved the state constitution, and once the state legislature ratified the Fourteenth Amendment, Congress would readmit the state into the Union. The Reconstruction Act of 1867 was far more radical than the Johnson program because it enfranchised blacks and disfranchised many ex-Confederates. Even then, however, it provided only temporary military rule, made no provisions to prosecute Confederate leaders for treason, and neither confiscated nor redistributed property.

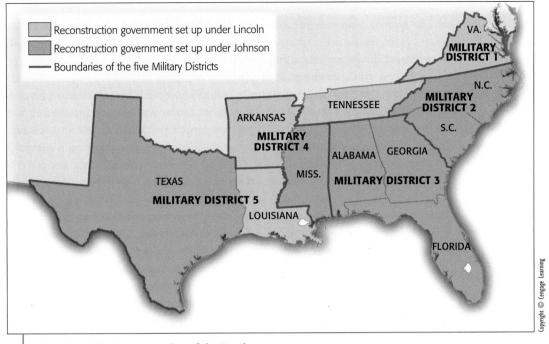

Map 16.1   The Reconstruction of the South

The Reconstruction Act of 1867 divided the former Confederate states, except Tennessee, into five military districts and set forth the steps by which new state governments could be created.

◉ Interactive Map

During the congressional debates, Radical Republican congressman Thaddeus Stevens had argued for the confiscation of large Confederate estates to "humble the proud traitors" and to provide for former slaves. He had proposed subdividing such confiscated property into forty-acre tracts to be distributed among the freedmen and selling the rest to pay off war debts. Stevens's land-reform bill won Radical support but never made progress; most Republicans held property rights sacred. Tampering with such rights, they feared, would endanger the rest of Reconstruction. Thus, land reform never came about. The "radical" Reconstruction acts were a compromise.

Congressional Reconstruction took effect in spring 1867, but Johnson impeded its enforcement by replacing pro-Radical military officers with conservative ones. Republicans seethed. More suspicious than ever, congressional moderates and Radicals again joined forces to block Johnson from further hampering Reconstruction.

The Impeachment Crisis, 1867–1868

In March 1867, Republicans in Congress passed two laws to curb presidential power. The **Tenure of Office Act** prohibited the president from removing civil officers without Senate consent. Its purpose was to bar Johnson from dismissing Secretary of War Edwin M. Stanton, a Radical ally. The other law barred the president from issuing military orders except through the commanding general, Ulysses S. Grant, who could not be removed without the Senate's consent.

Tenure of Office Act Law requiring the president to seek Senate consent before removing civil officers

The Radicals' enmity toward Johnson, however, went further: They began to seek grounds on which to impeach him. The House Judiciary Committee, aided by private detectives, could at first find no valid charges against Johnson. But Johnson again rescued his foes by providing the charges they needed.

In August 1867, Johnson suspended Stanton and, in February 1868, tried to remove him. The president's defiance of the Tenure of Office Act drove moderate Republicans back into alliance with the Radicals. The House approved eleven charges of impeachment, nine based on violation of the Tenure of Office Act. The other charges accused Johnson of being "unmindful of the high duties of the office," seeking to disgrace Congress, and not enforcing the Reconstruction acts.

Johnson's trial by the Senate, which began in March 1868, riveted public attention for eleven weeks. Seven congressmen, including leading Radicals, served as prosecutors, or "managers." Johnson's lawyers maintained that he was merely seeking a court test by violating the Tenure of Office Act, which he thought was unconstitutional. They also contended that the law did not protect Stanton, because Lincoln, not Johnson, had appointed him. Finally, they asserted, Johnson was guilty of no crime indictable in a regular court.

Congressional "managers" countered that impeachment was a political process, not a criminal trial, and that Johnson's "abuse of discretionary power" constituted an impeachable offense. Some Senate Republicans wavered, fearful that the removal of a president would destroy the balance of power within the federal government. They also distrusted Radical Republican Benjamin Wade, the president pro tempore of the Senate. Because there was no vice president, Wade would become president if Johnson were thrown out.

Ultimately, despite intense pressure, seven Republicans risked political suicide by voting with the Democrats against removal, and the Senate failed by one vote to convict Johnson. In so doing, they set a precedent: Their vote discouraged impeachment on political grounds for decades to come. But the anti-Johnson forces had also achieved their goal: Andrew Johnson had no future as president. Republicans in Congress, meanwhile, pursued their last major Reconstruction objective: to guarantee black male suffrage.

The Fifteenth Amendment and the Question of Woman Suffrage, 1869–1870

Black suffrage was the linchpin of congressional Reconstruction, since only with the black vote could Republicans secure control of the ex-Confederate states. The Reconstruction Act of 1867 had forced southern states to enfranchise black men in order to reenter the Union, but much of the North rejected black suffrage. The **Fifteenth Amendment,** proposed by Congress in 1869, sought to protect black suffrage in the South, and to enfranchise northern and border-state blacks, who would presumably vote Republican. The amendment prohibited the denial of suffrage by the states to any citizen on account of "race, color, or previous condition of servitude."

Fifteenth Amendment
Prevented states from denying the vote to any citizen on account of "race, color, or previous condition of servitude"

Democrats opposed the amendment on the grounds that it violated states' rights, but they did not control enough states to defeat the amendment, and it was ratified in 1870 (see Table 16.1). Some southerners appreciated the amendment's omissions: as a Richmond newspaper pointed out, it had "loopholes through which

Table 16.1 The Reconstruction Amendments

Amendment and Date of Congressional Passage	Provisions	Ratification
Thirteenth (January 1865)	Prohibited slavery in the United States	December 1865
Fourteenth (June 1866)	Defined citizenship to include all persons born or naturalized in the United States Provided proportional loss of congressional representation for any state that denied suffrage to any of its male citizens Disqualified prewar officeholders who supported the Confederacy from state or national office Repudiated the Confederate debt	July 1868, after Congress made ratification a prerequisite for readmission of ex-Confederate states to the Union
Fifteenth (February 1869)	Prohibited the denial of suffrage because of race, color, or previous condition of servitude	March 1870; ratification required of Virginia, Texas, Mississippi, and Georgia for readmission to the Union

a coach and four horses can be driven." For example, the Fifteenth Amendment neither guaranteed black officeholding nor prohibited voting restrictions such as property requirements and literacy tests. Such restrictions ultimately were used to deny blacks the vote.

The debate over black suffrage drew new participants into the fray. Women's rights advocates tried to promote both black suffrage and woman suffrage, but Radical Republicans rejected any linkage between the two, preferring to concentrate on black suffrage. Supporters of women's rights were themselves divided. Frederick Douglass argued that black suffrage had to receive priority. "If the elective franchise is not extended to the Negro, he is dead," explained Douglass. "Woman has a thousand ways by which she can attach herself to the ruling power of the land that we have not." But women's rights leaders Elizabeth Cady Stanton and **Susan B. Anthony** disagreed. In their view, the Fourteenth Amendment had disabled women by including the word "male." If the Fifteenth Amendment did not include women, they emphasized, it would increase women's disadvantages.

The battle over black suffrage and the Fifteenth Amendment split women's rights advocates into two rival suffrage associations, both formed in 1869. The Boston-based American Woman Suffrage Association sought state-by-state suffrage, whereas the more radical National Woman Suffrage Association, based in New York and led by Stanton and Anthony, promoted a constitutional amendment for woman suffrage.

Throughout the 1870s, the rival woman suffrage associations vied for constituents. In 1869 and 1870, independent of the suffrage movement, two territories, Wyoming and Utah, enfranchised women. But suffragists failed to sway legislators elsewhere. When Susan B. Anthony mobilized

Susan B. Anthony Women's rights advocate whose National Woman Suffrage Association called for a federal women suffrage amendment

Checking In

- Lincoln's somewhat lenient plan for Reconstruction died with him.

- President Johnson's even more tolerant plan for Reconstruction infuriated Radical Republicans.

- Congress overrode presidential vetoes of Reconstruction measures such as the Freedmen's Bureau and passed its own harsher version of Reconstruction legislation.

- The Fourteenth Amendment defined citizenship and guaranteed equal protection under the law, and the Fifteenth Amendment guaranteed the right of freedmen, but not of women, to vote.

- The attempt to impeach Johnson on political grounds failed by a narrow margin.

about seventy women to try to vote nationwide in 1872, she was indicted, convicted, and fined. In 1875 the Supreme Court ruled that a state could deny women the right to vote. Divided and rebuffed, woman suffrage advocates braced for a long struggle.

By 1870, when the Fifteenth Amendment was ratified, Congress could look back on five years of achievement. Since the start of 1865, three constitutional amendments had broadened the scope of American democracy by abolishing slavery, expanding civil rights, and prohibiting the denial of suffrage on the basis of race. Congress had also readmitted the former Confederate states into the Union. But after 1868, congressional momentum slowed, and the theater of action shifted to the South, where tumultuous change occurred.

RECONSTRUCTION GOVERNMENTS

What impact did federal Reconstruction policy have on the former Confederacy and ex-Confederates?

During the unstable years of presidential Reconstruction, 1865–1867, the southern states had to create new governments, revive the war-torn economy, and face the impact of emancipation. Crises abounded. Cities and factories lay in rubble, plantation labor systems disintegrated, and racial tensions flared as freedmen organized to protest ill treatment and demand equal rights. Race riots erupted in major southern cities. In May 1866, white crowds attacked black veterans in Memphis and rampaged through black neighborhoods, killing forty-six people.

Congressional Reconstruction, supervised by federal troops, took effect in the spring of 1867. The Johnson regimes were dismantled and voters elected new state governments, which Republicans dominated. By 1868 most former Confederate states had rejoined the Union, and within two years the process was complete.

But Republican rule did not long endure in the South. Opposition from southern Democrats, the landowning elite, vigilantes, and most white voters proved insurmountable. Nevertheless, the governments formed under congressional Reconstruction were unique because black men, including former slaves, participated in them. Slavery had ended in other societies, too, but only in the United States had freedmen gained democratic political rights.

A New Electorate   The Reconstruction laws of 1867–1868 transformed the southern electorate by temporarily disfranchising 10 to 15 percent of potential white voters and by enfranchising more than 700,000 freed slaves. Black voters outnumbered whites by 100,000 overall and held voting majorities in five states.

This new electorate provided a base for the Republican Party, which had never existed in the South. To scornful Democrats, the Republicans comprised three types of scoundrels: northern "carpetbaggers" who had come south for wealth and power; southern "scalawags," poor and ignorant whites, who sought to profit from Republican rule; and hordes of uneducated freedmen, who were easily manipulated.

Crossing class and racial lines, the hastily established Republican Party was in fact a loose coalition of diverse factions with often contradictory goals.

To northerners who moved south after the war, the former Confederacy was an undeveloped region, ripe with possibility. The carpetbaggers included many former Union soldiers who hoped to buy land, open factories, build railroads, or simply enjoy the warmer climate. Holding almost one in three state offices, they wielded disproportionate political power.

Although a handful of scalawags were old Whigs, most were small farmers from the mountain regions of North Carolina, Georgia, Alabama, and Arkansas. As former Unionists who had owned no slaves and felt no loyalty to the landowning elite, they sought to improve their economic position and lacked commitment to black rights. Most came from regions with small black populations and cared little whether blacks voted or not. Scalawags held the most political offices during Reconstruction, but they proved the least stable element of the southern Republican coalition; eventually, many drifted back to the Democratic fold.

Freedmen, the backbone of southern Republicanism, provided eight out of ten Republican votes. They sought land, education, civil rights, and political equality, and remained loyal Republicans. Although Reconstruction governments depended on

RADICAL·MEMBERS
OF THE S⁰. CA. LEGISLATURE.

The Museum of the Confederacy

Republicans in the South Carolina Legislature, ca. 1868
Only in South Carolina did blacks comprise a dominant majority in the legislature. This photographic collage of "Radical" legislators, black and white, suggests the extent of black representation. In 1874, blacks won the majority of seats in South Carolina's state senate as well.

African-American votes, freedmen held at most one in five political offices and constituted a legislative majority only in South Carolina, whose population was more than 60 percent black. A mere 6 percent of southern members of the House were African-American, and almost 50 percent came from South Carolina. No blacks became governor, and only two served in the U.S. Senate—the same number as served during the twentieth century.

Black officeholders on the state level formed a political elite. They often differed from black voters in background, education, and wealth. Many were literate blacks who had been free before the Civil War. In the South Carolina legislature, most black members came from large towns and cities; many had spent time in the North; and some were well-off property owners or even former slave owners. Color differences were evident as well: 43 percent of South Carolina's black legislators were of mixed race, compared to just 7 percent of the state's black population.

Black officials and black voters often had different priorities. Most freedmen cared mainly about their economic future, especially about acquiring land; black officeholders cared most about attaining equal rights. Still, both groups shared high expectations and prized enfranchisement. "We'd walk fifteen miles in wartime to find out about the battle," a Georgia freedman declared. "We can walk fifteen miles and more to find how to vote."

Republican Rule

Large numbers of African-Americans participated in government for the first time in the state constitutional conventions of 1867–1868. The South Carolina convention had a black majority, and in Louisiana half the delegates were freedmen. These conventions forged democratic changes. Delegates abolished property qualifications for officeholding, made many appointive offices elective, and established universal manhood suffrage.

However, no state instituted land reform. When proposals for land confiscation and redistribution arose at the state conventions, they fell to defeat, as they had in Congress. Hoping to attract northern investment, southern Republicans hesitated to threaten property rights or to adopt land-reform measures that northern Republicans had rejected. South Carolina did set up a commission to buy land and make it available to freedmen, and several states changed their tax structures to force uncultivated land onto the market, but in no case was ex-Confederate land confiscated.

Once civil power shifted to the new state governments, Republican administrations began ambitious programs of public works. They built roads and bridges, approved railroad bonds, and funded institutions to care for orphans, the insane, and the disabled. They also expanded state bureaucracies and formed state militias in which blacks often were heavily represented. Finally, they created public-school systems, which were almost nonexistent in the South until then. These reforms cost millions, and taxes skyrocketed. Although northern tax rates still exceeded southern tax rates, southerners, particularly landowners, resented the new levies.

To Reconstruction's foes, Republican rule was wasteful and corrupt, the "most stupendous system of organized robbery in history." Indeed, corruption did permeate some state governments, as in Louisiana and South Carolina. The main profiteers were government officials who accepted bribes and railroad promoters who doled them out. But neither group was exclusively Republican. In fact, corruption increasingly characterized government *nationally* in these years and was both more flagrant and more lucrative in the North.

Counterattacks

Ex-Confederates spoke with dread about black enfranchisement and the "horror of Negro domination." As soon as congressional Reconstruction took effect, former Confederates campaigned to undermine it. Democratic newspapers called Louisiana's constitution "the work of ignorant Negroes cooperating with a gang of white adventurers."

Democrats delayed mobilization until the southern states were readmitted to the Union, and then swung into action. At first, they pursued African-American votes; however, when that failed they tried other tactics. In every southern state the Democrats contested elections, backed dissident Republican factions, elected some Democratic legislators, and lured scalawags away from the Republican Party.

Vigilante efforts to reduce black votes bolstered Democratic campaigns to win white ones. Antagonism toward free blacks, long a motif in southern life, resurged after the war. In 1865, Freedmen's Bureau agents itemized a variety of outrages against blacks, including shooting, murder, rape, arson, roasting, and "inhuman beating." Vigilante groups sprang up in all parts of the former Confederacy, but one organization rose to dominance. In the spring of 1866, six young Confederate war veterans in Tennessee formed a social club, the **Ku Klux Klan,** distinguished by elaborate rituals, hooded costumes, and secret passwords. New Klan dens spread rapidly. By the election of 1868, the Klan had become a terrorist movement directed against potential African-American voters.

Ku Klux Klan Organization that used terrorism to prevent freedmen from voting and to reestablish white supremacy

The Klan sought to suppress black voting, reestablish white supremacy, and topple the Reconstruction governments. It attacked Freedmen's Bureau officials, white Republicans, black militia units, economically successful blacks, and black voters. Concentrated in areas where white and black populations were most evenly balanced and racial tensions were greatest, Klan dens adapted their tactics to local

The Ku Klux Klan

Disguised in long white robes and hoods, Ku Klux Klansmen sometimes claimed to be the ghosts of Confederate soldiers. The Klan, which spread rapidly after 1867, sought to end Republican rule, restore white supremacy, and obliterate, in one southern editor's words, "the preposterous and wicked dogma of Negro equality."

Tennessee State Archives

Enforcement Acts Series of laws to protect black voters passed in 1870 and 1871; banned the Klan and similar groups

CHECKING IN

- The Republican Party, with a large bloc of freedmen, temporarily dominated the South.
- Reconstruction governments instituted such reforms as public-school systems.
- To many southern whites, such reforms seemed a costly waste of money, aggravated by government corruption.
- The Ku Klux Klan and other groups used terrorism against freedmen and their white supporters in an effort to prevent black voting and restore white supremacy.
- The federal government passed laws against such activities but left too few troops in place to protect freedmen.

conditions. In Mississippi, the Klan targeted black schools; in Alabama, it concentrated on Republican officeholders. Some Democrats denounced Klan members as "cutthroats and riff-raff." But Klansmen included prominent ex-Confederates, among them General Nathan Bedford Forrest, the leader of the 1864 Fort Pillow massacre (see p. 354). Vigilantism united southern whites of different social classes; in areas where the Klan was inactive, other vigilante groups took its place.

Republican legislatures passed laws to outlaw vigilantism. However, when state militias could not enforce the laws, state officials turned to the federal government for help. Between May 1870 and February 1871 Congress passed three **Enforcement Acts,** each progressively more stringent. The First Enforcement Act protected black voters. The Second Enforcement Act provided for federal supervision of southern elections, and the Third Enforcement Act, or Ku Klux Klan Act, authorized the use of federal troops and the suspension of *habeas corpus* (HAY-bee-us KORP-us), the requirement that cause for detaining a prisoner be shown in court. Although thousands were arrested under the Enforcement Acts, most terrorists escaped conviction.

By 1872 the federal government had effectively suppressed the Klan, but vigilantism had served its purpose. A large military presence in the South could have protected black rights, but instead federal troop levels fell steadily. Congress allowed the Freedmen's Bureau to die in 1869; the Enforcement Acts thus became dead letters. The battle over Reconstruction was in essence a battle over the implications of emancipation, and it had begun as soon as the war ended.

THE IMPACT OF EMANCIPATION

How did the newly freed slaves reshape their lives after emancipation?

"The master he says we are all free," a South Carolina slave declared in 1865. "But it don't mean we is white. And it don't mean we is equal." Yet despite the daunting handicaps they faced—illiteracy, lack of property, meager skills—most former slaves found the exhilaration of freedom overwhelming. Emancipation gave them the right to their own labor and a new sense of autonomy. Under Reconstruction, they sought to cast off white control and shed the vestiges of slavery.

Confronting Freedom For former slaves, liberty meant mobility. Some moved out of the slave quarters; others fled the plantation completely. "The moment they see an opportunity to improve themselves, they will move on," diarist Mary Chesnut observed.

Emancipation stirred waves of migration within the former Confederacy. Some slaves headed to the Deep South, where desperate planters paid higher wages for labor, but more moved to towns and cities. Urban black populations doubled or tripled after emancipation. The desire to find lost family members prompted much of the movement. Parents sought children who had been sold; husbands and wives who had been separated reunited; and families reclaimed youngsters from masters' homes. The Freedmen's Bureau helped former slaves to get information about missing relatives and to travel to find them. Bureau agents also tried to resolve conflicts that arose when spouses who had been separated under slavery married other people.

However, reunification efforts often failed. Some fugitive slaves had died during the war or were untraceable. Still, success stories abounded. Once reunited, freed blacks quickly legalized unions formed under slavery, sometimes in mass ceremonies of up to seventy couples. Legal marriage had a tangible impact on family life. Men asserted themselves as household heads; wives of able-bodied men often withdrew from the work force to care for homes and families. "When I married my wife, I married her to wait on me and she has got all she can do right here for me and the children," a Tennessee freedman explained.

Severe labor shortages followed immediately after the war because women had made up half of all field workers. Still, by Reconstruction's end, many black women had returned to agricultural work as part of sharecropper families. Others took work in cities as laundresses, cooks, and domestic servants. (White women often sought employment as well, for the war had reduced the supply of future husbands and left families destitute.) However, former slaves continued to view stable, independent domestic life, especially the right to rear their own children, as a major blessing of freedom.

African-American Institutions

The freed blacks' desire for independence also led to the growth of black churches. The African Methodist Episcopal Church, founded by Philadelphia blacks in the 1790s, gained thousands of new southern members. Negro Baptist churches, their roots often in plantation "praise meetings" organized by slaves, sprouted everywhere.

Black churches offered a fervent, participatory experience. They also provided relief, raised funds for schools, and supported Republican policies. Black ministers assumed leading political roles until Reconstruction's end and then remained the main pillars of authority within African-American communities.

Schools, too, played a crucial role for freedmen as the ex-slaves sought literacy for themselves and, above all, for their children. At emancipation, blacks organized their own schools, which the Freedmen's Bureau soon supervised. Northern philanthropic societies paid the wages of instructors, about half of them women. In 1869, the bureau reported more than four thousand black schools were established in the former Confederacy. Within three years, each southern state had a public-school system, at least in principle, generally with separate schools for blacks and whites. The Freedmen's Bureau helped to establish Howard, Atlanta, and Fisk universities (1866–1867) and Hampton Institute (1868).

However, black education remained limited. Few rural blacks could reach the freedmen's schools located in towns. Underfunded black public schools held classes only for short seasons and sometimes drew vigilante attacks. At the end of Reconstruction, more than 80 percent of the black population was still illiterate, though literacy rose steadily among youngsters.

Hampton Institute
Founded in 1868, Hampton Institute in southeastern Virginia welcomed newly freed African-Americans to vocational programs in agriculture, teacher training, and homemaking. These students, photographed at the school's entrance around 1870, were among Hampton's first classes.

Civil Rights Act of 1875 Called for the desegregation of transportation facilities, juries, and public accommodations; invalidated by the Supreme Court in 1883

School segregation and other forms of racial separation were taken for granted. Even after the invalidation of the black codes, segregation continued on streetcars, steamboats, and trains as well as in churches, theaters, and restaurants. In honor of the late Republican senator Charles Sumner, Congress passed the **Civil Rights Act of 1875,** banning segregation except in schools. But in the 1883 *Civil Rights Cases,* the Supreme Court threw the law out. The Fourteenth Amendment did not prohibit discrimination by individuals, the Court ruled, only that perpetrated by the state.

White southerners rejected the prospect of racial integration, which they insisted would lead to racial amalgamation. "If we have social equality, we shall have intermarriage," one white southerner contended, "and if we have intermarriage, we shall degenerate." Urban blacks sometimes challenged segregation practices, but most freed blacks were less interested in "social equality" than in black liberty and community. Moreover, the new postwar elite—teachers, ministers, and politicians—served

Archival and Museum Collection/Hampton University

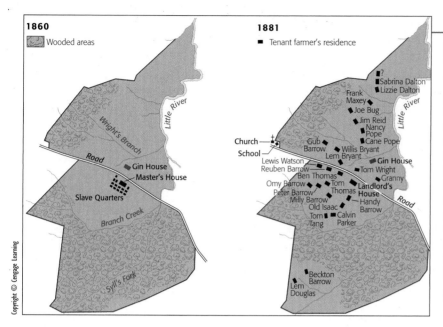

1860
🌳 Wooded areas

1881
■ Tenant farmer's residence

Wright's Branch

Little River

Road

Gin House

Master's House

Slave Quarters

Branch Creek

Syll's Fork

Copyright © Cengage Learning

Sabrina Dalton
Lizzie Dalton
Frank Maxey
Joe Bug
Jim Reid
Nancy Pope
Cane Pope
Church
Gub Barrow
Willis Bryant
School
Lem Bryant
Lewis Watson
Reuben Barrow
Gin House
Ben Thomas
Tom Wright
Granny
Omy Barrow
Tom Thomas
Landlord's House
Peter Barrow
Milly Barrow
Handy Barrow
Old Isaac
Tom Tang
Calvin Parker
Little River
Road
Beckton Barrow
Lem Douglas

Map 16.2   The Barrow Plantation, 1860 and 1881

The transformation of the Barrow plantation in Oglethorpe County, Georgia, illustrates the striking changes in southern agriculture during Reconstruction. After the war, the former slaves signed labor contracts with owner David Crenshaw Barrow and worked in squads under a hired foreman. But the freedman disliked the arrangement. By 1881, the old plantation had been subdivided into tenant farms of around thirty acres each. One out of four families was named Barrow.

💻 Interactive Map

black constituencies and thus had a vested interest in separate black institutions. Rural blacks, too, widely preferred all-black institutions, as they had little desire to mix with whites. In fact, they sought freedom from white control. Above all, they wanted to secure personal independence by acquiring land.

Land, Labor, and Sharecropping

"The sole ambition of the freedman," a New Englander wrote from South Carolina in 1865, "appears to be to become the owner of a little piece of land, there to erect a humble home, and to dwell in peace and security, at his own free will and pleasure." Indeed, to freed blacks everywhere, "forty acres and a mule" (a phrase that originated during the war as General William T. Sherman set aside land on the South Carolina Sea Islands for black settlement) promised emancipation from plantation labor, white domination, and cotton, the "slave crop."

However, the freedmen's visions of landownership failed to materialize, for, as we have seen, large-scale land reform never occurred. Some freedmen obtained land with the help of the Freedmen's Bureau or sometimes by pooling resources (see Map 16.2). In 1866, Congress passed the Southern Homestead Act, which set aside 44 million acres of public land in five southern states for freedmen and loyal whites. About four thousand blacks resettled on homesteads under the law. But the soil was poor and few former slaves had the resources to survive until their first harvest (poor whites fared little better). By Reconstruction's end, only a small minority of former slaves owned working farms. In Georgia in 1876, for example, blacks controlled a mere 1.3 percent of total acreage. Without large-scale land reform, obstacles to black landownership remained overwhelming.

What were these obstacles? First, freedmen lacked capital to buy land or tools. Furthermore, white southerners generally opposed selling land to blacks. Most important, planters sought to preserve a black labor force and took steps to ensure that black labor would remain available on the plantations.

During presidential Reconstruction, southern state legislatures tried to curb black mobility and preserve a captive labor force through the black codes. Under labor contracts in effect in 1865–1866, freedmen received wages, housing, food, and clothing in exchange for field work. With cash scarce, wages usually took the form of a very small share of the crop, often one-eighth or less, divided among the entire plantation work force. Freedmen's Bureau agents promoted the new labor system, seeing wage labor as a step toward economic independence. "You must begin at the bottom of the ladder and climb up," Freedmen's Bureau head O. O. Howard exhorted a group of Louisiana freedmen in 1865.

Problems arose immediately. Freedmen disliked the new wage system, especially the use of gang labor, which resembled the work pattern under slavery. Moreover, postwar planters had to compete for labor even as many scorned African-American workers as lazy or inefficient. One landowner estimated that workers accomplished only "two-fifths of what they did under the old system." As productivity fell, so did land values. Plummeting cotton prices and poor harvests compounded planters' woes. By 1867, an agricultural impasse had been reached: Landowners lacked labor, and freedmen lacked land.

sharecropping System in which a tenant farmer paid a share of the crop as rent to the landowner

Southerners began experimenting with new labor schemes, including the division of plantations into small tenancies. **Sharecropping,** the most widespread arrangement, evolved as a compromise. Under this system, landowners subdivided large plantations into farms of thirty to fifty acres, which they rented to freedmen under annual leases for a share of the crop, usually half. Freedmen preferred share-cropping to wage labor because it represented a step toward independence. Planters, meanwhile, retained control of their land. The most productive land thus remained in the hands of a small group of owners; in effect, sharecropping helped to preserve the planter elite.

Although the wage system continued on sugar and rice plantations, by 1870 the plantation tradition had yielded to sharecropping in the Cotton South (see Map 16.3). A severe depression in 1873 drove many blacks and independent white farmers into sharecropping. By 1880, 80 percent of the land in the cotton-producing states had been subdivided into tenancies, most of it farmed by share-croppers, both white and black. In fact, white sharecroppers outnumbered black, although a higher proportion of southern blacks, about 75 percent, were involved in the system. Changes in marketing and finance, meanwhile, made the sharecroppers' lot increasingly precarious.

Toward a Crop-Lien Economy

The postwar South's hundreds of thousands of tenant farmers and sharecroppers needed a local credit system to see them through the growing season until they could harvest their crops. Rural merchants advanced supplies to tenants and sharecroppers on credit and sold their crops to wholesalers. Because renters had no property to use as collateral, merchants secured their loans with a lien (leen), or claim, on each farmer's next crop. Exorbitant interest rates of 50 percent or more quickly forced many tenants and sharecroppers into a cycle of indebtedness. The sharecropper

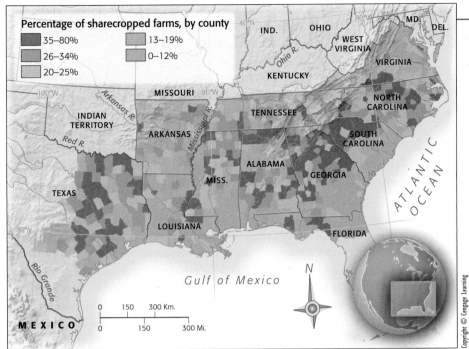

Percentage of sharecropped farms, by county
- 35–80%
- 26–34%
- 20–25%
- 13–19%
- 0–12%

Map 16.3 Southern Sharecropping, 1880

The depressed economy of the late 1870s caused poverty and debt, increased tenancy among white farmers, and forced many renters, black and white, into sharecropping. By 1880, the sharecropping system pervaded most southern counties, with highest concentrations in the Cotton Belt from South Carolina to eastern Texas.

■ Interactive Map

might well owe part of his crop to the landowner and another part (the rest of his crop, or more) to the merchant. Illiterate tenants who lost track of their financial arrangements often fell prey to unscrupulous merchants. Once a tenant's real or alleged debts exceeded the value of his crop, he was tied to the land, to cotton, and to sharecropping.

By Reconstruction's end, sharecropping and crop liens had bound the South to staple crops, such as cotton, and prevented crop diversification. Plunging prices, soil depletion, land erosion, and outmoded equipment soon locked much of the South into a cycle of poverty. Trapped in perpetual debt, tenant farmers became the chief victims of the new agricultural order. Cotton remained the only survival route open to poor farmers, regardless of race, but low income from cotton locked them into sharecropping and crop liens. African-American tenants saw their political rights dwindle as rapidly as their hopes for economic freedom. When Reconstruction ended, neither state governments nor the national government offered them protection, for northern politicians were preoccupied with their own problems.

CHECKING IN

- Tens of thousands of freedmen sought missing family members, and former slaves hastened to legalize the marriages they had made under slavery.

- Blacks formed their own communities, churches, and schools as segregation became firmly established in the South.

- Few former slaves achieved land ownership, and sharecropping became the dominant form of agricultural labor for blacks and many poor whites.

- Without economic status, blacks quickly saw their political rights erode.

NEW CONCERNS IN THE NORTH, 1868–1876

Why did northern concern about Reconstruction begin to wane?

The nomination of Ulysses S. Grant for president in 1868 launched a chaotic era in national politics. Grant's two terms in office saw political scandals, a party revolt, a massive depression, and a steady retreat from Reconstruction. By the mid-1870s, northern voters cared more about unemployment, labor unrest, and currency problems than about the "southern question." Responsive to the shift in popular mood, Republicans turned their backs on the freedmen.

Grantism

Republicans had good reason to nominate General Grant. A war hero, he was endorsed by veterans and admired throughout the North. To oppose Grant, the Democrats nominated New York Governor Horatio Seymour, arch-critic of the Lincoln administration in wartime and now a foe of Reconstruction. Grant ran on personal popularity more than issues. Although he carried all but eight states, the popular vote was close; in the South, newly enfranchised freedmen provided Grant's margin of victory.

A strong leader in war, Grant proved to be a passive president with little political skill. Many of his cabinet appointees were mediocre if not unscrupulous; scandals plagued his administration. In 1869 financier Jay Gould and his partner Jim Fisk tried to corner the gold market with the help of Grant's brother-in-law. When gold prices tumbled, investors were ruined and Grant's reputation suffered. Near the end of Grant's first term, his vice president, Schuyler Colfax, got caught up in the Crédit Mobilier (CRAY-dee MOH-bill-yay) scandal, a fraudulent scheme to skim off the profits of the Union Pacific Railroad. In 1875, Grant's personal secretary, Orville Babcock, was found guilty of accepting bribes from the "whiskey ring," distillers who bribed federal agents to avoid paying millions in taxes. And in 1876, voters learned that Grant's secretary of war, William E. Belknap, had taken bribes to sell lucrative Indian trading posts in Oklahoma.

Boss Tweed

Thomas Nast's cartoons in *Harper's Weekly* helped topple New York Democratic boss William M. Tweed, who, with his associates, embodied corruption on a large scale. The Tweed Ring had granted lucrative franchises to companies they controlled, padded construction bills, practiced graft and extortion, and exploited every opportunity to plunder the city's funds.

Brown Brothers

Harper's Weekly, 1871

Although uninvolved in the scandals, Grant defended his subordinates. To his critics, "Grantism" came to stand for fraud, bribery, and political corruption—evils that spread far beyond Washington. The New York City press revealed in 1872 that Democratic boss William M. Tweed, the leader of Tammany Hall, led a ring that had looted the city treasury and collected millions in kickbacks and payoffs. When Mark Twain and Charles Dudley Warner published their satiric novel *The Gilded Age* in 1873, readers recognized the book's speculators, self-promoters, and opportunists as familiar figures in public life. (The term "Gilded Age" has subsequently been used to refer to the decades from the 1870s to the 1890s.)

Grant did enjoy some foreign-policy successes. In 1872, his administration engineered the settlement of the *Alabama* claims with Britain. To compensate for damage done by Confederate-owned but British-built ships, an international tribunal awarded the United States $15.5 million. But Grant's administration faltered when it tried to add non-adjacent territory to the United States. In 1867, Johnson's secretary of state, William H. Seward, had negotiated a treaty to buy Alaska from Russia at the bargain price of $7.2 million. The purchase had rekindled expansionists' hopes, and in 1870, Grant decided to annex the eastern half of the Caribbean island of Santo Domingo (today called the Dominican Republic). Annexation, Grant believed, would promote Caribbean trade and provide a haven for persecuted southern blacks. Despite speculators' hopes for windfall profits, the Senate rejected the annexation treaty and further diminished Grant's reputation.

As the election of 1872 approached, dissident Republicans feared that "Grantism" would ruin the party. Former Radicals and other Republicans left out of Grant's "Great Barbecue" formed their own party, the **Liberal Republicans.**

Liberal Republicans Dissident political faction that opposed Grant and called for civil service reform and an end to congressional Reconstruction in the South

The Liberals' Revolt

The Liberal Republican revolt split the party and undermined Reconstruction. (The label "liberal" at the time meant support for economic doctrines such as free trade, the gold standard, and the law of supply and demand.) Liberals demanded civil service reform to bring the "best men" into government. They demanded an end to "bayonet rule" in the South and argued that blacks, now enfranchised, could fend for themselves. Corruption in government posed a greater threat than Confederate resurgence, the Liberals claimed, and they demanded that the "best men" in the South, ex-Confederates barred from holding office, be returned to government.

For president, the new party nominated *New York Tribune* editor Horace Greeley, who had inconsistently supported both a stringent Reconstruction policy and leniency toward former rebels. The Democrats endorsed Greeley as well; their campaign slogan was "Anything to Beat Grant." Horace Greeley campaigned so diligently that he worked himself to death making speeches from the back of a train, and died a few weeks after the election.

Grant carried 56 percent of the popular vote and won the electoral vote handily. But division among Republicans affected Reconstruction. To deprive the Liberals of a campaign issue, Grant Republicans in Congress passed the Amnesty Act, which allowed all but a few hundred ex-Confederate officials to hold office. In Grant's second term, Republican desires to discard the "southern question" mounted as depression gripped the nation.

The Panic of 1873

The postwar years brought accelerated industrialization, rapid economic growth, and frantic speculation as investors rushed to take advantage of seemingly boundless opportunities. Railroads led the speculative boom. The transcontinental line reached completion in 1869 (see Chapter 17). By 1873, almost four hundred railroads crisscrossed the Northeast. In addition to transforming the economy, the railroad boom led entrepreneurs to overspeculate, with drastic results.

In 1869 Philadelphia banker Jay Cooke took over a new transcontinental line, the Northern Pacific. Northern Pacific securities sold briskly for several years, but in 1873 construction costs outran bond sales. In September, Cooke defaulted on his obligations, and his bank, the largest in the nation, shut down. A financial panic began; other firms collapsed, as did the stock market. The Panic of 1873 plunged the nation into a five-year depression. Within two years, eighteen thousand businesses went bankrupt; 3 million people were unemployed by 1878. Wage cuts struck those still employed; labor protests mounted; and industrial violence spread. The depression of the 1870s revealed that conflicts born of industrialization had replaced sectional divisions.

The depression also fed a dispute over currency that had begun in 1865. During the Civil War, Americans had used greenbacks, a paper currency not backed by a specific weight in gold. "Sound money" supporters demanded the withdrawal of greenbacks from circulation as a means of stabilizing the currency. Their opponents, such as farmers and manufacturers dependent on easy credit who were known as "easy money" advocates, wanted to expand the currency by issuing additional greenbacks. The deepening depression created even more demand for easy money. The issue divided both major parties and was compounded by another one: how to repay the federal debt.

In wartime, the Union government had borrowed astronomical sums through the sale of war bonds. Bondholders wanted repayment in "coin," gold or silver, even though many of them had paid for the bonds in greenbacks. The Public Credit Act of 1869 promised payment in coin. Senator John Sherman, the author of the Public Credit Act, guided legislation through Congress that defined "coin" as gold only and swapped old short-term bonds for new ones payable over the next generation. Sherman's Specie Resumption Act of 1875 promised to put the nation back on the gold standard by 1879. His measures preserved the public credit, the currency, and Republican unity.

However, Sherman's measures did not satisfy the Democrats, who gained control of the House in 1875. Many Democrats and some Republicans demanded the restoration of the silver dollar in order to expand the currency and relieve the depression. The Bland-Allison Act of 1878 partially restored silver coinage by requiring the government to buy and coin several million dollars' worth of silver each month. In 1876, other expansionists formed the **Greenback Party,** which adopted the debtors' cause and fought to keep greenbacks in circulation, though with little success. As the depression receded in 1879, the clamor for "easy money" subsided, only to return in the 1890s (see Chapter 20). The controversial, but unresolved, "money question" of the 1870s gave politicians and voters another reason to forget about the South.

Greenback Party "Easy money" advocates who favored continued issuance of greenbacks and the free coinage of silver

Reconstruction and the Constitution

The Supreme Court of the 1870s also played a role in weakening northern support for Reconstruction as new constitutional questions surfaced. First, would the Court support laws to protect freedmen's rights? The decision in *Ex Parte Milligan* (1866) had suggested not. In *Milligan,* the Court had ruled that a military commission could not try civilians in areas where civilian courts were functioning. Thus, special military courts to enforce the Supplementary Freedmen's Bureau Act were doomed. Second, would the Court sabotage the congressional Reconstruction plan, as Republicans feared? In *Texas v. White* (1869), the Court had let Reconstruction stand, ruling that Congress had the power to ensure each state a republican form of government.

However, in the 1870s, the Court backed away from Reconstruction. In the *Slaughterhouse* case of 1873, the Court considered whether Louisiana had violated the constitutional rights of butchers excluded from a slaughterhouse monopoly established by the state in 1869. In ruling against the butchers, the Court ruled that the Fourteenth Amendment protected only the rights of *national* citizenship, such as the right to interstate travel, but not those rights that fell to citizens through *state* citizenship. The *Slaughterhouse* decision vitiated the intent of the Fourteenth Amendment—to secure freedmen's rights against state encroachment.

The Supreme Court again backed away from Reconstruction in two cases in 1876 involving the Enforcement Act of 1870, which were enacted to protect black suffrage. In *United States v. Reese* and *United States v. Cruikshank,* the Supreme Court undercut the act's effectiveness. Continuing its retreat from Reconstruction, the Supreme Court in 1883 invalidated both the Civil Rights Act of 1875 and the Ku Klux Klan Act of 1871. These decisions cumulatively dismantled the Reconstruction policies that Republicans had sponsored after the war and confirmed rising northern sentiment that Reconstruction's egalitarian goals could not be enforced.

Republicans in Retreat

The Republicans gradually disengaged from Reconstruction, beginning with the election of Grant as president in 1868. Grant believed in decentralized government and hesitated to assert federal authority in local and state affairs.

In the 1870s, Republican idealism waned. The Liberal Republican revolt of 1872 eroded what remained of radicalism. Commercial and industrial interests now dominated both wings of the party, and few Republicans wished to rekindle sectional strife. After the Democrats won the House in 1874, support for Reconstruction became a political liability.

By 1875, the Radical Republicans, so prominent in the 1860s, had vanished. Thaddeus Stevens and Charles Sumner were dead. Other Radicals had lost office or conviction. Republican leaders reported that voters were "sick of carpetbag government" and tiring of both the "southern question" and the "Negro question." It seemed pointless to continue the unpopular and expensive policy of military intervention in the South. Finally, Republican leaders and voters generally agreed that blacks, although worthy of freedom, were inferior to whites. The Republicans' retreat from Reconstruction set the stage for its demise in 1877.

CHECKING IN

- Grant's administration was riddled by corruption, mirroring politics in much of the country.
- The Panic of 1873 devastated the northern economy, plunging the nation into a deep depression.
- Through the 1870s the Supreme Court struck down basic legislation protecting freedmen's rights.
- Most Radical Republican leaders had died by the early 1870s, and commercial and industrial interests began to dominate the Republican Party.

RECONSTRUCTION ABANDONED, 1876–1877

What factors contributed to the end of Reconstruction in 1877?

"We are in a very hot political contest just now," a Mississippi planter wrote his daughter in 1875, "with a good prospect of turning out the carpetbag thieves by whom we have been robbed for the past six to ten years." Similar contests raged through the South in the 1870s, as the white resentment grew and Democratic influence surged. By 1876 Republican rule survived in only three southern states—South Carolina, Florida, and Louisiana. Democratic victories in state elections that year and political bargaining in Washington in 1877 ended what little remained of Reconstruction.

"Redeeming" the South

Republican collapse in the South accelerated after 1872. Congressional amnesty enabled virtually all ex-Confederate officials to regain office; divisions among the Republicans weakened their party's grip on the southern electorate; and attrition diminished Republican ranks. Carpetbaggers returned north or became Democrats. Scalawags deserted in even larger numbers. Tired of northern interference and seeing the possibility of "home rule," scalawags concluded that staying Republican meant going down with a sinking ship. Unable to win new white votes or retain the old ones, the fragile Republican coalition crumbled.

Meanwhile, Democrats mobilized once-apathetic white voters. The resurrected southern Democratic Party was divided. Businessmen who envisioned an industrialized "New South" opposed an agrarian faction called the Bourbons—the old planter elite. But Democrats shared one goal: to oust Republicans from office (see Table 16.2).

TABLE 16.2   THE DURATION OF REPUBLICAN RULE IN THE EX-CONFEDERATE STATES

FORMER CONFEDERATE STATES	READMISSION TO THE UNION UNDER CONGRESSIONAL RECONSTRUCTION	DEMOCRATS (CONSERVATIVES) GAIN CONTROL	DURATION OF REPUBLICAN RULE
Alabama	June 25, 1868	November 14, 1874	6½ years
Arkansas	June 22, 1868	November 10, 1874	6½ years
Florida	June 25, 1868	January 2, 1877	8½ years
Georgia	July 15, 1870	November 1, 1871	1 year
Louisiana	June 25, 1868	January 2, 1877	8½ years
Mississippi	February 23, 1870	November 3, 1875	5½ years
North Carolina	June 25, 1868	November 3, 1870	2 years
South Carolina	June 25, 1868	November 12, 1876	8 years
Tennessee	July 24, 1866[*]	October 4, 1869	3 years
Texas	March 30, 1870	January 14, 1873	3 years
Virginia	January 26, 1870	October 5, 1869[†]	0 years

Source: Reprinted by permission from John Hope Franklin, *Reconstruction After the Civil War* (Chicago: University of Chicago Press, 1962), 231.
[*]Admitted before the start of congressional Reconstruction.
[†]Democrats gained control before readmission.

Tactics varied by state. In several Deep South states Democrats resorted to violence. In Vicksburg, Mississippi, in 1874, rampaging whites slaughtered about three hundred blacks and terrorized thousands of potential voters. The "Mississippi plan" took effect in 1875; local Democratic clubs armed their members, who broke up Republican meetings, patrolled voter-registration locations, and marched through black areas. "The Republicans are paralyzed through fear and will not act," the anguished carpetbag governor of Mississippi wrote to his wife. "Why should I fight a hopeless battle?" In 1876, South Carolina's "Rifle Clubs" and "Red Shirts," armed groups that threatened Republicans, continued the scare tactics that had worked so well in Mississippi.

Terrorism did not completely squelch black voting, but it did deprive Republicans of enough black votes to win state elections. Throughout the South, economic pressures reinforced intimidation; labor contracts included clauses barring attendance at political meetings, and planters used eviction threats to keep sharecroppers in line. Together, intimidation and economic pressure succeeded.

"Redemption," the word that Democrats used to describe their return to power, brought sweeping changes. States rewrote constitutions, cut expenses, lowered taxes, eliminated social programs, limited the rights of tenants and sharecroppers, and shaped laws to ensure a stable black labor force. Legislatures restored vagrancy laws, strengthened crop-lien statutes, and rewrote criminal law. Local ordinances in heavily black counties often restricted hunting, fishing, gun carrying, and even dog ownership, drastically curtailing the ability of freedmen to live off the land. States passed severe laws against trespassing and theft; for example, stealing livestock or wrongly taking part of a crop became grand larceny with a penalty of up to five years at hard labor. By Reconstruction's end, black convict labor was commonplace.

For the freedmen, whose aspirations rose under Republican rule, redemption was devastating. The new laws, Tennessee blacks contended at an 1875 convention, would impose "a condition of servitude scarcely less degrading than that endured before the late civil war." In the late 1870s, as the political climate grew more oppressive, an "exodus" movement spread through the Deep South. Nearly fifteen thousand **"exodusters"** from the Deep South moved to Kansas and set up homesteads. But scarce resources left most of the freed slaves stranded. Mass movement of southern blacks to the North and Midwest would not gain momentum until the twentieth century.

"exodusters" Thousands of blacks who left the Deep South for homesteads in Kansas in the 1870s

The Election of 1876

By the autumn of 1876, with redemption almost complete, both parties moved to discard the animosity left by the war and Reconstruction. Republicans nominated Rutherford B. Hayes, three times Ohio's governor, for president. Untainted by the Grant-era scandals and popular with all factions in his party, Hayes presented himself as a "moderate" on southern policy. He favored "home rule" in the South and a guarantee of civil and political rights for all—two contradictory goals. The Democrats nominated Governor Samuel J. Tilden of New York, a political reformer known for his assaults on the Tweed Ring that had plundered New York City's treasury. Both candidates favored sound money, endorsed civil service reform, and decried corruption.

Tilden won the popular vote by a 3 percent margin and seemed destined to capture the 185 electoral votes needed for victory. But the Republicans challenged pro-Tilden returns from South Carolina, Florida, and Louisiana, and the Democrats challenged (on a technicality) one electoral vote from Oregon. Southern Republicans managed to throw out enough Democratic ballots in the contested states to proclaim Hayes the winner.

The nation now faced an unprecedented dilemma. Each party claimed victory, and each accused the other of fraud. In fact, both sets of southern votes were fraudulent: Republicans had discarded legitimate Democratic ballots, and Democrats had illegally prevented freedmen from voting. In January 1877, Congress created a special electoral commission—seven Democrats, seven Republicans, and one independent—to resolve the conflict. When the independent resigned, Congress replaced him with a Republican, and the commission gave Hayes the election by a vote of 8 to 7.

Congress now had to certify the new electoral vote. However, Democrats controlled the House, and some threatened to delay approval of the electoral vote. For many southern Democrats, regaining control of their states was far more important than preventing the election of a Republican president—*if* the new Republican administration would leave the South alone. Republican leaders, although sure of eventual triumph, were willing to bargain as well, for candidate Hayes desired not merely victory but southern approval. Informal negotiations followed, with both parties exchanging promises. Ohio Republicans and southern Democrats agreed that if Hayes won the election, he would remove federal troops from South Carolina and Louisiana, and Democrats could gain control of those states. Other negotiations led to the understanding that southerners would receive federal patronage, federal aid to railroads, and federal support for internal improvements. In turn, southerners promised to accept Hayes as president and to treat the freedmen fairly.

Congress thus ratified Hayes's election. Once in office, Hayes fulfilled some of the promises his Republican colleagues had made. He appointed a former Confederate as postmaster general and ordered federal troops who guarded the South Carolina and Louisiana statehouses back to their barracks. Republican rule toppled in Louisiana, South Carolina, and Florida. But some of the bargains struck in the **Compromise of 1877,** such as Democratic promises to treat southern blacks fairly, were forgotten, as were Hayes's pledges to ensure freedmen's rights. "When you turned us loose, you turned us loose to the sky, to the storm, to the whirlwind, and worst of all . . . to the wrath of our infuriated masters," Frederick Douglass charged at the 1876 Republican convention. "The question now is, do you mean to make good to us the promises in your Constitution?" By 1877 the answer was clear: "No."

Compromise of 1877 Deal that gave Republicans the presidency and restored Democrats to power in the South, ending Reconstruction

CHECKING IN

- The Republican collapse in the South accelerated after 1872.
- Democrats regained control of southern states.
- "Redeemers" ended reforms and limited or eliminated black rights.
- The election of 1876 resulted in challenges to some electoral votes and charges of fraud on both sides.
- The price of Republican victory in the election was the end of Reconstruction and the virtual abandonment of the freedmen.

Chapter Summary

How did Radical Republicans gain control of Reconstruction politics? (page 370)

Radical Republicans saw Johnson as too lenient on Reconstruction and passed a stringent congressional Reconstruction program over his veto. They even attempted to impeach the president for political reasons, but failed. The Fourteenth and Fifteenth Amendments, which Johnson opposed, were major triumphs for the Radicals.

KEY TERMS

Radical Republicans *(p. 370)*

Andrew Johnson *(p. 372)*

Presidential Reconstruction *(p. 372)*

What impact did federal Reconstruction policy have on the former Confederacy and ex-Confederates? (page 378)

Democrats and ex-Confederates were largely excluded from political power in the South, which fell to Republicans and freedmen. The Reconstruction governments passed costly reform measures, most of which were later abandoned or scaled back. Terrorist organizations such as the Ku Klux Klan flourished briefly. They were outlawed by the federal government but had already intimidated freedmen.

How did the newly freed slaves reshape their lives after emancipation? (page 382)

Former slaves sought missing family members, legalized marriages made under slavery, and created schools and churches in large numbers. However, without land reform most remained poor and ultimately were caught in the pernicious sharecropping system; their rights were soon eroded.

Why did northern concern about Reconstruction begin to wane? (page 387)

Other concerns soon began to preoccupy Republicans. Corruption, epitomized by the Grant administration, permeated the nation. The Panic of 1873 led to a major depression. The Supreme Court threw out important measures intended to protect freedmen's rights. Finally, with most Radical Republican leaders gone by the early 1870s, commercial and industrial interests began to dominate the Republican Party.

What factors contributed to the end of Reconstruction in 1877? (page 392)

Republican control of the South began to collapse in the early 1870s. As Democrats "redeemed" southern states, they curtailed reforms and eliminated black rights. The price of the Republican victory in the disputed presidential election of 1876 was the end of Reconstruction and the return of the South to Democratic control.

KEY TERMS continued

"black codes" *(p. 372)*
Civil Rights Act of 1866 *(p. 373)*
Fourteenth Amendment *(p. 373)*
Reconstruction Act of 1867 *(p. 374)*
Tenure of Office Act *(p. 375)*
Fifteenth Amendment *(p. 376)*
Susan B. Anthony *(p. 377)*
Ku Klux Klan *(p. 381)*
Enforcement Acts *(p. 382)*
Civil Rights Act of 1875 *(p. 384)*
sharecropping *(p. 386)*
Liberal Republicans *(p. 389)*
Greenback Party *(p. 390)*
"exodusters" *(p. 393)*
Compromise of 1877 *(p. 394)*

 **CourseMate**

Go to the CourseMate website at **www.cengagebrain.com** for additional study tools and review materials—including audio and video clips—for this chapter.

Appendix

DECLARATION OF INDEPENDENCE

IN CONGRESS, JULY 4, 1776

The Unanimous Declaration of the Thirteen United States of America

When, in the course of human events, it becomes necessary for one people to dissolve the political bands which have connected them with another, and to assume, among the powers of the earth, the separate and equal station to which the laws of nature and of nature's God entitle them, a decent respect to the opinions of mankind requires that they should declare the causes which impel them to the separation.

We hold these truths to be self-evident: That all men are created equal; that they are endowed by their Creator with certain unalienable rights; that among these are life, liberty, and the pursuit of happiness; that, to secure these rights, governments are instituted among men, deriving their just powers from the consent of the governed; that whenever any form of government becomes destructive of these ends, it is the right of the people to alter or to abolish it, and to institute new government, laying its foundation on such principles, and organizing its powers in such form, as to them shall seem most likely to effect their safety and happiness. Prudence, indeed, will dictate that governments long established should not be changed for light and transient causes; and accordingly all experience hath shown that mankind are more disposed to suffer, while evils are sufferable, than to right themselves by abolishing the forms to which they are accustomed. But when a long train of abuses and usurpations, pursuing invariably the same object, evinces a design to reduce them under absolute despotism, it is their right, it is their duty, to throw off such government, and to provide new guards for their future security. Such has been the patient sufferance of these colonies; and such is now the necessity which constrains them to alter their former systems of government. The history of the present King of Great Britain is a history of repeated injuries and usurpations, all having in direct object the establishment of an absolute tyranny over these states. To prove this, let facts be submitted to a candid world.

He has refused his assent to laws, the most wholesome and necessary for the public good.

He has forbidden his governors to pass laws of immediate and pressing importance, unless suspended in their operation till his assent should be obtained; and, when so suspended, he has utterly neglected to attend to them.

He has refused to pass other laws for the accommodation of large districts of people, unless those people would relinquish the right of representation in the legislature, a right inestimable to them, and formidable to tyrants only.

He has called together legislative bodies at places unusual, uncomfortable, and distant from the depository of their public records, for the sole purpose of fatiguing them into compliance with his measures.

He has dissolved representative houses repeatedly, for opposing, with manly firmness, his invasions on the rights of the people.

He has refused for a long time, after such dissolutions, to cause others to be elected; whereby the legislative powers, incapable of annihilation, have returned to the people at large for their exercise; the state remaining, in the mean time, exposed to all the dangers of invasions from without and convulsions within.

He has endeavored to prevent the population of these states; for that purpose obstructing the laws of naturalization of foreigners; refusing to pass others to encourage their migration hither, and raising the conditions of new appropriation of lands.

He has obstructed the administration of justice, by refusing his assent to laws for establishing judiciary powers.

He has made judges dependent on his will alone, for the tenure of their offices, and the amount and payment of their salaries.

He has erected a multitude of new offices, and sent hither swarms of officers to harass our people and eat out their substance.

He has kept among us, in times of peace, standing armies, without the consent of our legislatures.

He has affected to render the military independent of, and superior to, the civil power.

He has combined with others to subject us to a jurisdiction foreign to our constitution, and unacknowledged by our laws, giving his assent to their acts of pretended legislation:

For quartering large bodies of armed troops among us;

For protecting them, by a mock trial, from punishment for any murders which they should commit on the inhabitants of these states;

For cutting off our trade with all parts of the world;

For imposing taxes on us without our consent;

For depriving us, in many cases, of the benefits of trial by jury;

For transporting us beyond seas, to be tried for pretended offenses;

For abolishing the free system of English laws in a neighboring province, establishing therein an arbitrary government, and enlarging its boundaries, so as to render it at once an example and fit instrument for introducing the same absolute rule into these colonies;

For taking away our charters, abolishing our most valuable laws, and altering fundamentally the forms of our governments;

For suspending our own legislatures, and declaring themselves invested with power to legislate for us in all cases whatsoever.

He has abdicated government here, by declaring us out of his protection and waging war against us.

He has plundered our seas, ravaged our coasts, burned our towns, and destroyed the lives of our people.

He is at this time transporting large armies of foreign mercenaries to complete the works of death, desolation, and tyranny already begun with circumstances of cruelty and perfidy scarcely paralleled in the most barbarous ages, and totally unworthy of the head of a civilized nation.

He has constrained our fellow-citizens, taken captive on the high seas, to bear arms against their country, to become the executioners of their friends and brethren, or to fall themselves by their hands.

He has excited domestic insurrection among us, and has endeavored to bring on the inhabitants of our frontiers the merciless Indian savages, whose known rule of warfare is an undistinguished destruction of all ages, sexes, and conditions.

In every stage of these oppressions we have petitioned for redress in the most humble terms; our repeated petitions have been answered only by repeated injury. A prince, whose character is thus marked by every act which may define a tyrant, is unfit to be the ruler of a free people.

Nor have we been wanting in our attentions to our British brethren. We have warned them, from time to time, of attempts by their legislature to extend an unwarrantable jurisdiction over us. We have reminded them of the circumstances of our emigration and settlement here. We have appealed to their native justice and magnanimity; and we have conjured them by the ties of our common kindred, to disavow these usurpations, which would inevitably interrupt our connections and correspondence. They, too, have been deaf to the voice of justice and of consanguinity. We must, therefore, acquiesce in the necessity which denounces our separation, and hold them, as we hold the rest of mankind, enemies in war, in peace friends.

We, therefore, the representatives of the United States of America, in General Congress assembled, appealing to the Supreme Judge of the world for the rectitude of our intentions, do, in the name and by the authority of the good people of these colonies, solemnly publish and declare, that these United Colonies are, and of right ought to be, FREE AND INDEPENDENT STATES; that they are absolved from all allegiance to the British crown, and that all political connection between them and the state of Great Britain is, and ought to be, totally dissolved; and that, as free and independent states, they have full power to levy war, conclude peace, contract alliances, establish commerce, and do all other acts and things which independent states may of right do. And for the support of this declaration, with a firm reliance on the protection of Divine Providence, we mutually pledge to each other our lives, our fortunes, and our sacred honor.

JOHN HANCOCK *[President]*
[and fifty-five others]

CONSTITUTION OF THE UNITED STATES OF AMERICA

PREAMBLE

We the people of the United States, in order to form a more perfect union, establish justice, insure domestic tranquility, provide for the common defense, promote the general welfare, and secure the blessings of liberty to ourselves and our posterity, do ordain and establish this CONSTITUTION for the United States of America.

ARTICLE I

Section 1.   All legislative powers herein granted shall be vested in a Congress of the United States, which shall consist of a Senate and a House of Representatives.

Section 2.   The House of Representatives shall be composed of members chosen every second year by the people of the several States, and the electors in each State shall have the qualifications requisite for electors of the most numerous branch of the State Legislature.

No person shall be a Representative who shall not have attained to the age of twenty-five years, and been seven years a citizen of the United States, and who shall not, when elected, be an inhabitant of that State in which he shall be chosen.

Representatives and direct taxes shall be apportioned among the several States which may be included within this Union, according to their respective numbers, *which shall be determined by adding to the whole number of free persons, including those bound to service for a term of years and excluding Indians not taxed, three-fifths of all other persons.* The actual enumeration shall be made within three years after the first meeting of the Congress of the United States, and within every subsequent term of ten years, in such manner as they shall by law direct. The number of Representatives shall not exceed one for every thirty thousand, but each State shall have at least one Representative; *and until such enumeration shall be made, the State of New Hampshire shall be entitled to choose three, Massachusetts eight, Rhode Island and Providence Plantations one, Connecticut five, New York six, New Jersey four, Pennsylvania eight, Delaware one, Maryland six, Virginia ten, North Carolina five, South Carolina five, and Georgia three.*

When vacancies happen in the representation from any State, the Executive authority thereof shall issue writs of election to fill such vacancies.

Note: Passages no longer in effect are printed in italic type.

The House of Representatives shall choose their Speaker and other officers; and shall have the sole power of impeachment.

Section 3.   The Senate of the United States shall be composed of two Senators from each State, *chosen by the legislature thereof,* for six years; and each Senator shall have one vote.

Immediately after they shall be assembled in consequence of the first election, they shall be divided as equally as may be into three classes. The seats of the Senators of the first class shall be vacated at the expiration of the second year, of the second class at the expiration of the fourth year, and of the third class at the expiration of the sixth year, so that one-third may be chosen every second year; and if vacancies happen by resignation or otherwise, during the recess of the legislature of any State, the Executive thereof may make temporary appointments until the next meeting of the legislature, which shall then fill such vacancies.

No person shall be a Senator who shall not have attained to the age of thirty years, and been nine years a citizen of the United States, and who shall not, when elected, be an inhabitant of that State for which he shall be chosen.

The Vice President of the United States shall be President of the Senate, but shall have no vote, unless they be equally divided.

The Senate shall choose their other officers, and also a President *pro tempore,* in the absence of the Vice President, or when he shall exercise the office of the President of the United States.

The Senate shall have the sole power to try all impeachments. When sitting for that purpose, they shall be on oath or affirmation. When the President of the United States is tried, the Chief Justice shall preside: and no person shall be convicted without the concurrence of two-thirds of the members present.

Judgment in cases of impeachment shall not extend further than to removal from the office, and disqualification to hold and enjoy any office of honor, trust or profit under the United States; but the party convicted shall nevertheless be liable and subject to indictment, trial, judgment and punishment, according to law.

Section 4.   The times, places and manner of holding elections for Senators and Representatives shall be prescribed in each State by the legislature thereof; but the Congress may at any time by law make or alter such regulations, except as to the places of choosing Senators.

The Congress shall assemble at least once in every year, and such meeting *shall be on the first Monday in December, unless they shall by law appoint a different day.*

Section 5.   Each house shall be the judge of the elections, returns and qualifications of its own members, and a majority of each shall constitute a quorum to do business; but a smaller number may adjourn from day to day, and may be authorized to compel the attendance of absent members, in such manner, and under such penalties, as each house may provide.

Each house may determine the rules of its proceedings, punish its members for disorderly behavior, and with the concurrence of two-thirds, expel a member.

Each house shall keep a journal of its proceedings, and from time to time publish the same, excepting such parts as may in their judgment require secrecy; and the yeas and nays of the members of either house on any question shall, at the desire of one-fifth of those present, be entered on the journal.

Neither house, during the session of Congress, shall, without the consent of the other, adjourn for more than three days, nor to any other place than that in which the two houses shall be sitting.

Section 6.   The Senators and Representatives shall receive a compensation for their services, to be ascertained by law and paid out of the treasury of the United States. They shall in all cases except treason, felony and breach of the peace, be privileged from arrest during their attendance at the session of their respective houses, and in going to and returning from the same; and for any speech or debate in either house, they shall not be questioned in any other place.

No Senator or Representative shall, during the time for which he was elected, be appointed to any civil office under the authority of the United States, which shall have been created, or the emoluments whereof shall have been increased, during such time; and no person holding any office under the United States shall be a member of either house during his continuance in office.

Section 7.   All bills for raising revenue shall originate in the House of Representatives; but the Senate may propose or concur with amendments as on other bills.

Every bill which shall have passed the House of Representatives and the Senate, shall, before it become a law, be presented to the President of the United States; if he approve he shall sign it, but if not he shall return it with objections to that house in which it originated, who shall enter the objections at large on their journal, and proceed to reconsider it. If after such reconsideration two-thirds of that house shall agree to pass the bill, it shall be sent, together with the objections, to the other house, by which it shall likewise be reconsidered, and, if approved by two-thirds of that house, it shall become a law. But in all such cases the votes of both houses shall be determined by yeas and nays, and the names of the persons voting for and against the bill shall be entered on the journal of each house respectively. If any bill shall not be returned by the President within ten days (Sundays excepted) after it shall have been presented to him, the same shall be a law, in like manner as if he had signed it, unless the Congress by their adjournment prevent its return, in which case it shall not be a law.

Every order, resolution, or vote to which the concurrence of the Senate and House of Representatives may be necessary (except on a question of adjournment) shall be presented to the President of the United States; and before the same shall take effect, shall be approved by him, or being disapproved by him, shall be repassed by two-thirds of the Senate and House of Representatives, according to the rules and limitations prescribed in the case of a bill.

Section 8.   The Congress shall have power

To lay and collect taxes, duties, imposts, and excises, to pay the debts and provide for the common defense and general welfare of the United States; but all duties, imposts and excises shall be uniform throughout the United States;

To borrow money on the credit of the United States;

To regulate commerce with foreign nations, and among the several States, and with the Indian tribes;

To establish an uniform rule of naturalization, and uniform laws on the subject of bankruptcies throughout the United States;

To coin money, regulate the value thereof, and of foreign coin, and fix the standard of weights and measures;

To provide for the punishment of counterfeiting the securities and current coin of the United States;

To establish post offices and post roads;

To promote the progress of science and useful arts by securing for limited times to authors and inventors the exclusive right to their respective writings and discoveries;

To constitute tribunals inferior to the Supreme Court;

To define and punish piracies and felonies committed on the high seas and offenses against the law of nations;

To declare war, grant letters of marque and reprisal, and make rules concerning captures on land and water;

To raise and support armies, but no appropriation of money to that use shall be for a longer term than two years;

To provide and maintain a navy;

To make rules for the government and regulation of the land and naval forces;

To provide for calling forth the militia to execute the laws of the Union, suppress insurrections, and repel invasions;

To provide for organizing, arming, and disciplining the militia, and for governing such part of them as may be employed in the service of the United States, reserving to the States respectively the appointment of the officers, and the authority of training the militia according to the discipline prescribed by Congress;

To exercise exclusive legislation in all cases whatsoever, over such district (not exceeding ten miles square) as may, by cession of particular States, and the acceptance of Congress, become the seat of government of the United States, and to exercise like authority over all places purchased by the consent of the legislature of the State, in which the same shall be, for erection of forts, magazines, arsenals, dock-yards, and other needful buildings;—and

To make all laws which shall be necessary and proper for carrying into execution the foregoing powers, and all other powers vested by this Constitution in the government of the United States, or in any department or officer thereof.

Section 9. *The migration or importation of such persons as any of the States now existing shall think proper to admit shall not be prohibited by the Congress prior to the year 1808; but a tax or duty may be imposed on such importation, not exceeding $10 for each person.*

The privilege of the writ of habeas corpus shall not be suspended, unless when in cases of rebellion or invasion the public safety may require it.

No bill of attainder or ex post facto law shall be passed.

No capitation, or other direct, tax shall be laid, unless in proportion to the census or enumeration herein before directed to be taken.

No tax or duty shall be laid on articles exported from any State.

No preference shall be given by any regulation of commerce or revenue to the ports of one State over those of another; nor shall vessels bound to, or from, one State, be obliged to enter, clear, or pay duties in another.

No money shall be drawn from the treasury, but in consequence of appropriations made by law; and a regular statement and account of the receipts and expenditures of all public money shall be published from time to time.

No title of nobility shall be granted by the United States: and no person holding any office of profit or trust under them, shall, without the consent of the Congress, accept of any present, emolument, office, or title, of any kind whatever, from any king, prince, or foreign state.

Section 10. No State shall enter into any treaty, alliance, or confederation; grant letters of marque and reprisal; coin money; emit bills of credit; make anything but gold and silver coin a tender in payment of debts; pass any bill of attainder, ex post facto law, or law impairing the obligation of contracts, or grant any title of nobility.

No State shall, without the consent of Congress, lay any imposts or duties on imports or exports, except what may be absolutely necessary for executing its inspection laws: and the net produce of all duties and imposts, laid by any State on imports or exports, shall be for the use of the treasury of the United States; and all such laws shall be subject to the revision and control of the Congress.

No State shall, without the consent of Congress, lay any duty of tonnage, keep troops or ships of war in time of peace, enter into any agreement or compact with another State, or with a foreign power, or engage in war, unless actually invaded, or in such imminent danger as will not admit of delay.

ARTICLE II

Section 1.   The executive power shall be vested in a President of the United States of America. He shall hold his office during the term of four years, and, together with the Vice President, chosen for the same term, be elected as follows:

Each state shall appoint, in such manner as the legislature thereof may direct, a number of electors, equal to the whole number of Senators and Representatives to which the State may be entitled in the Congress; but no Senator or Representative, or person holding an office of trust or profit under the United States, shall be appointed an elector.

The electors shall meet in their respective States, and vote by ballot for two persons, of whom one at least shall not be an inhabitant of the same State with themselves. And they shall make a list of all the persons voted for, and of the number of votes for each; which list they shall sign and certify, and transmit sealed to the seat of government of the United States, directed to the President of the Senate. The President of the Senate shall, in the presence of the Senate and the House of Representatives, open all the certificates, and the votes shall then be counted. The person having the greatest number of votes shall be the President, if such number be a majority of the whole number of electors appointed; and if there be more than one who have such majority, and have an equal number of votes, then the House of Representatives shall immediately choose by ballot one of them for President; and if no person have a majority, then from the five highest on the list said house shall in like manner choose the President. But in choosing the President the votes shall be taken by States, the representation from each State having one vote; a quorum for this purpose shall consist of a member or members from two-thirds of the States, and a majority of all

the States shall be necessary to a choice. In every case, after the choice of the President, the person having the greatest number of votes of the electors shall be the Vice President. But if there should remain two or more who have equal votes, the Senate shall choose from them by ballot the Vice President.

The Congress may determine the time of choosing the electors and the day on which they shall give their votes; which day shall be the same throughout the United States.

No person except a natural-born citizen, *or a citizen of the United States at the time of the adoption of this Constitution,* shall be eligible to the office of President; neither shall any person be eligible to that office who shall not have attained to the age of thirty-five years, and been fourteen years a resident within the United States.

In case of the removal of the President from office or of his death, resignation, or inability to discharge the powers and duties of the said office, the same shall devolve on the Vice President, and the Congress may by law provide for the case of removal, death, resignation, or inability, both of the President and Vice President, declaring what officer shall then act as President, and such officer shall act accordingly, until the disability be removed, or a President shall be elected.

The President shall, at stated times, receive for his services a compensation, which shall neither be increased nor diminished during the period for which he shall have been elected, and he shall not receive within that period any other emolument from the United States, or any of them.

Before he enter on the execution of his office, he shall take the following oath or affirmation:—"I do solemnly swear (or affirm) that I will faithfully execute the office of the President of the United States, and will to the best of my ability preserve, protect and defend the Constitution of the United States."

Section 2.   The President shall be commander in chief of the army and navy of the United States, and of the militia of the several States, when called into the actual service of the United States; he may require the opinion, in writing, of the principal officer in each of the executive departments, upon any subject relating to the duties of their respective offices, and he shall have power to grant reprieves and pardons for offenses against the United States, except in cases of impeachment.

He shall have power, by and with the advice and consent of the Senate, to make treaties, provided two-thirds of the Senators present concur; and he shall nominate, and by and with the advice and consent of the Senate, shall appoint ambassadors, other public ministers and consuls, judges of the Supreme Court, and all other officers of the United States, whose appointments are not herein otherwise provided for, and which shall be established by law: but Congress may by law vest the appointment of such inferior officers, as they think proper, in the President alone, in the courts of law, or in the heads of departments.

The President shall have power to fill up all vacancies that may happen during the recess of the Senate, by granting commissions which shall expire at the end of their next session.

Section 3. He shall from time to time give to the Congress information of the state of the Union, and recommend to their consideration such measures as he shall judge necessary and expedient; he may, on extraordinary occasions, convene both houses, or either of them, and in case of disagreement between them, with respect to the time of adjournment, he may adjourn them to such time as he shall think proper; he shall receive ambassadors and other public ministers; he shall take care that the laws be faithfully executed, and shall commission all the officers of the United States.

Section 4. The President, Vice President and all civil officers of the United States shall be removed from office on impeachment for, and on conviction of, treason, bribery, or other high crimes and misdemeanors.

ARTICLE III

Section 1. The judicial power of the United States shall be vested in one Supreme Court, and in such inferior courts as the Congress may from time to time ordain and establish. The judges, both of the Supreme and inferior courts, shall hold their offices during good behavior, and shall, at stated times, receive for their services a compensation which shall not be diminished during their continuance in office.

Section 2. The judicial power shall extend to all cases, in law and equity, arising under this Constitution, the laws of the United States, and treaties made, or which shall be made, under their authority;—to all cases affecting ambassadors, other public ministers and consuls;—to all cases of admiralty and maritime jurisdiction;—to controversies to which the United States shall be a party;—to controversies between two or more States;—*between a State and citizens of another State;*—between citizens of different States;—between citizens of the same State claiming lands under grants of different States, and between a State, or the citizens thereof, and foreign states, citizens or subjects.

In all cases affecting ambassadors, other public ministers and consuls, and those in which a State shall be party, the Supreme Court shall have original jurisdiction. In all the other cases before mentioned, the Supreme Court shall have appellate jurisdiction, both as to law and fact, with such exceptions, and under such regulations, as the Congress shall make.

The trial of all crimes, except in cases of impeachment, shall be by jury; and such trial shall be held in the State where said crimes shall have been committed; but when not committed within any State, the trial shall be at such place or places as the Congress may by law have directed.

Section 3. Treason against the United States shall consist only in levying war against them, or in adhering to their enemies, giving them aid and comfort. No person shall be convicted of treason unless on the testimony of two witnesses to the same overt act, or on confession in open court.

The Congress shall have power to declare the punishment of treason, but no attainder of treason shall work corruption of blood, or forfeiture except during the life of the person attainted.

ARTICLE IV

Section 1. Full faith and credit shall be given in each State to the public acts, records, and judicial proceedings of every other State. And the Congress may by general laws prescribe the manner in which such acts, records, and proceedings shall be proved, and the effect thereof.

Section 2. The citizens of each State shall be entitled to all privileges and immunities of citizens in the several States.

A person charged in any State with treason, felony, or other crime, who shall flee from justice, and be found in another State, shall on demand of the executive authority of the State from which he fled, be delivered up, to be removed to the State having jurisdiction of the crime.

No person held to service or labor in one State, under the laws thereof, escaping into another, shall, in consequence of any law or regulation therein, be discharged from such service or labor, but shall be delivered up on claim of the party to whom such service or labor may be due.

Section 3.   New States may be admitted by the Congress into this Union; but no new State shall be formed or erected within the jurisdiction of any other State; nor any State be formed by the junction of two or more States, or parts of States, without the consent of the legislatures of the States concerned as well as of the Congress.

The Congress shall have power to dispose of and make all needful rules and regulations respecting the territory or other property belonging to the United States; and nothing in this Constitution shall be so construed as to prejudice any claims of the United States, or of any particular State.

Section 4.   The United States shall guarantee to every State in this Union a republican form of government, and shall protect each of them against invasion; and on application of the legislature, or of the executive (when the legislature cannot be convened); against domestic violence.

ARTICLE V

The Congress, whenever two-thirds of both houses shall deem it necessary, shall propose amendments to this Constitution, or, on the application of the legislatures of two-thirds of the several States, shall call a convention for proposing amendments, which, in either case, shall be valid to all intents and purposes, as part of this Constitution, when ratified by the legislatures of three-fourths of the several States, or by conventions in three-fourths thereof, as the one or the other mode of ratification may be proposed by the Congress; provided *that no amendments which may be made prior to the year one thousand eight hundred and eight shall in any manner affect the first and fourth clauses in the ninth section of the first article;* and that no State, without its consent, shall be deprived of its equal suffrage in the Senate.

ARTICLE VI

All debts contracted and engagements entered into, before the adoption of this Constitution, shall be as valid against the United States under this Constitution, as under the Confederation.

This Constitution, and the laws of the United States which shall be made in pursuance thereof; and all treaties made, or which shall be made, under the authority of the United States, shall be the supreme law of the land; and the judges in every State shall be bound thereby, anything in the Constitution or laws of any State to the contrary notwithstanding.

The Senators and Representatives before mentioned, and the members of the several State legislatures, and all executive and judicial officers, both of the United States and of the several States, shall be bound by oath or affirmation to support this Constitution; but no religious test shall ever be required as a qualification to any office or public trust under the United States.

ARTICLE VII

The ratification of the conventions of nine States shall be sufficient for the establishment of this Constitution between the States so ratifying the same.

Done in Convention by the unanimous consent of the States present, the seventeenth day of September in the year of our Lord one thousand seven hundred and eighty-seven and of the Independence of the United States of America the twelfth. In witness whereof we have hereunto subscribed our names.

[Signed by]
G° WASHINGTON
Presidt and Deputy from Virginia
[and thirty-eight others]

AMENDMENTS TO THE CONSTITUTION

AMENDMENT I*

Congress shall make no law respecting an establishment of religion, or prohibiting the free exercise thereof; or abridging the freedom of speech, or of the press; or the right of the people peaceably to assemble, and to petition the government for a redress of grievances.

AMENDMENT II

A well-regulated militia being necessary to the security of a free State, the right of the people to keep and bear arms shall not be infringed.

AMENDMENT III

No soldier shall, in time of peace, be quartered in any house without the consent of the owner, nor in time of war, but in a manner to be prescribed by law.

AMENDMENT IV

The right of the people to be secure in their persons, houses, papers, and effects, against unreasonable searches and seizures, shall not be violated, and no warrants shall issue but upon probable cause, supported by oath or affirmation, and particularly describing the place to be searched, and the persons or things to be seized.

AMENDMENT V

No person shall be held to answer for a capital, or otherwise infamous crime, unless on a presentment or indictment of a grand jury, except in cases arising in the land or naval forces, or in the militia, when in actual service in time of war or public danger; nor shall any person be subject for the same offense to be twice put in jeopardy of life or limb; nor shall be compelled in any criminal case to be a witness against himself, nor be deprived of life, liberty, or property, without due process of law; nor shall private property be taken for public use without just compensation.

* The first ten Amendments (Bill of Rights) were adopted in 1791.

AMENDMENT VI

In all criminal prosecutions, the accused shall enjoy the right to a speedy and public trial, by an impartial jury of the State and district wherein the crime shall have been committed, which district shall have been previously ascertained by law, and to be informed of the nature and cause of the accusation; to be confronted with the witnesses against him; to have compulsory process for obtaining witnesses in his favor, and to have the assistance of counsel for his defense.

AMENDMENT VII

In suits at common law, where the value in controversy shall exceed twenty dollars, the right of trial by jury shall be preserved, and no fact tried by a jury shall be otherwise reexamined in any court of the United States, than according to the rules of the common law.

AMENDMENT VIII

Excessive bail shall not be required, nor excessive fines imposed, nor cruel and unusual punishments inflicted.

AMENDMENT IX

The enumeration in the Constitution, of certain rights, shall not be construed to deny or disparage others retained by the people.

AMENDMENT X

The powers not delegated to the United States by the Constitution, not prohibited by it to the States, are reserved to the States respectively, or to the people.

AMENDMENT XI   [*Adopted 1798*]

The judicial power of the United States shall not be construed to extend to any suit in law or equity, commenced or prosecuted against one of the United States by citizens of another State, or by citizens or subjects of any foreign state.

AMENDMENT XII   [*Adopted 1804*]

The electors shall meet in their respective States, and vote by ballot for President and Vice President, one of whom, at least, shall not be an inhabitant of the same State with themselves; they shall name in their ballots the person voted for as President, and in distinct ballots the person voted for as Vice President, and they shall make distinct lists of all persons voted for as President, and of all persons voted for as Vice President, and of the number of votes for each, which lists they shall sign and certify, and transmit sealed to the seat of government of the United States, directed to the President of the Senate;—the President of the Senate shall, in the presence of the Senate and House of Representatives, open all the certificates and the votes shall then be counted;—the person having the greatest number of votes for President shall be the President, if such number be a majority of the whole number of electors appointed; and if no person have such majority, then from the persons having the highest numbers not exceeding three on the list of those voted for as President, the House of Representatives shall choose immediately, by ballot, the President. But in choosing the President, the votes shall be taken by States, the representation from each State having one vote; a quorum for this purpose shall consist of a member or members from two-thirds of the States, and a majority of all the States shall be necessary to a choice. And if the House of Representatives shall not choose a President whenever the right of choice shall devolve upon them, before *the fourth day of March* next following, then the Vice President shall act as President, as in the case of the death or other constitutional disability of the President.

The person having the greatest number of votes as Vice President shall be the Vice President, if such a number be a majority of the whole number of electors appointed; and if no person have a majority, then from the two highest numbers on the list the Senate shall choose the Vice President; a quorum for the purpose shall consist of two-thirds of the whole number of Senators, and a majority of the whole number shall be necessary to a choice. But no person constitutionally ineligible to the office of President shall be eligible to that of Vice President of the United States.

AMENDMENT XIII   [*Adopted 1865*]

Section 1.   Neither slavery nor involuntary servitude, except as a punishment for crime whereof the party shall have been duly convicted, shall exist within the United States, or any place subject to their jurisdiction.

Section 2.   Congress shall have power to enforce this article by appropriate legislation.

AMENDMENT XIV   [*Adopted 1868*]

Section 1.   All persons born or naturalized in the United States, and subject to the jurisdiction thereof, are citizens of the United States and of the State wherein they reside. No State shall make or enforce any law which shall abridge the privileges or immunities of citizens of the United States; nor shall any State deprive any person of life, liberty, or property, without due process of law; nor deny to any person within its jurisdiction the equal protection of the laws.

Section 2.   Representatives shall be apportioned among the several States according to their respective numbers, counting the whole number of persons in each State, excluding Indians not taxed. But when the right to vote at any election for the choice of Electors for President and Vice President of the United States, Representatives in Congress, the executive and judicial officers of a State, or the members of the legislature thereof, is denied to any of the male inhabitants of such State, being twenty-one years of age and citizens of the United States, or in any way abridged, except for participation in rebellion, or other crime, the basis of representation therein shall be reduced in the proportion which the number of such male citizens shall bear to the whole number of male citizens twenty-one years of age in such State.

Section 3.   No person shall be a Senator or Representative in Congress or Elector of President and Vice President, or hold any office, civil or military, under the United States, or under any State, who, having previously taken an oath, as a member of Congress, or as an officer of the United States, or as a member of any State legislature, or as an executive or judicial officer of any State, to support the Constitution of the

United States, shall have engaged in insurrection or rebellion against the same, or given aid and comfort to the enemies thereof. Congress may, by a vote of two-thirds of each house, remove such disability.

Section 4. The validity of the public debt of the United States, authorized by law, including debts incurred for payment of pensions and bounties for services in suppressing insurrection or rebellion, shall not be questioned. But neither the United States nor any State shall assume or pay any debt or obligation incurred in aid of insurrection or rebellion against the United States, or any claim for the loss or emancipation of any slave; but all such debts, obligations, and claims shall be held illegal and void.

Section 5. The Congress shall have the power to enforce, by appropriate legislation, the provisions of this article.

AMENDMENT XV   [*Adopted 1870*]

Section 1. The right of citizens of the United States to vote shall not be denied or abridged by the United States or by any State on account of race, color, or previous condition of servitude.

Section 2. The Congress shall have power to enforce this article by appropriate legislation.

AMENDMENT XVI   [*Adopted 1913*]

The Congress shall have power to lay and collect taxes on incomes, from whatever source derived, without apportionment among the several States, and without regard to any census or enumeration.

AMENDMENT XVII   [*Adopted 1913*]

Section 1. The Senate of the United States shall be composed of two Senators from each State, elected by the people thereof, for six years; and each Senator shall have one vote. The electors in each State shall have the qualifications requisite for electors of [voters for] the most numerous branch of the State legislatures.

Section 2. When vacancies happen in the representation of any State in the Senate, the executive authority

of such State shall issue writs of election to fill such vacancies: Provided, that the Legislature of any State may empower the executive thereof to make temporary appointments until the people fill the vacancies by election as the Legislature may direct.

Section 3. This amendment shall not be so construed as to affect the election or term of any Senator chosen before it becomes valid as part of the Constitution.

AMENDMENT XVIII   [*Adopted 1919; repealed 1933*]

Section 1. *After one year from the ratification of this article the manufacture, sale, or transportation of intoxicating liquors within, the importation thereof into, or the exportation thereof from the United States and all territory subject to the jurisdiction thereof, for beverage purposes, is hereby prohibited.*

Section 2. *The Congress and the several States shall have concurrent power to enforce this article by appropriate legislation.*

Section 3. *This article shall be inoperative unless it shall have been ratified as an amendment to the Constitution by the legislatures of the several States, as provided by the Constitution, within seven years from the date of the submission thereof to the States by the Congress.*

AMENDMENT XIX   [*Adopted 1920*]

Section 1. The right of citizens of the United States to vote shall not be denied or abridged by the United States or by any State on account of sex.

Section 2. The Congress shall have the power to enforce this article by appropriate legislation.

AMENDMENT XX   [*Adopted 1933*]

Section 1. The terms of the President and Vice President shall end at noon on the 20th day of January, and the terms of Senators and Representatives at noon on the 3d day of January, of the years in which such terms would have ended if this article had not been ratified; and the terms of their successors shall then begin.

Section 2. The Congress shall assemble at least once in every year, and such meeting shall begin at noon on the 3d day of January, unless they shall by law appoint a different day.

Section 3.   If, at the time fixed for the beginning of the term of the President, the President-elect shall have died, the Vice President-elect shall become President. If a President shall not have been chosen before the time fixed for the beginning of his term, or if the President-elect shall have failed to qualify, then the Vice President-elect shall act as President until a President shall have qualified; and the Congress may by law provide for the case wherein neither a President-elect nor a Vice President-elect shall have qualified, declaring who shall then act as President, or the manner in which one who is to act shall be selected, and such persons shall act accordingly until a President or Vice President shall have qualified.

Section 4.   The Congress may by law provide for the case of the death of any of the persons from whom the House of Representatives may choose a President whenever the right of choice shall have devolved upon them, and for the case of the death of any of the persons from whom the Senate may choose a Vice President whenever the right of choice shall have devolved upon them.

Section 5.   Sections 1 and 2 shall take effect on the 15th day of October following the ratification of this article.

Section 6.   This article shall be inoperative unless it shall have been ratified as an amendment to the Constitution by the Legislatures of three-fourths of the several States within seven years from the date of its submission.

AMENDMENT XXI   [*Adopted 1933*]

Section 1.   The eighteenth article of amendment to the Constitution of the United States is hereby repealed.

Section 2.   The transportation or importation into any State, Territory, or Possession of the United States for delivery or use therein of intoxicating liquors, in violation of the laws thereof, is hereby prohibited.

Section 3.   This article shall be inoperative unless it shall have been ratified as an amendment to the Constitution by conventions in the several States, as provided in the Constitution, within seven years from the date of submission thereof to the States by the Congress.

AMENDMENT XXII   [*Adopted 1951*]

Section 1.   No person shall be elected to the office of President more than twice, and no person who has held the office of President, or acted as President, for more than two years of a term to which some other person was elected President shall be elected to the office of President more than once. But this article shall not apply to any person holding the office of President when this article was proposed by the Congress, and shall not prevent any person who may be holding the office of President, or acting as President, during the term within which this article becomes operative from holding the office of President or acting as President during the remainder of such term.

Section 2.   This article shall be inoperative unless it shall have been ratified as an amendment to the Constitution by the legislatures of three-fourths of the several States within seven years from the date of its submission to the States by the Congress.

AMENDMENT XXIII   [*Adopted 1961*]

Section 1.   The District constituting the seat of Government of the United States shall appoint in such manner as the Congress may direct:

A number of electors of President and Vice President equal to the whole number of Senators and Representatives in Congress to which the District would be entitled if it were a State, but in no event more than the least populous State; they shall be in addition to those appointed by the States, but they shall be considered for the purposes of the election of President and Vice President, to be electors appointed by a State; and they shall meet in the District and perform such duties as provided by the twelfth article of amendment.

Section 2.   The Congress shall have the power to enforce this article by appropriate legislation.

AMENDMENT XXIV   [*Adopted 1964*]

Section 1.   The right of citizens of the United States to vote in any primary or other election for President or Vice President, for electors for President or Vice President, or for Senator or Representative in Congress, shall not be denied or abridged by the United States or any State by reason of failure to pay any poll tax or other tax.

Section 2.   The Congress shall have the power to enforce this article by appropriate legislation.

AMENDMENT XXV   [*Adopted 1967*]

Section 1.   In case of the removal of the President from office or of his death or resignation, the Vice President shall become President.

Section 2.   Whenever there is a vacancy in the office of the Vice President, the President shall nominate a Vice President who shall take office upon confirmation by a majority vote of both Houses of Congress.

Section 3.   Whenever the President transmits to the President pro tempore of the Senate and the Speaker of the House of Representatives his written declaration that he is unable to discharge the powers and duties of his office, and until he transmits to them a written declaration to the contrary, such powers and duties shall be discharged by the Vice President as Acting President.

Section 4.   Whenever the Vice President and a majority of either the principal officers of the executive departments or of such other body as Congress may by law provide, transmit to the President pro tempore of the Senate and the Speaker of the House of Representatives their written declaration that the President is unable to discharge the powers and duties of his office, the Vice President shall immediately assume the powers and duties of the office as Acting President.

Thereafter, when the President transmits to the President pro tempore of the Senate and the Speaker of the House of Representatives his written declaration that no inability exists, he shall resume the powers and duties of his office unless the Vice President and a majority of either the principal officers of the executive department[s] or of such other body as Congress may by law provide, transmit within four days to the President pro tempore of the Senate and the Speaker of the House of Representatives their written declaration that the President is unable to discharge the powers and duties of his office. Thereupon Congress shall decide the issue, assembling within forty-eight hours for that purpose if not in session. If the Congress, within twenty-one days after receipt of the latter written declaration, or, if Congress is not in session, within twenty-one days after Congress is required to assemble, determines by two-thirds vote of both Houses that the President is unable to discharge the powers and duties of his office, the Vice President shall continue to discharge the same as Acting President; otherwise, the President shall resume the powers and duties of his office.

AMENDMENT XXVI   [*Adopted 1971*]

Section 1.   The right of citizens of the United States, who are eighteen years of age or older, to vote shall not be denied or abridged by the United States or by any State on account of age.

Section 2.   The Congress shall have power to enforce this article by appropriate legislation.

AMENDMENT XXVII*   [*Adopted 1992*]

No law, varying the compensation for services of the Senators and Representatives, shall take effect, until an election of Representatives shall have intervened.

---

* Originally proposed in 1789 by James Madison, this amendment failed to win ratification along with the other parts of what became the Bill of Rights. However, the proposed amendment contained no deadline for ratification, and over the years other state legislatures voted to add it to the Constitution; many such ratifications occurred during the 1980s and early 1990s as public frustration with Congress's performance mounted. In May 1992 the Archivist of the United States certified that, with the Michigan legislature's ratification, the article had been approved by three-fourths of the states and thus automatically became part of the Constitution. But congressional leaders and constitutional specialists questioned whether an amendment that took 202 years to win ratification was valid, and the issue had not been resolved by the time this book went to press.

PRESIDENTIAL ELECTIONS, 1789–2008

YEAR	STATES IN THE UNION	CANDIDATES	PARTIES	ELECTORAL VOTE	POPULAR VOTE	PERCENTAGE OF POPULAR VOTE
1789	11	GEORGE WASHINGTON	No party designations	69		
		John Adams		34		
		Minor candidates		35		
1792	15	GEORGE WASHINGTON	No party designations	132		
		John Adams		77		
		George Clinton		50		
		Minor candidates		5		
1796	16	JOHN ADAMS	Federalist	71		
		Thomas Jefferson	Democratic-Republican	68		
		Thomas Pinckney	Federalist	59		
		Aaron Burr	Democratic-Republican	30		
		Minor candidates		48		
1800	16	THOMAS JEFFERSON	Democratic-Republican	73		
		Aaron Burr	Democratic-Republican	73		
		John Adams	Federalist	65		
		Charles C. Pinckney	Federalist	64		
		John Jay	Federalist	1		
1804	17	THOMAS JEFFERSON	Democratic-Republican	162		
		Charles C. Pinckney	Federalist	14		
1808	17	JAMES MADISON	Democratic-Republican	122		
		Charles C. Pinckney	Federalist	47		
		George Clinton	Democratic-Republican	6		
1812	18	JAMES MADISON	Democratic-Republican	128		
		DeWitt Clinton	Federalist	89		
1816	19	JAMES MONROE	Democratic-Republican	183		
		Rufus King	Federalist	34		
1820	24	JAMES MONROE	Democratic-Republican	231		
		John Quincy Adams	Independent Republican	1		
1824	24	JOHN QUINCY ADAMS	Democratic-Republican	84	108,740	30.5
		Andrew Jackson	Democratic-Republican	99	153,544	43.1
		William H. Crawford	Democratic-Republican	41	46,618	13.1
		Henry Clay	Democratic-Republican	37	47,136	13.2
1828	24	ANDREW JACKSON	Democratic	178	642,553	56.0
		John Quincy Adams	National Republican	83	500,897	44.0
1832	24	ANDREW JACKSON	Democratic	219	687,502	55.0
		Henry Clay	National Republican	49	530,189	42.4
		William Wirt	Anti-Masonic	7	33,108	2.6
		John Floyd	National Republican	11		

Because candidates receiving less than 1 percent of the popular vote are omitted, the percentage of popular vote may not total 100 percent.

Before the Twelfth Amendment was passed in 1804, the Electoral College voted for two presidential candidates; the runner-up became vice president.

PRESIDENTIAL ELECTIONS, 1789–2008 (*continued*)

YEAR	STATES IN THE UNION	CANDIDATES	PARTIES	ELECTORAL VOTE	POPULAR VOTE	PERCENTAGE OF POPULAR VOTE
1836	26	MARTIN VAN BUREN	Democratic	170	765,483	50.9
		William H. Harrison	Whig	73		
		Hugh L. White	Whig	26	739,795	49.1
		Daniel Webster	Whig	14		
		W. P. Mangum	Whig	11		
1840	26	WILLIAM H. HARRISON	Whig	234	1,274,624	53.1
		Martin Van Buren	Democratic	60	1,127,781	46.9
1844	26	JAMES K. POLK	Democratic	170	1,338,464	49.6
		Henry Clay	Whig	105	1,300,097	48.1
		James G. Birney	Liberty		62,300	2.3
1848	30	ZACHARY TAYLOR	Whig	163	1,360,967	47.4
		Lewis Cass	Democratic	127	1,222,342	42.5
		Martin Van Buren	Free Soil		291,263	10.1
1852	31	FRANKLIN PIERCE	Democratic	254	1,601,117	50.9
		Winfield Scott	Whig	42	1,385,453	44.1
		John P. Hale	Free Soil		155,825	5.0
1856	31	JAMES BUCHANAN	Democratic	174	1,832,955	45.3
		John C. Frémont	Republican	114	1,339,932	33.1
		Millard Fillmore	American	8	871,731	21.6
1860	33	ABRAHAM LINCOLN	Republican	180	1,865,593	39.8
		Stephen A. Douglas	Democratic	12	1,382,713	29.5
		John C. Breckinridge	Democratic	72	848,356	18.1
		John Bell	Constitutional Union	39	592,906	12.6
1864	36	ABRAHAM LINCOLN	Republican	212	2,206,938	55.0
		George B. McClellan	Democratic	21	1,803,787	45.0
1868	37	ULYSSES S. GRANT	Republican	214	3,013,421	52.7
		Horatio Seymour	Democratic	80	2,706,829	47.3
1872	37	ULYSSES S. GRANT	Republican	286	3,596,745	55.6
		Horace Greeley	Democratic	*	2,843,446	43.9
1876	38	RUTHERFORD B. HAYES	Republican	185	4,034,311	48.0
		Samuel J. Tilden	Democratic	184	4,288,546	51.0
		Peter Cooper	Greenback		75,973	1.0
1880	38	JAMES A. GARFIELD	Republican	214	4,453,295	48.5
		Winfield S. Hancock	Democratic	155	4,414,082	48.1
		James B. Weaver	Greenback-Labor		308,578	3.4
1884	38	GROVER CLEVELAND	Democratic	219	4,879,507	48.5
		James G. Blaine	Republican	182	4,850,293	48.2
		Benjamin F. Butler	Greenback-Labor		175,370	1.8
		John P. St. John	Prohibition		150,369	1.5

*When Greeley died shortly after the election, his supporters divided their votes among the minor candidates.

Because candidates receiving less than 1 percent of the popular vote are omitted, the percentage of popular vote may not total 100 percent.

PRESIDENTIAL ELECTIONS, 1789–2008 (*continued*)

Year	States in the Union	Candidates	Parties	Electoral Vote	Popular Vote	Percentage of Popular Vote
1888	38	BENJAMIN HARRISON	Republican	233	5,477,129	47.9
		Grover Cleveland	Democratic	168	5,537,857	48.6
		Clinton B. Fisk	Prohibition		249,506	2.2
		Anson J. Streeter	Union Labor		146,935	1.3
1892	44	GROVER CLEVELAND	Democratic	277	5,555,426	46.1
		Benjamin Harrison	Republican	145	5,182,690	43.0
		James B. Weaver	People's	22	1,029,846	8.5
		John Bidwell	Prohibition		264,133	2.2
1896	45	WILLIAM McKINLEY	Republican	271	7,102,246	51.1
		William J. Bryan	Democratic	176	6,492,559	47.7
1900	45	WILLIAM McKINLEY	Republican	292	7,218,491	51.7
		William J. Bryan	Democratic; Populist	155	6,356,734	45.5
		John C. Wooley	Prohibition		208,914	1.5
1904	45	THEODORE ROOSEVELT	Republican	336	7,628,461	57.4
		Alton B. Parker	Democratic	140	5,084,223	37.6
		Eugene V. Debs	Socialist		402,283	3.0
		Silas C. Swallow	Prohibition		258,536	1.9
1908	46	WILLIAM H. TAFT	Republican	321	7,675,320	51.6
		William J. Bryan	Democratic	162	6,412,294	43.1
		Eugene V. Debs	Socialist		420,793	2.8
		Eugene W. Chafin	Prohibition		253,840	1.7
1912	48	WOODROW WILSON	Democratic	435	6,296,547	41.9
		Theodore Roosevelt	Progressive	88	4,118,571	27.4
		William H. Taft	Republican	8	3,486,720	23.2
		Eugene V. Debs	Socialist		900,672	6.0
		Eugene W. Chafin	Prohibition		206,275	1.4
1916	48	WOODROW WILSON	Democratic	277	9,127,695	49.4
		Charles E. Hughes	Republican	254	8,533,507	46.2
		A. L. Benson	Socialist		585,113	3.2
		J. Frank Hanly	Prohibition		220,506	1.2
1920	48	WARREN G. HARDING	Republican	404	16,143,407	60.4
		James N. Cox	Democratic	127	9,130,328	34.2
		Eugene V. Debs	Socialist		919,799	3.4
		P. P. Christensen	Farmer-Labor		265,411	1.0
1924	48	CALVIN COOLIDGE	Republican	382	15,718,211	54.0
		John W. Davis	Democratic	136	8,385,283	28.8
		Robert M. La Follette	Progressive	13	4,831,289	16.6
1928	48	HERBERT C. HOOVER	Republican	444	21,391,993	58.2
		Alfred E. Smith	Democratic	87	15,016,169	40.9
1932	48	FRANKLIN D. ROOSEVELT	Democratic	472	22,809,638	57.4
		Herbert C. Hoover	Republican	59	15,758,901	39.7
		Norman Thomas	Socialist		881,951	2.2

Because candidates receiving less than 1 percent of the popular vote are omitted, the percentage of popular vote may not total 100 percent.

PRESIDENTIAL ELECTIONS, 1789–2008 (*continued*)

Year	States in the Union	Candidates	Parties	Electoral Vote	Popular Vote	Percentage of Popular Vote
1936	48	FRANKLIN D. ROOSEVELT	Democratic	523	27,752,869	60.8
		Alfred M. Landon	Republican	8	16,674,665	36.5
		William Lemke	Union		882,479	1.9
1940	48	FRANKLIN D. ROOSEVELT	Democratic	449	27,307,819	54.8
		Wendell L. Willkie	Republican	82	22,321,018	44.8
1944	48	FRANKLIN D. ROOSEVELT	Democratic	432	25,606,585	53.5
		Thomas E. Dewey	Republican	99	22,014,745	46.0
1948	48	HARRY S TRUMAN	Democratic	303	24,105,812	49.5
		Thomas E. Dewey	Republican	189	21,970,065	45.1
		Strom Thurmond	States' Rights	39	1,169,063	2.4
		Henry A. Wallace	Progressive		1,157,172	2.4
1952	48	DWIGHT D. EISENHOWER	Republican	442	33,936,234	55.1
		Adlai E. Stevenson	Democratic	89	27,314,992	44.4
1956	48	DWIGHT D. EISENHOWER	Republican	457	35,590,472	57.6
		Adlai E. Stevenson	Democratic	73	26,022,752	42.1
1960	50	JOHN F. KENNEDY	Democratic	303	34,227,096	49.7
		Richard M. Nixon	Republican	219	34,108,546	49.5
		Harry F. Byrd	Independent	15	502,363	.7
1964	50	LYNDON B. JOHNSON	Democratic	486	43,126,506	61.1
		Barry M. Goldwater	Republican	52	27,176,799	38.5
1968	50	RICHARD M. NIXON	Republican	301	31,770,237	43.4
		Hubert H. Humphrey	Democratic	191	31,270,533	42.7
		George C. Wallace	American Independent	46	9,906,141	13.5
1972	50	RICHARD M. NIXON	Republican	520	47,169,911	60.7
		George S. McGovern	Democratic	17	29,170,383	37.5
1976	50	JIMMY CARTER	Democratic	297	40,827,394	49.9
		Gerald R. Ford	Republican	240	39,145,977	47.9
1980	50	RONALD W. REAGAN	Republican	489	43,899,248	50.8
		Jimmy Carter	Democratic	49	35,481,435	41.0
		John B. Anderson	Independent		5,719,437	6.6
		Ed Clark	Libertarian		920,859	1.0
1984	50	RONALD W. REAGAN	Republican	525	54,451,521	58.8
		Walter F. Mondale	Democratic	13	37,565,334	40.5
1988	50	GEORGE H. W. BUSH	Republican	426	47,946,422	54.0
		Michael S. Dukakis	Democratic	112	41,016,429	46.0
1992	50	WILLIAM J. CLINTON	Democratic	370	43,728,275	43.2
		George H. W. Bush	Republican	168	38,167,416	37.7
		H. Ross Perot	Independent		19,237,247	19.0

Because candidates receiving less than 1 percent of the popular vote are omitted, the percentage of popular vote may not total 100 percent.

PRESIDENTIAL ELECTIONS, 1789–2008 *(continued)*

YEAR	STATES IN THE UNION	CANDIDATES	PARTIES	ELECTORAL VOTE	POPULAR VOTE	PERCENTAGE OF POPULAR VOTE
1996	50	WILLIAM J. CLINTON	Democratic	379	47,401,185	49.2
		Robert Dole	Republican	159	39,197,469	40.7
		H. Ross Perot	Reform		8,085,294	8.4
2000	50	GEORGE W. BUSH	Republican	271	50,456,141	47.9
		Albert Gore Jr.	Democratic	266	50,996,039	48.4
		Ralph Nader	Green		2,882,807	2.7
2004	50	GEORGE W. BUSH	Republican	286	60,608,582	51.0
		John Kerry	Democratic	252	57,288,974	48.0
		Ralph Nader	Independent		406,924	1.0
2008	50	BARACK OBAMA	Democratic	365	69,456,897	52.9
		John McCain	Republican	173	59,934,814	45.7

Because candidates receiving less than 1 percent of the popular vote are omitted, the percentage of popular vote may not total 100 percent.

Index

AAA. *See* Agricultural Adjustment Administration (AAA)

Abenaki Indians, 37

Abolition and abolitionists: African-Americans and, 170; during age of reform, 237–239; Fourteenth Amendment and, 374; Kansas crisis and, 324

Abortion, 217

Abstinence, birth control and, 217

Acadia, 71, 95

Acoma Indians, 31

Act for Religious Toleration (1649), 42

Actual representation, 99

Adams, Abigail, 131

Adams, Charles Francis, 351

Adams, Henry, 351

Adams, John, 113, 114, 129, 130; 1796 election, 161–162; 1800 election, 165; on Articles of Confederation, 135; Boston Massacre and, 107, 108; as first vice president, 148; Judiciary Act (1801) and, 177; Monroe Doctrine and, 195–196; view of women, 168; XYZ Affair and, 162

Adams, John Quincy, 221, 303; as president, 222–223; as secretary of state, 195; settlements and, 304

Adams, Samuel, 104, 107, 108, 111, 113

Adams-Onís (Transcontinental) Treaty (1819), 195, 295

Adena culture, 8

Administration of Justice Act, 112

AEF. *See* American Expeditionary Force (AEF)

Affluence. *See* Wealth

AFL. *See* American Federation of Labor (AFL)

Africa, 22; European voyages and, 20(map). *See also* West Africa

African-Americans, 282–283; after Revolutionary War, 131–133; black codes, 372–373; Civil Rights Act (1866) and, 373; colonization and, 237; free, in 19th-century North, 212–213; land ownership and, 385–386; in late 18th century, 170–172; liberty for, 111–112; marriage, 383; in public schools, 237; as Republicans, 379; soldiers in Union army, 354; suffrage, 370, 376–377. *See also under* Segregation; Slaves and slavery

African Methodist Episcopal Church, 213, 383

Agriculture: advancements in, 246–247; Eastern Woodlands peoples, 8; market economy and, 204; Native American,

3–4, 5, 6, 13; rise of, 204; in South, 268. *See also* Farmers and farming; Planters and plantations; Sharecropping

Alabama: Ku Klux Klan in, 382; Reconstruction and, 372; statehood for, 199

"Alabama fever," 204

Alabama (ship), 351, 389

Alamance Creek Battle, 110

Alamo, 83, 298

Alaska, 10, 11; expansion into, 389

Albany Congress, 93, 100

Albany Regency, 224

Alcott, Louisa May, 361

Aleut Indians, 2, 11

Algonquin Indians, 33

Alien Acts (1798), 162–164

Allen, Richard, 171

Almshouses, 241

American Colonization Society, 237

American Landscape Painting, 263

American Museum, 257

American Philosophical Society, 87, 175

American Railroad Journal, 248

American Red Cross, 361

American Renaissance, 257–258

American Republicans, 293

American Temperance Society, 236

American Woman Suffrage Association, 377

Americas, 4(map); France and, 80–81; Seven Years' War in, 92–95. *See also* Latin (South) America; North America

Ames, Fisher, 157

Amnesty Act, 389

Anaconda plan, 345

Anasazi culture, 7

Andros, Edmund, 68, 70

Anesthesia, 252–253

Anglicans. *See* Church of England

Anglo-French wars, 71

Anglo-Indian wars, 41(map)

Anglo-Powhatan Wars, 35, 36, 44

Anglo-Spanish War, 84

Anthony, Susan B., 361–362, 377–378

Anti-Catholicism, protest of, 293

Antietam, 347, 348

Antifederalists, 143–145, 144(map)

Anti-Masonry, 229

Antinomianism, 48–49

Antislavery movement, 132

Apache Indians, 2, 63, 83, 156

Appalachian Mountains, 75, 199

Appomattox Courthouse, 365

Archaic peoples, 2–5

Architecture, Anasazis, 7

Arguin, slaving station at, 25

Aristotle, 276

Arizona, Native peoples of, 7

Arkansas, 62; banks in, 231

Art, 263; commercialism and, 261–262; Mesoamerican influences, 7; Native American, 8–9

Articles of Confederation, 120, 135, 201

Artisans: of Benin, 17; industrialization and, 209, 211; middling classes and, 213; Shakers, 234–235; West African, 18

Asia, trade with, 26

Assassination, Abraham Lincoln, 365–66

Astor, John Jacob, 201, 212

Astor Place riot, 256

Asylums, 241

Atchison, David R., 324

Athapaskan speakers, 2

Atlantic Ocean region, European expansion in, 25–30

Attucks, Crispus, 107–108

Auburn system, for penitentiaries, 241

Augusta Powder Works, 339

Austin, Stephen F., 297

Authority, questioning of, 214–215

Awful Disclosures of the Hotel Dieu Nunnery in Montreal (Monk), 293

Aztecs of Mexico, 6; conquest of, 29

Babcock, Orville, 388

Bache, Sally Franklin, 131

Bacon, Nathaniel, 44

Bacon's Rebellion, 44–45

Balboa, Vasco Núñez de, 28

Baltimore, Lord, 39, 41, 42, 44

Bank of England, 73, 230

Bank of United States, 152–153, 206, 227; bank veto, 227, 228; Panic of 1837, 230–231; war on, 228–229

Bannekar, Benjamin, 170–171

Baptisms, in colonial New England, 51–52

Baptists, Great Awakening and, 89

Barbados, 50, 56

Barnum, P. T., 254, 256, 257

Barton, Clara, 361

Bathing, 252

Battles: Alamance Creek, 110; of Antietam, 347; of Bladensburg, 190; of Buena Vista, 306; Bull Run, 346; of Fallen Timbers, 159; of Fredericksburg, 345, 347; Lake Champlain, 33–34; of Mexican-American War, 308(map); of Monmouth, 126; of New Orleans, 192; of Princeton, 124; of Queenston, 188; of Saratoga, 124; Seven

Battles (*Continued*)
Days', 347; in Texas Revolution, 298(map); of the Thames, 189–190; of Tippecanoe, 187, 231; of Trenton, 123; of War of 1812, 189(map); of Yorktown, 129
Beaver fur trade, 32, 34, 37, 296
Beecher, Lyman, 236, 239, 318
Belknap, William E., 388
Bell, John, 333
Benin, 26; artisans of, 17
Bennett, James Gordon, 254, 255
Bering land bridge, 2
Berkeley, William, 44
Bible, 23, 87
Bible Riots, 293
Bickerdyke, Mary Ann, 360
Biddle, Nicholas, 227, 228
Bill of Rights, 143, 149–150
Bills of attainder, 149
Birch, William, 163
Birthrates, 217
Black codes, 372–373
Black Hawk, 203–204
Blacks. *See* African-Americans
Bland-Allison Act (1878), 390
Board of Customs Commissioners, 104–105
Board of Trade, 85
Bonaparte, Napoleon, 175, 178–179, 184–185
Bondage, 57
Book of Mormon, 234
Booth, John Wilkes, 365–366
Boston Manufacturing Company, 210
Boston Massacre, 91, 107–108
Boston Port Bill, 112
Boston Tea Party, 107, 111, 112
Bourbons, 392
Boyd, Belle, 361
Braddock, Edward, 93–94
Brandywine Creek, Pennsylvania, 124
Brant, Joseph, 121, 127, 137–138
Brazil, Portugal and, 27–28
Breckinridge, John C., 333
Breed's Hill battle, 114
Britain (England): 15th-century power in, 21; after the Treaty of Paris, 95; in Americas, 82(map); Civil War and, 351; colonial debt, 95–96; colonial populations, 73–76; expansion by, 81–83; explorers from, 27 and map; in Far West, 295; France and, 62; "Glorious Revolution" in, 69–70; immigrants from, 39–40, 43, 46, 55, 56; Navigation Acts, 72; North American colonies of, 34; Oregon and, 303–304; population growth in, 21–22; population of London, 21; Privy Council, 158; Reformation in, 23–24; Royal Navy, 158; slave trade by, 74(map); War of 1812, 175, 190
British America: immigration to, 47(map), 73, 75; Native Americans and, 81, 94–95;

public life in, 84–89; triumphs and tensions in, 92–97. *See also* Colonies and colonial era; *specific colony*
British-American Convention (1818), 195
British navy, in American Revolution, 121–122
British Royal Navy, 183
British Rule of 1756, 183
British West Indies, 55
Broken voyage, 183
Brook Farm, 242
Brooks, Preston, 326
Brown, Ezekiel, 123
Brown, John, 314, 325, 327, 331
Bryant, William Cullen, 263
Buchanan, James, 326, 327–328
Buffalo (bison) hunting, 10–11
Bunker Hill battle, 114
Burgoyne, John, 124
Burke, Edmund, 112
Burned-Over District, 233, 234
Burns, Anthony, 318
Burnside, Ambrose, 347
Burr, Aaron, 165, 179–180, 182
Business, railroads and, 249
Butler, Andrew, 326
Butler, Benjamin, 349
Butter, 247

Cabeza de Vaca, 31
Cabot, John, 27
Cahokia, 9
Cajuns, 95
Calhoun, John C., 186, 222–223, 225–227, 301, 309, 316
California, 10; American settlements in, 298; expansion and, 290; gold rush, 310–311; statehood for, 295; U.S. control over, 307
Callender, James, 175
Callender, Thomas, 164
Calvert, Cecilius, 41
Calvin, John, 23, 24
Calvinists (French Huguenots), 24, 32, 74
Camden, South Carolina, 127
Canada: France and, 31–34, 62, 94; mercantilism in, 72–73; War of 1812 and, 188–190
Canals, 7, 207 and map, 248–249
Cane Ridge, Kentucky, 232
Canning, George, 195–196
Cape of Good Hope, 25
Caribbean. *See* West Indies (Caribbean)
Carolina, Native Americans and, 57
Carpetbaggers, 392
Carson, Kit, 201
Cartier, Jacques, 31
Cass, Lewis, 310
Catawba Indians, 81

Catherine of Aragon, 24
Catholicism: in 15th-century Europe, 21; in 19th-century America, 212; in colonial New York, 68–69; Irish immigrants and, 293; in Maryland, 41–42; in Portugal, 23; Quebec Act and, 112; in Spain, 23
Catlin, George, 263
Central Park, 263
Cerro Gordo, 307
Chaco Canyon Indians, 7
Champlain, Samuel de, 32–34
Character, 277
Charbonneau, Toussaint, 181
Charles I (England), 24, 41, 47, 51
Charles II (England), 56, 59, 68, 69, 83–84
Charles Town, 57
Chase, Salmon P., 341, 363
Chase, Samuel, 177–178
Chauncy, Charles, 89
Checks and balances system, 141
Cherokee Indians, 81, 109, 121, 126–127, 147, 201, 203
Cherokee Nation v. Georgia, 203
Cherokee Phoenix, 201
Chesapeake Bay, 31, 40
Chesapeake-Leopard Affair, 183
Chesapeake region, 40–45; Bacon's Rebellion in, 44–45; death, gender, and kinship in, 43; expansion in, 41(map); slavery in, 45; state and church in, 40–42; tobacco in, 43–44. *See also* Maryland; Virginia
Chesnut, Mary Boykin, 272, 382
Chicago, growth of, 249
Chickasaw Indians, 81, 201, 203
Chiefdoms, 17
Child labor, in Europe, 22
Children: mulatto, 272; questioning parental authority, 215–216; rearing of, 216–217; slaves, 78; wages and, 250
Choctaw Indians, 80, 201, 203
Cholera, 212, 252, 282
Christianity: Columbus and, 26; Enlightenment and, 87; in Europe, 22–23; Native Americans and, 52, 62; Quakers and, 60; slaves and, 286. *See also* Catholicism
Church, for ex-slaves, 383
Church, Frederic, 263
Church of England (Anglicanism), 24; Great Awakening and, 89; Puritans and, 47; in Virginia, 41
Church of Jesus Christ of Latterday Saints, 234
Circular letter, 104
Cities, growth of, 208–209
City upon a hill, 47
Civil Disobedience (Thoreau), 259
Civil Rights Act (1866), 373
Civil Rights Act (1875), 384, 391

Civil Rights cases (1883), 384
Civil War, 337–367; 1864 election, 363; Appomattox Courthouse, 365–366; beginning of, 313–314; black soldiers in Union army, 354; crossing Union lines, 353; diplomatic war, 350–351; dissent and, 359–360; early years of, 343–345; eastern stalemate, 345–347; economic impact on North, 357–358; economic impact on South, 358–359; Emancipation Proclamation and, 352–353; financing, 340–341; impact of, 366; medical war, 360–361; naval war, 350–351; political leadership during, 341–342; recruitment and conscription, 338–339; securing Union borders, 342–343; Sherman's march, 364; slavery during, 354–355; soldier's war, 349–350; turning point (1863), 355–357; Union's victory, 362–363; war in the West, 347–349; women's rights and, 361–362
Clark, George Rogers, 127, 158
Clark, William, 181
Clarke, Elisha, 158
Clay, Cassius Marcellus, 276
Clay, Henry, 186, 192, 222–223, 227, 229, 301, 309, 316
Clergy and ministers, revivalism and, 214
Clermont, 206
Clinton, DeWitt, 191, 224
Clinton, George, 143, 180, 185
Clinton, Henry, 125–126, 127
Coahuila-Texas, 297
Coercive Acts, 112–113
Coitus interruptus, 217
Cole, Thomas, 262, 263
Colfax, Schuyler, 388
Colleges, 89
Colonies and colonial era: Chesapeake, 40–45; French Canada, 31–34; Middle, 58–61; New England, 36–37, 46–55; politics in, 84–86; statehood, 133–135
Colonization: African-Americans and, 237; in Middle and North Atlantic, 59(map)
Columbian exchange, 16, 29–30
Columbia Plateau, 10
Columbus, Christopher, 16
Comanche Indians, 81, 83, 156
Commercialism, art and, 261–262
Commercialization, of economy, 215
Commercial markets, 166
Committees of correspondence, 108, 110
Common Sense (Paine), 114–115
Commonwealth v. Hunt, 294
Compromise of 1850, 314–320
Compromise of 1877, 394
Compromise Tariff (1833), 226–227, 300
Concord, 114
Condoms, birth control and, 217
Conestoga Indians, 109

Confederate States of America, 313, 334; Civil War and, 337–367
"Confessions" (Turner), 266–272
Confiscation Acts, 352
Congregationalism, Great Awakening and, 88–89
Congress: election of 1876, 394; Reconstruction and, 370, 373–375, 378, 380
Connecticut colony, 46, 52
Connecticut River Valley, 52
Conquistadors, 28–29
Conscription, 338–339
Constitution: establishing, 138–145; implementing government, 148–149; Judiciary Act and Bill of Rights, 149–150; ratification of, 142–145; Reconstruction and, 391; state, 134; of United States, 141
Consumer revolution, 72, 96
Continental Army, 122
Continental Association, 113
Continental Congress, 113, 116, 123, 124
Continentals, 135–136
Coode, John, 70
Cooke, Jay, 390
Cooper, Anthony Ashley, 56, 57
Cooper, James Fenimore, 257, 258, 262
Copley, John Singleton, 147
Copperheads, 359–360
Corinth, Mississippi, 347
Corn (maize), 5, 7, 63, 204, 268
Cornwallis, Lord Charles, 127–129
Cortés, Hernán, 29
Cottage industries, 217
Cotton, 204, 230, 266–268, 387
Cotton gin, 172, 246
Counter-Reformation, 24
Coureurs de bois, 62
The Course of Empire (Cole), 263
Covenant Chain, 81
Crawford, William, 222–223
Crédit Mobilier scandal, 388
Creek Indians, 147, 156–157, 201, 202, 203
Creoles, 78–79
Crittenden, John J., 334
Crittenden plan, 335
Croatoan Indians, 34
Crop liens, 386–387
Crown Point, 115
Cuba, 29, 322
Culture, Native American diversity, 5–11
Curry, John, 279
Customs racketeering, 105

da Gama, Vasco, 25
Dairymaids, 166
Dance, African-American, 286–287
Daphne, 168
Dartmouth College v. Woodward, 192

Daughters of Liberty, 106
Davis, Jefferson, 332, 334, 341–342, 359, 363, 365
Dawes, William, 114
Death, slaves, 282
Death rate, in colonial Chesapeake region, 43
Debry, Theodore, 16
Debt: during Reconstruction, 374; from Revolutionary War, 135–136
Declaration of Independence, 116, 130, 132, 137
Declaratory Act (1766), 101
Dedham, Massachusetts, 52
Deere, John, 246
The Deerslayer (Cooper), 258
Deforestation, 76–77; colonial era, 52–53; Europe, 21
Deists, 87
Delaware Indians, 81, 94, 96, 109, 121, 137
Delaware Valley, 58
Democracy in America (Tocqueville), 232
Democratic Party: 1824 election, 222–223; 1828 election, 223–224; 1832 election, 227; Adams presidency, 222–223; bank controversy and second party system, 228–231; bank veto and, 227; beginning of, 224; election of 1860, 332–333; expansion and, 302–303; immigrants and, 294–295; Irish and, 229; Jackson in office, 223–225; nullification and, 225–227; political democratization, 221–222; in South, 392–393; Texas annexation and, 300–302
Deposit Act (1836), 228
Depression: in 1784, 139; of 1837, 230; after Panic of 1873, 390; in colonial Chesapeake region, 44
De Soto, Hernando, 31
Devil (Satan), 48, 54
Diaphragms, birth control and, 217
Días, Bartolomeu, 25
Dickens, Charles, 255
Dickinson, Emily, 261
Dickinson, John, 103, 113, 135
Diplomacy, Civil War and, 351
Discrimination, 283; of African-Americans, 213
Disease: cholera, 212, 252, 282; in colonial cities, 77; dysentery, 43, 282, 361; epidemics, 252; malaria, 43, 57, 282, 361; Native Americans, 52, 96, 133; slaves and, 282; smallpox, 29, 52, 58, 96; technology and, 252–254; typhoid, 43, 361; West Africans, 75; yellow fever, 57, 212, 252, 282
Divorce, 50; in early 19th century, 168
Dix, Dorothea, 220–221, 241, 360–361
Doeg Indians, 44
Dominican Republic, 179, 389

Dominion of New England, 68
Douglas, Stephen A., 316, 320, 321, 322, 327, 328, 329–331, 335
Douglass, Frederick, 238, 281, 284, 287, 352, 354, 377, 394
Downing, Andrew Jackson, 216
Drake, Francis, 34
Dred Scott decision, 327–328, 333, 374
Droughts, 63; Native Americans, 7–8
Dueling, 215, 277
Dunmore, Lord, 112
Durand, Asher, 263
Dwight, Timothy, 232
Dysentery, 43, 282, 361

Earl, Ralph, 225
Early, Jubal A., 363
Eastern Woodlands, Native peoples of, 8–10, 12(map)
East India Company, 110
East Indies, Portuguese in, 25
Eaton, John H., 226
Eclipse (boat), 206
Economy: colonial, 50–51, 71–80; commercialization of, 215; cotton and, 266–272; impact of Civil War on, 357–359; Panic of 1819, 206; regulation of, 22; technology and, 246–257
Education: for ex-slaves, 383–384; for girls, 168; Massachusetts, 48; Protestantism and, 23; public-school reform, 236–237; public schools, 383; in South, 269
Edwards, Jonathan, 88
Edward VI (England), 24
Eighth Amendment, 150
Elections: of 1796, 161–162; of 1800, 165; of 1804, 179–180; of 1824, 222–223; of 1828, 223–224, 224(map); of 1832, 227; of 1836, 229–230; of 1840, 300; of 1844, 301–302; of 1848, 309–310; of 1852, 320; of 1856, 326; of 1860, 332–333; of 1864, 363; of 1876, 393–394
Electoral College, 142, 148, 222
Elites: colonial Carolinas, 57; colonial era, 78–79, 85, 100, 101; common people and, 130; as loyalists, 121; New York colony, 59; planters, 271, 386, 392; political, 379; postwar, 384–385; in Quebec, 121; state governments and, 135
Elizabeth I (England), 24, 34
Emancipation, 352–353; African-American institutions, 383–385; confronting freedom, 382–383; crop-lien economy and, 386–387; land, labor, and sharecropping, 385–386; during Reconstruction, 369–372; Reconstruction and, 369, 372, 382–387
Emancipation Proclamation, 347, 351, 353
Embargo Act (1807), 175, 184–185, 191

Emerson, Ralph Waldo, 242, 246, 253, 257, 258–259, 261, 263, 314, 331
The Emigrant's Guide to the Gold Mines, 310
Empresarios, 297
Enclosure (England), 21–22
Encomiendas, 28
Enforcement Acts (1870–1871), 382, 391
England. *See* Britain (England)
Enlightenment, 67, 86–87
Enrollment Act (1863), 339
Enumerated goods, 72
Environment, deforestation, 21, 52–53, 76–77
Epidemic diseases, 252
Equality: between 1815 and 1840, 211; elites and, 130; urban, 211–214
"Era of Good Feelings" (1817–1824), 175, 192
Ericson, Leif, 11
Erie Canal, 207
Eskimo Indians, 2
Essay Concerning Human Understanding (Locke), 87
Ether, 252–253
Europe and Europeans: Africa and, 20(map); in Americas, 11, 33(map); Atlantic exploration and, 25–30; culture and society, 19, 21–22; occupation of North America, 82(map); reformation in, 24. *See also* Eastern Europe; *specific country*
Evangelicals, Southern, 278
Everett, Edward, 246
Exodusters, 393
Expansion and expansionism: by Britain, 75(map), 81–83; into California, New Mexico, and Oregon, 298, 303–304; Chesapeake region, 41(map); colonial New England, 52–53; Democratic Party and, 302–303; Far West, 295–297; Manifest Destiny and, 302–303; overland trails, 299–300; Texas Revolution, 297–298; toward West, 199–204; Tyler and Texas annexation, 301; Whig ascendancy, 300–301
Ex Parte Milligan (1866), 391
Ex post facto laws, 149
Extended families, 13
External taxes, 103

"The Fall of the House of Usher" (Poe), 261
Families: challenge to authority of, 215–216; Chesapeake poor, 43–44; colonial era, 76; in colonial New England, 49–50; extended, 13; Native American, 11, 13; nuclear, 11, 13, 22; slaves and, 280; West African, 18
Famine, in Europe, 21

Farmers and farming: after Revolutionary War, 139; colonial era, 49, 50, 51, 52, 76–77; debts of, 205–206; Native American, 5, 6, 8, 9–10; rising prices of, 204; scientific farming, 77; West African, 18; yeomen, 273
Farragut, David G., 349
Far West, 295–297; trails to, 296(map)
Federal debt, 390
Federalism and federalists, 141, 144(map); Constitution and, 143–145; Hartford Convention and, 191; party collapse, 175; Republicans and, 160–161
Fedoroff, Nina, 5
Ferdinand and Isabella (Spain), 21
Fiction-writing, 261–262
Fifteenth Amendment, 376–378
Fifth Amendment, 150, 327
Fillmore, Millard, 316, 317, 323, 326
Fink, Mike, 277
Finney, Charles Grandison, 233, 235, 236
First Amendment, 150
First Battle of Bull Run, 346
Fishing, fur trade and, 32
Fisk, Jim, 388
Fitzhugh, George, 276
Five Civilized Tribes, 201–202
Florida: Reconstruction and, 372; Spain in, 30, 31, 32, 63, 83–84, 195; Spanish settlement of, 64–65
Florida (ship), 351
Force Bill, 226–227
Forrest, Edwin, 256
Forrest, Nathan Bedford, 354, 382
Fort Duquesne, 93–94, 95
Fort Nassau, 37
Fort Pillow massacre (1864), 354, 382
Fort Stanwix, 124
Fort Sumter, 335
Fort Ticonderoga, 115, 124
Four Corners area, 7
Fourteenth Amendment, 373–374, 377, 384, 391
Fourth Amendment, 150
Fowler, Lorenzo, 253, 254
Fowler, Orson, 254
Fox, George, 60
France: 15th-century power in, 21; after Reformation, 24; in American Heartland, 80–81; Bonaparte, Napoleon and, 178–179; Canada and, 31–34, 59(map), 62, 82(map), 94; Caribbean colonies, 55–56; Civil War and, 351; in colonial America, 62–63; colonial populations, 73–76; explorers from, 27(map); Louisiana and, 80–81; mercantilism in, 72–73; Native Americans and, 80–81, 94–95; in North America, 95; Ohio Valley and, 81, 92; war with England, 91–95; XYZ Affair and, 162

Franciscan missionaries, 31
Franklin, Benjamin, 67, 75, 86–87, 108, 109, 129; at Philadelphia Convention, 139
Free African Society of Philadelphia, 171
Freedmen's Bureau, 373
Freedom dues, 75
Freeport doctrine, 330
Free soil, 321–322, 331, 335
Frelinghuysen, Theodore, 88, 302
Frémont, John C., 307, 326
French Revolution, 155; American Revolution and, 92; beginning of, 157
Freneau, Philip, 153
Fugitive Slave Act (1793), 315, 317
Fugitive Slave Law (1793), 171
Fuller, Margaret, 257, 259–260
Fulton, Robert, 206
Fundamental Constitutions of Carolina, 57
Fur trade, 44; beaver, 32, 34, 37, 296; Middle Colonies, 58; Native Americans, 52, 62; Russian, 156

Gabriel's rebellion, 171
Gadsden, James, 322
Gage, Thomas, 112, 114
Gallatin, Albert, 176
Galloway, Joseph, 113
Gangrene, 361
Gang system, 79
Gardner, Alexander, 341
Garrison, William Lloyd, 238, 319
Gates, Horatio, 124, 127
Gender: in colonial Chesapeake region, 43; Native Americans and, 11, 13; Revolutionary War and, 131
General Court, 51
Genêt, Edmond (Citizen), 158, 160
Genius of Universal Emancipation, 237–238
George III (England), 96, 102, 103, 105, 114, 116
Georgia: Britain in, 82–83; Reconstruction and, 372; slavery in, 83
Germany: after Reformation, 24; immigrants from, 74, 291–292
Gettysburg, 345, 355–357
Ghent, Treaty of (1814), 190–191, 195
Gibbons v. Ogden, 206
Gila River, 322
The Gilded Age (Warner), 389
"Glorious Revolution," 69–70
Gold, 72; in West Africa, 17
Gold Coast, 17
Gold rush, 29
Gold standard, 390
Goliad, 298
Gone with the Wind (movie), 271
Gordon, Thomas, 102
Gorgas, Josiah, 357
Gosnold, Bartholomew, 16

Gould, Jay, 388
Government: abolition and, 239; after Revolutionary War, 133–138; branches of, 141; colonial Carolinas, 56, 57; colonial era, 84–86; colonial New England, 68, 70; colonial Pennsylvania, 60–61; colonial Plymouth, 37; colonial Virginia, 36, 41; federal, and the West, 201; implementing, 148–149; Philadelphia Convention and, 139–142; Puritan, 47
Governor's Council (Virginia), 41
Graham, Sylvester, 253–254
Grand Banks, 32
Grant, Ulysses S., 307, 347–349, 354, 357, 362, 365, 375, 387–389, 391
Grantism, 388–389
Great Awakening, 88–89
Great Basin Indians, 10
Great Britain. See Britain (England)
Great Lakes region, Native Americans in, 9
Great Migration, 46
Great Plains, Indians, 10, 12(map)
Greeley, Horace, 255, 260, 389
Greenback Party, 390
Greenbacks, 340, 390
Greene, Nathanael, 128
Greenland, Norse in, 11
Green Mountain Boys, 110
Gregg, William, 269
Grenville, George, 99
Grimké, Angelina, 239
Grimké, Sarah, 239, 240
Guerrilla warfare, 122
Guinea, 17
Gulf of Mexico, 31

Habeus corpus, 342, 382
Haiti, 179
Half-Way Covenant, 51–52
Hall, Prince, 132
Hamilton, Alexander, 136; death of, 182; as Federalist, 144, 161; in The Federalist, 145; French Revolution and, 157; industrialization and, 167; national bank and, 152–153; national credit and, 150–152; partisanship and, 153–154; at Philadelphia Convention, 139; Whiskey Rebellion and, 154–155
Hancock, John, 105, 111
Handsome Lake, 170
Harpers Ferry, 331
Harrison, William Henry, 231, 300; Battle of the Thames, 189–190; Battle of Tippecanoe, 186–187
Hartford Convention, 191
Harvard College, 48
Hawthorne, Nathaniel, 242, 257, 260, 261
Hayes, Rutherford B., 393–394

Headrights, 36, 56
Health, of slaves, 281–282
Hemings, Sally, 175–176
Henrietta Maria (England), 41
Henry, Patrick, 100, 108, 113, 143
Henry the Navigator, 25
Henry VIII (England), 24, 27
Henson, Josiah, 284
Hessians, 121
Heth, Joice, 257
Higginson, Thomas Wentworth, 354
Hill, John William, 208
Hillsborough, Lord, 104
Hispanic people, 297
Hispaniola, 28
HMS Leopard, 183
Hogarth, William, 106
Hohokam culture, 7–8
Holmes, Oliver Wendell, Sr., 253
Holy Spirit, 60
Homestead Act (1862), 358
Honduras, 322
Honor, 277
Hood, John B., 363
Hooker, Joseph, 355
Hopewell culture, 8
Hopi Indians, 156
Horizontal allegiances, 217
"House Divided" speech (Lincoln), 329
House of Burgesses, 36, 41, 100, 123
The House of Seven Gables (Hawthorne), 260
Housing, 19th-century, 251
Houston, Sam, 290, 298
Howard, O. O., 373, 386
Howe, Elias Jr., 245
Howe, Richard, 123
Howe, William, 123, 124
Hudson, Henry, 37
Hudson River School, 263
Hudson's Bay Company, 295, 296
Huguenots, 32
Hull, Agrippa, 119–120
Hull, William, 188–190
Hunting, by Native peoples, 2, 3
Huron Indians, 33, 34, 37
Hutchinson, Anne, 48–49, 89
Hutchinson, Thomas, 100, 108, 111
Hydropathy, 253

Ice Age, 2
Illinois, 80; statehood for, 199
Illinois Central Railroad, 249
Immigrants and immigration: Anti-Catholicism, nativism, and labor protest, 293–294; British colonial, 75(map); Democratic Party and, 294–295; European, 73–74; expectations and realities, 290–291; Germans, 292;

Immigrants and immigration: (*Continued*) Irish, 292–293; to New France, 62; to New York colony, 59; poverty and, 212

Impeachment, 177–178; Johnson and, 376

Impressment, 158, 159, 183

Impressment Act (1863), 339

Inca of Peru, 6, 29

Indentured servants, 36, 55, 57, 74–75; in colonial Chesapeake region, 43

Independence, declaring, 115–116

Independence Hall, 139, 140

Independent Treasury Bill (1840), 230–231, 300

India, Portuguese in, 25

Indiana, statehood for, 199

Indian Removal Act (1830), 203

Indian Trade and Intercourse Acts, 169

Indirect taxes, 102–103

Indulgences, sale of, 23

Industrialization: American, 166–167; causes of, 209–210; in mid-19th century, 198; in mid-Atlantic cities, 211; New England textile towns, 210–211; rise of, 209; slavery and, 269; in South, 269; technology and, 247–248

Inflation, 341

Insane asylums, 241

Interchangeable parts, 248

Interposition, 164

Intolerable Acts, 112–113

Inuit Indians, 2

Ireland and Irish: Civil War and, 360; England and, 34; immigrants from, 74, 212, 291, 292–293

Iron, 72

Iroquois Indians, 13, 34, 37, 58, 62, 71, 81–82, 109, 121, 127, 137, 170

Irrigation, 6, 7

Irving, Washington, 257, 263

Italy, after Reformation, 24

Jackson, Andrew, 138, 192, 195; 1824 election, 222–223; 1828 election, 223–224; bank veto and 1832 election, 227; Native Americans and, 202–203; nullification and, 225–227; in office, 224–225; Treaty of Ghent, 190–191

Jackson, James, 154

Jackson, Thomas J. "Stonewall," 278, 347, 361

James I (England), 24, 35, 36, 37, 40

James II (England), 68, 69; colonial New York and, 59, 60

Jamestown, 35, 40, 44

Jay, John, 113, 129, 144, 158, 159; in *The Federalist*, 145

Jay's Treaty, 159, 162

Jefferson, Thomas, 108, 116, 137, 303; 1796 election, 161; 1800 election, 165; 1804 election, 179–180; Burr and, 182; Canada

and, 188; debt from Revolutionary War and, 152; Embargo Act (1807), 184–185; Enlightenment and, 87; French Revolution and, 157; Jeffersonianism and, 175–176; judiciary and, 176–178; land laws and, 205; Lewis and Clark expedition, 180–181; Louisiana Purchase, 178–179, 180(map); national bank and, 153; Randolph and, 182–183; Republicanism and, 160; "Revolution" of, 176; slaves and, 171; suppression of American trade and impressment, 183; Virginia and Kentucky Resolution, 164

Jenkins, Robert, 84

Jesuit missionaries, 62

Jews, in Europe, 22–23

Johnson, Andrew, 363, 366; presidential Reconstruction, 372–373; Tenure of Office Act (1867) and, 375–376

Johnson, Richard M., 186, 272

Johnson, William Tiler, 283

Johnston, Joseph, 363

Joint-stock companies, 22, 35, 41

Jolliet, Louis, 62

Jones, Absalom, 171

Judicial review, 177

Judiciary, Jefferson and, 176–178

Judiciary Act (1789), 149

Judiciary Act (1801), 177

Kampsville, Illinois, 3

Kansas: crisis in, 324–326; Lecompton constitution, 328–329; statehood for, 328–329

Kansas-Nebraska Act (1854), 321, 322

Kearny, Stephen, 306

Keayne, Robert, 51

Keelboats, 206

Kelley, Abby, 239, 240

Kentucky, 109; during Civil War, 342–343; revivals in, 232; statehood for, 199

Kentucky Resolutions, 225

Key, Francis Scott, 192

Kickapoo Indians, 81

Kiefft, Willem, 58

King, Charles Bird, 226

King, Rufus, 180, 185

King, William, 186

King Cotton, 266–268

King George's War, 84, 92

King Philip's War, 53

King William's War, 71

Kinship: in colonial Chesapeake region, 43; Native Americans and, 11, 13; slaves and, 281; West African, 18. *See also* Families

Kivas, 7, 63

Know-Nothing Party, 293, 323–324

Knox, Henry, 115

Kongo, 17

Kósciuszko, Thaddeus, 119

Ku Klux Klan, 381–382

Ku Klux Klan Act (1871), 391

Labor: problems after Reconstruction, 386; protest of, 293; strikes, 211; unions, 294

Labor unions, Civil War, 337–367

Lafayette, Marquis de, 124, 129

Lake Champlain, Battle of, 33–34

Lake Texcoco, 6

Lakota Sioux Indians, 81

Lalawéthica, 186

Land, for freedmen, 385–386

Land, Native American: Indian removal and, 201–204; treaties, 203–204

Land grants, 59, 83

Land policy, federal, 204–205

Land reform, 375, 380, 385

Landscapes, 263

Language, of slaves, 285

La Salle, Sieur de, 62–63

The Last of the Mohicans (Cooper), 258

Latin (South) America, Inca of, 6

Lawrence, Amos A., 318

Leaves of Grass (Whitman), 260

Lecompton constitution, 328–329

Lee, Ann, 234

Lee, Richard Henry, 108, 113, 143

Lee, Robert E., 307, 335, 339, 347, 355, 356, 357, 365

Legal Tender Act (1862), 340

Legree, Simon, 319

Leisler, Jacob, 70

Leisler's Rebellion, 70

Leisure and entertainment: American Renaissance, 258; art, 263; literature, 258–262; minstrel shows, 256; newspapers, 255; P.T. Barnum, 257; theater, 255–256

Letters from a Farmer in Pennsylvania, 103

Letters on the Condition of Women and the Equality of the Sexes (S. Grimké), 239

Letters to Catherine E. Beecher (A. Grimké), 239

Lewis, Meriwether, 180–181

Lewis and Clark expedition, 180–181

Lexington, 114

Liberal Republican, 389, 391

The Liberator, 238, 240

Liberty (ship), 105

Library of Congress, 175

Life expectancy, in colonial New England, 50

Lincoln, Abraham, 324, 332, 334; Civil War and, 313–314, 338–367; Lincoln-Douglas debates, 329–331; Reconstruction and, 371–372

Lincoln-Douglas debates, 329–331

Liquor, reform and, 235

Literacy, in 18th-century New England, 86

Literature, 258–262
Little Ice Age, 21
Livingston, Robert R., 179, 206
Locke, John, 57, 87, 101
Locofocos, 228–229
Locomotives. *See* Railroad
Log cabins, 231
Long, Crawford, 252
Lord Dunmore's War, 109
"Lost colony," 34
Louisiana, 63, 380; banks in, 231; colonial populations, 73; France in, 80–81; Poverty Point peoples, 8
Louisiana Purchase, 178–179, 180 (map), 201
Louis XIV (France), 62, 63, 71
Louis XVI (France), 124
L'Ouverture, Toussaint, 179
Lovejoy, Elijah P., 239
Lowell, Massachusetts, 198, 210–211
Lowell Offering, 199
Lower (Deep) South, 266
Loyalists (Tories), 113, 120–121, 127
Loyal Nine, 100
Lundy, Benjamin, 237–238
Luther, Martin, 23
Lutherans, 74
Luxuries, of mid-19th century, 251–252
Lyceums, 261
Lyon, Matthew, 164

McClellan, George B., 346–347, 363
McCormick, Cyrus, 247–248, 358
McCulloch v. Maryland, 193
McDowell, Irvin, 345–346
McGillivray, Alexander, 138
McGuffy readers, 237
Machinery, 247–248
McIntosh, William, 202
Macon's Bill No. 2, 185
Macready, William, 256
Madison, Dolley, 185, 190
Madison, James, 144; Bill of Rights and, 150; debt from Revolutionary War and, 152; in *The Federalist*, 145; French Revolution and, 157; vs. Marbury, 177; national bank and, 153; nationalism and "era of good feelings," 192; peaceable coercion and, 185; at Philadelphia Convention, 139; Republicanism and, 160; Second Bank of United States and, 193; Virginia and Kentucky Resolution, 164; Virginia Plan, 140; War of 1812, 188
Magellan, Ferdinand, 28
Maine, statehood for, 199
Maize-based farming, 5. *See also* Corn
Malaria, 43, 57, 282, 361
Mali, 17
Manassas Junction, Virginia, 345

Manhattan, 37
Manifest Destiny, 302–303, 322
Manitou, 14
Mann, Horace, 236–237
Manor system, in colonies, 41–42
Mansfield, William, 111
Manufacturing, 210
Manumission, 79
Manumit, 132
Marbury, William, 177
Marbury v. Madison, 177
Mardi (Melville), 260
Maritime revolution, 25. *See also* Ships and shipping
Market economy, 22, 204; effect on society, 214–218; federal land policy, 204–205; growth of cities, 208–209; panic of 1819, 205–206; speculators and squatters, 205; transportation revolution, 206–208
Marquette, Jacques, 62
Marriage: African-Americans, 383; in antebellum America, 215–216; in Chesapeake region, 43; colonial era, 76; communism and, 242; divorce and, 168; in New England, 49–50; between slaves, 279, 280–281, 282; West African, 18; wives and husbands, 216–217
Marshall, John, 177, 182, 192–193, 203, 206
Mary I (England), 24, 69–70
Maryland: Catholicism in, 41–42; in colonial era, 70; slavery in, 45; state and church in, 41–42; tobacco in, 43–44
Mason, George, 143
Mason, James, 351
Mason, John, 52
Massachusetts, as royal colony, 68
Massachusetts Bay colony, 46
Massachusetts Bay Company, 47
Massachusetts Government Act, 112
Massasoit, 37, 53
Mather, Increase, 54
Matrimonial Republican, 168
Maya Indians, 6
Mayflower Compact, 37
Meade, George G., 355
Melodramas, 256
Melville, Allan, 213
Melville, Herman, 213, 257, 260, 261
Mentally ill persons, 241; conditions of, 220–221
Mercantilism, 62, 71–73
Merchant marines, 72, 158
Merchants, 166; colonial New England, 60; industrialization and, 209; in New England, 51
Merrimac (ship), 350
Mesoamerica, 4, 5–6, 7
Mesquakie Indians, 81
Metacom, 53
Methodists, 232; Great Awakening and, 89

Mexican-American War, 304–311; battles of, 308(map); California gold rush, 310–311; effect on sectional conflict, 307–309; origins of, 304–306; Wilmot Proviso, 309
Mexican Revolution, 295
Mexico, 5–6; Far West expansion and, 295–297; silver from, 30
Mexico City, 29, 307
Miasmas, 252
Middle Colonies, 58–61, 116
Middle Passage, 75
Middling classes, 199, 213–214
Miller, William, 230
Mingo Indians, 94, 109
Minstrel shows, 256
Minuit, Peter, 37
Minutemen, 114
Missionaries, 63; Franciscan, 31; Jesuit, 62; New Light preachers as, 89; Spanish, 29, 31, 297
Mississippi: Democrats in, 393; Ku Klux Klan in, 382; Reconstruction and, 372
Mississippi plan, 393
Mississippi River region, 62–63; Native Americans in, 8–10; statehood for, 199
Missouri: during Civil War, 343; statehood for, 193, 199, 295
Missouri Compromise, 193–195, 308, 309, 314
Moby-Dick (Melville), 260, 261
Mohawk Indians, 33–34, 37, 62, 121, 127, 188–190
Molasses, 73
Molasses Act (1733), 72, 98
Monitor (ship), 350
Monk, Maria, 293
Monroe, James: 1816 election, 191; as Antifederalist, 143; "era of good feelings" and, 192; foreign policy under, 195; Louisiana Purchase, 179; Second Bank of United States and, 193
Monroe Doctrine, 195–196
Montagnais Indians, 33
Montcalm, Louis Joseph de, 94
Monterrey, 306
Monte Verde, Chile, 2
Morgan, William, 229
Mormonism, 234
Morrill Land Grant Act (1862), 358
Morris, Robert, 136
Morse, Samuel F. B., 248
Morton, William T. G., 252–253
Mott, Lucretia, 240
Mound-building cultures, 8–9
Moving frontier, 205
Mulatto children, 272
Murray, Judith Sargent, 168
Music, African-American, 286–287
Muslim, 17; in Europe, 22–23

Napoleonic Wars, 181, 195
Narragansett Bay, 48
Nast, Thomas, 388
Natchez, Mississippi, 182
Natchez Indians, 81
National bank, 152–153
National Bank Act (1863), 341
The National Gazette, 153
Nationalism: American, 191–196; in literature and art, 257–263
Nationalist perspective, 140
National Road, 201
National Union Party, 363
National Woman's Loyal League, 361–362
National Woman Suffrage Association, 377
Native Americans, 1–15; after Revolutionary War, 129, 133, 137; alcoholism, 53, 133, 170; in American society, 168–170; Archaic peoples, 2–5; British expansion and, 81–82; Carolinas and, 57; cultural diversity of, 5–11; diseases and, 29, 52, 96, 133; of Eastern Woodlands, 8–10, 12(map); enslavement of, 53; federal government and, 201; "Five Civilized Tribes," 201–202; France and, 94–95; fur trade, 52; homelands of, 12(map); land cessions, 169(map); in New England, 9, 13, 46, 52–53; in New Mexico colony, 63; nonfarming societies, 10–11; in paintings, 263; Plains Indians, 10–11; Quakers and, 61; reciprocity and, 2, 9, 11, 14; removal and, 201–204; slaves and, 284; Trail of Tears, 202(map), 203; US expansion and, 156–157; war in the West, 126(map), 126–127. *See also* Land, Native American; *specific tribal group*
Nativism, 293
Nat Turner rebellion, 283
Naturalization Act, 163
Natural rights, 101
Navajo Indians, 63, 156; ancestors of, 2
Navarro, José Antonio, 289–290
Navigation Acts, 72, 104
Navy, Civil War and, 350–351
Nebraska, 320, 321
Negro Baptist churches, 383
Neolin, 96
Netherlands (Dutch): after Reformation, 24; in North America, 31, 37; Puritans in, 37
New Amsterdam, 37
Newburgh Conspiracy, 136
New England: colonization of, 36–37; Native Americans in, 9, 13, 46, 52–53; Puritans of, 36–37
New England Non-Resistance Society, 239
New England Way, 47–49
Newfoundland, 27, 32; Norse in, 11
New France, 32
New Hampshire, 68
New Harmony, 242

New Haven colony, 46, 52
New Jersey, establishment of, 58–60
New Jersey Plan, 141
New Lights, 88, 89
New Mexico, 63; American settlements in, 298; Spain and, 31; statehood for, 295
New Netherland, 37, 49, 52, 58
New Orleans, 80
Newspapers, in mid-19th century, 255
New Sweden, 58
Newton, Isaac, 86
New York, establishment of, 58–60
New York Herald, 255, 362
New York Stabber, 255
New York Suspending Act, 103
New York Tribune, 255, 389
Nicaragua, 322
Nightingale, Florence, 361
Ninth Amendment, 150
Nomad populations, 11
Nonconsumption agreements, 106–107, 110
Nonimportation, 104
Non-Intercourse Act (1809), 185
Norse, in North America, 11, 26, 27(map)
North: divergence from South, 269, 271; Grantism, 388–389; Liberal's revolt, 389; Panic of 1873, 390; Reconstruction and Constitution, 391; Republicans in retreat, 391
North, Lord, 104, 108, 110, 112, 129
North America: Dutch in, 31; European footholds in, 30–37; European occupation of, 82(map); France in, 95; Indian homelands in, 12(map); Norse in, 26, 27(map)
North Carolina, Reconstruction and, 372
Northern Pacific Railroad, 390
Northwest Coast Indians, 10
Northwest Ordinance (1787), 136–138, 309
Northwest Territory, 137
Nova Scotia, 27, 71, 95
Noyes, John Humphrey, 242
Nuclear families, 11, 13, 22
Nueces River, 305
Nullification Crisis, 225–227
Nurses, 361

Oglethorpe, James, 82–83, 84
Ohio, statehood for, 199
Ohio Indians, 127
Ohio River, 109
Ohio River Valley, 81, 92; Native Americans in, 8
Old Deluder Act, 48
Old South: conflict and consensus, 274–275; evangelical values in, 278; pine barrens poor, 273–274; planter elite, 271–272; slavery argument, 275–277; small slaveholders, 272–273; social

relations, 274–278; violence, honor, and dueling in, 277; whites in, 271–274; yeomen, 272, 273
Olive Branch Petition, 114
Oliver, Andrew, 100
Olmec peoples (Mexico), 8
Olmsted, Frederick Law, 258, 263, 284
Omoo (Melville), 260
Oñate, Juan de, 31
Oneida Indians, 121, 127, 242
"On the Equality of the Sexes" (Murray), 168
Opechancanough, 36
Oppositionists, 102
Order of the Star-Spangled Banner, 293, 323
Ordinance of 1785, 136, 137, 204–205
Oregon: American settlements in, 298; expansion into, 290; Polk and, 303–304; statehood for, 295
Ostend Manifesto, 322, 326
O'Sullivan, John L., 302
Otis, James, 97–98, 99–100
Ottawa Indian, 96
Ottoman Empire, 23
Overland trails, 299
Owen, Robert, 242

Pacific Ocean region, Balboa in, 28
Pacific Railroad Act (1862), 358
Paelo-Indians, 2
Paine, Thomas, 114–115
Painters and painting, American, 263
Palmetto Guards, 313
Panama, Isthmus of, 28
Panic of 1819, 205–206
Panic of 1837, 230–231
Panic of 1873, 390
Paper money, 340–341. *See also* Greenbacks
Partisanship, after Revolutionary War, 153–154
Paterson, William, 140–141
The Pathfinder (Cooper), 258
Patting juba, 287
Patuxer Indians, 37
Pauperism, 212
Paxton Boys, 109
Peacable coercion, 175, 184, 186
Peale, Rembrandt, 190
Peasants, 21. *See also* Farmers and farming
Penitentiaries, 241
Penn, William, 60–61
Pennsylvania: conflict in, 108–109; Quakers, 60–61
Pennsylvania Journal, 105
Pennsylvania (separate) system, for penitentiaries, 241
Pennsylvania Society for the Encouragement of Manufactures and the Useful Arts, 166

Penny press, 254, 255
Pequot Indians, 52
Perry, Oliver Hazard, 189
Peru, Inca of, 6, 29
Philadelphia, 60
Philadelphia Convention, 139–142
Philippines, 28
Philosophy, 258
Phips, William, 54
Phrenology, 254
Pickering, John, 177
Pickett, George E., 356
Pidgin, 285
Piedmonts, 75
Pierce, Franklin, 318, 320, 322, 323
Pike, Zebulon, 201
Pilgrims, 37
Pinckney, Charles C., 180, 185
Pinckney, Thomas, 158–159
Pinckney's Treaty, 159
Pine barrens, 273–274
The Pioneers (Cooper), 258
Pitt, William, 95, 99, 102, 106
Plains Indians, 10, 12(map)
Planters and plantations, 268; black labor
   for, 386; in colonial era, 42, 43, 44; elites,
   386, 392; Enlightenment and, 87;
   maturing of, 278–279; of Old South,
   271–272; sharecropping, 386; slave labor
   for, 26; in West Indies, 55
Plato, 276
Plymouth colony, 37, 46, 53
Pocahontas, 35, 36
Pocket-veto, 372
Poe, Edgar Allen, 258, 260, 261
Political elite, 379
Politics: from 1857 to 1860, 327–332;
   Alien and Sedition Acts, 162–164;
   colonial era, 84–86; democratization,
   221–222; election of 1796, 161–162;
   election of 1800, 165; French crisis, 162;
   ideological confrontation, 160;
   Mexican-American War and, 307–308;
   during Reconstruction, 370–378;
   Republican Party, 160–161; in South,
   274–275
Polk, James K., 290, 301; Mexican-American
   War and, 306; Oregon and, 303–304;
   Wilmot Proviso and, 309
Ponce de León, Juan, 31
Pontiac, 96
Poor, in 19th century, 211–212
Poor Richard's Almanac, 86
Popé, 63
Popes and papacy, 23, 24. *See also*
   Catholicism
Popular sovereignty, 310, 328, 329
Population: colonial era, 43, 50, 57, 58,
   73–76; European, 21–22; growth of, 249;
   New France, 62

Portugal: Africa and, 20(map); after
   Reformation, 24; Brazil and, 27–28;
   Catholicism in, 23; early-17th-century
   empires, 29(map); explorers from,
   27(map); slave trade and, 25–26
Positive good, 275–276
Postwar elite, 384–385
Potato famine, 293
Potlatches, 10
Potomac River, 44
Pottawatomie Creek, 325
Potter, David, 319
Poverty: 19th-century Americans, 212; in
   colonial Chesapeake region, 44;
   colonial era, 77–78; cycle of, 387;
   France and, 73
Poverty Point, Louisiana, 8
Powhatan, 35, 36
Predestination, 23, 24
Preemption laws, 205
Pregnancy, control of, 217
Presbyterians, Great Awakening and, 89
President, powers of, 141
Presidential Reconstruction,
   372–373, 386
Prices, technology and, 250
Prince Henry the Navigator, 25
Print culture, 86
Prisoners, of Civil War, 361
Privy Council, 104, 158
Proclamation of 1763, 96–97, 169
Proclamation of Amnesty and
   Reconstruction (1863), 371, 372
Professions, attack on, 214–215
Prosser, Gabriel, 283
Protestantism: abolition and, 239;
   Catholics and, 41–42; evangelical,
   233; Great Awakening and, 89; Irish
   immigrants and, 293–294; Quebec Act
   and, 112; rebellions and, 70; Whigs
   and, 229
Protestant Reformation, 23–24
Providence, 48
Public Credit Act (1869), 390
Public domain, 201, 205
Public-school reform, 236–237
Public schools, 383
Public water systems, 251
Pueblo Indians, 7, 63–64, 83
Pueblo Revolt, 63–64, 81
Puerperal fever, 253
Puerto Rico, 31
Puritans: Church of England and, 47; "city
   upon a hill" and, 47; economic and
   religious tensions, 50–52; in Europe, 24;
   expansion and Native Americans, 46,
   52–53; in New England, 36–37; Salem
   witchcraft and, 53–55; towns, families,
   and farms, 49–50
Put-in-Bay, 189

Quakers, 60–61; Great Awakening and, 89;
   slavery and, 132
Quality of life, in mid-19th century,
   250–254
Quartering Act (1765), 102–103, 112
Quebec, 32
Quebec Act, 112–113
Queen Anne's War, 71
Quitman, John A., 322

Race and racism: in colonial Chesapeake
   region, 45; integration, 384; racial
   mixing, 30, 176; racial tensions, 79; in
   South Carolina, 79; toward Mexicans,
   307
Radical Republicans, 370, 371, 372, 373,
   375, 377, 391
Railroad, 208, 246; Douglas on, 321;
   postwar, 390; technology and, 248–250,
   249(map)
Raleigh, Walter, 34
Ranchos, 83
Randolph, John, 182–183
Ratification, 142
Recessions, in colonial era, 77
Reciprocity: in Europe, 22, 23; Native
   Americans, 2, 9, 11, 14, 32
Reconstruction, 369–395; congressional,
   374–375, 378, 380; Constitution and,
   373, 391; counterattacks, 380–382;
   emancipation and, 369, 372, 382–387;
   end of, 392–394; Fifteenth Amendment
   and, 376–378; Fourteenth Amendment
   and, 373–374, 377; impeachment crisis
   during, 375–376; Lincoln's plan for,
   371–372; northern concerns, 387–391;
   politics of, 370–378; presidential,
   372–373, 386; Republicans and, 378–379,
   380; of South, 375(map); state
   governments during, 372, 374, 378–381;
   Supreme Court and, 378, 384, 391
Reconstruction Acts (1867–1868), 372,
   374, 376
Redemption, Democratic, 393
Redemptioners, 74
Reform: for abolition, 237–239; land, 375,
   380, 385; for liquor, 235–236; for mental
   institutions, 220–221; for penitentiaries
   and asylums, 241; for public schools,
   236–237; utopian communities, 242; for
   women's rights, 240–241
Reformation, in Europe, 23–24
Regulators, 110
Religion: African-Americans, 285–286; in
   colonial New England, 47–49, 50–52;
   eastern revivals, 233; Enlightenment and,
   101; Great Awakening and, 88–89;
   Methodists, 232–233; in Middle
   Colonies, 58; Mormonism, 234; Native

Religion (*Continued*)
American, 8–9; Pennsylvania Quakers, 60–61; Reformation, 23–24; Salem witchcraft and, 54; Second Great Awakening, 214, 221, 232–233; Shakers, 234–235; slavery and, 276–277; Unitarians, 233–234; West African, 18–19; women and, 233
Renaissance, 19, 21
Report on National Bank, 152
Report on the Subject of Manufactures (1791) (Hamilton), 167
Reports on Public Credit, 150
Representation, 141
Republicanism, 134–135
Republican motherhood, 168
Republican Party: 1860 election, 332–333; beginning of, 224, 320; crisis in Kansas and, 324–326; *Dred Scott* decision, 327–328; Federalists and, 160–161; Reconstruction and, 380, 391–394; slavery and, 314; in the South, 378–379; split of, 1830s, 221
Restoration colonies, 56
Revenue Act (1767), 103
Revere, Paul, 91, 114
Revivalism and revivalists, 214, 232–233
Revolts and rebellions: Bacon's, 44–45; at Fort Sumter, 335; Gabriel's, 171; "Glorious Revolution," 69–70; Leisler's, 70; Liberal Republican, 389; Nat Turner's, 265–266, 283; Pueblo, 63–64, 81; Shays's Rebellion, 139; slave, 171; on slave ships, 75; Stono, 79
Revolutionary War, 119–146; African-Americans and, 121, 127, 131–133; casualties in, 114, 123, 124, 126–127, 129; debt from, 135–136, 150–152; French Revolution and, 92; loyalists (Tories) in, 113, 120–121, 126, 127; Native Americans and, 121, 122, 126–127, 129, 133; in North, 123–126; opposing sides, 121–123; social change and, 129–133; in South, 127–129; Treaty of Paris and, 129; in West, 126–127; Whiskey Rebellion, 154–155; white male equality in, 130; white women in, 130–131
Revolver, 246
Rhode Island colony, 46, 48
Rice cultivation, 57
Rio Grande, 305
Rio Grande Valley, 31
Rivers, 207(map); growing transportation on, 206–208
Roads, 207(map)
Roanoke colony, 34
Robards, Rachel, 224
Robinson, Harriet Jane Hanson, 198–199
Robinson, William Stevens, 198
Rolfe, John, 36

Romanticism, 258
Roosevelt, Franklin D., 320
Rosecrans, William S., 357
Ross, John, 203
Rotation in office, 224–225
Rowe, Katie, 369–370
Row houses, 251
Royal Society of London, 87
Ruffin, Edmund, 313–314
Rush-Bagot Treaty (1817), 195
Russia, 389; in Far West, 295

Sacajawea, 181
Sack of Lawrence, 325–326
St. Augustine, 31
Saint-Domingue, 157, 179
St. Lawrence Valley, 31, 62
St. Leger, Barry, 124
Salem witchcraft, 53–55
Samoset, 37
San Antonio de Bexar, 83
Sanitary Commission, U.S., 360
San Jacinto, 298
San Salvador, 16, 26
Santa Anna, 297–298, 307
Santo Domingo, 389
Savannah (grassland), 17–19
Scalawags, 378, 379, 381, 392
The Scarlet Letter (Hawthorne), 260, 261
Schools, for ex-slaves, 383. *See also* Education
Schudson, Michael, 255
Science, 87
Scientific farming, 77
Scorched earth policy, 34
Scott, Walter, 258
Scott, Winfield, 306, 307, 320, 323, 345
Scott's Great Snake, 345
Secession, 331–332, 333–334, 335
Second Amendment, 150
Second Bank of United States, 192, 205, 227
Second Battle of Bull Run, 347
Second Great Awakening, 214, 221, 232–233
Sedition Acts (1798), 163–164
Segregation, 372; in 19th-century America, 213; during Reconstruction, 384
Seminole Indians, 195, 201, 203
Seneca Falls, New York, 240–241
Senegambia, 17
Separate spheres, 216–217
Separation of powers, 141
Seven Days' Battles, 347
Seven Golden Cities of Cibola, 31
Seventh Amendment, 150
Seven Years' War, 92–95
Seward, William, 316, 323, 331, 332, 334, 389
Sewer systems, 252
Sewing machines, 245–246

Seymour, Horatio, 388
Shakers, 234–235
Shakespeare, William, 256
Sharecropping, 386–387
Shaw, Robert Gould, 354
Shawnee Indians, 81, 94, 109, 121, 137, 159, 186–187
Shays, Daniel, 139
Shays's Rebellion, 139
Sherman, John, 390
Sherman, William Tecumseh, 362, 364, 385
Shiloh Church, 348
Ships and shipping, 25; Navigation Acts, 72; Sugar Act and, 98. *See also* Navy
Shoshone Indian, 181
Sickle-cell anemia, 57
Silver, 72, 230, 390; from Mexico, 30
Singer, Isaac M., 245
Sixth Amendment, 150
Slash-and-burn agriculture, 10
Slater, Samuel, 166, 209, 210
Slaughterhouse case (1873), 391
Slaveocracy, 326, 327
Slave rebellion, 171, 179; fear of, 127, 283; Nat Turner's, 265–266
Slaves and slavery, 28, 278–284; abolition, 237–239; African origins of, 26; after Revolutionary War, 131–133; in Carolinas, 56–57; children, 78; colonial attitudes toward, 131–133; in colonial Chesapeake region, 45; colonial era, 78–79; in colonial Louisiana, 73; conflicts over, 314; in Constitution, 142; cotton cultivation and, 267–268; death rate, 282; disease, 282; Emancipation Proclamation, 352–353; families, 280–281; Fugitive Slave Law (1793), 171; industrialization and, 269; language of, 283–284; in late 18th century, 170–172; liberty for, 111–112; longevity, health, and diet, 281–282; marriage of, 279, 280–281, 282; Middle Passage, 75; in Missouri, 193–194; music and dance, 286–287; on plantations, 278–280; population, 79, 270(map), 279; Portuguese and, 25–26; proslavery argument, 275–277; racism and, 26; religion of, 285–286; resistance of, 283–284; Revolutionary War and, 121; Southern yeomen and, 272–273; spread of, 55–57; in towns, 282–283; *Uncle Tom's Cabin* (Stowe), 318–319; in wartime, 354–355; West African, 55, 75–76; in West Indies, 55–56
Slave trade: Portugal and, 25–26; West African, 25–26, 45
Slidell, John, 305, 351
Sloat, John D., 307
Smallpox, 29, 52, 58, 96
Smith, Jedediah, 201

Smith, John, 35
Smith, Joseph, 234
Smuggling, 98, 105, 110
Social class, after Revolutionary War, 130
Social improvement, as Adam's personal goal, 223
Society: attacks on professions, 214–215; challenge to family authority, 215–216; colonial, 71–80; revolutionism in, 214–218; voluntary associations and, 217–218; western customs and, 200; in white South, 271–278; wives and husbands, 216–217
Society for the Encouragement of Useful Manufactures, 166–167
Society of Friends, 60. *See also* Quakers
Soest, Gerard, 39
Somerset, James, 111
Sonoma, 307
Sons of Liberty, 100
South: divergence from North, 269, 271; Reconstruction of, 375(map); redeeming, 392–393
The South Alone Should Govern the South, 331
South America. *See* Latin (South) America
South Carolina, 57, 78, 110, 380; African-Americans in, 379; Democrats in, 393; Huguenots in, 32; Nullification Crisis and, 226; Reconstruction and, 372
South Carolina Exposition and Protest (Calhoun), 226
Southern Homestead Act (1866), 385
Southwest, Native peoples of, 7–8
Spain: after Reformation, 24; Armada of, 34; Catholicism in, 23; in colonial North America, 83–84; colonial populations, 73–76; colonies of, 29(map), 30; Columbus and, 16, 26–27, 28; exploration by, 30–31; in Far West, 295; in Florida, 30, 83–84, 195; mercantilism in, 72–73; missionaries, 297; Native Americans and, 28–29; in New World, 95; in North American colonies, 63–65; silver and inflation in, 30; slavery and, 26; unification of, 21; United States and, 138, 156
Spatial mobility, middling classes and, 214
Specie Circular (1836), 228
Specie Resumption Act (1875), 390
Speculation, 205
Spinning bees, 107
Spirituals, 287
Spoils system, 225
Sponslor, Mary Ann, 245
Squanto, 37
Squatters, 205
Squatter sovereignty, 310
Stamp Act (1765), 99–101, 102
Stamp Act Congress, 100–101
Stanton, Edwin M., 375, 376

Stanton, Elizabeth Cady, 240–241, 361–362, 377
Stanton, Henry, 352
"Star-Spangled Banner" (Key), 192
State banks, 205–206, 228
State constitutions, 134
State governments, Reconstruction and, 372, 374, 378–381
Steamboats, 206
Stephens, Alexander, 342, 372
Steuben, Friedrich von, 125
Stevens, Judith Sargent, 147
Stevens, Thaddeus, 341, 375, 391
Stone, Lucy, 240
Stone, William, 42
Stono Rebellion, 79
Stowe, Harriet Beecher, 258, 261, 318–319
Straits of Magellan, 28
Strauss, Levi, 292
Strikes, 211
Strong, Thomas W., 310
Stuart, Gilbert, 137–138
Stuart Restoration, 51
Stuyvesant, Peter, 58, 59
Suffolk Resolves, 113
Suffrage, 241; for African-Americans, 370, 376–377; for women, 377–378
Sugar Act (1764), 98
Sugar cane, in West Indies, 55
Sullivan, John, 127
Sumner, Charles, 325–326, 341, 384, 391
Sun Dance, 14
Sun Pyramid, 6
Supplementary Freedmen's Bureau Act (1866), 373
Supreme Court, 149, 192–193; *Civil Rights cases* (1883), 384; on interstate commerce, 206; Reconstruction and, 391
Susquehannock Indians, 44
Sutter, John, 295
Sweden, 58

Taino Indians, 16
Talleyrand, Charles de, 162
Tammany Hall, 294, 389
Taney, Roger B., 327, 343
Tariff of Abominations, 225
Tariffs, 98, 192, 225–227, 358
Task system, 79
Taxation: Aztecs, 6; colonial protests of, 98, 99–100; in colonial Virginia, 41; external, 103; indirect, 102–103; loyalists opposition to, 120; regulating trade through, 103; for Revolutionary War debt, 139; in South during Reconstruction, 380; on tea, 103, 104, 106; without representation, 104
Taylor, Zachary, 305, 306, 309, 316; election of 1848 and, 310; slavery and, 315–316

Tea, taxes on, 103, 104, 106
Tea Act (1773), 110–111
Technology, 246; agricultural advancement, 246–247; disease and health, 252–254; dwellings, 251–252; industrialization and, 210, 247–248; pastimes and, 254–257; railroad boom and, 248–250; rising prosperity and, 250
Tecumseh, 186–187, 188–190
Tehuacán, 5
Tejano, 289
Telegraph, 248
Temperance, 236, 294
Tenements, 251
Tennent, Gilbert, 88
Tennent, William, 88
Tennessee: redemption and, 393; revivals in, 232; statehood for, 199
Tenochtitlán, 6, 29
Tenskwatawa, 186
Tenth Amendment, 150
Tenure of Office Act (1867), 375–376
Teosinte, 5
Teotihuacán, 5–6
Tetanus, 361
Texas: annexation of, 301–302, 304–306; expansion toward, 290; Reconstruction and, 372; slavery and, 301; Spain in, 64–65, 83; statehood of, 295
Texas Revolution, 297–298
Texas v. White (1869), 391
Textile mills, 185, 198–199, 209, 210–211
Theater, in mid-19th century, 255–256
Third Amendment, 150
Thirteenth Amendment, 241, 363, 372, 377
Thomas, Gertrude Clanton, 337–338
Thomas, Jefferson, 337
Thomson, Samuel, 214
Thoreau, Henry David, 257, 259, 261, 263
Three-fifths clause, 142
Tilden, Samuel J., 393
Tippecanoe River, 187
Tituba, 54
Tobacco, 72, 266; in Chesapeake region, 43–44, 77; in Virginia, 36; in West Indies, 55
Tocqueville, Alexis de, 218, 232
Tom Thumb, 256, 257
Tordesillas, Treaty of (1494), 26–27, 29(map)
Tories. *See* Loyalists (Tories)
Townshend, Charles, 102, 103, 104
Townshend duties, 103
Trade: 1837 global economy and, 230; American, 159; with Asia, 26; with Britain, 185–186; British colonial laws, 72; in Canada, 62; far Western, 295–297; with France, 81, 185–186; Indian Trade and Intercourse Acts, 169; Native American, 5, 7, 8, 10, 32, 80; Portuguese,

Trade (*Continued*)
25; regulating through taxation, 103;
Sugar Act and, 98; suppression of, 183;
unions, 211; West African, 17
Trail of Tears, 202(map), 203
Transcendentalism, 242, 259
Transience, middling classes and, 214
Transcontinental (Adams-Onís) Treaty
(1819), 195, 295
Transcontinental railroad, 358, 390
Transportation revolution, 206–208; epidemic
diseases and, 252; railroads and, 248–250
Treaties: Adams-Onís (Transcontinental)
(1819), 195; of Fort Stanwix (1768), 109;
of Fort Wayne (1809), 186; of Ghent
(1814), 190–191, 195; of Greenville, 159;
of Guadalupe Hidalgo, 307; Jay-
Gardoqui, 138; Jay's, 159, 162; of New
Echota (1835), 203; of New York (1790),
157; of Paris (1763), 95, 129; Pinckney's,
159; Rush-Bagot (1817), 195; of San
Ildefonso, 178; of San Lorenzo, 159; of
Tordesillas (1494), 26–27, 29(map);
Webster-Ashburton (1842), 301
Tredegar Iron Works, 269, 339
Trenchard, John, 102
Trent (ship), 351
Treviño, Juan Francisco, 63
Tripolitan War, 174
Trumbull, John, 119
Truth, Sojourner, 240
Tubman, Harriet, 284
Turner, Nat, 265–266
Tuscarora Indians, 81, 121, 127
Twain, Mark, 256, 389
Tweed, William M., 388, 389
Twelfth Amendment, 180
Two-party system, collapse of, 320–326
Tyler, John, 231, 300–301
Typee (Melville), 260
Typhoid, 43, 361

Uncle Tom's Cabin (Stowe), 258, 261, 318–319
Underground railroad, 284
Unemployment, in colonial era, 77
Union Pacific Railroad, 388
Unions. *See* Labor unions
Unitarianism, 233–234
United Kingdom. *See* Britain (England)
United Order of Americans, 293
United States of America: challenges to,
158; creation of, 116; debt from
Revolutionary War, 135–136; expansion
by, 156–157; population, 199; Spain and,
156; War of 1812, 175
United States v. Cruikshank, 391
United States v. Reese, 391
Upper South, 266
Urban inequality, 211–214

Urbanization, 72, 77–78
Ursuline nuns, 62
USS *Chesapeake*, 183
Ute Indians, 83
Utopian communities, 242

Vallandigham, Clement L., 360
Valley Forge, 124
Van Buren, Martin, 223–224, 227, 229, 230,
231, 301; election of 1848 and, 310
Vanderlyn, Pieter, 67
Vaqueros, 83
Vargas, Diego de, 64
Vaux, Calvert, 263
Vera Cruz, 306
Vermont, statehood for, 199
Vertical allegiances, 217
Vesey, Denmark, 283, 286
Vespucci, Amerigo, 28
Vicksburg, 357
Vigilantism, 381–382
Vinland, Norse in, 11
Violence, in white South, 277
Virginia: Bacon's Rebellion in, 44–45;
colonization of, 35–36; House of
Burgesses, 36, 41, 100, 123; slavery in, 45;
state and church in, 40–41; tobacco in,
36, 43–44
Virginia and Kentucky Resolution, 164
Virginia Company of London, 35, 36
Virginia Company of Plymouth, 35
Virginia Plan, 140–141
Virginia Resolutions, 225
Virginia (ship), 350
Virtual representation, 99, 106
Voluntary associations, 217–218
Voting: 1830s rules for, 221–222; in colonial
era, 85; free blacks and, 212–213

Wabash River, 186
Wade, Benjamin, 376
Wade-Davis Bill (1864), 371–372
Wages, technology and, 250
Walden (Thoreau), 259
Walker, David, 237
Walker, William, 322
Wall Street, railroads and, 250
Waltham, Massachusetts, 210–211
Wampanoag Indians, 16, 37, 53
War and warfare: of 1812, 163; Anglo-
Spanish, 84; Cold War. *See* Cold War; by
England, 34; guerrilla, 122; King
George's War, 84; King William's War,
71; Lord Dunmore's War, 109; Mexican-
American War, 304–311; Napoleonic,
181, 195; Native Americans, 10, 39–40,
81; in New England colonies, 71; in
North, 125(map); Queen Anne's War, 71;

Seven Years' War, 92–95; in South,
127–129, 128(map); in West, 126(map)
See also specific war
War bonds, 340, 390
Ward, Nancy, 147–148
War hawks, 186
Warner, Charles Dudley, 389
Warner, Susan, 261
War of 1812: American nationalism after,
191–196; British offensive, 190; Canada
and, 188–190; Hartford Convention, 191;
Madison and, 188; major battles of,
189(map); Treaty of Ghent, 190–191
War of Jenkins' Ear, 84
War of the Austrian Succession, 84
War of the League of Augsburg, 71
Warren, Joseph, 102
War Woman, 147
Washington, George, 86, 92, 113, 114, 115,
119, 132; in army, 123, 124, 129;
expansion and, 156–157; as Federalist,
161; as first president, 148; national bank
and, 153; Newburgh Conspiracy and,
136; at Philadelphia Convention, 139;
Whiskey Rebellion and, 155
Washington, Martha, 172
Washington Temperance Society, 236
Wayne, Anthony, 159
Wealth: in 19th century, 211–212; in
colonial era, 78, 80; inheritance and, 76;
middling classes and, 199, 213–214
Webster, Daniel, 246, 301, 316
Webster-Ashburton Treaty (1842), 301
West: Civil War in, 347–349; expansion
toward, 199–204; government and, 201;
society and customs, 200
West Africa, 17–19; disease, 75; kinship in,
18; slave trade and, 26, 45, 55, 75–76;
sources of slaves from, 74(map)
West Indies (Caribbean): French trade and,
73; slavery in, 55–56; Spain in, 29
West Virginia, statehood for, 343
Wheat, 77, 80, 204, 246
Wheatley, Phillis, 131, 132
Whigs, 120, 221; 1840–42, 300–301;
disintegration of, 323; Fugitive Slave Act
and, 320; opposition to, 229
Whiskey Rebellion, 154–155
Whiskey ring, 388
White, John, 34
Whitefield, George, 67, 84, 88
Whitman, Walt, 250, 257, 258, 260
Whitney, Eli, 171–172, 204, 210, 246
Whittier, John Greenleaf, 239
The Wide, Wide World (Warner), 261
Wilkes, John, 105–106
Wilkinson, James, 156, 182
William of Orange, 69–70
Williams, Roger, 48
Wilmot, David, 309–310

Wilmot Proviso, 309
Winthrop, John, 47, 48, 51
Witchcraft, in Salem, 53–55
Women: abolition and, 239; antinomianism and, 48–49; in colonial Chesapeake region, 43; colonial era, 76, 85; colonial resistance and, 106–107; equality for, 240–241; Great Awakening and, 89; hydropathy and, 253; independence from families, 215–216; literature and, 261; Native American, 3, 13; in New England, 49–50; religion and, 233; rights of, war and, 361–362; Salem witchcraft and, 54; separate spheres and, 216–217; suffrage, 198, 241, 377–378; as teachers, 237; transcendentalism and, 259; urban colonial, 78; white, 130–131, 167–168; as wives, 216; writers, 262

Women, work of: after Reconstruction, 383; to aid Civil War soldiers, 360–361; dairymaids, 166; housecleaning, 252; indentured servants, 43; as mothers, 216–217; plantation wives, 272; textile mills, 210–211

Women in the Nineteenth Century (Fuller), 259–260
Worcester v. Georgia, 203
Workhouses, 241
Writers, 261–262; women, 262
Writ of assistance (1760), 97–98
Wyatt, Francis, 36

XYZ Affair, 162

Yamasee Indians, 81
Yazoo scandal, 182–183
Yellow fever, 57, 212, 252, 282
Yeomen, 272–273
Yerba Buena, 311
Young, Brigham, 290
Yuma Indians, 156

Zenger, John Peter, 86
Zuñi Indians, 31